미리 준비하는 중학생을 위한

중학 수능 특강

영어듣기

듣기 MP3 파일
바로듣기 & 다운로드

정답과 해설 및 듣기 MP3 파일은 EBS 중학사이트(mid.ebs.co.kr)에서 다운로드 받으실 수 있습니다.

| 교 재 내 용 문 의 | 교재 내용 문의는 EBS 중학사이트 (mid.ebs.co.kr)의 교재 Q&A 서비스를 활용하시기 바랍니다. | 교 재 정오표 공 지 | 발행 이후 발견된 정오 사항을 EBS 중학사이트 정오표 코너에서 알려 드립니다. 교재 검색 → 교재 선택 → 정오표 | 교 재 정 정 신 청 | 공지된 정오 내용 외에 발견된 정오 사항이 있다면 EBS 중학사이트를 통해 알려 주세요. 교재 검색 → 교재 선택 → 교재 Q&A |

필독

중학 국어로 수능 잡기

필독 중학 국어로 수능 잡기 시리즈

✦ 필독 중학 국어로 수능 잡기 시리즈

문학 — 비문학 독해 — 문법 — 교과서 시 — 교과서 소설

미리 준비하는 중학생을 위한

중학 수능 특강

영어듣기

이 책의 구성과 특징

PART I
수능유형 분석편

수능 유형들의 특징과 대비법을 소개하고, 유형을 체험해 볼 수 있는 대표 문제와 해결 전략을 제시합니다. 더불어 실제 시험에 등장했던 유형별 빈출 표현을 통해 수능 난이도를 체감할 수 있습니다. 이어 중3~고2 수준의 신규 문항과 연계교재 선별 문항으로 수능 대비 실력을 차곡차곡 쌓아갈 수 있습니다.

수능 유형별 대비법
수능에 꾸준히 출제되는 유형들의 특징과 대비법을 친절하게 설명

수능 유형 체험
수능 유형을 익힐 수 있는 대표 문제와 상세한 해결 전략 제시

유형 빈출 표현
수능과 모평에 등장했던 유형별 빈출 문장으로 수능 난이도 체감

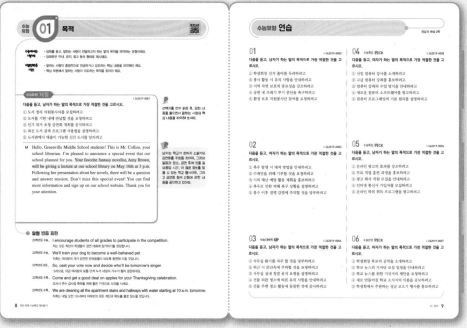

01~02번
중3 상위 수준부터 고1 수준의 문제로 본격적인 수능 유형 연습

03번
한 단계 업그레이드된 고1~2 수준의 문제로 수능 실전 체감 연습

04~06번
연계교재에서 선별한 수능 중하 수준의 문제로 수능 실전 대비 연습

단원명 옆에 있는 QR 코드를 이용해 MP3 파일을 바로듣기하거나 다운로드할 수 있습니다.

비교·분석 중학 영어듣기평가 vs. 수능 영어듣기평가

중학 영어듣기평가	
주관 기관	전국 16개 시·도 교육청 / 서울시
실시 시기	매년 4월, 9월
문항 수	20문항
대본 길이	대화문: 4~5 turn (중3 기준) 담화문: 60~90단어 (중3 기준)
시험 시간	20분 이내
출제 유형상의 특징	세부 정보를 묻는 유형이 많이 출제되며, 중1은 그림을 이용한 유형이, 중3은 말하기 유형이 상대적으로 많이 출제됨.
기타	학년에 따라 유형과 대본 길이에 차이가 있고, 같은 학년에서도 시기에 따라 출제 유형과 문항 순서에 변동이 있음.

본 교재는 중학 영어듣기에서 수능 영어듣기 실력으로의 도약을 위해 제작되었습니다. 교육과정에 부합하는 내용을 제시하는 동시에 수능 유형 체험과 수능 실전 연습을 위한 구성을 통해, 중3 수준에서 고1~2 및 수능 중 난이도 수준까지 3단계로 수능을 체감하며 연습할 수 있도록 구성하였습니다.

PART II
수능실전 대비편

수능 영어듣기평가와 동일한 형식의 모의고사 11회분으로 구성되어 수능 실전 감각을 익히고 충분히 연습할 수 있습니다. 고1 수준부터 수능 중간 난이도 수준의 신규 문항과 연계교재 선별 문항을 난이도에 따라 단계별로 풀어 볼 수 있어 수능 영어듣기에 대한 실전 감각뿐만 아니라 자신감도 키울 수 있습니다.

1~4회
고1 전국연합평가 수준의 신규 출제 문항과 연계교재 선별 문항으로 수능 실전 연습 돌입

5~9회
고2 전국연합평가 수준의 신규 출제 문항과 연계교재 선별 문항으로 수능 실전 연습 본격화

10~11회
수능 연계교재 수준의 100% 신규 출제 문항을 중심으로 수능 실전 연습 완성

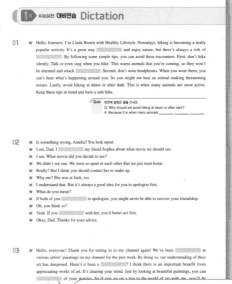

Dictation
수능실전 대비연습 문제에 등장하는 중요 표현들을 확인해 볼 수 있는 받아쓰기 연습

Dictation 활용 3 Steps
Dictation 코너를 100% 활용할 수 있는 Tip을 단계별로 제공하여 충분한 듣기 연습을 유도

빈칸으로 표시된 부분에 받아쓰기 할 내용은 한 단어가 아닌 발음상·내용상 중요 표현들입니다. 빈칸 개수로 받아 쓸 내용에 대한 힌트 없이 온전히 들리는 말에 집중해서 써 보세요.

수능 영어듣기평가	
주관 기관	한국교육과정평가원
실시 시기	매년 6월, 9월(모의평가), 11월(수능)
문항수	17문항
대본 길이	대화문: 6~7 turn 담화문: 100~120단어
시험 시간	25분 이내
출제 유형상의 특징	대의 파악, 세부 정보 파악, 말하기 유형이 골고루 출제될 뿐만 아니라, 하나의 긴 담화를 두 번 듣고 두 문항을 푸는 유형도 출제됨.
기타	출제 유형과 순서의 변동이 거의 없지만, 해당 연도의 모의평가 출제 경향에 따라 본 수능의 출제 방향이 정해지기도 함.

이 책의 차례

인공지능 DANCHOQ
푸리봇 문│제│검│색

EBS 중학사이트와 EBS 중학 APP 하단의
AI 학습도우미 푸리봇을 통해 문항코드를
검색하면 푸리봇이 해당 문제의 해설 강의를
찾아 줍니다.

문제별 문항코드 확인

242019-0001

[242019-0001]

1. 아래 그래프를 이해한 내용으로 가장 적절한 것은?

문항코드 검색

PART I

수능유형
분석편

수능에서는 이렇게!
- 담화를 듣고, 말하는 사람이 전달하고자 하는 말의 목적을 파악하는 유형이에요.
- 담화문은 안내, 공지, 광고 등의 형태로 제시돼요.

해결전략은 이것!
- 말하는 사람이 중점적으로 언급하거나 강조하는 핵심 내용을 파악해야 해요.
- 핵심 부분에서 말하는 사람이 의도하는 목적을 찾아야 해요.

수능유형 체험

▶ 242019-0001

다음을 듣고, 남자가 하는 말의 목적으로 가장 적절한 것을 고르시오.

① 도서 정리 자원봉사자를 모집하려고
② 도서를 기한 내에 반납할 것을 요청하려고
③ 인기 작가 초청 강연회 개최를 공지하려고
④ 최신 도서 검색 프로그램 사용법을 설명하려고
⑤ 도서관에서 대출이 가능한 신간 도서를 알리려고

M   Hello, Greenville Middle School students! This is Mr. Collins, your school librarian. I'm pleased to announce a special event that our school planned for you. Your favorite fantasy novelist, Amy Brown, will be giving a lecture at our school library on May 16th at 3 p.m. Following her presentation about her novels, there will be a question and answer session. Don't miss this special event! You can find more information and sign up on our school website. Thank you for your attention.

선택지를 먼저 읽은 후, 담화 내용을 들으면서 말하는 사람의 핵심 내용을 파악해 보세요.

남자는 학교가 판타지 소설가의 강연회를 주최할 것이며, 그것의 일정과 장소, 강연 후에 있을 질의응답 시간, 더 많은 정보를 찾을 수 있는 학교 웹사이트, 그리고 강연회 참석 신청에 관한 내용을 공지하고 있어요.

◎ 유형 빈출 표현

23학년도 수능_ I encourage students of all grades to participate in the competition.
저는 모든 학년의 학생들이 경연 대회에 참가하기를 권장합니다.

22학년도 수능_ We'll train your dog to become a well-behaved pet.
저희는 여러분의 개가 얌전한 반려동물이 되도록 훈련해 드릴 것입니다.

22학년도 9모_ So, cast your vote now and decide who'll be tomorrow's singer.
그러므로, 지금 여러분의 표를 던져 누가 내일의 가수가 될지 결정하세요.

23학년도 수특_ Come and get a good deal on apples for your Thanksgiving celebration.
오셔서 추수 감사절 축하를 위해 좋은 가격으로 사과를 사세요.

23학년도 수특_ We are cleaning all the apartment stairs and hallways with water starting at 10 a.m. tomorrow.
저희는 내일 오전 10시부터 아파트의 모든 계단과 복도를 물로 청소할 것입니다.

01

▶242019-0002

다음을 듣고, 남자가 하는 말의 목적으로 가장 적절한 것을 고르시오.

① 학생회장 선거 출마를 독려하려고
② 봉사 활동 시 유의 사항을 안내하려고
③ 지역 자연 보호의 중요성을 강조하려고
④ 공원 내 쓰레기 투기 중단을 촉구하려고
⑤ 환경 보호 자원봉사단 참여를 요청하려고

02

▶242019-0003

다음을 듣고, 여자가 하는 말의 목적으로 가장 적절한 것을 고르시오.

① 폭우 발생 시 대처 방법을 안내하려고
② 수재민을 위해 기부할 것을 요청하려고
③ 시의 재난 예방 활동 계획을 홍보하려고
④ 폭우로 인한 피해 복구 상황을 설명하려고
⑤ 홍수 이후 질병 감염에 주의할 것을 당부하려고

03 수능 대비력 **UP**

▶242019-0004

다음을 듣고, 남자가 하는 말의 목적으로 가장 적절한 것을 고르시오.

① 사무실 환기를 자주 할 것을 당부하려고
② 퇴근 시 문단속에 주의할 것을 요청하려고
③ 사무실 실내 청결 유지 요령을 설명하려고
④ 건물 외관 청소에 따른 유의 사항을 안내하려고
⑤ 건물 주변 청소 활동에 동참한 것에 감사하려고

04 수능특강 **PICK**

▶242019-0005

다음을 듣고, 여자가 하는 말의 목적으로 가장 적절한 것을 고르시오.

① 신임 컴퓨터 강사를 소개하려고
② 고급 컴퓨터 강좌를 홍보하려고
③ 컴퓨터 강좌의 수업 방식을 안내하려고
④ 새로운 컴퓨터 소프트웨어를 광고하려고
⑤ 컴퓨터 프로그래밍의 기본 원리를 설명하려고

05 수능특강 **PICK**

▶242019-0006

다음을 듣고, 남자가 하는 말의 목적으로 가장 적절한 것을 고르시오.

① 온라인 광고의 효과를 강조하려고
② 무료 직업 훈련 과정을 홍보하려고
③ 광고 회사 직원 모집을 안내하려고
④ 인터넷 통신사 가입자를 모집하려고
⑤ 온라인 학위 취득 프로그램을 광고하려고

06 수능완성 **PICK**

▶242019-0007

다음을 듣고, 여자가 하는 말의 목적으로 가장 적절한 것을 고르시오.

① 학생회장 후보의 공약을 소개하려고
② 학교 뉴스의 기자단 모집 일정을 안내하려고
③ 학교 뉴스를 위한 기삿거리 제안을 요청하려고
④ 새로 만들어질 학교 소식지의 이름을 공모하려고
⑤ 학생회에서 주관하는 성금 모으기 행사를 홍보하려고

- 대화 또는 담화를 듣고, 화자의 의견이나 주장, 요지가 무엇인지 파악하는 유형이에요.
- 대화 또는 담화에 제시된 상황에서 문제가 무엇인지 파악하는 것이 중요해요.

해결전략은
이것!
- 화자가 문제를 해결하기 위해 어떤 의견이나 주장, 요지를 담아 말하고 있는지에 주의해야 해요.
- 의견이나 주장, 요지에 해당되는 반복되는 표현을 찾으면 정확하게 이해할 수 있어요.

수능유형 체험

▶ 242019-0008

대화를 듣고, 남자의 의견으로 가장 적절한 것을 고르시오.

① 약속된 업무 일정을 철저하게 지켜야 한다.
② 건강을 먼저 회복해야 일을 더 잘할 수 있다.
③ 의사의 처방에 따라 약을 먹어야 안전하다.
④ 증상이 나타났을 때 즉시 병원 진료를 받아야 한다.
⑤ 무리하게 일을 하면 건강이 갑자기 악화할 수 있다.

선택지를 읽어 보면 어떤 소재와 관련된 대화가 나올지를 예상할 수 있어요.

M Honey, are you feeling okay? You don't look the greatest.
W I have a sore throat and I'm feeling a bit achy.
M Let me take a look. *[Pause]* Your forehead is really warm.
W I probably caught a cold.
M You'd better take a break and get some rest today.
W But I have so much work to do.
M Of course your work is important, but you need to put your health first. You can work better if you're feeling well.
W You're right. But I'm just worried about my report that's due on Friday.
M Don't worry. I'm sure you'll be able to get it done once you feel better.
W All right. I'll take some medicine and rest today.

여자는 몸 상태가 좋지 않지만, 이번 주 금요일까지 해야 할 보고서를 완성하기 위해 일을 하고 있고, 남자는 여자에게 건강이 좋아야 일을 더 잘할 수 있다고 조언하고 있어요.

◎ 유형 빈출 표현

23학년도 수능_ Apple peels can help improve our skin condition. 사과 껍질은 피부 상태 개선에 도움을 줄 수 있어요.

22학년도 수능_ I think you shouldn't plan too many things to do for a trip.
네가 여행에서 할 일을 너무 많이 계획해서는 안 될 것 같구나.

23학년도 9모_ But listening to the radio can increase your sense of happiness.
그러나 라디오를 듣는 것은 당신의 행복감을 증가시킬 수 있어요.

23학년도 수특_ I think people must stop warming up their car in the parking lot.
사람들이 주차장에서 차를 예열하는 것을 멈춰야 한다고 생각해요.

22학년도 수특_ Pet owners should be careful to respect others when they walk their pets.
반려동물 주인들은 자신의 반려동물을 산책시킬 때 다른 사람들을 배려하도록 주의해야 해.

01
▶ 242019-0009

대화를 듣고, 여자의 의견으로 가장 적절한 것을 고르시오.

① 위생을 위해 전자레인지 내부를 자주 청소해야 한다.
② 부엌에서 나는 악취의 원인을 찾아서 제거해야 한다.
③ 오렌지 껍질은 일상생활에서 유용하게 쓰일 수 있다.
④ 먹지 않고 남은 과일들을 요리 재료로 활용하면 좋다.
⑤ 오렌지는 우리 몸에 유용한 영양소를 많이 포함하고 있다.

02
▶ 242019-0010

대화를 듣고, 남자의 주장으로 가장 적절한 것을 고르시오.

① 상대의 기분을 파악하지 못한 채 농담을 하면 안 된다.
② 친구에게 실수를 저질렀을 때는 반드시 먼저 사과해야 한다.
③ 중요한 사항을 전달할 때는 상대방과 직접 통화를 해야 한다.
④ 상대방의 문자 메시지에 최대한 신속하게 답장을 보내야 한다.
⑤ 상대방이 오해하지 않도록 문자 메시지를 신중하게 작성해야 한다.

03 수능 대비력 UP
▶ 242019-0011

다음을 듣고, 남자가 하는 말의 요지로 가장 적절한 것을 고르시오.

① 음악 감상은 정서를 안정시키는 데 효과적이다.
② 악기 연주를 배우는 것이 삶을 더 활기차게 해 준다.
③ 어떤 악기든 배우려면 많은 시간과 노력이 필요하다.
④ 악기를 구입할 때 전문가의 조언을 구하는 것이 좋다.
⑤ 즐거운 마음으로 악기를 연주해야 더 좋은 소리가 난다.

04 수능특강 PICK
▶ 242019-0012

대화를 듣고, 남자의 의견으로 가장 적절한 것을 고르시오.

① 거실에 식물을 배치할 때 사람들의 동선을 고려해야 한다.
② 정원을 잘 가꾸기 위해서는 식물에 대한 공부가 필수적이다.
③ 식물을 적절히 배치하면 실내 공간이 넓어 보이게 할 수 있다.
④ 공기 정화의 측면에서 잎이 큰 식물을 키우는 것이 도움이 된다.
⑤ 실내 인테리어를 위해 식물을 사용하는 것에는 여러 장점이 있다.

05 수능완성 PICK
▶ 242019-0013

대화를 듣고, 여자의 의견으로 가장 적절한 것을 고르시오.

① 부모의 편식 습관은 자녀의 식습관 형성에 영향을 준다.
② 어린 시절의 편식 습관은 성인이 된 후에도 지속될 수 있다.
③ 자녀가 조리 과정에 참여하면 편식 습관 개선에 도움이 된다.
④ 유치원에서 조리 실습 수업을 할 때 사전 안전 교육이 필요하다.
⑤ 자녀의 식사 예절은 부모와 함께 식사하면서 자연스럽게 형성된다.

06 수능특강 PICK
▶ 242019-0014

대화를 듣고, 남자의 주장으로 가장 적절한 것을 고르시오.

① 미세 먼지가 심할 때 밖에서 캠페인 활동을 하면 안 된다.
② 미세 먼지 줄이기 실천에 대한 캠페인 활동을 강화해야 한다.
③ 미세 먼지가 심할 때는 마스크를 착용하고 외부 활동을 해야 한다.
④ 미세 먼지가 건강에 미치는 유해성에 대한 학생 교육을 강화해야 한다.
⑤ 미세 먼지로 인해 캠페인을 취소하려면 참가자들의 동의를 얻어야 한다.

수능에서는 이렇게!
- 대화를 듣고 두 사람의 관계를 추론하는 유형이에요.
- 대화자의 직업이나 대화가 이루어지고 있는 상황을 예측하기 위해 대화 시작 전에 선택지의 내용을 살펴보는 것이 도움이 돼요.

해결전략은 이것!
- 대화자가 처한 상황을 파악하고, 대화의 전체 흐름과 분위기를 파악해야 해요.
- 선택지에 제시되는 관계에 주목하여 그것들의 단서가 되는 표현에 집중해 듣도록 해요.

수능유형 체험

▶242019-0015

대화를 듣고, 두 사람의 관계를 가장 잘 나타낸 것을 고르시오.

① 모의 면접관 – 학생
② 에어컨 구매자 – 배달원
③ 상점 아르바이트생 – 손님
④ 구직자 – 중고 매장 운영자
⑤ 중고 물건 판매자 – 상점 직원

선택지의 내용을 먼저 살펴보면 중고 매장 및 구직과 관련된 대화가 오고 갈 것임을 예측할 수 있어요.

M Hello, I'm Jeremy Krull. I have an appointment with Ms. Green.

W I'm Ms. Green. Thank you for coming, Mr. Krull. Please take a seat.

M Thank you. *[Pause]* Your store is huge and has a wide variety of items.

W Yeah, nowadays many people are looking for second-hand goods. That's why we're hiring another delivery person.

M I actually bought a used air conditioner recently. As I'm sure you saw on my resume, I don't have much experience, but I think I can handle the job well.

W Okay. If you get the job, would you be able to start next week?

M Sure, I can do that.

W Great. Actually, I have two more interviews this afternoon. I'll make a decision by tomorrow and let you know.

M I understand. I look forward to seeing you again, Ms. Green.

W Same here.

중고 물건을 판매하는 상점을 방문한 남자에게 여자가 요즘 중고 물건을 찾는 사람이 많아서 배달원을 한 명 더 뽑는다고 말하고 있어요. 여자가 남자에게 일을 하게 되면 다음 주에 일을 시작할 수 있는지 물은 뒤 오후에 두 명을 더 면접하고 내일까지 결과를 알려 주겠다고 말하고 있어요.

◎ **유형 빈출 표현**

23학년도 수능_ I appreciate you taking the time to share your experience and knowledge.
선생님의 경험과 지식을 공유하기 위해 시간을 내 주셔서 감사합니다.

22학년도 수능_ Thanks for inviting me. 초대해 주셔서 감사합니다.

22학년도 6모_ Oh, thank you for interviewing me, Mr. Wilson. I'm a big fan of your magazine.
오, Wilson 선생님, 인터뷰해 주셔서 고맙습니다. 저는 선생님 잡지의 열렬한 팬입니다.

22학년도 수특_ Thank you for taking this time out for us after your overseas schedule, David.
해외 일정을 마치고 저희를 위해서 이렇게 시간을 내 주셔서 감사합니다, David.

21학년도 수특_ Do you have any particular model in mind? 특별히 마음에 두고 있는 모델이 있으세요?

01
▷ 242019-0016

대화를 듣고, 두 사람의 관계를 가장 잘 나타낸 것을 고르시오.

① 자원봉사자 – 수의사
② 동물 보호소 직원 – 교사
③ 반려동물용품 판매원 – 고객
④ 동아리 담당 교사 – 동아리 부원
⑤ 반려견 주인 – 반려견 입양 희망자

04 수능특강 **PICK**
▷ 242019-0019

대화를 듣고, 두 사람의 관계를 가장 잘 나타낸 것을 고르시오.

① 식당 주인 – 종업원
② 세입자 – 건물 주인
③ 경제학 교수 – 대학생
④ 인테리어 업자 – 의뢰인
⑤ 기업 경영자 – 영업 사원

02
▷ 242019-0017

대화를 듣고, 두 사람의 관계를 가장 잘 나타낸 것을 고르시오.

① 체육 교사 – 학생
② 테니스 코치 – 테니스 선수
③ 악기 수리공 – 수리 의뢰인
④ 스포츠 센터 직원 – 수강생
⑤ 스포츠용품 매장 직원 – 고객

05 수능특강 **PICK**
▷ 242019-0020

대화를 듣고, 두 사람의 관계를 가장 잘 나타낸 것을 고르시오.

① 꽃가게 주인 – 손님
② 식물원 직원 – 관람객
③ 사진작가 – 광고 기획자
④ 패션모델 – 잡지사 기자
⑤ 환경미화원 – 정원 관리자

03 수능 대비력 **UP**
▷ 242019-0018

대화를 듣고, 두 사람의 관계를 가장 잘 나타낸 것을 고르시오.

① 대학생 – 대학교수
② 관광객 – 여행 가이드
③ 박물관 직원 – 방문객
④ 여행사 대표 – 여행사 직원
⑤ 등산 동호회 회장 – 동호회 회원

06 수능완성 **PICK**
▷ 242019-0021

대화를 듣고, 두 사람의 관계를 가장 잘 나타낸 것을 고르시오.

① 의사 – 환자
② 수의사 – 반려동물 주인
③ 반려동물 미용사 – 고객
④ 사회복지사 – 자원봉사자
⑤ 방송 진행자 – 반려동물 훈련사

• 대화를 듣고 그림에서 두 사람이 말하는 내용과 일치하지 않는 부분을 찾는 유형이에요.

수능에서는 이렇게!
• 대화에서 묘사하는 사람, 동물, 사물의 모양, 위치, 개수 등이 그림과 일치하는지를 묻는다는 것을 기억하세요.

해결전략은 이것!
• 사진, 그림, 포스터 등이 그림으로 제시되고 이를 묘사하는 대화가 이루어지므로 그림의 세부적인 내용을 언급하는 부분을 집중해서 들어야 해요.
• 사람이나 사물의 외향적인 특징, 위치, 개수 등에 주목하여 그것을 묘사하는 표현을 주의하여 듣도록 해요.

수능유형 체험

▶ 242019-0022

대화를 듣고, 그림에서 대화의 내용과 일치하지 <u>않는</u> 것을 고르시오.

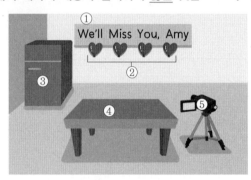

그림을 통해 Amy를 위한 송별회가 열린다는 것을 예측할 수 있어요.

W   Peter, the other club members will be arriving with Amy in 30 minutes. Is everything ready for her farewell party?

M   I think so. I hung a banner that says "We'll Miss You, Amy" on the wall.

W   Great! And the heart-shaped balloons under the banner are really lovely. By the way, where's the cake?

M   It's in the refrigerator in the corner. Should we take it out?

W   Let's do that right before they get here and put it on the round table in the center.

M   All right. That's a good idea.

W   What are the video camera and stand next to the table for?

M   I set up the video camera on the stand to record today's party and will later give Amy a copy of the video.

W   How thoughtful of you! I hope Amy likes the party we've prepared.

현수막에 적힌 글씨, 풍선의 위치와 모양, 냉장고의 위치, 테이블의 모양과 위치, 비디오카메라와 스탠드의 위치가 언급되고 있는데, 그림에는 직사각형 모양의 테이블이 있으나 대화에서는 둥근 테이블이라고 말하고 있어요.

◉ 유형 빈출 표현

23학년도 수능_ It's a picture I took at Grand Boulder National Park.
그것은 Grand Boulder 국립 공원에서 내가 찍은 사진이야.

23학년도 수능_ I like the bear statue wearing the check pattern jacket. 체크무늬 재킷을 입은 곰 조각상이 마음에 들어.

22학년도 9모_ Check out this picture I found on the Internet. 내가 인터넷에서 찾은 이 사진을 확인해 보세요.

22학년도 수특_ Is this you back there wearing a striped shirt? 줄무늬 셔츠를 입고 저 뒤쪽에 있는 이 사람이 너니?

01

▶ 242019-0023

대화를 듣고, 그림에서 대화의 내용과 일치하지 <u>않는</u> 것을 고르시오.

02

▶ 242019-0024

대화를 듣고, 그림에서 대화의 내용과 일치하지 <u>않는</u> 것을 고르시오.

03 수능 대비력 **UP**

▶ 242019-0025

대화를 듣고, 그림에서 대화의 내용과 일치하지 <u>않는</u> 것을 고르시오.

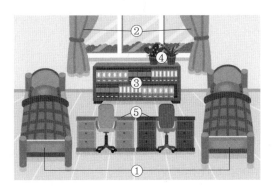

04 수능특강 **PICK**

▶ 242019-0026

대화를 듣고, 그림에서 대화의 내용과 일치하지 <u>않는</u> 것을 고르시오.

05 수능특강 **PICK**

▶ 242019-0027

대화를 듣고, 그림에서 대화의 내용과 일치하지 <u>않는</u> 것을 고르시오.

06 수능특강 **PICK**

▶ 242019-0028

대화를 듣고, 그림에서 대화의 내용과 일치하지 <u>않는</u> 것을 고르시오.

수능에서는 이렇게!
· 대화를 듣고 여자나 남자가 할 일 또는 상대방에게 부탁한 일을 파악하는 유형이에요.
· 선택지는 대화에서 언급되는 내용으로 만들어지기 때문에 대화를 듣기 전에 선택지의 내용을 빠르게 살펴보는 것도 중요하답니다.

해결전략은 이것!
· 대화의 상황을 파악하고, 특히 남자 또는 여자가 할 일이나 부탁하는 일과 관련하여 언급되는 내용에 집중하도록 해요.
· 대화 중 언급되는 여러 가지 일 중 문제에서 요구하는 것을 정확히 들어야 해요. 대화의 후반부에 정답과 관련된 결정적인 내용이 주로 언급된다는 것을 알아두세요.

수능유형 체험

▶ 242019-0029

대화를 듣고, 여자가 할 일로 가장 적절한 것을 고르시오.

① 배너 설치하기
② 홍보 전단 나눠 주기
③ 3D 프린터 확인하기
④ 동아리 부스 청소하기
⑤ 테이블과 의자 가져오기

선택지를 먼저 살펴보면 동아리 부스 설치 준비와 관련된 대화가 오고 갈 것임을 예측할 수 있어요.

W Wilson, I'm sorry for taking so long to print the flyers.

M It's okay. I just finished hanging the banner. Our club booth is almost ready now.

W You guys also set up the table and chairs while I was away. Thank you for your hard work.

M No problem. We just need to bring the 3D printer from the science lab tomorrow morning.

W We should also check if the printer is working properly.

M Mike and Rachel are doing that right now in the lab.

W Oh, great. Then I'll go and distribute the promotional flyers.

M Do you want me to help you?

W No, I can do it by myself.

M All right. I'll clean up the booth in the meantime.

W Okay. Thanks, Wilson. See you later.

동아리 부스를 준비하는 상황에서 홍보 전단을 인쇄하고 온 여자가 혼자서 전단을 배부하러 가겠다고 하자 그러는 동안 남자는 부스를 청소하겠다고 말하고 있어요.

유형 빈출 표현

23학년도 수능_ I'll do it now. 지금 할게요.

22학년도 9모_ I'll take care of it when they arrive. 그것들이 도착하면 제가 그것을 처리할게요.

23학년도 6모_ I'll put the posters up around the school and on social media as well.
내가 학교 주변과 소셜 미디어에도 포스터를 게시할게.

22학년도 수특_ Then could you pick out old books we don't need any more?
그럼 더 이상 필요 없는 헌책들을 골라 줄래요?

21학년도 수특_ Pam, sorry but can you do that for me? Pam, 미안하지만 날 위해 그걸 해 줄 수 있을까?

01
▶ 242019-0030

대화를 듣고, 여자가 할 일로 가장 적절한 것을 고르시오.

① 구직 면접 연습하기
② 지원서 양식 다운받기
③ 남자에게 에세이 보내기
④ 남자의 누나에게 전화하기
⑤ 인턴을 뽑는 회사 찾아보기

02
▶ 242019-0031

대화를 듣고, 여자가 남자에게 부탁한 일로 가장 적절한 것을 고르시오.

① 판매 부스 설치하기
② 입지 않는 옷 버리기
③ 벼룩시장 판매자 등록하기
④ 가게에서 비닐봉지 사 오기
⑤ 벼룩시장에서 물건 구입하기

03   수능 대비력 UP
▶ 242019-0032

대화를 듣고, 남자가 할 일로 가장 적절한 것을 고르시오.

① 이메일 확인하기
② 단어 카드 만들기
③ 말하기 연습 녹화하기
④ 말하기 대본 수정하기
⑤ 말하기 대회 신청하기

04   수능특강 PICK
▶ 242019-0033

대화를 듣고, 여자가 할 일로 가장 적절한 것을 고르시오.

① 기차표 구입하기
② 마이크 확인하기
③ 노트북 가져오기
④ 음료수 사러 가기
⑤ 발표 자료 수정하기

05   수능특강 PICK
▶ 242019-0034

대화를 듣고, 여자가 남자에게 부탁한 일로 가장 적절한 것을 고르시오.

① 인터뷰 질문 만들기
② 동아리 홍보 영상 올리기
③ 동아리 회의 자료 작성하기
④ 동아리 회원들에게 연락하기
⑤ 교실에 가서 동아리 홍보하기

06   수능특강 PICK
▶ 242019-0035

대화를 듣고, 남자가 할 일로 가장 적절한 것을 고르시오.

① 레몬 씻기
② 레몬 썰기
③ 설탕 사 오기
④ 유리병 끓이는 것 돕기
⑤ 온라인으로 설탕 주문하기

수능에서는
이렇게!
· 대화를 듣고 구매자가 지불해야 하는 금액을 파악하는 유형이에요.
· 대화문은 주로 상점에서 물건을 사거나 온라인에서 주문하는 상황의 형태로 제시돼요.

해결전략은
이것!
· 구매자가 어떤 물건을 몇 개씩 사려고 하는지를 우선 파악해야 해요.
· 대화의 후반부에 쿠폰이나 할인 조건 등이 등장하는 경우가 많기 때문에 메모를 하면서 빠르게 계산을 해야 한다는 것도 기억하세요.

수능유형 체험

▶242019-0036

대화를 듣고, 여자가 지불할 금액을 고르시오.

① $8

② $9

③ $10

④ $12

⑤ $15

발문과 두 사람의 첫 번째 대화를 통해 여자가 남자로부터 베이글을 구매하려는 상황임을 알수 있어요.

W Hi there, can I get some bagels to go?

M Of course. What can I get you?

W Are all the bagels the same price?

M Well, plain bagels are $2 each, and all the other flavors are $2.50.

W I see. Then let me have two plain bagels and two blueberry bagels, please.

M All right. So you'd like a total of four bagels, right?

W That's right. Also, I'd like to get some juice to go with the bagels. Do you have orange juice?

M Yes. It's $3 a bottle. How many would you like?

W I'll take two. That'll be all. Here's my credit card.

M Thank you. Please give me a moment.

여자는 개당 2달러인 일반 베이글 2개와 개당 2달러 50센트인 블루베리 베이글 두 개를 사면서 한 병에 3달러인 오렌지주스도 두 병 사겠다고 말하고 있어요.

◎ **유형 빈출 표현**

23학년도 수능_ It's $5 for a pack of vegetable sticks and $10 for a pack of sliced fruits.
야채 스틱 한 팩에 5달러, 얇게 썬 과일 한 팩에 10달러입니다.

23학년도 수능_ And I heard you're offering a 10% discount as an autumn promotional event.
그리고 가을 홍보 행사로 10퍼센트 할인해 주신다고 들었습니다.

23학년도 수능_ Here's my credit card. 여기 제 신용 카드가 있습니다.

23학년도 9모_ Can I get the 10% resident discount off the total price?
합계 금액에서 10%의 거주자 할인을 받을 수 있습니까?

22학년도 수특_ This one's on sale for $10. 이것은 10달러에 할인 판매 중이에요.

01
▶242019-0037

대화를 듣고, 여자가 지불할 금액을 고르시오.

① $40
② $50
③ $60
④ $80
⑤ $90

04 수능완성 **PICK**
▶242019-0040

대화를 듣고, 남자가 지불할 금액을 고르시오.

① $75
② $80
③ $85
④ $90
⑤ $95

02
▶242019-0038

대화를 듣고, 남자가 지불할 금액을 고르시오.

① $80
② $120
③ $160
④ $180
⑤ $220

05 수능특강 **PICK**
▶242019-0041

대화를 듣고, 여자가 지불할 금액을 고르시오.

① $54
② $66
③ $75
④ $99
⑤ $120

03 수능 대비력 **UP**
▶242019-0039

대화를 듣고, 여자가 지불할 금액을 고르시오.

① $62
② $64
③ $90
④ $92
⑤ $94

06 수능특강 **PICK**
▶242019-0042

대화를 듣고, 남자가 지불할 금액을 고르시오.

① $110
② $114
③ $120
④ $159
⑤ $165

수능에서는
이렇게!
- 대화를 듣고 여자[남자]가 어떤 행동을 하거나 하지 않은 이유를 파악하는 유형이에요.
- 실생활과 관련된 소재가 주로 출제되고 있으므로 상황을 가능한 한 구체적으로 파악하는 것이 중요해요.

해결전략은
이것!
- 발문에서 누구의 말에 초점을 맞춰야 하는지를 유념해야 해요.
- 대화에서 제시되는 여러 정보 중에서 주요한 이유에 해당하는 정보를 정확히 찾아야 해요.
- 대화 후반부에 정답과 관련된 단서가 나오는 경우가 많다는 것도 알아두세요.

수능유형 체험

▶ 242019-0043

대화를 듣고, 남자가 바이올린 수업에 갈 수 <u>없는</u> 이유를 고르시오.

① 손을 다쳐서
② 과제를 해야 해서
③ 선생님이 몸이 아파서
④ 봉사 활동에 참여해야 해서
⑤ 친구 생일 파티에 가야 해서

선택지의 내용을 먼저 살펴보고 바이올린 수업에 갈 수 없는 여러 가지 이유를 확인하세요.

W Henry, are you done with your homework?
M Yes, Mom. It was pretty easy.
W That's good. Don't forget you have your violin lesson this evening.
M Oh, I'm afraid I won't be able to go to it.
W Why's that? Does your hand still hurt from falling yesterday?
M No, it's fine.
W Then, why can't you go to your lesson?
M Actually, my friend John's birthday party is this evening.
W Oh, how come you never mentioned that to me!
M Sorry, Mom. I was so busy with school and volunteer work all week.
W I understand. Then I'll contact your violin teacher to let him know you won't be going.

여자가 남자와 대화를 주고받는 과정에서 남자가 과제도 다 했고, 손도 아프지 않지만, 바이올린 수업에 갈 수 없는 이유는 친구 생일 파티에 가야 하기 때문이라고 밝히고 있어요.

◎ **유형 빈출 표현**

23학년도 수능_ But I can't come to the festival. 그런데 난 그 페스티벌에 갈 수 없어.

22학년도 수능_ Actually, I'm on my way to volunteer at the school library.
사실은 내가 학교 도서관에 자원봉사하러 가는 길이라서.

21학년도 수능_ We usually have to walk a bit to get to the campsite.
우리가 보통 캠핑장에 가려면 조금 걸어야만 하거든.

20학년도 수완_ But I think the camp is more important to me. 하지만 나는 캠프가 내게 더 중요하다고 생각해.

21학년도 수특_ The problem is I have to leave before the contest begins.
문제는 내가 대회가 시작되기 전에 떠나야 한다는 거야.

01
▶242019-0044

대화를 듣고, 여자가 요리 잡지 구독을 중단한 이유를 고르시오.

① 음식을 자주 배달시켜서
② 채식 위주의 내용이어서
③ 잡지 가격이 인상되어서
④ 온라인을 더 많이 활용해서
⑤ 좋은 조리법이 실리지 않아서

02
▶242019-0045

대화를 듣고, 여자가 스웨터를 반품하지 <u>못한</u> 이유를 고르시오.

① 할인 품목이어서
② 가격표를 떼어서
③ 이미 입어 버려서
④ 30일 기한이 지나서
⑤ 영수증을 잃어버려서

03 수능 대비력 **UP**
▶242019-0046

대화를 듣고, 여자가 파티 장소를 바꾸려는 이유를 고르시오.

① 주변 경관이 좋지 않아서
② 식당 예약이 중복되어서
③ 회사에서 거리가 멀어서
④ 회사 일정이 변경되어서
⑤ 참석자가 너무 많아져서

04 수능특강 **PICK**
▶242019-0047

대화를 듣고, 남자가 자동차를 구입하려는 이유를 고르시오.

① 캠핑용 차가 필요해서
② 장거리 통근을 해야 해서
③ 아들이 사 달라고 요청해서
④ 타고 다니던 차가 고장이 나서
⑤ 사업상 많은 장비를 싣고 다녀야 해서

05 수능특강 **PICK**
▶242019-0048

대화를 듣고, 남자가 트랙 달리기를 하지 <u>못한</u> 이유를 고르시오.

① 트랙이 보수 중이어서
② 역사 공부하느라 바빠서
③ 동영상을 편집해야 해서
④ 식사 준비를 도와야 해서
⑤ 학습 계획표를 짜야 해서

06 수능완성 **PICK**
▶242019-0049

대화를 듣고, 남자가 워크숍에 끝까지 참석할 수 <u>없는</u> 이유를 고르시오.

① 치과 예약이 있어서
② 도서관에 들러야 해서
③ 친척 병문안을 가야 해서
④ 밀린 업무가 너무 많아서
⑤ 자녀를 태우러 가야 해서

수능유형 체험

▶ 242019-0050

대화를 듣고, Global Habitat Trip에 관해 언급되지 <u>않은</u> 것을 고르시오.

① 목적
② 방문 국가
③ 활동
④ 경비
⑤ 체류 기간

W Max. Do you have any plans for this summer?

M I'm going to attend the "Global Habitat Trip" this summer.

W What's that?

M It's a house-building program. Its goal is to assist poor people in other countries.

W That's cool. Which country are you going to?

M I'm going to Mongolia.

W What exactly will you do there?

M Well, I'll be mainly helping out with repairing houses and bridges, and digging wells for water.

W That's wonderful! How long will you be there?

M I'll be there exactly a month. I can't wait!

W I'm looking forward to hearing about it.

발문과 선택지를 먼저 보고 소재와 관련하여 언급될 수 있는 사항들을 확인하세요. 그리고 대화의 흐름대로 선택지를 보며 세부 정보를 파악해 보세요.

남자와 여자가 대화를 주고받는 과정에서 목적(to assist poor people), 국가(Mongolia), 활동(repairing houses and bridges, and digging wells for water), 기간(exactly a month)을 말하고 있어요.

◎ 유형 빈출 표현

23학년도 수능_ How long will it take to shoot the photos? 사진을 찍는 데 얼마나 걸릴까요?

22학년도 수능_ So, to register, I should send an email to the address on the flyer.
그래서 등록하려면 전단지에 적힌 주소로 이메일을 보내야 해요.

21학년도 수능_ It's located in Greenfalls, Hillside. 그것은 Hillside의 Greenfalls에 위치해 있어요.

20학년도 수완_ What exactly does the foundation do? 재단이 하는 일이 정확하게 무엇인가요?

21학년도 수특_ Could you tell me about the programs available?
이용할 수 있는 프로그램에 관해 말씀해 주실 수 있나요?

01
▶242019-0051

대화를 듣고, Super Computing Youth Camp에 관해 언급되지 않은 것을 고르시오.

① 팀 인원수
② 참가 팀 수
③ 신청 방법
④ 개최 기간
⑤ 지역 예선 장소

02
▶242019-0052

대화를 듣고, Art Appreciation Program에 관해 언급되지 않은 것을 고르시오.

① 행사 장소
② 행사 내용
③ 신청 자격
④ 신청 마감일
⑤ 신청 방법

03 수능 대비력 UP
▶242019-0053

대화를 듣고, Student Short Video Contest에 관해 언급되지 않은 것을 고르시오.

① 제출 마감일
② 제출 자료
③ 상품
④ 심사 기준
⑤ 심사 위원

04 수능특강 PICK
▶242019-0054

대화를 듣고, Animals-in-Need Marathon에 관해 언급되지 않은 것을 고르시오.

① 개최 목적
② 참가비
③ 주관 단체
④ 참가 등록 마감일
⑤ 마라톤 코스

05 수능특강 PICK
▶242019-0055

대화를 듣고, Northeast Spring Fashion Show에 관해 언급되지 않은 것을 고르시오.

① 개최일
② 개최 장소
③ 참가국
④ 주제
⑤ 입장료

06 수능완성 PICK
▶242019-0056

대화를 듣고, Survival Camp에 관해 언급되지 않은 것을 고르시오.

① 기간
② 장소
③ 모집 인원
④ 활동
⑤ 참가 대상

수능유형 체험

▶ 242019-0057

Moonlight Sonata Concert에 관한 다음 내용을 듣고, 일치하지 <u>않는</u> 것을 고르시오.

① 일 년에 한 번 개최된다.
② 11월 23일 오후 7시에 열릴 것이다.
③ 베토벤의 작품을 연주할 것이다.
④ 좌석은 300명에게 한정되어 있다.
⑤ 공연은 세 시간 동안 진행된다.

W   Hello, listeners and all classical music lovers! The Moonlight Sonata Concert is finally coming to our town. This classical music concert is held annually. This year it's November 23rd at 7:00 p.m., so mark your calendars! This year's concert is at Steinway and will feature musicians performing the great works of Beethoven. Their amazing performance will surely be a delight to your ears. Seating is limited to only 300 people, so don't miss your chance to attend this extraordinary two-hour musical experience. Get your tickets today!

발문과 선택지를 먼저 보고 어떤 성격의 행사에 대한 담화일지 예측하세요. 그리고 언급 순서에 따라 선택지를 확인하세요.

여자가 청취자와 클래식 음악 애호가들에게 Moonlight Sonata Concert를 홍보하면서 개최 주기(annually), 일시(November 23rd at 7:00 p.m.), 레퍼토리(great works of Beethoven), 좌석 수(seating), 공연 시간(two-hour musical experience) 등 세부적인 관련 정보를 직접적으로 말하고 있어요.

◎ 유형 빈출 표현

23학년도 수능_ I'm here to announce that the expo will run for three days starting on March 17th, 2023.
2023년 3월 17일부터 3일간 엑스포가 진행됨을 알려 드리고자 합니다.

22학년도 수능_ We'll also give out a children's science magazine for free.
우리는 또한 어린이 과학 잡지를 무료로 나눠줄 것입니다.

21학년도 수능_ It'll be broadcast live on our website starting from 9 a.m.
그것은 오전 9시부터 저희 웹사이트를 통해 생중계됩니다.

20학년도 수완_ Over the course of the semester, we'll be studying the ancient civilizations of China.
한 학기 과정 동안, 우리는 중국의 고대 문명을 공부할 것입니다.

21학년도 수특_ Those who are invited will be given a poster at the theater.
초대받은 분들은 극장에서 포스터를 받게 될 것입니다.

01
▶ 242019-0058

영화 Super Rabbit Princess에 관한 다음 내용을 듣고, 일치하지 <u>않는</u> 것을 고르시오.

① 5월 24일에 개봉한다.
② 판타지 코미디 영화이다.
③ 주인공이 춤추는 장면이 나온다.
④ 유명한 가수가 주인공 목소리로 출연한다.
⑤ 이번 주 금요일까지 예매하면 무료 포스터를 받는다.

02
▶ 242019-0059

Lantern Festival에 관한 다음 내용을 듣고, 일치하지 <u>않는</u> 것을 고르시오.

① 중국 전통문화를 기리는 행사이다.
② 1월 13일부터 3일 동안 열린다.
③ 거리마다 깃털로 만든 등으로 장식될 것이다.
④ 퍼즐 풀이에 참여할 수 있다.
⑤ 중국 음식이 판매될 것이다.

03 수능 대비력 UP
▶ 242019-0060

Clean-up Campaign에 관한 다음 내용을 듣고, 일치하지 <u>않는</u> 것을 고르시오.

① 다음 주 토요일 오후에 개최된다.
② 30분 동안 공원을 살펴볼 것이다.
③ 참가자들에게 장갑을 지급할 것이다.
④ 쓰레기 유형별로 지정된 봉투나 용기를 사용한다.
⑤ 공원 내 지정된 장소에 쓰레기를 모아야 한다.

04 수능특강 PICK
▶ 242019-0061

Ashley's Tea Class에 관한 다음 내용을 듣고, 일치하지 <u>않</u>는 것을 고르시오.

① Rosehill 호텔에서 열린다.
② 이번 달 수업은 3월 20일에 열릴 것이다.
③ 이번 달에는 꽃차를 선보일 것이다.
④ 수강생들은 네 가지 다른 종류의 차를 맛보게 된다.
⑤ 수강 인원은 20명으로 한정된다.

05 수능특강 PICK
▶ 242019-0062

Urban Design Competition에 관한 다음 내용을 듣고, 일치하지 <u>않는</u> 것을 고르시오.

① 등록하려면 온라인으로 제안서를 제출해야 한다.
② 등록 마감일은 9월 10일이다.
③ 네 팀이 결선에 진출할 것이다.
④ 결선 진출 팀이 제안서를 발표한 날 우승팀이 공지될 것이다.
⑤ 우승 팀은 5백 달러의 상금을 받는다.

06 수능완성 PICK
▶ 242019-0063

Early Childhood Fair에 관한 다음 내용을 듣고, 일치하지 <u>않는</u> 것을 고르시오.

① 아동 건강과 발달에 관한 정보를 제공한다.
② 취학 전 아동을 위한 프로그램에 등록할 수 있다.
③ 먼저 도착한 50명의 아동은 무료 선물을 받는다.
④ 5시간 동안 진행된다.
⑤ 참가비는 무료이다.

수능유형 체험

▶ 242019-0064

다음 표를 보면서 대화를 듣고, 여자가 구매할 휴지통을 고르시오.

Office Wastebaskets

	Model	Price	Material	Capacity (Gallons)	Lid
①	A	$7	Plastic	8	×
②	B	$12	Metal	3	○
③	C	$15	Ceramic	7	×
④	D	$17	Metal	4	×
⑤	E	$21	Metal	6	○

M Welcome to Uptown Office Essentials. How may I help you today?

W Hi, I'm looking for an office wastebasket.

M All right. These are the ones we have. What's your budget?

W I can spend up to $20.

M Okay. And what about the material?

W I don't like ceramic. It's heavy.

M I see. How about the capacity? Are you looking for a certain size?

W Well, it needs to fit under my desk. So I think it should be under 5 gallons.

M Got it. Lastly, do you want a wastebasket with a lid?

W Yes, I prefer that.

M Then this is the one for you.

W Thank you. I'll take it.

표를 먼저 훑어보면 여자가 휴지통을 구매할 것이고, 기준 항목은 가격, 재료, 용량, 뚜껑임을 예측할 수 있어요.

여자는 가격이 20달러까지이고 도자기로 된 것이 아니면서 용량은 5갤런보다 작고 뚜껑이 있는 모델을 골랐어요. 표에 제시된 순서대로 언급되었으므로 대화를 따라가면서 20달러보다 비싼 모델, 도자기로 된 모델, 용량이 5갤런보다 큰 모델, 뚜껑이 없는 모델을 지워 나가야 해요. 여자가 도자기로 된 모델을 선호하지 않는다고 말했으므로 도자기를 선택에서 제외해야 함에 유의하세요.

◎ 유형 빈출 표현

22학년도 수능_ Should we choose a study room with a projector? 프로젝터가 있는 스터디 룸을 선택해야 할까?

23학년도 수능_ I want a case that's at least 50 inches long. 저는 적어도 50인치 길이의 케이스를 원합니다.

20학년도 수완_ I prefer not to spend more than $400. 400달러 넘게는 쓰고 싶지 않아요.

23학년도 수특_ It's for children aged 10 and up. Jimmy is only 8.
그것은 열 살 이상 어린이를 위한 거예요. Jimmy는 겨우 여덟 살이에요.

23학년도 수특_ Then you should consider choosing either plastic or carbon fiber.
그렇다면 플라스틱이나 탄소 섬유 중 하나를 선택하는 것을 고려하셔야 합니다.

01

▷242019-0065

다음 표를 보면서 대화를 듣고, 두 사람이 주문할 천장 선풍기를 고르시오.

Ceiling Fans

	Model	Width (Inches)	Price	Material	Remote Control
①	A	36	$98	Plastic	×
②	B	40	$121	Wooden	×
③	C	45	$188	Metal	×
④	D	50	$156	Wooden	○
⑤	E	55	$210	Plastic	○

02

▷242019-0066

다음 표를 보면서 대화를 듣고, 남자가 구매할 아트 프린트를 고르시오.

Art Prints for Sale

	Model	Price	Size	Subject Matter	Frame
①	A	$48	Medium	Landscape	×
②	B	$55	Small	Animal	○
③	C	$75	Medium	Still Life	○
④	D	$90	Large	Still Life	×
⑤	E	$115	Large	Animal	○

03 수능 대비력 UP

▷242019-0067

다음 표를 보면서 대화를 듣고, 여자가 예약할 파티 패키지를 고르시오.

Happy Playzone Party Packages

	Package	Duration (Hours)	Number of Kids	Arcade Game Credits	Snacks
①	A	1.5	8	40	×
②	B	2	8	60	○
③	C	2	12	80	×
④	D	3	12	120	×
⑤	E	3	16	140	○

04 수능특강 PICK

▷242019-0068

다음 표를 보면서 대화를 듣고, 두 사람이 아들을 데리고 갈 프로그램을 고르시오.

Georgia Zoo Programs

	Program	Age	Days Offered	Time
①	Penguin Beach Tour	5 years & older	Tue. / Wed. / Thu.	2:00 p.m.
②	Elephant Encounter	5 years & older	Sat. / Sun.	1:15 p.m.
③	Rhino Encounter	7 years & older	Sat.	9:30 a.m.
④	Red Panda Tour	7 years & older	Fri. / Sat.	9:00 a.m.
⑤	Galapagos Tortoise Feed and Encounter	10 years & older	Thu. / Fri. / Sat.	10:15 a.m.

05 수능완성 PICK

▷242019-0069

다음 표를 보면서 대화를 듣고, 두 사람이 구입할 휴대용 바비큐 그릴을 고르시오.

Portable Barbecue Grills

	Model	Price	Cooking Surface (square inches)	Fuel Type	Grate Material
①	A	$29	100	Gas	Aluminum
②	B	$46	150	Gas	Aluminum
③	C	$67	150	Gas	Steel
④	D	$85	180	Charcoal	Aluminum
⑤	E	$116	200	Charcoal	Steel

06 수능특강 PICK

▷242019-0070

다음 표를 보면서 대화를 듣고, 여자가 주문할 크레용 세트를 고르시오.

Animal Character Crayon Sets

		Number of Crayons	Animal Character	Price	Washable
①	A	12	Koala	$8	×
②	B	24	Bear	$12	○
③	C	24	Puppy	$14	○
④	D	32	Rabbit	$17	×
⑤	E	32	Kitten	$22	○

수능에서는 이렇게!
• 짧은 대화를 듣고, 마지막 말에 대한 적절한 응답을 고르는 유형이에요.
• 대화의 마지막 말은 의문문이 될 수도 있고, 평서문이 될 수도 있어요.

해결전략은 이것!
• 대화의 전체적인 흐름을 파악해야 해요.
• 대화의 마지막 말을 집중해서 듣고 어떤 응답이 필요한지 생각해야 해요.

수능유형 체험

▶242019-0071

대화를 듣고, 남자의 마지막 말에 대한 여자의 응답으로 가장 적절한 것을 고르시오.

① Don't worry. Brainstorm before you start writing.
② That's right. We succeeded due to our teamwork.
③ Awesome! You seem to have chosen a great topic.
④ Good idea. Let's meet up at the library after school.
⑤ Never mind. I already finished the essay assignment.

M Cassidy, have you finished the essay assignment yet?
W No, Daniel. I haven't even started. I'm struggling to think of a good topic.
M Me, too. Sometimes it helps to brainstorm ideas with someone else. How about working on it together?
W Good idea. Let's meet up at the library after school.

대화의 전체적인 흐름상 에세이 과제에 대해 이야기하고 있어요.

남자가 마지막 말에서 에세이 과제 작업을 같이 하는 게 어떤지 제안하고 있으므로, 이에 대한 여자의 응답으로 가장 적절한 것은 남자의 제안에 대해 찬성하고 같이 만날 장소를 정하는 답변이에요.

◎ **유형 빈출 표현**

23학년도 수능_ Then why don't we join him?
그럼 우리가 그와 같이 가는 게 어때요?

22학년도 수능_ How long do you think it'll take?
얼마나 걸릴 것 같은가요?

23학년도 9모_ I'll be available any day after next Monday.
저는 다음 주 월요일 이후에는 언제든지 가능합니다.

23학년도 수특_ I wonder how I can learn to cook like you.
어떻게 하면 너처럼 요리를 배울 수 있을지 궁금하네.

23학년도 수특_ Actually, I don't think we'll have enough pamphlets for tomorrow.
실은 내일 쓸 팸플릿이 충분하지 않을 거라고 생각해요.

정답과 해설 **38**쪽

01
▶ 242019-0072

대화를 듣고, 여자의 마지막 말에 대한 남자의 응답으로 가장 적절한 것을 고르시오.

① Sorry. I recommend that you revise it a little.
② Good choice. I'd be glad to lend you the book.
③ You're right. The book was a bit disappointing.
④ Not sure. I haven't finished writing the ending yet.
⑤ I really liked it. It was a great way to finish the story.

02
▶ 242019-0073

대화를 듣고, 남자의 마지막 말에 대한 여자의 응답으로 가장 적절한 것을 고르시오.

① Great idea. I'll reserve a table at a restaurant.
② Okay. Let's find another movie to watch instead.
③ I don't think so. The movie was absolutely fantastic.
④ I agree. It's better to watch the movie and then eat.
⑤ No way. I'm not skipping dinner to see an earlier show.

03 수능 대비력 UP
▶ 242019-0074

대화를 듣고, 여자의 마지막 말에 대한 남자의 응답으로 가장 적절한 것을 고르시오.

① I know of a few. I'll send you the links to them.
② Not really. I'm surprised you prefer taking in-person classes.
③ Thanks. I'll take a look and see which one suits me best.
④ Absolutely. I'll try to take a class at the local language school.
⑤ No. Your learning style doesn't affect how you learn a language.

04 수능완성 PICK
▶ 242019-0075

대화를 듣고, 남자의 마지막 말에 대한 여자의 응답으로 가장 적절한 것을 고르시오.

① I'll drive you home after choir practice.
② You did your best to win the competition.
③ Okay. I'll knock on your door at six o'clock.
④ Thanks for inviting me to the choir competition.
⑤ Working out early in the morning is good for you.

05 수능특강 PICK
▶ 242019-0076

대화를 듣고, 여자의 마지막 말에 대한 남자의 응답으로 가장 적절한 것을 고르시오.

① Then I'll ask my dad if the hotel is hiring.
② You can join me when my dad teaches me.
③ Well, I have never cooked anything myself.
④ I don't think you should get a job at a hotel.
⑤ My dad asks me to cook on special occasions.

06 수능특강 PICK
▶ 242019-0077

대화를 듣고, 남자의 마지막 말에 대한 여자의 응답으로 가장 적절한 것을 고르시오.

① Actually, I already booked our train tickets.
② I'd love to, but I can't go to your parents' with you.
③ Sure, I'll check a website with cheap flights I know of.
④ Yes, I'll book my parents' flight tickets online right now.
⑤ Well, I'm not sure if there are any train tickets available on their website.

수능유형 체험

▶ 242019-0078

대화를 듣고, 남자의 마지막 말에 대한 여자의 응답으로 가장 적절한 것을 고르시오.

Woman: _____

① No worries. I'm sure I can bake it on my own.
② Okay. Let's look for the recipe book in the attic.
③ Trust me. You know I'm a really good cook, too.
④ Thanks. I can't wait to bring back grandma's pie.
⑤ Sorry. I don't really feel like cooking a pie right now.

W Dad, look what I found in the attic!

M What is it?

W It's grandma's old recipe book. It has all of her secret recipes.

M Oh, yeah. She used to cook amazing meals from that book.

W Here's her apple pie recipe. I heard it was so delicious. I wish I could recreate it.

M You should give it a try. It would be a meaningful experience.

W Well, I'm afraid I'd mess it up. I'm not confident in my cooking skills.

M Don't worry. I'm sure you'll do a fine job if you just follow the recipe.

W Maybe, but can you help me out?

M Sure! Let's make it together this weekend. I'll help you shop for the ingredients, too.

W Thanks. I can't wait to bring back grandma's pie.

선택지를 먼저 훑어보면 요리에 관한 대화가 오고 갈 것임을 예측할 수 있어요.

대화의 흐름상 여자는 다락방에서 할머니의 요리법 책을 찾아내고, 남자에게 할머니의 사과파이를 다시 만들어 보고 싶지만 요리에 자신이 없다고 말해요. 남자가 마지막 말에서 이번 주말에 함께 만들어 보자고 하고 재료 구입도 도와주겠다고 제안하고 있으므로, 이에 대한 여자의 응답으로 가장 적절한 것은 제안에 감사하고 기대를 표현하는 답변이에요.

🎯 유형 빈출 표현

23학년도 수능_ That'd be great. Peter might come as well if his favorite grandpa invites him.
그러면 좋을 거예요. Peter 또한 자기가 가장 좋아하는 할아버지가 초대하면 올 수도 있어요.

23학년도 9모_ Then, what about the 8 p.m. class? 그럼, 오후 8시 수업은 어떻습니까?

23학년도 9모_ I think it would be good if you told her that you didn't mean to miss it.
그녀에게 그걸 놓칠 생각은 없었다고 말해 주면 좋을 것 같아요.

23학년도 수특_ How about looking for an organization that supports a good cause you're interested in?
네가 관심이 있는 좋은 목적을 지지하는 단체를 찾아보는 게 어때?

01
▶242019-0079

대화를 듣고, 여자의 마지막 말에 대한 남자의 응답으로 가장 적절한 것을 고르시오.

Man: _____

① It's no wonder. The food there is amazing.

② Okay. Let's head to the bookstore first then.

③ Maybe not. There's no cafe near the restaurant.

④ Too bad. I really wanted to try the new restaurant.

⑤ No problem. I'll find another restaurant that's open.

02
▶242019-0080

대화를 듣고, 남자의 마지막 말에 대한 여자의 응답으로 가장 적절한 것을 고르시오.

Woman: _____

① Yes. We need to watch more videos to get better ideas.

② Exactly. That way, we can include a variety of content.

③ That's right. It was thoughtful of you to share the video online.

④ I heard what you said. Your idea shined through in the debate.

⑤ Not really. Let's not accept suggestions from the other members.

03 수능 대비력 UP
▶242019-0081

대화를 듣고, 여자의 마지막 말에 대한 남자의 응답으로 가장 적절한 것을 고르시오.

Man: _____

① I don't think so. I prefer taking a walk every day.

② Good luck. I hope your family will enjoy the walk.

③ Don't worry. I'll try my best to get used to the route.

④ Sorry. I need to focus on my family rather than work.

⑤ You're right. It'll definitely help us reconnect as a family.

04 수능특강 PICK
▶242019-0082

대화를 듣고, 남자의 마지막 말에 대한 여자의 응답으로 가장 적절한 것을 고르시오.

Woman: _____

① Of course. I'll call and ask if the book is there.

② Yes, I do. We can order the book over the phone.

③ I'm afraid I don't. I'll ask for their number when they move in.

④ No, I don't. I'm sure the delivery driver knows the address though.

⑤ Sure. They called just now and said they'd come pick up the book.

05 수능완성 PICK
▶242019-0083

대화를 듣고, 여자의 마지막 말에 대한 남자의 응답으로 가장 적절한 것을 고르시오.

Man: _____

① Yes. This is why he does not eat vegetables.

② Sorry. I only have a small vegetable garden.

③ Sure. You can grow vegetables in my backyard.

④ You need gardening tools if you're going to do it.

⑤ Okay. I'll let you know if my son starts eating vegetables.

06 수능특강 PICK
▶242019-0084

대화를 듣고, 남자의 마지막 말에 대한 여자의 응답으로 가장 적절한 것을 고르시오.

Woman: _____

① That was a meaningful event for animal rights.

② You can raise money to make the oceans cleaner.

③ Then, try to find some products that help animals.

④ I'm so glad to know you've helped those organizations.

⑤ Your research was helpful for my social studies project.

수능에서는 이렇게!
- 상황에 대한 설명을 듣고, 그 상황에서 특정 인물이 할 말을 고르는 유형이에요.
- 대화가 아닌 담화로 등장인물이 처한 상황을 자세히 설명해 줘요.

해결전략은 이것!
- 등장인물 사이의 관계와 그들이 처한 상황을 파악해야 해요.
- 마지막 부분에서 특정 인물이 하고 싶어 하는 말을 설명해 주므로 그 부분을 잘 들어야 해요.

수능유형 체험

▶ 242019-0085

다음 상황 설명을 듣고, Ellie가 학생들에게 할 말로 가장 적절한 것을 고르시오.

Ellie: _____

① Would you please turn off your mobile devices?
② I kindly ask that everyone turn their cameras on.
③ Could everyone increase their mic volume a little bit?
④ Please ensure that you have a stable internet connection.
⑤ I'd like to request that all of you observe my body language.

등장인물 Ellie는 의사소통에 관한 온라인 과정을 가르치고, 그 과정을 듣는 학생들이 있음을 파악할 수 있어요.

W Ellie is teaching an online course on communication. For today's lesson, she's teaching the importance of body language in communication. As she starts the lesson, she notices that some students have their cameras turned off. One of the main activities she has planned focuses on the students observing and interpreting each other's body language. In order to do this activity, they need to be able to see each other on the screen. So Ellie wants to respectfully request the students turn on their cameras. In this situation, what would Ellie most likely say to the students?

Ellie I kindly ask that everyone turn their cameras on.

마지막 부분에서 Ellie가 학생들에게 카메라를 켜 달라고 정중히 요청하고 싶다고 했으므로 이에 해당하는 답을 찾아야 해요.

◎ **유형 빈출 표현**

23학년도 수능_ So Katie wants to suggest to Jacob that next time he should plan more than one activity.
그래서 Katie는 Jacob에게 다음번에는 한 가지 이상의 활동을 계획해야 한다고 제안하고 싶어 합니다.

22학년도 수능_ Jason is a sculptor and Sarah is the head of a local library.
Jason은 조각가이고 Sarah는 지역 도서관장입니다.

23학년도 6모_ So, Tom wants to tell Alice that she needs to make use of negative reviews to improve her business.
그래서 Tom은 Alice에게 그녀의 사업을 개선하기 위해 부정적인 리뷰를 활용해야 한다고 말하고 싶어 합니다.

23학년도 수특_ William has been traveling around Seoul the past week, and today he flies back home.
William은 지난주 서울 여기저기를 여행했고, 오늘 그는 비행기를 타고 집으로 돌아갑니다.

23학년도 수특_ In this situation, what would Ms. White most likely say to the camper?
이런 상황에서 White 씨는 야영객에게 뭐라고 말하겠습니까?

수능유형 연습

01
▶ 242019-0086

다음 상황 설명을 듣고, Jason이 Amy에게 할 말로 가장 적절한 것을 고르시오.

Jason: _____

① Each child has their own learning speed.
② Solving math problems every day is important.
③ You should consider talking to his math teacher.
④ Focus on building a positive attitude toward math.
⑤ Setting clear and achievable goals is important for academic success.

02
▶ 242019-0087

다음 상황 설명을 듣고, Sarah가 Eric에게 할 말로 가장 적절한 것을 고르시오.

Sarah: _____

① I'm sure that there will be another chance.
② You're already the star player on the team.
③ You should accept the offer and join the team.
④ Keep practicing and maybe they'll ask you to join.
⑤ It would be better to just stay on your current team.

03 수능 대비력 UP
▶ 242019-0088

다음 상황 설명을 듣고, Sam이 Audrey에게 할 말로 가장 적절한 것을 고르시오.

Sam: _____

① How about meeting up more often this week?
② Let's divide the tasks and do them separately.
③ I think we should conduct more in-depth research.
④ Why don't we narrow our topic before doing the research?
⑤ There's plenty of time left to prepare for the presentation.

04 수능특강 PICK
▶ 242019-0089

다음 상황 설명을 듣고, Ms. White가 야영객에게 할 말로 가장 적절한 것을 고르시오.

Ms. White: _____

① Well, you should look for a better place to camp.
② Sorry, but you're not allowed to sleep in the park.
③ Excuse me, making a fire in the park is prohibited.
④ Actually, there's a limit to the number of daily visitors.
⑤ Remember it's required for you to carry a fire extinguisher.

05 수능특강 PICK
▶ 242019-0090

다음 상황 설명을 듣고, William이 호텔 직원에게 할 말로 가장 적절한 것을 고르시오.

William: _____

① Can I possibly get a late checkout tomorrow?
② Would you recommend shopping malls nearby?
③ Is it possible to extend my stay for another day?
④ Could I store my luggage here after checking out?
⑤ Do you provide a hotel-to-airport luggage delivery service?

06 수능완성 PICK
▶ 242019-0091

다음 상황 설명을 듣고, Andy가 Jack에게 할 말로 가장 적절한 것을 고르시오.

Andy: _____

① Don't worry about your leg. Just trust yourself.
② If you don't mind, I want to run together with you.
③ It'll take quite some time before you can walk again.
④ Your leg looks okay, so you can run at normal speed.
⑤ You'd better not run until your leg has fully recovered.

수능유형 체험

▶242019-0092

[01~02] 다음을 듣고, 물음에 답하시오.

01 남자가 하는 말의 주제로 가장 적절한 것은?

① origins of various fruit names
② delicious foods made with fruits
③ benefits of eating fruit every day
④ differences between fruits and vegetables
⑤ English expressions that include fruit names

02 언급된 과일이 <u>아닌</u> 것은?

① cherries ② grapes ③ bananas ④ oranges ⑤ apples

담화 초반에 오늘은 과일 이름을 포함하는 영어 표현을 배울 것이라고 말하고, 이어서 예를 들어 설명하고 있으므로, 담화 전체의 주제를 파악할 수 있어요.

M Good morning, listeners! Welcome back to Andy's Daily English. In the last lesson, I introduced you to some English expressions with animal names. I hope you've had a chance to use them. Today, I'm going to do the same thing except with fruit names. The first one is "cherry-pick." This expression means to select the best option. It may have originated from people carefully choosing ripe cherries. Next, we have "sour grapes." This popular expression comes from one of Aesop's fables. It means wanting something really badly that you can't have. Let's move on to "go bananas." This phrase can be used when you're feeling angry. The last expression is "the apple of my eye." It's used to represent something or someone that you value more than anything or anyone else. In fact, you are all the apples of my eye, my dear listeners. English expressions including fruit names are really fun, aren't they? Want to learn more fun and informative expressions? Then see you next time!

화자가 과일 이름을 포함하는 영어 표현을 하나씩 언급하면서 설명하고 있으니, 선지에서 하나씩 지워 나가면 오렌지가 언급되지 않았음을 알 수 있어요.

◎ 유형 빈출 표현

23학년도 수능_ Today, we're going to discuss the contribution of metals to the development of civilization.
오늘, 우리는 문명 발전에 대한 금속의 기여에 관해 토론할 거예요.

23학년도 9모_ First, plants communicate to call for help. 첫째, 식물들은 도움을 요청하기 위해 의사소통을 합니다.

23학년도 수능_ In fact, eating a balanced diet with the right nutrients can benefit your hair.
사실, 적절한 영양소가 포함된 균형 잡힌 식사를 하는 것은 여러분의 모발에 도움이 될 수 있습니다.

[01~02] 다음을 듣고, 물음에 답하시오.

01

▶242019-0093

여자가 하는 말의 주제로 가장 적절한 것은?

① the origin of some traditional dances
② the benefits of learning how to dance
③ the characteristics of traditional dances
④ the most popular international dance songs
⑤ the influence of world dances on classical music

02

▶242019-0094

언급된 나라가 <u>아닌</u> 것은?

① Spain   ② France   ③ Brazil
④ Argentina   ⑤ Australia

[03~04] 다음을 듣고, 물음에 답하시오.

03

▶242019-0095

남자가 하는 말의 주제로 가장 적절한 것은?

① unique ways that reptiles survive
② reptiles' amazing interactive ability
③ reasons that people like reptiles as pets
④ responsibilities of raising reptiles as pets
⑤ common characteristics that reptiles share

04

▶242019-0096

언급된 파충류가 <u>아닌</u> 것은?

① lizards   ② turtles   ③ chameleons
④ snakes   ⑤ iguanas

[05~06] 다음을 듣고, 물음에 답하시오.

수능특강 **PICK**

05

▶242019-0097

여자가 하는 말의 주제로 가장 적절한 것은?

① eating habits for healthier teeth
② benefits of using natural toothpaste
③ natural ways to whiten teeth at home
④ reasons that bacteria grow in the mouth
⑤ foods that can cause teeth to turn yellow

06

▶242019-0098

언급된 재료가 <u>아닌</u> 것은?

① 코코넛오일   ② 베이킹 소다   ③ 사과 식초
④ 녹차   ⑤ 허브 가루

[07~08] 다음을 듣고, 물음에 답하시오.

수능특강 **PICK**

07

▶242019-0099

남자가 하는 말의 주제로 가장 적절한 것은?

① how to organize after-work schedules
② differences between work and home stress
③ some disadvantages of doing activities alone
④ what to do to meet daily expenses on a tight budget
⑤ ways of relieving work stress through rewarding oneself

08

▶242019-0100

언급된 일이 <u>아닌</u> 것은?

① 혼자 영화 보기   ② 아이스크림 사서 먹기
③ 새 옷이나 액세서리 사기   ④ 뜨거운 물에 목욕하기
⑤ 미용실 가기

PART II

수능실전
대비편

수능완성 **PICK** ▶ 242019-0101

01 다음을 듣고, 여자가 하는 말의 목적으로 가장 적절한 것을 고르시오.

① 야생 동물 구조 방법을 알려 주려고
② 안전한 산행을 위한 필수 장비를 소개하려고
③ 공원에서의 반려동물 산책 규칙을 공지하려고
④ 야생 동물 서식지 보호의 중요성을 강조하려고
⑤ 하이킹 시 야생 동물을 피하는 방법을 안내하려고

수능특강 **PICK** ▶ 242019-0102

02 대화를 듣고, 남자의 의견으로 가장 적절한 것을 고르시오.

① 사과는 진정한 마음으로 해야 한다.
② 상대방이 사과하면 기꺼이 받아야 한다.
③ 의견 충돌이 있는 경우 말을 자제해야 한다.
④ 우정을 회복하기 위해서는 먼저 사과해야 한다.
⑤ 상대방의 말을 경청한 후 자기 의견을 말해야 한다.

▶ 242019-0103

03 다음을 듣고, 여자가 하는 말의 요지로 가장 적절한 것을 고르시오.

① 미술 작품 활동은 매우 유익한 취미이다.
② 그림 그리기는 집중력 향상에 도움이 된다.
③ 미술 감상은 마음을 정화해 주는 이점이 있다.
④ 학교에서의 미술 감상 교육이 증대되어야 한다.
⑤ 예술품 감상을 위해서 기본적인 지식이 필요하다.

수능완성 **PICK** ▶ 242019-0104

04 대화를 듣고, 그림에서 대화의 내용과 일치하지 <u>않는</u> 것을 고르시오.

수능완성 **PICK** ▶ 242019-0105

05 대화를 듣고, 남자가 할 일로 가장 적절한 것을 고르시오.

① 음료 준비하기
② 집 안 청소하기
③ 식료품 사 오기
④ 저녁 식사 차리기
⑤ 보드게임 세트 가져오기

수능특강 **PICK** ▶ 242019-0106

06 대화를 듣고, 여자가 지불한 금액을 고르시오. [3점]

① $20 ② $36 ③ $40
④ $52 ⑤ $60

▶ 242019-0107

07 대화를 듣고, 남자가 블루투스 이어폰을 오늘 구매하지 <u>않은</u> 이유를 고르시오.

① 제품이 모두 판매되어서
② 건강 상태가 좋지 않아서
③ 제품 할인 기간이 끝나서
④ 신용 카드를 안 가져가서
⑤ 제품이 사용하기 불편해서

수능완성 **PICK** ▶ 242019-0108

08 대화를 듣고, Mexican cooking class에 관해 언급되지 <u>않은</u> 것을 고르시오.

① 요리 종류
② 수강료
③ 수업 시간
④ 수강 인원
⑤ 수업 장소

▶ 242019-0109

09 Dream Future Program에 관한 다음 내용을 듣고, 일치하지 않는 것을 고르시오.

① 15개의 특강을 포함한다.
② 이번 주 금요일까지 등록할 수 있다.
③ 5일 동안 진행될 것이다.
④ 제한 인원은 강의당 30명이다.
⑤ 강의 후에 보고서를 작성해야 한다.

▶242019-0110

10 다음 표를 보면서 대화를 듣고, 두 사람이 선택한 주차장을 고르시오.

Amsterdam Parking Lots

	Parking Lot	Walking Time and Distance to City Center	Average Rating	Refundable	Total Price (per day)
①	A	6 min (0.4 km)	★★☆☆☆ (2.5)	×	€32
②	B	7 min (0.5 km)	★★★★☆ (4.5)	×	€40
③	C	8 min (0.6 km)	★★★★☆ (4.5)	×	€38
④	D	9 min (0.7 km)	★★★★☆ (4.0)	○	€42
⑤	E	13 min (1.1 km)	★★★★☆ (4.0)	○	€22

▶242019-0111

11 대화를 듣고, 남자의 마지막 말에 대한 여자의 응답으로 가장 적절한 것을 고르시오.

① I can lend it to you if you want.
② I'm going to buy it online tomorrow.
③ How about going to another library?
④ Get the textbook at the campus bookstore.
⑤ That's why you should learn speed reading.

▶242019-0112

12 대화를 듣고, 여자의 마지막 말에 대한 남자의 응답으로 가장 적절한 것을 고르시오.

① Let's take his literature class next semester.
② When is the deadline for our literature report?
③ The new literature teacher is known to be very strict.
④ Why don't we have a surprise party for him tomorrow?
⑤ All of his students attended the farewell party yesterday.

▶242019-0113

13 대화를 듣고, 남자의 마지막 말에 대한 여자의 응답으로 가장 적절한 것을 고르시오.

Woman: _____

① Yes, it's my fault. I should've kept my promise.
② No, you shouldn't. Your health is more important.
③ Oh, that would be great. I'll talk to him tomorrow.
④ Wow, that was awesome! Your presentation was perfect.
⑤ Don't worry. I feel comfortable doing it by myself tomorrow.

▶242019-0114

14 대화를 듣고, 여자의 마지막 말에 대한 남자의 응답으로 가장 적절한 것을 고르시오. [3점]

Man: _____

① No. The role of mass media should differ from the past.
② Okay. I'll be sure to create questions that are not partial.
③ Right. You should be cautious before answering questions.
④ Sure. Surveys are very effective in getting reliable information.
⑤ Thanks. I was able to avoid making a big mistake thanks to you.

▶242019-0115

15 다음 상황 설명을 듣고, Sally가 John에게 할 말로 가장 적절한 것을 고르시오. [3점]

Sally: _____

① Do you want some cookies with the tea?
② Can I get the cookies from your bakery?
③ Do your customers buy a lot of cookies from you?
④ Do you think I'll get more customers at my flower shop?
⑤ Will you be able to buy some cookies and flowers on the way?

[16~17] 다음을 듣고, 물음에 답하시오.

▶242019-0116

16 남자가 하는 말의 주제로 가장 적절한 것은?

① jobs in which statistics is useful
② career choices in the digital age
③ forecasts of global industrial trends
④ factors that influence job satisfaction
⑤ ways to collect data for statistical purposes

▶242019-0117

17 언급된 직업이 아닌 것은?

① business owner
② financial manager
③ weather forecaster
④ military recruiter
⑤ medical researcher

01 W Hello, listeners. I'm Linda Brown with Healthy Lifestyle. Nowadays, hiking is becoming a really popular activity. It's a great way _____ and enjoy nature, but there's always a risk of _____. By following some simple tips, you can avoid these encounters. First, don't hike silently. Talk or even sing when you hike. This warns animals that you're coming, so they won't be alarmed and attack _____. Second, don't wear headphones. When you wear them, you can't hear what's happening around you. So you might not hear an animal making threatening noises. Lastly, avoid hiking at dawn or after dark. This is when many animals are most active. Keep these tips in mind and have a safe hike.

> **Quiz** 빈칸에 알맞은 말을 쓰시오.
> Q: Why should we avoid hiking at dawn or after dark?
> A: Because it is when many animals _____ _____ _____.

02 M Is something wrong, Amelia? You look upset.

   W I am, Dad. I _____ my friend Sophia about what movie we should see.

   M I see. What movie did you decide to see?

   W We didn't see one. We were so upset at each other that we just went home.

   M Really? But I think you should contact her to make up.

   W Why me? She was at fault, too.

   M I understand that. But it's always a good idea for you to apologize first.

   W What do you mean?

   M If both of you _____ to apologize, you might never be able to recover your friendship.

   W Oh, you think so?

   M Yeah. If you _____ with her, you'd better act first.

   W Okay, Dad. Thanks for your advice.

03 W Hello, everyone! Thank you for tuning in to my channel again! We've been _____ at various artists' paintings on my channel for the past week. By doing so, our understanding of their art has deepened. Hasn't it been a _____? I think there is an important benefit from appreciating works of art. It's clearing your mind. Just by looking at beautiful paintings, you can _____ of your worries. So if you go on a trip to the world of art with me, you'll be stress-free with a clear mind!

04

W   David, I've finished designing the photo zone poster for our club campaign.

M   Cool. Let me see.

W   I wrote the campaign title, 'See the World,' in the box at the top.

M   It's very eye-catching. I like the picture of the Earth you put on the right side of the poster.

W   I added it because nowadays there are a lot of issues that ▢▢▢▢▢.

M   Good point. I also like how you put the three kids standing hand in hand on top of the Earth.

W   I wanted to express ▢▢▢▢▢ and cooperation with each other, even with nature. That's why I also drew the three bees in the middle, just under the title.

M   Wonderful. And the balloon with stars on it on the left side of the poster looks good.

W   I wanted to add ▢▢▢▢▢.

M   Really nice. I'm sure people will love taking photos in front of your poster.

05

W   Honey, your aunt and uncle will be here in a couple hours.

M   It's our first time having them over since we got married.

W   Yeah. We're basically ready, right?

M   Well, I finished cooking dinner, but I think we need to ▢▢▢▢▢.

W   I forgot to tell you. I bought some lemonade at the grocery store this morning.

M   Oh, perfect. And I vacuumed while you were ▢▢▢▢▢. By the way, what should we do after dinner?

W   How about playing board games together?

M   That's a good idea. Do you know where the board game sets are?

W   Yeah. I put them ▢▢▢▢▢.

M   All right. I'll go and bring them down now.

W   Okay. I'll be in the living room.

> **Quiz**   빈칸에 알맞은 말을 쓰시오.
> Q: What are they going to do after dinner?
> A: They are going to _____ _____ _____ _____.

06

M   Welcome to Papyrus Stationery Store. What can I help you with?

W   Hi, where are ▢▢▢▢▢?

M   Right over here. We sell them in sets.

W   That's exactly what I want.

M   Okay. Here they are. How about this set? It has 18 colors. It's on sale for $5 per set.

W   Great. I'll take four sets. And I also ▢▢▢▢▢.

M   Those are right behind you.

W All right. This one looks pretty good. Let's see.... It's $20. Umm.... The paper in the sketchbook is a little thicker than I want.

M Oh, then here. This one ▢▢▢▢▢. It's normally $16, but it's 50% off right now, so it's only $8.

W Perfect. I'll buy two of them.

M Okay. Do you need anything else besides the four sets of colored pencils and two sketchbooks?

W Nope. And here's my credit card.

07

W Hey, honey. Did you go to the shopping mall today?

M Yeah. And while I was there, I started getting a headache. So I ▢▢▢▢▢ a little while ago.

W I'm sorry to hear that. Weren't you going to get the Bluetooth earphones you've been thinking about buying?

M Yeah. But I didn't ▢▢▢▢▢ them.

W Why not? I hope you didn't forget to take the credit card.

M That's not it.

W Oh, were they sold out? Or were they not on sale anymore?

M No. In fact, when I tried them on, they weren't that comfortable.

W Oh, I see.

M So I'm going to ▢▢▢▢▢ to buy.

08

W Hi, Tony. Are you interested in Mexican food?

M Yes. Why do you ask?

W I found this flyer about a Mexican cooking class. It says you get to make various kinds of foods like tacos and burritos.

M Sounds interesting. How much is the class?

W It's 65 dollars per person.

M Isn't it ▢▢▢▢▢?

W The cost includes a class, menu design and printable recipes, so I think it's quite reasonable.

M Maybe. How long is the class?

W 4 hours.

M Where is the class taking place?

W ▢▢▢▢▢ located in the River City Mall.

M It's an easy drive from my house. Hmm, ▢▢▢▢▢ to call the studio and find out more about the class.

W Yeah. Let's make a call right away.

Quiz 두 사람이 대화 직후에 할 일로 가장 적절한 것은?

① 멕시코 음식 요리하기　　　② River City Mall 방문하기　　　③ 요리 스튜디오에 전화하기

09

M Hello, students! This is your vice principal, Mr. Davis. I'm happy to ▢▢▢▢▢ the upcoming Dream Future Program. The program includes 15 special lectures related to a variety of jobs. You can ▢▢▢▢▢ individually on the school website until 6 p.m. this Friday. It will be three days long, starting from the 5th of next month. Please note that there's a limit of 30 participants for each lecture. After attending the lectures, you will be required to write a report about what you learned. Don't ▢▢▢▢▢ this informative program!

10

W Honey, what are you looking at?

M A website for Amsterdam parking lots. We should ▢▢▢▢▢ for tomorrow.

W Good idea. It's going to be really crowded, so it's going to be hard to find a spot.

M Yeah, which lot should we choose?

W We'll have the kids with us, so this one's too far from the city center. We should choose one of these ▢▢▢▢▢.

M Okay. Then how about this one? It's only a 6-minute walk.

W It has such a low rating, though. Under three stars.

M Yeah, let's choose one with ▢▢▢▢▢.

W All right. We won't need to cancel it, will we?

M I doubt it. Let's get one of these non-refundable options. They're cheaper.

W Okay. Then it's between these two places.

M They are not much different.

W Yeah. Then let's just get the cheaper one.

M Okay. Good choice.

11

M Christina, what are you reading?

W This is John Brown's ▢▢▢▢▢, *Tomorrow*. It's so interesting that I can't ▢▢▢▢▢.

M Oh, I didn't know he had a new novel. I think I should read it.

12

W   Roy, tomorrow's literature class is Mr. Kane's last class at our school.

M   I know. That's too bad. But it's good for him _____ at a college next semester.

W   Yeah, definitely. I think we should _____ in his last class.

13

M   Lily, why do you look so down?

W   Dad, it's because of my friend Kate. We talked on the phone earlier.

M   And? _____ between the two of you?

W   Yeah. We're supposed to make a geography presentation tomorrow, but she won't be at school tomorrow.

M   Oh no! Is there a problem?

W   She said she caught a bad cold.

M   She _____. So you're probably worried about your presentation tomorrow.

W   Right. I don't think I can do it without her.

M   Then why don't you _____ about it tomorrow?

W   What do you think he can actually do to help though?

M   He might be able to let you do it later.

14

W   Hi, Daniel. Is something wrong?

M   Hey, Claudia. Yeah, actually I _____ about the presentation I gave this morning.

W   What presentation?

M   It was for my sociology class. It was about the influence of mass media on society.

W   Did you make a mistake or something?

M   Well, the main part of the presentation went smoothly, but something happened during the Q&A session.

W   Were you asked a question you couldn't answer?

M   No. But some people pointed out that one of _____ in my presentation wasn't reliable.

W   Why?

M   They said the question I asked was biased, prompting the respondents to answer in a specific way. I hadn't realized that, but they were right.

W   I see. Don't worry too much. Just be more careful in the future _____ the same mistake.

> **Quiz** 밑줄 친 단어와 의미가 가장 가까운 것은?
> One of the survey results in my presentation wasn't <u>reliable</u>.
> ① optimistic   ② credible   ③ positive

15　W　Sally runs a flower shop downtown and her friend John owns a bakery _____. These days Sally is worried about the decrease in the number of her customers. So she's trying to find _____. Today she comes up with the idea of selling tea at her flower shop. People who come for tea could buy flowers. Sally tells John about that and he says it's a good idea. John suggests that she also sell _____. Sally likes his tip a lot and wants to ask if she can buy them from him. In this situation, what would Sally most likely say to John?

16~17　M　Hello, students. Last class, we talked about the origin and history of statistics. Today we'll move on to the present day. As information technology opens new worlds of possibilities, statistics greatly helps people _____. Here are some examples. Firstly, when it comes to running a small business, the business owner needs to make important decisions such as how much product to purchase. Statistical analysis helps him or her _____. Also, financial managers who work at a bank or insurance company should have advanced statistical knowledge. This is because financial institutions forecast future economic conditions and those forecasts are heavily dependent on statistical sampling. Next, military recruiters _____ to forecast how many people will join the military in the future. Lastly, biostatistics is critical to medical researchers for conducting research. Statisticians are involved in these efforts and many more.

Dictation 빠른답

01 ☐ to be outside ☐ dangerous wildlife encounters ☐ from feeling threatened

02 ☐ had an argument with ☐ wait too long ☐ value your friendship

03 ☐ taking a look ☐ very rewarding experience ☐ clear your mind

04 ☐ affect the whole world ☐ the importance of harmony ☐ some bright accents

05 ☐ get some drinks ☐ at the grocery store ☐ in the attic

06 ☐ the colored pencils ☐ need two sketchbooks ☐ has thinner paper

07 ☐ took some medicine ☐ end up buying ☐ look for another model

08 ☐ a bit expensive ☐ In a cooking studio ☐ it wouldn't hurt

09 ☐ tell you about ☐ register for the lectures ☐ miss out on

10 ☐ reserve a spot ☐ under 10 minutes away ☐ more than three stars

11 ☐ latest novel ☐ put it down

12 ☐ to start teaching ☐ do something for him

13 ☐ Is there something wrong ☐ must be pretty sick ☐ talk to your teacher

14 ☐ can't stop thinking ☐ the survey results ☐ to avoid making

15 ☐ several blocks away ☐ ways to attract customers ☐ cookies with the tea

16~17 ☐ carry out their work ☐ make these decisions ☐ rely on statistics

---

Quiz 01 are most active **05** play board games together **08** ③ **09** ③ **14** ②

▶242019-0118

01 다음을 듣고, 여자가 하는 말의 목적으로 가장 적절한 것을 고르시오.

① 설탕을 대체할 수 있는 식재료를 소개하려고
② 건강 관리를 도와주는 영상 채널을 홍보하려고
③ 음료의 당분 함량을 확인하는 법을 설명하려고
④ 설탕 섭취가 건강에 미치는 위험성을 경고하려고
⑤ 체중 관리를 도와주는 운동 프로그램을 추천하려고

수능특강 **PICK**　▶242019-0119

02 대화를 듣고, 여자의 주장으로 가장 적절한 것을 고르시오.

① 자전거 도로를 더 확충해야 한다.
② 자전거 도로의 선을 뚜렷하게 그려야 한다.
③ 자전거 도로 표지판을 더 많이 설치해야 한다.
④ 여러 대의 자전거가 옆으로 늘어서서 가서는 안 된다.
⑤ 자전거 전용 도로의 보행 금지 규정을 준수해야 한다.

수능완성 **PICK**　▶242019-0120

03 대화를 듣고, 두 사람의 관계를 가장 잘 나타낸 것을 고르시오.

① 고객 – 가전제품 판매원
② 판매 사원 – 가구점 매니저
③ 의뢰인 – 인테리어 디자이너
④ 공사 감독관 – 건축 설계사
⑤ 출판사 직원 – 서점 주인

수능완성 **PICK**　▶242019-0121

04 대화를 듣고, 그림에서 대화의 내용과 일치하지 <u>않는</u> 것을 고르시오.

수능완성 **PICK**　▶242019-0122

05 대화를 듣고, 남자가 여자에게 부탁한 일로 가장 적절한 것을 고르시오.

① 피자 주문하기
② 두통약 구입하기
③ 과제물 출력하기
④ 책상 서랍 정리하기
⑤ 잉크 카트리지 사 오기

▶242019-0123

06 대화를 듣고, 여자가 지불할 금액을 고르시오.

① $20　　② $25　　③ $30
④ $35　　⑤ $40

▶242019-0124

07 대화를 듣고, 남자가 시상식에 참석하지 <u>못하는</u> 이유를 고르시오.

① 출장이 예정되어 있어서
② 저녁 식사 약속이 있어서
③ 수영 대회에 나가야 해서
④ 아내와 모임에 가야 해서
⑤ 선생님과 상담을 해야 해서

수능특강 **PICK**　▶242019-0125

08 대화를 듣고, Greenhill Light Festival에 관해 언급되지 <u>않은</u> 것을 고르시오.

① 개최 기간　　② 개최 장소
③ 입장료　　　④ 참가 기념품
⑤ 주차장

▶242019-0126

09 Poetry Writing Competition에 관한 다음 내용을 듣고, 일치하지 <u>않는</u> 것을 고르시오.

① 기말고사 바로 다음 주에 개최된다.
② 학생이면 누구나 참가할 수 있다.
③ 사회 문제에 관한 시를 쓰는 것이 가능하다.
④ 제출된 시는 외부 초청 시인들이 심사할 것이다.
⑤ 우승자들은 서점에서 쓸 수 있는 상품권을 받게 된다.

10 수능특강 **PICK** ▶242019-0127

다음 표를 보면서 대화를 듣고, 남자가 구입할 마이크를 고르시오.

Bluetooth Wireless Microphones

	Model	Price	LED Lights	Color	Battery Life
①	A	$27	×	Gray	3 hours
②	B	$33	○	Silver	4 hours
③	C	$38	○	Pink	4 hours
④	D	$42	○	Yellow	5 hours
⑤	E	$47	×	Gold	5 hours

11 수능특강 **PICK** ▶242019-0128

대화를 듣고, 남자의 마지막 말에 대한 여자의 응답으로 가장 적절한 것을 고르시오.

① No, thanks. I feel great after taking a hot bath.
② Well, it'll take at least five hours to drive there.
③ Not at all. I've never heard about the hot spring.
④ Wow! I didn't realize the hot springs were so close.
⑤ Sounds awesome! I can't wait to enjoy the hot spring.

12 수능특강 **PICK** ▶242019-0129

대화를 듣고, 여자의 마지막 말에 대한 남자의 응답으로 가장 적절한 것을 고르시오.

① No, I won't. I'll check in about half an hour.
② You don't have to. I've already parked our car.
③ Thank you. Then I'll get out with the kids first.
④ Sounds good. I'll go there after parking the car.
⑤ Right. We can go to the hotel by airport shuttle bus.

13 수능특강 **PICK** ▶242019-0130

대화를 듣고, 남자의 마지막 말에 대한 여자의 응답으로 가장 적절한 것을 고르시오. [3점]

Woman: _____

① Of course. I'll find you a good travel agent.
② I'm sorry. I won't skip working out from now on.
③ You're right. We should've worked out on our trip.
④ Exactly. Our different travel styles made me regret this trip.
⑤ No. My friend was different the last time we traveled together.

14 수능특강 **PICK** ▶242019-0131

대화를 듣고, 여자의 마지막 말에 대한 남자의 응답으로 가장 적절한 것을 고르시오. [3점]

Man: _____

① All right. I'll change my seat on the flight.
② Really? Then we can sit next to each other.
③ I see. I should take this picture down right away.
④ No way. We'll have to cancel our flight reservation.
⑤ Don't worry. I have another app that scans bar codes.

15 ▶242019-0132

다음 상황 설명을 듣고, Adam이 Cassie에게 할 말로 가장 적절한 것을 고르시오. [3점]

Adam: _____

① I don't know where I put my flashcards.
② Let's take French class together this semester.
③ It'd be better for you to study another language.
④ You should use more accurate words when you speak.
⑤ Utilizing flashcards will help you memorize words easily.

16 수능완성 **PICK**

[16~17] 다음을 듣고, 물음에 답하시오. ▶242019-0133

16 여자가 하는 말의 주제로 가장 적절한 것은?

① designs of socks for special purposes
② basic features of modern footwear design
③ accessories that add an accent to an outfit
④ changes in the materials and designs of socks
⑤ technological innovation that affected fashion

17 ▶242019-0134

언급된 재료가 <u>아닌</u> 것은?

① animal skins   ② linen
③ wool   ④ cotton
⑤ nylon

01

W Good morning, everyone. Welcome to *One-Minute Health*. How often do you eat _____? Maybe very often. Now is the best time _____. According to studies, consuming too much sugar can have serious negative health effects. High sugar intake is strongly related to obesity, diabetes, heart disease, and even certain types of cancer. To protect your health, avoid sugary beverages and snacks, and replace them with _____, such as fruits. Your health matters, so let's make smart decisions to safeguard your bodies. Come back tomorrow to hear another useful health tip. Have a great day!

02

M Hey, Jennifer. Let's walk on the new sidewalk.

W It's not actually a sidewalk, and it's not meant for pedestrians. It's _____.

M You mean this is for cyclists only?

W Yes. We're not supposed to walk on this path. There's a sign on the path up ahead.

M Does that mean people can't walk there at all?

W You got that right.

M I didn't know that.

W Well, the city is building more and more bike paths to encourage more people _____.

M That's good. But there aren't _____.

W We still shouldn't walk on the bike path. It's the law.

M I see.

03

[Cell phone rings.]

M Hello, Ms. Elliot. How are you?

W Hello, Mr. Rogers. I'm good. How can I help you?

M I'd like to change _____ that we discussed.

W What would you like to change?

M I planned on moving the TV to my bedroom, but now I'd rather _____.

W But if you leave the TV in the living room, you can't put a standing bookshelf along the entire wall like you wanted to.

M I know. How about putting two compact bookshelves at both ends of the TV, instead? Do you think they can hold all of my books?

W No, I don't think they can hold that many.

M Maybe it's best I go back to the original plan.

W Well, a wall-mounted bookshelf and storage cabinets may be a good solution. That will make your living room look stylish, as well as give you _____.

M Sounds perfect! You're such a creative thinker.

W I'm glad you like my idea.

M And would you keep the new design within my budget?

W Sure. Not a problem.

> **Quiz** 빈칸에 알맞은 말을 대화에서 찾아 쓰시오.
> Q: What is the woman's solution to the problem of not being able to hold all of the man's books?
> A: She suggests installing _____.

04

W How was your weekend, Benjamin?

M Great, Ms. Green. I went to an ice skating show. Here's a picture I took.

W Wow, the stage looks fantastic. I like _____ in the background.

M Me, too. I also loved _____ on the doors between them.

W It makes the stage look more interesting.

M The show was about a magic castle. Do you see the snowman at the top of the steps?

W Yes.

M He used to be the king, but a witch _____. The female skater is his daughter, the princess.

W Sounds interesting. The male skater must be a prince.

M Yes. He lifted the female skater above his head.

W And look, even with her arms together, she was able to balance.

M Yeah. It was a wonderful show with a lot to see.

05

[Cell phone rings.]

W Hi, Justin. What's up?

M Mom, are you on your way home?

W Not yet, but I'm leaving work soon. You're going to see a movie with Kevin this evening, right?

M Well, he just called and said he can't go because he has a bad headache.

W Sorry to hear that, but now we can have dinner together.

M Well, then, how about _____?

W That sounds good to me. I think I'll be home around seven.

M Okay, then I'll order a pizza around 6:30.

W Perfect.

M One more thing, Mom. I have _____ for my homework, but the printer says the ink cartridge is empty.

W There might be an extra cartridge in the desk drawer. Have you looked?

M Yeah, but there isn't one there. Can you get one for me?

W Okay. Then I'll stop by _____ next to my work.

M Thanks, Mom. See you soon.

> **Quiz** Kevin이 남자와 영화를 보러 갈 수 없는 이유는?
> ① 두통이 심해서   ② 숙제가 많아서   ③ 엄마와 저녁을 먹기로 해서

06

M   Good morning, Ms. Gibson.

W   Hello, Mr. Turner. I'm here ⬚⬚⬚⬚⬚⬚ I dropped off a few days ago.

M   Yes, just a moment, please. *[Pause]* Here it is.

W   It looks perfect. Thank you. You said the cost was $20, didn't you?

M   That's right.

W   Okay. I'd also like to ⬚⬚⬚⬚⬚⬚.

M   All right. How many pairs?

W   I have two pairs. How much ⬚⬚⬚⬚⬚⬚?

M   It's $5 a pair.

W   Oh, that's cheap. Please charge the fees for the skirt and the shoes to this credit card.

M   Okay. Thanks.

07

W   Dad, I've got great news.

M   What is it, Julia?

W   Ms. Evans told me that I won first place ⬚⬚⬚⬚⬚⬚ I participated in last month.

M   Really? Congratulations! I'm so proud of you!

W   Thanks, Dad. She said ⬚⬚⬚⬚⬚⬚ is next Saturday at the City Hall.

M   What time is it at? You have your swimming lessons on Saturday mornings.

W   I know. Fortunately, the ceremony is at 2 p.m., so I can make it. Can you come?

M   I'm really sorry, but I have ⬚⬚⬚⬚⬚⬚.

W   Ah, that's okay. Mom said she would come.

M   That's good. I'll treat you to a fancy dinner on Saturday evening to celebrate.

W   Sounds great, Dad.

> **Quiz** 밑줄 친 표현과 의미가 같은 것은?
> Fortunately, the ceremony is at 2 p.m., so I can go there on time.
> ① make it   ② watch it   ③ pick it up

08

W   Honey, what are you looking at on your smartphone?

M   The Greenhill Light Festival website. Do you want to go again this year?

W   Sure, I'd love to. When is it?

M   It's from December 11th to the 20th.

W   Will it be held at Greenhill Gardens again this year?

M   Yes, but it looks bigger this year.

W   How much does it cost?

M   Adult tickets are $10, with ⬚⬚⬚⬚⬚⬚.

W Good. Our girls will love the festival. Have they ▭?

M Yeah. It's now 3 km long, and it even goes through a tunnel. And there are now over a million twinkling lights.

W Awesome!

M And it says they're going to open up ▭ nearby for extra parking.

W That's good. They'll need it.

09 **M** Attention, everyone! This is Mr. Anderson, the school literature teacher. I'm excited to tell you about the school Poetry Writing Competition coming up the week right ▭. All students can enter the competition ▭ through poetry. Poems can be about anything: love, the beauty of nature, social issues, or anything else that you're passionate about. Each student can enter one poem, and you must submit your poem by June 3rd. The poems will be ▭, and the top three winners will receive a $100 gift certificate for the downtown bookstore. For more information, please visit the teachers' office on the 3rd floor. I eagerly anticipate a lot of you participating in this competition. Thank you.

10 **W** Good afternoon. Can I help you find something?

M Yes. I'm looking for a Bluetooth wireless microphone for my son's birthday party.

W Okay, we have various Bluetooth microphones. Do you have ▭?

M Well, I'd like to ▭ $45.

W All right. How about a microphone with LED lights? Kids really like ones with colorful LED lights.

M Perfect. It'll be fun to use at the birthday party.

W Right. And what color do you think your son will like?

M Definitely not pink. He'd like either of the other two colors.

W Okay. Well, this one has ▭.

M I'll take it, then. Here's my credit card.

11 **M** Emily, we finally made it to the hot spring. That was ▭.

W Yeah. But it'll be worth driving all the way here. A lot of people told me this hot spring is really nice.

M I also heard the water is really hot and clean, and there are ▭.

Quiz 우리말과 같도록 빈칸에 알맞은 말을 쓰시오.
이 고전 소설은 읽을 만한 가치가 있을 것이다.
This classic novel will _____ _____ _____.

12

W Honey, finally we're at the airport. Do you know where the parking lot is?

M Yes, I do. It's a little ▨▨▨▨▨▨, so I'll drop off you and the kids first ▨▨▨▨▨▨.

W Okay. Shall I wait for you at the check-in counter?

13

M Hi, Sophia. It's been a long time since I've seen you at the gym.

W Hey, Tyler. I went to Canada with a friend for two weeks, so I couldn't come ▨▨▨▨▨▨.

M Oh, I see. How was your trip to Canada?

W It wasn't that good. It would've been much better if I'd traveled alone.

M Why do you say that?

W I'd never traveled with others before, but I thought it'd be okay to travel ▨▨▨▨▨▨. But I was wrong.

M What happened?

W Nothing specific. Our styles are just so different. I like to always be doing something and want to go to as many places as possible when I travel.

M Ah, but your friend likes to just ▨▨▨▨▨▨.

14

W Jason, you're back! How was your trip to Cuba?

M It was great! You should go there someday.

W I'd love to. Do you have any pictures?

M Sure! I posted pictures on social media during my trip. Let me show you. *[Pause]* Here.... This is a photo of me ▨▨▨▨▨▨ to Cuba.

W Your boarding pass is completely visible! You shouldn't ▨▨▨▨▨▨!

M Why not?

W Because the bar code printed on your boarding pass can be used to get private information about you.

M But I didn't have any problems at all during my trip.

W That's good, but let me show you what I mean. Watch, using the bar code scanning app on my phone I'll scan your bar code. Look!

M Oh, wow! It shows my name and ▨▨▨▨▨▨ of my ticket!

W Right. If someone accessed this, they could steal your flight or change your seats. They could do a lot.

15   **M**   This semester, Adam and Cassie are taking French class together. Cassie is very interested in French and studies really hard, but recently she's been struggling with memorizing French words. So she'd like to learn about _____. She knows that Adam always does really well on the vocabulary quizzes in their French class, so she _____ on how he's able to learn French words quickly. Adam takes flashcards out of his backpack and wants to tell Cassie that making and using her own could greatly help her _____. In this situation, what would Adam mostly likely say to Cassie?

16~17   **W**   Good morning, everybody. Today, let's talk about the most overlooked part of an outfit. Our socks. The clothing item that _____ has been around since the Stone Age, long before the concept of pants existed. The first socks were made from animal skins and tied around the ankle. Then, the first knit socks were made in Ancient Egypt. During the Middle Ages, the length of trousers was extended and the sock became a tight, brightly-colored cloth covering the lower part of the leg. They were made _____ and looked like today's leggings. In the late 17th century cotton became a popular choice for many clothing items including socks. As trousers became longer and socks became shorter, the term 'socks' started to refer to what was previously known as stockings. The next revolution in sock-making came with _____ in 1938. The strength and elasticity of socks made from cotton-nylon blends led to a natural step forward in manufacturing. Since then, sock designs have remained almost the same but various materials have been experimented with.

Dictation 빠른답

수능특강 PICK ▶242019-0135

01 다음을 듣고, 남자가 하는 말의 목적으로 가장 적절한 것을 고르시오.

① 지하철 운행 시간 변경을 공지하려고
② 출퇴근 시 자전거 이용을 권장하려고
③ 대중교통 체계 개선의 필요성을 알리려고
④ 지하철 자전거 휴대승차 규정을 안내하려고
⑤ 지하철역 자전거 무료 대여 서비스를 홍보하려고

▶242019-0136

02 대화를 듣고, 여자의 의견으로 가장 적절한 것을 고르시오.

① 좋아하는 스포츠 활동을 하는 것은 학교생활에 활력을 준다.
② 본인이 좋아하는 것과 관련된 동아리를 선택하는 것이 좋다.
③ 동아리를 선택하기 전에 지도교사와 상담하는 것이 도움이 된다.
④ 동아리를 고를 때 학업과 관련된 것을 꼭 선택할 필요는 없다.
⑤ 동아리 활동 시 부원들의 의견을 존중하는 태도를 갖춰야 한다.

수능특강 PICK ▶242019-0137

03 대화를 듣고, 두 사람의 관계를 가장 잘 나타낸 것을 고르시오.

① 기자 – 작곡가　　② 무대 감독 – 가수
③ 교사 – 뮤지컬 배우　　④ 수강생 – 연극 강사
⑤ 극장 매표소 직원 – 관객

수능특강 PICK ▶242019-0138

04 대화를 듣고, 그림에서 대화의 내용과 일치하지 않는 것을 고르시오.

수능특강 PICK ▶242019-0139

05 대화를 듣고, 여자가 할 일로 가장 적절한 것을 고르시오.

① 남자 대신 수업 등록하기
② 방학 강좌 전단 구해 오기
③ 토요일 오전 약속 취소하기
④ 태권도 수업 시간 변경하기
⑤ 남자를 코딩 수업에 데려다주기

수능특강 PICK ▶242019-0140

06 대화를 듣고, 남자가 지불한 금액을 고르시오. [3점]

① $43　　② $45　　③ $48
④ $49　　⑤ $52

▶242019-0141

07 대화를 듣고, 여자가 Jane 대신 계주에 참가할 수 없는 이유를 고르시오.

① 발목 통증이 심해서
② 달리기를 잘하지 못해서
③ 중국어 말하기 대회가 있어서
④ 방과 후에 연습을 할 수가 없어서
⑤ 다른 친구가 먼저 참가하기로 해서

수능완성 PICK ▶242019-0142

08 대화를 듣고, Riverside Bike Ride에 관해 언급되지 않은 것을 고르시오.

① 출발 장소　　② 코스 길이
③ 소요 예상 시간　　④ 행사 일시
⑤ 신청 방법

수능특강 PICK ▶242019-0143

09 Stand-up Comedy with Funny Glen 프로그램에 관한 다음 내용을 듣고, 일치하지 않는 것을 고르시오.

① 강사는 5년 경력을 가진 지역의 코미디언이다.
② 20세 이상의 성인이 참가할 수 있다.
③ 매주 목요일에 수업이 있을 것이다.
④ 온라인이나 커뮤니티 센터에서 등록할 수 있다.
⑤ 등록비에 워크북이 포함되어 있다.

10 수능완성 **PICK** ▶ 242019-0144

다음 표를 보면서 대화를 듣고, 여자가 주문할 태블릿 케이스를 고르시오.

Tablet Cases

	Model	Material	Color	Stylus Pen	Price
①	A	nylon	pink	×	$30
②	B	plastic	blue	×	$35
③	C	plastic	black	○	$38
④	D	leather	brown	○	$45
⑤	E	leather	yellow	○	$52

11 수능특강 **PICK** ▶ 242019-0145

대화를 듣고, 남자의 마지막 말에 대한 여자의 응답으로 가장 적절한 것을 고르시오.

① Right. You can find clothes there that'll fit you.
② I don't think so. We need to return these clothes.
③ Then put them with my clothes. I'll take them, too.
④ Okay. Just let me know when you'll be downtown.
⑤ Good. Next time you go there, you should donate mine.

12 수능특강 **PICK** ▶ 242019-0146

대화를 듣고, 여자의 마지막 말에 대한 남자의 응답으로 가장 적절한 것을 고르시오.

① I go for a morning run before work.
② Don't work out on an empty stomach.
③ You'll see good results if you don't give up.
④ Swimming is fun, and is a great way to meet people.
⑤ It's not easy to lose weight in a short period of time.

13 수능특강 **PICK** ▶ 242019-0147

대화를 듣고, 남자의 마지막 말에 대한 여자의 응답으로 가장 적절한 것을 고르시오. [3점]

Woman: _____

① Okay. You can use my key card from now on.
② Don't worry. I don't need the key card anymore.
③ Really? I'm relieved that you're not far from here.
④ Sorry, but I'm afraid I can't go with you at that time.
⑤ Come on. I'm eager to hear about the interview results.

14 수능특강 **PICK** ▶ 242019-0148

대화를 듣고, 여자의 마지막 말에 대한 남자의 응답으로 가장 적절한 것을 고르시오.

Man: _____

① Great. Then I'd like to get a refund on it.
② Okay. Then I'll pay the difference in cash.
③ All right. In that case I'll buy the bag as well.
④ Sure. I'll just look for another hat in my size.
⑤ I see. I'll have to find a climbing bag that isn't on sale.

15 수능완성 **PICK** ▶ 242019-0149

다음 상황 설명을 듣고, Jason이 호텔 프런트 사무원에게 할 말로 가장 적절한 것을 고르시오. [3점]

Jason: _____

① It seems that this room key is not working.
② How much does it cost to upgrade my room?
③ Do you have any vacancies for this weekend?
④ I'd like to switch to another nonsmoking room.
⑤ I have to cancel my reservation for next weekend.

[16~17] 다음을 듣고, 물음에 답하시오.

▶ 242019-0150

16 남자가 하는 말의 주제로 가장 적절한 것은?

① good exercises for people with back pain
② benefits of maintaining an active lifestyle
③ the importance of stretching before exercising
④ reasons why a lot of people suffer from back pain
⑤ helpful activities for people suffering from depression

▶ 242019-0151

17 언급된 운동이 <u>아닌</u> 것은?

① swimming　　　② cycling
③ golf　　　④ running
⑤ yoga

01 W   Good morning. I'm Jim Rogan, the chief of public transit of Summerville. Last week, we started a policy to allow passengers to bring bikes on the subway _____. If you plan on bringing your bike on the subway, please follow these rules for _____. First, take the elevator with your bike, not the escalator. And do not ride your bike in the station or on the platform. Also, when you board a subway car, use only the first or last car since the middle cars are usually _____. Your observance of these rules will be much appreciated. I hope you enjoy your ride!

02 M   Elizabeth, have you been thinking about joining a school club this year?

     W   Yeah. I'm going to join the book club. How about you, Walter?

     M   I'd like to join a club, but I haven't decided _____.

     W   Well, what are you interested in?

     M   Nowadays I've become really interested in sports.

     W   Then why don't you join _____? I'm sure it's something you'll enjoy.

     M   That makes sense.

     W   I joined the book club because I love reading. It's best to choose a club based on what you like.

     M   Right. Baseball is my favorite sport, so I think I'll _____.

     W   That sounds like a great choice.

03 W   Hello, Mr. White. Thank you for coming. It's really nice to meet you.

     M   My pleasure. Thank you for inviting me, Ms. Adams.

     W   It's my honor to talk to you in person. I'm _____.

     M   I'm glad to be here. I always love working with students.

     W   Great! As I mentioned, the students in my music class are going to perform Fantasy at our school festival this year.

     M   Oh, yes. That's one of my favorite musicals. I enjoyed playing _____ in it.

     W   I saw your performance in the musical last year. It was awesome!

     M   Thanks. I _____ your students and get started.

     W   Let me show you around the auditorium. That's the stage where the students will perform.

     M   Wow, that's a nice stage.

     W   Thanks. Let's go backstage where the students are. I'll introduce you to them.

     M   Okay.

> **Quiz** 빈칸에 알맞은 것은?
> Q: Where is the conversation taking place?
> A: At the school _____.
> ① auditorium   ② gymnasium   ③ music room

04

W   Dad, we're approaching the island!

M   Yes, it's beautiful! The water is so clear.

W   And look at all of the fish swimming in the sea. I can't wait to go snorkeling.

M   Me, neither. But be careful when you walk on the sea walkway to the beach. It _____ .

W   All right. So we have to go through the log cabin at the end of the walkway to _____ ?

M   Yes. Then we're going to check in to our rooms.

W   Are we staying in one of those houses behind the trees?

M   Yeah. I think we can enjoy the ocean view from the house.

W   Cool! And there are tables _____ on the beach. One of them is free. Let's spend the afternoon there today.

M   That's a great idea.

05

M   Mom, take a look at this flyer.

W   What is it about?

M   It's about summer vacation classes. Do you think I can take one?

W   Of course! Which one would you like to take?

M   I'm thinking about _____ . What do you think?

W   That sounds good. But I heard that the coding class is difficult to enter because _____ is really small. When is the registration?

M   It starts at 10 a.m. this Saturday. It's online and it's on a first-come, first-served basis.

W   You have Taekwondo class at that time, right?

M   Right. So I _____ register at that time.

W   Then I'll do it for you. Don't worry.

M   Really? Thank you so much, Mom.

> **Quiz** 우리말과 같도록 빈칸에 알맞은 말을 대화에서 찾아 쓰시오.
> 콘서트 입장권은 무료이지만, 선착순이다.
> Admission to the concert is free, but it is on a _____, _____ _____.

06

W   Hello. May I help you?

M   Yes. I'd like to buy some souvenir T-shirts.

W   You've come to the right place! That blue T-shirt with an ocean painting on it is very popular.

M   That's a nice picture. How about _____ ?

W   Oh, yes. That one has _____ . It's $2 more expensive than our regular T-shirts, so $12.

M   They're both nice. I'll take one of each, so one blue and one yellow.

W   Okay. Can I interest you in any of our local food products?

M   Yeah, how much are these packages of dried mango?

W   They're $3 a package, but if you buy   , you get 10% off.

M   Then I'll take 10 packages. Here's my credit card.

W   Sounds good. I'll check you out over at the counter.

07

M   Hi, Karen. How's your day going?

W   Hey, Jacob. It's going well. I heard that you've been practicing   for Sports Day.

M   Yeah. We've been practicing every day after school.

W   That's good. By the way, I heard that Jane   .

M   Yeah. We didn't think it would be that bad, but she just texted me that she won't be able to participate in the relay.

W   Oh, no! That's too bad.

M   I know. Actually, can you run in the relay instead of Jane?

W   Gosh, I'd like to, but I won't be at school because I have a Chinese speaking contest that day.

M   Oh, I see. I'll ask someone else then.

W   Ask Amy. She's   .

M   Really? I'll talk to her then. Thanks.

W   No problem.

> **Quiz** 빈칸에 알맞은 것은?
> Q: Why can't Jane participate in the relay race for Sports Day?
> A: Because _____.
> ① she twisted her ankle
> ② she can't practice every day after school
> ③ she has to participate in the Chinese speaking contest

08

W   Joshua, what are you looking at?

M   A flyer for the Riverside Bike Ride, which is coming up.

W   Oh, cool. Is it nearby?

M   Yeah. It's going to be held   . The ride starts at River Port Plaza.

W   Great. That's not far from here. Look, the event follows the Riverside Bike Trail for 15 kilometers.

M   Plus, it says it's not a competition,   .

W   Then, it'll take about one hour if we take our time.

M   It also says the trail has been recently   .

W The trail must be in good condition.

M For sure. And the timing is perfect! It's on November 27th, at 3 p.m.

W Terrific! It's just after the final exams. Why don't we sign up?

M Let's do it. How about asking Linda and Steve to join us?

W Great idea!

09

W Attention, please. I'm Emma Jones, program coordinator at the Midtown Community Center. I'd like to tell you about a new program we're having: Stand-up Comedy with Funny Glen. Funny Glen is _____ with 5 years of teaching experience. Stand-up Comedy with Funny Glen is a 6-week program open to adults _____. Participants will learn the art of stand-up comedy, including writing and telling jokes. The class will meet once a week, on Thursdays. The first class is Thursday, July 9th. You may register online or _____. The registration fee is $60, which doesn't include the workbook. We hope to see you there!

10

M What are you doing on your smartphone, Annie?

W Oh, hey, Andy. I'm looking for _____. My current one is falling apart.

M Where are you going to buy a new one?

W Well, here. These five are on sale right now. I've ordered from this site before, so I'm thinking about getting one of those.

M Oh, they all look good. Do you have anything in mind?

W I like how this one looks, but it's nylon, _____.

M Then, get one of the others. Which color do you want?

W Any of these would be okay except for yellow. That'd be hard to keep clean.

M Okay. These ones come with _____. Do you have one?

W No, but I've always wanted one. I'll get one of these that come with a stylus pen.

M Then there are two options left. Which one do you prefer?

W Hmm, they both look good. I was hoping to keep it less than $40, so I'll get the cheaper one.

M I think that's a good choice.

Quiz Annie가 선택한 태블릿 케이스에 관해 언급되지 <u>않은</u> 것은?
① 재질   ② 색상   ③ 크기

11

M Honey, what are you going to do _____?

W I'm going to donate them to the homeless shelter downtown. They don't _____.

M That's a good idea. I have a lot of clothes that I don't wear often, too.

12

W Hi, Mike. Long time no see. Wow, you've lost ▨▨▨▨▨. You look great!

M Thanks. I ▨▨▨▨▨ and started exercising a lot.

W What kind of exercise? I know you're always busy.

13

[Cell phone rings.]

M Hello, Grandma?

W Daniel, where are you now? You're not at home.

M I'm on my way now. Don't you remember I told you in the morning that I was supposed to ▨▨▨▨▨?

W Right. I remember now. I forget a lot these days. By the way, I have a problem.

M You have a problem? What is it?

W I forgot to take the apartment complex key card when I went out for a walk. So I can't ▨▨▨▨▨.

M Did you call the security office to open it?

W Sure, I did. But nobody answered.

M All right. Don't worry. I'm almost there.

W How long do you think it'll take ▨▨▨▨▨?

M Well, I'll be there in just about 5 minutes.

14

W Hi. Can I help you, sir?

M Yes. I got this climbing hat as a gift, but it ▨▨▨▨▨.

W Let me see it. *[Pause]* Oh, it's our brand.

M Yes. I can exchange it without a receipt, right?

W Sure. If it's our brand, we can do that. Would you like to change it ▨▨▨▨▨?

M No, actually I have several hats. Can I change it to other items?

W Yes, you can. What did you have in mind?

M I'd like to change it to a climbing bag over there.

W Does it matter that it's more expensive than the hat?

M No. By the way, I saw a discount sign. Does the discount ▨▨▨▨▨?

W Let me see. *[Typing sound]* Yeah, you can get 10% off the marked price.

15 W Jason is on the first day of a three-day trip by himself. He has booked a hotel with a beautiful beachfront view and is looking forward to getting ▢▢▢▢▢▢. After checking in at the hotel, he goes to his room ▢▢▢▢▢▢. He opens his hotel room door, but all he can smell is a thick smell of cigarettes. He specifically booked a nonsmoking room. He feels it is his right to ask for ▢▢▢▢▢▢. So, he directly goes down to the front desk to ask for it. In this situation, what would Jason most likely say to the hotel front desk agent?

16~17 M Hello, everyone. I'm Dr. Johansson from the Salvia Medical Center. Many people with back pain believe that they ▢▢▢▢▢▢, but that's not completely true. There are some exercises that are good for individuals with back pain. First is swimming. This is a great exercise for people with back pain because it's low-impact, ▢▢▢▢▢▢ on the body. Cycling is also a low-impact activity that's good for individuals with back pain. It even helps strengthen the muscles around the back. Moving on, golf is great because it not only helps promote flexibility but also ▢▢▢▢▢▢. And finally is yoga, which combines gentle movements and stretching, so it is an ideal choice. So even if your back hurts, you can safely stay active by doing these exercises.

Dictation 빠른답

01 ☐ to promote bike use ☐ a smooth and safe ride
☐ the most crowded

02 ☐ which one yet ☐ one of the sports clubs
☐ join the baseball club

03 ☐ a big fan of yours ☐ the leading role ☐ can't wait to meet

04 ☐ has no rail ☐ get on the island ☐ under the trees

05 ☐ the coding class ☐ the class size ☐ won't be able to

06 ☐ the yellow one ☐ handcrafted beads on it
☐ more than five

07 ☐ for the relay race ☐ twisted her ankle
☐ a really good runner

08 ☐ near our school ☐ just a leisurely ride
☐ renovated and repaved

09 ☐ a local comedian ☐ aged 20 and over
☐ at the community center

10 ☐ a case for my tablet ☐ which falls apart easily
☐ a stylus pen

11 ☐ with those clothes ☐ fit me anymore

12 ☐ a lot of weight ☐ went on a diet

13 ☐ have a job interview ☐ get into our apartment
☐ to get here

14 ☐ doesn't fit me ☐ to a bigger hat ☐ apply to this bag

15 ☐ some nice rest and relaxation ☐ with great anticipation
☐ a room change

16~17 ☐ should avoid exercising ☐ with minimal stress
☐ includes gentle stretching

Quiz 03 ① **05** first-come, first-served basis **07** ① **10** ③ **15** right to ask for

01 ▶242019-0152

다음을 듣고, 남자가 하는 말의 목적으로 가장 적절한 것을 고르시오.

① 음식점에서 일할 직원을 채용하려고
② 집 없는 사람들을 위한 기부를 요청하려고
③ 급식 봉사소에서 일할 요리사를 채용하려고
④ 무료 식사 나눔을 도울 봉사자를 모집하려고
⑤ 식당 휴무일이 일요일로 변경됨을 공지하려고

02 수능특강 **PICK** ▶242019-0153

대화를 듣고, 여자의 의견으로 가장 적절한 것을 고르시오.

① 타인의 기분을 상하게 한 경우 먼저 사과를 해야 한다.
② 건전한 취미 활동은 스트레스를 해소하는 데 도움이 된다.
③ 다른 사람이 찍은 사진을 무단으로 사용하는 것은 불법이다.
④ 허락 없이 상대방의 사진을 찍으면 그 사람이 불편해할 수도 있다.
⑤ 친구와의 심한 갈등은 시간을 두고 대화를 통해 푸는 것이 좋다.

03 수능특강 **PICK** ▶242019-0154

대화를 듣고, 두 사람의 관계를 가장 잘 나타낸 것을 고르시오.

① 면접관 – 지원자
② 집주인 – 집수리 기사
③ 부동산 중개인 – 고객
④ 인테리어업자 – 의뢰인
⑤ 건축 설계사 – 건설업자

04 ▶242019-0155

대화를 듣고, 그림에서 대화의 내용과 일치하지 <u>않는</u> 것을 고르시오.

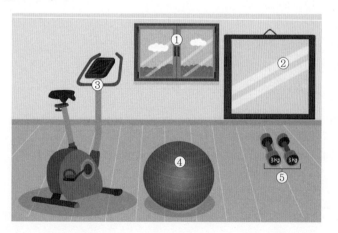

05 수능완성 **PICK** ▶242019-0156

대화를 듣고, 남자가 할 일로 가장 적절한 것을 고르시오.

① 옷 수선 맡기기
② 드레스 찾아오기
③ 드레스 주문하기
④ 딸을 집으로 데려오기
⑤ 옷가게 위치 알려 주기

06 수능특강 **PICK** ▶242019-0157

대화를 듣고, 여자가 지불할 금액을 고르시오. [3점]

① $44   ② $49   ③ $52
④ $54   ⑤ $57

07 수능특강 **PICK** ▶242019-0158

대화를 듣고, 남자가 야구팀을 그만둔 이유를 고르시오.

① 독서 동아리에 가입해야 해서
② 야구 장비 가격이 너무 비싸서
③ 야구팀 선수들과 사이가 나빠져서
④ 이사로 방과 후 연습에 갈 수 없어서
⑤ 주말에 도서관 봉사 활동을 가야 해서

08 ▶242019-0159

대화를 듣고, Riverville Run에 관해 언급되지 <u>않은</u> 것을 고르시오.

① 개최 빈도   ② 개최일   ③ 출발지
④ 등록 방법   ⑤ 참가비

09 수능완성 **PICK** ▶242019-0160

GW Handwriting Contest에 관한 다음 내용을 듣고, 일치하지 <u>않는</u> 것을 고르시오.

① 매년 개최되는 대회이다.
② 연령에 따라 3개의 범주로 나뉜다.
③ 참가자에게 옮겨 적을 글이 제공된다.
④ 연령 범주별 우승자에게는 상금과 트로피가 수여된다.
⑤ 수상작은 3월 31일까지 웹사이트에 게시된다.

10 수능특강 PICK ▶242019-0161

다음 표를 보면서 대화를 듣고, 여자가 주문할 선물 세트를 고르시오.

Mother's Day Gift Sets

	Set	Items	Price	Delivered by	Customer Rating (out of 5)
①	A	Silk Pillowcase & Sleeping Mask	$39	May 4	4.5
②	B	Smart Mug & Plate	$35	May 2	4.6
③	C	Scarf & Gloves	$49	May 5	4.7
④	D	Adult Coloring Book & Colored Pencils	$30	May 3	4.2
⑤	E	Candle & Diffuser	$25	May 6	4.8

11 수능완성 PICK ▶242019-0162

대화를 듣고, 남자의 마지막 말에 대한 여자의 응답으로 가장 적절한 것을 고르시오.

① Yes. Put the medicine in the first-aid kit.
② No. You need to take a couple more pills.
③ Right. You should keep track of your dose.
④ Look! The thermometer says he has a fever.
⑤ Sure. Let me bring the medicine to you, too.

12 ▶242019-0163

대화를 듣고, 여자의 마지막 말에 대한 남자의 응답으로 가장 적절한 것을 고르시오.

① You're just as outgoing as I am.
② I'm always too busy to feel bored.
③ Going camping seems like a great plan.
④ Four days was too short to make any plans.
⑤ I took some rest at home during the weekend.

13 수능특강 PICK ▶242019-0164

대화를 듣고, 남자의 마지막 말에 대한 여자의 응답으로 가장 적절한 것을 고르시오. [3점]

Woman: _____

① I didn't know about that. I'm sure I'll go to the expo.
② No problem. I'm good at researching on the Internet.
③ It's okay. Check another library for the books you need.
④ I agree. You'll be able to do well since you started early.
⑤ Your knowledge of AI will help me with the exhibition.

14 수능특강 PICK ▶242019-0165

대화를 듣고, 여자의 마지막 말에 대한 남자의 응답으로 가장 적절한 것을 고르시오. [3점]

Man: _____

① No. I don't like taking crowded subways.
② Definitely. You can walk there from here.
③ I'm sorry. I've never been to the museum before.
④ You're right. You need to have change for bus fare.
⑤ Then I guess you should use the bus, not the subway.

15 ▶242019-0166

다음 상황 설명을 듣고, Jeremy가 Emma에게 할 말로 가장 적절한 것을 고르시오.

Jeremy: _____

① Try to stop eating such a large breakfast.
② It's important that you pay attention in class more.
③ You should have been careful not to make mistakes.
④ Make sure you don't skip breakfast to concentrate better.
⑤ Remember that grades aren't the most important thing in your school life.

수능특강 PICK

[16~17] 다음을 듣고, 물음에 답하시오. ▶242019-0167

16 여자가 하는 말의 목적으로 가장 적절한 것은?

① 새로운 사물 인터넷 기술을 제안하려고
② 사물 인터넷 기술의 문제점을 제기하려고
③ 사물 인터넷 제품의 작동 원리를 설명하려고
④ 사물 인터넷 기술을 활용한 제품들을 소개하려고
⑤ 사물 인터넷 제품 사용 시 유의 사항을 안내하려고

17 ▶242019-0168
언급된 제품이 <u>아닌</u> 것은?

① refrigerator   ② coffee maker
③ air purifier   ④ washing machine
⑤ alarm clock

01

M Hello, my name is George Thompson, and I'm the owner of J&J Restaurant downtown. For over a year, we have been ▨▨▨▨▨▨ for homeless people at the restaurant once a month. This has become more and more popular, so we need to ▨▨▨▨▨▨ to help us out. Volunteers will help prepare meals, serve, and clean up. No prior experience is required. So if you're interested in helping people in need, please visit our homepage and apply. Your support can make a difference in the lives of ▨▨▨▨▨▨ in our community. Together, let's make a positive impact! Thank you.

02

W Ian, can I talk to you for a minute?

M Sure, Emily. What's up?

W I'm not sure if it's okay to tell you this, but since we're all friends I feel like I should. Did you know that Jane is upset with you?

M Really? I didn't know that. Why is that?

W You took a picture of her the other day, right?

M Yeah. But as you know, I always ▨▨▨▨▨▨ when we hang out. What's the problem?

W Well, some people may feel uncomfortable about having their photo taken ▨▨▨▨▨▨.

M Hmm, I haven't thought of that.

W You and I don't mind ▨▨▨▨▨▨, but some people don't like being photographed, especially without their permission.

M Ah, so that's why Jane is upset.

W Right. She just hasn't told you directly because she doesn't want to offend you.

M I see. Thanks for telling me. I'll talk to her about it.

03

M Hello, Ms. Anderson. Nice to see you again.

W Hello, Mr. Davis.

M Have you talked to your family about the three houses that you looked at last time?

W Yes. Thanks again for showing them to me.

M No problem. I feel very rewarded by ▨▨▨▨▨▨. What do you think about them? I thought the one on the hill would be best for you.

W I love its interior design and the yard is beautiful. But its price is too high for our budget.

M Oh, I see. Then how do you like the one near the beach? That's ▨▨▨▨▨▨, right?

W Yes. The house is nice too and ▨▨▨▨▨▨. But I wish it had more bedrooms.

M Okay. Then how about the one with four bedrooms?

W I think that one is spacious enough, but it's too old. It needs lots of work to fix it up.

M I see. Would you like to see any of them again?

W   Yes, the beach house. I'd like to see if I could possibly add space to it by remodeling.

M   Great. I'll call the house owner and tell them we would like to stop by soon.

W   Sounds good.

> ○ **Quiz**   밑줄 친 표현과 의미가 같은 것은?
> I'll tell them we would like to stop by soon.
> ① speak up   ② drop by   ③ drive away

04

M   So, Claudia, this is my home gym.

W   Wow, this is awesome! It even has windows.

M   Yeah. So I open them up and let fresh air in [   ].

W   That's good. I like the mirror next to the windows.

M   It helps to make sure I use the right form when exercising. And I just got [   ] a few days ago. It has a monitor so I can watch TV while riding it.

W   Awesome. What do you do with the gym ball next to the bicycle?

M   I use it for stretching.

W   That's good. So how much do these dumbbells in front of the mirror weigh?

M   They're 5 kg each. They're not too heavy, but they're good enough for the exercises I do.

W   This room is a perfect place [   ].

M   Exactly. Would you like to try the bicycle?

W   Sure.

05

[Cell phone rings.]

M   Hello?

W   Honey, when do you get off work today?

M   Pretty soon. Why? What's up?

W   Well, Jill just messaged me and said her violin lesson is going to run a little late. She needs some extra practice for her performance tomorrow.

M   Okay. So do you want me to [   ] on my way home?

W   No. I can take care of that.

M   Then is there anything else you want me to do?

W   Yes. I [   ] at the dry cleaner's. Can you pick it up?

M   Sure, no problem.

W   Thanks. Do you know where the dry cleaner's is?

M   I think so. It's the one across from the library, right?

W   Yes. The dress is [   ]. I'll pick up Jill after her violin practice.

M   Okay. See you at home.

06

W Honey, can you come here for a moment? I'm shopping online for what we need to repot the plant in the living room.

M Okay.

W What do you think about this large white pot? It's $30.

M Hmm.... I think this brown one is better.

W I agree. But it's $40.

M It's $10 more, but [＿＿＿＿＿＿].

W Okay. I'll buy it. And we need some potting soil, too.

M How much is a bag?

W $5 each. I think [＿＿＿＿＿＿].

M Okay, let's get two bags. And let's get a bag of pebbles to put on the soil. Look here. They're $4 a bag.

W That's a good idea. Pebbles will look nice. I'll get a bag of pebbles.

M Okay. What's the shipping fee for all of them?

W Normally it's $3, but I just got a membership, so the [＿＿＿＿＿＿]. I'll pay for them by my credit card now.

> **Quiz** 괄호 안에서 알맞은 것을 고르시오.
> Q: How did the woman get the shipping free?
> A: By getting [a coupon / a membership].

07

W What's up, Jeremy?

M Hey, Olivia. Where are you coming from?

W I was volunteering. My fellow book club members and I read books to kids at the library every Saturday.

M Wow, that's really thoughtful.

W Thank you. By the way, what's all that?

M Just stuff [＿＿＿＿＿＿]. I don't need these things anymore.

W You don't need your baseball glove? Aren't you on the school baseball team?

M Well, this glove is really old. And I'm [＿＿＿＿＿＿].

W Really? Did something happen between you and the other players by any chance?

M No. It's because I'm [＿＿＿＿＿＿] next week, so it'd be hard to make it to practice after school.

W Oh, are you? I didn't know that. So are you changing schools?

M No. I'm staying at the same school. My dad will give me a ride to school on his way to work.

W That's nice.

> **Quiz** 빈칸에 알맞은 것은?
> Q: What does the woman do every Saturday?
> A: She ＿＿＿＿＿＿＿＿＿＿＿＿＿＿.
> ① plays baseball at school　　② reads books to kids at the library
> ③ meets her friends in the school baseball team

08

M Judy, check out this flyer for the Riverville Run.

W Oh, it's this year. It's held every two years.

M Right. It's on Saturday, May 11th this year.

W I'd love to ▨▨▨▨▨. How about you?

M Sure. Let's do it together.

W Great! It should be fun. By the way, is the starting point ▨▨▨▨▨ in the past?

M Yeah. It begins in front of the downtown library. It's a 10-kilometer loop, so the end is also at the library.

W Okay. When is ▨▨▨▨▨?

M Next Friday. Let's register now. We just have to scan this QR code to register.

W Perfect. I'll get my phone.

M All right.

09

W Good morning, listeners! I'd like to tell you about the University of Greenwood's upcoming annual GW Handwriting Contest. The contest is open to all Greenwood residents, and there are three age categories: 12 and younger, ages 13–16, and ages 17 and older. Contestants will be given ▨▨▨▨▨, and their submissions will be judged on the style, neatness, and layout of their handwriting. The ▨▨▨▨▨ is March 31. Winners in each category will win a $200 cash prize and a trophy. The award-winning works will be ▨▨▨▨▨ until April 30, 2019. For the official rules and the text to be copied, visit www.gwhc.org. Thank you.

10

W Dad, please come help me.

M Okay. What's up?

W I want to buy Mom a Mother's Day present from this online store, but I don't know which of these five gift sets to choose.

M Let's see. All of them look nice. But I don't think your mom would use this silk pillowcase and sleeping mask.

W That's good to know. I'll buy one of these four sets then. Oh, I like this one, but it's ▨▨▨▨▨.

M What's your budget?

W I don't think I can spend more than $40.

M Then you have to choose one of these three. What do you think of this set?

W Oh, look at the delivery date. I want it ▨▨▨▨▨ May 5 just in case. Mother's Day falls on May 8 this year.

M These two options are left then. I think your mom will like either of them. Why don't you go for the one with ▨▨▨▨▨?

W Okay, I'll order it. Thanks for your help.

M No problem.

11

M Excuse me, I'd like to know if you have a thermometer on this plane. My son ▨▨▨▨▨▨▨.

W We should have one in the first-aid kit. I'll go bring it to you ▨▨▨▨▨▨▨.

M Thank you. And could I get some fever-reducing pills for children, too?

> **Quiz** 빈칸에 알맞은 말을 대화에서 찾아 쓰시오.
> Q: What did the man ask the woman to bring?
> A: He asked her to bring a _____ and some _____ _____.

12

W Honey, we have a 4-day weekend at the end of this month. Is there anything special you'd like to do ▨▨▨▨▨▨▨?

M Well, it'd be nice to do something outdoors. It'd be boring ▨▨▨▨▨▨▨ for four days.

W I agree. Let me know if you have anything in mind.

13

M Hey, Mary. What are you going to do after school?

W Hi, Daniel. I'm going to ▨▨▨▨▨▨ for my science class presentation.

M What's the presentation topic?

W It's about AI and the Fourth Industrial Revolution. I want to add realistic pictures of the products used in everyday life besides the information online.

M You've already ▨▨▨▨▨▨, right?

W Yes, I went there, but I couldn't find the pictures I was looking for.

M That's too bad. Oh, when is your presentation? The 2022 AI Expo is at the civic center downtown this weekend, which exhibits many AI products.

W Really? The presentation is next Friday, so it sounds like ▨▨▨▨▨▨ for my presentation.

M Yeah. They even allow you to take pictures of the exhibits.

> **Quiz** 우리말과 같도록 빈칸에 알맞은 말을 대화에서 찾아 쓰시오.
> 이번 미술 워크숍에서는 강사가 여러분이 작품을 만지는 것을 허용할 것이다.
> In this art workshop, the instructor will _____ _____ _____ touch the artworks.

14

W Excuse me. I'm touring the city and was wondering if I could ask you something.

M Sure. Go ahead.

W Can I ▨▨▨▨▨▨ which goes to the Pine Museum?

M Yes, you should take the number 10 bus and change buses at Oak Street.

W How many stops are there from here to Oak Street?

M About 15 stops. It ▨▨▨▨▨▨.

W Oh, I see. And how much is the fare?

M It's 1 dollar and 50 cents.

W Thank you.

M No problem. But you know you could also take the subway to the museum. You don't even have to transfer lines.

W Really? Can you tell me where the subway station is?

M It's simple. Just walk about ten minutes that way.

W Oh my! I've been walking around all day. I ＿＿＿＿＿ anymore.

15 **M** Emma is a high school student and she receives poor grades ＿＿＿＿＿. She didn't study that hard, which she regrets, so she decides to start studying hard. She begins waking up early every morning to study, but she has difficulty ＿＿＿＿＿. She tells her friend Jeremy about her problem. Jeremy knows that Emma always skips breakfast, which he thinks is why she can't focus in the morning. He explains to Emma that eating breakfast is related to ＿＿＿＿＿. Now Jeremy wants to suggest that Emma eat something in the morning to help her study. In this situation, what would Jeremy most likely say to Emma?

16~17 **W** Good afternoon, everyone. Last time, we talked about IoT, the Internet of Things, which refers to the connection of everyday objects to the Internet. Today, let me give you some ＿＿＿＿＿ that use IoT technology. ＿＿＿＿＿ can create grocery lists and link to smartphone apps, allowing users to control the temperature remotely. Another example is a smart coffee maker, which makes it easy to schedule, monitor, and modify users' coffee brewing from anywhere. The next example is a smart washing machine. It can easily specify when ＿＿＿＿＿. Finally, a recently launched smart alarm clock, hidden in a stylish lamp, offers a refreshing wake-up experience through changing light and customized music. With these products, we can experience the IoT technology every day.

Dictation 빠른답

01 ☐ providing free lunches ☐ recruit some volunteers ☐ the less fortunate	**09** ☐ a text to copy and submit ☐ submission deadline ☐ posted on our website
02 ☐ take pictures ☐ without their permission ☐ having our picture taken	**10** ☐ out of my budget ☐ to be delivered earlier than ☐ a higher customer rating
03 ☐ helping people find the right house ☐ within your budget range ☐ its location is amazing	**11** ☐ seems to have a fever ☐ in a minute
	12 ☐ during the holiday ☐ to just stay inside
04 ☐ while working out ☐ this indoor bike ☐ to exercise alone	**13** ☐ find some visual material ☐ checked the school library ☐ the expo could be helpful
05 ☐ pick her up ☐ had her dress dry-cleaned ☐ under my name	**14** ☐ catch a bus here ☐ takes about 30 minutes ☐ don't feel like walking
06 ☐ I think it's worth it ☐ we need two of them ☐ shipping is free	**15** ☐ on her first exams ☐ focusing on studying ☐ brain activity and concentration
07 ☐ I'm throwing out ☐ not on the team this year ☐ moving a little far away	**16~17** ☐ examples of smart home appliances ☐ A smart refrigerator ☐ users need their laundry done
08 ☐ run in it ☐ the same as ☐ the registration deadline	

Quiz 03 ② **06** a membership **07** ② **11** thermometer, fever-reducing pills **13** allow you to

01 수능특강 **PICK** ▶242019-0169

다음을 듣고, 남자가 하는 말의 목적으로 가장 적절한 것을 고르시오.

① 자녀를 위한 책 배달 서비스를 홍보하려고
② 도서관 책 대출 서비스가 중단됨을 공지하려고
③ 부모를 위한 자녀 독서 지도 강좌를 소개하려고
④ 아동 서적 구매 시 주의해야 할 점을 조언하려고
⑤ 어린이를 위한 책 읽어 주기 프로그램을 추천하려고

02 ▶242019-0170

대화를 듣고, 남자의 주장으로 가장 적절한 것을 고르시오.

① 며칠 뒤 일기 예보는 바뀌는 경우가 적지 않다.
② 날씨에 대비해 워크숍 장소를 변경하는 것이 좋다.
③ 우천 시 하이킹은 위험하므로 행사를 취소해야 한다.
④ 워크숍 장소는 직원들이 선호하는 장소로 골라야 한다.
⑤ 업무가 많더라도 점심시간에는 잠시 휴식을 취해야 한다.

03 수능특강 **PICK** ▶242019-0171

대화를 듣고, 두 사람의 관계를 가장 잘 나타낸 것을 고르시오.

① 잡지 기자 – 사육사
② 동물 사진작가 – 수강생
③ 반려동물 보호자 – 수의사
④ 동물원 관람객 – 동물원 직원
⑤ 방송 진행자 – 반려동물 훈련사

04 수능완성 **PICK** ▶242019-0172

대화를 듣고, 그림에서 대화의 내용과 일치하지 않는 것을 고르시오.

05 ▶242019-0173

대화를 듣고, 남자가 여자에게 부탁한 일로 가장 적절한 것을 고르시오.

① 책 대신 반납하기
② 발표 연습 도와주기
③ 발표 날짜 바꿔 주기
④ 미술 대회 용품 사다 주기
⑤ 선생님께 결석 여부 전달하기

06 ▶242019-0174

대화를 듣고, 남자가 지불할 금액을 고르시오.

① $80   ② $85   ③ $90
④ $95   ⑤ $100

07 수능특강 **PICK** ▶242019-0175

대화를 듣고, 남자가 온라인 IT 학회에 늦은 이유를 고르시오.

① 스마트폰이 고장 나서
② 학회 일정을 잘못 알아서
③ 접속 대기 시간이 오래 걸려서
④ 다른 온라인 강의 시간과 겹쳐서
⑤ 노트북 자동 업데이트가 오래 걸려서

08 수능특강 **PICK** ▶242019-0176

대화를 듣고, Doggy Palace에 관해 언급되지 않은 것을 고르시오.

① 위치   ② 이용 요금   ③ 시설
④ 영업시간   ⑤ 예약 방법

09 ▶242019-0177

robot racing competition에 관한 다음 내용을 듣고, 일치하지 않는 것을 고르시오.

① 로봇은 30미터를 경주하게 된다.
② 개인 또는 팀으로 참가가 가능하다.
③ 로봇의 크기나 형태에는 제한이 없다.
④ 가장 빠른 로봇 하나가 전국 대회에 참가하게 된다.
⑤ 참가 신청 마감은 다음 주 월요일이다.

▶242019-0178

10 다음 표를 보면서 대화를 듣고, 남자가 선택할 자외선 차단제를 고르시오.

Sunscreens

	Product	Brand	UV Index Scale	Type	Amount
①	A	Green Life	4	Gel	150 ml
②	B	Charming Soon	5	Spray	150 ml
③	C	Bright Skin	8	Gel	170 ml
④	D	Healthy Bodies	10	Stick	180 ml
⑤	E	Romance	12	Spray	250 ml

수능특강 **PICK** ▶242019-0179

11 대화를 듣고, 남자의 마지막 말에 대한 여자의 응답으로 가장 적절한 것을 고르시오.

① Okay. I'll repair the zipper on your pants now.

② For sure. I can wash my school uniform by myself.

③ Then, I'll go to the repair shop and pick up your pants.

④ Well, I couldn't find your pants anywhere in your room.

⑤ I'm sorry. I'll drop off your pants at the repair shop later.

수능특강 **PICK** ▶242019-0180

12 대화를 듣고, 여자의 마지막 말에 대한 남자의 응답으로 가장 적절한 것을 고르시오.

① We need to find the fastest way to go to work.

② You'd better go around the mountain to be safe.

③ I think that will cut my commuting time in half.

④ The road is blocked due to new tunnel construction.

⑤ There's a lot of traffic in the tunnel during rush hour.

▶242019-0181

13 대화를 듣고, 남자의 마지막 말에 대한 여자의 응답으로 가장 적절한 것을 고르시오. [3점]

Woman: _____

① Good telescopes tend to be more expensive.

② I'll bring some telescopes from home for you.

③ The sky should be clear enough to observe stars.

④ You should have some knowledge about stargazing first.

⑤ I already showed you the proper way to use this telescope.

수능특강 **PICK** ▶242019-0182

14 대화를 듣고, 여자의 마지막 말에 대한 남자의 응답으로 가장 적절한 것을 고르시오. [3점]

Man: _____

① No problem. I'm happy to show him around the school.

② All right. I'll call him and ask if we can meet next week.

③ You're welcome. I think he's familiar with our school now.

④ I'm grateful to him, too. He helps me study every weekend.

⑤ Yeah. I'm so excited to move to a new school and make new friends.

수능완성 **PICK** ▶242019-0183

15 다음 상황 설명을 듣고, Greg가 Juan에게 할 말로 가장 적절한 것을 고르시오. [3점]

Greg: _____

① Do you mind if I ride with you tomorrow?

② Could you drop me off on your way home?

③ I'll assign a driver to take you to the stadium.

④ Why don't we share a taxi to school tomorrow?

⑤ Okay. I'll call my parents to drive us to the game.

[16~17] 다음을 듣고, 물음에 답하시오.

▶242019-0184

16 남자가 하는 말의 주제로 가장 적절한 것은?

① ways to avoid being bitten by mosquitoes

② household products that keep mosquitoes away

③ substances that should not be applied to itchy skin

④ good foods to eat to build immunity to mosquito bites

⑤ natural solutions for reducing itchiness from mosquito bites

▶242019-0185

17 언급된 물질이 <u>아닌</u> 것은?

① aloe vera gel　　② witch hazel

③ tea tree oil　　④ honey

⑤ ground oatmeal

01

M Hello, parents! Do you want your child to ░░░░░░░░░░? Then ░░░░░░░░░░ the Little Fun Reading Club. Every month your child will receive a Little Fun Reading Club box containing three books. The books are matched to your child's age and interests that you check in the initial enrollment form. The books are selected through a rigorous review process, considering the subjects, authors, awards, and book reviews. And all the books are read and discussed by the Little Fun Reading Club experts before they are included in a ░░░░░░░░░░ for any age category. For only $16.95 a month, give your child the meaningful gift of reading!

> **Quiz** Little Fun Reading Club에 관해 언급되지 않은 것은?
> ① 매달 받게 되는 책의 수   ② 책 배달 날짜   ③ 한 달 구독료

02

M Ms. Ellis, have you checked the weather forecast for this Saturday?

W No. That's the day of ░░░░░░░░░░. We're going hiking.

M Right. But it seems like it might rain that day.

W Really? Let me check. *[Pause]* Oh, no. There's ░░░░░░░░░░ rain right now, but it could change. It's only Monday.

M That's true. But in case it does rain, we won't be able to go hiking.

W Hmm, you're right. Maybe we should plan something else.

M Yeah, we'd better change the place. It's better to ░░░░░░░░░░.

W Right. Let's talk about it together after lunch.

M Okay. Then we won't have to worry about whether it's going to rain or not.

W Exactly. I'll inform the others that we're going to meet at 1:30.

M Sounds good.

03

W Hello. I'm Sharon Baker. We talked on the phone yesterday.

M Hi, Ms. Baker. Come on in.

W Thanks for taking time out of your day for me. What were you doing?

M I was just cleaning up one of the cages, and now I'm getting food ready for the animals. I'm glad to have a chance to talk about my job with your readers.

W They'll love it. A lot of our young readers asked us to write about what it's like ░░░░░░░░░░.

M I'm so happy to let them know.

W Me, too. This will be in an article in the ░░░░░░░░░░. Can I ask what the pills in this bowl are? Are they medicine for animals?

M They're animal vitamins. We put them in their food.

W Oh, I never knew that there were animal vitamins. Can I go with you when you ░░░░░░░░░░?

M Of course. I'll show you how it's done.

W Great! I'll take some pictures.

04

M Look at our baby room, honey. I can't wait to see our baby.

W I can't believe we're going to be parents soon.

M Me, neither. Those stars [____] make this room look peaceful.

W Yes. They look nice.

M Right. When our baby sees this drawing of a smiling sun on the wall, he will surely smile, too.

W It makes me so happy to picture our baby smiling in his bed. Honey, did you put this cushion in the bed? I haven't seen it before.

M Yes, I did. Look! The letter "C" written on the cushion stands for "Chris", our baby's name.

W Good choice! And I like the [____] on the wall near the bed.

M I'm going to put our baby's first photo in the frame.

W I hope to see our baby crawl to the [____] next to the bed and play with it soon.

05

M Charlotte, can I talk to you for a moment?

W Sure, Ivan. Is it about the book I borrowed from you? I'm almost [____].

M No, it's not about that. You can keep it for as long as you need it.

W Okay. Then what's up?

M You're scheduled to give [____] next week, right?

W Yeah. And aren't you the week after me?

M Yeah. But I was asked to participate in an art competition, which is [____] as my presentation.

W Oh, so you need to change the date.

M Right. So could you switch presentation dates with me?

W Sure. No problem.

M Thank you so much. I'll tell the teacher about it.

W Okay. I hope you do well in the art competition.

M Thanks, Charlotte.

> **Quiz** 남자가 역사 발표일을 바꾸려는 이유는?
> ① 다른 과목 발표와 겹쳐서　　　② 미술 대회에 참가해야 해서　　　③ 발표에 필요한 책을 다 못 읽어서

06

W Hello, how can I help you?

M Hi. Are all of the shoes you have out on the floor?

W No, we have some [____].

M Okay. Do you have this shoe in a size 7?

W Let me check the system. [Pause] I'm sorry, we don't. But I can order it for you though. You should get it in about 3 days.

M Is it possible to have the shoes [____]?

W   Yes, but there's a $5 ▨▨▨.

M   That's okay. And the shoes are $90, right?

W   Yes.

M   I have this $5-off coupon. Can I use it for the shoes?

W   I'm sorry, but the coupon can't be used on any new items like these shoes.

M   No problem. I'll take the shoes and have them delivered to my house. Here's my credit card.

W   Thank you. Just a moment.

07

W   Hi, Ben. I didn't think I saw you at the online IT conference. Were you there?

M   Yes, but I was late, so I missed the first session.

W   Oh, it's too bad you missed it. That was the best part of the conference. Did you forget the start time?

M   No. I added a reminder on my phone with the right date and time. And I also made sure I ▨▨▨ before the conference.

W   Then why were you late?

M   I had a computer issue.

W   Was there ▨▨▨?

M   No. Just when I turned on my laptop, it ▨▨▨. It took around 30 minutes!

W   Oh, no! And you can't restart your laptop while it's updating.

M   Right. So I had to just sit and wait.

W   Sorry to hear that. But I heard they're going to upload a video of the entire conference later.

M   Oh, good. I can watch the first session later then.

08

M   Hi, Debbie. I heard you're taking a family trip.

W   Yes, next week. But I still haven't found anyone to ▨▨▨.

M   Why don't you use a dog boarding service at Doggy Palace?

W   What's that?

M   It's a place that looks after dogs. I took my dog there last month when I was out of town on business.

W   That sounds good. Where is it?

M   It's on 42nd Avenue, just ▨▨▨.

W   That's convenient. Do you remember the rates?

M   It's $40 per night and $150 per week.

W   Not bad. Are the facilities nice?

M   Yes. It's really clean, and they have a large outdoor park for the dogs to play in.

W　How can I use the service?

M　You can make a reservation ▨▨▨▨▨▨▨▨▨.

W　Great! That's where I'll take my dog. Thanks!

Quiz 밑줄 친 표현과 의미가 같은 것은?
It's a place that <u>looks after</u> dogs.
① trains　　②takes care of　　③looks forward to

09　M　Hello, robot lovers! I'm Mr. Rodriguez, the school science teacher, with an announcement about the school ▨▨▨▨▨▨▨. It's going to be held on Saturday, July 6th. Students build robots and race them in a 30-meter race. All students can participate, either individually or ▨▨▨▨▨▨▨. There are no restrictions on the size or shape of the robots. The three fastest robots will qualify to race ▨▨▨▨▨▨▨ in August. The deadline to enter is next Monday, and you can enter by ▨▨▨▨▨▨▨ located on the 1st floor to me. I look forward to your passionate participation!

10　W　Honey, are you shopping for sunscreen?

M　Yeah. Which one in this list do you think I should get?

W　Didn't you have Green Life sunscreen before?

M　Yeah. It felt ▨▨▨▨▨▨▨, which I didn't like. I'll try a different brand this time.

W　Okay. Look at this one's UV index. You should get one with a UV index of ▨▨▨▨▨▨▨.

M　Definitely. And this one is gel type. I don't like that.

W　I agree. It can feel sticky. So ▨▨▨▨▨▨▨ would be better.

M　Right. The difference between these last two is the amount.

W　How about buying the larger one?

M　That makes sense. I'm sure I'll use it a lot this summer.

W　Then this is the sunscreen you should get.

M　Right. I'll order it now.

11　M　Mom, did you get the zipper on my school uniform pants repaired?

W　I ▨▨▨▨▨▨▨ at the repair shop yesterday. And I got a message a little while ago that they're ▨▨▨▨▨▨▨. What's wrong?

M　My other pair of pants got too dirty to wear to school tomorrow.

12

W Todd, did you hear the news that the city's going to [____] through Albany Mountain?

M Yes. It's always [____] all the way to work due to the mountain.

W When the tunnel is completed, you'll be able to go right through it.

Quiz 괄호 안에서 알맞은 것을 고르시오.

Q: What problem does Albany Mountain cause for the man?

A: It causes the [traffic congestion / limited visibility] problem.

13

M Ms. Green, can I ask you something?

W Sure, Peter. Is it about today's class?

M No, it's about stargazing. I've become really interested in it recently.

W That's cool. I [____] when I was young, too.

M That's what I thought since you're a science teacher. Could you [____] for me to buy?

W Hmm. Well, there's a wide variety of them with different functions and prices.

M I noticed that. I'm guessing that the more expensive, the better, right?

W Yes, in general. But for beginners like you, there's no need to buy an expensive one.

M That's what I thought.

W So how about using some of my telescopes first to find out which one [____]?

M Oh, really? That'd be really helpful in making my decision.

14

W Paul, do you have a minute?

M Yes, Ms. Brown.

W A new student named Ben Jones is transferring to our school next week.

M Oh, that's great.

W So, I wonder if you can [____] sometime before next Monday.

M Sure, I'd love to. When would be good?

W Ben said any time this weekend is possible. When is [____]?

M Saturday morning is good. I work at the library in the afternoon. And I'm going on a picnic with my family on Sunday.

W Okay. Saturday morning should be fine with Ben. Could you make plans with him? I'll give you his phone number.

M Sure. I'll call him to [____] to meet up.

W That'd be great. He'll really appreciate your help.

15 **W** Greg and Juan are neighborhood friends who go to the same college. They both play on the college football team and they have an early game tomorrow at a college about an hour away. Because ▩▩▩▩, the football players have to find their own way to the game. However, Greg is worried about driving to the game because he ▩▩▩▩, so he's not used to driving long distances. Luckily, he finds out that Juan is planning to drive to the game. So, he wants to ask Juan if he can ▩▩▩▩. In this situation, what would Greg most likely say to Juan?

> **Quiz** 우리말과 같도록 빈칸에 알맞은 말을 담화에서 찾아 쓰시오.
> 그는 처음에는 긴장했지만, 이제는 고속 도로에서 운전하는 것에 익숙하다.
> He was nervous at first, but now he's _____ _____ _____ on the highway.

16~17 **M** Hi, everyone! When the weather gets warmer, annoying mosquitoes come out. And with mosquitoes come ▩▩▩▩! So today I'd like to talk about natural substances you can apply to mosquito bites. First of all, you can try aloe vera. Known for ▩▩▩▩, aloe vera gel can provide instant relief to your itchiness. You can also use witch hazel, which has cooling effects and can reduce itchiness. Apply it directly to mosquito bites using a cotton pad. Surprisingly, honey can also soothe skin irritated by mosquito bites and even prevent infection. Apply a little on the bites and leave it on for a while before rinsing. Lastly, soaking in an oatmeal bath or applying a paste of ground oatmeal mixed with water can provide relief from itching and promote healing. So the next time you become ▩▩▩▩, skip going to the pharmacy and instead try these natural substances for some needed relief. Thank you for listening!

Dictation 빠른답

01 ☐ learn the enjoyment of reading ☐ enroll them in ☐ subscription box

02 ☐ the company workshop ☐ a high chance of ☐ be safe than sorry

03 ☐ working with animals at a zoo ☐ October issue of our magazine ☐ feed the animals

04 ☐ hanging from the ceiling ☐ round photo frame ☐ stuffed toy dog

05 ☐ done with it ☐ your history presentation ☐ on the same day

06 ☐ in the storeroom ☐ delivered to my house ☐ delivery fee for that

07 ☐ had the right access link ☐ something wrong with your computer ☐ automatically started updating

08 ☐ take care of our dog ☐ a few minutes from the airport

09 ☐ robot racing competition ☐ as a team ☐ in the national competition ☐ submitting a registration form

10 ☐ a bit sticky ☐ at least 7 ☐ either stick or spray

11 ☐ dropped them off ☐ ready to be picked up

12 ☐ make a tunnel ☐ bumper-to-bumper

13 ☐ got into stargazing ☐ recommend a good telescope ☐ suits you best

14 ☐ give him a school tour ☐ convenient for you ☐ figure out the time and place

15 ☐ the team bus broke down ☐ recently just got his driver's license ☐ go to the game with him

16~17 ☐ itchy mosquito bites ☐ its soothing effect ☐ a victim of mosquitoes

---

Quiz 01 ② **05** ② **08** ② **12** traffic congestion **15** used to driving

▶242019-0186

01 다음을 듣고, 여자가 하는 말의 목적으로 가장 적절한 것을 고르시오.

① 새로운 교복 규정을 설명하려고
② 동아리 단체복 제작을 공지하려고
③ 옷 제작 동아리 가입을 권유하려고
④ 동아리 패션쇼를 할 장소를 섭외하려고
⑤ 남성복 리폼 판매 행사 일정을 안내하려고

▶242019-0187

02 대화를 듣고, 남자의 의견으로 가장 적절한 것을 고르시오.

① 추운 날씨는 건강에 이롭다.
② 청결이 감기 예방에 중요하다.
③ 건강을 위해 충분히 자야 한다.
④ 부상 치료는 제때에 해야 한다.
⑤ 적정 체온을 항상 유지해야 한다.

▶242019-0188

03 대화를 듣고, 두 사람의 관계를 가장 잘 나타낸 것을 고르시오.

① 안무가 – 무용수   ② 사회자 – 마술사
③ 전시 기획자 – 화가   ④ 사진작가 – 패션모델
⑤ 코치 – 리듬체조 선수

수능특강 **PICK**   ▶242019-0189

04 대화를 듣고, 그림에서 대화의 내용과 일치하지 않는 것을 고르시오.

수능특강 **PICK**   ▶242019-0190

05 대화를 듣고, 여자가 할 일로 가장 적절한 것을 고르시오.

① 프로젝터와 스크린 챙기기   ② 담요 가져오기
③ 영화 선택하기   ④ 접이식 의자 구매하기
⑤ 짐을 차에 싣기

수능특강 **PICK**   ▶242019-0191

06 대화를 듣고, 남자가 지불할 금액을 고르시오. [3점]

① $72   ② $81   ③ $90
④ $108   ⑤ $120

▶242019-0192

07 대화를 듣고, 여자가 영화관에 갈 수 없는 이유를 고르시오.

① 아르바이트를 해야 해서
② 컴퓨터 시험을 봐야 해서
③ 영화 비평문을 써야 해서
④ 책을 사러 서점에 가야 해서
⑤ 취업 면접 특강을 들어야 해서

수능특강 **PICK**   ▶242019-0193

08 대화를 듣고, 상자 배달에 관해 언급되지 않은 것을 고르시오.

① 배달지 주소   ② 배달 물품
③ 비용 산정 방법   ④ 배달 소요 시간
⑤ 배달 운송 수단

▶242019-0194

09 Tom's Double Pizza에 관한 다음 내용을 듣고, 일치하지 않는 것을 고르시오.

① 5월 1일에 출시되었다.
② 매운 소스로 맛을 냈다.
③ 토마토가 토핑으로 올라간다.
④ 5월에 포장해 가면 주문 금액에서 10% 할인받는다.
⑤ 배달 주문하면 정확히 20분 안에 도착한다.

수능특강 **PICK**   ▶242019-0195

10 다음 표를 보면서 대화를 듣고, 남자가 구입할 무선 포인터를 고르시오.

King Wireless Pointers

	Model	Price	Control Distance	Laser Color	Battery Life
①	A	$20	10 m	Green	36 hours
②	B	$25	30 m	Red	36 hours
③	C	$30	30 m	Green	48 hours
④	D	$35	50 m	Red	72 hours
⑤	E	$45	60 m	Red	72 hours

▶242019-0196

11 대화를 듣고, 남자의 마지막 말에 대한 여자의 응답으로 가장 적절한 것을 고르시오.

① It's so pity. I really wanted you to make it this time.

② That's awesome! As a big fan of his, I have all of his albums.

③ I'm sorry. I hope you will get the music CD by next weekend.

④ Good luck. I'm sure you will definitely get a chance to debut.

⑤ You're right. I'll find a way to look into it without revealing the surprise.

수능완성 **PICK**   ▶242019-0197

12 대화를 듣고, 여자의 마지막 말에 대한 남자의 응답으로 가장 적절한 것을 고르시오.

① Please look again. I'm sure I gave it to you.

② You're right. Eye ointments are more effective than pills.

③ I'm sorry, but you can't purchase it without a prescription.

④ Sure. Just drop off your prescription and come back later.

⑤ Don't worry. This ointment is safe to use with contact lenses.

▶242019-0198

13 대화를 듣고, 남자의 마지막 말에 대한 여자의 응답으로 가장 적절한 것을 고르시오.

Woman: _____

① I'm really sorry. I never did it on purpose.

② That's a wonderful idea. I'm proud of you.

③ Okay. Keep your word. I'll be watching you.

④ Thank God. Let's get this back to the owner.

⑤ I still don't get it. Let me have an example.

수능완성 **PICK**   ▶242019-0199

14 대화를 듣고, 여자의 마지막 말에 대한 남자의 응답으로 가장 적절한 것을 고르시오. [3점]

Man: _____

① Then, we should rent hanboks and take some pictures.

② Hmm, the line is long even though it's just a normal day.

③ Well, I think the Korean Folk Village is the best place to visit.

④ No problem! We're wearing hanboks, so we can get a discount.

⑤ Don't worry. We got here early, so I think we can sit in the front row.

▶242019-0200

15 다음 상황 설명을 듣고, Danny가 Clara에게 할 말로 가장 적절한 것을 고르시오. [3점]

Danny: _____

① Sorry. I can't come to your house for the history report as we planned.

② Right. I'll just keep looking for a better place to study history together.

③ Too bad. I hope your baby sister makes the full and immediate recovery.

④ Unbelievable. How can your parents put up with such rude behavior like that?

⑤ Exactly. I'll ask the teacher to reschedule the deadline for the history report.

수능완성 **PICK**

[16~17] 다음을 듣고, 물음에 답하시오.

▶242019-0201

16 여자가 하는 말의 주제로 가장 적절한 것은?

① countries with identical national flowers

② misconceptions about national identities

③ unexpected meanings of national flowers

④ the importance of having national symbols

⑤ reasons why national heritage should be preserved

▶242019-0202

17 언급된 나라가 아닌 것은?

① England   ② India   ③ Egypt

④ Belgium   ⑤ France

01 W Hello, Ariel High School freshmen. I'm Jeanie Morrison, the president of the Teen Designer Club. Are you interested in designing clothes? Well, the Teen Designer Club offers a fantastic opportunity to pursue your passion. You'll get to _____ that fit you perfectly. You might be wondering if it's more difficult and expensive _____. Well, the answer is no! And not only is it cheaper, it's really fun and easy to learn. And hey, boys, don't worry! Our club warmly welcomes everybody! So if you're interested, feel free to _____ through our website, www.teendesigners.com, or just give us a call. Thank you!

02 M Look, it's snowing. I love winter weather so much.

W Not me! _____. It's so cold!

M Probably you don't know that cold weather can be good for you.

W No way! It always gives me a cold and makes me feel gloomy.

M Of course, you can catch a cold, but cold weather can _____.

W How's that?

M The cold can kill harmful bacteria, which can boost your overall health.

W Oh, I didn't know that. That sounds similar to cold therapy, which is commonly used to treat injuries.

M Exactly. The cold can _____ and regulate body temperature, leading to deeper and more restful sleep.

W Wow. I guess I should try to start appreciating the cold weather in the winter.

> **Quiz** 빈칸에 알맞은 것은?
> Q: Why does the woman dislike cold weather?
> A: Because _____.
> ① she catches a cold easily and feels gloomy
> ② she can't work out outside
> ③ she has to wear too many clothes

03 M Good morning! How are you today?

W Couldn't be better. I'm so happy to be working with you.

M Likewise. We have _____ planned for today's shoot.

W I can't wait to get started.

M Me too. And if you have any ideas or preferences, please let me know.

W I appreciate that. I'll definitely share my thoughts during the shoot.

M Perfect. Remember, when you're _____, show off your unique style and personality.

W Okay, I'll _____ that bring the outfits to life.

M Fantastic! Let's get started. Get ready to shine, and I will capture your brilliance.

W Yeah! Let's create some magic!

04

W   Dad, come and see how I've rearranged my study area.

M   Okay, Sally. Oh, you put your desk under the window.

W   Right. Now I can [   ].

M   That's nice. And you put your new laptop on the right side of the desk.

W   Yeah. I'm so happy to have my own laptop.

M   I bet! Oh, the lamp on the left side of the desk is also new.

W   Right. It's adjustable.

M   Good. Your pencil holder next to it [   ]. It looks like a soccer ball. That's really cool.

W   Isn't it? My friend Jennifer gave it to me for my birthday.

M   Oh, where did you put all your books that used to be on the bookshelf? It's almost empty now.

W   I put most of them on the bookshelf in the living room. Only these two books are [   ].

M   Well, I really like what you've done here.

05

M   Honey, I'm so excited about going camping tomorrow.

W   Me, too. I especially like our plan of [   ] by the campfire.

M   Absolutely! I think it's a great idea.

W   It's going to be so romantic. Did you pack the projector and screen?

M   Of course. I've put them in the car.

W   Great. Thanks.

M   Shall we take some blankets just [   ] in the evening?

W   I've already packed them in our luggage.

M   Good. Oh, we haven't decided which movie we're going to watch tomorrow. Could you pick one?

W   Sure. I'll choose a movie.

M   Thanks. Do you know [   ]?

W   I think I last saw them in the trunk.

M   Alright. I'll check when I'm putting the luggage in the car.

W   Great. I cannot wait for tomorrow!

○ **Quiz** 빈칸에 알맞은 말을 대화에서 찾아 쓰시오.

Q: What do they take just in case it gets cold in the evening?

A: They take _____ _____ .

06

W Hello. How may I help you?

M Hello. Could I book some activities here in this resort?

W Sure. For how many people? And what activities are you thinking of?

M There are three of us, and we'd like to go sea kayaking, tomorrow morning if possible. How much is that?

W Sure, no problem. It's   , and it starts at 8 a.m.

M Perfect. And how much are tickets for the aquarium and virtual reality game room?

W They're   and $10 for the virtual reality game room.

M The virtual reality game room sounds exciting. How long would we get in the virtual reality game room?

W One hour.

M Okay. I'll take 3 tickets for that, too. Oh! I have   .

W Okay. So 3 tickets for sea kayaking and 3 tickets for the virtual reality game room. And you get 10% off the total price.

M Yes. Here's my credit card.

07

M Hi, Jenny. How did your computer test go?

W Not very well. I studied a lot too. It's frustrating.

M I understand how you feel. It sounds like you could   . How about going to the movies tonight?

W Thanks for the offer, but I'm afraid I can't.

M Why not? Do you have your part-time job tonight?

W No, I   .

M I see. Well, if anything changes and you can go, let me know. There are some really good movies playing right now.

W Thanks, but I'm   on job interviews at the career center tonight.

M Oh, I see. That'll be really useful. I'll probably just go to the bookstore and look around.

W That sounds like a good plan.

08

[Telephone rings.]

W Blue Quick Delivery Service. How can I help you?

M Hi. I'd like to have a small package delivered to San Francisco, California.

W All right. Can you please give me   ?

M Sure. John Faulk and 4512 West River Road, San Francisco, California.

W Thanks. And where can we pick up your package?

M   1414 University Ave., here in Berkeley.

W   Okay. May I ask ▮▮▮▮▮▮▮▮?

M   It's a camera.

W   All right. I'll send somebody over to pick it up. He should be there in about an hour.

M   Thank you. How much will it cost?

W   Well, we have to weigh your package to decide the charge.

M   I see. (A) How long will it take for the package to be delivered?

W   It'll ▮▮▮▮▮▮▮▮, I think.

M   Okay, thanks.

> **Quiz** 밑줄 친 (A)를 우리말로 해석하시오.
> _____

09

M   Tom's pizza just got better! We just introduced our brand-new creation, Tom's Double Pizza, on May 1st! Prepare yourself for an explosion of fiery flavors with our ▮▮▮▮▮▮▮▮. Topped with mouthwatering bacon, fresh tomatoes, and black olives, every bite will take you to pizza heaven. And ▮▮▮▮▮▮▮▮ in May, you get a 15% off your order and a free soft drink. Or ▮▮▮▮▮▮▮▮, your pizza will arrive at your doorstep within just 20 minutes! So, don't wait to enjoy the incredible taste of the new Tom's Double Pizza.

10

W   Honey, why are you looking at wireless pointers on the Internet? Are you going to buy one?

M   Yes. I ▮▮▮▮▮▮▮▮ next week.

W   Have you ever used one before?

M   No. I'm not sure which one to get. But I don't want to spend more than $40.

W   I know a little about them. I suggest you get one ▮▮▮▮▮▮▮▮ of at least 30 meters.

M   Okay. Then I won't get this one.

W   Do you have any preference for the laser color? Well, how about green?

M   That'd be okay, but red is usually better for people to see.

W   You might be right. How about battery life?

M   I don't think I need this one ▮▮▮▮▮▮▮▮. I know I won't use it that often. I'll get this one.

W   I think that's a good choice.

11

M   Peggy, have you ▮▮▮▮▮▮▮▮ for your coworker yet?

W   Yes. I bought a music CD. It's his favorite band's debut album.

M   That's cool. But I think ▮▮▮▮▮▮▮▮ if he already has it.

12

W Excuse me, but I think you forgot to include the eye ointment.

M Let me check. Well, the eye ointment is _____.

W Oh, my doctor must have forgotten to add it to the prescription. Can I _____?

> **Quiz** 우리말과 같도록 빈칸에 알맞은 말을 대화에서 찾아 쓰시오.
> 그는 수도꼭지를 잠그는 것을 잊어버린 것이 틀림없다.
> He _____ _____ _____ to turn off the faucet.

13

W Hey, Brian. I saw _____ yesterday.

M What did you see?

W I saw it in the park. Can you guess?

M Hmm. I'm not sure. Just tell me.

W I saw _____.

M Oh... I don't like when people throw trash.

W Right? And actually, that boy was you!

M You saw that? I just... I couldn't find a trash can anywhere. There should be more trash cans in the park.

W I understand but there might be better alternatives. You know our park is getting dirtier these days.

M It's not like I litter all the time. It was just a few times. I promise _____.

14

W Hey, Joe. It's a perfect day to _____, isn't it?

M Yeah. I'm so glad we came here today.

W Me too. Do you know where the ticket booth is?

M It's over there. Wow, _____.

W Oh, it looks like there's a special event today.

M Really?

W Yeah. See the sign. There's a special festival related to the Joseon Dynasty today.

M That sounds really cool!

W Yeah! Let's get in line and get our tickets.

M All right. Hey, do you see those people inside the village wearing hanboks?

W Yeah. I wonder _____ here.

M Let's ask the person at the ticket booth.

W What if they say yes?

15 **W** Danny and Clara are middle school friends and classmates who are taking history class together. Their history teacher, Mr. Davidson, ＿＿＿＿＿＿. Danny and Clara decided to work on it together, and made plans to meet at Clara's house the next evening to work on it. However, after Danny told his parents about the meeting at Clara's house, his parents informed him that ＿＿＿＿＿＿ for the next evening, so he needs to stay home and ＿＿＿＿＿＿ that evening. Consequently, he wants to inform Clara that he cannot make it that day. In this situation, what would Danny most likely say to Clara?

○ **Quiz** 밑줄 친 표현과 의미가 같은 것은?
He needs to <u>take care of</u> his baby sister.
① brush aside ② look after ③ take on

16~17 **W** Hello, students. Last class, ＿＿＿＿＿＿. National identity can be formed through national symbols. Every country in the world has numerous national symbols, such as a national anthem, flag, bird or flower. Today we're going to ＿＿＿＿＿＿. A large number of countries across the globe have national floral emblems. Some of them are chosen by the governments, while others are selected through public polls. Interestingly, some countries share ＿＿＿＿＿＿. Do you know what is the official flower in both the United States and England? The answer is the rose. Also, the tulip is the national flower of both Turkey and the Netherlands. And India and Egypt have the lotus as their national flower. The red poppy is the national flower for Belgium and Albania. Now let's take a look at some photos of floral emblems.

Dictation 빠른답

01 ☐ create your own custom clothes
☐ compared to buying regular clothes
☐ reach out to us

02 ☐ I can't stand winter ☐ help make you stronger
☐ provide relief for certain conditions

03 ☐ some amazing outfits and locations
☐ in front of my camera ☐ try to take poses

04 ☐ look outside when I study ☐ has a unique shape
☐ the ones I need nowadays

05 ☐ watching a movie outdoors ☐ in case it gets cold
☐ where the folding chairs are

06 ☐ $20 per person ☐ $30 for the aquarium
☐ a 10% off coupon

07 ☐ use a break to recharge ☐ only work during the week
☐ going to a special lecture

08 ☐ the receiver's name and address ☐ what you are sending
☐ take about two hours

09 ☐ super spicy special garlic sauce ☐ if you order takeout
☐ if you order for delivery

10 ☐ need one for my presentation ☐ with a control distance
☐ with a longer battery life

11 ☐ bought a surprise birthday present ☐ you need to check

12 ☐ not included in your prescription
☐ buy it over the counter

13 ☐ something that bothered me ☐ a boy littering in the park
☐ I'll never do it again

14 ☐ visit the Korean Folk Village ☐ look at the long line
☐ if we can rent hanboks

15 ☐ gave them a history report to do ☐ they have a plan
☐ take care of his baby sister

16~17 ☐ we learned about national identity
☐ focus on national flowers ☐ the same national flower

Quiz **02** ① **05** some blankets **08** 포장한 상품이 배달되는 데 얼마나 걸릴까요? **12** must have forgotten **15** ②

수능완성 PICK ▶242019-0203

01 다음을 듣고, 남자가 하는 말의 목적으로 가장 적절한 것을 고르시오.

① 학교 축제 일정에 대해 공지하려고
② 원활한 행사 진행을 위한 협조를 부탁하려고
③ 학년 회장의 미이행 공약 실행을 촉구하려고
④ 학년 회장 선거의 후보 등록 절차를 안내하려고
⑤ 학년 회장으로 출마한 친구에 대해 지지를 호소하려고

수능완성 PICK ▶242019-0204

02 대화를 듣고, 여자의 의견으로 가장 적절한 것을 고르시오.

① 세계화에 따른 열린 마음을 가져야 한다.
② 자신의 경제 상황에 맞는 여행 계획이 필요하다.
③ 가난한 지역의 사람들에 대한 편견을 버려야 한다.
④ 문명이 발달한 곳에 가야 안전한 여행을 할 수 있다.
⑤ 낯선 나라에서의 문화 체험은 시야와 견문을 넓혀 준다.

▶242019-0205

03 다음을 듣고, 남자가 하는 말의 요지로 가장 적절한 것을 고르시오.

① 과도한 동영상 시청은 아이들의 상상력을 제한한다.
② 아이들이 동영상을 직접 제작하도록 가르쳐야 한다.
③ 동영상은 책 내용을 간결하게 요약하는 데 유용하다.
④ 동영상을 통한 외국어 학습은 아이들에게 효과가 있다.
⑤ 발달 단계에 맞춘 동영상 자료는 아동 교육에 필수적이다.

수능완성 PICK ▶242019-0206

04 대화를 듣고, 그림에서 대화의 내용과 일치하지 않는 것을 고르시오.

05 대화를 듣고, 여자가 할 일로 가장 적절한 것을 고르시오.

① 역에 마중 가기
② 선물 목록 만들기
③ 전화로 꽃 주문하기
④ 버스 관광 예약하기
⑤ 음식점 위치 파악하기

▶242019-0208

06 대화를 듣고, 여자가 지불할 금액을 고르시오 [3점]

① $28   ② $34   ③ $42
④ $46   ⑤ $50

수능완성 PICK ▶242019-0209

07 대화를 듣고, 남자가 토요일에 여자와 함께 갈 수 없는 이유를 고르시오.

① 의학 지식이 부족해서
② 누나 결혼식이 있어서
③ 실험실 근무를 해야 해서
④ 프랑스어를 잘하지 못해서
⑤ 새로운 프로젝트로 바빠서

수능특강 PICK ▶242019-0210

08 대화를 듣고, 방과 후 학교 수학 수업에 관해 언급되지 않은 것을 고르시오.

① 수강 대상   ② 시작 날짜   ③ 수강료
④ 교재   ⑤ 강사

수능특강 PICK ▶242019-0211

09 Vegan Dessert Contest에 관한 다음 내용을 듣고, 일치하지 않는 것을 고르시오.

① 우유, 버터, 달걀을 사용하지 말아야 한다.
② 요리법과 요리 사진을 4월 21일까지 보내야 한다.
③ 웹사이트 방문자들은 가장 좋아하는 후식에 투표할 수 있다.
④ 요리사들의 평가가 심사에 반영될 것이다.
⑤ 우승자는 1,000달러를 받게 될 것이다.

▶ 242019-0212

10 다음 표를 보면서 대화를 듣고, 두 사람이 주문할 반려견 목줄을 고르시오.

Dog Leashes for Small Dogs

	Model	Length (feet)	Price	Padded Handle	Material
①	A	4	$6	○	Nylon
②	B	4	$8	○	Leather
③	C	6	$10	×	Nylon
④	D	6	$17	○	Leather
⑤	E	8	$17	×	Nylon

수능특강 **PICK**　　　▶ 242019-0213

11 대화를 듣고, 남자의 마지막 말에 대한 여자의 응답으로 가장 적절한 것을 고르시오.

① Too late. Someone already picked it up.
② Well, I'll give you a call when it's done.
③ I'm sorry. I don't know why the button's stuck.
④ It started yesterday after I dropped the camera.
⑤ Not for long. I've had the camera for only a month.

수능특강 **PICK**　　　▶ 242019-0214

12 대화를 듣고, 여자의 마지막 말에 대한 남자의 응답으로 가장 적절한 것을 고르시오.

① No problem. I can relax and breathe deeply.
② Of course. I cleaned the windows yesterday.
③ Don't worry. I've already washed my hands.
④ Good. I'll spray it on my window to clean it.
⑤ You're right. I'll open the window right away.

▶ 242019-0215

13 대화를 듣고, 남자의 마지막 말에 대한 여자의 응답으로 가장 적절한 것을 고르시오.

Woman: _____

① Don't eat too much. You'll get a stomachache.
② I can't eat any more. Let's take the leftovers to go.
③ I really want to go to Vietnam. I've never been there.
④ Thanks. The pho you recommended was delicious.
⑤ Okay, let's go. I hope it's as delicious as you say.

▶ 242019-0216

14 대화를 듣고, 여자의 마지막 말에 대한 남자의 응답으로 가장 적절한 것을 고르시오. [3점]

Man: _____

① Yes. You can connect through a pen pal program.
② No. I don't have any friends to help me with my essay.
③ No. You can't get much without using any smart devices.
④ Yes. You can make a new friend and get help with your essay.
⑤ Yes. I'll text you my email so you can pass it along to her.

수능특강 **PICK**　　　▶ 242019-0217

15 다음 상황 설명을 듣고, Joshua가 Maya에게 할 말로 가장 적절한 것을 고르시오. [3점]

Joshua: _____

① Don't forget the plant needs sunlight to survive.
② Try not to water the plant too much or it will die.
③ You should put the plant in a cool, shaded place.
④ Be sure to give the plant fresh air as often as possible.
⑤ You need to trim the plant to prevent it from overgrowing.

[16~17] 다음을 듣고, 물음에 답하시오.

▶ 242019-0218

16 남자가 하는 말의 주제로 가장 적절한 것은?

① various ways to prevent catching a cold
② habits that are dangerous to people's health
③ common signs and symptoms of colds and flu
④ environmental factors that threaten human life
⑤ importance of having a regular exercise routine

▶ 242019-0219

17 언급된 행동이 <u>아닌</u> 것은?

① avoiding extreme diets
② washing hands
③ exercising
④ controlling house temperature
⑤ getting enough sleep

01

M Good morning, everyone. Thank you for the warm welcome. I'm standing here today _____ the strongest presidential candidate for our grade, Mark Jenson. The reasons I support him are simple. This year, there are two major events for us as seniors. First is the school festival and the second is the dance party at the end of the school year. They're the biggest and most important events of our high school lives, and they require a tremendous amount of _____. So, we need a leader who can meet that challenge. And I think Mark _____ to be able to plan and put on these two major events. He has shown leadership in class, and he will do the same for the school if we elect him. So vote for Mark. Thank you.

> **Quiz** 빈칸에 알맞은 말을 담화에서 찾아 쓰시오.
> Q: What are two major events for them as seniors?
> A: _____.

02

W Hi, Tom. Where are you headed?

M Hi, Lily. I'm going to meet Jimmy and Tyler to _____.

W Where are you guys going?

M We haven't decided yet. Jimmy wants to travel to Rome again while Tyler firmly insists that we go to a country that we have not been to before like Nepal.

W Why does Jimmy want to go to Rome again?

M Because when we went there last time, we didn't have time to do everything we wanted.

W What's Tyler's argument?

M He thinks that _____ doesn't challenge us enough. What do you think?

W Hmm. If I had a vote, I'd go with Tyler.

M Why is that?

W First of all, when _____, any experiences you have of the new culture will broaden your horizon.

M Hmm, interesting.

W Also, I think you'll learn a lot from a journey into a new country you've never been to.

03

M Hello, I'm Steve Jennings from Ace Parents Academy. Kids can learn a lot from watching videos, but that doesn't mean watching videos is always beneficial for them. Above all, _____ that could be spent on reading books and prevents them from developing an interest in it. As a consequence, _____. When children read, they engage in imagining characters and scenes, which enhances their creativity. However, with videos such as movies and cartoons, everything is presented visually, so _____. Excessive video consumption can hinder their imaginative abilities, leaving minimal space for creative thinking.

04

W Hi, Mr. White. I'm Nancy Blake, Elin's mom.

M Nice to meet you, Ms. Blake. Have a seat, please.

W Thank you.

M Last week I asked my students to draw a picture, and this is Elin's.

W Oh, it's nice. She put the sun in the corner.

M It's a common thing among kids. What is interesting is that Elin drew _____.

W You're right. Smoke is coming out of it. Does it mean anything special?

M A smoking chimney means an expression of warmth and affection within the family.

W That's a good sign.

M And the wide-open door leading to the pathway _____ to the outside world.

W That makes sense. The girl who is jumping rope must be Elin.

M Yes, I think so. And take a look at this tree. She drew _____. It means she has a well-rounded nature.

W It's very interesting that we can read her mind just with a picture.

M I hope it helps you understand a part of her psychological state.

> **Quiz** 괄호 안에서 알맞은 것을 고르시오
> Q: What could Mr. White learn about Elin from her drawing?
> A: He could gain insight into her [psychological / physiological] state.

05

W Honey, do you remember that my cousin, Amy, will be arriving at the station at 10:00 a.m. this Saturday?

M Sure. I'm going to pick her up. We haven't seen her for a long time since we moved here.

W Yeah. She is going to stay with us all weekend. Let's _____ for her.

M Okay. Like I told you, I've already made a reservation at a fancy restaurant for her.

W That's sweet. And let's decorate the house for her arrival.

M Good idea. _____. I'll take care of that.

W Perfect. There's a nice flower shop near your workplace.

M Exactly. I'll call them to see what they have. Also, I'll book a city bus tour before dinner on Saturday.

W Sounds like a great plan. I wonder if there's anything I can do.

M Let's get her a small gift to celebrate her first visit to our home.

W Good idea. I'll make _____ for her.

M Let's show Amy how much we're looking forward to seeing her.

06

M Hello. Is there anything I can help you with today?

W Hi. Actually, yes. Do you have this shirt in a smaller size? I only see larges here.

M Yes, there are smalls and mediums in the back. What size would you like?

W A medium, please. And is it part of the sale?

M Yes. It's _____. It's now $28.

W Great! I'll buy it. What are other things on sale?

M _____. Would you like me to show you where they are?

W Yes, please. My son actually needs a hat.

M Here they are. They're all on sale.

W Oh, this one is perfect for my son. How much is it?

M _____. But you get 10% off.

W It's not expensive. I'll buy that, too.

07

W Hey, Matthew. I've found a young French biomedical engineer.

M Oh? That's great.

W Yes. I believe she can _____ in completing our company's new major project. So I want her to join our team.

M How are you going to get her to join us?

W I will go to Daejeon to meet her this Saturday. She is working in a lab there.

M Did you _____ to meet her?

W Yes. I sent her an email and she said she could meet me on Saturday.

M I see. But do you think she will be interested?

W I think I am going to have to persuade her to work with us.

M Oh, really?

W Yeah. But the biggest problem is she doesn't speak Korean well, and I only speak a little French.

M Oh, that's a problem.

W So, could you go see her with me? _____, don't you?

M Yes, I do. But I'm afraid I can't. My older sister is getting married this Saturday.

W Oh, I forgot. Anyway, I need to find someone to help me out.

○ **Quiz** 우리말과 같도록 빈칸에 알맞은 말을 대화에서 찾아 쓰시오.
교사들은 더 많은 학생이 그들과 함께 일하도록 설득할 방법이 필요하다.
Teachers need ways to _____ more students _____ _____ with them.

08

W   Excuse me, Mr. Smith. May I talk to you for a minute?

M   Sure. What is it?

W   I'd like to get more [_____] math class you mentioned yesterday.

M   Okay. It's targeted for students who are struggling in math.

W   I see. When does the class start?

M   [_____]. And it'll meet after school on Mondays, Wednesdays, and Fridays.

W   All right. And how much does it cost?

M   Don't worry. It's free.

W   That's great. I have one more question. Who's going to teach it?

M   Probably a university student who [_____].

W   Okay, Mr. Smith. Thank you so much for the detailed information.

M   You're welcome. Come to me anytime if you need my help.

09

W   Have you always wanted to show off your cooking skills? Think of a delicious dessert that is [_____], and enter the Vegan Dessert Contest. Send us your recipe and a photo of your dish by April 21st. After all entries have been uploaded, visitors to our website can [_____]. Last year, chefs assessed the entries, but this year is different. The winner will be chosen based only on the total number of votes each entry receives. The winner will receive $1,000, and will [_____]. Be creative and show us your best desserts for vegans!

10

M   Honey, it looks like you're shopping for something online.

W   I am. I'm [_____] for Walnut. His leash is coming apart.

M   Good idea. I noticed that too. Have you found a good site?

W   Yeah. Here's a site selling leashes. What length do you think we should get?

M   This one seems too long. I think under 7 feet would be good.

W   I agree. And this one is too expensive. There's no need to [_____].

M   Right. And look, these two have padded handles. Do you think that's necessary?

W   We go for long walks, so that would be much more comfortable.

M   Good point. So [_____]. What do you think about this one?

W   Hmm. Well, I think nylon comes apart pretty easily.

M   You're right. Let's order the other one then.

Quiz 밑줄 친 표현과 의미가 같은 것은?
I think nylon <u>comes apart</u> pretty easily.
① blows up   ② sticks together   ③ splits up

11
M Hi. The button on my digital camera is stuck. Would you be able to fix it?

W Let me have a look. *[Pause]* I see what's wrong. I can fix it later today.

M Okay. [_____] to pick it up?

12
W Jack, what did you spray in your room? The smell is really strong.

M It's antibacterial spray. Mike, my friend, gave it to me. He said I should spray it to keep my room clean.

W Yeah, but you should [_____] so you're not breathing so much of it in.

13
W We finally finished the project!

M It feels so good! Now I'm as hungry as a bear. Let's [_____].

W Yeah. I [_____]! What do you want to eat?

M How about pho?

W Pho? What's that?

M It's a Vietnamese noodle soup dish. You need to try it.

W Well, it sounds good, but will that be enough? I normally don't get full off of just noodles.

M But pho is different. There's [_____] in it.

W Oh, meat? Then it definitely sounds like it'd be enough.

M There are also different vegetables in it. I'm sure you'll love it.

14
M Hey, Gloria. You look really busy.

W Yes. I have to [_____] without the help of the internet, and it's driving me crazy.

M Singapore? Do you know a lot about it?

W No. That's the problem.

M Then why do you have to write about it?

W The teacher randomly gave us our topic. There's so much research I need to do.

M If you want, I can [_____]?

W Who's Tracy?

M She's my Singaporean pen pal. Maybe she can help you.

W Oh, that would be great. So is she your girlfriend?

M No, she's just a friend. She's really nice. And she even [_____] like you.

W Cool! Can she become my friend too?

Quiz 남자의 마지막 말과 같은 상황을 표현할 수 있는 영어 속담을 쓰시오.
Killing _____.

15 **W** Joshua and Maya are friends. Joshua is good at taking care of plants. Whenever Maya visits his house, she compliments him on all of his nice houseplants. So Joshua decides to ▓▓▓▓▓ for her birthday. After a few weeks, Maya notices some of the leaves on the plant turning yellow. She's worried and asks Joshua ▓▓▓▓▓. After asking her how she's taken care of the plant, Joshua concludes that ▓▓▓▓▓. Joshua wants to tell Maya that if she keeps doing that, it could be deadly. In this situation, what would Joshua most likely say to Maya?

16~17 **M** Hello, Class. The cold season is just around the corner. Nine out of ten people catch a cold once a year, and during the change of seasons, people catch colds more easily. So, what can we do to ▓▓▓▓▓? Let's talk about some basic rules to do. First, maintain a balanced diet. Extreme diets weaken your body, which can make you catch a cold more easily. Second, strengthen your immune system through exercise. ▓▓▓▓▓, you're less likely to catch a cold. Third, lower the temperature of your house by 9 to 11 degrees Fahrenheit. Temperatures that are too high or too low can have a bad effect on your body's defense. Lastly, be sure to ▓▓▓▓▓. You're more likely to catch a cold when you're tired, so enough rest and sleep are extremely important. Keep all of this in mind for the upcoming winter season!

Dictation 빠른답

01 ☐ on behalf of ☐ time and planning to organize
☐ is the most qualified candidate

02 ☐ plan for our summer trip
☐ traveling in developed countries
☐ the culture is totally different

03 ☐ it takes away time from children
☐ it can limit their imagination
☐ kids seldom use their imagination

04 ☐ a house with a chimney ☐ shows her open mind
☐ branches and leaves on the tree

05 ☐ plan a fun weekend ☐ Let's get some flowers
☐ a list of thoughtful presents

06 ☐ on sale for 30% off ☐ All of the hats are 10% off
☐ It's originally $20

07 ☐ play a big role ☐ set up a time ☐ You speak French

08 ☐ information about the after school
☐ it begins on May 3rd ☐ graduated from our school

09 ☐ free of milk, butter, and eggs ☐ vote for their favorites
☐ be announced on May 5th

10 ☐ looking for a dog leash ☐ spend more than $15
☐ it's down to these two

11 ☐ What time shall I come

12 ☐ open the window

13 ☐ grab something to eat ☐ could eat a horse
☐ meat and other ingredients

14 ☐ write an essay about Singapore
☐ introduce you to Tracy ☐ enjoys collecting coins

15 ☐ give Maya a potted houseplant
☐ what could be the problem
☐ Maya is overwatering the plant

16~17 ☐ prevent catching a cold
☐ With a strong immune system
☐ get enough rest and sleep

Quiz 01 First is the school festival and the second is the dance party **04** psychological **07** persuade, to work **10** ③ **14** two birds with one stone

▶242019-0220

01 다음을 듣고, 여자가 하는 말의 목적으로 가장 적절한 것을 고르시오.

① 접수된 도색 관련 민원을 소개하려고
② 주차장 정기 안전 점검을 공지하려고
③ 확장된 주차장 사용에 대해 안내하려고
④ 주차장 재도색 작업 시행을 알려 주려고
⑤ 장애인 주차 구역 이용 규칙을 설명하려고

▶242019-0221

02 대화를 듣고, 남자의 주장으로 가장 적절한 것을 고르시오.

① 동아리 활동을 통해 건전한 취미를 확보해야 한다.
② 기회가 될 때마다 사람들을 적극적으로 도와야 한다.
③ 주변의 사람들에게는 늘 즐거움을 주려 노력해야 한다.
④ 책을 꾸준히 읽어서 긍정적인 인생관을 형성해야 한다.
⑤ 삶의 태도를 바꾸려는 결심에 흔들림 없이 전념해야 한다.

수능완성 **PICK** ▶242019-0222

03 대화를 듣고, 두 사람의 관계를 가장 잘 나타낸 것을 고르시오.

① 의사 – 환자
② 기자 – 연예인
③ 지휘자 – 연주자
④ 체육 교사 – 학부모
⑤ 심사 위원 – 무용수

수능완성 **PICK** ▶242019-0223

04 대화를 듣고, 그림에서 대화의 내용과 일치하지 않는 것을 고르시오.

▶242019-0224

05 대화를 듣고, 여자가 남자에게 부탁한 일로 가장 적절한 것을 고르시오.

① 초대장 만들기
② 포토 부스 설치하기
③ 연극 의상 빌려오기
④ 음식 주문할 식당 찾기
⑤ 실내에서 할 게임 조사하기

▶242019-0225

06 대화를 듣고, 여자가 지불할 금액을 고르시오.

① $12   ② $13   ③ $14
④ $15   ⑤ $16

▶242019-0226

07 대화를 듣고, 남자가 동아리 활동에 참여할 수 없는 이유를 고르시오.

① 한국에 체류해야 해서
② 역사 연구 활동을 해야 해서
③ 연구 제안서를 제출하지 못해서
④ 대표 학생과 사이가 좋지 못해서
⑤ 동물 보호소 봉사 활동을 해야 해서

▶242019-0227

08 대화를 듣고, 영어 시험에 관해 언급되지 않은 것을 고르시오.

① 실시 요일   ② 시험 범위   ③ 시험 시간
④ 총문항 수   ⑤ 에세이 주제

▶242019-0228

09 Kensington World Festival에 관한 다음 내용을 듣고, 일치하지 않는 것을 고르시오.

① 여러 나라의 학생들이 프로그램을 준비했다.
② 도서관에서 나라별 책 전시 부스가 열린다.
③ 학생 식당에서 아시아 음식을 무료로 제공한다.
④ 오후 2시에 아프리카 전통 패션쇼가 있을 예정이다.
⑤ 20개국의 학생들이 함께 음악과 춤 공연을 할 예정이다.

▶242019-0229

10 다음 표를 보면서 대화를 듣고, 여자가 구입할 스마트폰을 고르시오.

Cell Zone Smartphones

	Model	Storage	Number of Camera Lense	Color	Price
①	A	32 GB	3	Black or Gray	$400
②	B	64 GB	3	Black or Gray	$500
③	C	128 GB	4	Black or Gray	$600
④	D	256 GB	4	White or Gold	$850
⑤	E	512 GB	5	White or Gold	$950

▶242019-0230

11 대화를 듣고, 남자의 마지막 말에 대한 여자의 응답으로 가장 적절한 것을 고르시오.

① I told you. The umbrella is not easy to get.
② No, I didn't. I packed the raincoats instead.
③ No worries. It's not raining as hard as it was.
④ Yeah, the weather was perfect for watching a game.
⑤ Sure. You should have checked the weather forecast.

▶242019-0231

12 대화를 듣고, 여자의 마지막 말에 대한 남자의 응답으로 가장 적절한 것을 고르시오.

① I can't believe it. You got over your cold so quickly.
② That's good. Don't forget to get enough rest, too.
③ That's right. I seldom catch a cold these years.
④ That's too bad. It's not easy to find an open hospital.
⑤ No way. Painkillers are better for relieving headaches.

▶242019-0232

13 대화를 듣고, 남자의 마지막 말에 대한 여자의 응답으로 가장 적절한 것을 고르시오. [3점]

Woman: _____

① No problem. She'll draw a cartoon if you ask.
② I agree. You should get your article done on time.
③ No way. She's not at all responsible for this article.
④ Don't worry. You can print the school newspaper right away.
⑤ Not at all. She won't mind making some changes to her article.

▶242019-0233

14 대화를 듣고, 여자의 마지막 말에 대한 남자의 응답으로 가장 적절한 것을 고르시오. [3점]

Man: _____

① I want to talk to you about your recent bad performance.
② Don't you think you should go and apologize to her first?
③ Oh, no. Everybody has the right to express their own opinion.
④ You should have made a fair evaluation of Ellen's annual report.
⑤ Why don't you have an honest talk with Ellen about the problem?

▶242019-0234

15 다음 상황 설명을 듣고, Austin이 계산대 직원에게 할 말로 가장 적절한 것을 고르시오. [3점]

Austin: _____

① Can you go to the grocery store for me?
② Excuse me, have you seen a wallet here?
③ I think you should put it in the lost and found.
④ I forgot to take my milk when I was here earlier.
⑤ What should I do with this wallet I found on the floor?

[16~17] 다음을 듣고, 물음에 답하시오.

▶242019-0235

16 여자가 하는 말의 주제로 가장 적절한 것은?

① ways to improve food production
② foods threatened by climate change
③ nutritional benefits of eating organic food
④ effects of climate change on human health
⑤ global trends of climate change and sea level rise

▶242019-0236

17 언급된 식품이 아닌 것은?

① coffee　　② peanuts　　③ wheat
④ rice　　⑤ salmon

01

W Hello, residents! I'm Jennifer Jones, the apartment maintenance office manager, and I have an important announcement about the repainting of the parking lot. It's scheduled for June 18th. We _____ to improve the parking lot's appearance and functionality. And this time, we're also painting the expanded parking area _____. During the painting process, some areas of the parking lot _____. If you have any concerns or require assistance, please contact the management office. We're here to help. Thank you for your attention, and have a wonderful day!

> **Quiz** 주차장 도색 작업에 관해 언급되지 않은 것은?
> ① 예정일　　　② 목적　　　③ 색상

02

W Hey, Mark, I saw you in front of the library in a group of people yesterday. You were all wearing green shirts.

M Yeah. We met there and then went to McCalister Park.

W What did you do there?

M We _____. It's an activity of the volunteer club I'm in. We do it every week.

W That's great. How long have you been in the club?

M I actually just joined a few weeks ago.

W That's so cool. I didn't think you were interested in doing anything like that.

M I wasn't until I read a book about _____ a couple months ago. It really changed me.

W Awesome! So, you must feel really happy while passing out food.

M Definitely. You should actively engage in helping people whenever you have the opportunity.

W Absolutely. Your story actually encourages me to explore similar opportunities.

M I'm glad to hear that! Trust me. Don't miss the chances _____.

W Okay. I will.

03

W Are you ready, Mr. Simpson?

M I'm pretty nervous, but yes, I'm ready.

W Just relax and do your best.

M Thank you. Could I _____ first?

W Sure. Begin when you are ready.

M Okay, I'm ready. I'll start now.

W *[Pause]* Oh, that was wonderful!

M Thank you.

W You performed it so smoothly even _____.

M My ankle is still sore from performing in Swan Lake in the international dance festival last week.

W   Part of being a dancer is performing through the pain, and you just did that. You moved so effortlessly that I couldn't even tell your ankle was hurting.

M   Once I start to dance, I don't even notice the pain.

W   Based on your audition today, I can tell [   ] and dedicated.

M   Thank you for saying that. If I get the part, I will do my best to put on a great production.

04

W   Honey, look at the picture in this interior design book. I want to decorate Mike's room like this.

M   Let me see. Wow, it's wonderful. The first thing that gets my attention is [   ].

W   I think world maps are great because they allow us to dream of far-off places.

M   This big bookshelf beside the window is nice. It would make organizing all of Mike's books easier.

W   Yes, it would. I like how the desk is placed [   ].

M   Me, too. Let's move Mike's desk like that. It'll be a more comfortable place for him to do his homework.

W   And look how they have storage boxes under the bed. That's a good way to create more storage.

M   If we do that, we could stop worrying about him leaving his stuff all over the room.

W   That'd be great. And look at [   ]. Some greenery in a room is always a mood booster.

M   Right. Plants can have a positive effect on a child's emotional well-being.

W   I can't wait to start redecorating his room.

05

W   Ted. I'm really excited about having my own studio in our new house.

M   That's going to be really nice. So have you thought about when [   ]?

W   Yeah. How about in two weekends?

M   That works. Then I'll start writing the invitations.

W   Sounds good. And how about [   ] so people can take funny pictures.

M   I love that idea! I'll see if we can borrow some fun costumes from the local theater.

W   That's sounds awesome! Everybody will have so much fun dressing up.

M   And as far as food goes, let's just keep it simple and get [   ].

W   Good idea! Can you look for a restaurant that we can order from?

M   Sure. I'll find a few places that we can choose from.

W   And I'll also do some research to find different indoor games for us to play.

M   Great. I can't wait for the housewarming party.

Quiz 빈칸에 알맞은 것은?

Q: Where does Ted borrow the costumes for the photo booth?

A: He borrows some fun costumes from _____.

① the local theater   ② the elementary school   ③ his workplace

06

M   Good morning! How may I help you?

W   I'm looking for some flowers for my mom. Can you give me some suggestions?

M   Certainly! How about these charming egg cup roses? They're adorable.

W   Oh, they're lovely. How much are they?

M   They're ▒▒▒▒▒▒▒.

W   Then I'll take one egg cup rose.

M   I recommend these carnations too. ▒▒▒▒▒▒▒.

W   That's good. And can I choose different colors?

M   Of course! You can mix and match the colors as you like.

W   Perfect. I'll ▒▒▒▒▒▒▒: three red and two pink.

M   Would you like them arranged as a bouquet? It's free.

W   Thank you very much. Here's my credit card.

07

M   Hi, Monica! Have you heard that our club is organizing a special camp this summer?

W   Oh, really? I don't know that. What's the plan for the camp?

M   They're ▒▒▒▒▒▒▒, which exhibits Korean traditional things. They'll do historical research there.

W   I'd really like to go. How can I apply?

M   Just talk to the club president. But ▒▒▒▒▒▒▒ you should know about.

W   What's that?

M   You need to submit a research proposal related to the theme of the camp.

W   No problem. There're so many things that I really want to know about Asian history. And what's your research topic?

M   Unfortunately, I won't be able to participate this time. I've already ▒▒▒▒▒▒▒ at an animal shelter.

W   Still, volunteering at an animal shelter is a wonderful thing. It's going to be a rewarding experience.

○ Quiz 빈칸에 알맞은 말을 대화에서 찾아 쓰시오.

Q: What is the requirement Monica should know about to apply for the camp?

A: She needs to _____.

08

W   Hey, Evan. Why don't you stop drawing and study for the English test on Friday?

M   Wait, what? There's an English test on Friday? Isn't it next week?

W   ▒▒▒▒▒▒▒.

M   Oh my gosh. I must not have been paying attention when the teacher told us that. So the test is this Friday?

W   Yes. ▮▮▮▮▮▮ and lasts for an hour and a half.

M   How many questions are there?

W   The test has 25 simple questions and one essay writing task.

M   So, ▮▮▮▮▮▮. What is the essay about?

W   You can choose between two topics: friends and your future.

M   Great. I'll choose the topic of my best and kindest friend, you.

W   Stop joking around. This test is really important for this term. You'd better start studying.

M   I know, you're right. I'm going to start studying hard today.

09

M   Welcome to Kensington World Festival. I'm Larry Johnson, the head organizer of the festival. This festival is a celebration of various cultures and traditions. This year, students from different countries have prepared exciting programs. First, there will be ▮▮▮▮▮▮, where students will exhibit books from their countries at each booth. Lunch will be from 11 to 1. In the student cafeteria, various kinds of Asian foods will be served, all for free! After lunch, ▮▮▮▮▮▮, there will be a fashion show featuring traditional African clothing in the student hall. At 4, there will be a traditional music performance in the Kensington Concert Hall. ▮▮▮▮▮▮ will showcase their incredible musical and dancing skills together. I hope you have a great time at the festival.

10

M   Honey, what are you looking at?

W   A website that sells smartphones. It's about time to get a new one.

M   I agree. Yours is ancient! Let's see those. What do you think about this model?

W   It's good, but I want at least ▮▮▮▮▮▮.

M   Yeah, right. Oh, these models have a lot of camera lenses. That'd be good for taking pictures for social media.

W   Right. I want ▮▮▮▮▮▮ or more.

M   And I'm sure when it comes to color you don't want black or gray.

W   Yeah. You know me. I like bright colors.

M   Then, it comes down to these two models. What's your price range?

W   I'd like to ▮▮▮▮▮▮.

M   Then, this is the one to choose.

W   Yup. I'll get it.

11

M Honey, are you ready to leave for Jenny's soccer game?

W Yeah, let's go. _____, is it?

M Not now. But the weather forecast said it might rain later. Did you put the umbrellas in the car?

12

W Oh, gosh. I don't feel well at all. My coughing is _____.

M Sorry to hear that. Are you taking any medicine?

W Yes. I've been _____ for the past couple days.

13

M Olivia, here's the first draft of the school newspaper. I just got it from the print shop.

W Nice. How does it look?

M Pretty good, but Ms. Manning's article _____.

W It's her article about being a cartoonist, right?

M Yeah. It's really good, but it's almost two whole pages.

W That's because she included _____.

M Hmm, they seem important, so I don't think we should take them out.

W Then should we ask the print shop to make the font size smaller?

M That's one option, but it's already pretty small. If _____, it'd be perfect.

W That'd work. How about asking her? She's really nice. You have her email address.

M I could. But do you think she'd find that a little impolite?

14

M Agnes, you look upset. Is there something wrong?

W Yes. Benny, can we _____?

M Of course. What's the matter?

W Well... actually, it's about Ellen. She seems to have some type of misunderstanding about me.

M Really? What do you mean?

W She seems to think she _____ on her last annual report because of me.

M What? That's not true, you know.

W That's what I mean. I can't believe she's been making those false claims without talking to me first.

M That's strange. She's usually _____. If she had thought you were the reason for her bad evaluation, she would've discussed it with you.

W I think so, too. I don't know what to do.

> **Quiz** 괄호 안에서 알맞은 것을 고르시오.
> Q: What was Benny's option of Ellen?
> A: Benny thought Ellen to be usually communicative and [sensitive / sensible].

15   **M**   Austin stops at a grocery store on his way home to pick up some milk. To pay for the milk, he takes his wallet out of his pocket and hands the cashier his credit card. The cashier gives Austin his credit card back, and Austin puts his wallet in his pocket. When he gets home, he puts his hand in his pocket to take out his wallet. Suddenly, he realizes that his wallet   . He searches his other pockets and can't find it. He thinks about when he last used his wallet and remembers it   , so he quickly goes back to the store. At the grocery store, Austin wants to ask the cashier if   . In this situation, what would Austin most likely say to the cashier?

16~17   **W**   Hello, everyone. Last class, we learned about the causes of climate change. Today we're going to talk about how climate change will have   . (A) <u>Endangered lists are no longer just for animals.</u> The following foods are so-called "endangered foods." One of them is coffee. Coffee plantations in South America, Africa, and `Hawaii are being   and unstable rainfall patterns. Second, peanuts require consistently warm temperatures and 20 to 40 inches of rain over five months. Because of long-term droughts, these plants are finding it very difficult to stay alive. Third, wheat is becoming endangered, too. In the coming decades, at least one-quarter of the world's wheat production will be lost. Lastly,   the world's aquaculture as well. As the water temperature rises, salmon populations will decline because they depend on cold water for reproduction. Now let's have a look at some graphs of recent global changes in temperature.

> **Quiz**   밑줄 친 (A)를 우리말로 해석하시오.

Dictation 빠른답

01 ☐ do this every four years ☐ for the disabled
☐ may be temporarily unavailable

02 ☐ handed out food to homeless people
☐ the happiness of helping people
☐ to help out in your community

03 ☐ take a quick sip of water ☐ with your ankle bandaged up
☐ you are extremely talented

04 ☐ the world map on the wall ☐ in front of the window
☐ the plant hanging from the ceiling

05 ☐ we should have our housewarming party
☐ setting up a photo booth ☐ a variety of finger foods

06 ☐ four dollars each ☐ They're two dollars each
☐ take five carnations then

07 ☐ planning to visit the City Museum
☐ there's one requirement
☐ committed to a volunteering opportunity

08 ☐ There is a test this Friday ☐ It starts at 1 p.m.
☐ a total of 26 questions

09 ☐ a book display in the library ☐ starting at 1:30
☐ Students from twenty countries

10 ☐ 64 GB of storage ☐ a smartphone with four lenses
☐ spend less than $900

11 ☐ It's not raining outside

12 ☐ getting worse and worse ☐ taking some cold medicine

13 ☐ seems a little long ☐ some of her illustrations
☐ she could cut about 200 words

14 ☐ talk for a moment ☐ received the poor evaluation
☐ communicative and sensible

15 ☐ isn't in his pocket ☐ was at the grocery store
☐ he has seen his wallet

16~17 ☐ a negative impact on our food production
☐ threatened by rising air temperatures
☐ climate change is affecting

Quiz 01 ③   **05** ①   **07** submit a research proposal related to the theme of the camp   **14** sensible   **16~17** 멸종 위기 목록은 더 이상 동물에게만 해당하지 않습니다.

9회 수능실전 대비연습

▶ 242019-0237

수능특강 PICK

01 다음을 듣고, 남자가 하는 말의 목적으로 가장 적절한 것을 고르시오.

① 스쿨버스 승하차 시 질서 유지의 필요성을 설명하려고
② 스쿨버스 안전 수칙 관련 설문지 응답을 요청하려고
③ 학교 안전사고 예방 교육 참가를 독려하려고
④ 스쿨버스 이용 시간 변경을 공지하려고
⑤ 스쿨버스 탑승 규칙을 안내하려고

수능특강 PICK

▶ 242019-0238

02 대화를 듣고, 여자의 의견으로 가장 적절한 것을 고르시오.

① 다양한 신체 활동을 통해 아이들의 인지 학습 능력이 향상된다.
② 부모와 함께 그림을 그림으로써 자녀는 정서적 안정감을 느낀다.
③ 아이의 상상력을 기르기 위해 자연 관찰의 기회가 많이 필요하다.
④ 그림을 잘 그리기 위해 유명한 작품을 모사하는 연습을 해야 한다.
⑤ 그림을 그려 주는 대신 아이가 느낀 것을 스스로 표현하게 도와야 한다.

수능특강 PICK

▶ 242019-0239

03 대화를 듣고, 두 사람의 관계를 가장 잘 나타낸 것을 고르시오.

① 택시 기사 – 승객
② 응급실 의사 – 환자
③ 응급 구조사 – 간호사
④ 병원 직원 – 환자 보호자
⑤ 응급 환자 신고자 – 환자 가족

수능특강 PICK

▶ 242019-0240

04 대화를 듣고, 그림에서 대화의 내용과 일치하지 않는 것을 고르시오.

▶ 242019-0241

05 대화를 듣고, 남자가 할 일로 가장 적절한 것을 고르시오.

① 전시 구역 확인하기
② 안내 표지판 게시하기
③ 오디오 장비 설치하기
④ 전시 테이블 구입하기
⑤ 자원봉사 학생 모집하기

▶ 242019-0242

06 대화를 듣고, 여자가 지불할 금액을 고르시오.

① $36   ② $40   ③ $45
④ $50   ⑤ $55

수능특강 PICK

▶ 242019-0243

07 대화를 듣고, 남자가 체육관에 가는 이유를 고르시오.

① 농구 연습을 해야 해서
② 취업 박람회를 둘러보려고
③ 체육 실기 시험을 준비하러
④ 축구 동아리에 가입하기 위해
⑤ 축구 장비를 가지러 가야 해서

▶ 242019-0244

08 대화를 듣고, Old Town Trolley Tour에 관해 언급되지 않은 것을 고르시오.

① 경유지
② 소요 시간
③ 요금
④ 참가 가능 인원수
⑤ 예약 방법

▶ 242019-0245

09 Benton Cheese Village Experience에 관한 다음 내용을 듣고, 일치하지 않는 것을 고르시오.

① 8월부터 매주 토요일에 진행된다.
② 치즈 만들기를 직접 해 보는 체험으로 하루가 시작된다.
③ 참가자는 동물들에게 먹이를 줄 수 있다.
④ 점심 식사로 피자가 제공된다.
⑤ 입장권은 온라인 예매와 현장 구매 모두 가능하다.

10 수능특강 **PICK** ▶242019-0246

다음 표를 보면서 대화를 듣고, 남자가 주문할 창문 블라인드를 고르시오.

Window Blinds

	Model	Material	Price	Type	Light-blocking
①	A	Paper	$25	Vertical	×
②	B	Plastic	$35	Horizontal	○
③	C	Fabric	$45	Vertical	○
④	D	Wood	$55	Horizontal	○
⑤	E	Metal	$65	Vertical	×

11 ▶242019-0247

대화를 듣고, 남자의 마지막 말에 대한 여자의 응답으로 가장 적절한 것을 고르시오.

① Not really. Just regular ones will do.
② Yes. The farmers' market is open today.
③ Great. I'll make sure to get you large ones.
④ No way. I don't feel like eggs for breakfast.
⑤ Never mind. I've never tried these ones before.

12 ▶242019-0248

대화를 듣고, 여자의 마지막 말에 대한 남자의 응답으로 가장 적절한 것을 고르시오.

① Awesome! I'm glad the laptop is working properly.
② Too bad. You need to go to a repair shop immediately.
③ Why not? Your new laptop is better than your old one.
④ That's frustrating. Maybe you should ask for a replacement.
⑤ Don't worry. I'm sure the repairs will only take a couple of days.

13 수능완성 **PICK** ▶242019-0249

대화를 듣고, 남자의 마지막 말에 대한 여자의 응답으로 가장 적절한 것을 고르시오. [3점]

Woman: _____

① That's right. I can join you next week.
② It's my fault. I'll find another hotel soon.
③ It's possible. I'll take care of the kids for you.
④ There are a few available. I'll make a reservation.
⑤ I'm sorry. I'm not interested in farm stay programs.

14 수능특강 **PICK** ▶242019-0250

대화를 듣고, 여자의 마지막 말에 대한 남자의 응답으로 가장 적절한 것을 고르시오. [3점]

Man: _____

① Of course. It's more convenient to buy things online.
② Never mind. I'll watch the documentary myself soon.
③ Don't worry. We can resell the items for a higher price.
④ Right. Inventing stories about the objects must be tough.
⑤ For sure. They show the power of storytelling in marketing.

15 수능특강 **PICK** ▶242019-0251

다음 상황 설명을 듣고, Cathy가 Carpenter 선생님에게 할 말로 가장 적절한 것을 고르시오. [3점]

Cathy: _____

① What college do you think has the best physics program?
② Do you think the online course will be too difficult for me?
③ Can you let me know the textbook for your physics course?
④ Could you tell me how to take the online advanced physics course?
⑤ What should I do to get better results in the advanced physics course?

[16~17] 다음을 듣고, 물음에 답하시오.

▶242019-0252

16 여자가 하는 말의 주제로 가장 적절한 것은?

① how plants adapt to different environments
② how plants protect themselves from animals
③ what to do to keep your houseplants healthy
④ why plants are important for the environment
⑤ why outdoor plants grow better than indoor plants

▶242019-0253

17 언급된 식물이 <u>아닌</u> 것은?

① water lilies   ② aloes   ③ mangroves
④ maple trees   ⑤ Joshua trees

01 M Hello, students. I'm John Edwards from the school office. We're always trying to find ways to improve your safety during your school bus commute. So we would appreciate it if you could ▢▢▢▢ about your ▢▢▢▢. The survey sheet has been mailed to your home. It consists of 20 questions that ask about your perception of safety rules related to waiting for the bus, boarding the bus, being on the bus, and getting off the bus. Your answers will be very helpful in determining how we can ▢▢▢▢. After filling out the survey, please submit it to your homeroom teacher. Thank you for your cooperation.

> **Quiz** 스쿨버스 안전 수칙 관련 설문에 관해 언급되지 <u>않은</u> 것은?
> ① 질문 개수   ② 제출 기한   ③ 제출 방법

02 W Alex, how's your son these days?

M He's into drawing, so he often asks me to draw pictures. This morning I drew trees for him.

W I don't think it's a good idea to draw pictures for him. Instead, you should ▢▢▢▢ for himself.

M What do you mean?

W Children learn the world through direct experiences by exploring with their eyes, their hands, and their senses.

M Right. But I still don't understand why drawing trees for him is a problem.

W Imagine how children will feel the tree. Leaves, trunks, branches.... Each child will feel the tree ▢▢▢▢.

M You mean the tree the child experiences is different from the tree I draw?

W Exactly. When you draw a tree for him, he'll practice imitating his father's tree, not the tree he felt.

M You've got a point.

W The next time he asks you to draw something, encourage him to ▢▢▢▢ instead of saying "yes."

M I got it.

03 [Cell phone rings.]

M Hello?

W Hello. May I speak to Mark Green?

M Speaking. May I ask who's calling?

W My name is Amy. You're the ▢▢▢▢ who fainted on the street and reported it to 911, right?

M Yes, I'm him.

W I'm ▢▢▢▢. I called 911 and found out your phone number because I really wanted to thank you.

M Oh, I'm glad to have helped. How is your husband?

W   He's okay thanks to you. The doctor said my husband [   ] if he had arrived a little later.

M   I'm glad to hear he's better.

W   My husband also wants to send you a thank-you gift.

M   He doesn't have to do that. I just did what I had to do.

W   Hmm, really?

M   Of course. I just hope your husband keeps getting better.

04

W   Tommy, we made it back to the foot of the mountain. That was a fun hike, wasn't it?

M   Yeah, I loved it. Now I'm starving. How about eating at this restaurant?

W   Okay. They have a menu on the outside wall. They serve various kinds of food.

M   That's great. And there is a tree in the dining area. It seems to block out the sun.

W   Yes. Why don't we take the [   ] surrounding the tree?

M   All right. Look, the [   ] is holding a welcome sign.

W   The statue is fitting because there used to be a lot of bears in this area.

M   I didn't know that. Look at the [   ] with the fence. They probably cook with what they grow here.

W   The food must be really fresh.

M   Yeah, I can't wait to try it. Let's get seated at the table now.

W   Okay.

05

M   Hi, Ms. Kane. How's everything going for tomorrow's science fair?

W   Hi, Mr. Anderson. I just finished [   ] with the school administration.

M   Would you like me to help you with anything?

W   That'd be fantastic. Thanks. There are still a few more things that need to be done.

M   Okay. Have the tables for the project displays been set up yet?

W   Not yet. But some students are going to do that later today.

M   All right. I noticed that none of the signs directing people where to go have been put up. Should I [   ]?

W   I'll take care of that. Actually, it'd be really helpful if you could [   ] for the presentations.

M   Sure, I can handle that.

W   Great! Thanks so much for the help!

> **Quiz** 밑줄 친 표현과 의미가 같은 것은?
> Have the tables for the project displays been <u>set up</u> yet?
> ① arranged   ② repaired   ③ upgraded

06

M   Welcome to the Lindenberg Animation Center. Do you need tickets?

W   Hi. Yes, I do. I need three tickets. How much are they?

M   ⬚⬚⬚⬚⬚⬚ tickets are $10 for adults and $15 for children under 13.

W   I need two adult tickets and one child ticket.

M   All right, so that's three tickets in total.

W   Yes. We're also interested in the Stop Motion Animation Workshop. Is that ⬚⬚⬚⬚⬚⬚?

M   No, it's not. It's an extra $5 per person.

W   Okay. I'd also like ⬚⬚⬚⬚⬚⬚.

M   All right. So, two adult and one child general admission tickets, and three workshop tickets, right?

W   Yes, that's correct. Here's my credit card.

07

W   Hi, Jack. Where are you going?

M   Hi, Sandra. I'm ⬚⬚⬚⬚⬚⬚ the school gym.

W   Oh, for your basketball club?

M   No. I actually quit the basketball club.

W   Really? I thought you really liked basketball.

M   I did. And I still like it. But I quit ⬚⬚⬚⬚⬚⬚. I recently realized how much I love playing soccer.

W   That's cool. Then why are you going to the gym?

M   There's a ⬚⬚⬚⬚⬚⬚. Don't you know about it?

W   Oh, yeah, that's right. I know about it.

M   I just want to see what it's like. Maybe I'll find something I'm interested in.

W   That's a good idea. I'd also like to go, but I have to finish a big history report by Monday.

M   I see. See you later.

> **Quiz** 빈칸에 알맞은 말을 대화에서 찾아 쓰시오.
> Q: Why can't the woman go to the job fair?
> A: Because she has _____.

08

W   Honey, since we're going to Queen's City next week, I was thinking it'd be fun to take the Old Town Trolley Tour.

M   That's a fantastic idea! Do you have any details about the tour?

W   Yeah, I checked their website. The tour covers the ⬚⬚⬚⬚⬚⬚ Queen's City. It takes you around the historic downtown area, the waterfront, and other popular landmarks.

M   Cool! How long does the tour last?

W   It lasts about 90 minutes.

M   That's perfect. And how much ⬚⬚⬚⬚⬚⬚?

W   Tickets are $50 per person.

M That's not bad at all. How do we get tickets for the tour?

W We can book them [＿＿＿＿＿]. Should we do that now?

M Sure! I'm already looking forward to the tour!

09

W Attention, everyone! I'm Sarah Lee, the manager of Benton Cheese Village, and I'm excited to tell you about our Benton Cheese Village Experience. Starting in August, we're inviting you to join us every Saturday for an exciting adventure. The day starts off with a [＿＿＿＿＿] where you'll learn how to milk the cows and mold the cheese! Sounds fun, right? But that's not all! You'll also have a chance to [＿＿＿＿＿] in our village. Delicious pizza will be provided for lunch, and you'll be able to try a variety of our cheeses. Wondering how to get tickets? You must book them online. Tickets are [＿＿＿＿＿]. So visit our website at www.bentoncheesevillage.com, today!

10

M Hi, Amy. I'm trying to buy window blinds for my bedroom on this website. Can you help me?

W Sure. Do you have a [＿＿＿＿＿]?

M Not really. I just don't want wood. It's weak to moisture and humidity.

W I agree. It can also split over time. And [＿＿＿＿＿]?

M I don't want to spend more than $60.

W Okay. And there are two types, horizontal or vertical. It depends on the size of your window and how it opens.

M My bedroom window is really big and wide, and it slides open.

W A vertical one will be better, then.

M Okay. I'll go with a [＿＿＿＿＿].

W Do you think you need light-blocking blinds?

M Definitely. I want to be able to keep my bedroom dark in the morning.

W Then you should go with this model.

M Good. I'll order it right now. Thanks.

> **Quiz** 밑줄 친 go with와 같은 의미로 쓰인 것은?
> I'll go with a vertical type.
> ① Does the skirt go with this shirt?
> ② A lot of responsibilities go with this job.
> ③ Let's go with salads for a light meal.

11

M Sandy, I'm going to [＿＿＿＿＿] the farmers' market in a little bit. Is there anything you need?

W Oh, actually, there is. Would you mind picking up some eggs for me?

M Not at all. Any [＿＿＿＿＿] eggs you prefer?

12

W I've had nothing but problems with my new laptop. It keeps ▢▢▢▢▢▢.

M Really? And you just got it a few weeks ago. Have you taken it to a ▢▢▢▢▢▢?

W Yes, I have. But they said they couldn't find any issues with it and said it's functioning properly.

13

W Honey, come and look at this ad. It's about ▢▢▢▢▢▢.

M Let me see. Oh, the farm is not far from here.

W Yeah. Moreover, this overnight program costs only $300 per family, including 3 meals.

M Sounds great! What can we do there?

W We can dig out sweet potatoes, pick corn, make cheese, and so on. Also, we can catch fish in the nearby river.

M Perfect! Our kids will like it.

W Yeah. They'll have lots of fun there and learn to enjoy nature.

M I'm sure they will. Honey, why don't we apply for the program for this Saturday and Sunday?

W Okay. Let me check on the Internet if there's room left. *[Typing sound]* Hmm.... It's ▢▢▢▢▢▢.

M Would you check if there are any places left ▢▢▢▢▢▢?

14

W Dave, I saw a really good documentary on TV last night.

M Oh, really? What was the name of it?

W The Age of Storytelling. It was about an experiment ▢▢▢▢▢▢. It was super interesting.

M What was the experiment about?

W Well, a journalist bought some objects, like a little toy, a mug, and an old pepper shaker, for about $1 each.

M They are cheap objects.

W Right. And he had creative writers invent stories about them. Then he resold the items online ▢▢▢▢▢▢ on a website.

M Ah, so he gave the items a special meaning.

W Yeah. And he could resell the items for a much higher price than he bought them for. He sold one of the items for more than $100!

M Wow! That's so amazing!

W I think the results of the experiment ▢▢▢▢▢▢.

Quiz 빈칸에 알맞은 말을 대화에서 찾아 쓰시오.

In the documentary mentioned above, the journalist sold cheap _____ for a much higher price than he bought them for by creating _____ about them.

15　**M** Cathy's family recently moved to a new house, so she had to transfer to a new high school. Her new friends are really kind, so she's happy. But there's ▢▢▢▢▢▢ about her new school. She likes physics and wants to major in it when she goes to college, but her new school doesn't have ▢▢▢▢▢▢ she wants to take. One day, she tells Mr. Carpenter, her science teacher, about her disappointment. He tells her that the city provides online courses for students, including advanced physics courses. Cathy decides to sign up for the online advanced physics course, so she wants to ask Mr. Carpenter ▢▢▢▢▢▢ . In this situation, what would Cathy most likely say to Mr. Carpenter?

16~17　**W** Hello, students. Have you ever wondered how plants can survive in extreme conditions? Today, we're going to explore the amazing ways in which plants ▢▢▢▢▢▢ . First, water lilies have adapted to live in aquatic habitats. Their wide leaves and air-filled spaces allow them to float, while their roots absorb nutrients from the water. Second, aloes are plants that thrive in dry conditions. They have ▢▢▢▢▢▢ in their thick leaves, allowing them to survive long periods of drought. Third, mangroves are trees that grow in saltwater environments along coastlines. They have roots that can tolerate ▢▢▢▢▢▢ and specialized structures to get oxygen from soil soaked with water. Lastly, Joshua trees can be found in vast, extremely dry deserts. With reduced leaves and an extensive root system, Joshua trees can efficiently collect water from deep underground. Now let's watch a short video about these amazing plants.

Dictation 빠른답

01 ▢ fill out a survey ▢ school bus experience
▢ make riding the bus safer for you

02 ▢ help him express what he feels ▢ in his own way
▢ express his feelings for himself

03 ▢ taxi driver who found the man ▢ his wife
▢ might have been in big trouble

04 ▢ empty round table ▢ bear statue ▢ vegetable garden

05 ▢ confirming the project display areas ▢ put them up
▢ set up the audio equipment

06 ▢ General admission ▢ included with general admission
▢ three tickets to the workshop

07 ▢ on my way to ▢ to join the soccer club
▢ job fair today and tomorrow

08 ▢ main attractions of ▢ does it cost ▢ on their website

09 ▢ hands-on cheese-making experience
▢ feed the adorable animals ▢ not sold on site

10 ▢ particular material in mind ▢ what's your budget
▢ vertical type

11 ▢ head over to ▢ specific type of

12 ▢ shutting down unexpectedly ▢ repair shop

13 ▢ a farm stay program ▢ all booked up for this weekend
▢ next weekend

14 ▢ a journalist conducted ▢ with their stories posted
▢ provide insights into marketing

15 ▢ one disappointing thing ▢ advanced physics classes
▢ the way she can take the course

16~17 ▢ adjust and thrive in various environments
▢ adapted by storing water ▢ high salt concentrations

Quiz 01 ② **05** ① **07** to finish a big history report by Monday　**10** ③　**14** objects, stories

▶242019-0254

01 다음을 듣고, 남자가 하는 말의 목적으로 가장 적절한 것을 고르시오.

① 화학 물질을 만졌을 경우 대처 방법을 전달하려고
② 새로운 해충 방제 회사 선정을 위한 의견을 수렴하려고
③ 단지 내 산책 시 벌레 퇴치제를 지참할 것을 조언하려고
④ 살충제 선택 시 주의 사항과 올바른 사용법을 설명하려고
⑤ 살충제를 뿌린 단지 주변의 수목을 만지지 말 것을 요청하려고

▶242019-0255

02 대화를 듣고, 남자의 의견으로 가장 적절한 것을 고르시오.

① 목표는 가능하면 구체적으로 세우는 것이 좋다.
② 운동하기 전에 스트레칭을 하면 부상을 줄일 수 있다.
③ 목표를 중간에 포기하지 않으려면 굳은 결심이 필요하다.
④ 독서와 운동은 조금씩이라도 매일 하는 것이 효과적이다.
⑤ 목표를 눈에 보이는 곳에 적어 두면 실천하는 데 도움이 된다.

▶242019-0256

03 다음을 듣고, 여자가 하는 말의 요지로 가장 적절한 것을 고르시오.

① 부모가 책 읽기를 즐겨야 아이도 책을 좋아하게 된다.
② 독서는 아이부터 어른까지 평생 즐길 수 있는 취미이다.
③ 좋아하는 책을 마음껏 읽게 해야 아이가 책을 즐기게 된다.
④ 지나치게 수준이 높은 책은 책에 대한 흥미를 잃게 만든다.
⑤ 여러 장르의 책을 읽는 것이 독해력 향상에 도움이 된다.

▶242019-0257

04 대화를 듣고, 그림에서 대화의 내용과 일치하지 않는 것을 고르시오.

▶242019-0258

05 대화를 듣고, 여자가 할 일로 가장 적절한 것을 고르시오.

① 발표 내용 수정하기
② 삼촌과 통화해 보기
③ 삼촌 연구실 방문하기
④ 로봇에 관한 자료 보내기
⑤ 로봇에 관한 자료 찾아주기

▶242019-0259

06 대화를 듣고, 남자가 지불할 금액을 고르시오. [3점]

① $360   ② $380   ③ $420
④ $550   ⑤ $610

▶242019-0260

07 대화를 듣고, 여자가 오늘 테니스 연습을 하러 갈 수 없는 이유를 고르시오.

① 심한 감기에 걸려서
② 무릎 치료를 받아야 해서
③ 수학 시험공부를 해야 해서
④ 피아노 콘서트에 가야 해서
⑤ 댄스 공연 연습을 해야 해서

▶242019-0261

08 대화를 듣고, Bently Drama Festival에 관해 언급되지 않은 것을 고르시오.

① 개최 기간   ② 참가 팀 수   ③ 장소
④ 상품   ⑤ 후원 기관

▶242019-0262

09 World Spirit Music Concert에 대한 다음 내용을 듣고, 일치하지 않는 것을 고르시오.

① 작년에는 개최되지 않았다.
② 올해 12개 국가의 전통 음악단이 공연할 것이다.
③ 저녁 7시부터 세 시간 동안 열릴 것이다.
④ 마지막 순서로 개최국이 단독 공연을 할 것이다.
⑤ 웹사이트에서 관람권을 살 수 있다.

▶242019-0263

10 다음 표를 보면서 대화를 듣고, 남자가 주문할 딸기잼을 고르시오.

Strawberry Jams

	Product	Service Size (g)	Price	Consumer Rating	Container
①	A	200	$15	4.8	Jar
②	B	230	$18	4.6	Tube
③	C	250	$17	4.8	Tube
④	D	280	$23	4.7	Jar
⑤	E	330	$19	4.7	Jar

▶242019-0264

11 대화를 듣고, 남자의 마지막 말에 대한 여자의 응답으로 가장 적절한 것을 고르시오.

① Thank you. Your sweater helped keep me warm.

② That's terrific! It was a very exciting experience.

③ I'm sure. We'll go swimming in the lake to cool off.

④ I will. I'm going to bring a really warm sleeping bag.

⑤ Don't worry. We'll buy enough food for our camping trip.

▶242019-0265

12 대화를 듣고, 여자의 마지막 말에 대한 남자의 응답으로 가장 적절한 것을 고르시오.

① Sounds great. I'll see you at lunch today.

② Exactly. I really enjoyed having lunch with you.

③ Okay. Sorry you had to cancel your family plans.

④ I don't think so. My schedule is already full today.

⑤ All right. I'll check my calendar and get back to you.

▶242019-0266

13 대화를 듣고, 남자의 마지막 말에 대한 여자의 응답으로 가장 적절한 것을 고르시오. [3점]

Woman: _____

① Exactly. He said he was too busy to meet us today.

② I don't know. There is no need for me to apologize.

③ Right. The meeting today was really informative and useful.

④ I will. Just make sure that you don't forget our meeting again.

⑤ Okay. I'll go see him now to apologize and discuss a new meeting time.

▶242019-0267

14 대화를 듣고, 여자의 마지막 말에 대한 남자의 응답으로 가장 적절한 것을 고르시오. [3점]

Man: _____

① Yes. Let's figure out all three stages of your habit loop.

② Sorry. Having good habits is important for success in life.

③ No. Being bored sometimes gives the brain the rest it needs.

④ Sure. You have to find something else to remove your boredom.

⑤ Exactly. It can lead to weight gain and increase the risk of obesity.

▶242019-0268

15 다음 상황 설명을 듣고 Andy가 Kelly에게 할 말로 가장 적절한 것을 고르시오.

Andy: _____

① Let's change the channel, Mom. This news is boring.

② Unbelievable, Mom. The wildfire is going out so easily.

③ I'm so angry, Mom. How could people let that happen?

④ That's absurd, Mom. You shouldn't ask such questions.

⑤ I'm quite embarrassed, Mom. I didn't think before I acted.

[16~17] 다음을 듣고, 물음에 답하시오.

▶242019-0269

16 남자가 하는 말의 주제로 가장 적절한 것은?

① reason humans reject superstitions

② tips for dealing with difficulties in life

③ warning of the dangers of superstition

④ superstitions related to good and bad luck

⑤ ways to appropriately use household objects

▶242019-0270

17 언급된 물건이 <u>아닌</u> 것은?

① horseshoe   ② mirror   ③ ladder

④ candle   ⑤ umbrella

01

M Attention, residents. This is Klaudio Rodriguez from the maintenance office. Due to the recent unusually wet and hot weather, we've noticed an increase in the number of ▨▨▨▨▨▨ within the apartment complex. To deal with this problem, we've hired a pest control company to spray pesticide around the complex. This will take place next Monday during the day. Pesticides are chemicals that can be harmful if taken in or ▨▨▨▨▨▨. Therefore, we kindly ask that ▨▨▨▨▨▨ any flowers, trees, or other vegetation for a couple of days after the spraying. Your cooperation is greatly appreciated. If you have any questions or concerns, don't hesitate to contact us. Thank you.

02

M Stacy, what have you been up to lately?

W Hi, Tom. I've been planning to start an exercise routine because I've been feeling ▨▨▨▨▨▨.

M Oh, what exercises are you thinking of?

W I'm thinking of doing a 30-minute stretch routine every day, but I'm not sure if I'll be able to ▨▨▨▨▨▨.

M Try not to doubt yourself like that. You can do it.

W Thanks, but I've set similar goals in the past and ▨▨▨▨▨▨. I really hope I can stick to it this time.

M I know of a method you should try. I used it to develop a habit of reading.

W Oh, what is it?

M You write down your goal on pieces of paper and place them around your house where you can see them.

W Ah, that way I'll constantly be reminded of my plan.

M Exactly. Wherever you go, you'll see those papers and remember to take action right away.

W That's a great idea. Thank you.

03

W Hello, I'm Jane Brown, a librarian with over 20 years of experience in various schools. A lot of parents have told me they're concerned that their children don't ▨▨▨▨▨▨. One key characteristic I've noticed in people who love reading is that they read ▨▨▨▨▨▨. This goes against what I see some parents do: they force their children to read particular genres or topics of books. This usually leads to negative outcomes. Instead, it's important to encourage your children ▨▨▨▨▨▨, whatever they are. I believe that this is the best way to turn your kids into lifelong readers.

Quiz 여자가 하는 말의 목적으로 알맞은 것은?

① 독서 교육에 대해 조언하려고　　② 독서 교육 특강을 추천하려고　　③ 책 읽기 프로그램 등록을 권유하려고

04

M　Hey, Ms. Anderson, did you have a good weekend?

W　Hi, Mr. Robinson. Yeah, my family visited my parents' house.

M　Ah, you said your parents live ⬚⬚⬚⬚⬚⬚.

W　Yes. In fact, here's a picture from the weekend.

M　Oh, cool. Your parents have a pond in the yard. And there are even fish in it.

W　Yeah. My son is the boy wearing a hat, ⬚⬚⬚⬚⬚⬚.

M　He must have loved it! These two big trees in the yard must be really old. I'm sure they provide ⬚⬚⬚⬚⬚⬚.

W　Right. That's why my parents set up the hammock between the trees. The person lying on the hammock is my husband.

M　It looks so relaxing.

W　We also put up this tent in front of the pond to sleep in at night, but it got pretty chilly at night, so we didn't actually sleep in it.

M　I see. Your parents' place is really cool.

W　Yeah, we love visiting there.

05

W　Hey, Justin, how are the preparations for the presentation going?

M　They're going fine. How about your group?

W　We've decided on everybody's roles and ⬚⬚⬚⬚⬚⬚.

M　It sounds like your group is making progress. Actually, our team is having some difficulties.

W　Ah, is someone in your group causing problems?

M　That's not it. We're doing a presentation on robots, and surprisingly, we haven't been able to find ⬚⬚⬚⬚⬚⬚ that we're looking for.

W　You've tried searching online, right?

M　Of course. It seems that we're looking for things that aren't very common.

W　I see. Actually, my uncle is a robot engineer. He might know about ⬚⬚⬚⬚⬚⬚. I could ask him if he could help.

M　Oh, could you do that? It'd be really helpful if I could talk to him.

W　Sure. I'll talk to him over the phone and let you know.

M　Thank you so much, Amy.

> ○ **Quiz** 빈칸에 알맞은 것은?
> Q: What is the problem the man's group has?
> A: They have difficulty _____.
> ① deciding on each member's role
> ② choosing their presentation topic
> ③ finding examples of unusual robots

06

W Welcome to King's Fitness Center. How can I help you today?

M Hi, I'd like ⬚⬚⬚⬚⬚ a PT course.

W Okay. We have a 3-month course and a 6-month course.

M How much does each course cost?

W The 3-month course is $400, and the 6-month course is $600.

M The 6-month course is ⬚⬚⬚⬚⬚. I'll go with that one.

W Sounds good. And you'll get 10% off the PT course as a new member.

M That's great. I'd also like to buy this fitness center running shirt. How much is it?

W It's normally $20, but it's $10 off ⬚⬚⬚⬚⬚.

M Good. I'll take it. Here's my credit card.

W Thank you.

07

M Hi, Kate. How did your math test go yesterday?

W Not very good. I didn't study enough for it.

M Was there ⬚⬚⬚⬚⬚?

W Well, I caught a cold last week and had a hard time concentrating.

M Sorry to hear that. So are you going to tennis practice after school today?

W I'd like to, but I can't.

M Why? Did your knee ⬚⬚⬚⬚⬚?

W No. Ever since I saw the doctor, it's been a lot better.

M That's good to hear. So, do you have to practice for your school festival performance with the dance team?

W No. I'm meeting my cousin after school. We're going to a piano concert together.

M I see. Sounds like fun. Have a great time.

W Thanks! I'll definitely ⬚⬚⬚⬚⬚ the next tennis practice.

> **Quiz** 우리말과 같도록 빈칸에 알맞은 말을 대화에서 찾아 쓰시오.
> 우리는 집중하는 데 어려움을 겪었다.
> We ＿＿＿＿ ＿＿＿＿ ＿＿＿＿ ＿＿＿＿ concentrating.

08

M Ms. Anderson, what are you busy with these days?

W Hello, Mr. Smith. I'm in charge of organizing the Bently Drama Festival this year, so I've been ⬚⬚⬚⬚⬚.

M Ah, I see. That's the annual citywide student drama festival, right?

W Right. It starts next Wednesday, and it lasts three days.

M I see. How many teams are participating?

W There are nine teams participating this year, with three teams performing on each day.

M And where will it take place?

W ▢▢▢▢▢▢ wasn't easy, but fortunately, I was able to reserve the auditorium at the city's education office.

M That's a perfect place for the festival.

W I agree. And I'm happy because I just found out this morning that two high schools are going to sponsor the festival along with a local shopping mall.

M I'm also glad to hear that. Sounds like you've done an amazing job with ▢▢▢▢▢▢.

W Thank you, Mr. Smith.

09

M Hello, listeners! I'm David Richardson from the National Traditional Music Center, and I'm thrilled to announce the World Spirit Music Concert, ▢▢▢▢▢▢ focusing on traditional music from around the world! After the concert was not held last year, ▢▢▢▢▢▢ to participate this year. So, this year there will be traditional bands from 12 countries performing. The concert's next Friday from 7 to 10 p.m. at the National Traditional Music Concert Hall. At the end, all the music bands will join together for an amazing harmonious finale. To ▢▢▢▢▢▢, simply purchase tickets on our website. Don't miss out on this unique event combining traditional cultures around the world!

10

W Honey, we're completely out of strawberry jam.

M I know. I'll order some online right now. Take a look. Which one of these should we buy?

W Let me see. *[Pause]* This one's pretty big. Do we need that much?

M I don't think so. It's over 300 g. That's a lot. Let's ▢▢▢▢▢▢.

W All right. Whoa, look at this one. It's over $20!

M Oh, that's too pricey.

W I agree. Let's choose one of the other three options.

M Look at the customer ratings. These two have a ▢▢▢▢▢▢ than this one.

W Then let's get one with a higher customer rating.

M Okay. How about we try a tube this time?

W Sounds good. It should be ▢▢▢▢▢▢.

M Right. Then I'll go ahead and order this one.

11

M Hey, Cathy, do you have any plans for the ▢▢▢▢▢▢?

W Yeah. I'm going camping with my friend at Mt. Emerton.

M Sounds fun! But it's supposed to be ▢▢▢▢▢▢, so make sure you prepare for that.

Quiz 우리말과 같도록 빈칸에 알맞은 말을 대화에서 찾아 쓰시오.
너는 그곳에서 매우 추운 날씨에 대비해야 해.
You should _____ _____ very cold weather there.

12

W Chris, I'm terribly sorry, but could we _____? I won't be able to make it today.

M Of course. I was really looking forward to our lunch though. Is everything all right?

W Unfortunately, a _____ came up. I should be free to meet any day after Tuesday.

13

[Cell phone rings.]

W Hi, Mark.

M Sarah, why didn't you answer your phone when I called a little while ago?

W Sorry. I _____ because I was studying. What's up?

M Remember our meeting with Mr. Stevens about our science project today? It was supposed to start an hour ago. We waited for you in his office for 20 minutes before canceling the meeting.

W Oh, no. I completely forgot about it. I'm so sorry.

M It's disappointing that you forgot. We've been preparing for this meeting for weeks!

W I know. I've just been so overwhelmed with exams that _____. I sincerely apologize.

M Well, I accept your apology. But Mr. Stevens was pretty let down.

W I should personally apologize to him right away.

M I agree. And you should ask him if he's willing to _____ for some time next week.

> **Quiz** 우리말과 같도록 빈칸에 알맞은 말을 대화에서 찾아 쓰시오.
> 그는 파티 때문에 너무나도 신이 나서 전날 밤에 잠을 잘 수 없었다.
> He was _____ excited about the party _____ he couldn't sleep the night before.

14

M Emily, you just had dinner a little while ago, and now you're eating something again.

W Dad, I've been snacking too much lately. I want to stop.

M I can help you with that. Have you _____?

W No. What is it?

M It's the basic structure of every habit. It consists of three parts: the cue, the routine, and the reward. Identifying the parts can help you break your habit.

W Okay, I assume the routine is eating snacks.

M Exactly. So then you need to figure out _____.

W Hmm. I tend to eat snacks when I have nothing else to do or when I'm really busy. I usually don't eat snacks otherwise.

M It sounds like your cue is an emotional state.

W You're right. I eat snacks because I feel bored.

M Right. So now let's _____. I think the reward is that you feel less bored when you're eating snacks.

W That's true. So, do you know of a plan to help me break my snacking habit?

15 **W** Kelly and Andy are a mother and son with a strong _____. They are currently watching a news report on TV about intense wildfires in another region of the country. The news states that the wildfires have burned over one million acres of land and are still spreading, _____ of wildlife and their habitats. The news reporter attributes the cause of the wildfire to reckless logging by humans. Andy is deeply upset about the way _____. He wants to express his anger to Kelly. In this situation, what would Andy most likely say to Kelly?

16~17 **M** Welcome to the Jacky-Wicky horror show! I'm Taylor. Have you ever wondered why on some days nothing goes your way, while on others _____? People have varying reasons as to why. In our show, we take a look at the mysteries of superstitions passed down through the ages. Let's begin learning about different situations. First is wearing a rabbit's foot, which is believed _____. Hanging up a horseshoe is thought of similarly, as it's a way to collect good luck for future use. However, if you hang it upside down, all the luck will pour out, leaving you with none! Breaking a mirror is also believed to bring seven years of bad luck! Walking underneath a ladder may lead to something unfortunate. And it's often advised not to open an umbrella indoors, _____ for the rest of the day. Throughout our show, you will learn about more beliefs and warnings that people follow.

Dictation 빠른답

01 ☐ insects and pests ☐ absorbed through the skin ☐ you avoid touching

02 ☐ a little stiff ☐ stick to it ☐ ended up giving up

03 ☐ enjoy reading books ☐ whatever interests them ☐ to read their favorite books

04 ☐ in the countryside ☐ feeding the fish ☐ some nice shade

05 ☐ started gathering materials ☐ examples of robots ☐ uncommon robots

06 ☐ to register for ☐ a better deal ☐ for new members

07 ☐ any particular reason ☐ start hurting again ☐ make it to

08 ☐ working on that ☐ Finding a proper place ☐ organizing the festival

09 ☐ a spectacular concert ☐ many countries reached out ☐ attend the concert

10 ☐ get a smaller size ☐ higher customer rating ☐ convenient to use

11 ☐ upcoming long weekend ☐ pretty cold this weekend

12 ☐ reschedule our lunch appointment ☐ family emergency

13 ☐ had it on silent ☐ it slipped my mind ☐ reschedule the meeting

14 ☐ heard of the habit loop ☐ what triggers your snack eating ☐ focus on the reward

15 ☐ passion for protecting the Earth ☐ leading to the death and destruction ☐ humans are harming the environment

16~17 ☐ everything goes our way ☐ to bring good luck ☐ unless you want bad luck

----

Quiz 03 ① **05** ③ **07** had a hard time **11** prepare for **13** so, that

▶ 242019-0271

01 다음을 듣고, 여자가 하는 말의 목적으로 가장 적절한 것을 고르시오.

① 퍼레이드 시간 연장을 알리려고
② 퍼레이드 이동 동선을 안내하려고
③ 놀이 기구 수리 일정을 공지하려고
④ 놀이공원 캐릭터 교체를 설명하려고
⑤ 놀이공원 고객의 질서 유지를 당부하려고

▶ 242019-0272

02 대화를 듣고, 여자의 의견으로 가장 적절한 것을 고르시오.

① 그룹 운동은 동기 부여 효과가 크다.
② 운동은 꾸준히 해야 실력이 향상한다.
③ 일상생활에서 칼로리 소모량을 높여야 한다.
④ 음악을 들으면서 걷기 운동을 하면 지루하지 않다.
⑤ 음악을 들으면서 줄넘기하는 것이 체중 감량에 좋다.

▶ 242019-0273

03 다음을 듣고, 남자가 하는 말의 요지로 가장 적절한 것을 고르시오.

① 다양한 경험을 하면 직업에서 성공할 가능성이 크다.
② 아침에 일의 우선순위를 정하면 능률을 유지할 수 있다.
③ 자신이 진정으로 좋아하는 일을 직업으로 선택해야 한다.
④ 직장 생활과 여가 생활의 균형을 찾으려고 노력해야 한다.
⑤ 한 번에 한 가지 일에 집중하면 과업의 완성도가 높아진다.

▶ 242019-0274

04 대화를 듣고, 그림에서 대화의 내용과 일치하지 <u>않는</u> 것을 고르시오.

▶ 242019-0275

05 대화를 듣고, 남자가 할 일로 가장 적절한 것을 고르시오.

① 케이크 굽기
② 꽃집에 전화하기
③ 테이블 빌려오기
④ 메뉴 마무리하기
⑤ 가족사진 가져오기

▶ 242019-0276

06 대화를 듣고, 여자가 지불할 금액을 고르시오. [3점]

① $60 ② $90 ③ $100
④ $110 ⑤ $140

▶ 242019-0277

07 대화를 듣고, 남자가 하이킹을 갈 수 <u>없는</u> 이유를 고르시오.

① 딸의 학교에 방문해야 해서
② 중간고사 준비를 해야 해서
③ 지도 교수와 면담이 있어서
④ 육아 워크숍에 참석해야 해서
⑤ 연구 프로젝트 작업을 해야 해서

▶ 242019-0278

08 대화를 듣고, 가족 춤 활동에 관해 언급되지 <u>않은</u> 것을 고르시오.

① 장소 ② 시작 시간 ③ 춤의 종류
④ 참가비 ⑤ 현장 등록 가능 여부

▶ 242019-0279

09 Sanford School Video Contest에 관한 다음 내용을 듣고, 일치하지 <u>않는</u> 것을 고르시오.

① 모든 연령대의 학생이 참가할 수 있다.
② 동영상은 30초 이하로 제작해야 한다.
③ 수상자는 상금으로 100달러를 받을 것이다.
④ 한 사람이 여러 개의 동영상을 제출할 수 있다.
⑤ 영상 제출 마감일은 9월 1일이다.

▶242019-0280

10 다음 표를 보면서 대화를 듣고, 두 사람이 자녀를 위해 선택한 여름 캠프를 고르시오.

Summer Camp Programs

	Camp	Theme	Age	Price	Lunch Included
①	A	Art	8 to 11	$160	○
②	B	Science	5 to 9	$170	○
③	C	Storybook	5 to 9	$180	×
④	D	Sports	8 to 13	$220	○
⑤	E	Nature	8 to 11	$190	×

▶242019-0281

11 대화를 듣고, 남자의 마지막 말에 대한 여자의 응답으로 가장 적절한 것을 고르시오.

① Yeah. Your pasta was great and cooked to perfection.

② I don't think so. But let's use the tomato sauce instead.

③ Of course. We'll need some ripe tomatoes for the salad.

④ Too bad. We don't have any tomatoes left in the refrigerator.

⑤ Not really. We can just follow a recipe I found in a magazine.

▶242019-0282

12 대화를 듣고, 여자의 마지막 말에 대한 남자의 응답으로 가장 적절한 것을 고르시오.

① Thanks. I'll wait for the new one then.

② Don't worry. The discount will increase sales.

③ Never mind. We'll have more in stock next week.

④ That sounds fair. I'll take it even with the scratch.

⑤ That's right. Thanks for getting rid of the scratch.

▶242019-0283

13 대화를 듣고, 남자의 마지막 말에 대한 여자의 응답으로 가장 적절한 것을 고르시오. [3점]

Woman: _____

① No thanks. I'll recycle the bottle myself.

② Sure. Congratulations on opening the new store.

③ Sorry. I'd rather go to the zero-waste store in town.

④ Perfect. I'll get that sustainable cleaning spray there.

⑤ I don't think so. The store doesn't sell cleaning products.

▶242019-0284

14 대화를 듣고, 여자의 마지막 말에 대한 남자의 응답으로 가장 적절한 것을 고르시오. [3점]

Man: _____

① Sounds good. I'm sorry I didn't read it last week.

② Thanks. I'll make sure to read it before the meeting.

③ I see. Let me know if you find the right club for me.

④ I got it. Let's see if I can write a good article about it.

⑤ No need to worry. I'll correct any mistakes and return it.

▶242019-0285

15 다음 상황 설명을 듣고, Jim이 Adrian에게 할 말로 가장 적절한 것을 고르시오.

Jim: _____

① Why don't we plan some outdoor activities?

② I think we need to cancel his academy lessons.

③ Let's go to a different shopping mall for lunch.

④ We should ask Ethan about what he wants to do.

⑤ How about moving to a house in the countryside for Ethan?

[16~17] 다음을 듣고, 물음에 답하시오.

▶242019-0286

16 여자가 하는 말의 주제로 가장 적절한 것은?

① effects of climate change on marine species

② tourism practices to conserve marine species

③ challenges in saving endangered marine species

④ technological innovations for marine conservation

⑤ threats of foreign animal species to marine ecosystems

▶242019-0287

17 언급된 동물이 <u>아닌</u> 것은?

① marine turtles   ② whale sharks

③ sea lions   ④ seahorses

⑤ dolphins

01 W Hello, Blue Moon Amusement Park visitors. Based on the cheers and laughs we're hearing, it sounds like you're having a great time at the park today! And we want to enhance your joy and excitement even more! Starting today, we're ▓▓▓▓▓ from 30 minutes to 45 minutes, giving you more time to enjoy it. So, grab your spot along the parade route and ▓▓▓▓▓ by the outstanding performers and beloved characters filling the streets with music and magic ▓▓▓▓▓. I hope you enjoy the rest of your day here at Blue Moon Amusement Park!

02 W Hi, Jeremy. It seems like ▓▓▓▓▓.

M I have lost a little. Thanks for noticing.

W That's great to hear! What have you been doing?

M I've been taking daily walks. But honestly, it's pretty boring, so I want to find something else to do.

W How about jumping rope? It can be a great exercise for weight loss.

M Really? It can be?

W Yeah. It's a high-intensity exercise that burns calories quickly, which helps lose weight.

M I see. But that sounds pretty boring and monotonous.

W That's why it's good to ▓▓▓▓▓. You jump to the beat of the music, so it's way more enjoyable.

M Ah, that could keep me motivated.

W Absolutely! Jumping rope to music is ▓▓▓▓▓.

M I'll definitely give it a shot. Thanks for the recommendation!

> **Quiz** 빈칸에 알맞은 말을 대화에서 찾아 쓰시오.
> In the conversation, the man has been _____ _____ _____, but will try _____ _____ to music to lose weight.

03 M Hello, viewers! Thank you for tuning in to my video channel. As you might know, I juggle multiple roles as a content creator, freelance writer, and fitness instructor. I'm often asked how I ▓▓▓▓▓ with such a busy schedule. My secret is ▓▓▓▓▓. Let's say you have to study for a math test, deal with urgent emails, and prepare for a school club meeting. In that case, it's a good idea to create a to-do list in your head and ▓▓▓▓▓. This way, you can stay efficient and might even have some spare time to do things you love. Thanks again for watching!

04

M　Hey, Ellie. What are you looking at on your phone?

W　Hey, Sebastian. It's a picture of my brother Sean and me at Wheeler State Park.

M　Let me see. *[Pause]* Wow, there's a ⬚⬚⬚⬚⬚⬚⬚ .

W　Pretty cool, right?

M　Yeah. And I really like the bench ⬚⬚⬚⬚⬚⬚⬚ . It's a cozy place to sit.

W　Do you see the teddy bear on the bench? It's Sean's. He accidentally left it there, so we had to go back and get it.

M　Thank goodness nobody took it! I see you and Sean in a boat.

W　We rented it. It was fun, and I wore ⬚⬚⬚⬚⬚⬚ because it was really sunny.

M　Oh, look. These two ducks were swimming behind you.

W　Aren't they adorable? They followed us the whole time we were in the boat. It was a great time.

05

M　Mom, I'm really excited for grandma's birthday party tomorrow.

W　Me, too. It's going to be fun. I just ⬚⬚⬚⬚⬚⬚ with the caterer.

M　That's good. As far as the cake, are you baking one?

W　No. I ordered one from the bakery.

M　That's easier. Is there anything I can do to help? I could ⬚⬚⬚⬚⬚⬚ .

W　That's not necessary. Your dad will take care of that later today.

M　Okay. I think it'd be nice to decorate the table with flowers and family photos.

W　That's a great idea. We can use the family photos in the master bedroom.

M　Yeah. I'll ⬚⬚⬚⬚⬚⬚ right now.

W　Perfect! While you do that, I'll call the flower shop.

Quiz　괄호 안에서 알맞은 것을 고르시오.
Q: What are they going to do with the family photos?
A: They are going to decorate [the table / the master bedroom] with them.

06

M Welcome to Aqua Splash Water Park.

W Hi, I need _____. How much are they?

M They're $30 for adults and $20 for children under 12.

W Okay. I'll take two adult tickets and two child tickets, please.

M All right. Would you like to rent a locker as well? It's a secure way to store your belongings while you enjoy the park.

W How much does it cost?

M It's $10 to _____.

W Sounds good. I'll rent one locker.

M So, that's two adult tickets, two child tickets, and one locker rental, correct?

W That's right. Oh, and I saw something on your social media about a 10%-off promotional event.

M I'm sorry, but _____.

W I see. No problem. Here's my credit card.

07

W Hey, Sam. How have you been?

M Pretty good. But busy. Being a dad and a graduate student isn't easy.

W I can only imagine. But you've been doing really great in our classes. Now that our mid-terms are over, John and I are planning to _____. Would you like to join us?

M I wish I could, but I can't.

W Why not? Are you going to start _____?

M No. Since it's not due until the end of the semester, I plan on starting it sometime next week.

W Then why can't you come?

M It's about my daughter.

W Do you have to visit her school on Friday?

M No. I'm attending a _____ Dr. Paul Johnson.

W Oh, he's a parenting expert, right?

M Yeah. I think it's going to be really informative.

W I'm sure it will be.

> **Quiz** 우리말과 같도록 빈칸에 알맞은 말을 대화에서 찾아 쓰시오.
> 이제 나는 숙제를 끝냈으니, 휴식을 취하고 TV를 좀 볼 수 있다.
> _____ _____ I have finished my homework, I can relax and watch some TV.

08

[Telephone rings.]

W Hello, Gardner Community Center. How may I help you?

M Hi, I'd like to get some information about your family dance activity.

W You mean the one held in Gardner Park?

M That's right. _____?

W It's every Saturday, starting at 10 a.m.

M Great! ▨▨▨▨▨ does it focus on?

W It focuses on a variety of dance styles, including hip-hop and salsa. Everybody I've talked to who's attended the activity said it's really fun.

M That sounds fantastic! Can I just show up, or do I need to ▨▨▨▨▨?

W We encourage participants to sign up in advance, but but on-site registration is also possible.

M That's good to know. Thank you for the information.

W You're welcome. Have a great day. Bye.

09 W Hello, students. I'm Melanie Brown, director of the Sanford Public School Foundation. This year, we have something exciting for you: the Sanford School Video Contest! It's a fantastic opportunity ▨▨▨▨▨. We're seeking short videos, ▨▨▨▨▨, showcasing your school. You can create a video of fun moments you've recorded throughout your school years, introduce your teachers, or capture new memories with your friends. Multiple winners will be selected, and each of them will receive a cash prize of $100. Each person is allowed to ▨▨▨▨▨, and the submission deadline is September 1st. For more information, please visit our website at www.sanfordpsf.org.

10 W Honey, it's time to decide on a summer camp for Annie and Tom.

M You're right. *[Typing Sound]* Let me pull up the website that shows the summer camps in town.

W All right. Let's see. Which theme sounds best?

M I think ▨▨▨▨▨ would be okay. They did the science camp last summer.

W Yeah, they wouldn't want to do that again. And we want them to attend the same camp, so we need to consider their ages too.

M Right. We need a camp for both 8- and 10-year-olds. Then there's the price.

W Since there's the two of them, let's ▨▨▨▨▨ $200.

M Okay. Hmm. Then should we choose this camp that includes lunch?

W No, I'll ▨▨▨▨▨. I'm concerned about Annie's allergies.

M Good point. Then in that case, let's choose this camp.

W All right. I'm sure they'll like it.

11 M Oh, no. We're all ▨▨▨▨▨. I was planning to cook pasta for dinner.

W Don't worry. We have tomatoes in the refrigerator. We can ▨▨▨▨▨.

M I've never done that. Do you think it's difficult?

Quiz 밑줄 친 표현과 의미가 같은 것은?
We can <u>make it from scratch</u>.
① adjust it to suit our taste preferences
② add necessary ingredients to it
③ prepare it using raw ingredients

12

W Did you find everything okay, sir?

M Well, I'd like to purchase a bag like this, but ⬛⬛⬛⬛⬛ right here. Do you happen to have a new one?

W I'm sorry, but that's ⬛⬛⬛⬛⬛. But I can offer you a 15% discount.

13

M Hi, Janet. What are you doing on your phone?

W I'm trying to find an ⬛⬛⬛⬛⬛.

M Have you heard about the zero-waste store in town? They have sustainable alternatives for everyday items.

W No, I haven't. What exactly is a zero-waste store?

M It's a store that tries to minimize packaging waste and promote reusable products.

W That's great! I've been ⬛⬛⬛⬛⬛ climate change lately. It's really serious.

M Absolutely. It's important we make sustainable choices in our daily lives.

W Definitely. So do they have cleaning products at the zero-waste store?

M Yes. I actually bought a cleaning spray with a reusable aluminum bottle last week.

W That's exactly what I'm looking for. Can you tell me ⬛⬛⬛⬛⬛?

M Of course. We can even go there together. I'm planning on going there tomorrow.

14

W What are you reading, Jay?

M Hi, Irene. It's a ⬛⬛⬛⬛⬛.

W I didn't know you enjoyed reading such news articles.

M Yeah, I do. But sometimes they're a little challenging to understand. I wish I had some people to talk to about them.

W I had no idea you were interested in something like that. You should join the school International Relations Club. I'm in it.

M Oh, do you discuss news articles about international affairs?

W Yeah. We meet every Thursday. It'd be a great chance for you ⬛⬛⬛⬛⬛.

M That's perfect. So I can join the club?

W Of course! You should come this week. I can send you the ⬛⬛⬛⬛⬛ so you can read it in advance.

M Sounds good. What's the article about?

W It's about Korea's diplomatic strategy. I'll send it to you right away.

15

M Jim and Adrian are married and have a 15-year-old son named Ethan. They're currently ⬛⬛⬛⬛⬛ for the upcoming weekend. Adrian suggests they go to a nearby shopping mall to have lunch and enjoy the indoor amusement park there. These days, Jim is concerned about Ethan's ⬚⬚⬚⬚⬚. Basically, all Ethan has been doing lately is spending most of his time indoors studying for his mid-term exams and attending academies. Jim thinks it's really important for him to connect with nature, breathe in some fresh air, and experience the beauty of the natural surroundings. So Jim wants to suggest to Adrian that they ⬚⬚⬚⬚⬚. In this situation, what would Jim most likely say to Adrian?

16~17 **W** Hello, everyone. While encountering sea animals during vacation is extremely exciting, it's important that these animals be protected. So today we're going to talk about ⬚⬚⬚⬚⬚ to protect some of these animals. First, in Costa Rica, tour operators are working together to protect the nesting beaches of marine turtles. They ensure there are minimal disturbances to the nesting turtles during tours. Next, in the Maldives, educational sessions are provided for visitors to ⬚⬚⬚⬚⬚. Tourists are taught how to prevent any direct contact with them that could harm them. Moving on, there are travel measures that emphasize protecting seahorses' habitats in the Philippines. Tourists are encouraged to not disturb seahorse habitats, such as coral reefs and seagrass beds. Lastly, in New Zealand, dolphin watching tours operate under strict guidelines to ⬚⬚⬚⬚⬚. Also, marine research institutions often work closely with tour operators to develop guidelines that prioritize the well-being of dolphins. Now let's watch a short video.

> ○ **Quiz** 빈칸에 알맞은 말을 대화에서 찾아 쓰시오.
> Q: What are tourists in the Maldives taught?
> A: They are taught _____ with whale sharks.

Dictation 빠른답

01 ☐ extending the parade time ☐ get ready to be amazed
☐ for an extended duration

02 ☐ you've lost some weight
☐ jump rope while listening to music
☐ great for losing weight

03 ☐ manage to stay efficient
☐ prioritizing tasks in the morning
☐ set your priorities in the morning

04 ☐ windmill in the background ☐ between the trees
☐ my striped hat

05 ☐ finalized the menu ☐ vacuum the floors ☐ go grab them

06 ☐ four admission tickets ☐ rent a locker for the day
☐ that event ended last week

07 ☐ go hiking this Friday ☐ working on your research project
☐ parenting workshop conducted by

08 ☐ When is it held ☐ What types of dances
☐ sign up in advance

09 ☐ for students of all ages ☐ thirty seconds or less
☐ submit only one video

10 ☐ all of them except science ☐ keep it under
☐ pack their lunches

11 ☐ out of tomato sauce ☐ make it from scratch

12 ☐ this one is scratched ☐ the last one we have in stock

13 ☐ eco-friendly cleaning product
☐ getting more concerned about ☐ where the store is

14 ☐ news article about international affairs
☐ to have meaningful conversations
☐ article that we'll talk about

15 ☐ planning some family activities
☐ lack of exposure to nature
☐ arrange some things to do outside

16~17 ☐ responsible travel measures being used
☐ raise awareness about whale sharks
☐ maintain a safe distance from dolphins

Quiz 02 taking daily walks, jumping rope **05** the table **07** Now that **11** ③ **16~17** how to prevent any direct contact

PART Ⅰ | 수능유형 분석편

01 목적
본문 8~9쪽

수능유형 체험 | ③

수능유형 연습 | 01 ⑤ 02 ② 03 ④ 04 ② 05 ⑤ 06 ③

02 의견 / 주장 / 요지
본문 10~11쪽

수능유형 체험 | ②

수능유형 연습 | 01 ③ 02 ⑤ 03 ② 04 ⑤ 05 ③ 06 ①

03 관계
본문 12~13쪽

수능유형 체험 | ④

수능유형 연습 | 01 ② 02 ⑤ 03 ② 04 ② 05 ② 06 ②

04 그림 내용 일치
본문 14~15쪽

수능유형 체험 | ④

수능유형 연습 | 01 ⑤ 02 ⑤ 03 ⑤ 04 ④ 05 ⑤ 06 ④

05 할 일/부탁한 일
본문 16~17쪽

수능유형 체험 | ②

수능유형 연습 | 01 ③ 02 ④ 03 ③ 04 ③ 05 ④ 06 ③

06 숫자 정보
본문 18~19쪽

수능유형 체험 | ⑤

수능유형 연습 | 01 ② 02 ③ 03 ⑤ 04 ③ 05 ① 06 ②

07 이유
본문 20~21쪽

수능유형 체험 | ⑤

수능유형 연습 | 01 ③ 02 ① 03 ⑤ 04 ① 05 ① 06 ①

08 언급 유무
본문 22~23쪽

수능유형 체험 | ④

수능유형 연습 | 01 ③ 02 ③ 03 ④ 04 ③ 05 ⑤ 06 ③

09 담화 내용 일치
본문 24~25쪽

수능유형 체험 | ⑤

수능유형 연습 | 01 ④ 02 ③ 03 ③ 04 ④ 05 ④ 06 ④

10 도표
본문 26~27쪽

수능유형 체험 | ②

수능유형 연습 | 01 ④ 02 ③ 03 ⑤ 04 ④ 05 ③ 06 ③

11 짧은 대화의 응답
본문 28~29쪽

수능유형 체험 | ④

수능유형 연습 | 01 ⑤ 02 ① 03 ① 04 ④ 05 ② 06 ③

12 긴 대화의 응답
본문 30~31쪽

수능유형 체험 | ④

수능유형 연습 | 01 ② 02 ② 03 ⑤ 04 ① 05 ⑤ 06 ③

13 상황에 적절한 말
본문 32~33쪽

수능유형 체험 | ②

수능유형 연습 | 01 ① 02 ③ 03 ② 04 ③ 05 ④ 06 ⑤

14 복합 이해
본문 34~35쪽

수능유형 체험 | 01 ⑤ 02 ④

수능유형 연습 | 01 ③ 02 ⑤ 03 ③ 04 ④ 05 ③ 06 ④
07 ⑤ 08 ④

PART Ⅱ | 수능실전 **대비편**

MEMO

하루 한 장으로 중학 수학 실력 UP↑

인터넷·모바일·TV
무료 강의 제공

1(상) | 1(하) | 2(상) | 2(하) | 3(상) | 3(하)

중학 수학은
한 장 수학으로
이렇게!

하나!

하루 한 장으로
가볍게 **습관 들이기**

둘!

기초부터 시작해서
문제로 **완성**하기

셋!

서술형·신유형 문항도
빠짐없이 연습하기

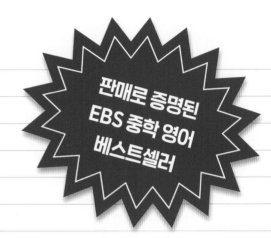

판매로 증명된
EBS 중학 영어
베스트셀러

MY COACH

중학 내신 영어 해결사

NEW

GOOD DAY!

문법, 독해부터 단어, 쓰기까지
내신 시험도 대비하는 **중학 영어 특화 시리즈**

GRAMMAR	GRAMMAR 내신기출 N제	READING	WRITING 내신서술형	VOCA

중 | 학 | 도 | 역 | 시 **EBS**

듣기 MP3 파일
바로듣기 & 다운로드

미리 준비하는 중학생을 위한

중학 수능특강

중학 영어듣기에서
수능 영어듣기 실력으로의 도약

PART Ⅰ 수능유형 분석편
수능 유형의 대표 문제와 해결 전략

PART Ⅱ 수능실전 대비편
수능 실전 감각을 익히는 모의고사 11회분

정답과 해설

 인터넷·모바일·TV
무료 강의 제공

영어듣기

중학 수능특강 **영어듣기**

정답과 해설

수능 유형

01 목적

수능유형 **체험** | ③

수능유형 **연습** | 01 ⑤ 02 ② 03 ④ 04 ② 05 ⑤ 06 ③

수능유형 체험   작가 초청 강연회 개최 공지   [정답] ③

남   안녕하세요, Greenville 중학교 학생 여러분! 저는 여러분의 학교 도서관 사서인 Collins 선생님입니다. 우리 학교에서 여러분을 위해 기획한 특별 행사를 발표하게 되어 기쁩니다. 여러분이 가장 좋아하는 판타지 소설가 Amy Brown이 5월 16일 오후 3시에 우리 학교 도서관에서 강연할 것입니다. 그녀의 소설에 관한 발표 후에, 질의응답 시간이 있을 것입니다. 이 특별한 행사를 놓치지 마세요! 여러분은 우리 학교 웹사이트에서 더 많은 정보를 찾을 수 있고 신청할 수 있습니다. 관심을 가져 주셔서 감사합니다.

문제 해설   남자는 학교에서 학생들이 가장 좋아하는 판타지 소설가를 초청하여 강연회를 개최할 것이라고 말하며, 학생들에게 일시, 장소, 일정 등에 관해 공지하고 있다. 따라서 남자가 하는 말의 목적으로 가장 적절한 것은 ③이다.

어휘&어구   librarian (도서관의) 사서   announce 알리다   lecture 강연, 강의   session 시간, 기간   sign up 신청하다

수능유형 연습

01 환경 보호 자원봉사단 참여   [정답] ⑤

M   Hello, everyone. I'm James Wright, your student council president. We all love Silver Lake Park, as it provides a great natural space near our school. However, as you're likely aware, there's recently been news about a growing problem in the park because visitors throw their trash on the ground. Therefore, our student council has decided to organize an environmental protection volunteer group for the park. I'd like to ask all of you to join us and help keep the park clean. If you're interested, stop by the student council room anytime. Let's work together to keep our favorite park in good shape!

남   안녕하세요, 여러분. 저는 여러분의 학생회장 James Wright입니다. Silver Lake 공원이 우리 학교 근처에서 훌륭한 자연 공간을 제공하므로 우리는 모두 그것을 사랑합니다. 하지만, 여러분도 알다시피, 방문객들이 바닥에 쓰레기를 버려서 문제가 심해진다는 뉴스가 최근에 있었습니다. 그래서, 우리 학생회는 공원을 위한 환경 보호 자원봉사단을 조직하기로 결정했습니다. 저는 여러분 모두에게 우리와 함께해 공원을 깨끗하게 유지하는 것을 돕도록 요청하고 싶습니다. 관심이 있다면 언제든지 학생회실에 들르세요. 우리가 가장 좋아하는 공원을 좋은 상태로 유지하기 위해 함께 노력합시다!

문제 해설   남자는 학교 근처에 있는 공원에서 방문객들이 쓰레기를 버려서 문제가 된다는 뉴스가 있었음을 말하고, 이에 학생회에서 환경 보호 자원봉사단을 조직하기로 했으니 봉사단에 참여하기를 요청한다고 했다. 따라서 남자가 하는 말의 목적으로 가장 적절한 것은 ⑤이다.

어휘&어구   student council president 학생회장   provide 제공하다   recently 최근에   trash 쓰레기   environmental 환경의   protection 보호   volunteer group 자원봉사단   stop by ~에 들르다   in good shape 상태가 좋은, 건강한

02 수재민을 위한 기부   [정답] ②

W   Hello, listeners in the Edington area! This is Cathy Martin from Edington City Hall. Unfortunately, the heavy rain last weekend caused damage throughout the city, flooding many residents' houses. Without a place to live, a lot of residents are currently living in

여   안녕하세요, Edington 지역 청취자 여러분! 저는 Edington 시청의 Cathy Martin입니다. 유감스럽게도, 지난 주말 폭우로 인해 도시 전역에 피해가 발생하여 많은 주민의 집이 침수되었습니다. 살 곳이 없어 현재 많은 주민이 임시 대피소에서 생활하고 있습니다. 저희가 그분들을 지원하기 위해 할 수 있는 모든 것을 하는 동안,

temporary shelters. While we're doing everything we can to support them, small donations from you can make a big difference in their lives. I kindly request that you consider making a donation. For more information, please visit the city hall website. Now's the perfect time to show your compassion and support for our fellow citizens in need. Thank you for your consideration.

여러분의 작은 기부가 그분들의 삶에 큰 변화를 가져올 수 있습니다. 기부하는 것을 고려해 주시기를 정중히 요청합니다. 더 많은 정보를 원하시면, 시청 웹사이트를 방문해 주세요. 지금이 도움이 필요한 우리의 이웃 시민들에 대한 연민과 지지를 보여 줄 완벽한 때입니다. 여러분의 배려에 감사합니다.

문제 해설 여자는 폭우에 의한 침수로 인해 집을 떠나 임시 대피소에서 생활하고 있는 많은 이웃 시민을 위해 기부에 동참할 것을 요청하고 있다. 따라서 여자가 하는 말의 목적으로 가장 적절한 것은 ②이다.

어휘&어구 listener 청취자 resident 주민, 거주자 temporary 임시의 shelter 대피소, 거처 donation 기부 request 요청하다 compassion 연민 citizen 시민 in need 도움이 필요한 consideration 배려

03 건물 외관 청소에 따른 유의 사항
[정답] ④

M Good morning, everyone! This is John Smith from the building management office. As you know, our regular building exterior cleaning is scheduled for tomorrow. It's a necessary part of our maintenance plan to ensure a safe and clean environment for all the offices in the building. During the cleaning process, we kindly ask that you keep your windows closed to prevent water from entering your offices. Also, please make sure to remove any items from your windowsills and also move any equipment or furniture away from the window. If you have any questions regarding this matter, please contact our office. Your cooperation is greatly appreciated.

남 안녕하세요, 여러분! 저는 건물 관리실의 John Smith입니다. 아시다시피, 저희의 정기적인 건물 외관 청소가 내일로 예정되어 있습니다. 그것은 건물 내의 모든 사무실들을 위한 안전하고 깨끗한 환경을 보장하려는 저희의 유지 보수 계획의 필수적인 부분입니다. 청소 진행 중에는 물이 사무실에 들어가지 않도록 창문을 꼭 닫아 주시기를 부탁드립니다. 또한 물건들을 반드시 창턱에서 치워 주시고 장비나 가구도 창문에서 멀리 옮겨 주십시오. 이 문제와 관련하여 궁금한 사항이 있으시면 우리 사무실로 문의해 주시기를 바랍니다. 협조해 주셔서 대단히 감사합니다.

문제 해설 남자는 내일로 예정된 정기적인 건물 외관 청소를 알리면서, 창문을 닫을 것, 물건을 창턱에서 치울 것 등 유의 사항을 안내하고 있다. 따라서 남자가 하는 말의 목적으로 가장 적절한 것은 ④이다.

어휘&어구 management office 관리실 regular 정기적인 exterior 외관의, 외부의 maintenance 유지 보수, 정비 ensure 보장하다 prevent ... from -ing …이 ~하지 않게 하다 remove 치우다, 제거하다 windowsill 창턱 cooperation 협조 appreciate 감사하다

04 컴퓨터 강좌
[정답] ②

W Well, today is the last day of our intermediate computer programming class. You've all done a great job over the past six months. And now you're one step closer to becoming an expert computer programmer. If you want to elevate your skills to the next level, I encourage you to take the advanced course. As you may have seen on the bulletin board, three very experienced computer programming professionals will instruct you with brand-new computers in the computer lab on the third floor. The course begins on the first Thursday of next month. You need to sign up for it on our education center website by next Friday. This is a great opportunity to take another step towards your goal. I hope many of you sign up. Thank you.

여 음, 오늘은 우리 중급 컴퓨터 프로그래밍 수업의 마지막 날입니다. 여러분은 모두 지난 6개월 동안 잘해 왔습니다. 그리고 이제 여러분은 전문적인 컴퓨터 프로그래머가 되는 데 한발 더 가까워졌습니다. 만일 여러분이 다음 단계로 여러분의 기술을 높이고 싶으시면, 저는 여러분이 고급 강좌를 수강하시기를 권합니다. 아마도 여러분이 게시판에서 보셨을 수도 있는데, 세 분의 매우 경험이 풍부한 컴퓨터 프로그래밍 전문가들이 여러분을 3층 컴퓨터실에서 신제품 컴퓨터로 지도할 것입니다. 그 강좌는 다음 달 첫 번째 목요일에 시작됩니다. 여러분은 우리 교육 센터 웹사이트에서 그 강좌를 다음 주 금요일까지 신청해야 합니다. 이것은 여러분이 목표를 향해 또 한발 다가갈 수 있는 좋은 기회입니다. 여러분 중 많은 분이 신청하길 바랍니다. 감사합니다.

문제 해설 여자는 중급 컴퓨터 프로그래밍 수업의 마지막 날에 다음 수준의 강좌인 고급 강좌를 수강할 것을 권하며, 경험이 많은 전문 강사와 신제품 컴퓨터가 있는 교실, 강좌 시작일, 신청 방법 등에 대해 알리고 있다. 따라서 여자가 하는 말의 목적으로 가장 적절한 것은 ②이다.

어휘&어구 intermediate 중급의 expert 전문적인; 전문가 advanced 고급의 experienced 경험이 풍부한 instruct 지도하다, 가르치다 brand-new 신제품의 sign up for ~을 신청하다

05 온라인 학위 취득 프로그램 [정답] ⑤

M Hello, listeners. Are you looking for better career opportunities while you're still employed? Then it's time to consider enrolling in the Central Burbank College online degree program. Our more than 80 career-focused online programs provide the same quality education as our on-campus programs with greater flexibility in class scheduling. Earn a master's degree in your own time, at your own pace while working full-time. You can study at home or wherever you can connect to the Internet. Our interactive courses and dynamic instructional videos make it easy for you to immerse yourself in our curriculum. Check out our online degree programs and dream for a new tomorrow! Visit CBConline.edu for more information. Thank you.

남 안녕하세요, 청취자 여러분. 여러분은 여전히 취업한 상태로 더 나은 직업 기회를 찾고 계신가요? 그러면 Central Burbank 대학의 온라인 학위 프로그램에 등록하는 것을 고려하실 때입니다. 저희의 80개가 넘는 직업 중심의 온라인 프로그램은 저희의 대학 내 프로그램과 똑같은 우수한 교육을 수업 일정 관리에 있어서 더 융통성 있게 제공합니다. 전일제로 직장에 다니면서 여러분이 편할 때, 여러분의 속도에 맞게 석사 학위를 취득하세요. 여러분은 집에서든 혹은 인터넷에 접속할 수 있는 어느 곳에서든 공부할 수 있습니다. 저희 쌍방향 강좌들과 역동적인 교육 동영상은 여러분이 저희 교육 과정에 몰두하는 것을 쉽게 만들어 줍니다. 저희 온라인 학위 프로그램을 확인해 보시고 새로운 미래를 꿈꾸세요! 더 많은 정보를 원하시면, CBConline.edu를 방문하세요. 감사합니다.

문제 해설 남자는 Central Burbank 대학의 온라인 학위 취득 프로그램의 특징을 설명하면서 직장에 다니면서 더 나은 직업 기회를 찾을 수 있도록 온라인으로 학위를 취득할 수 있는 프로그램에 등록을 고려해 보라고 말하고 있다. 따라서 남자가 하는 말의 목적으로 가장 적절한 것은 ⑤이다.

어휘&어구 enroll 등록하다 career-focused 직업 중심의 quality 우수한, 양질의; 품질 flexibility 융통성, 유연성 earn 취득하다 interactive 쌍방향의 dynamic 역동적인 immerse oneself in ~에 몰두하다

06 학교 뉴스 제보 [정답] ③

W Hello, students! I am Sophia Brown, president of the student council. Many things happen in our daily school lives. You hear things from your friends or teachers but your curiosity may not be fully satisfied. The student council is planning to broadcast weekly school news. You can be the source of the news as well as the audience. If there's an event that you want to share or learn more about, please let us know. News on anything such as a club fundraiser or a class field trip is welcome. There is a suggestion box in front of the student council room. Write about what has happened and put it in the box. We hope this can help you feel more aware of and involved in what goes on every day in our school.

여 안녕하세요, 학생 여러분! 저는 학생회장인 Sophia Brown입니다. 우리의 일상적인 학교생활에서 많은 일이 일어납니다. 여러분은 친구나 선생님으로부터 무언가를 듣지만 여러분의 호기심은 완전히 충족되지 않을 수도 있습니다. 학생회는 매주 학교 뉴스를 방송할 계획입니다. 여러분은 청취자뿐만 아니라 뉴스의 원천도 될 수 있습니다. 여러분이 공유하고 싶거나 더 알고 싶은 사건이 있으면, 저희에게 알려 주세요. 동아리 기금 모금 행사나 학급 현장 체험 학습과 같이 어떤 것에 관한 뉴스라도 환영합니다. 학생회실 앞에 제안함이 있습니다. 무슨 일이 일어났는지 써서 상자에 넣어 주세요. 저희는 이것이 여러분이 우리 학교에서 매일 일어나는 일에 더 많이 알고 참여하고 있다고 느끼도록 도울 수 있기를 바랍니다.

문제 해설 학생회에서 매주 학교 뉴스를 방송할 계획이며 공유하고 싶거나 더 알고 싶은 사건이 있으면 무슨 일이 일어났는지 써서 학생회실 앞의 제안함에 넣어 달라고 요청하는 내용이므로, 여자가 하는 말의 목적으로 가장 적절한 것은 ③이다.

어휘&어구 student council 학생회 curiosity 호기심 satisfy 충족시키다, 만족시키다 broadcast 방송하다, 널리 알리다 fundraiser (기금) 모금 행사 suggestion 제안, 제의 involved 참여[관여]하는, 관련된

수능 유형

02 의견 / 주장 / 요지

수능유형 체험 | ②
수능유형 연습 | 01 ③ 02 ⑤ 03 ② 04 ⑤ 05 ③ 06 ①

수능유형 체험 | 건강이 좋지 않을 때 일하기 [정답] ②

남 여보, 괜찮아요? 당신은 아주 좋아 보이지 않아요.

여 목이 아프고 몸이 좀 아파요.

남 제가 좀 볼게요. [잠시 후] 이마가 정말로 열이 있어요.

여 아마 감기에 걸린 것 같아요.

남 오늘은 일을 그만하고 좀 쉬는 게 좋겠어요.

여 하지만 할 일이 너무 많아요.

남 물론 일도 중요하지만, 건강을 최우선으로 생각해야 해요. 건강이 좋으면 일을 더 잘할 수 있는 거예요.

여 맞아요. 하지만 금요일까지 제출해야 하는 제 보고서가 걱정돼요.

남 걱정하지 마세요. 당신이 건강해지면 그것을 해낼 수 있을 거예요.

여 좋아요. 오늘은 약을 먹고 쉴게요.

문제 해설 여자는 건강이 좋지 않지만, 금요일까지 제출해야 하는 보고서 때문에 일을 하고 있고, 남자는 그런 여자에게 일을 그만하고 쉴 것을 권유하면서, 건강이 좋아야 일을 더 잘할 수 있다고 말하고 있다. 따라서 남자의 의견으로 가장 적절한 것은 ② '건강을 먼저 회복해야 일을 더 잘할 수 있다.'이다.

어휘&어구 sore 아픈, 쓰린 throat 목, 목구멍 achy 아픈 medicine 약

수능유형 연습

01 오렌지 껍질의 유용성 [정답] ③

W Honey, wait! Are you throwing away those orange peels?

M Yes. Why? They're just peels.

W Don't do that. I'd like to use them for cleaning glass.

M Really? You can clean glass with them?

W Yeah. If you use them to wipe windows, they leave them perfectly clean.

M Wow. I didn't know that.

W You can even use them to clean the microwave, to get rid of any food smells.

M That's amazing.

W Orange peels can be quite useful in our daily lives.

M Then I won't be throwing them away anymore.

W Sounds good.

여 여보, 잠깐만요! 당신은 그 오렌지 껍질들을 버리는 건가요?

남 네. 왜요? 그냥 껍질일 뿐이에요.

여 그러지 마세요. 유리를 닦는 데 그것들을 사용하고 싶어요.

남 정말이요? 그것들로 유리를 닦을 수 있어요?

여 네. 창문을 닦을 때 그것들을 사용하면, 창문을 완전히 깨끗하게 해 줘요.

남 와. 몰랐어요.

여 전자레인지를 청소하고 음식 냄새를 없애기 위해 그것들을 사용할 수도 있어요.

남 정말 놀랍군요.

여 오렌지 껍질은 우리의 일상생활에서 꽤 유용할 수 있거든요.

남 그럼 앞으로는 그것들을 버리지 않을게요.

여 좋아요.

문제 해설 오렌지 껍질을 버리려는 남자를 제지하면서, 여자가 유리를 닦는 데 그것들을 사용하고 싶다고 했다. 게다가 여자는 오렌지 껍질이 창문이나 전자레인지를 닦고, 음식 냄새를 없애기 위해 사용할 수도 있다고 하면서 그것들이 일상생활에서 유용하다고 말하고 있다. 따라서 여자의 의견으로 가장 적절한 것은 ③ '오렌지 껍질은 일상생활에서 유용하게 쓰일 수 있다.'이다.

어휘&어구 throw away ~을 버리다 peel 껍질 microwave 전자레인지 get rid of ~을 없애다

---

02 문자 메시지에 대한 오해 [정답] ⑤

M Cindy, is something bothering you?

W Well, I've been thinking about my friend Kate.

남 Cindy, 무슨 안 좋은 일이 있니?

여 음, 내 친구 Kate에 대해 생각하고 있었어.

M	Did she do something to upset you?	남	그 애가 너를 화나게 할 무슨 일을 했니?
W	She sent me a text message with her usual jokes, but this time it felt like she was making fun of me.	여	그 애는 평소에 하던 농담과 함께 문자 메시지를 내게 보냈는데, 이번에는 마치 나를 놀리는 것 같았어.
M	Oh, dear. I'm sure she didn't mean it that way. Maybe you misunderstood what she was trying to say.	남	아, 저런. 그런 뜻은 아니었을 거야. 아마도 너는 그 애가 말하려는 것을 오해했을 거야.
W	I guess I could have. It was difficult to understand her intention from the text.	여	그럴 수도 있었을 것 같아. 문자에서 그 애의 의도를 이해하는 것이 어려웠어.
M	That's why we have to be careful when we write text messages.	남	그래서 우리는 문자 메시지를 작성할 때 신중해야 하는 거야.
W	You're so right.	여	네 말이 맞아.
M	Text messages can often be misunderstood by the receiver.	남	문자 메시지는 종종 받는 사람이 오해할 수가 있거든.
W	That's true. I'll choose to believe that Kate didn't mean to hurt my feelings.	여	맞아. Kate가 내 감정을 상하게 할 의도는 없었다고 믿을게.
M	I think that's a wise decision.	남	그것이 현명한 결정이라고 생각해.

문제 해설　여자가 친구 Kate가 보낸 문자 메시지가 자신을 놀리는 것으로 느껴졌다고 말하자, 남자는 그런 뜻은 아니었을 거라고 하면서, 문자 메시지를 받는 사람이 메시지를 오해하기 쉬우므로, 작성할 때 신중해야 한다고 말한다. 따라서 남자의 주장으로 가장 적절한 것은 ⑤ '상대방이 오해하지 않도록 문자 메시지를 신중하게 작성해야 한다.'이다.

어휘&어구　bother 언짢게 하다, 성가시게 하다　make fun of ~을 놀리다　misunderstand 오해하다　intention 의도　receiver 받는 사람, 수령인　decision 결정

03 악기 연주를 배우는 것의 이점 　　　　　　　　　　　　　　　　　　[정답] ②

M	Hello, everyone! I'm Kevin Johnson, a jazz pianist. Do you like music? Yes. Everybody loves listening to music, but few people actually know how to play a musical instrument. This is unfortunate because playing an instrument is a really enjoyable experience! Fortunately, however, more and more people are learning to play musical instruments these days, and they experience the fun of it. Just imagine yourself playing the piano, the violin, or the guitar. Isn't that a cool thought? Learning a musical instrument gets you out of your daily routine for a while, and it will be a source of pleasure in your life. So I encourage you to learn how to play a musical instrument. I'm sure it will make your life more lively!

남　여러분, 안녕하세요! 저는 재즈 피아니스트 Kevin Johnson입니다. 여러분은 음악을 좋아하세요? 네. 모든 사람들이 음악 듣는 것을 좋아하지만, 실제로 악기를 연주할 줄 아는 사람은 거의 없습니다. 악기를 연주하는 것은 정말 즐거운 경험이기 때문에 이것은 불행한 일입니다! 하지만 다행히도, 요즘 점점 더 많은 사람들이 악기 연주를 배우고 있고, 그들은 악기 연주의 재미를 경험합니다. 피아노, 바이올린 또는 기타를 연주하는 여러분 자신을 그저 상상해 보세요. 멋진 생각 아닌가요? 악기를 배우는 것은 여러분을 일상에서 잠시 벗어나게 해 주고, 그것은 여러분의 삶에서 즐거움의 원천이 될 것입니다. 그래서 저는 여러분이 악기를 연주하는 법을 배우길 권합니다. 저는 그것이 여러분의 삶을 더 활기차게 만들어 줄 거라고 확신합니다!

문제 해설　남자는 악기 연주를 배우는 것이 일상에서 잠시 벗어나게 해 주고, 삶에서 즐거움의 원천이 되며, 삶을 더 활기차게 만들어 준다고 말하고 있다. 따라서 남자가 하는 말의 요지로 가장 적절한 것은 ② '악기 연주를 배우는 것이 삶을 더 활기차게 해 준다.'이다.

어휘&어구　musical instrument 악기　unfortunate 불행한　enjoyable 즐거운　daily routine (반복적인) 일상　source 원천　pleasure 즐거움

04 식물을 활용한 실내 인테리어 　　　　　　　　　　　　　　　　　　[정답] ⑤

W	Honey, what is that?	여	여보, 그게 무엇이에요?
M	It's a sketch of my ideas for updating our living room. I'm thinking of decorating it with houseplants.	남	우리 거실을 개조하기 위한 내 생각에 관한 스케치예요. 나는 실내용 화초로 그것을 꾸미는 것에 관해 생각 중이에요.
W	Really? What types do you have in mind?	여	정말요? 어떤 종류의 것들을 생각하고 있나요?
M	I'm thinking of putting some flowerpots on the floor and hanging some others near the windows. Here, like this.	남	나는 바닥에 몇몇 화분을 놓고 창문 근처에 몇몇 다른 화분을 걸어 두는 것에 대해 생각 중이에요. 여기, 이렇게 말이에요.

W	Oh, I see. Why do you want so many plants?	여	아, 알겠어요. 왜 이렇게 많은 식물들을 원하는 것이에요?
M	They'll make the living room feel cleaner and fresher.	남	그것들이 거실을 더 깨끗하고 더 산뜻하게 느껴지도록 만들어 줄 거예요.
W	How is that?	여	어떻게 그렇게 되죠?
M	Because they're alive and they help purify the air.	남	그것들이 살아 있고 공기를 정화하는 데 도움을 주기 때문이에요.
W	I see what you mean.	여	당신이 하는 말이 무엇인지 알겠어요.
M	There are also other benefits of having houseplants. They help reduce stress and anxiety and even increase productivity.	남	실내용 화초를 두는 것의 다른 장점들도 있어요. 그것들은 스트레스와 불안감을 줄이고 심지어 생산성을 높이는 데에도 도움을 줘요.
W	Wow, I didn't know that.	여	와, 그것은 몰랐어요.
M	So, what do you think about my idea of adding plants to the living room?	남	그러면 거실에 식물을 추가하자는 내 생각에 대해 어떻게 생각해요?
W	I love it!	여	정말 좋아요!

문제 해설 남자는 거실을 새롭게 꾸미는 데 실내용 화초를 사용하자고 제안하며, 화초의 다양한 장점에 대해 설명하고 있다. 따라서 남자의 의견으로 가장 적절한 것은 ⑤ '실내 인테리어를 위해 식물을 사용하는 것에는 여러 장점이 있다.'이다.

어휘&어구 houseplant 실내용 화초 flowerpot 화분 purify 정화하다 anxiety 불안감

05 조리 과정 참여를 통한 편식 습관 개선
[정답] ③

M	Honey, what are you looking for on the Internet?	남	여보, 인터넷에서 뭘 찾고 있는 거예요?
W	Well, I'm looking for a dish that Jimmy and I can cook together.	여	음, Jimmy와 함께 조리할 수 있는 요리를 찾고 있어요.
M	Are you going to cook with him? Is it a kindergarten assignment?	남	아이와 함께 조리한다고요? 유치원 과제인가요?
W	Not really. Jimmy's been such a picky eater these days.	여	그런 건 아니에요. Jimmy가 요즘 편식이 심해졌어요.
M	Right. He hasn't been eating his vegetables. But how's that related to cooking together?	남	맞아요. 요즘 아이가 채소를 안 먹고 있어요. 하지만 그것이 함께 조리하는 것과 어떤 관련이 있나요?
W	I think cooking with Jimmy can make him more interested in food ingredients.	여	나는 Jimmy와 함께 조리하는 것이 아이가 음식 재료에 더 관심을 갖게 할 수 있다고 생각해요.
M	Sounds interesting, but do you really think it will reduce his picky eating?	남	흥미롭긴 한데요, 그것이 정말로 아이의 편식 습관을 줄일 것이라고 생각하나요?
W	Yes, there's a report that if you handle the ingredients yourself, you grow to like their taste.	여	네, 재료를 직접 다루면 그 재료의 맛을 더 좋아하게 된다는 보고가 있어요.
M	Oh, that makes sense. Is there anything I can do for you?	남	아, 그럴 수 있겠네요. 내가 뭐 도와줄 일이라도 있나요?
W	Nothing for you to do. Just enjoy whatever Jimmy makes.	여	당신이 할 일은 없어요. 그냥 Jimmy가 만드는 것이면 무엇이든 먹으면 돼요.
M	What? Anything?	남	뭐라고요? 어떤 것이라도요?
W	Of course. It's to help Jimmy.	여	물론이죠, Jimmy를 돕기 위해서예요.

문제 해설 여자는 음식 재료를 직접 다루면 그 재료의 맛을 좋아하게 된다는 보고서를 근거로 어린 아들의 편식 습관을 개선하기 위해 어린 아들을 음식 조리 과정에 참여시킬 수 있는 요리를 찾는다고 했으므로 여자의 의견으로 가장 적절한 것은 ③ '자녀가 조리 과정에 참여하면 편식 습관 개선에 도움이 된다.'이다.

어휘&어구 look for ~을 찾다 dish 요리, 접시 kindergarten 유치원 assignment 과제, 임무 picky eater 편식가 food ingredient 음식 재료 reduce 줄이다 handle 다루다, 만지다

06 미세 먼지와 캠페인 활동
[정답] ①

W	Mr. Anderson, our club members are really looking forward to the Respect Life Campaign this Saturday.	여	Anderson 선생님, 우리 동아리 부원들은 이번 토요일에 있을 '생명 존중 캠페인'을 정말 기대하고 있어요.

M That's good. How many of your club members are participating?

W Everyone. We've finished making our signs.

M Great. But I don't think it's a good idea to campaign outside if there's a lot of fine dust. I'm afraid it'll be bad this Saturday.

W Really? But it'll be difficult to reschedule it.

M I understand. But the forecast says the fine dust will be very bad this weekend. It won't be good for your health if you stay outside.

W What if we all wear masks?

M Masks don't really help when you're outside for hours and the fine dust is really bad. You're going to run the campaign all day, aren't you?

W Yes, we are. Can we do it indoors?

M I guess that could be an option. Would you like to do that?

W I'll talk to the other members and let you know.

남 좋아. 너희 동아리 부원들 중 몇 명이 참가할 거니?

여 전부요. 저희는 홍보판을 다 만들었어요.

남 잘했네. 하지만 미세 먼지가 심하면 밖에서 캠페인을 하는 것이 좋지 않다고 생각해. 이번 토요일은 미세 먼지가 심할 것 같아.

여 정말요? 하지만 일정을 변경하기는 어려울 거예요.

남 알아. 하지만 예보에 따르면 이번 주말에 미세 먼지가 매우 심할 거래. 밖에 머무르면 건강에 좋지 않을 거야.

여 저희 모두 마스크를 쓰면 어때요?

남 장시간 야외에 있는데 미세 먼지가 정말 심할 때는 마스크가 그다지 도움이 안 돼. 너희는 온종일 그 캠페인을 할 거지, 그렇지?

여 네, 그래요. 저희가 그것을 실내에서 할 수 있을까요?

남 그렇게 선택할 수도 있겠구나. 그렇게 하고 싶니?

여 다른 부원들과 이야기해 보고 알려 드릴게요.

문제 해설 남자는 동아리 부원들과 토요일에 '생명 존중 캠페인'을 할 예정인 여자에게 토요일은 미세 먼지가 심할 것이므로 밖에서 캠페인을 해서는 안 된다고 말하며, 일정 변경이 어렵다는 여자의 말에 건강에 해로우니 미세 먼지가 심할 때는 밖에서 캠페인을 해서는 안 된다고 강조하고 있다. 따라서 남자의 주장으로 가장 적절한 것은 ① '미세 먼지가 심할 때 밖에서 캠페인 활동을 하면 안 된다.'이다.

어휘&어구 look forward to ~을 기대하다 participate 참가하다 fine dust 미세 먼지 reschedule 일정을 변경하다 option 선택 사항

---

03 관계

수능유형 체험	④
수능유형 연습	01 ② 02 ⑤ 03 ② 04 ② 05 ② 06 ②

본문 12~13쪽

수능유형 체험 중고 매장 배달원 면접 [정답] ④

남 안녕하세요, 저는 Jeremy Krull입니다. Green 씨와 약속이 있어서요.

여 제가 Ms. Green입니다. 와 주셔서 감사드려요, Krull 씨. 앉으세요.

남 감사합니다. [잠시 후] 매장이 크고 물건들이 정말 다양하네요.

여 네. 요즘 중고품을 찾는 분들이 많으세요. 그래서 저희가 또 다른 배달원을 고용하는 것입니다.

남 실은 저도 최근에 중고 에어컨을 샀습니다. 물론 제 이력서에서 보셨겠지만, 제가 경험은 많지 않지만, 그 일을 잘할 수 있을 겁니다.

여 알겠습니다. 일을 하시게 되면 다음 주에 시작하실 수 있으세요?

남 물론입니다. 그렇게 할 수 있습니다.

여 좋습니다. 실은 오늘 오후에 면접이 두 개 더 있습니다. 제가 내일까지 결정을 내리고 알려 드리겠습니다.

남 이해합니다. 다시 만나 뵙기를 기대하겠습니다, Green 씨.

여 저도요.

문제 해설 중고품을 판매하는 여자가 매장에 필요한 배달원을 고용하기 위해 남자를 면접하는 상황이다. 여자가 남자에게 다음 주에 일을 시작할 수 있는지 물으면서 두 명을 더 면접한 뒤에 내일까지 결과를 알려 주겠다고 말하고 있다. 따라서 두 사람의 관계를 가장 잘 나타낸 것은 ④ '구직자 - 중고 매장 운영자'이다.

어휘&어구 appointment 약속 huge 거대한, 큰 a variety of 다양한 second-hand 중고의 delivery 배달 resume 이력서 look forward to ~을 기대하다

01 동물 보호소 봉사 활동

[정답] ②

[Telephone rings.]

W This is Ms. Robinson. How may I help you?

M Hello, I'm Kevin Brown from Wellington High School. I have a few questions.

W I'll be happy to try to answer them.

M Thanks. Actually, I'm in charge of the school's animal club. I was wondering if my students could volunteer at your shelter next Saturday.

W Absolutely. We're actually planning a big cleanup, so we need some volunteers.

M That's great. There will be ten of us, including myself.

W That's wonderful. Could you come by around 10 a.m.? The cleaning should take about 3 hours.

M All right. Also, we'd like to donate some dog food and blankets that could be useful during the winter. Would that be okay?

W Sure. We'd appreciate that. I'll see you next Saturday then.

M Great. See you then.

[전화벨이 울린다.]

여 Ms. Robinson입니다. 어떻게 도와드릴까요?

남 안녕하세요, 저는 Wellington 고등학교에서 일하는 Kevin Brown이라고 합니다. 몇 가지 여쭤보려고 합니다.

여 기꺼이 답변해 드리도록 하겠습니다.

남 감사합니다. 사실은 제가 학교 동물 동아리를 맡고 있습니다. 제 학생들이 다음 주 토요일에 보호소에서 봉사 활동을 할 수 있는지 궁금합니다.

여 물론입니다. 우리가 실은 대청소를 계획 중이라서 자원봉사자가 몇 분 필요합니다.

남 잘됐네요. 저를 포함해 10명이 될 것입니다.

여 아주 좋네요. 대략 오전 10시까지 오시겠습니까? 청소는 약 3시간 정도 소요될 것입니다.

남 알겠습니다. 또한 우리는 개 사료와 겨울철에 유용할 수 있는 담요를 좀 기부하고 싶습니다. 그래도 괜찮을까요?

여 물론이죠. 감사합니다. 그러면 다음 주 토요일에 뵙겠습니다.

남 좋습니다. 그때 뵙겠습니다.

문제 해설 고등학교 동물 동아리 담당 교사인 남자가 동물 보호소에 전화를 걸어 학생들과 봉사 활동을 하러 갈 수 있는지 묻자 여자가 허락하면서 다음 토요일에 와서 대청소를 도와달라고 부탁하고 있다. 따라서 두 사람의 관계를 가장 잘 나타낸 것은 ② '동물 보호소 직원 – 교사'이다.

어휘&어구 in charge of ~을 담당하는 shelter 보호소 cleanup 대청소 donate 기부하다 blanket 담요 appreciate 고마워하다

02 테니스 라켓 수리

[정답] ⑤

M Hello. How can I help you, ma'am?

W Hello. I'm here to pick up my tennis racket. I received a text message saying that the repair is done.

M Okay. What's your name?

W Ellen Miller.

M Just a moment, please. *[Pause]* Here it is.

W Wow, it's like brand-new. Thank you. How much do I owe you for this?

M You bought the racket here last month, right? It comes with a 2-month warranty, so the repair is free.

W That's great. And I saw something about a special promotion on tennis balls on your social media.

M That's right. All our tennis balls are 30% off this week.

W That's an amazing deal. I'll take 20 balls. Here's my credit card.

M Thank you.

남 안녕하세요. 어떻게 도와드릴까요, 부인?

여 안녕하세요. 제 테니스 라켓을 찾으러 왔습니다. 수리가 끝났다는 문자를 받았습니다.

남 네. 성함이 어떻게 되시죠?

여 Ellen Miller입니다.

남 잠시만요. *[잠시 후]* 여기 있습니다.

여 와, 새것 같네요. 감사합니다. 제가 얼마를 지불하면 될까요?

남 지난달에 여기에서 라켓을 사셨네요, 그렇죠? 2개월 보증이 제공되니 수리는 무료입니다.

여 잘됐네요. 그리고 제가 상점의 소셜 미디어에서 테니스공 특별 프로모션에 관한 것을 봤어요.

남 맞습니다. 이번 주에 우리의 모든 테니스공이 30퍼센트 할인됩니다.

여 아주 좋은 가격이네요. 공 20개를 사겠습니다. 여기 제 신용 카드가 있습니다.

남 감사합니다.

문제 해설 수리를 맡긴 테니스 라켓을 찾으러 온 여자가 남자의 상점에서 테니스공 특별 할인 행사를 하자 테니스공을 20개 구매하겠다고 말하고 있다. 따라서 두 사람의 관계를 가장 잘 나타낸 것은 ⑤ '스포츠용품 매장 직원 – 고객'이다.

어휘&어구   text message 문자   repair 수리   warranty 보증

03 박물관 관광 중 친구 만나기   [정답] ②

W Mr. Muncy, today's hiking tour was fantastic. Thank you.

M I'm glad you enjoyed it. The weather was perfect, so you were able to experience amazing views.

W Your explanations during the tour were also very helpful.

M Thank you. Tomorrow's museum tour will be equally enjoyable.

W Can I ask you something? The museum we're visiting tomorrow is near Peterson University, right?

M Yes, it's right next to the university.

W My best friend works as a professor at Peterson University, so I'd really like to meet her. Would it be okay for me to do that while the other tourists are touring the museum?

M Sure. We're leaving the hotel at 9 a.m. and arriving at the museum around 10 a.m.

W Then I'll make plans to meet my friend near the museum.

M Sounds good. Have a good rest tonight and see you tomorrow.

W See you tomorrow.

여 Muncy 씨, 오늘 하이킹 투어는 환상적이었어요. 감사합니다.

남 즐거우셨다니 기쁘네요. 날씨가 완벽해서 멋진 경치들을 경험하실 수 있으셨네요.

여 투어 중 해 주셨던 설명도 큰 도움이 되었습니다.

남 고맙습니다. 내일 박물관 투어도 마찬가지로 즐거울 것입니다.

여 뭐 좀 여쭤봐도 될까요? 우리가 내일 방문하는 박물관이 Peterson 대학 근처에 있는 것이 맞지요?

남 네, 그곳은 그 대학교 바로 옆입니다.

여 저의 가장 친한 친구가 Peterson 대학에서 교수로 일하고 있어서 그녀를 정말 만나고 싶거든요. 다른 관광객들이 박물관 투어를 하는 동안 제가 그렇게 해도 괜찮을까요?

남 물론입니다. 우리는 오전 9시에 호텔을 떠나서 오전 10시쯤 박물관에 도착할 것입니다.

여 그러면 박물관 근처에서 제 친구를 만날 계획을 세우도록 하겠습니다.

남 좋습니다. 오늘 밤 푹 쉬시고 내일 뵙겠습니다.

여 내일 뵙겠습니다.

문제 해설 설명과 함께 하이킹 투어를 제공했던 남자에게 여자가 내일 있을 박물관 투어에 다른 관광객들이 박물관을 구경하는 동안 박물관 근처 대학에서 교수로 일하는 자신의 친구를 만나도 되는지를 묻고 있다. 따라서 두 사람의 관계를 가장 잘 나타낸 것은 ② '관광객 – 여행 가이드'이다.

어휘&어구 view 경치   explanation 설명   enjoyable 즐거운   professor 교수

04 임대료 삭감   [정답] ②

W Hello, Mr. Robinson.

M Hello, Ms. Baker. Do you have a minute to talk about your restaurant's rent?

W Sure. As you know, business has been really slow since a few restaurants opened up in the neighborhood recently.

M I know. That's why you were a week late paying this month's rent, right?

W Yes. I've been working hard, but I just haven't been making as much money.

M I understand. It's very competitive and this building is really in need of some renovations.

W Right. Have you considered renovating it?

M Yes, I have. But it costs too much right now. But to help out, I can reduce the rent by 5% starting next month.

W That's great. It'll help out a lot.

여 안녕하세요, Robinson 씨.

남 안녕하세요, Baker 씨. 당신의 식당 임대료에 대해 잠시 얘기할 수 있을까요?

여 물론이죠. 아시다시피, 최근에 주변에 몇몇 식당들이 문을 연 이후로 장사가 정말로 잘 안 됐어요.

남 알아요. 그래서 이번 달 임대료를 일주일 늦게 내셨군요, 그렇죠?

여 맞아요. 열심히 일했지만, 돈을 그렇게 많이 벌지는 못했어요.

남 이해합니다. 상황은 매우 경쟁적이고 이 건물은 정말로 약간의 개조가 필요하지요.

여 맞아요. 건물을 개조할 생각을 해 보셨어요?

남 네, 해 봤어요. 하지만 지금 당장은 비용이 너무 많이 들어요. 하지만 도움을 드리기 위해서, 다음 달부터 가게 임대료를 5퍼센트 낮출 수 있어요.

여 잘됐네요. 그것이 도움이 많이 될 거예요.

남 좋아요. 당신의 식당 사업이 곧 살아나길 바랄게요.

M Good. I hope business picks up in your restaurant soon.
W Thank you, Mr. Robinson.

여 감사합니다, Robinson 씨.

여자는 주변에 식당들이 문을 열어서 돈이 잘 벌리지 않는다고 말했고, 남자는 건물의 개조를 생각해 봤지만 비용이 너무 많이 들어서, 차라리 다음 달부터 임대료를 5퍼센트 낮춰 주겠다고 말했으므로 두 사람의 관계를 가장 잘 나타낸 것은 ② '세입자 – 건물 주인'이다.

rent 임대료   neighborhood 주변, 이웃   competitive 경쟁적인   renovation 개조, 수리, 혁신   pick up 살아나다, 회복하다

05 식물원 직원과 관람객의 대화 [정답] ②

W Excuse me, sir. Are we allowed to eat around the gardens?
M No, ma'am. To protect the gardens, we no longer allow people to eat anywhere around the gardens. The number of visitors has just increased too much.
W Where can I eat then?
M There's a picnic area next to the rose garden. That's the only place where you can eat.
W All right. By the way, I heard that you expanded the gardens last year, right?
M Yes. The newest garden has wild flowers from Africa. Make sure you see it if you haven't yet.
W Okay, thank you. Actually, I work for a fashion magazine, and this seems like a great place for a photo shoot. Would that be possible?
M Sure. But you need permission first. After seeing the gardens, stop by the management office, where I work. I'll help you.
W I will. Thank you.
M You're welcome.

여 실례합니다. 정원 주변에서 음식을 먹는 것이 허용되나요?
남 안 됩니다, 부인. 정원들을 보호하기 위해 저희는 더 이상 사람들이 정원 주변 어디에서도 음식을 먹는 것을 허용하지 않습니다. 방문객 수가 너무 많이 증가해서요.
여 그러면 제가 어디에서 음식을 먹을 수 있을까요?
남 장미 정원 옆에 피크닉장이 있습니다. 그곳이 음식을 먹을 수 있는 유일한 장소입니다.
여 알겠습니다. 그런데, 작년에 정원들을 확장하셨다고 들었습니다, 그렇죠?
남 네. 가장 최근에 생긴 정원에는 아프리카에서 온 야생화가 있습니다. 아직 못 보셨으면 꼭 보세요.
여 네, 고맙습니다. 실은 제가 패션 잡지사에서 일하는데, 이곳은 사진 촬영을 하기에 훌륭한 장소인 것 같습니다. 그것이 가능할까요?
남 물론입니다. 하지만 우선 허가가 필요합니다. 정원들을 보신 후에 제가 일하는 관리 사무소에 들러 주세요. 제가 도와드리겠습니다.
여 그러겠습니다. 감사합니다.
남 천만에요.

이 장소의 관리 사무소에서 일하는 남자는 음식을 먹어도 되는지 묻는 여자에게 답을 하고, 아프리카 야생화를 볼 것을 추천하고 있다. 이곳에서 사진 촬영이 가능한지를 묻는 여자에게 도와줄 테니 관리소에 들르라고 남자가 말하고 있는 것으로 보아, 두 사람의 관계를 가장 잘 나타낸 것은 ② '식물원 직원 – 관람객'이다.

be allowed to ~하도록 허락[허용]되다   anywhere 어디에서도   expand 확장하다   permission 허가, 허락   management office 관리 사무소

06 동물병원 방문 [정답] ②

W Hello. This puppy's cute! What's its name?
M Her name is April. Actually, I adopted her today.
W Where did you adopt her from?
M I brought her from the animal shelter where I've been volunteering.
W You must have grown attached to her while volunteering.
M Yeah. When I went to volunteer at the shelter in April last year, she came there the same day. I even gave her the name, April.
W Do you have any records of vaccination from the shelter?

여 안녕하세요. 이 강아지가 귀엽네요! 애 이름이 뭐예요?
남 애 이름은 April이에요. 사실, 제가 오늘 얘를 입양했어요.
여 어디서 얘를 입양했어요?
남 제가 자원봉사를 해 오고 있는 동물 보호소에서 얘를 데려왔어요.
여 자원봉사를 하면서 얘한테 애착을 갖게 된 것이 틀림없네요.
남 네. 지난해 4월 보호소 봉사 활동을 갔을 때, 같은 날 얘가 왔어요. 제가 April이라는 이름까지 지어 줬어요.
여 보호소에서 예방 접종한 기록을 갖고 있나요?
남 여기 있어요. 얘가 기본적인 예방 접종을 다 했다고 들었습니다.
여 [잠시 후] 그러네요. 그럼 제가 종합 건강 검진을 해야겠네요.
남 그래요, 부탁드릴게요.

M　Here you go. I heard she got all the basic vaccinations.

W　*[Pause]* Right. Then I'll have to do a general health check-up.

M　Yes, please.

W　Let me look inside her ears first. Could you hold April?

M　Okay.

여　제가 먼저 얘 귀 안을 보겠습니다. April을 붙잡아 주시겠어요?

남　알겠습니다.

문제 해설　남자는 강아지를 오늘 입양하였다고 했으므로 강아지의 주인임을 알 수 있다. 여자는 강아지의 예방 접종 기록을 확인하고, 강아지의 귓속을 들여다보는 것부터 종합 건강 검진을 시작하겠다고 했으므로 수의사임을 알 수 있다. 따라서 두 사람의 관계를 가장 잘 나타낸 것은 ② '수의사 – 반려동물 주인'이다.

어휘&어구　adopt 입양하다　shelter 보호소　volunteer 자원봉사하다　attached 애착을 가진　vaccination 예방 접종　check-up 검진, 건강 진단

04　그림 내용 일치

수능유형 체험 |　④

수능유형 연습 |　01 ⑤　02 ⑤　03 ⑤　04 ④　05 ⑤　06 ④

본문 14~15쪽

수능유형 체험　**동아리 친구 송별회**　　　　[정답] ④

여　Peter, 다른 동아리 회원들이 Amy랑 30분 후에 도착할 거야. 그녀의 송별회 준비가 다 됐니?

남　그런 것 같아. 내가 'We'll Miss You, Amy'라고 적힌 현수막을 벽에 걸었어.

여　좋네! 그리고 현수막 아래 하트 모양의 풍선들이 정말 사랑스러워. 그런데 케이크는 어디 있니?

남　그것은 구석에 있는 냉장고 안에 있어. 그것을 꺼내야 할까?

여　애들이 여기 도착하기 직전에 꺼내서 중앙에 있는 둥근 테이블 위에 놓자.

남　알겠어. 좋은 생각이야.

여　테이블 옆에 비디오카메라와 스탠드는 무엇을 위한 것이니?

남　오늘 파티를 녹화하고 나중에 Amy에게 영상 한 부를 주려고 내가 스탠드 위에 비디오카메라를 설치했어.

여　너는 정말 사려 깊구나! Amy가 우리가 준비한 파티를 좋아하면 좋겠다.

문제 해설　동아리 친구인 Amy의 송별회를 준비하면서 중앙에 둥근 테이블이 있다고 했는데 그림에서는 직사각형 모양의 테이블이 있으므로, 그림에서 대화의 내용과 일치하지 않는 것은 ④이다.

어휘&어구　arrive 도착하다　farewell party 송별회　hang 걸다　refrigerator 냉장고　set up ~을 설치하다　thoughtful 사려 깊은, 배려심 있는

수능유형 연습

01　카라반 캠핑　　　　[정답] ⑤

M　Hey, Tina, how was your weekend?

W　Hey, Oliver. It was fun. I went camping with my parents. Look at this photo.

M　Wow, does your family own this caravan?

W　No, we rented it. It was our first time sleeping in a caravan, and it was actually really comfortable.

M　It's a really nice one. Is this man with glasses in front of the caravan your dad?

W　Yes. He posed for me while I took the photo.

남　안녕, Tina, 주말 어땠니?

여　안녕, Oliver. 재미있었어. 부모님이랑 캠핑을 갔었어. 이 사진을 봐.

남　와, 이 카라반은 너희 가족 것이니?

여　아니야, 우리는 그것을 대여했어. 우리가 카라반에서 잔 건 처음이었는데, 실제로 정말 편했어.

남　정말 좋은 거구나. 카라반 앞에 안경 쓴 이 남자분이 네 아버지시니?

여　응. 내가 사진을 찍을 때 날 위해 포즈를 취하셨어.

남　파라솔이 있는 테이블이 좋구나.

M The table with the parasol is nice.

W It was quite sunny, so the parasol provided some much-needed shade.

M I see. Oh, there is a fire next to the table. Did you make a fire at night?

W Yeah. We sat in the two camping chairs around the fire, and sang along.

M It seems like you had a wonderful time.

여 햇빛이 꽤 내리쫴서 그 파라솔이 절실하게 필요한 그늘을 좀 제공했어.

남 그랬구나. 아, 테이블 옆에 불이 있구나. 밤에 불을 피웠니?

여 응. 우리는 불 주위에 두 개의 캠핑 의자에 앉아서 노래를 따라 불렀어.

남 네가 멋진 시간을 보낸 거 같구나.

문제 해설 대여한 카라반으로 갔던 캠핑에서 불 주위에 두 개의 캠핑 의자에 앉아 노래를 따라 불렀다고 했는데 그림에서는 캠핑 의자가 세 개이므로, 그림에서 대화의 내용과 일치하지 않는 것은 ⑤이다.

어휘&어구 rent 대여하다, 빌리다 comfortable 편안한 parasol 파라솔 much-needed 절실하게[대단히] 필요한 shade 그늘 sing along 노래를 따라 부르다

02 패스트푸드 안 먹기 캠페인 [정답] ⑤

W Hey, Jackson, what are you drawing?

M Hey, Elaine. This is a poster for a campaign encouraging students to eat no fast food.

W Ah, that's what "No Junk Food" written on the top means.

M Right. And you can see the hamburger and other fast foods I drew in the center of the poster.

W I think it's great. And this child on the left side of the poster making an X shape with his arms fits perfectly.

M I thought it'd strengthen the message. And that's why I also wrote "Say No" on the right side.

W It's really convincing. So what happens if I scan this QR code at the bottom of the poster?

M It'll automatically send you to the registration for the campaign.

W That's so simple. I'm sure a lot of students will sign up.

M That's what I'm hoping for.

여 안녕, Jackson, 무엇을 그리고 있니?

남 안녕, Elaine. 이건 학생들이 패스트푸드를 먹지 않도록 장려하는 캠페인용 포스터야.

여 아, 위쪽에 적힌 'No Junk Food'가 그런 의미구나.

남 맞아. 그리고 포스터 가운데에 내가 그린 햄버거와 다른 패스트푸드를 볼 수 있어.

여 아주 좋은 거 같아. 그리고 팔로 X자 표시를 하고 있는 포스터 왼쪽에 있는 이 아이가 딱 맞아.

남 나는 그것이 메시지를 강화해 준다고 생각했어. 그리고 그것이 내가 오른쪽에 'Say No'라고 쓴 이유이기도 해.

여 그것이 정말 설득력이 있어. 그런데 내가 포스터 하단에 있는 이 QR 코드를 스캔하면 어떻게 되니?

남 그것이 자동으로 너를 캠페인 등록으로 연결해 줄 거야.

여 아주 간단하네. 분명히 많은 학생들이 등록할 거야.

남 그것이 내가 바라는 거야.

문제 해설 패스트푸드 덜 먹기 캠페인용 포스터에서 포스터 하단에 QR 코드를 스캔하면 자동으로 캠페인 등록이 된다고 남자가 말했는데 그림에서는 포스터 하단에 참가를 위한 웹사이트 주소가 적혀 있으므로, 그림에서 대화의 내용과 일치하지 않는 것은 ⑤이다.

어휘&어구 encourage 장려하다, 격려하다 fit 맞다 strengthen 강화하다 convincing 설득력 있는 automatically 자동으로 registration 등록

03 쌍둥이 방의 새로운 배치 [정답] ⑤

M Hi, honey, what's that?

W Since each of our twins will have their own bed, I drew up a new layout of their room.

M I see. So you're thinking of placing two single beds on each side of the room.

W Right. And we can get curtains for the windows.

M I like that idea. It'll keep the room warm. I see you think we should keep the bookcase under the window.

남 안녕, 여보, 그게 뭐예요?

여 우리 쌍둥이 각자가 자기 침대를 가지게 될 거여서 내가 그들 방의 새로운 배치도를 그렸어요.

남 그렇군요. 그래서 당신은 싱글 침대 두 개를 방의 양쪽에 각각 배치할 생각이군요.

여 맞아요. 그리고 우리는 창문에 커튼을 달 수 있어요.

남 그 아이디어가 좋네요. 그것이 방을 따뜻하게 유지할 거예요. 당신이 책장을 창문 아래에 계속 두어야 한다고 생각한다는 것을 알겠네요.

W   Yeah. And wouldn't it be cool to put two houseplants on top of the bookcase?

M   Good idea. The twins will like that. But don't you think having the two desks in the middle of the room like this will be a little uncomfortable?

W   Well, that's what they want. They said that having the two desks face each other like this will give them each some privacy.

M   That makes sense. I'm sure they'll like your layout.

W   I hope so. Then why don't we go buy the new beds this weekend?

M   Okay. Let's do that.

여   네. 그리고 책장 위에 실내용 화초를 두 개 올려놓으면 멋지지 않을까요?

남   좋은 생각이에요. 쌍둥이가 그것을 좋아할 거예요. 그런데 책상 두 개를 이렇게 방 가운데 두면 조금 불편하지 않을까요?

여   음, 그게 아이들이 원하는 거예요. 책상 두 개를 이렇게 서로 마주 보게 두면 사생활이 어느 정도 보장될 거라고 하더라고요.

남   말이 되네요. 분명히 아이들이 당신의 배치도를 좋아할 거예요.

여   그랬으면 좋겠네요. 그러면 우리가 이번 주말에 새 침대를 사러 가는 게 어때요?

남   좋아요. 그렇게 해요.

문제 해설   쌍둥이의 방 배치를 새로 하기 위해 그린 배치도에 따르면 사생활 보호를 위해 책상 두 개를 서로 마주 보게 배치한다고 했는데 그림에서는 책상이 나란히 붙어 있으므로, 그림에서 대화의 내용과 일치하지 않는 것은 ⑤이다.

어휘&어구   layout 배치, 배치도   uncomfortable 불편한   privacy 사생활

04 생일 파티를 위한 그림   [정답] ④

M   Honey, William's birthday is already coming up. Can you believe he's almost three?

W   I know. Time really flies. I actually created a picture for his birthday party and printed it out. What do you think of it?

M   Wow, it's great! I like the triangular flags hanging on the string.

W   I thought it looked festive.

M   Definitely. Same with the balloons in the middle of the picture.

W   Every party needs balloons!

M   Yeah. And you put candies under the balloons.

W   You know, William loves candies.

M   I also like how you put a heart-shaped cake in the right bottom corner of the picture.

W   I wanted to express our love for him. And how do you like William wearing the cap?

M   He looks so cute. Great picture, honey.

W   Thanks.

남   여보, William의 생일이 벌써 다가오고 있어요. 당신은 그가 거의 세 살이라는 것을 믿을 수 있으세요?

여   알고 있어요. 시간이 정말 빠르게 지나가요. 제가 실은 그의 생일 파티를 위해 그림을 그려서 그것을 출력했어요. 어떤가요?

남   와, 아주 멋져요! 줄에 걸려 있는 삼각 깃발들이 마음에 들어요.

여   그것이 축제 분위기를 띠게 한다고 생각했어요.

남   물론이지요. 그림 중앙의 풍선들도 마찬가지예요.

여   모든 파티에는 풍선이 필요해요!

남   네. 그리고 당신은 풍선 밑에 사탕을 두었군요.

여   아시다시피, William이 사탕을 좋아하잖아요.

남   저는 또한 당신이 하트 모양의 케이크를 그림의 오른쪽 아래 구석에 넣은 것이 마음에 들어요.

여   그에 대한 우리의 사랑을 표현하고 싶었어요. 그리고 모자를 쓰고 있는 William은 어때요?

남   그는 정말 귀여워 보여요. 아주 좋은 그림이에요, 여보.

여   고마워요.

문제 해설   대화에서 여자가 아들에 대한 사랑을 표현하고 싶어서 하트 모양의 케이크를 그렸다고 했는데, 그림에서는 케이크가 둥근 모양이므로, 그림에서 대화의 내용과 일치하지 않는 것은 ④이다.

어휘&어구   fly (시간이) 아주 빨리 가다   actually 실은   print out ~을 출력하다   triangular 삼각형의   flag 깃발   string 끈, 줄   festive 축제 분위기의   express 표현하다

05 야외 수영장에 놀러 간 가족   [정답] ⑤

W   David, did you have a good time at the outdoor pool on Sunday?

M   Yes. My family played and ate delicious food all day long. Would you like to see a picture?

여   David, 일요일에 야외 수영장에서 즐거운 시간 보냈어요?

남   네. 우리 가족은 하루 종일 놀고 아주 맛있는 음식을 먹었어요. 사진 볼래요?

여   물론이죠.

W	Of course.
M	See this water slide with a picture of a dolphin on it? My son loved it.
W	It's good that no one was waiting in line on the water slide stairs.
M	Yeah. The boy coming down the slide wearing the swimming goggles is my son Peter. He went up and down the slide all day.
W	Haha, I can imagine. What were you doing in the water?
M	I was standing at the end of the slide waiting for Peter to come down.
W	That's fun! It's nice there are sunbeds to rest on.
M	Yeah, but unfortunately they don't have parasols.
W	I see. But it looks like you had a great time there.
M	We sure did. You should go there sometime.

남	돌고래 사진이 있는 이 물 미끄럼틀 보여요? 우리 아들이 그것을 좋아하더라고요.
여	물 미끄럼틀 계단에 줄 서서 기다리는 사람이 아무도 없으니 좋네요.
남	네. 물안경을 쓰고 미끄럼틀을 내려오는 남자애가 내 아들 Peter예요. 그 애는 온종일 미끄럼틀을 오르내렸어요.
여	하하, 상상이 돼요. 물속에서 뭘 하고 있었어요?
남	Peter가 내려오기를 기다리면서 미끄럼틀 끝에 서 있었어요.
여	재미있네요! 위에서 쉴 선베드가 있으니 좋네요.
남	네, 하지만 안타깝게도 파라솔이 없어요.
여	그렇군요. 그래도 그곳에서 좋은 시간을 보냈던 거 같네요.
남	확실히 그랬죠. 언젠가 그곳에 가 보세요.

문제 해설 남자는 야외 수영장에 선베드는 있으나 안타깝게도 파라솔은 없다고 했는데 그림에서는 선베드와 파라솔이 있으므로, 그림에서 대화의 내용과 일치하지 않는 것은 ⑤이다.

어휘&어구 slide 미끄럼틀 swimming goggles 물안경 sunbed 선베드 unfortunately 안타깝게도 parasol 파라솔

06 영화 촬영 현장   [정답] ④

W	Chris, look at this photo. I took it at the park yesterday. Some people were filming a movie.
M	Wow, cool! Why is the man next to the bench holding a round plate over his head?
W	The plate is reflective. He's lighting up the actors. See the actress wearing the sunglasses sitting on the bench? Who do you think she looks like?
M	She kind of looks like Ms. Jacobson, our math teacher.
W	Doesn't she? See the man in the center holding the stick over his head? What he's holding is a boom microphone.
M	That looks like a tough job.
W	Yeah. The man with the beard sitting on the stool was the cameraman. He had a more difficult job because he had to hold the camera on his shoulder the whole time.
M	His shoulder must have been sore.
W	Yeah. And this woman behind the cameraman was the director. She just sat in that chair holding the megaphone telling people what to do.
M	It's cool you saw this.

여	Chris, 이 사진 좀 봐. 내가 어제 공원에서 찍었어. 몇몇 사람들이 영화를 찍고 있었어.
남	와, 멋지다! 벤치 옆의 이 남자는 왜 둥근 판을 머리 위로 들고 있는 거니?
여	그 판은 빛을 반사해. 그 사람은 배우들에게 빛을 비춰 주고 있는 거야. 벤치에 앉아서 선글라스를 끼고 있는 여배우 보이지? 그녀가. 누구를 닮은 것 같아?
남	우리 수학 교사인 Jacobson 선생님을 약간 닮은 것 같아.
여	그렇지? 머리 위로 막대기를 들고 있는 중앙의 이 남자 보이지? 그 사람이 들고 있는 것은 붐 마이크야.
남	그것은 고된 일처럼 보인다.
여	맞아. 의자에 앉아 있는 턱수염을 기른 남자는 카메라맨이었어. 그는 어깨에 카메라를 내내 메고 있어야 해서 하는 일이 더 힘들었어.
남	틀림없이 그의 어깨가 아팠을 거야.
여	응. 그리고 카메라맨 뒤에 있는 이 여자가 감독이었어. 그녀는 메가폰을 들고 사람들에게 무엇을 해야 할지 말하면서 저 의자에 앉아 있었어.
남	네가 이걸 봤다니 멋지다.

문제 해설 여자가 카메라맨이 카메라를 어깨에 메고 있었다고 말했는데, 그림에는 카메라가 삼각대 위에 얹혀 있다. 따라서 그림에서 대화의 내용과 일치하지 않는 것은 ④이다.

어휘&어구 film 촬영하다 reflective 빛을 반사하는 light up (빛을) 비추다 boom microphone 붐 마이크(마이크를 낚싯대같이 생긴 장대 끝에 매단 장치) stool (등받이와 팔걸이가 없는) 의자 sore 아픈

수능 유형 05 할 일/부탁한 일

수능유형 체험 | ②

수능유형 연습 | 01 ③ 02 ④ 03 ③ 04 ③ 05 ④ 06 ③

수능유형 체험 동아리 부스 설치

[정답] ②

여 Wilson, 전단을 인쇄하는 데 시간이 너무 오래 걸려서 미안해.

남 괜찮아. 현수막 거는 것을 내가 막 끝냈어. 우리 동아리 부스가 이제 거의 준비가 됐어.

여 내가 없는 동안 너희들이 테이블과 의자들도 설치했구나. 수고해 줘서 고마워.

남 괜찮아. 우리가 내일 아침에 과학 실험실에서 3D 프린터를 가져오기만 하면 돼.

여 우리는 프린터가 제대로 작동하는지 확인도 해야 해.

남 Mike와 Rachel이 실험실에서 지금 그것을 하는 중이야.

여 아, 좋아. 그러면 내가 가서 홍보 전단을 나누어 줄게.

남 내가 널 도와줄까?

여 아니야. 그건 내가 혼자 할 수 있어.

남 알겠어. 그동안에 내가 부스를 청소할게.

여 알겠어. 고마워, Wilson. 나중에 봐.

문제 해설 동아리 부스를 준비하는 과정에서 남자가 Mike와 Rachel이 내일 사용할 3D 프린터를 과학 실험실에서 확인하는 중이라고 하자 여자는 혼자서 홍보 전단을 나누어 주겠다고 했으므로, 여자가 할 일로 가장 적절한 것은 ② '홍보 전단 나눠 주기'이다.

어휘&어구 flyer 전단 lab 실험실 properly 제대로 distribute 나누어 주다 promotional 홍보[판촉]의 in the meantime 그동안[사이]에

수능유형 연습

01 방학 중 인턴십 지원하기

[정답] ③

M Amanda, do you have any special plans for the upcoming vacation?

W I'll apply for an internship at Grand Electronics. They're looking for college students to work during the summer vacation.

M Oh, I'm familiar with that company.

W Really? How come?

M My sister works there. She actually interned there in her last year of college.

W Wow, that's impressive. I really want to get an internship there, but it's really competitive.

M What's the selection process like?

W I first have to submit an application and essay, and if I pass that step, there's an interview. I finished writing my essay last night, but I'm not sure how good it is.

M If you want, I can ask my sister to take a look at your essay.

W Really? That'd be amazing. I'll email it to you when I get home. Thank you so much.

M I'm happy to help.

남 Amanda, 다가오는 방학 동안에 어떤 특별한 계획 있니?

여 나는 Grand Electronics 인턴십에 지원할 거야. 그곳에서 여름 방학 동안 일할 대학생들을 찾고 있거든.

남 아, 나는 그 회사가 익숙해.

여 정말? 어떻게?

남 내 누나가 그곳에서 일해. 그녀는 실제로 대학교 마지막 해에 그곳에서 인턴을 했어.

여 와, 인상적이야. 나는 그곳에서 인턴십을 정말 하고 싶은데, 경쟁이 정말 치열하거든.

남 선발 과정이 어떻게 되니?

여 나는 지원서와 에세이를 우선 제출해야 하고, 내가 그 단계를 통과하면 면접이 있어. 나는 어젯밤에 에세이를 다 썼는데, 얼마나 잘 쓴 건지 잘 모르겠어.

남 네가 원하면 누나에게 에세이를 봐 달라고 내가 부탁할 수 있어.

여 정말이니? 그러면 정말 좋겠어. 내가 집에 가면 그것을 너에게 이메일로 보낼게. 정말 고마워.

남 도와주게 돼서 기뻐.

02 벼룩시장에서 물건 팔기

[정답] ④

W	Hi, honey, I heard there's a flea market downtown this weekend.
M	Oh, is there something specific you're planning to buy there?
W	Not really. Actually, I'm thinking of selling some things there.
M	Oh, what do you want to sell?
W	We have so many clothes that the kids no longer wear, so I thought we could sell them.
M	That's a great idea. But can anyone sell things at the flea market?
W	Yeah, but you have to register online first.
M	That's what I thought. Do you want me to do that?
W	Thanks, but I can do it. While I'm doing that, could you go buy some large plastic bags from the store so we can sort out the clothes?
M	Sure thing.
W	Thank you, honey.

여	안녕, 여보, 이번 주말에 시내에서 벼룩시장이 열린다고 들었어요.
남	아, 당신이 거기서 사려고 하는 특별한 것이 있어요?
여	꼭 그렇지는 않아요. 사실은 거기서 물건을 팔까 생각 중이에요.
남	아, 무엇을 팔고 싶어요?
여	아이들이 더 이상 입지 않는 옷이 너무 많아서 그것들을 팔 수 있을 거 같아요.
남	그거 좋은 생각이네요. 그런데 누구나 벼룩시장에서 물건을 팔 수 있어요?
여	네, 하지만 우선 온라인으로 등록을 해야 해요.
남	나도 그렇게 생각했어요. 내가 그것을 할까요?
여	고마워요, 하지만 그건 내가 할 수 있어요. 내가 그것을 하는 동안 우리가 옷을 분류할 수 있게 가게에서 큰 비닐봉지 좀 사다 줄래요?
남	물론이죠.
여	고마워요, 여보.

03 말하기 대회 연습 영상 찍기

[정답] ③

M	Ms. Tiffin, thank you for your feedback on my speech draft.
W	You're welcome, Tom. As I mentioned in my email, it's excellent. Your vocabulary has clearly improved a lot.
M	Thank you. I've been using flashcards as you suggested, and it's been really effective.
W	I'm glad to hear that. The Spanish speaking contest is next week, right?
M	Yes, there are only 7 days left until the contest, so I'm getting a little nervous.
W	Try not to worry too much. Just continue practicing as much as you can, as if it were the real contest.
M	That's my plan. But it's not easy to pretend like it's real.

남	Tiffin 선생님, 제 말하기 원고에 대해 피드백을 주셔서 감사합니다.
여	천만에, Tom. 내 이메일에서 언급했듯이 원고가 훌륭해. 네 어휘력이 확실히 많이 향상되었어.
남	감사합니다. 제안해 주셨듯이 플래시 카드를 사용해 왔는데, 그것이 정말 효과적이었어요.
여	그 말을 들으니 기쁘구나. 스페인어 말하기 대회가 다음 주구나, 맞지?
남	네, 대회까지 7일밖에 남지 않아서 조금 긴장이 되네요.
여	너무 걱정하지는 마. 진짜 대회인 것처럼 네가 할 수 있는 만큼 그냥 연습을 계속해.
남	그것이 제 계획입니다. 하지만 실제인 척을 하는 것이 쉽지는 않습니다.

W Well, how about recording yourself speaking and sending it to me? Then I can watch it and give you feedback.

M Really? Thanks. That would be so helpful, Ms. Tiffin. I'll make a recording as soon as I get home today.

W My pleasure.

여 음, 네가 말하는 것을 녹화해서 그것을 나에게 보내면 어때? 그러면 내가 그것을 보고 피드백을 줄 수 있어.

남 정말요? 감사합니다. 그것이 정말 도움이 될 것 같습니다, Tiffin 선생님. 오늘 제가 집에 가자마자 녹화를 하겠습니다.

여 천만에.

문제 해설 스페인어 말하기 대회를 앞두고 걱정하는 남자에게 여자는 실제인 것처럼 연습하라고 하면서 남자가 말하는 것을 녹화해서 보내 주면 보고 피드백을 주겠다고 하자, 남자가 고마움을 표시하면서 집에 가자마자 녹화를 하겠다고 했으므로, 남자가 할 일로 가장 적절한 것은 ③ '말하기 연습 녹화하기'이다.

어휘&어구 draft 원고, 초안   mention 언급하다   improve 향상시키다, 나아지다   effective 효과적인   pretend ~인 척하다

04 강의 준비   [정답] ③

W Hello, Mr. Shaw. Thank you for coming to give our students a lecture.

M It's my pleasure. I highly value this opportunity.

W The students are really looking forward to your talk. How was your train ride?

M Great. The scenery was really beautiful.

W Good. Feel free to relax before your lecture.

M Thank you. My lecture starts at 2 o'clock, right?

W Yes. A microphone and a projector are set up for you.

M Thank you. I'm sorry to bother you, but is there a laptop I can use right now?

W Sure, I'll get you one right away.

M Thank you so much. I'd like to revise my presentation slides a little.

W I see. Is there anything else you need, like something to drink?

M No, thanks. I had some coffee on the way here.

여 안녕하세요, Shaw 선생님. 우리 학생들에게 강의를 하러 와 주셔서 감사합니다.

남 제가 기쁩니다. 전 이 기회가 매우 가치 있다고 생각하고 있거든요.

여 학생들이 오늘 선생님의 강의를 듣기를 정말 고대하고 있어요. 기차 타시는 건 어떠셨나요?

남 좋았습니다. 경치가 정말 아름다웠어요.

여 다행입니다. 강의하시기 전에 마음 편히 쉬세요.

남 감사합니다. 제 강의가 2시에 시작하죠, 맞나요?

여 네. 마이크와 프로젝터는 설치돼 있습니다.

남 감사합니다. 귀찮게 해 드려 죄송합니다만, 제가 바로 지금 쓸 수 있는 노트북이 있나요?

여 물론이죠, 지금 바로 하나 갖다 드릴게요.

남 정말 감사합니다. 제 발표 슬라이드를 약간 수정하고 싶어서요.

여 그렇군요. 뭐 더 필요하신 것은 없으세요, 마실 거라든지?

남 아니요, 괜찮습니다. 이곳에 오는 길에 커피를 좀 마셨어요.

문제 해설 남자가 강의 시작 전, 여자에게 자신이 사용할 수 있는 노트북이 있는지 물었고 여자는 바로 노트북을 하나 가져다주겠다고 말하고 있다. 따라서 여자가 할 일로 가장 적절한 것은 ③ '노트북 가져오기'이다.

어휘&어구 lecture 강의   highly 매우, 높이 평가하여   value 가치 있게 생각하다   opportunity 기회   look forward to ~을 고대하다   scenery 풍경   feel free to *do* 편하게 ~하다   relax 쉬다, 휴식을 취하다   microphone 마이크   projector 프로젝터   set up ~을 설치하다   bother 귀찮게 하다   laptop 노트북   revise 수정하다

05 동아리 홍보 활동   [정답] ④

W Mark, how's preparing for the interview going? Have you finished making interview questions for the new club members?

M Yeah, I completed making them yesterday. Have you uploaded the club's promotional video on the bulletin board at our school website?

W Yes. It's been up for a week, but it hasn't gotten many views.

M Maybe it's because students don't use the bulletin board much.

여 Mark, 인터뷰 준비는 어떻게 되어 가고 있니? 너는 새 동아리 회원을 위한 인터뷰 질문 만들기를 끝냈니?

남 응, 어제 질문 만들기를 마무리 지었어. 너는 학교 웹사이트 게시판에 동아리 홍보 동영상을 업로드했어?

여 응. 일주일 동안 게시해 놓았는데, 별로 조회 수가 많지 않았어.

남 아마도 학생들이 게시판을 많이 사용하지 않기 때문일 거야.

여 네 말이 맞는 것 같아.

남 그럼 우리 동아리에 관해 학생들에게 알려 줄 또 다른 방법을 찾아보려고 시도해야겠다.

여 우리 동아리의 모든 회원들이 그것을 홍보하기 위해 교실을 방문하

W	I think you're right.
M	Then we should try to find another way to let students know about our club.
W	Why don't all our club members visit classrooms to promote it?
M	That's a good idea. Then we can share our personal club experiences with the students.
W	Yeah. Let's have a club meeting later today and talk about it.
M	Okay.
W	So, could you contact the members and tell them to come to the club room after school? I'll make handouts for the meeting.
M	Alright. I'll tell them it starts at 4 p.m.
W	Great. Thanks.

는 것은 어떨까?

남	그거 좋은 생각이다. 그럼 우리는 학생들과 우리의 개인적인 동아리 경험을 공유할 수 있을 거야.
여	응. 오늘 이따가 동아리 회의를 하면서 그것에 관해 이야기하자.
남	좋아.
여	그러면, 네가 회원들에게 연락해서 방과 후에 동아리실로 오라고 말해 줄 수 있니? 나는 회의를 위해 유인물을 만들게.
남	좋아. 내가 회원들에게 회의가 오후 4시에 시작한다고 말할게.
여	훌륭해. 고마워.

문제 해설   여자가 동아리 홍보를 위해 동아리 회원들이 교실을 방문하는 것이 어떨지 남자에게 묻자 남자가 좋은 생각이라며 동의한다. 이에 여자가 동아리 회의에서 그에 관해 이야기하자고 말하며, 남자에게 동아리 회원들에게 연락해서 방과 후에 동아리실로 오라고 말해 달라고 부탁하자, 남자가 이를 수락한다. 따라서 여자가 남자에게 부탁한 일로 가장 적절한 것은 ④ '동아리 회원들에게 연락하기'이다.

어휘&어구   complete 마무리 짓다, 완료하다   bulletin board 게시판   handout 유인물, 인쇄물

06 레몬청 만들기
[정답] ③

M	Mom, what are you doing with all those lemons? Are you making your special lemon preserve for tea?
W	Yes.
M	Awesome! I love your lemon tea. It looks like you're making a lot.
W	Yeah, because I'm going to give some away as gifts for the upcoming holiday.
M	Good idea. Whoever you give it to will love it. Let me know if you need any help. I can wash the lemons for you.
W	I already washed them. I was just about to clean the glass jars I'll put the lemons in.
M	You mean by boiling them, right?
W	Yes, that's the best way.
M	Well, then while you do that, I can slice up the lemons.
W	Thanks, but I'll do that when I'm done with the jars. Actually, I don't think there's enough sugar.
M	Okay, I'll go out and get some now. I can pick it up at the supermarket on the corner, right?
W	Sure. Thank you.

남	엄마, 그 레몬들을 다 가지고 뭐 하고 계세요? 차를 위한 엄마의 특별한 레몬청을 만들고 있는 거예요?
여	그래.
남	아주 좋아요! 저는 엄마의 레몬차가 정말 좋아요. 많이 만드시는 것 같아요.
여	그래, 다가오는 휴일에 선물로 좀 나누어 줄 예정이라서.
남	좋은 생각이에요. 엄마가 누구에게 주든지 다 그것을 좋아할 거예요. 도움이 필요하면 알려 주세요. 제가 레몬을 씻어 줄 수 있어요.
여	내가 벌써 씻었어. 나는 방금 레몬을 넣을 유리병을 깨끗이 하려던 참이었어.
남	끓여서 그렇게 한다는 뜻이죠, 맞죠?
여	그래, 그게 가장 좋은 방법이야.
남	그럼, 엄마가 그것을 하는 동안, 제가 레몬을 썰 수 있어요.
여	고맙지만, 내가 병을 끓이는 일을 끝내고 그것을 할게. 실은, 설탕이 충분하지 않은 것 같아.
남	알았어요, 제가 지금 나가서 사 올게요. 모퉁이에 있는 슈퍼마켓에서 살 수 있죠, 맞죠?
여	물론이지. 고마워.

문제 해설   레몬청을 만들고 있는 여자가 설탕이 부족하다고 하자 남자가 지금 나가서 사 오겠다고 했으므로, 남자가 할 일로 가장 적절한 것은 ③ '설탕 사 오기'이다.

어휘&어구   preserve 설탕 절임   give away 나누어 주다   upcoming 다가오는   boil 끓이다   slice up (얇게) 썰다

수능유형 체험 베이글과 주스 사기 [정답] ⑤

여 안녕하세요, 가져갈 베이글 좀 살 수 있을까요?

남 물론이죠. 어떤 것으로 드릴까요?

여 모든 베이글이 다 같은 가격인가요?

남 음, 일반 베이글은 개당 2달러이고, 다른 맛은 모두 2달러 50센트입니다.

여 그렇군요. 그러면 일반 베이글 2개랑 블루베리 베이글 2개 주세요.

남 알겠습니다. 그러면 총 4개의 베이글 맞으시죠?

여 맞습니다. 베이글과 함께 먹을 주스도 좀 사고 싶습니다. 오렌지주스가 있나요?

남 네. 한 병에 3달러입니다. 몇 개 드릴까요?

여 두 병 할게요. 그게 전부입니다. 제 신용 카드 여기 있습니다.

남 감사합니다. 잠시만요.

문제 해설 여자는 개당 2달러인 일반 베이글 2개와 개당 2달러 50센트인 블루베리 베이글 2개와 함께 한 병에 3달러인 오렌지주스도 두 병 사겠다고 했다. 따라서 여자가 지불할 금액은 ⑤ '15달러'이다.

어휘&어구 plain 보통의 flavor 맛 bottle 병

수능유형 연습

01 중고 선풍기 사기 [정답] ②

M Hello, are you looking for something specific?

W Yes, I'm in search of a used fan in good condition.

M All right. We have a couple available. Let me show them to you. *[Pause]* Here they are. Both are in excellent condition.

W How much are they?

M This one is $40, and this one is $50. It's more expensive because it comes with a remote control.

W It'd be nice to have a remote control, so I'll go with the more expensive one. Can you deliver it to Old Town?

M Yes, but there will be a $10 fee for the delivery service.

W In that case, I'll just take it with me.

M All right. I'll pack it up nicely to make it easy to carry.

W Thank you. Here's my credit card.

M Thank you. Wait a moment, please.

남 안녕하세요, 특별히 찾으시는 게 있으세요?

여 네, 상태가 좋은 중고 선풍기를 찾고 있습니다.

남 알겠습니다. 두 개가 있습니다. 그것들을 손님께 보여 드리겠습니다. *[잠시 후]* 여기 있습니다. 둘 다 상태가 훌륭합니다.

여 얼마인가요?

남 이것은 40달러이고, 이것은 50달러입니다. 이것에는 리모컨이 딸려 있어서 더 비쌉니다.

여 리모컨이 있으면 좋을 것 같으니 더 비싼 것으로 하겠습니다. 그것을 Old Town까지 배달해 주실 수 있나요?

남 네, 그런데 배달 서비스에는 10달러의 비용이 있을 것입니다.

여 그렇다면 제가 그냥 그것을 가져가겠습니다.

남 알겠습니다. 가져가기 쉽게 잘 포장해 드리겠습니다.

여 감사합니다. 제 신용 카드가 여기 있습니다.

남 감사합니다. 잠시만 기다려 주세요.

문제 해설 여자는 리모컨이 딸린 50달러짜리 중고 선풍기를 사겠다고 하면서 선풍기 배달 비용이 10달러라고 하자 그냥 직접 가져가겠다고 말했다. 따라서 여자가 지불할 금액은 ② '50달러'이다.

어휘&어구 specific 특정한 come with ~이 딸려 있다 deliver 배달하다 pack 포장하다

W	Hello, how can I help you?
M	Hi, I'm interested in the schedule for the cooking classes offered here, at the Midland Community Center.
W	We have classes on Wednesdays at 10 a.m., and Saturdays at 10 a.m.
M	Are there any differences between the two classes?
W	Yes. The Wednesday class focuses on vegetarian options, while the Saturday class focuses on desserts. The tuition for both classes is $100 per session.
M	I see. Is it possible to take both classes?
W	Sure, if you enroll in both classes, you'll get a 10% discount on the total tuition fee.
M	Great. I'll enroll in both Wednesday and Saturday classes.
W	Okay. Are you a community center member? If so, you'll receive an additional 10% discount.
M	Yes, I am. My name is John Remington.
W	Just a moment. *[Typing sound]* All right. Then you'll get a 20% off on the total tuition fee.
M	Thank you. Here's my credit card.

여	안녕하세요, 어떻게 도와드릴까요?
남	안녕하세요. 여기 Midland Community Center에서 제공되는 요리 수업 일정에 관심이 있습니다.
여	수요일 오전 10시와 토요일 오전 10시에 수업이 있습니다.
남	두 수업에 차이점이라도 있나요?
여	네. 토요일 수업은 디저트에 중점을 두는 반면에, 수요일 수업은 채식 옵션에 중점을 둡니다. 두 수업의 수업료는 세션당 100달러입니다.
남	그렇군요. 두 과목 모두 수강하는 것이 가능한가요?
여	물론입니다, 두 수업을 모두 등록하시면 전체 수업료에서 10퍼센트 할인을 받으실 겁니다.
남	좋네요. 수요일과 토요일 수업 모두 등록하겠습니다.
여	알겠습니다. 커뮤니티 센터 회원이신가요? 그렇다면 10퍼센트 추가 할인을 받게 되실 겁니다.
남	네, 맞습니다. 제 이름은 John Remington입니다.
여	잠시만요. *[타자 치는 소리]* 알겠습니다. 그러면 총 수업료에서 20퍼센트 할인을 받으실 겁니다.
남	감사합니다. 제 신용 카드가 여기 있습니다.

문제 해설 남자가 세션당 수업료가 100달러인 수요일과 토요일 수업 두 개를 모두 듣겠다고 하자 여자는 10퍼센트 할인이 제공된다고 하면서 커뮤니티 센터 회원에게는 10퍼센트 추가 할인이 제공된다고 말했다. 결국 총수업료에서 20퍼센트 할인을 남자가 받게 된다고 말했으므로, 남자가 지불할 금액은 ③ '160달러'이다.

어휘&어구 offer 제공하다 vegetarian 채식주의자 enroll in ~에 등록하다 tuition fee 수업료 additional 추가의

M	Welcome to Dreamer's Zoo. How can I help you?
W	Hi. I'd like to buy admission tickets for one adult and two children. How much will that be?
M	Admission tickets are $30 each, regardless of age. And children under 5 are free of charge.
W	Oh, my kids are both teenagers.
M	In that case, you'll have to purchase three admission tickets.
W	Okay. Here's my credit card. By the way, are we allowed to feed the animals in the zoo?
M	Yes, but only with specific food that we sell. Would you like to buy some food packets?
W	Yes. How much are they?
M	They're $2 a packet. How many would you like?

남	Dreamer's Zoo에 오신 것을 환영합니다. 어떻게 도와드릴까요?
여	안녕하세요. 어른 1명과 어린이 2명의 입장권을 구매하고 싶습니다. 금액이 얼마인가요?
남	입장권은 연령에 관계없이 한 장당 30달러입니다. 그리고 5세 미만의 어린이는 무료입니다.
여	아, 우리 아이들은 둘 다 십 대입니다.
남	그렇다면 입장권을 3장 구매하셔야 합니다.
여	알겠습니다. 여기 제 신용 카드가 있습니다. 그런데 우리가 동물원 동물에게 먹이를 주는 것이 허용되나요?
남	네, 하지만 우리가 판매하는 특정한 먹이로만 줄 수 있습니다. 먹이 꾸러미를 구매하시겠습니까?
여	네. 얼마인가요?
남	꾸러미당 2달러입니다. 몇 개 드릴까요?
여	두 꾸러미 주세요.

W　Two packets, please.

M　Here you go. So I'll charge both the admission tickets and the food packets to this credit card.

W　All right, thanks.

남　여기 있습니다. 그러면 이 신용 카드에 입장권과 음식 꾸러미 비용을 모두 청구하겠습니다.

여　네, 감사합니다.

문제 해설　한 장당 30달러인 동물원 입장권을 3장 구매하는 여자가 꾸러미당 2달러인 동물 먹이도 두 꾸러미 구매하겠다고 남자에게 말했으므로, 여자가 지불할 금액은 ⑤ '94달러'이다.

어휘&어구　admission ticket 입장권　regardless of ~에 관계없이, ~에 상관없이　free of charge 무료의　feed 먹이를 주다　packet 꾸러미, 통, 곽

04 현대 미술관 입장권 구매　　　　　　　　　　　　　　　　[정답] ③

W　Hello, sir. Welcome to the Modern Art Museum.

M　Hello. How much are the admission tickets?

W　They're $10 for adults and $5 for children. How many of you are there?

M　Eight adults and four children. Could you give us a group discount?

W　We give a 25 percent discount for large groups, but it applies to a group of more than fifteen people.

M　That's too bad. Oh well, nothing can be done about that.

W　Do you have a Modern Art Museum membership by any chance?

M　No. Does it have any benefits?

W　Yes. For this month you can get 20 percent off your admission ticket. Besides, the same applies to those accompanying you. The annual membership fee is $5.

M　Great. I want a one-year membership and admission tickets.

W　Okay. I'll help you with one annual membership, and eight adult and four children's tickets. The 20 percent discount applies to all tickets.

M　Thanks.

여　안녕하십니까, 고객님. Modern Art Museum에 오신 것을 환영합니다.

남　안녕하세요. 입장권은 얼마입니까?

여　성인은 10달러, 어린이는 5달러입니다. 몇 분이세요?

남　어른 8명, 아이 4명입니다. 단체 할인이 가능한가요?

여　인원이 많은 단체에 대해서는 25퍼센트 할인해 주지만, 15명이 넘는 단체에 적용됩니다.

남　그렇다니 유감이네요. 어 그럼, 어쩔 수 없네요.

여　혹시 Modern Art Museum 회원권이 있으신가요?

남　아니요. 무슨 혜택이 있나요?

여　네. 이번 달은 입장권을 20퍼센트 할인받을 수 있습니다. 게다가, 귀하와 동행한 사람들에게 똑같이 적용됩니다. 연회비는 5달러입니다.

남　좋네요. 1년 회원권과 입장권을 주세요.

여　알겠습니다. 연간 회원권 하나와 성인 8명, 아동 4명의 입장권을 도와드리겠습니다. 20퍼센트 할인은 모든 입장권에 적용됩니다.

남　고맙습니다.

문제 해설　성인용 10달러짜리 입장권 8개, 아동용 5달러짜리 입장권 4개를 구입하기로 하여 100달러를 지불해야 하는데, 5달러를 추가로 지불하고 구매하는 연간 회원권으로 입장권 금액(100달러)의 20퍼센트(20달러)를 할인받을 수 있다. 따라서 남자가 지불할 금액은 ③ '85달러'이다.

어휘&어구　admission ticket 입장권　apply to ~에 적용되다　by any chance 혹시, 혹시라도　benefit 혜택　accompany 동행하다　annual 연간의

05 신발 재고품 염가 판매　　　　　　　　　　　　　　　　[정답] ①

M　Hello. Can I help you?

W　Yes. I saw your shoe clearance sale ad on the flyer.

M　Yeah. We're offering discounts on all our shoes. It's the best chance to buy your favorite shoes at a low price.

W　Great! [Pause] How much are these sneakers? I like their design.

M　Their regular price is $90, but they're on sale for 50%

남　안녕하세요. 도와드릴까요?

여　네. 전단에서 신발 재고품 염가 판매 광고를 봤어요.

남　네. 저희는 모든 신발에 대해 할인을 제공하고 있습니다. 저렴한 가격으로 손님이 마음에 드는 신발을 구매할 수 있는 가장 좋은 기회입니다.

여　잘됐군요! [잠시 후] 이 운동화는 얼마인가요? 디자인이 마음에 들어요.

off right now.	남 정가는 90달러지만 지금은 50% 할인 판매 중입니다.
W Wow, really? Let me try them on. Do you have a size 8?	여 와, 정말요? 신어 볼게요. 8 사이즈 있나요?
M Let me see. *[Pause]* Here you are.	남 어디 봅시다. *[잠시 후]* 여기 있습니다.
W Oh, they fit me well. I'll buy a pair of these sneakers. And how much are these slippers?	여 오, 잘 맞네요. 이 운동화 한 켤레를 살게요. 그리고 이 슬리퍼는 얼마예요?
M They're originally $30, but on sale for 70% off.	남 원래는 30달러인데, 70% 할인 판매 중입니다.
W Great. Do you have my size?	여 좋군요. 제 사이즈 있나요?
M Sure. *[Pause]* Here you are.	남 그럼요. *[잠시 후]* 여기 있습니다.
W Oh, I like them. I'll take a pair of them, too. Here's my credit card.	여 오, 마음에 들어요. 그것 한 켤레도 살게요. 여기 제 신용 카드가 있습니다.
M Thanks.	남 감사합니다.

문제 해설 여자는 정가가 90달러인데 50% 할인 중인 운동화와 원래 가격이 30달러인데 70% 할인 중인 슬리퍼를 사겠다고 말했다. 따라서 여자가 지불할 금액은 ① '54달러'이다.

어휘&어구 clearance sale 재고품 염가 판매 flyer 전단 originally 원래

06 유아용 세제와 비누 구입

[정답] ②

W Hi. Can I help you with anything?	여 안녕하세요. 뭐 좀 도와드릴까요?
M Yes. I'd like to buy some baby-safe detergent. Could you recommend one?	남 네. 유아에게 안전한 세제를 사려고 합니다. 하나 추천해 주시겠습니까?
W Sure. *[Pause]* This one's really good. It's non-toxic and chemical-free.	여 물론이지요. *[잠시 후]* 이것은 정말로 좋아요. 무독성이고 화학 물질이 없어요.
M My son has sensitive skin, so that'll be perfect. How much is it?	남 제 아들은 피부가 민감해서 그것이 딱 맞겠네요. 얼마인가요?
W It's $20 for a small bottle, and $90 for a big one.	여 작은 병은 20달러이고, 큰 병은 90달러입니다.
M I'll take three small bottles.	남 작은 병 세 개를 살게요.
W Okay. Is there anything else I can help you find?	여 알겠습니다. 찾으시는 걸 도와드릴 그 밖에 다른 것이 있나요?
M Yeah. I'm also looking for a good baby soap.	남 네. 괜찮은 아기용 비누를 또한 찾고 있어요.
W That's right over here. *[Pause]* It's $6 a bar, and if you buy five or more bars, you can get 10% off the price of the soap.	여 그것은 바로 이쪽에 있습니다. *[잠시 후]* 한 개에 6달러인데, 5개 이상 구입하시면 비누 금액에서 10% 할인을 받으십니다.
M Oh, great. I'll take ten bars.	남 오, 좋네요. 10개를 살게요.
W All right. I can check you out over here.	여 알겠습니다. 이쪽에서 계산해 드릴게요.
M Okay. Here's a credit card.	남 네. 여기 신용 카드가 있습니다.

문제 해설 남자는 한 병에 20달러인 아기 전용 세제 작은 병 세 개와 한 개에 6달러인 비누 10개를 사겠다고 했고 비누의 경우 10% 할인이 된다. 따라서 남자가 지불할 금액은 ② '114달러'이다.

어휘&어구 baby-safe 유아에게 안전한 detergent 세제 recommend 추천하다 non-toxic 무독성의 chemical-free 화학 물질이 없는 sensitive 민감한

수능 유형 07 이유

수능유형 **체험** | ⑤

수능유형 **연습** | 01 ③ 02 ① 03 ⑤ 04 ① 05 ① 06 ①

본문 20~21쪽

수능유형 체험 바이올린 수업 불참 사유 [정답] ⑤

여 Henry, 숙제 다 했니?
남 네, 엄마. 꽤 쉬웠어요.
여 좋아. 오늘 저녁에 바이올린 수업 있는 거 잊지 마.
남 음, 아무래도 수업에 못 갈 것 같아요.
여 왜 그러니? 어제 넘어져서 손이 아직 아프니?
남 아니요, 손은 괜찮아요.

여 그럼, 왜 수업에 갈 수가 없니?
남 실은 제 친구 John의 생일 파티가 오늘 저녁에 있어요.
여 아, 어째서 그것에 대해 아무 말도 안 했던 거야!
남 죄송해요, 엄마. 학교와 자원봉사 활동으로 일주일 내내 정말 바빴어요.
여 이해해. 그러면 내가 바이올린 선생님께 연락드려서 네가 가지 않을 거라고 알려 드려야겠다.

문제 해설 숙제를 다 끝냈다는 남자에게 여자가 저녁에 바이올린 수업이 있는 걸 잊지 말라고 말하자 남자는 친구의 생일 파티에 가야 해서 수업에 갈 수 없다고 했으므로, 남자가 바이올린 수업에 갈 수 없는 이유는 ⑤ '친구 생일 파티에 가야 해서'이다.

어휘&어구 hurt 아프다 how come 어째서 mention 말하다, 언급하다 volunteer work 자원봉사 활동 contact 연락하다

수능유형 연습

01 요리 잡지 구독 중단 이유 [정답] ③

M Honey, I'm thinking about ordering some food.
W But I've already cooked dinner, cabbage steak.
M A vegetarian dish again?
W Yes. We agreed that we'd start to eat healthier.
M That's true. But... did you find the recipe in your cooking magazine?
W No. Actually, I canceled my subscription to it last month.
M Why? It has many good recipes, doesn't it?
W Yes, it does.
M Then why did you stop your subscription?
W The price has gone up a lot recently. It's a bit expensive.
M I see. I'm sure you can find good recipes online.

남 여보, 음식을 좀 시켜 먹을까 생각 중이에요.
여 그런데 내가 양배추 스테이크로 벌써 저녁 식사를 준비했어요.
남 또 채식 요리라고요?
여 그럼요. 우리 더 건강하게 먹기 시작하자고 합의했잖아요.
남 그렇긴 하죠. 그런데… 당신의 요리 잡지에서 조리법을 찾았나요?
여 아니요. 실은 나는 지난달에 그 잡지 구독을 취소했어요.
남 왜요? 좋은 조리법이 많이 있잖아요, 그렇죠?
여 네, 그래요.
남 그러면 왜 구독을 중단했어요?
여 최근에 가격이 많이 올랐어요. 조금 비싸요.
남 알겠어요. 분명 온라인에서도 좋은 조리법을 찾을 수 있을 거예요.

문제 해설 양배추 스테이크를 저녁 식사로 준비한 여자에게 남자가 요리 잡지에서 찾은 조리법이냐고 묻자 여자는 최근에 가격이 많이 올라서 잡지 구독을 중단했다고 말했으므로, 여자가 요리 잡지 구독을 중단한 이유는 ③ '잡지 가격이 인상되어서'이다.

어휘&어구 cabbage 양배추 vegetarian 채식의 recipe 조리법 subscription 구독

---

02 스웨터 반품 불가 이유 [정답] ①

M Hey, honey, you look great in that sweater.

남 안녕, 여보, 그 스웨터 당신한테 잘 어울려요.

W	Thanks. But, honestly, I don't really like it.	여	고마워요, 그런데, 솔직히, 나는 그게 별로 마음에 안 들어요.
M	Why's that?	남	왜 그러는데요?
W	It's a little small on me. I tried to return it, but I couldn't.	여	나한테는 조금 작아서요. 그것을 반품하려고 했는데, 할 수 없었어요.
M	Why not? Had you already worn it or did you lose the receipt?	남	왜 안 되었어요? 그 옷을 이미 입었거나 아니면 영수증을 잃어버렸어요?
W	No. I hadn't even removed the price tag and I still have the receipt.	여	아니요. 나는 심지어 가격표도 떼지 않았고 영수증도 아직 가지고 있어요.
M	Oh, had it been over 30 days since you bought it?	남	아, 그럼 그것을 구매한 지 30일이 지났어요?
W	No. I tried returning it just a week after I got it.	여	아니요. 산 지 한 주 만에 반품하려고 했어요.
M	Then what was the problem?	남	그럼 뭐가 문제였지요?
W	Well, I bought the sweater on sale, and they have a no-refund policy for sale items.	여	글쎄, 그 스웨터를 할인해서 샀는데, 할인 품목에 대해서는 환불이 안 되는 방침이 있었어요.
M	Yeah, a lot of stores do.	남	그래요, 많은 상점들이 그렇게 하죠.

문제 해설 남자가 스웨터를 왜 반품하지 못했냐고 여자에게 묻자 여자는 스웨터를 할인해서 구매했는데 업체에는 할인 품목에 대해서는 환불이 안 되는 방침이 있어서라고 답하고 있다. 따라서 여자가 스웨터를 반품하지 못한 이유는 ① '할인 품목이어서'이다.

어휘&어구 return 반품하다, 환불하다 receipt 영수증 price tag 가격표 policy 방침, 정책

03 회사 창립 기념일 파티 장소 변경 이유

[정답] ⑤

W	Hi, David. You're a little late today.	여	안녕, David. 오늘은 좀 늦었네요.
M	Yeah, you know I moved, right? My new house is a bit farther from work, and I haven't fully adjusted to the commute yet.	남	네, 제가 이사를 했다는 건 알죠, 그렇죠? 새집이 직장에서 좀 더 멀어져서 아직 출퇴근에 완전히 적응하지 못했어요.
W	You'll get used to it soon enough. By the way, did you hear about the problem with the company's anniversary party?	여	금방 충분히 그것에 익숙해질 거예요. 그런데, 회사의 창립 기념 파티에 문제가 있다는 소식은 들었나요?
M	No, I haven't. Do we need to change the date?	남	아니요, 못 들었어요. 우리가 날짜를 바꿔야 하나요?
W	No, the date is fine. The problem is with the location.	여	아니요, 날짜는 괜찮아요. 문제는 장소에 있어요.
M	Oh, was it double-booked?	남	아, 예약이 겹쳤어요?
W	No. It ends up that the restaurant is too small for us because more people have recently said they were coming.	여	아니요. 최근 더 많은 사람이 참석한다고 해서 결국 그 레스토랑이 우리에게 너무 좁아지고 말았어요.
M	So we need a new place with more space. Do you have any suggestions?	남	그럼 더 넓은 공간이 있는 새로운 장소가 필요하겠군요. 제안할 곳이 있나요?
W	How about using the rooftop of the company building? It's big and we can use it for free.	여	회사 건물 옥상을 사용하는 건 어떨까요? 거긴 크고 우리가 무료로 그것을 사용할 수 있잖아요.
M	What a great idea! And the view from up there is fantastic.	남	정말 좋은 생각이군요! 그리고 거기서의 전망도 환상적이죠.
W	Absolutely! It would be perfect for our anniversary party.	여	정말 그렇죠! 거긴 우리 창립 기념 파티에 완벽한 곳일 거예요.

문제 해설 여자는 회사 창립 기념 파티 장소에 문제가 생겼다고 남자에게 말하며 그 이유로 파티에 참석한다고 말하는 사람이 많아져서 예약한 식당이 너무 협소해졌다고 말하고 있다. 따라서 여자가 파티 장소를 바꾸려는 이유는 ⑤ '참석자가 너무 많아져서'이다.

어휘&어구 get used to ~에 익숙해지다 anniversary (해마다의) 기념일 location 장소 end up 결국 ~하게 되다

04 캠핑용 차량 구입

[정답] ①

W	Hi, Matthew. What are you looking at?	여	안녕하세요, Matthew. 뭘 보고 있어요?
M	Oh, hi, April. It's a car catalog.	남	아, 안녕하세요, April. 자동차 카탈로그예요.
W	Are you looking to buy a car?	여	차를 사려고 보고 있는 거예요?
M	Yes. I need a new one.	남	네, 새 차가 필요해요.
W	But didn't you buy one last year when your wife started to commute to work?	여	하지만 작년에 당신 부인이 직장으로 통근하기 시작했을 때 하나 구입하지 않았었나요?
M	Yes, I did. I bought a small used car.	남	그래요, 구입했어요. 전 작은 중고차를 샀죠.
W	Is there anything wrong with it?	여	그 차에 무슨 문제가 있나요?
M	No, it runs perfectly.	남	아뇨, 지극히 잘 굴러가요.
W	Don't tell me your son convinced you to buy him a car.	여	설마 당신 아들이 차를 사 달라고 당신을 설득한 건 아닐 텐데요.
M	No. I don't think he needs one yet. We recently started camping as a family, but our car isn't great for that.	남	아니에요. 아직은 그가 차가 필요하다고 생각하지 않아요. 최근에 우리는 가족이 함께 캠핑을 시작했는데, 우리 차는 그것을 하기에 그다지 좋지 않아요.
W	I see. So you want one for off-road travel with more space for camping equipment?	여	그렇군요. 그러니까 캠핑 장비를 싣기 위한 더 큰 공간이 있는 오프로드 여행을 위한 차를 원하는 거죠?
M	Exactly. That's what I'm looking for.	남	맞아요. 그게 제가 찾고 있는 거예요.

문제 해설 남자는 자기 가족이 최근에 캠핑을 시작했는데 현재 가진 차는 캠핑에 적합하지 않아서 차량을 구입하려고 한다고 말하고 있으므로, 남자가 자동차를 구입하려는 이유는 ① '캠핑용 차가 필요해서'이다.

어휘&어구 commute 통근하다   used car 중고차   convince 설득하다   off-road 오프로드의, 일반 도로에서가 아닌   equipment 장비

05 트랙 달리기

[정답] ①

M	Mom, I'm home.	남	엄마, 다녀왔어요.
W	Hi, Michael. How was your history presentation? I was worried because you stayed up almost all night working on it.	여	어서 오렴, Michael. 네 역사 발표는 어땠니? 네가 그것을 작업하느라 거의 밤을 새워서 걱정했었어.
M	It was good. The teacher praised my presentation.	남	좋았어요. 선생님께서 제 발표를 칭찬해 주셨어요.
W	Great. Your hard work paid off. Did your classmates like the video clip you made?	여	잘됐구나. 네가 열심히 한 보람이 있었구나. 반 친구들이 네가 만든 동영상을 좋아했니?
M	Yes. They really liked it. Some classmates told me so after class.	남	네. 반 친구들이 정말로 그것을 좋아했어요. 몇몇 친구들은 수업 후에 제게 그렇게 말해 주었어요.
W	I'm happy to hear that. Well, did you go for a run around the track after school?	여	그 말을 들으니 기쁘구나. 참, 방과 후에 트랙 달리기를 했니?
M	That's what I was planning on doing, but I couldn't.	남	그렇게 하려고 계획했었는데, 그럴 수 없었어요.
W	Why? Do you have something to study for?	여	왜? 공부해야 할 거라도 있니?
M	No, Mom. I couldn't use the track because it is being renovated.	남	아뇨, 엄마. 트랙이 보수 중이어서 그것을 사용할 수 없었어요.
W	I see. Well, do you want something to eat?	여	그렇구나. 음, 뭐 좀 먹고 싶니?
M	Yeah, I'm starving.	남	네, 몹시 배고파요.
W	Then I'll make you a sandwich.	여	그러면 내가 샌드위치를 만들어 줄게.
M	Thanks, Mom.	남	고마워요, 엄마.

문제 해설 방과 후에 트랙 달리기를 했냐는 여자의 질문에 남자는 트랙이 보수 중이어서 트랙을 사용할 수 없었다고 말하고 있다. 따라서 남자가 트랙 달리기를 하지 못한 이유는 ① '트랙이 보수 중이어서'이다.

어휘&어구 stay up all night 밤을 새우다, 온밤을 꼬박 새우다   praise 칭찬하다   pay off 보람이 있다, 성공하다   track 트랙   renovate 보수하다, 개조하다   starve 몹시 배고프다

[Cell phone rings.]

W Hi, Sam. What's up?

M I'm calling about our schedule for tomorrow. We were supposed to drive to the workshop together, remember?

W Oh, yeah. Thanks for calling. I'm really excited about the workshop tomorrow. When and where should we meet?

M Why don't we meet in front of the city library at 9 a.m.?

W Good.

M By the way, are you planning to attend all the sessions?

W Yes, I want to.

M Well, I won't be able to stay until the end, so you might need to look for a ride back home.

W You're not going to stay for the whole workshop?

M No, I can't. I have a dentist's appointment. I'm sorry to inconvenience you.

W That's okay. Unfortunately you'll miss some really good workshop sessions.

M I know, but I couldn't reschedule the appointment. The dentist will be out of the office the day after tomorrow for a week to attend a conference.

W I see. So you would have to wait at least a week if you postponed this appointment.

M That's right. And my tooth aches so much that I can't wait another week.

[휴대 전화가 울린다.]

여 안녕, Sam. 무슨 일인가요?

남 내일 우리 일정 때문에 전화했어요. 우리는 워크숍에 함께 차를 타고 가기로 되어 있어요, 기억해요?

여 아, 네. 전화해 줘서 고마워요. 내일 워크숍 때문에 정말 들떠 있어요. 언제 어디서 만날까요?

남 오전 9시에 시립도서관 앞에서 만나는 게 어때요?

여 좋아요.

남 그런데, 모든 활동 시간에 참석할 계획인가요?

여 네, 그러고 싶어요.

남 음, 저는 끝날 때까지 머물 수 없을 테니, 집으로 오는 차편을 알아보셔야겠어요.

여 워크숍에 내내 머물 작정이 아니군요?

남 네, 그럴 수 없어요. 치과 예약이 있어요. 불편하게 해 드려 미안해요.

여 괜찮아요. 유감스럽게도 당신은 몇몇 정말 좋은 워크숍 활동 시간을 놓치실 거예요.

남 알아요, 그렇지만 예약 일정을 변경할 수 없었어요. 치과 의사가 학회에 참석하기 위해서 모레부터 일주일 동안 진료실을 비울 거예요.

여 알겠어요. 그래서 당신이 이 예약을 연기하면 적어도 일주일을 기다려야 하겠군요.

남 맞아요. 그리고 이가 너무 아파서 일주일을 더 기다릴 수는 없어요.

문제 해설 남자의 치과 의사가 모레부터 일주일 동안 진료하지 못하는 상황이어서, 남자는 내일 치과에 꼭 가야 한다. 따라서 남자가 워크숍에 끝까지 참석할 수 없는 이유는 ① '치과 예약이 있어서'이다.

어휘&어구 session 활동 시간   inconvenience 불편하게 하다   reschedule 일정을 변경하다   conference 학회   postpone 연기하다

수능 유형

08 언급 유무

수능유형 체험	④					본문 22~23쪽
수능유형 연습	01 ③	02 ③	03 ④	04 ③	05 ⑤	06 ③

수능유형 체험   Global Habitat Trip 활동   [정답] ④

여 Max, 올해 여름에 어떤 계획이 있어요?

남 저는 올여름에 'Global Habitat Trip'에 참여할 거예요.

여 그게 무엇이에요?

남 그건 집 짓기 프로그램이에요. 그 목적은 다른 나라의 가난한 사람들을 돕는 것이에요.

여 멋지군요. 어느 나라로 갈 건가요?

남 전 몽골로 갈 거예요.

여 거기서 정확히 무엇을 할 건가요?

남 음, 주로 주택과 다리를 수리하고 물을 얻기 위해 우물을 파는 데 도움을 줄 거예요.

여 정말 대단하군요! 거기에 얼마나 오래 있을 건가요?

남 정확히 한 달 동안 있을 거예요. 정말 기대돼요!

여 그것에 대한 소식 듣기를 고대하고 있을게요.

문제 해설   대화에서 Global Habitat Trip에 관해 목적, 방문 국가, 활동, 체류 기간은 언급되었지만, ④ '경비'는 언급되지 않았다.

어휘&어구   attend 참석하다   assist 돕다   repair 수리하다   dig 파다   well 우물   look forward to ~을 고대하다

수능유형 **연습**

01 Super Computing Youth Camp 참가 [정답] ③

M	Hey, Sally. I came across something called the Super Computing Youth Camp on social media this morning.
W	Sounds interesting. What is it?
M	It's a camp for high schoolers where they form teams of three and make and present a project using a super computer.
W	Wow, cool!
M	It's a national camp. Only 30 teams can advance through the regional qualifiers.
W	That sounds interesting. When is it taking place?
M	It's scheduled from July 15 to July 21. Would you like to sign up with me?
W	Sure. Luckily, I'm free that week.
M	Great! The qualifiers will be held at the Science and Technology Center in our city.
W	I can't wait. It sounds like a unique opportunity.

남   안녕, Sally. 오늘 아침 소셜 미디어에서 Super Computing Youth Camp라는 것을 우연히 발견했어.
여   흥미롭게 들리네. 그게 뭐야?
남   그것은 세 명으로 팀을 이루고, 슈퍼컴퓨터를 사용하여 프로젝트를 만들고 발표하는 고등학생을 위한 캠프야.
여   와, 멋있다!
남   그것은 전국 규모 캠프야. 30개 팀만이 지역 예선을 통과할 수 있어.
여   그거 흥미로워 보인다. 언제 열리는데?
남   7월 15일부터 7월 21일까지 예정이야. 나랑 함께 신청할래?
여   물론이지. 다행히 그 주에는 시간이 있어.
남   좋아! 우리 시에서는 과학기술 센터에서 예선이 열릴 거야.
여   정말 기대돼. 독특한 기회 같거든.

문제 해설   대화에서 Super Computing Youth Camp에 관해 팀 인원수, 참가 팀 수, 개최 기간, 지역 예선 장소는 언급되었지만, ③ '신청 방법'은 언급되지 않았다.

어휘&어구   come across ~을 우연히 발견하다   schooler 학생   present 발표하다   national 전국적인, 국가의   sign up 신청하다, 등록하다   be held 열리다   opportunity 기회

02 Art Appreciation Program 소개 및 신청 [정답] ③

	[Cell phone rings.]
W	Hey, Ken.
M	Hey, Angela. What are you up to this weekend?
W	I'm going to participate in the Art Appreciation Program at the Kingston City Gallery.
M	Sounds interesting. What's planned for the program?
W	Participants will view their current exhibit and then talk with the artists.
M	How cool! I've always wanted to do something like that. Is it too late to sign up for it?

[휴대 전화가 울린다.]
여   안녕, Ken.
남   안녕, Angela. 이번 주말에 어떤 계획 있어?
여   나 Kingston 시립 갤러리에서 Art Appreciation Program에 참여할 거야.
남   흥미로운데. 그 프로그램에 어떤 내용이 계획되어 있니?
여   참여자들이 현재 전시 중인 작품들을 관람한 뒤 작가들과 대화할 거야.
남   정말 멋지네! 나도 항상 그런 경험을 해 보고 싶었어. 신청하기엔 너무 늦었을까?

W No, but you'd better hurry because the sign-up deadline is this Thursday.

M I'll do it right away. How can I sign up?

W You just have to fill out a form on the gallery's website.

M Thanks. I'll call you back once I'm done.

여 아니, 하지만 신청 마감이 이번 주 목요일까지니 서둘러야 해.

남 지금 바로 신청해 볼게. 어떻게 신청하면 되지?

여 갤러리 웹사이트에서 서식을 작성하기만 하면 돼.

남 고마워. 다 신청하고 나면 너에게 다시 전화할게.

문제 해설 대화에서 Art Appreciation Program에 관해 행사 장소, 행사 내용, 신청 마감일, 신청 방법은 언급되었지만, ③ '신청 자격'은 언급되지 않았다.

어휘&어구 gallery 갤러리(미술품 전시실) current 현재의 exhibit 전시품 deadline 마감, 기한 fill out a form 서식을 작성하다

03 Student Short Video Contest 준비   [정답] ④

M Amy, are you still busy with the Student Short Video Contest?

W Yes, Dad. The deadline is coming up.

M Oh, when is the deadline for submission?

W It's August 8th. So I'm running out of time.

M Only three days left. Do you need to submit just the video?

W I need to submit the script too. But I haven't even edited the video yet.

M Really? Then I think you'd better work on it all weekend.

W That's my plan. I want to win because the winners receive a ticket to the International Youth Film Festival.

M Wow! I really hope you win!

W Thanks. And there's something really special about the contest.

M What is it?

W Jean Cook, the famous movie director, is the judge.

M That's so cool! I know she's your favorite. Good luck, Amy!

W Thanks, Dad.

남 Amy, 아직도 학생 단편 영상 대회로 바쁘니?

여 네, 아빠. 마감이 다가와요.

남 아, 제출 마감일은 언제야?

여 8월 8일이에요. 그래서 시간이 없어요.

남 단 사흘밖에 남지 않았네. 영상만 제출하면 되는 거야?

여 대본도 제출해야 해요. 그런데 영상 편집도 아직 안 했어요.

남 정말? 그럼 주말 내내 작업해야겠구나.

여 그게 제 계획이에요. 수상자들은 국제 청소년 영화제 입장권을 받기 때문에 저는 수상하고 싶어요.

남 와! 정말로 수상하길 바랄게!

여 고마워요. 그리고 이 대회에 정말 특별한 점이 있어요.

남 그게 뭐니?

여 유명 영화감독인 Jean Cook이 심사 위원이에요.

남 정말 멋진걸! 그녀가 네가 가장 좋아하는 감독이라는 거 알고 있단다. 행운을 빌게, Amy!

여 고마워요, 아빠.

문제 해설 대화에서 Student Short Video Contest에 관해 제출 마감일, 제출 자료, 상품, 심사 위원은 언급되었지만, ④ '심사 기준'은 언급되지 않았다.

어휘&어구 submission 제출 submit 제출하다 run out of time 시간이 없다 script (극·영화·방송극 등의) 대본

04 Animals-in-Need 마라톤 참가   [정답] ③

W Hi, Matt. I heard that you're training for a marathon nowadays.

M Yeah. I'm running the Animals-in-Need Marathon. It's my second marathon.

W Oh, I've heard of that event. It's to raise money for

여 안녕, Matt. 네가 요즘 마라톤 훈련을 하고 있다고 들었어.

남 응. Animals-in-Need 마라톤을 뛸 거야. 이번이 나의 두 번째 마라톤이야.

여 아, 그 행사에 대해 들어 본 적 있어. 동물 보호소를 위한 기금을 마련하기 위한 거지, 그렇지 않니?

animal shelters, isn't it?

M Right. The $50 entry fee gets donated to support abandoned, homeless animals.

W That's a great cause. I've never run a marathon before, but I've always wanted to.

M Then why don't you join me?

W Is it still possible to register?

M Yes. The registration deadline is May 5.

W Okay. What is the marathon course?

M It starts downtown in front of the Central Building and goes around Lake Middleton twice.

W All right. Do you have to bring your own water?

M There will be water stations every kilometer, so there's no need to bring your own.

W Great! I'll sign up for it tonight.

남 맞아. 50달러의 참가비는 버려진, 집 없는 동물들을 지원하기 위해 기부돼.

여 그건 훌륭한 목적인걸. 난 전에 마라톤은 한 번도 해 본 적이 없지만, 항상 하고 싶었어.

남 그럼 나랑 함께하지 않을래?

여 아직도 등록할 수 있어?

남 응. 등록 마감일은 5월 5일이야.

여 알았어. 마라톤 코스는 어디야?

남 시내의 Central 빌딩 앞에서 시작해서 Middleton 호수를 두 번 돌아.

여 알았어. 물을 직접 가져가야 하나?

남 킬로미터마다 급수대가 있을 거니까 자신의 것을 가져갈 필요는 없어.

여 좋아! 오늘 밤에 그것을 신청할게.

문제 해설 두 사람이 Animals-in-Need 마라톤에 관해 대화를 나누고 있는데, 개최 목적, 참가비, 참가 등록 마감일, 마라톤 코스는 언급되었지만, ③ '주관 단체'는 언급되지 않았다.

어휘&어구 raise (자금 등을) 모으다 entry fee 참가비 donate 기부하다 abandoned 버려진 cause 목적, 대의 register 등록하다 deadline 마감일

---

05 Northeast Spring Fashion Show
[정답] ⑤

W Hi, Darin. What are you looking at?

M I'm looking at the website of the Northeast Spring Fashion Show. It's on Saturday, April 6.

W I heard about that. Are you going to the show?

M Yes. I got a ticket from my uncle. It'll be the first show I've ever attended.

W You must be excited. It's held at the same place as the job fair we went to last year, right?

M Yes, the Golden Convention Center. The website says three countries are going to participate.

W Cool! What countries?

M Italy, France, and Korea. And the theme of the fashion show is really cool, too.

W What's the theme?

M It's "Green Future." All of their pieces will be hand-stitched and upcycled from recycled materials.

W That's great! You'll have so much fun.

여 안녕, Darin. 뭘 보고 있는 거야?

남 Northeast Spring Fashion Show 웹사이트를 보고 있어. 그것이 4월 6일 토요일에 있거든.

여 그것에 대해 들었어. 그 쇼에 갈 거니?

남 응. 삼촌한테 표를 한 장 받았어. 그건 내가 처음 참석해 보는 쇼가 될 거야.

여 신나겠다. 그게 작년에 우리가 갔던 취업 박람회와 같은 장소에서 열리지, 맞지?

남 응, Golden Convention Center야. 웹사이트에 3개국이 참가할 것이라고 적혀 있어.

여 멋진데! 어느 나라야?

남 이탈리아, 프랑스, 그리고 한국이야. 그리고 패션쇼의 주제도 정말 근사해.

여 주제가 뭔데?

남 '녹색의 미래'야. 그들의 모든 작품이 재활용된 재료로, 손으로 꿰매고 업사이클이 된 거야.

여 너무 멋지다! 정말 재미있겠구나.

문제 해설 Northeast Spring Fashion Show에 관해 개최일, 개최 장소, 참가국, 주제는 언급되었으나 ⑤ '입장료'는 언급되지 않았다.

어휘&어구 attend 참석하다 job fair 취업 박람회 theme 주제 hand-stitched 손으로 꿰맨 upcycled 업사이클된(재활용품을 더 나은 것으로 만든) material 재료

W	Ben, have you read the notice about Survival Camp at Mt. Smokey?	여	Ben, Smokey 산에서 있을 Survival Camp에 관한 안내문을 읽었니?
M	No, what's that?	남	아니, 그게 뭐니?
W	You probably don't know because you transferred here this year. Our school has a survival camp every summer. It started in 2010.	여	네가 올해 이곳으로 전학을 왔기 때문에 아마 모를 거야. 우리 학교는 매년 여름에 생존 캠프를 해. 그것은 2010년에 시작되었어.
M	That sounds kind of cool. How long is it?	남	그거 다소 멋진 것 같은데. 기간이 얼마 동안이니?
W	Five days, from the first Monday of July.	여	7월의 첫 번째 월요일부터 5일간이야.
M	Where does it take place?	남	어디에서 열리지?
W	In the Mt. Smokey Campground in Belleville.	여	Belleville에 있는 Smokey 산 야영지에서야.
M	I know where that is. It's not too far. What do students do at the camp?	남	그곳이 어디인지 알아. 그리 멀지 않네. 캠프에서 학생들은 뭘 하니?
W	Since it's a survival camp, they learn basic survival skills.	여	생존 캠프여서, 기본적인 생존 기술을 배워.
M	Really? That sounds like fun.	남	정말? 재미있겠는데.
W	There are also survival games where you need to use the skills you learn to win.	여	이기려면 네가 배우는 기술을 사용해야 하는 서바이벌 게임도 있어.
M	Is the camp for all students?	남	캠프엔 모든 학생이 참가할 수 있니?
W	No, it's just for sophomores.	여	아니, 그건 2학년생만을 위한 거야.
M	Ah! How much does it cost?	남	아하! 비용은 얼마니?
W	It's $50. Do you want to apply?	여	50달러야. 지원하고 싶니?
M	Sure. It sounds fun.	남	물론이지. 재미있을 것 같아.

문제 해설 Survival Camp에 관해 기간, 장소, 활동, 참가 대상은 언급되었지만, ③ '모집 인원'은 언급되지 않았다.

어휘&어구 notice 안내문, 공고문 survival 생존 transfer 전학하다 sophomore 2학년생

수능 유형

09 담화 내용 일치

수능유형 체험	⑤	본문 24~25쪽
수능유형 연습	01 ④ 02 ③ 03 ③ 04 ④ 05 ④ 06 ④	

수능유형 체험 Moonlight Sonata Concert 홍보 [정답] ⑤

여 안녕하세요, 청취자 여러분과 모든 클래식 음악 애호가 여러분! 'Moonlight Sonata Concert'가 드디어 우리 시에 옵니다. 이 클래식 음악 콘서트는 일 년에 한 번 개최됩니다. 올해는 11월 23일 오후 7시에 열리니 여러분 달력에 표시해 주세요! 올해 콘서트는 Steinway에 서 진행되며, 베토벤의 위대한 작품들을 연주하는 음악가들이 출연합니다. 그들의 놀라운 연주는 여러분의 귀에 즐거움을 선사할 것입니다. 좌석은 단 300명에게만 한정되어 있으니, 이 특별한 두 시간 동안의 음악 체험에 참석할 기회를 놓치지 마세요. 오늘 티켓을 구매하세요!

| 문제 해설 | 여자는 클래식 음악 공연인 Moonlight Sonata Concert가 두 시간 동안의 특별한 음악 체험이라고 했으므로, 담화의 내용과 일치하지 않는 것은 ⑤ '공연은 세 시간 동안 진행된다.'이다. |
| 어휘&어구 | annually 일 년에 한 번, 연 1회 mark 표시를 하다 feature 출연하다 performance 연주, 공연 delight 즐거움을 주는 것 seating 좌석 (수) extraordinary 대단한, 비범한 |

수능유형 **연습**

01 Super Rabbit Princess 홍보   [정답] ④

W Hello, viewers. I'm Sam, a regular film critic on this channel. Today I'm talking about *Super Rabbit Princess*, which will be released on May 24. It's a fantasy, comedy movie that seems like it will be a delight to watch. It features entertaining dance scenes by the main character, Rita Rabbit. Directed by Steve Woods, this movie features the talented comedian Mary Jones as the voice of Rita Rabbit. And let me tell you about a special offer! If you book your ticket on the website www.superrabbitprincess.com by this Friday, you will receive a free movie poster. So grab this chance as soon as you can.

여 안녕하세요, 시청자 여러분. 저는 이 채널의 고정 영화 평론가인 Sam입니다. 오늘은 5월 24일에 개봉할 영화 *Super Rabbit Princess*에 관해 이야기하려고 합니다. 그것은 판타지 코미디 영화로, 그것을 관람하는 것은 큰 즐거움이 되리라 생각됩니다. 이 영화는 주인공 Rita Rabbit의 재미있는 춤 장면이 특징입니다. Steve Woods가 감독하였으며, 이 영화에서는 재능 있는 코미디언 Mary Jones가 Rita Rabbit의 목소리로 출연합니다. 그리고 특별한 혜택에 대해 알려 드리겠습니다! 이번 주 금요일까지 웹사이트인 www.superrabbitprincess.com에서 영화표를 예매하면, 여러분은 무료 영화 포스터를 받게 될 것입니다. 그러니 가능한 한 빨리 이 기회를 잡으세요.

| 문제 해설 | 여자는 5월 24일에 개봉하는 영화인 Super Rabbit Princess에서 코미디언인 Mary Jones가 주인공인 Rita Rabbit의 목소리를 연기했다고 했으므로, 담화의 내용과 일치하지 않는 것은 ④ '유명한 가수가 주인공 목소리로 출연한다.'이다. |
| 어휘&어구 | regular 일상의, 상시적인 critic 평론가 release (영화를) 개봉하다 feature 특징으로 하다, 주연으로 하다 direct (영화·연극 따위를) 감독하다 book 예매하다, 예약하다 |

02 Lantern Festival 홍보   [정답] ③

M Hello, River Town residents! I'm Brian Johnson from the River Town Cultural Association. I'm delighted to announce the upcoming Lantern Festival. This festival is a cherished annual tradition that celebrates a fascinating aspect of Chinese culture. It will take place over three days, starting on January 13th. Throughout the festival, our streets will be decorated with various colorful paper lanterns. And there will be fun puzzles on the lanterns that you and your family can try to solve! Lastly, I encourage you not to miss out on the delicious Chinese foods available for purchase at the event. See you there!

남 안녕하세요, River Town 주민 여러분! River Town 문화 협회에서 온 Brian Johnson입니다. 다가오는 Lantern Festival에 관해 안내하게 되어 기쁩니다. 이 축제는 중국 문화의 흥미로운 한 면을 기리는 소중한 연례행사입니다. 그것은 1월 13일에 시작하여 3일 동안 열릴 예정입니다. 축제 동안 내내 우리 거리는 다양한 색상의 종이 등으로 장식될 것입니다. 그리고 등에는 여러분과 여러분의 가족이 함께 풀어 볼 수 있는 재미있는 퍼즐이 있을 것입니다! 마지막으로, 행사에서 판매되는 맛있는 중국 음식을 놓치지 않도록 권장합니다. 그곳에서 뵙겠습니다!

| 문제 해설 | 남자는 중국 문화를 기리는 연례행사인 Lantern Festival에서 거리가 종이 등으로 장식될 것이라고 했으므로, 담화의 내용과 일치하지 않는 것은 ③ '거리마다 깃털로 만든 등으로 장식될 것이다.'이다. |

03 Clean-up Campaign 안내

[정답] ③

W Good morning, students! This is your vice principal, Ms. Taylor, with a brief announcement about the upcoming Clean-up Campaign. It takes place at city park next Saturday afternoon at 2 p.m. We'll first walk around and survey the park for 30 minutes. After that, we'll begin cleaning up the park by picking up garbage. To make this a successful experience, please keep the following precautions in mind. Remember to bring and wear your own gloves. And please use the designated trash bags or containers for different types of waste. Please be sure to collect all the waste in the designated area within the park. Let's work together to keep our precious environment clean.

여 학생 여러분, 좋은 아침입니다! 저는 여러분의 교감 선생님인 Taylor 선생님인데, 다가오는 Clean-up 캠페인에 관한 간단한 안내 말씀을 드리려고 합니다. 청소 캠페인은 다음 주 토요일 오후 2시에 city park에서 개최됩니다. 우리는 먼저 공원을 30분 동안 돌아다니며 살펴볼 것입니다. 그 후에는 쓰레기를 주워 공원을 청소하기 시작할 것입니다. 이것을 성공적인 경험으로 만들 수 있도록 다음의 사전 주의 사항을 명심해 주세요. 자기 장갑을 가져와서 착용하는 것을 잊지 마세요. 그리고 쓰레기의 여러 유형마다 지정된 쓰레기봉투나 용기를 사용하세요. 반드시 모든 쓰레기를 공원 내 지정된 구역에 모아 주세요. 소중한 환경을 깨끗하게 유지하기 위해 함께 노력합시다.

문제 해설 여자는 다음 주 토요일 공원에서 쓰레기를 줍는 Clean-up Campaign에서 자기 장갑을 가져와서 착용하라고 했으므로, 담화의 내용과 일치하지 않는 것은 ③ '참가자들에게 장갑을 지급할 것이다.'이다.

어휘&어구 brief 간단한 take place 개최되다 garbage 쓰레기 precaution 사전 주의 사항 designated 지정된 container 용기 precious 소중한

04 Ashley's Tea Class

[정답] ④

M Hello. I'm Ashley Thompson, a tea specialist. Are you interested in tea? Then come to Ashley's Tea Class. Ashley's tea workshops are educational yet full of fun with a combination of tea tasting and preparation activities. We hold a new class with a seasonal theme each month for two hours at Rosehill Hotel. This month's class will be held from 2 p.m. to 4 p.m. on March 20. The content of each class varies based on the season. This month we'll be featuring flower teas to celebrate the spring. During our hands-on classes, attendees taste three different kinds of tea and learn about their processing methods. Each class costs $50 per person. Space is limited to 20 attendees, so hurry up and reserve your spot. I hope to see you in class!

남 안녕하세요. 저는 차 전문가 Ashley Thompson입니다. 차에 관심이 있으십니까? 그러시다면 Ashley의 다도 수업에 오십시오. Ashley의 다도 워크숍은 교육적이지만 차 시음 및 준비 활동이 어우러져 아주 재미있습니다. 저희는 Rosehill 호텔에서 두 시간 동안 매달 계절에 맞는 주제를 가지고 새로운 수업을 엽니다. 이번 달 수업은 3월 20일 오후 2시부터 4시까지 열릴 것입니다. 각 수업의 내용은 계절에 따라 다릅니다. 이번 달에 저희는 봄을 기념하기 위해 꽃차를 특별히 선보일 것입니다. 체험 수업 중에 수강생들은 세 가지 다른 종류의 차를 맛보고 가공 방법에 대해 배웁니다. 각 수업 비용은 1인당 50달러입니다. 수강 인원이 20명으로 한정되어 있으니 서둘러 자리를 예약하십시오. 수업에서 만나기를 바랍니다!

문제 해설 남자는 Ashley's Tea Class를 홍보하면서 수업에서 수강생들이 세 가지 다른 종류의 차를 맛보게 된다고 했으므로, 담화의 내용과 일치하지 않는 것은 ④ '수강생들은 네 가지 다른 종류의 차를 맛보게 된다.'이다.

어휘&어구 specialist 전문가 educational 교육적인 combination 조합, 결합 theme 주제 content 내용 vary 다르다, 다양하다 feature 특징으로 하다 hands-on 체험의, 실습의, (말만 하지 않고) 직접 해 보는 attendee 수강생, 참석자

05 Urban Design Competition

[정답] ④

W Hello, Radio 22 listeners. I'm Emma Johnson from the Urban Development Corporation. I'm glad to announce the upcoming Urban Design Competition. In the competition, teams of students will compete to find the best way to use land. To register, teams need to submit an online proposal with their ideas of how to use land efficiently. The registration deadline is September 10th. The competition jury will select four finalist teams. Each finalist team will present their proposals to the jury on October 20th, and the jury will announce the winning team the next day. The winning team will receive $500, and the three other finalist teams will receive $200 each. For more information, visit our website. Thanks!

여 안녕하세요, Radio 22 청취자 여러분. 저는 Urban Development Corporation의 Emma Johnson입니다. 다가오는 Urban Design Competition을 알려 드리게 되어 기쁩니다. 경연 대회에서 학생들로 구성된 팀들이 토지를 사용할 최선의 방법을 찾기 위해 경쟁할 것입니다. 등록하려면 팀들은 어떻게 토지를 효율적으로 사용할 것인지에 대한 아이디어와 함께 온라인 제안서를 제출할 필요가 있습니다. 등록 마감일은 9월 10일입니다. 대회 심사 위원단이 결선에 진출할 네 팀을 선정할 것입니다. 각각의 결선 진출 팀은 10월 20일에 제안서를 심사 위원단에게 발표할 것이고, 심사 위원단은 다음 날 우승 팀을 공지할 것입니다. 우승 팀은 5백 달러를 받을 것이며, 나머지 결선 진출 세 팀은 각각 2백 달러를 받을 것입니다. 더 많은 정보를 원하시면, 저희 웹사이트를 방문해 주십시오. 감사합니다!

문제 해설 여자는 결선 진출 팀이 제안서를 발표한 다음 날 우승 팀이 공지될 것이라고 말했으므로, 담화의 내용과 일치하지 않는 것은 ④ '결선 진출 팀이 제안서를 발표한 날 우승 팀이 공지될 것이다.'이다.

어휘&어구 urban 도시의 corporation 회사 announce 알리다, 공지하다 upcoming 다가오는 competition (경연) 대회 register 등록하다 submit 제출하다 proposal 제안서 efficiently 효율적으로 deadline 마감 일자, 기한 jury 심사 위원단 finalist 결선 진출자

06 유아기 박람회

[정답] ④

M Good morning, Green City residents! I'm Darcy Young, activity director at the Green City Community Center. Do you have a child under the age of 5? If so, you don't want to miss the Early Childhood Fair. There, you'll be able to get information about early childhood education, child health and development, and community programs for children. You'll even be able to sign up for the programs for preschoolers. The first 50 children to arrive will receive a free gift, and there will be fun activities for children. And come hungry; there will be free snacks! The Early Childhood Fair will be held on October 24 from 11:00 a.m. to 1:00 p.m. at Larson Preschool. And the best part is the fair is free to attend! See you there!

남 좋은 아침입니다, Green City 주민 여러분! Green City 지역 사회 센터의 활동 담당자 Darcy Young입니다. 5살 미만의 아이가 있습니까? 그렇다면 유아기 박람회를 놓치지 마세요. 그곳에서, 여러분은 유아기 교육, 아동 건강과 발달, 그리고 아동을 위한 지역 사회 프로그램에 관한 정보를 얻을 수 있을 것입니다. 여러분은 심지어 취학 전 아동을 위한 프로그램에 등록할 수도 있을 것입니다. 먼저 도착한 50명의 아동은 무료 선물을 받게 될 것이고, 아동들을 위한 재미있는 활동도 있을 것입니다. 그리고 배고픈 상태로 오세요. 무료 간식이 있을 예정이니까요! 유아기 박람회는 10월 24일 오전 11시부터 오후 1시까지 Larson 유치원에서 열릴 것입니다. 그리고 가장 좋은 부분은 박람회에 무료로 참석할 수 있다는 것입니다! 거기서 뵙겠습니다!

문제 해설 유아기 박람회는 10월 24일 오전 11시부터 오후 1시까지 열린다고 했으므로 2시간 동안 진행된다. 따라서 담화의 내용과 일치하지 않는 것은 ④ '5시간 동안 진행된다.'이다.

어휘&어구 early childhood 유아기 sign up for ~에 등록하다 preschooler 취학 전의 아동 free 무료의

수능 유형 10 도표

수능유형 체험 | 사무실용 휴지통 구매

[정답] ②

남 Uptown Office Essentials에 오신 것을 환영합니다. 오늘 어떻게 도와드릴까요?

여 안녕하세요, 사무실 휴지통을 찾고 있는데요.

남 좋습니다. 이것들이 우리가 가지고 있는 것들입니다. 예산이 얼마나 됩니까?

여 20달러까지 쓸 수 있어요.

남 네. 그리고 소재는요?

여 저는 도자기를 좋아하지 않아요. 무거워서요.

남 그렇군요. 용량은 어떻습니까? 특정 크기를 찾으시나요?

여 음, 그것은 제 책상 밑에 맞아야 해요. 그래서 저는 5갤런 미만이어야 한다고 생각합니다.

남 알겠습니다. 마지막으로, 뚜껑이 있는 휴지통을 원하십니까?

여 네, 저는 그게 더 좋아요.

남 그럼 이것이 손님을 위한 것이네요.

여 감사합니다. 그걸로 살게요.

문제 해설 여자는 가격이 20달러까지이고 도자기로 된 것이 아니면서 용량이 5갤런보다 작고 뚜껑이 있는 모델을 골랐으므로, 여자가 구매할 휴지통은 ②이다.

어휘&어구 wastebasket 휴지통 budget 예산 material 소재, 물질 ceramic 도자기

수능유형 연습

01 천장 선풍기 구매

[정답] ④

M Honey, I think we should get a new ceiling fan for the living room.

W I agree. Let's look for one online.

M Sounds good. *[Typing sound]* How about this website? These ones are nice.

W I'm sure one of them will work. Well, I think the width should be at least 40 inches.

M I think so, too. And how much should we spend?

W Let's keep it under $200. What about the material?

M These wooden ones are really cool.

W Yeah. Either one would look great in the living room.

M Hmm. This one comes with a remote control. I think it would be better.

W Okay. Let's order it.

남 여보, 거실에 천장 선풍기를 새로 사야 할 것 같아요.

여 맞아요. 온라인으로 하나 찾아봅시다.

남 좋아요. *[타자 치는 소리]* 이 웹사이트는 어때요? 이것들이 좋네요.

여 그것들 중 하나가 틀림없이 도움이 될 거 같아요. 음, 나는 너비가 적어도 40인치는 되어야 한다고 생각해요.

남 나도 그렇게 생각해요. 그리고 우리가 얼마를 써야 하죠?

여 200달러보다 싼 것으로 해요. 소재는요?

남 이 나무로 된 것들이 정말 멋져요.

여 네. 둘 중 어느 것이라도 거실에 있으면 멋질 것 같아요.

남 음. 이것은 리모컨이 딸려 있어요. 그게 더 나을 것 같아요.

여 좋아요. 그걸로 주문합시다.

문제 해설 두 사람은 너비가 적어도 40인치이고, 200달러보다 싼 것이면서, 나무로 된 것이고, 리모컨이 딸려 있는 것을 골랐으므로, 두 사람이 주문할 천장 선풍기는 ④이다.

어휘&어구 ceiling fan 천장 선풍기 remote control 리모컨

---

02 아트 프린트 구매

[정답] ③

W Welcome to Johnson Art Gallery. What can I help you find today?

여 Johnson Art Gallery에 오신 것을 환영합니다. 오늘 무엇을 찾는 것을 도와드릴까요?

M	Hi, I'm looking for an art print for my living room.	남	안녕하세요, 거실에 놓을 아트 프린트를 찾고 있어요.
W	Great! Here, let me show you the ones we have in stock. Do you have a budget?	여	좋습니다! 여기, 재고가 있는 것들을 보여 드리겠습니다. 예산이 있나요?
M	Yes. I'd like to keep it under $100.	남	네. 100달러 미만으로 하고 싶습니다.
W	Okay. What size are you looking for?	여	네. 어떤 크기를 찾고 계시나요?
M	Something in the medium or large range.	남	중간 또는 큰 범위에 있는 것으로요.
W	All right. How about the subject matter?	여	알겠습니다. 주제는요?
M	I already have a landscape print in my bedroom, so I'd like something different.	남	제 침실에 이미 풍경화 프린트가 있어서, 저는 다른 것을 원해요.
W	Great. Would you like it to be framed?	여	좋습니다. 그것을 액자에 넣어 드릴까요?
M	Yes.	남	네.
W	In that case, this print is the one for you.	여	그렇다면, 이 프린트가 당신을 위한 것입니다.
M	Perfect! I'll take it.	남	완벽해요! 그걸로 살게요.

문제 해설 남자는 100달러 미만이면서, 크기는 중간 또는 큰 범위에 있고, 풍경화가 아니면서, 액자에 넣는 것을 골랐으므로, 남자가 구매할 아트 프린트는 ③이다.

어휘&어구 in stock 재고가 있는 budget 예산 range 범위 subject matter 주제 landscape 풍경(화)

03 파티 패키지 예약 [정답] ⑤

W	Hey, sweetie, I'm on the Happy Playzone website to reserve a party package for your birthday.	여	안녕, 얘야, 나는 Happy Playzone 웹사이트에서 네 생일을 위한 파티 패키지를 예약하려고 한단다.
M	Thank you so much, Mom.	남	정말 고마워요, 엄마.
W	No problem. How long would you like the party to last?	여	그래. 파티가 얼마나 오래 지속되기를 원하니?
M	Can it be at least two hours?	남	적어도 두 시간으로 할 수 있을까요?
W	Sure. How many friends are you inviting?	여	물론이야. 얼마나 많은 친구들을 초대할 거니?
M	I'm inviting at least 10.	남	적어도 10명은 초대할 거예요.
W	Okay. Then we'd better choose a package for 12 kids or more.	여	좋아. 그러면 12명 이상의 아이들을 위한 패키지를 선택해야겠구나.
M	And my friends and I love arcade games, so can we get a package with a lot of credits?	남	그리고 제 친구들과 저는 아케이드 게임을 정말 좋아하니까, 크레딧이 많이 있는 패키지를 살 수 있을까요?
W	Of course. How many credits would you like?	여	물론이야. 몇 크레딧이면 좋겠니?
M	Hmm. Can we have at least 100?	남	음. 적어도 100크레딧을 가질 수 있을까요?
W	Absolutely. All the party packages include pizza and drinks, but should we get one that also has snacks?	여	그럼. 모든 파티 패키지에는 피자와 음료가 포함되어 있는데, 간식도 포함된 것으로 할까?
M	Yeah. That'd be great!	남	네. 그거 정말 좋을 것 같아요!
W	All right. Let's reserve this one!	여	좋아. 이걸로 예약하자!

문제 해설 여자는 파티 시간이 적어도 두 시간이고, 12명 이상의 아이들을 위한 것으로, 게임 크레딧이 적어도 100개이고, 간식이 포함된 패키지를 골랐으므로, 여자가 예약할 파티 패키지는 ⑤이다.

어휘&어구 reserve 예약하다 last 지속되다 arcade game 아케이드 게임(오락실[게임 센터]에 있는 비디오[컴퓨터] 게임)

04 Georgia 동물원 프로그램 [정답] ④

W	Honey, what are you looking at?	여	여보, 뭘 보고 있어요?
M	The Georgia Zoo website. They have some really interesting programs for kids.	남	Georgia 동물원 웹사이트예요. 아이들을 위한 정말 흥미로운 프로그램들이 좀 있어요.
W	Oh, cool. Let me have a look. We should take our son Jimmy to one.	여	오, 좋아요. 내가 한번 볼게요. 우리 아들 Jimmy를 한 프로그램에 데리고 가야 해요.

M That's what I was thinking. Which one do you think seems best?

W We've done something similar to this elephant one before. Let's choose one of the others.

M Okay. Oh, Jimmy would like this one.

W But it's for children aged 10 and up. Jimmy is only 8.

M I didn't see that. So it's down to these three. I think going on a weekday would be better since it's summer vacation.

W I agree. Now we have these two options left.

M All right. Then how about the one in the afternoon?

W Well, I think the morning one would be better. It gets hot in the afternoon.

M You're right. Let's take Jimmy to that one.

남 나도 그렇게 생각하고 있었어요. 어떤 게 가장 좋을 것 같아요?

여 우리는 전에 이 코끼리 프로그램과 비슷한 것을 해 봤어요. 다른 것 중에서 하나를 고릅시다.

남 알겠어요. 오, Jimmy는 이것을 좋아할 거예요.

여 하지만 그것은 열 살 이상 어린이를 위한 거예요. Jimmy는 겨우 여덟 살이에요.

남 나는 그것을 못 봤어요. 그럼 이 세 가지가 남았네요. 여름 방학이라 평일에 가는 게 좋을 것 같아요.

여 동의해요. 이제 우리에게 이 두 개의 선택 사항이 남았네요.

남 좋아요. 그럼 오후에 있는 게 어때요?

여 음, 나는 오전 것이 더 나을 것 같아요. 오후에는 더워져요.

남 당신 말이 맞아요. Jimmy를 그 프로그램에 데려갑시다.

문제 해설 두 사람은 아들 Jimmy를 데리고 갈 프로그램으로 코끼리 관련 프로그램은 제외하고, 8세인 아들이 참여 가능하며, 평일 프로그램 중 오전에 있는 것으로 골랐으므로, 두 사람이 아들을 데리고 갈 프로그램은 ④이다.

어휘&어구 encounter 만남, 조우 tortoise 거북 feed 먹이, 사료

05 휴대용 바비큐 그릴 구입

[정답] ③

M Honey, I found a website that sells portable barbecue grills. We need one for our family camping trip next week.

W Okay, good. But remember we're on a tight budget.

M I know. That's why I'm not considering getting this one over $100.

W Yeah, that's too pricey. How big do you think the grill should be?

M I think we need one with a cooking surface of at least 150 square inches. We'll be cooking for 8 people.

W You're right.

M Should we get a gas or charcoal grill?

W I prefer charcoal because it adds a nice smoky flavor.

M But gas would be much easier and cleaner to use. And we wouldn't have to carry around a heavy bag of charcoal.

W That's true. Let's go with your opinion.

M Okay. Then between these remaining two, we need to choose the type of cooking grate. How about the one with an aluminum grate?

W Well, let's choose the other one. As far as I know, aluminum is not as strong as steel.

M All right.

남 여보, 휴대용 바비큐 그릴을 파는 웹사이트를 찾았어요. 다음 주에 가족 캠핑 여행을 위해 하나 필요해요.

여 그래요, 좋아요. 하지만 우리가 예산이 빠듯하다는 것을 기억해요.

남 나도 알아요. 그래서 100달러가 넘는 이걸 사는 건 고려하지 않고 있어요.

여 네, 그건 너무 비싸요. 그릴이 얼마나 커야 할 것 같아요?

남 조리면이 적어도 150평방인치인 것이 필요하다고 생각해요. 우리는 8인분 요리를 할 거잖아요.

여 당신 말이 맞아요.

남 가스 그릴로 할까요, 아니면 숯 그릴로 할까요?

여 나는 좋은 훈제 맛을 더해 주어서 숯을 선호해요.

남 하지만 가스가 사용하기 훨씬 더 쉽고 더 깨끗할 거예요. 그리고 무거운 숯 포대를 들고 다니지 않아도 될 거예요.

여 그 말이 맞아요. 당신 의견대로 합시다.

남 좋아요. 그러면 이 남은 둘 중에서, 우리는 조리용 불판의 종류를 선택해야 해요. 알루미늄 불판이 있는 것은 어때요?

여 음, 다른 쪽을 선택하죠. 내가 아는 한 알루미늄은 철만큼 강하지 않아요.

남 좋아요.

문제 해설 100달러가 넘지 않으면서 조리면의 크기는 적어도 150평방인치이고 가스 그릴이면서 알루미늄 불판이 아닌 것을 선택한다고 했으므로, 두 사람이 구입할 휴대용 바비큐 그릴은 ③이다.

어휘&어구 on a tight budget 예산이 빠듯한, 돈이 없는 grate 불판, 쇠살대

06 동물 캐릭터가 있는 크레용 세트

[정답] ③

M	Lisa, why are you looking at crayon sets online?
W	I'm buying my cousin a birthday present. She's turning 5. Which set do you think I should get?
M	Let's see. I think this one with 12 crayons is too small. There aren't enough crayons.
W	I agree. More is better.
M	Do you think she'll be happy with any of the animal characters?
W	Come to think of it, I doubt she'd like the set with bears. I'll get one of the others.
M	Okay. And this one is more expensive than the others.
W	Yeah, it's too expensive, so I'll buy one of these two.
M	Then the main difference is washable or not. Your cousin is pretty young, so maybe the washable set would be better.
W	I think you're right. She did draw on the wall once. So I'll order this one. Thanks for helping me.
M	No problem.

남	Lisa, 온라인으로 크레용 세트를 왜 보고 있는 거니?
여	사촌에게 생일 선물을 사 주려고. 그 아이는 5살이 되거든. 어떤 세트를 사야 할까?
남	어디 보자. 12개의 크레용이 있는 이건 너무 작은 것 같아. 크레용이 충분하지 않아.
여	나도 그렇게 생각해. 더 많은 것이 더 좋지.
남	그 애가 동물 캐릭터라면 어떤 것이라도 좋아할 것 같니?
여	생각해 보니, 그 애가 곰이 있는 세트를 좋아할 것 같지 않아. 다른 것 중 하나를 사야겠어.
남	알겠어. 그리고 이건 다른 것들보다 더 비싸구나.
여	그래, 그건 너무 비싸니까, 이 두 개 중 하나를 사야겠어.
남	그럼 주된 차이는 세척이 가능한지 아닌지야. 네 사촌은 꽤 어리기 때문에 세척이 가능한 세트가 더 나을 것 같아.
여	네 말이 맞는 것 같아. 그 애는 정말로 언젠가 벽에 그림을 그렸거든. 그럼 이것을 주문해야겠다. 도와줘서 고마워.
남	천만에.

문제 해설 여자는 사촌 동생을 위한 선물로 크레용 세트를 고르면서, 크레용이 12개 넘게 들어 있는 것, 곰 캐릭터가 아닌 것, 다른 것들보다 비싸지 않은 것, 그리고 세척이 가능한 것을 선택했다. 따라서 여자가 주문할 크레용 세트는 ③이다.

어휘&어구 come to think of it 생각해 보니   washable 세척이 가능한

수능 유형 11 짧은 대화의 응답

수능유형 **체험** | ④

수능유형 **연습** | 01 ⑤   02 ①   03 ①   04 ③   05 ②   06 ③

본문 28~29쪽

수능유형 체험 에세이 숙제

[정답] ④

남	Cassidy, 에세이 과제는 끝냈니?
여	아니, Daniel. 아직 시작도 안 했어. 좋은 주제를 생각하려고 애쓰고 있어.

남	나도 그래. 때때로 다른 사람과 아이디어에 관해 브레인스토밍을 하는 게 도움이 돼. 같이 작업하는 게 어때?
여	좋은 생각이야. 방과 후에 도서관에서 만나자.

문제 해설 여자가 아직 에세이 과제를 시작도 못 했고 좋은 주제를 생각하려고 애쓰고 있다고 하자, 이에 남자가 다른 사람과 아이디어에 관해 브레인스토밍을 하는 게 도움이 된다며 같이 작업하자고 제안하였으므로, 이에 대한 여자의 응답으로 가장 적절한 것은 ④ '좋은 생각이야. 방과 후에 도서관에서 만나자.'이다.
① 걱정하지 마. 글을 쓰기 전에 브레인스토밍을 해.
② 맞아. 우리는 팀워크 덕분에 성공했어.
③ 멋지다! 너는 멋진 주제를 선택한 것 같아.
⑤ 신경 쓰지 마. 나는 이미 에세이 과제를 마쳤어.

어휘&어구 assignment 과제   struggle to *do* ~하려고 애쓰다   brainstorm 브레인스토밍하다(다른 사람과 머리를 모으고 이야기를 나누다)

01 책의 결말

[정답] ⑤

W David, have you finished reading the book I lent you last week?

M Yes, I have. I really enjoyed it. Thanks for lending it to me.

W I'm glad you liked it. What did you think about the ending?

M I really liked it. It was a great way to finish the story.

여 David, 제가 지난주에 빌려준 책 다 읽었어요?

남 네, 다 읽었어요. 정말 재미있었어요. 빌려주셔서 감사합니다.

여 마음에 드셨다니 다행이에요. 결말에 대해 어떻게 생각했어요?

남 정말 좋았어요. 그것은 이야기를 끝내는 훌륭한 방법이었어요.

문제 해설 여자가 빌려준 책을 다 읽고 마음에 들었다고 말하는 남자에게 여자가 결말에 대해 어떻게 생각했는지 물어보았으므로, 이에 대한 남자의 응답으로 가장 적절한 것은 ⑤ '정말 좋았어요. 그것은 이야기를 끝내는 훌륭한 방법이었어요.'이다.

① 죄송해요. 저는 당신이 그것을 조금 수정하기를 권해요.
② 잘 선택했어요. 기꺼이 그 책을 빌려드릴게요.
③ 맞아요. 그 책은 조금 실망스러웠어요.
④ 확실하지 않아요. 저는 아직 결말을 다 쓰지 못했어요.

어휘&어구 lend 빌려주다 ending 결말

02 영화 관람 전 저녁 식사

[정답] ①

M Honey, how about going to see the movie, "Tommy's Adventure" today?

W I'd love to, but the only available tickets are for the late show.

M That works out perfectly. We can have a nice dinner before the movie.

W Great idea. I'll reserve a table at a restaurant.

남 여보, 오늘 영화 '토미의 모험'을 보러 가는 건 어때요?

여 그러고 싶지만, 이용 가능한 표는 늦은 시간 상영표뿐이에요.

남 그거 완벽하게 들어맞는데요. 우리가 영화 보기 전에 맛있는 저녁을 먹을 수 있어요.

여 좋은 생각이에요. 음식점에 자리를 예약할게요.

문제 해설 영화를 보러 가자고 제안하는 남자에게 여자는 영화를 보고 싶지만 늦은 시간에 상영하는 표밖에 없다고 하고, 이에 남자가 좋아하며 영화 보기 전에 맛있는 저녁을 먹을 수 있다고 했으므로, 이에 대한 여자의 응답으로 가장 적절한 것은 ① '좋은 생각이에요. 음식점에 자리를 예약할게요.'이다.

② 알겠어요. 대신 볼 다른 영화를 찾아봅시다.
③ 아닌 것 같아요. 그 영화는 정말 환상적이었어요.
④ 동의해요. 영화를 보고 나서 그다음에 식사를 하는 게 더 나아요.
⑤ 말도 안 돼요. 저는 더 일찍 상영하는 걸 보기 위해 저녁을 거르지 않을 거예요.

어휘&어구 available 이용 가능한 work out (일이) 들어맞다, 잘 풀리다

03 온라인 언어 학습

[정답] ①

W I'm interested in learning a new language, but I'm not sure where to start.

M What fits your learning style better: taking a class in person or learning online?

W I prefer online learning. I wonder if there are any websites that offer free language courses.

M I know of a few. I'll send you the links to them.

여 저는 새로운 언어를 배우는 것에 관심이 있지만, 어디서부터 시작해야 할지 잘 모르겠어요.

남 수업을 직접 듣는 것과 온라인으로 배우는 것 중에 당신의 학습 스타일에 더 잘 맞는 것은 무엇인가요?

여 저는 온라인 학습을 선호해요. 무료 어학 강좌를 제공하는 웹사이트가 있는지 궁금해요.

남 제가 몇 군데 알아요. 거기로 연결되는 링크를 보내 줄게요.

문제 해설 여자는 온라인으로 무료 어학 강좌를 제공하는 웹사이트가 있는지 궁금해하였으므로, 이에 대한 남자의 응답으로 가장 적절한 것은 ① '제가 몇 군데 알아요. 거기로 연결되는 링크를 보내 줄게요.'이다.

② 그렇지는 않아요. 당신이 직접 수업을 듣는 것을 선호하다니 놀랍군요.

③ 고마워요. 제가 보고 어떤 것이 저에게 가장 잘 어울리는지 알아볼게요.

④ 물론이에요. 지역 어학원에서 수업을 들을 수 있도록 노력할게요.

⑤ 아니요. 당신의 학습 스타일은 당신이 언어를 배우는 방법에 영향을 주지 않아요.

어휘&어구 fit ~에 맞다   in person 직접   prefer 선호하다

---

04 합창 대회 연습
[정답] ③

M Mom, could you wake me up at 6, instead of 7, tomorrow morning? I have to leave home at 7.	**남** 엄마, 내일 아침에 7시 대신 6시에 저를 깨워 주실 수 있나요? 7시에 집에서 출발해야 해요.
W Why do you need to go to school that early?	**여** 왜 그렇게 일찍 학교에 가야 하니?
M The school choir competition is next week, so I have to go to school an hour earlier than usual for choir practice.	**남** 학교 합창 대회가 다음 주에 있어서, 합창 연습을 위해서 평소보다 한 시간 더 일찍 학교에 가야 해요.
W Okay. I'll knock on your door at six o'clock.	**여** 알았어. 6시에 네 방문을 두드릴게.

문제 해설 남자는 여자에게 학교에 일찍 가기 위해서 6시에 깨워 달라고 부탁했으므로, 이에 대한 여자의 응답으로 가장 적절한 것은 ③ '알았어. 6시에 네 방문을 두드릴게.'이다.

① 합창 연습 후에 너를 차로 집까지 데려다줄게.

② 너는 대회에서 우승하기 위해서 최선을 다했어.

④ 합창 대회에 나를 초대해 주어서 고마워.

⑤ 아침 일찍 운동하는 것은 너에게 좋아.

어휘&어구 choir competition 합창 대회

---

05 요리 배우기
[정답] ②

W Oliver, dinner was delicious. I had no idea you were such a good cook.	**여** Oliver, 저녁이 아주 맛있었어. 네가 그렇게 훌륭한 요리사인 줄 전혀 몰랐어.
M I'm glad you liked it. I've been learning how to cook from my dad recently. He's a chef at a hotel restaurant.	**남** 네가 그것이 좋았다니 기뻐. 최근에 아빠한테 요리하는 법을 배우고 있어. 아빠가 호텔 식당의 요리사이시거든.
W That's so cool. I wonder how I can learn to cook like you.	**여** 그거 아주 멋지네. 어떻게 하면 너처럼 요리를 배울 수 있을지 궁금하네.
M You can join me when my dad teaches me.	**남** 아빠가 나를 가르치실 때 네가 나랑 함께 해도 돼.

문제 해설 남자가 호텔 식당의 요리사인 아빠에게서 최근에 요리하는 법을 배우고 있다고 하자, 여자는 남자처럼 요리를 배울 수 있는지 궁금하다고 말하고 있으므로, 이에 대한 남자의 응답으로 가장 적절한 것은 ② '아빠가 나를 가르치실 때 네가 나랑 함께 해도 돼.'이다.

① 그러면 내가 아빠에게 호텔에서 (사람을) 고용하는지 여쭤볼게.

③ 음, 내가 직접 어떤 것도 요리한 적이 없어.

④ 너는 호텔에 취직하지 말아야 한다고 생각해.

⑤ 아빠는 특별한 경우에 나에게 요리를 부탁하셔.

어휘&어구 delicious 아주 맛있는   recently 최근에   hire 고용하다   occasion 경우, 행사

---

06 저렴한 항공편 찾아보기
[정답] ③

M Honey, I tried to book train tickets to visit your parents next weekend, but they're sold out.	**남** 여보, 다음 주말에 당신 부모님을 방문하기 위해 기차표를 예매하려고 했는데, 매진이에요.
W Then how about flying? I'm sure there are flights available and tickets are really cheap nowadays.	**여** 그럼 비행기로 가는 것은 어때요? 틀림없이 항공편을 구할 수 있을 것이고 요즘은 표도 정말 저렴해요.
M Good idea. Can you look for some?	**남** 좋은 생각이에요. 당신이 좀 찾아봐 줄 수 있어요?
W Sure, I'll check a website with cheap flights I know of.	**여** 물론이죠, 내가 알고 있는 저렴한 항공편이 있는 웹사이트를 확인해 볼게요.

12 긴 대화의 응답

본문 30~31쪽

수능유형 체험 | ④

수능유형 연습 | 01 ② 02 ② 03 ⑤ 04 ① 05 ⑤ 06 ③

수능유형 체험 할머니의 요리법

[정답] ④

여 아빠, 제가 다락방에서 뭘 찾았는지 보세요!

남 뭐니?

여 할머니의 오래된 요리법 책이에요. 할머니의 모든 비밀 요리법이 들어 있어요.

남 아, 그래. 그 책으로 놀라운 음식을 요리하시곤 했지.

여 여기 할머니의 사과파이 요리법이에요. 너무 맛있었다고 들었어요. 제가 그걸 재현할 수 있으면 좋겠어요.

남 한번 해 봐. 의미 있는 경험이 될 거야.

여 음, 제가 망칠까 봐 걱정이에요. 저는 제 요리 실력에 자신이 없어요.

남 걱정하지 마. 네가 그저 요리법만 따르면 잘 해낼 것이라고 확신해.

여 그럴지도 모르지만, 절 좀 도와주시겠어요?

남 물론이지! 이번 주말에 함께 만들자. 내가 재료 구입도 도와줄게.

여 감사해요. 할머니의 파이를 빨리 되살리고 싶어요.

문제 해설 여자는 다락방에서 찾은 할머니의 요리법 책으로 할머니의 사과파이를 재현해 보고 싶어 하지만 요리 실력에 자신이 없어서 남자에게 도움을 요청한다. 이에 남자가 이번 주말에 함께 만들자고 하고 재료 구입도 도와주겠다고 했으므로, 이에 대한 여자의 응답으로 가장 적절한 것은 ④ '감사해요. 할머니의 파이를 빨리 되살리고 싶어요.'이다.

① 걱정하지 마세요. 제가 혼자 구울 수 있다고 확신해요.

② 좋아요. 다락방에서 레시피 책을 찾아봐요.

③ 절 믿으세요. 저도 요리 정말 잘하는 거 아시잖아요.

⑤ 죄송해요. 지금은 정말 파이를 만들고 싶지 않아요.

어휘&어구 recipe 요리법   meal 음식   recreate 재현하다   give it a try 한번 해 보다, 시도하다   meaningful 의미 있는   confident 자신이 있는   ingredient 재료

수능유형 연습

01 서점 방문

[정답] ②

W Honey, I feel like having Mexican food. Do you know of any good restaurants?

M I heard there's a new Mexican restaurant downtown.

W I'd love to try it! Shall we go there now?

M Let me check.... Oh, it looks like they're on break until 5 p.m.

W It's only 4 now.

여 여보, 나는 멕시코 음식이 먹고 싶어요. 아는 괜찮은 식당이 있나요?

남 시내에 새로운 멕시코 음식점이 있다고 들었어요.

여 꼭 가 보고 싶어요! 지금 거기로 가 볼까요?

남 확인해 볼게요…. 아, 그 음식점이 오후 5시까지 쉬는 것 같아요.

여 이제 겨우 4시예요.

남 영업하고 있는 음식점에 대신 갈까요?

여 아니요. 그 새로운 음식점에 꼭 가 보고 싶어요.

M	Shall we go to a restaurant that's open instead?	남	그럼 기다리는 동안 식당 근처에 있는 서점에 가는 게 어때요?
W	No. I really want to try the new restaurant.	여	좋은 생각이에요.
M	Then how about we go to the bookstore near the restaurant while we wait?	남	네. 시간을 보내는 재미있는 방법일 거예요.
W	That's a great idea.	여	좋은 계획이네요. 그리고 우리는 읽을 흥미로운 책을 발견할 수도 있어요.
M	Yeah. That should be a fun way to pass the time.	남	<u>좋아요. 그럼 서점으로 먼저 갑시다.</u>
W	Sounds like a plan. And we might discover an interesting book to read.		
M	Okay. Let's head to the bookstore first then.		

문제 해설 여자는 새로운 멕시코 음식점에 가 보고 싶어 하지만 아직 영업이 시작하기까지는 한 시간 정도 남은 상황으로, 남자가 기다리는 동안 식당 근처 서점으로 가는 게 어떤지 제안하고, 이에 여자가 좋은 계획이라고 말했으므로, 이에 대한 남자의 응답으로 가장 적절한 것은 ② '좋아요. 그럼 서점으로 먼저 갑시다.'이다.
① 놀랄 일도 아니에요. 거기 음식은 정말 맛있어요.
③ 아닐 거예요. 식당 근처에 카페가 없어요.
④ 안됐군요. 정말로 그 새로운 식당에 가 보고 싶었어요.
⑤ 문제없어요. 영업하는 다른 식당을 찾아볼게요.

어휘&어구 on break 쉬는   pass the time 시간을 보내다   discover 발견하다

02 토론 동아리 동영상

[정답] ②

M	I'm worried that our debate club hasn't attracted many new members lately.	남	최근에 우리 토론 동아리에 새로운 회원들이 많이 모이지 않아서 걱정이에요.
W	Me too. I think students think it sounds boring.	여	저도요. 학생들은 그게 지루하게 들린다고 생각하는 것 같아요.
M	I think you're right. Then how about creating a funny video about our club?	남	당신 말이 맞는 것 같아요. 그럼 우리 동아리에 대한 재미있는 동영상을 만들어 보는 건 어때요?
W	That's a great idea! We can include some of the funny moments we've had during debates.	여	좋은 생각이에요! 토론하는 동안 있었던 재미있는 순간들을 포함할 수 있어요.
M	Yeah, and we can share the video on social media.	남	네, 그리고 우리는 소셜 미디어에서 동영상을 공유할 수 있죠.
W	Perfect! And we can all share it with our friends, too.	여	완벽해요! 그리고 우리 모두가 그것을 친구들과 공유할 수도 있어요.
M	It'll help spread the word. Then what clips should we include in the video?	남	그건 입소문을 내는 데 도움이 될 거예요. 그럼 동영상에 어떤 클립을 넣을까요?
W	How about discussing that at the club meeting next week instead of deciding it ourselves?	여	그건 우리가 직접 결정하지 말고 다음 주 동아리 회의에서 논의하는 게 어때요?
M	Why?	남	왜요?
W	That way, we can gather other members' ideas, too.	여	그래야 다른 회원들의 아이디어도 모을 수 있어요.
M	Good point. So, you mean two heads are better than one, right?	남	좋은 지적이에요. 그러니까, 백지장도 맞들면 낫다는 뜻이죠, 그렇죠?
W	<u>Exactly. That way, we can include a variety of content.</u>	여	<u>맞아요. 그렇게 하면 다양한 콘텐츠를 포함할 수 있어요.</u>

문제 해설 토론 동아리에 새로운 회원이 많이 모이지 않아서 걱정인 남자와 여자가 동아리에 대한 재미있는 동영상을 만들어서 공유할 계획을 세운다. 동영상에 어떤 클립을 넣을지 묻는 남자에게 여자는 다음 주 동아리 회의에서 논의해서 다른 회원의 아이디어도 모을 수 있다고 말하고, 이에 남자가 좋은 지적이라고 하며 백지장도 맞들면 낫다는 뜻인지 물었으므로, 이에 대한 여자의 응답으로 가장 적절한 것은 ② '맞아요. 그렇게 하면 다양한 콘텐츠를 포함할 수 있어요.'이다.
① 네. 더 좋은 아이디어를 얻기 위해서는 더 많은 동영상을 봐야 해요.
③ 맞아요. 당신이 그 동영상을 온라인으로 공유한 건 사려 깊었어요.
④ 당신이 한 말을 들었어요. 당신의 생각은 토론에서 빛났어요.
⑤ 그렇지는 않아요. 다른 회원들의 제안을 받아들이지 맙시다.

어휘&어구 debate 토론   attract (사람을) 끌어들이다   spread the word 입소문을 내다   clip 클립(필름 중 일부만 따로 떼어서 보여 주는 부분)   Two heads are better than one. 백지장도 맞들면 낫다.[한 사람이 하는 것보다는 두 사람이 하는 것이 낫다.]

03 가족과의 산책　　　　　　　　　　　　　　　　　　　　[정답] ⑤

W	Hey, Joe. Is something on your mind?
M	Yeah, I've been worrying about my family lately. We're not as close as we used to be.
W	Why is that?
M	It's mainly because of our busy schedules. Everyone's caught up in their own routines.
W	I understand how that can be tough. Maybe you should plan regular family activities together.
M	That's a good idea, but it's so hard to find a suitable time.
W	Then how about starting with something simple like taking a walk after dinner?
M	That sounds nice. But every day sounds like a lot.
W	Well, you could make it a weekly tradition. Try taking a walk after dinner every Sunday.
M	That's a good compromise. And maybe we can walk different routes each week to keep it interesting.
W	Right. It'll be a great way to talk with each other and enjoy spending time together.
M	You're right. It'll definitely help us reconnect as a family.

여	안녕하세요, Joe. 무슨 마음에 걸리는 일이라도 있으세요?
남	네, 저는 최근 가족에 대해 걱정해 왔어요. 우리는 예전만큼 가깝지 않아요.
여	왜 그런가요?
남	주로 우리의 바쁜 일정 때문이죠. 모든 사람들이 각자의 일과에 사로잡혀 있어요.
여	그게 얼마나 힘든지 이해해요. 아마도 당신은 규칙적인 가족 활동을 함께 계획해야 해요.
남	좋은 생각이지만, 적당한 시간을 찾기가 너무 어려워요.
여	그럼 저녁 식사 후에 산책하는 것과 같은 간단한 것부터 시작하는 게 어때요?
남	좋네요. 하지만 매일은 많은 것 같아요.
여	음, 주간 전통으로 만들 수도 있어요. 매주 일요일 저녁 식사 후에 산책을 해 보세요.
남	좋은 절충안이군요. 그리고 흥미를 유지하기 위해 우리가 매주 다른 길을 걸을 수도 있어요.
여	네. 서로 이야기하고 함께 시간 보내는 것을 즐기는 좋은 방법이 될 거예요.
남	맞아요. 우리가 가족으로서 다시 연결되는 데 그것이 분명히 도움이 될 거예요.

문제 해설 가족이 서로 멀어진 것에 대해 걱정하는 남자에게 여자는 가족과 함께 매주 일요일 저녁 식사 후에 산책을 해 볼 것을 제안하고, 이에 남자가 수긍한다. 여자가 그것이 서로 이야기하고 함께 시간 보내는 것을 즐기는 좋은 방법이 될 것이라고 말했으므로, 이에 대한 남자의 응답으로 가장 적절한 것은 ⑤ '맞아요. 우리가 가족으로서 다시 연결되는 데 그것이 분명히 도움이 될 거예요.'이다.
① 아닌 것 같아요. 저는 매일 산책하는 것을 더 좋아해요.
② 행운을 빌어요. 저는 당신의 가족이 산책을 즐기길 바랍니다.
③ 걱정하지 마세요. 그 길에 익숙해지도록 최선을 다할게요.
④ 죄송합니다. 저는 일보다는 가족에게 집중해야 해요.

어휘&어구 on one's mind 마음에 걸리는　lately 최근　be caught up in ~에 사로잡히다　suitable 적당한　tradition 전통　compromise 절충안, 타협　route 길, 경로

04 옛 주소로 배달된 책　　　　　　　　　　　　　　　　　[정답] ①

M	Mom, did I get a package delivered today?
W	No, you didn't. What did you order?
M	A book for my physics class. I need it for the first day of class next Monday.
W	When did you order it?
M	I ordered it last week, so it should've arrived by now.
W	Are you sure you didn't order it to our old address? It hasn't been long since we moved into this house.
M	I don't think so.
W	Check the website where you ordered the book.
M	Okay. [Typing sound] Oh, no. I added the new address in my profile, but I didn't select it when I ordered.
W	Oh, dear. The book must have been delivered to our old house. Do you want me to check with the people living there?

남	엄마, 오늘 저한테 배달된 소포가 있나요?
여	아니, 없어. 뭘 주문했니?
남	제 물리 수업 교재예요. 다음 월요일 수업 첫날에 필요해요.
여	언제 주문했니?
남	지난주에 주문했으니까, 지금쯤 도착했어야 해요.
여	너는 그것을 우리 옛 주소로 주문하지 않은 것이 확실하니? 우리가 이 집으로 이사 온 지 얼마 안 됐잖아.
남	그런 것 같지 않아요.
여	네가 책을 주문한 웹사이트를 확인해 봐.
남	알았어요. [타자 치는 소리] 오, 이런. 제 프로필에 새 주소를 추가했는데, 주문할 때 그것을 선택하지 않았어요.
여	오, 저런. 그 책이 우리 옛집으로 배달된 것이 틀림없어. 그곳에 사는 사람들에게 확인해 줄까?
남	그게 좋을 것 같아요. 만약 그분들이 그것을 가지고 있다면, 제가 그것을 가지러 갈게요. 엄마가 그분들의 전화번호를 가지고 있어요?

M That'd be great. If they have it, I'll go pick it up. Do you have their phone number?

W Of course. I'll call and ask if the book is there.

여 물론이지. 내가 전화해서 책이 거기 있는지 물어볼게.

문제 해설 남자가 주문한 책이 옛집으로 배달되었고, 여자가 옛집에 지금 사는 사람들에게 확인해 준다고 하자 남자는 그 사람들의 전화번호를 알고 있는지 묻고 있다. 따라서 남자의 마지막 말에 대한 여자의 응답으로 가장 적절한 것은 ① '물론이지. 내가 전화해서 책이 거기 있는지 물어볼게.'이다.

② 응, 있어. 우리는 전화로 그 책을 주문할 수 있어.

③ 나한테는 없는 것 같아. 그들이 이사를 오면 내가 그들의 전화번호를 물어볼게.

④ 아니, 없어. 하지만 배달 기사가 주소를 알고 있다고 확신해.

⑤ 물론이지. 그들이 방금 전화해서 책을 가지러 오겠다고 했어.

어휘&어구 package 소포, 꾸러미, 포장물 deliver 배달하다 profile 프로필, 개요, 약력 select 선택하다

05 자녀가 야채를 좋아하게 하는 방법   [정답] ⑤

W Peter, is everything okay? It looks like something's on your mind.

M Hi, Jennifer. Yeah, I've been trying to get my son to eat more vegetables, but nothing has worked.

W Have you tried gardening together?

M No. Do you think that'll work?

W It could. My son didn't like vegetables when he was young. So I started a small vegetable garden in our backyard that we worked on and he started to eat them.

M That's good.

W He even started working in the garden when I wasn't home.

M But I live in an apartment, without a yard.

W Then, you can make a small garden on your apartment balcony.

M Oh, that's a good idea. Maybe I should try that.

W Why not? Just try it and tell me if it works out or not.

M Okay. I'll let you know if my son starts eating vegetables.

여 Peter, 괜찮아요? 뭔가 걱정거리가 있는 것 같아요.

남 안녕하세요, Jennifer. 그래요, 제 아들에게 야채를 더 먹이려고 애써 왔는데, 아무것도 효과가 없었어요.

여 함께 텃밭 가꾸기를 해 본 적이 있나요?

남 아뇨. 그것이 효과가 있을까요?

여 그럴 수도 있어요. 제 아들이 어렸을 때 야채를 좋아하지 않았거든요. 그래서 저는 뒤뜰에 우리가 작업하는 작은 야채 텃밭을 시작했고 그는 야채를 먹기 시작했어요.

남 그거 좋네요.

여 제가 집에 없을 때, 그는 심지어 텃밭에서 일하기 시작했어요.

남 하지만 저는 아파트에 살아서 뜰이 없어요.

여 그러면, 아파트 발코니에 작은 텃밭을 만들 수 있어요.

남 오, 그거 좋은 생각이군요. 시도해 봐야겠네요.

여 그러세요. 한번 해 보고 좋게 진행되는지 아닌지를 말해 줘요.

남 좋아요. 제 아들이 야채를 먹기 시작하면 알려 줄게요.

문제 해설 아들에게 야채를 더 먹일 수 있는 방법에 대해 고민하는 남자에게 여자는 아들과 함께 텃밭 가꾸기를 시도한 후 좋게 진행되는지 아닌지를 말해 줄 것을 요청했으므로, 이에 대한 남자의 응답으로 가장 적절한 것은 ⑤ '좋아요. 제 아들이 야채를 먹기 시작하면 알려 줄게요.'이다.

① 네. 이것이 그가 야채를 먹지 않는 이유예요.

② 미안해요. 저는 단지 작은 야채 텃밭을 가지고 있어요.

③ 물론이죠. 당신은 제 뒤뜰에서 야채를 기를 수 있어요.

④ 당신이 그것을 하려고 한다면 텃밭용 도구가 필요해요.

어휘&어구 yard 뜰, 마당

06 좋은 목적을 위한 쇼핑   [정답] ③

M Hi, Jane. I like your new sunglasses.

W Thanks. They're made of plastic waste gathered from the ocean. I bought them from a non-profit organization.

M Wow, they make sunglasses from trash? That's amazing.

W The organization uses the profits to clean up ocean waste.

남 안녕, Jane. 네 새 선글라스가 마음에 든다.

여 고마워. 이건 바다로부터 모은 플라스틱 쓰레기로 만들어졌어. 비영리 단체에서 그것을 구입했지.

남 와, 쓰레기로 선글라스를 만든다고? 그거 놀랍다.

여 그 단체는 이윤을 해양 쓰레기를 청소하는 데 사용해.

남 그거 멋진데! 그러니까 넌 구매를 해서 좋은 목적을 지지하는 거구

M	That's cool! So you're supporting a good cause by making your purchase. How did you find that organization?
W	From my social studies class. I learned about some organizations that make products that support good causes, so I searched on my own and found this one.
M	Great! You know how much I love shopping. If I can donate to a good cause and shop at the same time, I'll love it even more.
W	I know what you mean. How about looking for an organization that supports a good cause you're interested in?
M	Great idea. I'm interested in animal rights.
W	Then, try to find some products that help animals.

나. 그 단체는 어떻게 알았니?

여 사회 수업을 통해서. 좋은 목적을 지지하는 제품을 만드는 단체들에 대해 좀 알게 돼서, 스스로 조사해 보고 이것을 발견했어.

남 훌륭하다! 넌 내가 쇼핑을 얼마나 좋아하는지 알지. 좋은 목적에 기부하는 일과 쇼핑을 동시에 할 수 있다면 난 그걸 훨씬 더 좋아하게 될 거야.

여 무슨 말인지 알아. 네가 관심이 있는 좋은 목적을 지지하는 단체를 찾아보는 게 어때?

남 좋은 생각이야. 난 동물 권리에 관심이 있어.

여 그럼, 동물을 돕는 제품들을 좀 찾아봐.

문제 해설 남자가 여자로부터 좋은 목적을 지지하는 제품을 만드는 비영리 단체들에 대한 이야기를 듣고, 기부하는 일과 쇼핑을 동시에 할 수 있다면 훨씬 더 좋으며 자신은 동물의 권리에 관심이 있다고 말하고 있다. 따라서 남자의 마지막 말에 대한 여자의 응답으로 가장 적절한 것은 ③ '그럼, 동물을 돕는 제품들을 좀 찾아봐.'이다.

① 그것은 동물의 권리를 위한 의미 있는 행사였어.

② 넌 바다를 더 깨끗하게 만들기 위한 기금을 모금할 수 있어.

④ 네가 그런 단체들을 도와왔다는 걸 알게 돼서 정말 기뻐.

⑤ 너의 연구가 내 사회 수업 프로젝트에 도움이 됐어.

어휘&어구 non-profit 비영리의 organization 단체 trash 쓰레기 profit 이윤 support 지지하다 cause 목적, 대의 purchase 구매 social studies (학교 교과로서의) 사회 donate 기부하다 raise 모으다, 모금하다

수능 유형

(13) 상황에 적절한 말

본문 32~33쪽

수능유형 체험 | ②

수능유형 연습 | 01 ① 02 ③ 03 ② 04 ③ 05 ④ 06 ⑤

수능유형 체험 온라인 과정 진행

[정답] ②

여 Ellie는 의사소통에 관한 온라인 과정을 가르치고 있습니다. 오늘 수업에서 그녀는 의사소통에 있어 몸짓 언어의 중요성에 관해 가르칩니다. 수업을 시작할 때, 그녀는 몇몇 학생들이 카메라를 끈 것을 알아차립니다. 그녀가 계획한 주요 활동 중 하나는 학생들이 서로의 몸짓 언어를 관찰하고 해석하는 것에 초점을 맞추고 있습니다. 이 활동을 하기 위해서, 그들은 화면에서 서로를 볼 수 있어야 합니다. 그래서 Ellie는 학생들에게 카메라를 켜 달라고 정중히 요청하기를 원합니다. 이런 상황에서 Ellie는 학생들에게 뭐라고 말하겠습니까?

Ellie 모두 카메라를 켜 주시길 정중히 부탁드립니다.

문제 해설 의사소통에 관한 온라인 과정을 가르치는 Ellie가 카메라를 끈 학생들에게 카메라를 켜 달라고 정중히 요청하고 싶어 하는 상황이다. 따라서 Ellie가 학생들에게 할 말로 가장 적절한 것은 ② '모두 카메라를 켜 주시길 정중히 부탁드립니다.'이다.

① 모바일 기기를 꺼 주시겠습니까?

③ 모두 마이크 볼륨을 조금만 높여 주시겠습니까?

④ 인터넷이 안정적으로 연결되어 있는지 확실히 해 주십시오.

⑤ 여러분 모두 제 몸짓 언어를 관찰해 주시길 요청하고 싶습니다.

어휘&어구 communication 의사소통 notice 알아차리다 observe 관찰하다 interpret 해석하다 respectfully 정중히 request 요청하다

01 아이의 학습 속도
[정답] ①

M Amy has a 10-year-old son named Nicholas. She is concerned because he's not making much progress in math. She often compares his abilities to those of other children his age, which worries her even more. Amy shares her concerns with her friend Jason, who is an elementary school teacher. He has a really good understanding of child development. He thinks that Amy doesn't have to worry because children have different learning styles and strengths and that she shouldn't compare Nicholas to others. So Jason wants to tell Amy that all children learn at their own pace. In this situation, what would Jason most likely say to Amy?

Jason Each child has their own learning speed.

남 Amy에게는 Nicholas라는 이름의 10살짜리 아들이 있습니다. 그녀는 그가 수학에서 많은 발전을 이루지 못하고 있기 때문에 걱정하고 있습니다. 그녀는 종종 그의 능력을 그의 또래의 다른 아이들의 능력과 비교하는데, 이것은 그녀를 더욱더 걱정스럽게 합니다. Amy는 초등학교 선생님인 친구 Jason과 자신의 고민을 공유합니다. 그는 아동 발달에 대한 이해가 정말 뛰어납니다. 그는 아이들은 학습 스타일과 강점이 서로 다르기 때문에 Amy가 걱정할 필요가 없고 그녀가 Nicholas를 다른 아이들과 비교하면 안 된다고 생각합니다. 그래서 Jason은 Amy에게 모든 아이들이 자신만의 속도로 배운다고 말하고 싶어 합니다. 이런 상황에서 Jason은 Amy에게 뭐라고 말하겠습니까?

Jason <u>모든 아이에게는 자신만의 학습 속도가 있어요.</u>

문제 해설 아들인 Nicholas가 수학 학습이 느린 것을 걱정하며 그를 다른 아이들과 종종 비교하는 Amy에게 Jason이 모든 아이들이 자신만의 속도로 배운다고 말하고 싶어 하는 상황이다. 따라서 Jason이 Amy에게 할 말로 가장 적절한 것은 ① '모든 아이에게는 자신만의 학습 속도가 있어요.'이다.
② 매일 수학 문제를 푸는 것은 중요해요.
③ 그의 수학 선생님과 대화해 보는 것을 고려해 보셔야 해요.
④ 수학에 대한 긍정적인 태도를 기르는 데 집중하세요.
⑤ 명확하고 달성 가능한 목표를 세우는 것은 학업의 성공에 중요해요.

어휘&어구 make progress 발전하다 ability 능력 concern 걱정 development 발달 strength 강점 at one's own pace 자신만의 속도로

02 야구팀 합류
[정답] ③

W Sarah and Eric are co-workers. Eric loves playing baseball and often plays in a local park on weekends. Their supervisor, who also loves playing baseball and plays in a local baseball league, hears about Eric's passion for baseball. So one day, the supervisor asks Eric if he'd like to join the supervisor's baseball team. Eric is hesitant to join the team because he doesn't think he's very good. When Sarah hears about this, she thinks he should join the team because it could offer him new opportunities to improve and socialize. So Sarah wants to encourage Eric to take on the new challenge and give it a try. In this situation, what would Sarah most likely say to Eric?

Sarah You should accept the offer and join the team.

여 Sarah와 Eric은 직장 동료입니다. Eric은 야구하는 것을 좋아하고 종종 주말에 지역 공원에서 경기를 합니다. 야구를 좋아하고 지역 야구 리그에서 뛰고 있는 그들의 상사가 Eric의 야구에 대한 열정에 대해 듣습니다. 그래서 어느 날, 상사는 Eric에게 자신의 야구팀에 합류하겠는지 물어봅니다. Eric은 자신이 매우 잘하지 못한다고 생각하기 때문에 팀에 합류하는 것을 주저합니다. Sarah는 그 이야기를 듣고 그가 팀에 합류해야 한다고 생각하는데, 왜냐하면 그것이 그에게 발전하고 사람들과 사귈 새로운 기회를 제공할 수 있기 때문입니다. 그래서 Sarah는 Eric에게 새로운 도전을 받아들이고 시도하도록 격려하고 싶어 합니다. 이런 상황에서 Sarah는 Eric에게 뭐라고 말하겠습니까?

Sarah <u>제안을 받아들여서 팀에 합류해야 해.</u>

문제 해설 상사에게 지역 야구 리그 팀에 합류하라는 제안을 받은 Eric이 망설이자, Sarah가 그에게 도전을 받아들이고 시도하도록 격려하고 싶어 하는 상황이다. 따라서 Sarah가 Eric에게 할 말로 가장 적절한 것은 ③ '제안을 받아들여서 팀에 합류해야 해.'이다.
① 나는 다른 기회가 있을 거라고 확신해.
② 너는 이미 팀의 스타 선수야.
④ 계속 연습하면 아마 그들이 너에게 합류하라고 요청할 거야.
⑤ 그냥 현재 네 소속 팀에 있는 게 좋을 것 같아.

03 과학 프로젝트 분업

[정답] ②

M Sam and Audrey are taking the same science class at school. For their science project, they're working together as a team to give a presentation. They've been working on it for the last week but haven't made much progress. They've only worked on it when they've had time to work together, which has limited how much they've been able to work on it. Their presentation is in only a few days. Sam doesn't think they'll be ready for it if they keep on only working together. So Sam wants to suggest to Audrey that they split up what needs to be done and work on it individually. In this situation, what would Sam most likely say to Audrey?

Sam Let's divide the tasks and do them separately.

남 Sam과 Audrey는 학교에서 같은 과학 수업을 듣고 있습니다. 과학 프로젝트를 위해, 그들은 발표를 하기 위해 팀으로 함께 일하고 있습니다. 그들은 지난 일주일 동안 그것을 작업해 왔지만 별로 진전이 없었습니다. 그들은 함께 일할 시간이 있을 때만 작업을 해 왔고, 이것은 그들이 작업할 수 있는 양을 제한했습니다. 발표까지 며칠 안 남았습니다. Sam은 그들이 계속해서 함께 일한다면 그것에 대한 준비가 되지 않을 것이라고 생각합니다. 그래서 Sam은 Audrey에게 해야 할 일을 나눠서 개별적으로 작업하자고 제안하고 싶어 합니다. 이런 상황에서 Sam은 Audrey에게 뭐라고 말하겠습니까?

Sam 과업을 나누어서 각자 하자.

문제 해설 과학 프로젝트 준비하면서 함께 일할 시간이 있을 때 작업을 하는 바람에 속도가 나지 않고 있는 상황이다. Sam은 Audrey에게 해야 할 일을 나눠서 개별적으로 작업하자고 제안하고 싶어 하므로, Sam이 Audrey에게 할 말로 가장 적절한 것은 ② '과업을 나누어서 각자 하자.'이다.
① 이번 주에 더 자주 만나는 게 어때?
③ 우리가 좀 더 심층적인 연구를 해야 한다고 생각해.
④ 조사를 하기 전에 주제를 좁히는 게 어때?
⑤ 발표를 준비할 시간이 많이 남았어.

어휘&어구 give a presentation 발표를 하다 make progress 진전이 있다 limit 제한하다 split up ~을 나누다 individually 개별적으로

04 국립 공원 내 불 사용 금지 규정

[정답] ③

W Ms. White has worked as a national park manager for a long time. Recently, as many people have become interested in camping, the number of visitors to the park has increased, so she has more work to do. She believes that it's a good thing that more people are enjoying nature, but she's worried because there are more and more people not following the park rules. One day while driving around the park, Ms. White sees a camper trying to make a fire, which is against the park rules. So she wants to inform the camper of the rules. In this situation, what would Ms. White most likely say to the camper?

Ms. White Excuse me, making a fire in the park is prohibited.

여 White 씨는 오랫동안 국립 공원 관리자로 일했습니다. 최근 많은 사람이 캠핑에 관심을 가지면서 공원 방문객 수가 증가했고, 그래서 그녀는 할 일이 더 많습니다. 그녀는 더 많은 사람이 자연을 즐기는 것은 좋은 일이라고 생각하지만, 공원 규칙을 따르지 않는 사람들이 점점 많아져 걱정입니다. 어느 날 운전하면서 공원을 돌아다니던 중, White 씨는 한 야영객이 불을 피우려고 하는 것을 보는데, 그것은 공원 규칙에 어긋납니다. 그래서 그녀는 야영객에게 그 규칙을 알려 주고 싶습니다. 이런 상황에서 White 씨는 야영객에게 뭐라고 말하겠습니까?

Ms. White 실례지만, 공원에서 불을 피우는 것은 금지되어 있습니다.

문제 해설 국립 공원 관리자인 White 씨는 공원 규칙을 지키지 않는 사람들이 많아져 걱정하던 중 한 야영객이 불을 피우려고 하는 것을 목격하고 그것이 공원 규칙에 어긋난다는 것을 알려 주고 싶어 하는 상황이다. 따라서 White 씨가 야영객에게 할 말로 가장 적절한 것은 ③ '실례지만, 공원에서 불을 피우는 것은 금지되어 있습니다.'이다.
① 음, 캠핑하기 더 좋은 장소를 찾아보셔야 합니다.
② 죄송하지만 공원에서는 잠자는 것이 허락되지 않습니다.
④ 사실, 일일 방문객 수에는 제한이 있습니다.
⑤ 당신이 소화기를 가지고 다닐 것이 요구됨을 기억하세요.

어휘&어구 national park 국립 공원 make a fire 불을 피우다 inform 알리다 prohibit 금지하다 limit 제한 fire extinguisher 소화기

05 호텔 체크아웃 후 짐 보관 가능 여부 묻기 [정답] ④

M William has been traveling around Seoul the past week, and today he flies back home. It's 11:30 a.m. now, and he's in his hotel room. He goes to the front desk to check out. However, since his flight is at 8 p.m., he still has some time to do some last-minute shopping near his hotel. After checking out, he'll have to carry around his heavy luggage with him. But he knows that some hotels allow guests to keep their luggage at the hotel for a little while after checking out. So he wants to ask the hotel staff if they provide that service. In this situation, what would William most likely say to the hotel staff?

William Could I store my luggage here after checking out?

남 William은 지난주 서울 여기저기를 여행했고, 오늘 그는 비행기를 타고 집으로 돌아갑니다. 지금은 오전 11시 30분이고, 그는 호텔 객실에 있습니다. 그는 체크아웃을 하기 위해 호텔의 프런트로 갑니다. 하지만 그의 항공편은 밤 8시에 있기 때문에 자신의 호텔 근처에서 마지막 쇼핑을 할 시간이 좀 있습니다. 체크아웃 후에 그는 무거운 짐을 가지고 다녀야 할 것입니다. 하지만 그는 일부 호텔에서는 체크아웃 후에 고객들이 자신의 짐을 잠시 호텔에 두는 것을 허용한다는 것을 알고 있습니다. 그래서 그는 호텔 직원에게 그들이 그 서비스를 제공하는지 묻고 싶습니다. 이런 상황에서 William은 호텔 직원에게 뭐라고 말하겠습니까?

William 체크아웃 후에 제 짐을 여기에 보관할 수 있습니까?

문제 해설 William은 호텔 체크아웃 후에 비행기 시간까지 시간이 남아서 쇼핑을 더 하고 싶은데 무거운 짐을 가지고 다녀야 해서 호텔 직원에게 체크아웃 후에 짐을 호텔에 보관할 수 있는지 물어보고 싶어 하는 상황이다. 이런 상황에서 William이 호텔 직원에게 할 말로 가장 적절한 것은 ④ '체크아웃 후에 제 짐을 여기에 보관할 수 있습니까?'이다.
① 혹시 내일 늦은 체크아웃을 할 수 있습니까?
② 근처의 쇼핑몰을 추천해 주시겠어요?
③ 제 체류를 하루 더 연장하는 것이 가능할까요?
⑤ 호텔-공항 간 수하물 배달 서비스를 제공하나요?

어휘&어구 past 지난 fly back 비행기를 타고 돌아가다 front desk (호텔의) 프런트 last-minute 마지막 순간의, 막바지의 carry around ~을 가지고 다니다 luggage (여행용) 짐, 수하물 staff 직원 possibly 혹시, 아마 extend 연장하다 stay 체류

06 다리 부상으로 인한 마라톤 연습 중단 [정답] ⑤

W Andy and Jack like marathons very much. They are dreaming of becoming marathon runners in the future. They practice really hard every day. But unfortunately, Jack injured his leg recently and stopped running for about a month. He's been so depressed while staying at home. But as soon as he can walk again, he puts on his running shoes and practices running, even though his leg hasn't fully healed yet. On seeing this, Andy is worried that Jack's injury might worsen. He'd like to tell Jack that he has to wait until his leg gets completely better. In this situation, what would Andy most likely say to Jack?

Andy You'd better not run until your leg has fully recovered.

여 Andy와 Jack은 마라톤을 무척 좋아합니다. 그들은 장래 마라톤 선수가 되기를 꿈꾸고 있습니다. 그들은 매일 정말 열심히 연습합니다. 하지만 불행히도, Jack이 최근에 다리를 다쳐 약 한 달 동안 달리기를 중단했습니다. 그는 집에 있는 동안 무척 우울했습니다. 하지만 다시 걸을 수 있게 되자마자, 그는 다리가 아직 완전히 낫지 않았는데도 운동화를 신고 달리기 연습을 합니다. 이것을 보자마자, Andy는 Jack의 부상이 악화되지 않을까 걱정합니다. 그는 Jack에게 그의 다리가 완전히 나아질 때까지 기다려야 한다고 말하고 싶습니다. 이런 상황에서 Andy는 Jack에게 뭐라고 말하겠습니까?

Andy 네 다리가 완전히 나을 때까지 달리지 않는 게 좋아.

문제 해설 다리가 아직 완전히 낫지 않았는데도 운동화를 신고 달리기 연습을 하는 Jack을 보고 Andy는 그에게 다리가 완전히 나아질 때까지 기다려야 한다고 말하고 싶다고 했다. 따라서 Andy가 Jack에게 할 말로 가장 적절한 것은 ⑤ '네 다리가 완전히 나을 때까지 달리지 않는 게 좋아.'이다.
① 네 다리에 대해서 걱정하지 마. 그저 너 자신을 믿어.
② 네가 괜찮다면, 너와 함께 달리고 싶어.
③ 네가 다시 걸을 수 있으려면 시간이 꽤 걸릴 거야.
④ 네 다리가 괜찮아 보이니까, 정상 속도로 달리면 돼.

어휘&어구 depressed 우울한 heal 낫다 worsen 악화되다 completely 완전히

수능 유형
⑭ 복합 이해

본문 34~35쪽

수능유형 체험 | 01 ⑤ 02 ④

수능유형 연습 | 01 ③ 02 ⑤ 03 ③ 04 ④ 05 ③ 06 ④
07 ⑤ 08 ④

수능유형 체험 과일 이름을 포함하는 영어 표현들

[정답] 01 ⑤ 02 ④

남 안녕하세요, 청취자 여러분! Andy의 Daily English에 다시 오신 것을 환영합니다. 지난 수업에서, 저는 여러분에게 동물 이름이 있는 몇 가지 영어 표현을 소개했습니다. 저는 여러분이 그것들을 사용할 기회가 있었기를 바랍니다. 오늘은 과일 이름이라는 것만 제외하고 똑같은 것을 할 것입니다. 첫 번째는 'cherry-pick'입니다. 이 표현은 최상의 선택을 고르라는 의미입니다. 그것은 사람들이 잘 익은 체리를 신중하게 고르는 것에서 유래했을 수도 있습니다. 다음은 'sour grapes'입니다. 이 잘 알려진 표현은 이솝 우화 중의 하나에서 나온 것입니다. 그

것은 여러분이 가질 수 없는 무언가를 정말 몹시 원한다는 것을 의미합니다. 다음은 'go bananas'입니다. 이 문구는 여러분이 화가 날 때 사용될 수 있습니다. 마지막 표현은 'the apple of my eye'입니다. 그것은 여러분이 다른 그 어떤 것이나 다른 누구보다도 더 소중하게 여기는 어떤 것이나 누군가를 나타내기 위해 사용됩니다. 사실, 여러분은 모두 제 눈의 사과입니다. 나의 사랑하는 청취자분들. 과일 이름을 포함한 영어 표현은 정말 재미있어요, 그렇지 않나요? 더 재미있고 유익한 표현을 배우고 싶으십니까? 그러면 다음에 뵙겠습니다!

문제 해설 01 남자는 과일 이름을 포함하는 영어 표현들을 예로 들면서 의미를 설명하고 있다. 따라서 남자가 하는 말의 주제로 가장 적절한 것은 ⑤ '과일 이름을 포함한 영어 표현들'이다.
① 다양한 과일 이름의 기원들
② 과일로 만든 맛있는 음식들
③ 매일 과일을 먹는 것의 이점들
④ 과일과 채소의 차이점들
02 남자가 과일 이름을 포함한 영어 표현들을 설명하면서 체리, 포도, 바나나, 사과는 언급되었지만, ④ '오렌지'는 언급되지 않았다.

어휘&어구 expression 표현 select 고르다 option 선택, 선택 사항 originate 유래하다 fable 우화 phrase 문구, 구절 represent 나타내다 value 소중하게 여기다; 가치 informative 유익한

수능유형 **연습**

01~02 전통 무용의 특징들

[정답] 01 ③ 02 ⑤

W Hello, everyone. In the last class, we explored the unique characteristics of traditional songs. Today, I'd like to turn to the distinctive features of traditional dances from various countries. First, try to think of a traditional dance from Spain. I'm guessing that many of you thought of flamenco, a delightful dance with passionate movements that describe the art of bullfighting. Moving on to France, we find the popular cancan. In this lively dance, performers elegantly kick their legs up high. Next up is Brazil, which is famous for its traditional dance called samba. The dance is characterized by vigorous hip movements. This dance is so beloved that there's an annual international samba festival. Finally, let's move on to the traditional dance of Argentina, tango, a two-person dance which is celebrated for its graceful

여 안녕하세요, 여러분. 지난 수업에서, 우리는 우리의 전통 노래들의 독특한 특징을 탐구했습니다. 오늘은 다양한 나라들의 전통 무용 특유의 특징으로 넘어가고자 합니다. 먼저, 스페인의 전통 무용을 생각해 보세요. 저는 여러분 중 많은 사람들이 투우의 기술을 묘사하는 열정적인 움직임을 가진 즐거운 춤인 플라멩코를 생각했을 것이라고 추측합니다. 프랑스로 넘어가면, 우리는 인기 있는 캉캉을 발견합니다. 이 활기찬 춤에서, 공연자들은 우아하게 다리를 높이 차올립니다. 다음은 브라질인데, 삼바라고 불리는 전통 무용으로 유명합니다. 그 춤은 격렬한 골반 부위의 움직임이 특징입니다. 이 춤은 매년 국제 삼바 축제가 열릴 정도로 사랑을 받고 있습니다. 마지막으로, 우아하고 낭만적인 스타일로 유명한 아르헨티나의 전통 무용이자 두 사람이 추는 춤인 탱고로 넘어갑시다. 이 춤에서 남자와 여자는 리듬에 맞춰 스텝을 조화시킵니다. 이제, 이러한 전통 무용들을 보여 주는 동영상을 봅시다.

and romantic style. In this dance, a man and a woman harmonize their steps to the rhythm. Now, let's watch a video that showcases these traditional dances.

문제 해설 01 여자는 다양한 나라들의 전통 무용의 특징을 예를 들며 설명하고 있다. 따라서 여자가 하는 말의 주제로 가장 적절한 것은 ③ '전통 무용의 특징들'이다.
① 몇몇 전통 무용의 기원들
② 춤을 배우는 것의 이점들
④ 가장 인기 있는 국제 무용 노래들
⑤ 세계 무용의 클래식 음악에 대한 영향

02 여자가 전통 무용의 특징들에 대해 설명하는 과정에서 스페인, 프랑스, 브라질, 아르헨티나는 언급했지만, ⑤ '호주'는 언급하지 않았다.

어휘&어구 explore 탐구하다 unique 독특한 characteristic 특징 distinctive 특유의 feature 특징 delightful 즐거운 passionate 열정적인 bullfighting 투우 lively 활기찬 performer 공연자 elegantly 우아하게 characterize 특징짓다 vigorous 격렬한 annual 매년의 be celebrated for ~로 유명하다 graceful 우아한 harmonize 조화시키다 showcase 보여 주다

03~04 사람들이 파충류를 반려동물로 좋아하는 이유 [정답] 03 ③ 04 ④

M Good afternoon, viewers! Welcome back to my channel, *Ryan's Life*. I'm sure many of you have dogs or cats as pets. But how about reptiles? There are many reasons why people love reptiles as pets. Let's begin with lizards. Lizards can be easily tamed, and they provide endless entertainment with their cute behavior. Their presence enhances the mood of your home. Moving on to turtles, we find a reptile that offers a sense of peacefulness. Watching them swim brings a sense of peace, making them perfect for those seeking a calming presence. Chameleons also make attractive pets. These masters of disguise have an amazing ability to change color and blend in with their surroundings. And their captivating displays of adaptation serve as a reminder of nature's brilliance. Lastly, iguanas are fascinating reptiles that can form strong bonds with their owners. They offer an interactive pet experience, allowing gentle handling, and they even respond to their name. With various reasons, reptiles enrich our lives in remarkable ways!

남 안녕하세요, 시청자 여러분! 제 채널 *Ryan's Life*에 다시 오신 것을 환영합니다. 여러분 중 많은 사람들이 개나 고양이를 반려동물로 기르고 있을 것입니다. 하지만 파충류는 어떨까요? 사람들이 파충류를 반려동물로 좋아하는 많은 이유들이 있습니다. 도마뱀부터 시작해 보죠. 도마뱀은 쉽게 길들일 수 있고, 그것들은 귀여운 행동으로 끝없는 즐거움을 제공합니다. 그것들의 존재는 여러분 집의 분위기를 향상시킵니다. 거북이로 넘어가면, 우리는 평온함을 제공하는 파충류를 발견하게 됩니다. 그것들이 수영하는 것을 보는 것은 평온함을 가져다주며, 그것들은 고요하게 해 주는 존재를 찾는 사람들에게 완벽한 것이 됩니다. 카멜레온도 매력적인 반려동물이 됩니다. 이 변장의 달인들은 색깔을 바꾸고 주변 환경과 조화를 이루는 능력을 가지고 있습니다. 그리고 그것들의 매혹적인 적응의 표현은 자연의 찬란함을 상기시키는 역할을 합니다. 마지막으로, 이구아나는 주인과 강한 유대감을 형성할 수 있는 매혹적인 파충류입니다. 그것들은 상호 작용의 반려동물 경험을 제공하여 부드럽게 만지는 것을 허락하고 심지어 이름에 반응하기도 합니다. 다양한 이유로, 파충류는 놀라운 방법으로 우리의 삶을 풍요롭게 합니다!

문제 해설 03 남자는 몇몇 파충류를 예로 들어 말하면서, 사람들이 파충류를 반려동물로 좋아하는 이유에 대해 설명하고 있다. 따라서 남자가 하는 말의 주제로 가장 적절한 것은 ③ '사람들이 파충류를 반려동물로 좋아하는 이유'이다.
① 파충류가 생존하는 독특한 방법
② 파충류의 놀라운 상호 작용 능력
④ 파충류를 반려동물로 기르는 책임
⑤ 파충류가 공유하는 공통적인 특징

04 남자가 사람들이 파충류를 반려동물로 좋아하는 이유를 설명하면서, 도마뱀, 거북이, 카멜레온, 이구아나는 언급했지만, ④ '뱀'은 언급하지 않았다.

어휘&어구 reptile 파충류 lizard 도마뱀 tame 길들이다 endless 끝없는 entertainment 즐거움, 오락 presence 존재 enhance 향상시키다 sense of peace 평온함 calming 고요하게 해 주는 attractive 매력적인 disguise 변장 blend in with ~과 조화를 이루다 surroundings 주변, 환경 captivating 매혹적인 adaptation 적응 reminder 상기시켜 주는 것 brilliance 찬란함 fascinating 매혹적인 bond 유대감 interactive 상호 작용의 enrich 풍요롭게 하다 remarkable 놀라운

W Hello, everyone. I'm Lois Griffin with Healthy Life TV! Do you want to have shiny white teeth? Then listen up for some natural home remedies to whiten your teeth. First, try using coconut oil. Gargle 1 to 2 teaspoons of coconut oil for 10 to 15 minutes. This helps to remove plaque from and kill bacteria in the mouth, which helps to whiten teeth. Baking soda is another option. It's not harsh, and it can help scrub away surface stains on teeth. Mix 1 teaspoon of baking soda with water to make a paste to brush with. You can also try apple cider vinegar. Dilute a very small amount of it with water and use it as a mouthwash. Herbs also have teeth-whitening properties. Just grind herbs and apply the powder to your teeth. Let that sit for 5 minutes and then brush your teeth. It may be best to try a few of these treatments and rotate them throughout the week to see which ones are best for you. Join me tomorrow for more tips on healthy living!

여 안녕하세요, 여러분. Healthy Life TV의 Lois Griffin입니다. 여러분은 빛나는 하얀 치아를 갖기를 원하시나요? 그러면 여러분의 치아를 하얗게 하기 위한 몇 가지 자연 가정 치료법을 잘 들어 주세요. 첫째, 코코넛오일을 사용해 보세요. 하나에서 두 찻숟가락의 코코넛오일로 10분에서 15분 동안 입안을 행구세요. 이것은 입으로부터 나오는 치태를 제거하고 입안에 있는 박테리아를 죽여 치아를 하얗게 하는 데 도움이 됩니다. 베이킹 소다는 또 다른 선택 사항입니다. 그것은 불쾌하지 않고 치아 표면의 얼룩을 문질러 씻어 내는 데 도움이 될 수 있습니다. 베이킹 소다 한 찻숟가락을 물에 섞어 반죽을 만들어 그것으로 칫솔질을 하세요. 여러분은 또한 사과 식초를 사용할 수 있습니다. 아주 소량의 사과 식초를 물과 희석하여 그것을 구강 청정제로 사용하세요. 허브 또한 치아 미백 속성이 있습니다. 허브를 갈아서 그 가루를 치아에 발라만 주세요. 그것을 5분 동안 그대로 두고 그러고 나서 칫솔질을 하세요. 이러한 치료법 중 몇 가지를 해 보고 어떤 것이 여러분에게 가장 적합한지 알아보기 위해 한 주 내내 그것들을 교대로 해 보는 것이 가장 좋을 수 있습니다. 건강한 생활에 관한 더 많은 정보를 위해 내일도 함께해 주세요!

문제 해설

05 여자는 빛나는 하얀 치아를 갖기를 원한다면 치아를 하얗게 하기 위한 몇 가지 자연 가정 치료법을 잘 들어 달라고 하면서 그것에 관한 몇 가지 방법을 이야기하고 있으므로, 여자가 하는 말의 주제로 가장 적절한 것은 ③ '가정에서 치아를 하얗게 하는 자연적인 방법'이다.
① 더 건강한 치아를 위한 식습관
② 천연 치약 사용의 이점
④ 입안에서 박테리아가 자라는 이유
⑤ 치아를 노랗게 변하게 할 수 있는 음식

06 코코넛오일, 베이킹 소다, 사과 식초, 허브 가루는 언급되었으나 ④ '녹차'는 언급되지 않았다.

어휘&어구 shiny 빛나는, 반짝거리는   remedy 치료법, 치료   gargle 입안을 행구다   teaspoon 찻숟가락   plaque 치태   harsh (맛·냄새 따위가) 불쾌한, 쓴   scrub away 문질러 없애다   stain 얼룩, 때   paste 반죽   brush 칫솔질[솔질]을 하다   dilute 희석하다   properties 특성, 속성   grind (곡식 등을 잘게) 갈다, 빻다   apply (페인트·크림 등을) 바르다

M Hello, listeners! Welcome to the Balanced Life podcast. Today, I'd like to introduce some of my favorite things to do when feeling down because of stress from work. If you're busy working nonstop, then you may feel tired and underappreciated. So why not reward yourself? You're worth it! It'll boost your spirits, making you feel good and ultimately lowering your work stress. Here are some things you can do to treat yourself. First, go and see a movie by yourself. There's something relaxing and peaceful about seeing a film without anybody else. Second, buy your favorite ice cream on your way home from work and spend time enjoying it while watching TV. Third, buy yourself a new outfit, or at least a new accessory. If you are on a tight budget, visit charity shops or hold a clothes-swapping event with friends. Lastly,

남 안녕하세요, 청취자 여러분! Balanced Life 팟캐스트에 오신 것을 환영합니다. 오늘, 저는 업무로 인한 스트레스 때문에 마음이 울적할 때, 제가 하는 몇 가지 좋아하는 일을 소개하고 싶습니다. 만일 여러분이 쉬지 않고 일하느라 바쁘다면, 그러면 여러분은 피곤하거나 제대로 인정받고 있지 못하다고 느낄 수 있습니다. 그럼 여러분 자신에게 보상하는 것은 어떨까요? 여러분은 그럴 가치가 있습니다! 그것은 여러분의 기분을 좋게 하고, 궁극적으로 업무 스트레스를 낮추면서 기운을 북돋아 줄 것입니다. 여기 여러분이 자신을 대접하기 위해 할 수 있는 몇 가지 것들이 있습니다. 첫째, 혼자 가서 영화를 보세요. 다른 어떤 사람도 없이 영화를 보는 것에는 뭔가 마음을 느긋하게 해 주고 평화로운 것이 있습니다. 둘째, 직장에서 집으로 가는 길에 좋아하는 아이스크림을 사서 TV를 보는 동안 그것을 즐기면서 시간을 보내세요. 셋째, 자신에게 새 옷이나, 또는 적어도 새 액세서리를 사 주세요. 만일 예산이 빠듯하다면, 중고품 가게를 방문하거나 친구들과 함께 옷을 교환하는 행사를 개최해 보

you can also forget all the stresses of work by going to the hairdresser. Rewards don't have to be expensive or time-consuming. Even the smallest treat will help you feel better!

세요. 마지막으로, 여러분은 또한 미용실에 감으로써 업무의 스트레스를 모두 잊을 수 있습니다. 보상은 값이 비싸거나 시간이 많이 걸릴 필요가 없습니다. 아무리 작은 특별한 것이라도 여러분이 더 기분 좋게 느끼도록 도와줄 것입니다!

문제 해설

07 남자는 쉬지 않고 일하느라 바쁘다면, 그러면 피곤하거나 제대로 인정받고 있지 못하다고 느낄 수 있을 거라고 하면서, 업무 스트레스를 잊기 위해 자기 자신에게 보상할 수 있는 몇 가지 방법을 언급하고 있다. 따라서 남자가 하는 말의 주제로 가장 적절한 것은 ⑤ '업무 스트레스를 경감하기 위한 자기 보상 방법'이다.
① 퇴근 후의 일정을 정리하는 방법
② 업무 스트레스와 가정 스트레스 간의 차이점
③ 혼자 활동하는 것의 몇 가지 단점
④ 빠듯한 예산으로 일일 경비를 충당하기 위해 해야 할 일

08 혼자 영화 보기, 아이스크림 사서 먹기, 새 옷이나 액세서리 사기, 미용실 가기는 언급되었지만, ④ '뜨거운 물에 목욕하기'는 언급되지 않았다.

어휘&어구 underappreciated 제대로 인정받지 못하는, 저평가된   spirit 기분, 마음   treat 대접하다; 특별한 것[선물]   outfit 옷   accessory 액세서리   charity shop 중고품 가게   swap 교환하다, 바꾸다

1회 수능실전 **대비연습**

본문 38~39쪽

01 ⑤	02 ④	03 ③	04 ⑤	05 ⑤	06 ②	07 ⑤	08 ④	09 ③	10 ③	11 ①	12 ④	13 ③	14 ②
15 ②	16 ①	17 ③											

01 하이킹 시 야생 동물을 피하는 방법

[정답] ⑤

W Hello, listeners. I'm Linda Brown with Healthy Lifestyle. Nowadays, hiking is becoming a really popular activity. It's a great way to be outside and enjoy nature, but there's always a risk of dangerous wildlife encounters. By following some simple tips, you can avoid these encounters. First, don't hike silently. Talk or even sing when you hike. This warns animals that you're coming, so they won't be alarmed and attack from feeling threatened. Second, don't wear headphones. When you wear them, you can't hear what's happening around you. So you might not hear an animal making threatening noises. Lastly, avoid hiking at dawn or after dark. This is when many animals are most active. Keep these tips in mind and have a safe hike.

여 청취자 여러분, 안녕하세요. Healthy Lifestyle의 Linda Brown 입니다. 요즘 하이킹이 정말 인기 있는 활동이 되고 있습니다. 그것은 야외에 나가 자연을 즐기기에 좋은 방법이지만, 위험한 야생 동물과 마주칠 위험성이 항상 있습니다. 몇 가지 간단한 조언을 따르면 여러분은 이러한 마주침을 피할 수 있습니다. 첫째, 조용히 하이킹하지 마세요. 하이킹할 때 말하거나 심지어 노래도 부르세요. 이것은 동물들에게 여러분이 오고 있다는 경고를 해서 그것들이 불안해하지도 않을 것이고 위협을 받는다고 느끼기 때문에 공격하지도 않을 것입니다. 둘째, 헤드폰을 끼지 마세요. 여러분이 그것을 끼면 여러분 주변에서 무슨 일이 일어나는지 들을 수 없습니다. 따라서 여러분은 동물이 위협적인 소리를 내는 것을 듣지 못할지도 모릅니다. 마지막으로, 새벽이나 어두워진 후에 하이킹하는 것을 피하세요. 이때가 많은 동물들이 가장 활동적인 때입니다. 이러한 조언을 명심하고 안전한 하이킹을 하세요.

문제 해설 여자는 하이킹할 때 위험한 야생 동물과 마주치는 것을 피할 수 있는 방법을 알려 주고 있다. 그러므로 여자가 하는 말의 목적으로 가장 적절한 것은 ⑤ '하이킹 시 야생 동물을 피하는 방법을 안내하려고'이다.

어휘&어구 encounter 마주침, 뜻밖의 만남 alarm 불안하게[두렵게] 만들다 dawn 새벽

02 먼저 사과해야 할 필요성

[정답] ④

M Is something wrong, Amelia? You look upset.

W I am, Dad. I had an argument with my friend Sophia about what movie we should see.

M I see. What movie did you decide to see?

W We didn't see one. We were so upset at each other that we just went home.

M Really? But I think you should contact her to make up.

W Why me? She was at fault, too.

M I understand that. But it's always a good idea for you to apologize first.

W What do you mean?

M If both of you wait too long to apologize, you might never be able to recover your friendship.

W Oh, you think so?

M Yeah. If you value your friendship with her, you'd better act first.

W Okay, Dad. Thanks for your advice.

남 무슨 문제라도 있니, Amelia? 화가 나 보이네.

여 그래요, 아빠. 친구 Sophia와 무슨 영화를 볼 건지에 관해 말다툼을 했어요.

남 그렇구나. 무슨 영화를 보기로 결정했니?

여 아무것도 보지 못했어요. 서로에게 너무 화가 나 그냥 집으로 갔어요.

남 그래? 하지만 화해하기 위해 네가 그녀와 연락해야만 한다고 생각해.

여 왜 제가요? 그 애도 잘못했어요.

남 이해해. 하지만 네가 먼저 사과하는 것이 항상 좋은 생각이야.

여 무슨 말씀이세요?

남 너희 둘이 너무 오래 기다리다가 사과하지 못한다면, 너희들의 우정을 결코 회복할 수 없을 수도 있단다.

여 아, 그렇게 생각하세요?

남 그래. 그 애와의 우정을 소중히 여긴다면, 먼저 행동하는 것이 좋단다.

여 알겠어요, 아빠. 조언해 주셔서 감사합니다.

문제 해설 친구와 말다툼을 하고 화가 나 있는 여자(딸)에게 남자는 잘못이 누구에게 있든 먼저 사과하는 것이 우정 회복에 필요하다고 조언하고 있다. 따라서 남자의 의견으로 가장 적절한 것은 ④ '우정을 회복하기 위해서는 먼저 사과해야 한다.'이다.

어휘&어구 argument 말다툼, 논쟁   contact 연락하다   make up 화해하다   apologize 사과하다   recover 회복하다   value 소중히 여기다

03 미술 감상의 이점
[정답] ③

W	Hello, everyone! Thank you for tuning in to my channel again! We've been taking a look at various artists' paintings on my channel for the past week. By doing so, our understanding of their art has deepened. Hasn't it been a very rewarding experience? I think there is an important benefit from appreciating works of art. It's clearing your mind. Just by looking at beautiful paintings, you can clear your mind of your worries. So if you go on a trip to the world of art with me, you'll be stress-free with a clear mind!	**여**	안녕하세요, 여러분! 다시 제 채널에 맞춰 주셔서 감사합니다! 우리는 지난 한 주 동안 제 채널에서 다양한 예술가들의 그림을 보았습니다. 그렇게 함으로써, 그들의 미술 작품에 대한 우리의 이해가 깊어졌습니다. 그것은 매우 보람 있는 경험이 아니었나요? 저는 미술 작품을 감상하여 얻는 중요한 이점이 있다고 생각합니다. 마음을 맑게 해 주는 것이죠. 아름다운 그림을 보는 것만으로도, 여러분은 마음속의 걱정을 없앨 수 있습니다. 그러니 저와 함께 미술의 세계로 여행을 간다면, 맑은 마음으로 스트레스가 없어질 것입니다!

문제 해설 여자는 미술 작품을 감상하여 얻는 중요한 이점이 있다고 하면서, 그것은 마음을 맑게 해 주는 것이라고 했고, 자신과 함께 미술 감상을 계속하면 맑은 마음으로 스트레스가 없어질 것이라고 했다. 따라서 여자가 하는 말의 요지로 가장 적절한 것은 ③ '미술 감상은 마음을 정화해 주는 이점이 있다.'이다.

어휘&어구 tune in to (채널을) ~에 맞추다   take a look at ~을 보다   deepen 깊어지다   rewarding 보람 있는   benefit 이점, 혜택   appreciate 감상하다   stress-free 스트레스가 없는

04 포토 존 포스터 디자인
[정답] ⑤

W	David, I've finished designing the photo zone poster for our club campaign.	**여**	David, 우리 동아리 캠페인을 위한 포토 존 포스터 디자인을 끝냈어.
M	Cool. Let me see.	**남**	좋아. 어디 보자.
W	I wrote the campaign title, 'See the World,' in the box at the top.	**여**	나는 'See the World'라는 캠페인 제목을 맨 위에 있는 네모 칸 안에 썼어.
M	It's very eye-catching. I like the picture of the Earth you put on the right side of the poster.	**남**	그건 아주 눈길을 끌어. 나는 네가 포스터 오른쪽에 넣은 지구 그림이 마음에 들어.
W	I added it because nowadays there are a lot of issues that affect the whole world.	**여**	요즘 전 세계에 영향을 미치는 이슈들이 많아서 그것을 추가했어.
M	Good point. I also like how you put the three kids standing hand in hand on top of the Earth.	**남**	좋은 지적이야. 나는 네가 그 지구 위에 서로 손을 잡고 서 있는 세 명의 어린이들을 넣은 것도 마음에 들어.
W	I wanted to express the importance of harmony and cooperation with each other, even with nature. That's why I also drew the three bees in the middle, just under the title.	**여**	나는 서로, 심지어 자연과도, 조화를 이루고 협력하는 것의 중요성을 표현하고 싶었어. 그래서 제목 바로 아래, 가운데에 꿀벌 세 마리를 또한 그린 거야.
M	Wonderful. And the balloon with stars on it on the left side of the poster looks good.	**남**	멋지다. 그리고 포스터 왼쪽에 있는 별이 그려진 풍선도 좋아 보여.
W	I wanted to add some bright accents.	**여**	눈에 띄게 하는 밝은 것을 좀 더하고 싶었거든.
M	Really nice. I'm sure people will love taking photos in front of your poster.	**남**	정말 좋아. 사람들이 네 포스터 앞에서 사진 찍는 것을 좋아할 거라고 확신해.

대화에서는 포스터 왼쪽에 별이 그려진 풍선이 있다고 하였으나 그림에서는 풍선에 줄무늬가 그려져 있으므로, 대화의 내용과 일치하지 않는 것은 ⑤이다.

어휘&어구 eye-catching (단번에) 눈길을 끄는 hand in hand 서로 손을 잡고 cooperation 협력, 협동 accent (장식·요리 따위에서) 눈에 띄게[두드러지게] 하는 것, 억양

05 이모와 삼촌의 첫 방문
[정답] ⑤

W	Honey, your aunt and uncle will be here in a couple of hours.
M	It's our first time having them over since we got married.
W	Yeah. We're basically ready, right?
M	Well, I finished cooking dinner, but I think we need to get some drinks.
W	I forgot to tell you. I bought some lemonade at the grocery store this morning.
M	Oh, perfect. And I vacuumed while you were at the grocery store. By the way, what should we do after dinner?
W	How about playing board games together?
M	That's a good idea. Do you know where the board game sets are?
W	Yeah. I put them in the attic.
M	All right. I'll go and bring them down now.
W	Okay. I'll be in the living room.

여 여보, 당신의 이모와 삼촌이 두어 시간 후에 여기에 오실 거예요.
남 우리가 결혼한 이후로 그분들을 초대한 건 이번이 처음이에요.
여 네. 우리는 기본적으로 준비가 되어 있어요. 그렇죠?
남 음, 내가 저녁 식사 준비를 끝냈는데, 음료를 좀 사 와야 할 것 같아요.
여 말하는 것을 잊었네요. 내가 오늘 아침에 식료품점에서 레모네이드를 좀 샀어요.
남 오, 완벽해요. 그리고 당신이 식료품점에 가 있는 동안 내가 진공청소기로 청소했어요. 그런데, 저녁 식사 후에 우리가 무엇을 해야 할까요?
여 보드게임을 함께 하는 거 어때요?
남 좋은 생각이에요. 보드게임 세트가 어디에 있는지 알아요?
여 네. 내가 그것들을 다락방에 두었어요.
남 좋아요. 내가 지금 가서 그것들을 가지고 내려올게요.
여 네. 나는 거실에 있을게요.

문제 해설 이모와 삼촌의 방문에 대비하면서 저녁 식사 후에 보드게임을 하자는 여자의 제안에 남자는 좋은 생각이라고 하면서 보드게임 세트가 있는 곳을 물었고, 이에 여자가 그것들을 다락방에 두었다고 대답하자, 남자가 가서 가지고 내려오겠다고 말했으므로, 남자가 할 일로 가장 적절한 것은 ⑤ '보드게임 세트 가져오기'이다.

어휘&어구 have ~ over ~을 초대하다 grocery store 식료품점 vacuum 진공청소기로 청소하다 attic 다락방

06 학용품 구입
[정답] ②

M	Welcome to Papyrus Stationery Store. What can I help you with?
W	Hi, where are the colored pencils?
M	Right over here. We sell them in sets.
W	That's exactly what I want.
M	Okay. Here they are. How about this set? It has 18 colors. It's on sale for $5 per set.
W	Great. I'll take four sets. And I also need two sketchbooks.
M	Those are right behind you.
W	All right. This one looks pretty good. Let's see.... It's $20. Umm.... The paper in the sketchbook is a little thicker than I want.

남 Papyrus 문구점에 오신 것을 환영합니다. 무엇을 도와드릴까요?
여 안녕하세요, 색연필이 어디에 있나요?
남 바로 이쪽에 있습니다. 그것들은 세트로 판매하고 있어요.
여 그것이 정확히 제가 원하는 거예요.
남 알겠습니다. 그것들이 여기에 있어요. 이 세트는 어떠세요? 열여덟 가지 색이에요. 세트당 5달러에 할인 판매 중이고요.
여 아주 좋아요. 네 세트를 살게요. 그리고 저는 스케치북 두 개도 필요해요.
남 그것은 당신 바로 뒤에 있어요.
여 좋아요. 이것이 꽤 좋아 보이는군요. 어디 보자…. 20달러네요. 음…. 이 스케치북의 종이는 제가 원하는 것보다 조금 두껍네요.
남 아, 그러면 여기를 보세요. 이것은 종이가 더 얇아요. 보통 때는 16달러지만 지금은 50% 할인 중이어서 단지 8달러예요.

M Oh, then here. This one has thinner paper. It's normally $16, but it's 50% off right now, so it's only $8.

W Perfect. I'll buy two of them.

M Okay. Do you need anything else besides the four sets of colored pencils and two sketchbooks?

W Nope. And here's my credit card.

여 완벽해요. 그것 두 개를 살게요.

남 좋아요. 네 세트의 색연필과 두 개의 스케치북 외에 다른 필요하신 것이 있나요?

여 아니요. 그리고 여기 제 신용 카드가 있습니다.

문제 해설 여자가 한 세트당 5달러에 할인 판매 중인 색연필 네 세트와, 50% 할인 중이어서 한 개에 8달러인 스케치북 두 개를 구입했으므로, 여자가 지불할 금액은 ② '36달러'이다.

어휘&어구 stationery store 문구점   thin 얇은   normally 보통 때는   besides ~ 외에

---

07 블루투스 이어폰을 구매하지 않은 이유   [정답] ⑤

W Hey, honey. Did you go to the shopping mall today?

M Yeah. And while I was there, I started getting a headache. So I took some medicine a little while ago.

W I'm sorry to hear that. Weren't you going to get the Bluetooth earphones you've been thinking about buying?

M Yeah. But I didn't end up buying them.

W Why not? I hope you didn't forget to take the credit card.

M That's not it.

W Oh, were they sold out? Or were they not on sale anymore?

M No. In fact, when I tried them on, they weren't that comfortable.

W Oh, I see.

M So I'm going to look for another model to buy.

여 안녕, 여보. 오늘 쇼핑몰에 갔어요?

남 네. 그리고 그곳에 있는 동안, 머리가 아프기 시작했어요. 그래서 조금 전에 약을 먹었어요.

여 그런 말을 들으니 안타깝군요. 당신이 사려던 블루투스 이어폰을 사러 간 것이 아니었어요?

남 네. 하지만 나는 그것들을 결국 사지 않았어요.

여 왜요? 신용 카드를 가져가는 것을 잊지 않았기를 바라요.

남 그게 아니에요.

여 아, 그것들이 모두 팔렸나요? 아니면 더 이상 세일을 하지 않았나요?

남 아니요. 사실, 내가 그것들을 착용해 봤더니, 그렇게 편하지 않았어요.

여 아, 그렇군요.

남 그래서 살 만한 다른 모델을 찾아보려고요.

문제 해설 쇼핑몰에 갔지만 사길 원했던 블루투스 이어폰을 사지 않았다고 남자가 말하자 여자는 그 이유를 물었고, 이에 남자는 그것들을 착용해 봤더니 그렇게 편하지 않았다고 하면서 다른 모델을 찾아보려 한다고 했으므로, 남자가 블루투스 이어폰을 오늘 구매하지 않은 이유는 ⑤ '제품이 사용하기 불편해서'이다.

어휘&어구 headache 두통   medicine 약   end up -ing 결국 ~하다   sold out 모두 판매된, 매진된   comfortable 편한, 편안한

---

08 멕시코 요리 수업   [정답] ④

W Hi, Tony. Are you interested in Mexican food?

M Yes. Why do you ask?

W I found this flyer about a Mexican cooking class. It says you get to make various kinds of foods like tacos and burritos.

M Sounds interesting. How much is the class?

W It's 65 dollars per person.

M Isn't it a bit expensive?

W The cost includes a class, menu design and printable recipes, so I think it's quite reasonable.

여 안녕, Tony. 멕시코 음식에 관심이 있니?

남 응. 왜 물어보는 거야?

여 멕시코 요리 수업에 관한 이 전단지를 발견했어. 타코와 부리토 같은 다양한 종류의 음식을 만들게 될 거야.

남 재미있겠다. 수강료는 얼마야?

여 1인당 65달러야.

남 좀 비싸지 않아?

여 그 비용에는 수업, 메뉴 디자인, 인쇄 가능한 조리법이 포함되어 있으니까, 내 생각에는 꽤 적정한 것 같아.

남 글쎄. 수업은 얼마나 길어?

M	Maybe. How long is the class?	여	4시간이야.
W	4 hours.	남	수업은 어디서 하니?
M	Where is the class taking place?	여	River City Mall에 위치한 요리 스튜디오에서 해.
W	In a cooking studio located in the River City Mall.	남	우리 집에서 편하게 운전해서 갈 수 있는 거리야. 음, 스튜디오에
M	It's an easy drive from my house. Hmm, it wouldn't hurt to call the studio and find out more about the class.		전화해서 수업에 대해 더 알아보는 것도 나쁠 건 없을 것 같다.
W	Yeah. Let's make a call right away.	여	맞아. 지금 바로 전화하자.

문제 해설 요리 종류(various kinds of foods like tacos and burritos), 수강료(65 dollars per person), 수업 시간(4 hours), 수업 장소(a cooking studio located in the River City Mall)는 언급되었지만, ④ '수강 인원'은 언급되지 않았다.

어휘&어구 flyer 전단지   reasonable (가격이) 적정한, 비싸지 않은

09 Dream Future Program 안내
[정답] ③

M	Hello, students! This is your vice principal, Mr. Davis. I'm happy to tell you about the upcoming Dream Future Program. The program includes 15 special lectures related to a variety of jobs. You can register for the lectures individually on the school website until 6 p.m. this Friday. It will be three days long, starting from the 5th of next month. Please note that there's a limit of 30 participants for each lecture. After attending the lectures, you will be required to write a report about what you learned. Don't miss out on this informative program!	남	안녕하세요, 학생 여러분! 저는 여러분의 교감인 Davis 선생님입니다. 다가오는 Dream Future Program에 대해 알려 드리게 되어 기쁩니다. 프로그램에는 다양한 직업과 관련된 15개의 특강이 포함되어 있습니다. 여러분은 이번 주 금요일 오후 6시까지 학교 웹사이트에서 강의를 개별적으로 등록할 수 있습니다. 그것은 다음 달 5일부터 시작해서 3일간 진행될 것입니다. 각 강의에는 30명의 참가자 제한이 있다는 점에 유의하십시오. 강의에 참석한 후에, 여러분은 배운 것에 관한 보고서를 작성해야 할 것입니다. 이 유익한 프로그램을 놓치지 마세요!

문제 해설 Dream Future Program은 5일부터 시작해 3일간 진행될 것이라고 말했으므로, 담화의 내용과 일치하지 않는 것은 ③ '5일 동안 진행될 것이다.'이다.

어휘&어구 vice principal 교감 선생님   upcoming 다가오는   a variety of 다양한   register for ~에 등록하다   individually 개별적으로   note 유의하다, 주목하다   participant 참가자   attend 참석하다   miss out on ~을 놓치다   informative 유익한

10 주차장 온라인 예약
[정답] ③

W	Honey, what are you looking at?	여	여보, 뭘 보고 있어요?
M	A website for Amsterdam parking lots. We should reserve a spot for tomorrow.	남	Amsterdam 주차장 웹사이트요. 내일을 위해 자리를 예약해야 해요.
W	Good idea. It's going to be really crowded, so it's going to be hard to find a spot.	여	좋은 생각이네요. 정말 붐벼서 자리를 찾는 데 어려울 텐데요.
M	Yeah, which lot should we choose?	남	네. 어느 주차장을 선택해야 할까요?
W	We'll have the kids with us, so this one's too far from the city center. We should choose one of these under 10 minutes away.	여	우리는 아이들이 있어서 이곳은 도심에서 매우 멀어요. 10분 미만으로 떨어진 이 중에서 하나를 선택해야 할 것 같아요.
M	Okay. Then how about this one? It's only a 6-minute walk.	남	알겠어요. 그러면 이곳은 어때요? 단지 걸어서 6분이에요.
W	It has such a low rating, though. Under three stars.	여	하지만 아주 낮은 평가를 받았어요. 별이 3개 미만이에요.
M	Yeah, let's choose one with more than three stars.	남	네, 별이 3개보다 많은 곳을 선택해요.
W	All right. We won't need to cancel it, will we?	여	알겠어요. 우리는 이걸 취소할 필요는 없을 거 같아요, 그렇죠?
M	I doubt it. Let's get one of these non-refundable options.	남	없을 거 같아요. 환불 불가 선택 사항 중에 하나를 해요. 그것들이 더 저렴해요.
		여	그래요. 그러면 이 두 곳 중이네요.
		남	그것들은 크게 다르지 않아요.

They're cheaper.

W Okay. Then it's between these two places.

M They are not much different.

W Yeah. Then let's just get the cheaper one.

M Okay. Good choice.

여 네. 그러면 그냥 더 저렴한 곳으로 해요.

남 알겠어요. 좋은 선택이에요.

문제 해설 두 사람은 주차장을 예약하는데, 도심에서 걸어서 10분 미만으로 떨어진 곳이어야 하고, 평가에서 별을 3개보다 많이 받은 곳이면서 환불이 안 되는 곳 중에서 더 저렴한 곳을 하자고 했다. 따라서 두 사람이 선택한 주차장은 ③이다.

어휘&어구 spot 자리, 장소 crowded 붐비는, 복잡한 rating 평가, 순위 cancel 취소하다 non-refundable 환불 불가의

---

11 신작 소설　　　　　　　　　　　　　　　　　　　　　　　　　[정답] ①

M Christina, what are you reading?

W This is John Brown's latest novel, *Tomorrow*. It's so interesting that I can't put it down.

M Oh, I didn't know he had a new novel. I think I should read it.

W I can lend it to you if you want.

남 Christina, 뭐 읽고 있니?

여 이거 John Brown의 최신 소설 *Tomorrow*야. 정말 재밌어서 내려놓을 수가 없어.

남 아, 그가 새 소설을 쓴 줄 몰랐네. 나 그거 읽어 봐야겠다.

여 네가 원하면 그것을 빌려줄 수 있어.

문제 해설 John Brown의 새 소설을 재미있게 읽고 있는 여자에게 남자가 그의 새 소설이 나온 것을 몰랐다며 자신도 그 소설을 읽어 봐야겠다고 말하고 있다. 따라서 여자의 응답으로 가장 적절한 것은 ① '네가 원하면 그것을 빌려줄 수 있어.'이다.

② 나는 내일 그것을 온라인으로 살 거야.

③ 다른 도서관에 가 보는 게 어때?

④ 구내 서점에서 그 교재를 사.

⑤ 그것이 네가 속독을 배워야 하는 이유야.

어휘&어구 put down ~을 내려놓다

---

12 대학교수가 된 선생님 축하해 드리기　　　　　　　　　　　　　[정답] ④

W Roy, tomorrow's literature class is Mr. Kane's last class at our school.

M I know. That's too bad. But it's good for him to start teaching at a college next semester.

W Yeah, definitely. I think we should do something for him in his last class.

M Why don't we have a surprise party for him tomorrow?

여 Roy, 내일 문학 수업은 Kane 선생님의 우리 학교에서의 마지막 수업이야.

남 나도 알아. 아쉽다. 하지만 선생님이 다음 학기에 대학에서 강의를 시작하는 것은 좋은 일이잖아.

여 그래, 물론이지. 난 우리가 선생님의 마지막 수업에서 선생님을 위해 무언가를 해야 한다고 생각해.

남 우리가 내일 선생님을 위해 깜짝 파티를 여는 게 어때?

문제 해설 남자가 문학 선생님이 대학 강의를 시작하게 된 것이 좋은 일이라고 말하자, 여자는 선생님의 마지막 수업 시간에 무언가를 해야 한다고 말했다. 따라서 여자의 마지막 말에 대한 남자의 응답으로 가장 적절한 것은 ④ '우리가 내일 선생님을 위해 깜짝 파티를 여는 게 어때?'이다.

① 다음 학기에 선생님의 문학 수업을 듣기로 하자.

② 우리의 문학 보고서 마감일은 언제니?

③ 새 문학 선생님은 매우 엄격하다고 알려져 있어.

⑤ 그의 모든 학생들이 어제 송별회에 참석했어.

어휘&어구 literature 문학 semester 학기 deadline 마감일, 마감 시간 strict 엄격한 farewell party 송별회

M	Lily, why do you look so down?	남	Lily, 너는 왜 그렇게 울적해 보이는 거니?
W	Dad, it's because of my friend Kate. We talked on the phone earlier.	여	아빠, 제 친구 Kate 때문이에요. 우리는 아까 전화 통화를 했거든요.
M	And? Is there something wrong between the two of you?	남	그리고? 너희 둘 사이에 무슨 문제라도 있니?
W	Yeah. We're supposed to make a geography presentation tomorrow, but she won't be at school tomorrow.	여	네. 우리는 내일 지리 발표를 하기로 했는데, 그 애가 내일 학교에 오지 않을 거예요.
M	Oh no! Is there a problem?	남	아, 이런! 무슨 문제가 있는 거니?
W	She said she caught a bad cold.	여	그 애는 심한 감기에 걸렸다고 말했어요.
M	She must be pretty sick. So you're probably worried about your presentation tomorrow.	남	그 애가 꽤 아픈가 보구나. 그래서 너는 아마 내일 발표에 대해 걱정이 되겠구나.
W	Right. I don't think I can do it without her.	여	맞아요. 저는 그 애 없이는 그것을 할 수 없을 것 같아요.
M	Then why don't you talk to your teacher about it tomorrow?	남	그럼 내일 선생님께 그것에 대해 말씀드리는 게 어떠니?
W	What do you think he can actually do to help though?	여	하지만 선생님께서 실제로 무엇을 도와주실 수 있다고 생각하세요?
M	He might be able to let you do it later.	남	너희가 나중에 그것을 하게 해 주실 수도 있을 거야.
W	Oh, that would be great. I'll talk to him tomorrow.	여	아, 그것참 좋겠군요. 제가 내일 선생님께 말씀드릴게요.

문제 해설 친구가 아파서 내일 있을 지리 발표를 제대로 할 수 없다는 여자의 말에 남자는 선생님께 그것에 대해 말씀드리라고 조언했고, 이에 여자가 선생님께서 어떤 도움을 줄 수 있겠냐고 되묻자, 남자는 발표를 나중에 하게 해 주실 수 있을 거라고 말했다. 따라서 남자의 마지막 말에 대한 여자의 응답으로 가장 적절한 것은 ③ '아, 그것참 좋겠군요. 제가 내일 선생님께 말씀드릴게요.'이다.
① 네, 그건 제 잘못이에요. 제가 약속을 지켰어야 했어요.
② 아니요, 그러면 안 돼요. 아빠의 건강이 더 중요해요.
④ 와, 정말 멋졌어요! 아빠의 발표는 완벽했어요.
⑤ 걱정하지 마세요. 내일 제가 혼자 그것을 하는 게 편해요.

어휘&어구 geography 지리　presentation 발표

W	Hi, Daniel. Is something wrong?	여	안녕, Daniel. 무슨 일 있니?
M	Hey, Claudia. Yeah, actually I can't stop thinking about the presentation I gave this morning.	남	안녕, Claudia. 응, 실은 내가 오늘 오전에 했던 발표에 대한 생각을 멈출 수가 없어.
W	What presentation?	여	무슨 발표였는데?
M	It was for my sociology class. It was about the influence of mass media on society.	남	그것은 내 사회학 수업을 위한 것이었어. 대중 매체가 사회에 미치는 영향에 관한 것이었어.
W	Did you make a mistake or something?	여	실수를 하거나 그랬니?
M	Well, the main part of the presentation went smoothly, but something happened during the Q&A session.	남	음, 그 발표의 중요 부분은 잘 진행됐는데, 질의응답 시간에 어떤 일이 생겼어.
W	Were you asked a question you couldn't answer?	여	네가 답을 할 수가 없었던 질문을 받았니?
M	No. But some people pointed out that one of the survey results in my presentation wasn't reliable.	남	아니야. 그런데 어떤 사람들이 내 발표의 설문 결과들 중 하나가 신뢰할 수가 없다고 지적했어.
W	Why?	여	왜?
M	They said the question I asked was biased, prompting the respondents to answer in a specific way. I hadn't realized that, but they were right.	남	내가 했던 질문이 편향되어 있어서 응답자들이 특정한 방식으로 답하도록 유도한다고 그들이 말하더라고. 깨닫지 못했었는데, 그들이 옳았어.
W	I see. Don't worry too much. Just be more careful in the future to avoid making the same mistake.	여	그렇구나. 너무 걱정하지는 마. 똑같은 실수를 하지 않도록 나중에 더 조심하기만 하면 돼.
M	Okay. I'll be sure to create questions that are not partial.	남	알겠어. 나는 반드시 편파적이지 않은 질문들을 만들 거야.

문제 해설 남자가 사회학 수업 발표에서 발표에 포함된 설문 조사 질문이 응답자들이 특정한 방식으로 답하도록 유도해 신뢰할 수가 없다고 지적받았다고 하자 여자가 위로하면서 똑같은 실수를 하지 않도록 조심하라고 말했으므로, 이에 대한 남자의 응답으로 가장 적절한 것은 ② '알겠어. 나는 반드시 편파적이지 않은 질문들을 만들 거야.'이다.
① 아니야. 대중 매체의 역할은 과거와는 달라야만 해.
③ 맞아. 질문에 답하기 전에 너는 신중해야만 해.
④ 물론이야. 설문은 신뢰할 수 있는 정보를 얻는 데 매우 효과적이야.
⑤ 고마워. 나는 네 덕분에 크게 실수하는 것을 피할 수가 있었어.

어휘&어구 sociology 사회학 mass media 대중 매체 point out ~을 지적하다 survey result 설문 결과 reliable 신뢰할 수 있는 biased 편향된, 선입견이 있는 prompt 유도하다 respondent 응답자 partial 편파적인

---

15 꽃집 고객 유치하기 [정답] ②

W Sally runs a flower shop downtown and her friend John owns a bakery several blocks away. These days Sally is worried about the decrease in the number of her customers. So she's trying to find ways to attract customers. Today she comes up with the idea of selling tea at her flower shop. People who come for tea could buy flowers. Sally tells John about that and he says it's a good idea. John suggests that she also sell cookies with the tea. Sally likes his tip a lot and wants to ask if she can buy them from him. In this situation, what would Sally most likely say to John?

Sally Can I get the cookies from your bakery?

여 Sally는 시내에서 꽃집을 운영하고, 그녀의 친구 John은 몇 블록 떨어진 곳에서 제과점을 소유하고 있습니다. 요즘 Sally는 고객 수가 줄어들어 걱정하고 있습니다. 그래서 그녀는 고객을 끌어들이기 위한 방법을 찾기 위해 애쓰고 있습니다. 오늘 그녀는 자신의 꽃집에서 차를 파는 아이디어를 생각해 냅니다. 차를 마시러 오는 사람들이 꽃을 살 수도 있을 것입니다. Sally는 John에게 그것에 대해 말하고 그는 그것이 좋은 생각이라고 말합니다. John은 그녀가 차와 함께 쿠키도 팔라고 제안합니다. Sally는 그의 조언이 아주 마음에 들어서 그에게서 그것들을 살 수 있는지 묻고 싶어 합니다. 이런 상황에서 Sally는 John에게 뭐라고 말하겠습니까?

Sally 네 제과점에서 쿠키를 살 수 있니?

문제 해설 꽃집을 운영하는 Sally는 고객 수가 줄어들어서 꽃과 함께 차를 파는 아이디어를 생각해 내고, 이것을 들은 제과점 주인인 친구 John은 차와 함께 쿠키도 팔 것을 제안하여, Sally는 John에게서 쿠키를 살 수 있는지 묻고 싶어 하는 상황이다. 따라서 Sally가 John에게 할 말로 가장 적절한 것은 ② '네 제과점에서 쿠키를 살 수 있니?'이다.
① 차와 함께 쿠키를 먹고 싶니?
③ 네 고객들이 너에게서 많은 쿠키를 사니?
④ 내 꽃집에 더 많은 고객이 올 것이라고 생각하니?
⑤ 오는 길에 쿠키와 꽃을 좀 사서 올 수 있겠니?

어휘&어구 run 운영하다 own 소유하다 decrease 감소 attract 끌어들이다 come up with ~을 생각해 내다, ~을 떠올리다

16~17 통계학의 다양한 활용 [정답] 16 ① 17 ③

M Hello, students. Last class, we talked about the origin and history of statistics. Today we'll move on to the present day. As information technology opens new worlds of possibilities, statistics greatly helps people carry out their work. Here are some examples. Firstly, when it comes to running a small business, the business owner needs to make important decisions such as how much product to purchase. Statistical analysis helps him or her make these

남 안녕하세요, 학생 여러분. 지난 수업 시간에 우리는 통계의 기원과 역사에 대해 이야기했습니다. 오늘은 지금 시대로 옮겨 가겠습니다. 정보 기술이 새로운 가능성의 세계를 열면서, 통계는 사람들이 자신의 일을 수행하는 데 큰 도움을 줍니다. 여기 몇 가지 예가 있습니다. 첫째, 소규모 기업 운영에 관해 말하자면, 사업주는 얼마만큼의 제품을 구매해야 하는지와 같은 중요한 결정을 내려야 합니다. 통계 분석은 그 사람이 이러한 결정을 내리는 데 도움을 줍니다. 또한, 은행이나 보험 회사에서 일하는 금융 관리자들은 고도의

decisions. Also, financial managers who work at a bank or insurance company should have advanced statistical knowledge. This is because financial institutions forecast future economic conditions and those forecasts are heavily dependent on statistical sampling. Next, military recruiters rely on statistics to forecast how many people will join the military in the future. Lastly, biostatistics is critical to medical researchers for conducting research. Statisticians are involved in these efforts and many more.

통계 지식을 갖춰야 합니다. 이는 금융 기관이 미래의 경제 상황을 예측하고, 그러한 예측은 통계 표본에 대단히 의존하기 때문입니다. 다음으로, 군대의 신병 모집자들은 미래에 얼마나 많은 사람이 군에 입대할 것인지를 예측하기 위해 통계에 의존합니다. 마지막으로, 생물 통계학은 의학 연구자들에게 연구를 수행하는 데 있어 매우 중요합니다. 통계 전문가들은 이러한 노력과 더욱 많은 것에 관여합니다.

문제 해설 16 지난 수업 시간에 통계학의 기원과 역사를 학습했다고 말한 후, 현재는 통계학이 정보 기술의 발전으로 다양한 분야에서 응용되고 있음을 각 분야의 사례를 제시하면서 설명하고 있다. 따라서 남자가 하는 말의 주제로 가장 적절한 것은 ① '통계가 도움이 되는 직업'이다.
② 디지털 시대의 직업 선택
③ 세계 산업 동향의 예측
④ 직업 만족도에 영향을 미치는 요인
⑤ 통계 목적으로 데이터를 수집하는 방법
17 사업주, 금융 관리자, 군대의 신병 모집자, 의학 연구원은 언급되었지만, ③ '기상 예보자'는 언급되지 않았다.

어휘&어구 statistics 통계, 통계학 purchase 구입하다 analysis 분석 financial 금융의, 재무의 insurance 보험 institution 기관 forecast 예측하다, 예보하다 recruiter 신병 모집자 biostatistics 생물 통계학

2회 수능실전 대비연습

본문 46~47쪽

01 ④ 02 ⑤ 03 ③ 04 ⑤ 05 ⑤ 06 ③ 07 ① 08 ④ 09 ④ 10 ④ 11 ⑤ 12 ④ 13 ④ 14 ③
15 ⑤ 16 ④ 17 ②

01 지나친 설탕 섭취의 위험성

[정답] ④

W Good morning, everyone. Welcome to *One-Minute Health*. How often do you eat sweet drinks or candy? Maybe very often. Now is the best time to break this unhealthy habit. According to studies, consuming too much sugar can have serious negative health effects. High sugar intake is strongly related to obesity, diabetes, heart disease, and even certain types of cancer. To protect your health, avoid sugary beverages and snacks, and replace them with natural sources of sweetness, such as fruits. Your health matters, so let's make smart decisions to safeguard your bodies. Come back tomorrow to hear another useful health tip. Have a great day!

여 좋은 아침입니다, 여러분. *One-Minute Health*에 오신 것을 환영합니다. 여러분께서는 단 음료나 사탕을 얼마나 자주 드시나요? 아마도 매우 자주일 것입니다. 지금이 이 건강에 해로운 습관을 끊기에 가장 좋은 때입니다. 연구들에 따르면 설탕을 너무 많이 섭취하는 것은 건강에 심각한 부정적인 영향을 미칠 수 있습니다. 높은 설탕 섭취는 비만, 당뇨, 심장병, 심지어는 특정 유형의 암과 밀접한 관련이 있습니다. 여러분의 건강을 보호하려면 설탕이 든 음료와 스낵을 피하고 그것들을 과일과 같은 자연적인 단맛으로 대체하십시오. 여러분의 건강은 중요하므로, 여러분의 몸을 보호하기 위해 현명한 결정을 내리세요. 내일도 오셔서 또 다른 유용한 건강 팁을 들으세요. 좋은 하루 보내세요!

문제 해설　여자는 지나친 설탕 섭취가 비만, 당뇨, 심장병, 암과 같은 질병을 일으킬 수 있으므로 건강을 위해 설탕이 든 음료와 스낵을 피하라고 말하고 있다. 따라서 여자가 하는 말의 목적으로 가장 적절한 것은 ④ '설탕 섭취가 건강에 미치는 위험성을 경고하려고'이다.

어휘&어구　negative 부정적인　intake 섭취(량)　obesity 비만　diabetes 당뇨　sugary 설탕이 든　replace A with B A를 B로 대체하다
safeguard 보호하다

02 자전거 전용 도로 보행 금지 규정 준수 [정답] ⑤

M	Hey, Jennifer. Let's walk on the new sidewalk.
W	It's not actually a sidewalk, and it's not meant for pedestrians. It's a bike-only path.
M	You mean this is for cyclists only?
W	Yes. We're not supposed to walk on this path. There's a sign on the path up ahead.
M	Does that mean people can't walk there at all?
W	You got that right.
M	I didn't know that.
W	Well, the city is building more and more bike paths to encourage more people to ride their bikes.
M	That's good. But there aren't any cyclists around.
W	We still shouldn't walk on the bike path. It's the law.
M	I see.

남	어이, Jennifer. 새 보도로 걷자.
여	그것은 실제로 보도가 아니야. 그리고 그것은 보행자용으로 만들어진 게 아니야. 그것은 자전거 전용 도로야.
남	네 말은 이것은 자전거 타는 사람들만을 위한 것이라는 뜻이니?
여	그래. 우리는 이 길에서 걸어서는 안 돼. 길 위 저 앞에 표지가 있네.
남	그것은 사람들이 거기서 절대 걸어서는 안 된다는 뜻이니?
여	네 말이 맞아.
남	난 그것을 몰랐어.
여	음, 이 도시는 더 많은 사람들이 자전거를 타도록 권장하기 위해서 점점 더 많은 자전거 도로를 건설 중이야.
남	좋은 일이네. 하지만 주변에 자전거 타는 사람이 한 명도 없잖아.
여	그래도 우리는 자전거 도로 위에서 걸어서는 안 돼. 그것은 법이야.
남	알겠어.

문제 해설　여자는 남자에게 자전거 전용 도로를 보행자가 이용해서는 안 되며, 주변에 자전거 타는 사람이 없더라도 자전거 도로에서 걸으면 안 되며, 그것은 법이라고 말했다. 따라서 여자의 주장으로 가장 적절한 것은 ⑤ '자전거 전용 도로의 보행 금지 규정을 준수해야 한다.'이다.

어휘&어구　sidewalk 보도, 인도　pedestrian 보행자　path 길　sign 표지(판)　You got that right. 네 말이 맞아.　encourage 권장하다

03 인테리어 변경 요청 [정답] ③

	[Cell phone rings.]
M	Hello, Ms. Elliot. How are you?
W	Hello, Mr. Rogers. I'm good. How can I help you?
M	I'd like to change some of the design elements that we discussed.
W	What would you like to change?
M	I planned on moving the TV to my bedroom, but now I'd rather leave it as it is.
W	But if you leave the TV in the living room, you can't put a standing bookshelf along the entire wall like you wanted to.
M	I know. How about putting two compact bookshelves at both ends of the TV, instead? Do you think they can hold all of my books?

	[휴대 전화가 울린다.]
남	안녕하세요, Elliot 씨. 어떻게 지내세요?
여	안녕하세요, Rogers 씨. 잘 지내고 있어요. 무엇을 도와드릴까요?
남	저희가 의논한 디자인 요소 중 일부를 변경하고 싶어요.
여	어느 부분을 변경하고 싶으신가요?
남	TV를 제 침실로 옮기려고 계획했으나, 지금은 그대로 두고 싶어요.
여	그런데 TV를 거실에 둔다면, 당신이 원하셨던 대로 스탠드형 책장을 (거실) 벽면 전체에 나란히 둘 수가 없어요.
남	알아요. 대신에, TV 양쪽에 소형 책장 두 개를 놓는 것은 어떤가요? 그 책장들에 제 책이 전부 들어갈 수 있을 것 같나요?
여	아니요, 그 책장들에는 그렇게 많은 책이 들어가지는 못할 것 같아요.
남	어쩌면 원래 계획으로 되돌아가는 것이 최선일 수 있겠네요.
여	글쎄요, 벽걸이형 책장과 보관장이 좋은 해결책이 될 것 같아요. 그

W No, I don't think they can hold that many.	렇게 하면 보관 공간이 더 확보될 뿐만 아니라, 거실이 멋지게 보일 거예요.
M Maybe it's best I go back to the original plan.	남 완벽한 것 같아요! 당신은 정말 창의적으로 사고하는 사람이에요.
W Well, a wall-mounted bookshelf and storage cabinets may be a good solution. That will make your living room look stylish, as well as give you more storage space.	여 제 아이디어를 마음에 들어 하시니 기쁘네요.
M Sounds perfect! You're such a creative thinker.	남 그리고 새로운 디자인을 예산 내로 해 주시겠어요?
W I'm glad you like my idea.	여 물론이죠. 문제없어요.
M And would you keep the new design within my budget?	
W Sure. Not a problem.	

문제 해설 남자가 여자에게 자신의 거실 실내 디자인 일부를 변경해 달라고 요청하고 있으므로 의뢰인임을 알 수 있다. 여자는 남자의 요청 사항을 듣고 나은 디자인 대안을 제시하고 있으므로 인테리어 디자이너임을 알 수 있다. 따라서 두 사람의 관계를 가장 잘 나타낸 것은 ③이다.

어휘&어구 element 요소, 부분 plan on -ing ~하는 것을 계획하다 bookshelf 책장, 책꽂이 compact 소형의 wall-mounted 벽걸이형의, 벽에 고정된[부착된] budget 예산

04 아이스 스케이팅 쇼 　　　　　　　　　　　　　　　　　　　　　[정답] ⑤

W How was your weekend, Benjamin?	여 주말은 어땠니, Benjamin?
M Great, Ms. Green. I went to an ice skating show. Here's a picture I took.	남 좋았어요, Green 선생님. 저는 아이스 스케이트 쇼에 갔어요. 여기 제가 찍은 사진이 있어요.
W Wow, the stage looks fantastic. I like the two towers in the background.	여 와, 무대가 정말 멋져 보이는구나. 배경에 있는 두 개의 탑이 마음에 든다.
M Me, too. I also loved the diamond pattern on the doors between them.	남 저도요. 저는 그것들 사이의 문에 있는 다이아몬드 무늬도 정말 마음에 들었어요.
W It makes the stage look more interesting.	여 그게 무대를 더 흥미롭게 보이게 하는구나.
M The show was about a magic castle. Do you see the snowman at the top of the steps?	남 그 쇼는 마법의 성에 관한 거였어요. 계단 맨 위에 눈사람이 보이시나요?
W Yes.	여 그래.
M He used to be the king, but a witch turned him into a snowman. The female skater is his daughter, the princess.	남 그는 왕이었는데, 마녀가 그를 눈사람으로 만들었어요. 여자 스케이터는 그의 딸인 공주예요.
W Sounds interesting. The male skater must be a prince.	여 흥미롭구나. 남자 스케이터가 틀림없이 왕자겠지.
M Yes. He lifted the female skater above his head.	남 네. 그는 자신의 머리 위로 여자 스케이터를 들어 올렸어요.
W And look, even with her arms together, she was able to balance.	여 그리고 봐, 그녀는 양팔을 모으고도 균형을 잡을 수 있었구나.
M Yeah. It was a wonderful show with a lot to see.	남 네. 볼거리가 많은 멋진 쇼였어요.

문제 해설 대화에서 여자 스케이터가 양팔을 모으고 있다고 하였으나, 그림에서 여자 스케이터는 양팔을 벌리고 있으므로, 대화의 내용과 일치하지 않는 것은 ⑤이다.

어휘&어구 balance 균형을 잡다

05 잉크 카트리지 구입 부탁하기 　　　　　　　　　　　　　　　　　　[정답] ⑤

[Cell phone rings.]	[휴대 전화가 울린다.]
W Hi, Justin. What's up?	여 안녕, Justin. 무슨 일이니?
M Mom, are you on your way home?	남 엄마, 집에 오시는 길이세요?

W Not yet, but I'm leaving work soon. You're going to see a movie with Kevin this evening, right?	**여** 아직 아니지만, 곧 퇴근할 거야. 오늘 저녁에 Kevin이랑 영화 보러 가지, 그렇지?
M Well, he just called and said he can't go because he has a bad headache.	**남** 음, 걔가 방금 전화해서 두통이 심해서 못 간다고 했어요.
W Sorry to hear that, but now we can have dinner together.	**여** 유감이지만, 그러면 이제 우리가 저녁을 같이 먹을 수 있겠구나.
M Well, then, how about ordering a pizza?	**남** 음, 그러면 피자를 주문하면 어때요?
W That sounds good to me. I think I'll be home around seven.	**여** 그거 좋은 생각이구나. 7시쯤에 집에 도착할 것 같아.
M Okay, then I'll order a pizza around 6:30.	**남** 알겠어요, 그럼 6시 30분쯤에 피자를 주문할게요.
W Perfect.	**여** 좋아.
M One more thing, Mom. I have something to print out for my homework, but the printer says the ink cartridge is empty.	**남** 한 가지 더요, 엄마. 숙제 때문에 출력할 것이 있는데, 프린터에 잉크 카트리지가 비어 있다고 나와요.
W There might be an extra cartridge in the desk drawer. Have you looked?	**여** 책상 서랍에 여분의 카트리지가 있을지도 몰라. 찾아봤니?
M Yeah, but there isn't one there. Can you get one for me?	**남** 네, 하지만 거기에 없어요. 하나 사다 주실래요?
W Okay. Then I'll stop by the office supply store next to my work.	**여** 알았어. 그러면 회사 옆 사무용품 판매점에 들를게.
M Thanks, Mom. See you soon.	**남** 고마워요, 엄마. 곧 봐요.

문제 해설 남자는 여자에게 집에 오는 길에 잉크 카트리지를 사다 줄 수 있는지 묻고 있으므로, 남자가 여자에게 부탁한 일로 가장 적절한 것은 ⑤ '잉크 카트리지 사 오기'이다.

어휘&어구 cartridge 카트리지 drawer 서랍 office supply store 사무용품 판매점

06 운동화 세탁 맡기기 [정답] ③

M Good morning, Ms. Gibson.	**남** 안녕하세요, Gibson 씨.
W Hello, Mr. Turner. I'm here to pick up the skirt I dropped off a few days ago.	**여** 안녕하세요, Turner 씨. 제가 며칠 전에 맡겼던 치마를 찾으러 왔습니다.
M Yes, just a moment, please. *[Pause]* Here it is.	**남** 네, 잠시만요. *[잠시 후]* 여기 있습니다.
W It looks perfect. Thank you. You said the cost was $20, didn't you?	**여** 완벽해 보이네요. 감사합니다. 비용이 20달러라고 하셨죠?
M That's right.	**남** 맞습니다.
W Okay. I'd also like to have these running shoes cleaned.	**여** 좋아요. 이 운동화들도 세탁하고 싶습니다.
M All right. How many pairs?	**남** 알겠습니다. 몇 켤레죠?
W I have two pairs. How much does a shoe cleaning cost?	**여** 두 켤레입니다. 신발 세탁은 얼마입니까?
M It's $5 a pair.	**남** 한 켤레에 5달러입니다.
W Oh, that's cheap. Please charge the fees for the skirt and the shoes to this credit card.	**여** 아, 싸네요. 이 신용 카드에 치마와 신발 비용을 청구해 주세요.
M Okay. Thanks.	**남** 알겠습니다. 감사해요.

문제 해설 치마에 대한 비용은 20달러이고 운동화 세탁비는 켤레 당 5달러인데 두 켤레를 가져왔다고 했으므로, 여자가 지불할 금액은 ③ '30달러'이다.

어휘&어구 running shoes 운동화 charge 청구하다

07 미술 대회 시상식 참석 [정답] ①

W Dad, I've got great news.	**여** 아빠, 좋은 소식이 있어요.
M What is it, Julia?	**남** 뭐니, Julia?
W Ms. Evans told me that I won first place at the art competition I participated in last month.	**여** Evans 선생님께서 지난달에 참가한 미술 대회에서 제가 1등을 했다고 말씀하셨어요.

M	Really? Congratulations! I'm so proud of you!	남	정말? 축하해! 네가 정말 자랑스럽구나!
W	Thanks, Dad. She said the award ceremony is next Saturday at the City Hall.	여	고마워요, 아빠. 그녀는 시상식이 다음 주 토요일에 시청에서 열린 다고 말씀하셨어요.
M	What time is it at? You have your swimming lessons on Saturday mornings.	남	몇 시에 열리니? 너는 토요일 아침에 수영 수업이 있잖아.
W	I know. Fortunately, the ceremony is at 2 p.m., so I can make it. Can you come?	여	알고 있어요. 다행히 시상식은 오후 2시여서 갈 수 있어요. 오실 수 있어요?
M	I'm really sorry, but I have a business trip that day.	남	정말 미안하지만 내가 그날 출장이 있구나.
W	Ah, that's okay. Mom said she would come.	여	아, 괜찮아요. 엄마가 오실 거라고 하셨어요.
M	That's good. I'll treat you to a fancy dinner on Saturday evening to celebrate.	남	잘됐구나. 축하하기 위해 내가 토요일 저녁에 너에게 멋진 저녁을 사 줄게.
W	Sounds great, Dad.	여	좋아요, 아빠.

문제 해설 지난달에 참가한 미술 대회에서 1등을 해 토요일에 시상식에 참석해야 하는 여자가 아빠인 남자에게 올 수 있는지를 묻자 남자가 그날 출장이 있어 갈 수가 없다고 했으므로, 남자가 시상식에 참석하지 못하는 이유는 ① '출장이 예정되어 있어서'이다.

어휘&어구 be proud of ~을 자랑스러워하다 award ceremony 시상식 make it 참석하다, 시간 맞춰 가다 business trip 출장 celebrate 축하하다

08 Greenhill 불빛 축제　　　　　　　　　　　　　　　　　　　　　　　[정답] ④

W	Honey, what are you looking at on your smartphone?	여	여보, 스마트폰으로 무엇을 보고 있어요?
M	The Greenhill Light Festival website. Do you want to go again this year?	남	Greenhill 불빛 축제의 웹사이트요. 올해 다시 가고 싶지요?
W	Sure, I'd love to. When is it?	여	물론이죠, 가고 싶어요. 그것은 언제예요?
M	It's from December 11th to the 20th.	남	12월 11일부터 20일까지예요.
W	Will it be held at Greenhill Gardens again this year?	여	올해도 Greenhill Gardens에서 다시 열리나요?
M	Yes, but it looks bigger this year.	남	네, 하지만 그것이 올해는 더 커 보이네요.
W	How much does it cost?	여	그것(입장료)은 얼마인가요?
M	Adult tickets are $10, with discounts for children.	남	성인 입장권은 10달러이고, 아이들은 할인돼요.
W	Good. Our girls will love the festival. Have they extended the trail?	여	좋네요. 우리 딸들이 그 축제를 좋아할 거예요. 코스를 연장했나요?
M	Yeah. It's now 3 km long, and it even goes through a tunnel. And there are now over a million twinkling lights.	남	네. 그것이 이제는 거리가 3킬로미터이고, 심지어 터널을 통과해요. 그리고 지금은 반짝거리는 전등이 백만 개가 넘어요.
W	Awesome!	여	굉장하네요!
M	And it says they're going to open up a public parking lot nearby for extra parking.	남	그리고 추가 주차를 위해서 근처에 공용 주차장을 개장할 거라고 나와 있어요.
W	That's good. They'll need it.	여	그거 잘됐네요. 그것이 필요할 거예요.

문제 해설 Greenhill 불빛 축제에 관해 개최 기간, 개최 장소, 입장료, 주차장은 언급되었지만, ④ '참가 기념품'은 언급되지 않았다.

어휘&어구 light 불빛, 전등 extend 연장하다 trail (특정 목적을 위해 따라가는) 코스, 오솔길 go through ~을 통과하다 twinkle 반짝거리다, 반짝반짝 빛나다 awesome 굉장한, 멋진

09 교내 시 쓰기 대회　　　　　　　　　　　　　　　　　　　　　　　[정답] ④

M	Attention, everyone! This is Mr. Anderson, the school literature teacher. I'm excited to tell you about the school Poetry Writing Competition coming up the week right after final exams. All students can enter the competition to show off their creativity through poetry. Poems can	남	주목해 주세요, 여러분! 저는 학교의 문학 교사인 Mr. Anderson 입니다. 기말고사 바로 다음 주에 열릴 교내 Poetry Writing Competition에 대해 말씀드리게 되어 기쁩니다. 모든 학생들이 시를 통해 창의력을 뽐내기 위해 대회에 참가할 수 있습니다. 시는 사랑, 자연의 아름다움, 사회 문제 또는 여러분이 열정을 가지고

be about anything: love, the beauty of nature, social issues, or anything else that you're passionate about. Each student can enter one poem, and you must submit your poem by June 3rd. The poems will be judged by our school teachers, and the top three winners will receive a $100 gift certificate for the downtown bookstore. For more information, please visit the teachers' office on the 3rd floor. I eagerly anticipate a lot of you participating in this competition. Thank you.

있는 다른 어떤 것에 관한 것일 수 있습니다. 각 학생이 한 편의 시를 출품할 수 있는데, 6월 3일까지 시를 제출해야 합니다. 시는 본교 교사들이 심사할 것이며, 상위 3명의 우승자는 시내 서점에서 사용할 수 있는 100달러짜리 상품권을 받게 될 것입니다. 더 많은 정보를 위해서는 3층에 있는 교무실을 방문하기 바랍니다. 이번 대회에 여러분 중 많은 사람이 참가하기를 많이 기대하겠습니다. 감사합니다.

문제 해설 Poetry Writing Competition에서 학생들이 제출한 시는 본교 교사들이 심사할 것이라고 했으므로, 담화의 내용과 일치하지 않는 것은 ④ '제출된 시는 외부 초청 시인들이 심사할 것이다.'이다.

어휘&어구 literature 문학 poetry 시 show off ~을 뽐내다, ~을 자랑하다 creativity 창의력 passionate 열정적인 judge 심사하다 gift certificate 상품권

10 아들 생일 파티용 블루투스 마이크 구입 [정답] ④

W Good afternoon. Can I help you find something?

M Yes. I'm looking for a Bluetooth wireless microphone for my son's birthday party.

W Okay, we have various Bluetooth microphones. Do you have a budget in mind?

M Well, I'd like to keep it under $45.

W All right. How about a microphone with LED lights? Kids really like ones with colorful LED lights.

M Perfect. It'll be fun to use at the birthday party.

W Right. And what color do you think your son will like?

M Definitely not pink. He'd like either of the other two colors.

W Okay. Well, this one has a longer battery life.

M I'll take it, then. Here's my credit card.

여 안녕하세요. 어떤 걸 찾고 계신지 좀 도와드릴까요?

남 네. 제 아들 생일 파티를 위한 블루투스 무선 마이크를 찾고 있어요.

여 알겠습니다, 다양한 블루투스 마이크가 있습니다. 생각해 두신 예산이 있나요?

남 음, 45달러 미만으로 돈을 쓰고 싶어요.

여 알겠습니다. LED 조명이 있는 마이크는 어때요? 아이들은 알록달록한 LED 조명이 있는 것을 정말 좋아해요.

남 완벽해요. 생일 파티에서 사용하면 재미있을 거예요.

여 맞아요. 그리고 아드님이 무슨 색을 좋아할 거라고 생각하세요?

남 분명히 분홍색은 아닙니다. 나머지 두 가지 색들 중에서는 어느 것이든 좋아할 거예요.

여 알겠습니다. 음, 이것이 배터리 수명이 더 길어요.

남 그럼, 그것을 살게요. 여기 제 신용 카드가 있습니다.

문제 해설 남자는 아들 생일 파티를 위해 사려고 하는 블루투스 무선 마이크로 가격은 45달러 미만이며, LED 조명이 있고 분홍색이 아니며 배터리 수명이 더 긴 것을 사겠다고 말했다. 따라서 남자가 구입할 마이크는 ④이다.

어휘&어구 wireless 무선의 budget 예산 colorful 알록달록한, 다채로운 definitely 분명히

11 온천 방문 [정답] ⑤

M Emily, we finally made it to the hot spring. That was a long drive.

W Yeah. But it'll be worth driving all the way here. A lot of people told me this hot spring is really nice.

M I also heard the water is really hot and clean, and there are beautiful mountain views.

W Sounds awesome! I can't wait to enjoy the hot spring.

남 Emily, 우리 마침내 온천에 도착했어요. 그것은 장거리 운전이었어요.

여 그래요. 하지만 여기까지 내내 운전해서 올 가치가 있을 거예요. 많은 사람들이 이 온천이 매우 좋다고 말해 주었어요.

남 물이 정말 뜨겁고 깨끗하고, 산의 전망이 아름답다고도 들었어요.

여 정말 멋질 것 같아요! 난 온천을 빨리 즐기고 싶어요.

문제 해설 여자가 온천이 매우 좋은 곳으로 알려져 있다고 말하자, 남자도 물이 뜨겁고 깨끗하고, 산의 전망이 아름답다고 들었다고 말했다. 따라서 남자의 마지막 말에 대한 여자의 응답으로 가장 적절한 것은 ⑤ '정말 멋질 것 같아요! 난 온천을 빨리 즐기고 싶어요.'이다.
① 아니요, 고마워요. 뜨거운 목욕을 하고 나니 기분이 좋아요.
② 음, 거기까지 운전하려면 적어도 5시간은 걸릴 거예요.

③ 전혀 그렇지 않아요. 나는 그 온천에 대해서 들어 본 적이 없어요.

④ 와! 온천이 이렇게 가까운 데 있을 줄 몰랐네요.

make it to ~에 도착하다 hot spring 온천 be worth -ing ~할 가치가 있다

---

12 공항에서 주차하기

[정답] ④

W Honey, finally we're at the airport. Do you know where the parking lot is?

M Yes, I do. It's a little far from here, so I'll drop off you and the kids first in front of the entrance.

W Okay. Shall I wait for you at the check-in counter?

M Sounds good. I'll go there after parking the car.

여 여보, 드디어 공항에 도착했어요. 주차장이 어디 있는지 알아요?

남 네, 알아요. 여기서 좀 머니까 당신과 아이들을 입구 앞에서 먼저 내려 줄게요.

여 좋아요. 내가 탑승 수속 창구에서 당신을 기다릴까요?

남 좋을 것 같아요. 나는 차를 주차한 후에 그곳에 갈게요.

남자는 공항에 도착하자, 주차장이 머니까 입구 앞에서 여자와 아이들을 먼저 내려 주겠다고 말했고, 이에 여자는 남자에게 자신이 탑승 수속 창구에서 기다리고 있을지 물었다. 따라서 여자의 마지막 말에 대한 남자의 응답으로 가장 적절한 것은 ④ '좋을 것 같아요. 나는 차를 주차한 후에 그곳에 갈게요.'이다.

① 아니요, 그러지 않을 거예요. 나는 30분쯤 후에 체크인할 거예요.

② 그럴 필요 없어요. 난 이미 우리 차를 주차했거든요.

③ 고마워요. 그럼 내가 먼저 우리 애들과 함께 내릴게요.

⑤ 맞아요. 우리는 공항 셔틀버스로 호텔에 갈 수 있어요.

entrance 입구 check-in counter (공항의) 탑승 수속 창구

---

13 여행 스타일이 다른 친구와의 여행

[정답] ④

M Hi, Sophia. It's been a long time since I've seen you at the gym.

W Hey, Tyler. I went to Canada with a friend for two weeks, so I couldn't come to work out.

M Oh, I see. How was your trip to Canada?

W It wasn't that good. It would've been much better if I'd traveled alone.

M Why do you say that?

W I'd never traveled with others before, but I thought it'd be okay to travel with my best friend. But I was wrong.

M What happened?

W Nothing specific. Our styles are just so different. I like to always be doing something and want to go to as many places as possible when I travel.

M Ah, but your friend likes to just stay in one place.

W Exactly. Our different travel styles made me regret this trip.

남 안녕, Sophia. 체육관에서 본 이후로 오랜만이야.

여 안녕, Tyler. 친구랑 2주 동안 캐나다에 가 있어서 운동하러 올 수가 없었어.

남 아, 그렇구나. 캐나다 여행은 어땠어?

여 그렇게 좋지는 않았어. 혼자 여행을 했으면 훨씬 더 좋았을 것 같아.

남 왜 그렇게 말하니?

여 내가 전에 다른 사람들과 여행을 해 본 적이 없었지만, 가장 친한 친구와 여행하는 것은 괜찮다고 생각했거든. 하지만 내가 틀렸어.

남 무슨 일이 있었니?

여 특별한 일은 없었어. 우리 스타일이 그저 너무 달라. 여행할 때 나는 항상 무언가를 하는 것이 좋고 가능한 한 많은 장소를 가 보고 싶거든.

남 아, 하지만 네 친구는 한곳에 그냥 머무르는 것을 좋아하는구나.

여 맞아. 우리의 다른 여행 스타일이 내가 이 여행을 후회하게 만들었어.

여자가 가장 친한 친구와 여행을 갔었지만 서로 여행 스타일이 달라서 아쉬웠다고 하면서 자신은 항상 무언가를 하고 많은 장소에 가 보고 싶어 한다고 하자 남자가 '네 친구는 한곳에 머무르는 것을 좋아하는구나'라고 말했으므로, 이에 대한 여자의 응답으로 가장 적절한 것은 ④ '맞아. 우리의 다른 여행 스타일이 내가 이 여행을 후회하게 만들었어.'이다.

① 물론이지. 내가 좋은 여행사 직원을 찾아 줄게.

② 미안해. 지금부터 운동하는 것을 거르지 않을게.

③ 맞는 말이야. 우리는 여행 중에 운동을 했어야만 했어.

⑤ 아니야. 우리가 지난번에 함께 여행했을 때 내 친구는 달랐어.

work out 운동하다 travel agent 여행사 직원 skip 거르다 regret 후회하다

14 탑승권을 인터넷에 올리지 말아야 하는 이유

[정답] ③

W	Jason, you're back! How was your trip to Cuba?
M	It was great! You should go there someday.
W	I'd love to. Do you have any pictures?
M	Sure! I posted pictures on social media during my trip. Let me show you. *[Pause]* Here.... This is a photo of me boarding the plane to Cuba.
W	Your boarding pass is completely visible! You shouldn't upload that online!
M	Why not?
W	Because the bar code printed on your boarding pass can be used to get private information about you.
M	But I didn't have any problems at all during my trip.
W	That's good, but let me show you what I mean. Watch, using the bar code scanning app on my phone I'll scan your bar code. Look!
M	Oh, wow! It shows my name and the booking reference of my ticket!
W	Right. If someone accessed this, they could steal your flight or change your seats. They could do a lot.
M	I see. I should take this picture down right away.

여	Jason, 너 돌아왔구나! 쿠바 여행은 어땠어?
남	멋졌어! 언젠가 너 거기 가 봐.
여	그러고 싶어. 사진을 좀 찍었니?
남	물론이지! 여행하는 동안 소셜 미디어에 사진을 게시했어. 너에게 보여 줄게. *[잠시 후]* 여기…. 쿠바로 가는 비행기에 탑승하는 내 사진이야.
여	네 탑승권이 완전하게 보이잖아! 그걸 온라인에 올리면 안 돼!
남	왜 안 돼?
여	네 탑승권에 인쇄된 바코드가 너의 개인 정보를 찾는 데 사용될 수 있어.
남	하지만 난 여행 동안 내내 어떠한 문제도 없었는걸.
여	다행이지만, 내가 무슨 말을 하는지 너에게 보여 줄게. 봐, 내 전화기에 있는 바코드를 스캔하는 앱을 이용해서 내가 너의 바코드를 스캔해 볼게. 봐!
남	오, 와! 내 이름과 내 항공권의 예약 번호잖아.
여	맞아. 누군가가 여기에 접근한다면, 그들이 너의 항공권을 훔치거나 너의 좌석을 바꿔 놓을 수 있어. 그들은 많은 것을 할 수 있을 거야.
남	알겠어. 지금 바로 이 사진을 내려야겠어.

문제 해설 쿠바로 여행을 다녀온 남자가 자신의 소셜 미디어에 올린 탑승권 사진을 여자에게 보여 주자 여자는 탑승권에 인쇄된 바코드를 스캔하면 개인 정보를 찾는 데 사용될 수 있음을 알려 주면서 전화기로 바코드를 스캔하여 보여 주면서 많은 것을 할 수 있다고 말하고 있다. 따라서 여자의 마지막 말에 대한 남자의 응답으로 가장 적절한 것은 ③ '알겠어. 지금 바로 이 사진을 내려야겠어.'이다.
① 알겠어. 내가 항공편에서 내 좌석을 바꿀게.
② 정말? 그러면 우리 서로 나란히 앉을 수 있어.
④ 절대 안 돼. 우리 항공편 예약을 취소해야겠어.
⑤ 걱정하지 마. 바코드를 스캔하는 또 다른 앱이 있어.

어휘&어구 post 게시하다 boarding pass (여객기의) 탑승권 visible (눈에) 보이는 booking reference 예약 번호 flight 항공편, 여행

15 프랑스어 단어 암기 비법

[정답] ⑤

M	This semester, Adam and Cassie are taking French class together. Cassie is very interested in French and studies really hard, but recently she's been struggling with memorizing French words. So she'd like to learn about effective memorization techniques. She knows that Adam always does really well on the vocabulary quizzes in their French class, so she asks him for advice on how he's able to learn French words quickly. Adam takes flashcards out of his backpack and wants to tell Cassie that making and using her own could greatly help her memorize French words. In this situation, what would Adam mostly likely say to Cassie?
Adam	Utilizing flashcards will help you memorize words easily.

남	이번 학기에 Adam과 Cassie는 프랑스어 수업을 함께 듣습니다. Cassie는 프랑스어에 매우 관심이 많고 정말 열심히 공부하지만, 그녀는 최근에 프랑스어 단어를 암기하는 데 어려움을 겪고 있습니다. 그래서 그녀는 효과적인 암기 기법에 대해 배우고 싶습니다. 그녀는 Adam이 항상 프랑스어 수업에서 어휘 퀴즈 시험에서 정말 잘한다는 것을 알고 있어서, 그에게 프랑스어 단어를 빨리 배울 수 있는 방법에 대한 조언을 구합니다. Adam은 자신의 백팩에서 플래시 카드를 꺼내 Cassie에게 그녀 자신의 플래시 카드를 만들어서 사용하면 프랑스어 단어를 암기하는 데 큰 도움이 될 수 있다고 말하고 싶습니다. 이런 상황에서 Adam은 Cassie에게 뭐라고 말하겠습니까?
Adam	플래시 카드를 활용하면 네가 단어를 쉽게 외우는 데 도움이 될 거야.

문제 해설 프랑스어 수업을 듣는 Cassie가 효과적인 단어 암기 기법을 알고 싶어 항상 어휘 퀴즈 시험에서 정말 잘하는 Adam에게 조언을 구하자,

Adam은 자신의 플래시 카드를 보여 주면서 플래시 카드를 만들어 사용하면 단어 암기에 도움이 된다고 말하고 싶어 하는 상황이다. 따라서 Adam이 Cassie에게 할 말로 가장 적절한 것은 ⑤ '플래시 카드를 활용하면 네가 단어를 쉽게 외우는 데 도움이 될 거야.'이다.

① 내 플래시 카드를 어디에 뒀는지 모르겠어.

② 이번 학기에 프랑스어 수업을 같이 듣자.

③ 너는 다른 언어를 공부하는 것이 더 좋을 거야.

④ 너는 말할 때 더 정확한 단어를 사용해야 해.

어휘&어구 struggle 어려움을 겪다, 투쟁하다 memorize 암기하다 memorization 암기 backpack 백팩, 배낭 accurate 정확한 utilize 활용하다

16~17 양말

[정답] 16 ④ 17 ②

W Good morning, everybody. Today, let's talk about the most overlooked part of an outfit. Our socks. The clothing item that covers the feet and ankles has been around since the Stone Age, long before the concept of pants existed. The first socks were made from animal skins and tied around the ankle. Then, the first knit socks were made in Ancient Egypt. During the Middle Ages, the length of trousers was extended and the sock became a tight, brightly-colored cloth covering the lower part of the leg. They were made of wool or silk and looked like today's leggings. In the late 17th century cotton became a popular choice for many clothing items including socks. As trousers became longer and socks became shorter, the term 'socks' started to refer to what was previously known as stockings. The next revolution in sock-making came with the invention of nylon in 1938. The strength and elasticity of socks made from cotton-nylon blends led to a natural step forward in manufacturing. Since then, sock designs have remained almost the same but various materials have been experimented with.

여 안녕하세요, 여러분. 오늘은 의상에서 가장 경시된 부분에 관해 이야기해 봅시다. 우리 양말입니다. 우리의 발과 발목을 감싸는 의류는 바지라는 개념이 존재하기 훨씬 전인 석기시대부터 존재했습니다. 최초의 양말은 동물 가죽으로 만들어졌고 발목 주위에서 묶였습니다. 그런 다음 실로 짠 첫 번째 양말이 고대 이집트에서 만들어졌습니다. 중세에, 바지의 길이는 길어졌고 양말은 다리의 아래쪽을 감싸는 꽉 끼는 밝은색의 천이 되었습니다. 그것들은 모나 견으로 만들어졌고 오늘날의 레깅스처럼 보였습니다. 17세기 후반에 면이 양말을 포함한 많은 의류를 위한 인기 있는 선택이 되었습니다. 바지가 더 길어지고 양말이 더 짧아지면서, '양말'이라는 용어는 예전에 스타킹이라고 알려졌던 것을 지칭하기 시작했습니다. 양말 제작의 다음 혁명은 1938년의 나일론 발명과 함께 왔습니다. 면과 나일론의 혼방으로 만들어진 양말의 튼튼함과 탄성은 제조법의 자연스러운 발전으로 이어졌습니다. 그때 이후, 양말 디자인은 거의 동일하게 유지되었지만 다양한 재료가 실험되어 왔습니다.

문제 해설 16 여자는 양말의 역사와 다양한 재료의 변천에 관해 설명하고 있다. 그러므로 여자가 하는 말의 주제로 가장 적절한 것은 ④ '양말 재료와 디자인의 변화'이다.

① 특별한 목적을 위한 양말의 디자인

② 현대 신발 디자인의 기본적인 특징

③ 의상에 강조점을 더하는 액세서리

⑤ 패션에 영향을 미친 기술 혁신

17 동물의 가죽(animal skins), 모(wool), 면(cotton), 나일론(nylon)은 언급되었지만 ② '아마[리넨]'는 언급되지 않았다.

어휘&어구 overlooked 경시된 ankle 발목 extend 길게 하다 elasticity 탄성

3회 수능실전 대비연습

본문 54~55쪽

01 지하철 자전거 휴대승차 규정 안내

[정답] ④

M Good morning. I'm Jim Rogan, the chief of public transit of Summerville. Last week, we started a policy to allow passengers to bring bikes on the subway to promote bike use. If you plan on bringing your bike on the subway, please follow these rules for a smooth and safe ride. First, take the elevator with your bike, not the escalator. And do not ride your bike in the station or on the platform. Also, when you board a subway car, use only the first or last car since the middle cars are usually the most crowded. Your observance of these rules will be much appreciated. I hope you enjoy your ride!

남 안녕하세요. 저는 Summerville의 대중교통 국장인 Jim Rogan입니다. 지난주, 저희는 자전거 사용을 장려하기 위해 승객들이 지하철에 자전거를 가지고 탈 수 있도록 허용하는 정책을 시작했습니다. 여러분이 자전거를 가지고 지하철을 타실 계획이라면, 순조롭고 안전하게 탈 수 있도록 이 규정들을 따라 주십시오. 먼저, 자전거를 가지고 에스컬레이터를 타지 마시고 엘리베이터를 타십시오. 그리고 역이나 플랫폼에서 자전거를 타지 마십시오. 또한, 지하철 차량에 탑승하실 때는, 중간 차량이 보통 가장 붐비니 지하철의 첫 번째 차량이나 마지막 차량만 이용하십시오. 여러분께서 이 규정들을 준수해 주신다면 매우 감사하겠습니다. 즐겁게 여행하시기 바랍니다!

문제 해설 남자는 지하철에 자전거를 가지고 탈 경우 지켜야 할 규정을 구체적으로 안내하고 있다. 따라서 남자가 하는 말의 목적으로 가장 적절한 것은 ④ '지하철 자전거 휴대승차 규정을 안내하려고'이다.

어휘&어구 public transit 대중교통 policy 정책 passenger 승객 promote 장려하다 smooth 순조로운, 원활한 crowded 붐비는 observance 준수 appreciate 감사하다

02 동아리 선택 기준

[정답] ②

M Elizabeth, have you been thinking about joining a school club this year?

W Yeah. I'm going to join the book club. How about you, Walter?

M I'd like to join a club, but I haven't decided which one yet.

W Well, what are you interested in?

M Nowadays I've become really interested in sports.

W Then why don't you join one of the sports clubs? I'm sure it's something you'll enjoy.

M That makes sense.

W I joined the book club because I love reading. It's best to choose a club based on what you like.

M Right. Baseball is my favorite sport, so I think I'll join the baseball club.

W That sounds like a great choice.

남 Elizabeth, 올해 학교 동아리에 가입하는 것에 대해 생각해 봤니?

여 응. 나는 도서 동아리에 가입할 거야. 넌 어때, Walter?

남 동아리에 가입하고 싶은데, 아직 어느 동아리를 가입할지는 결정하지 않았어.

여 음, 넌 무엇에 관심이 있니?

남 요즘 나는 스포츠에 정말 관심이 생겼어.

여 그러면 스포츠 동아리 중 하나에 가입하는 게 어때? 분명히 네가 즐길 수 있는 것일 거야.

남 말이 되네.

여 나는 책 읽기를 좋아해서 도서 동아리에 가입했어. 네가 좋아하는 것에 기초하여 동아리를 선택하는 것이 가장 좋아.

남 맞아. 야구가 내가 가장 좋아하는 스포츠니까 야구 동아리에 가입할 것 같아.

여 훌륭한 선택인 것 같구나.

문제 해설 어떤 동아리에 가입할지 고민하는 남자에게 여자는 자신이 좋아하는 것에 기초하여 동아리를 선택하는 것이 가장 좋다고 조언하고 있다. 따라서 여자의 의견으로 가장 적절한 것은 ② '본인이 좋아하는 것과 관련된 동아리를 선택하는 것이 좋다.'이다.

어휘&어구 make sense 말이 되다, 타당하다 based on ~에 기초하여

03 뮤지컬 수업

[정답] ③

W Hello, Mr. White. Thank you for coming. It's really nice to meet you.

M My pleasure. Thank you for inviting me, Ms. Adams.

W It's my honor to talk to you in person. I'm a big fan of yours.

M I'm glad to be here. I always love working with students.

여 안녕하세요, White 씨. 와 주셔서 감사해요. 만나서 정말 반갑습니다.

남 저도 기쁩니다. 절 초대해 주셔서 감사드립니다, Adams 씨.

여 직접 말씀을 나누게 되어 영광이네요. 저는 선생님의 열렬한 팬이에요.

남 이곳에 오게 되어 기쁘네요. 전 늘 학생들과 작업하는 것을 좋아합니다.

W	Great! As I mentioned, the students in my music class are going to perform Fantasy at our school festival this year.	여	잘됐네요! 제가 말씀드렸듯이, 제 음악 수업을 듣는 학생들이 올해 우리 학교 축제에서 Fantasy를 공연할 거예요.
M	Oh, yes. That's one of my favorite musicals. I enjoyed playing the leading role in it.	남	아, 그래요. 그건 제가 가장 좋아하는 뮤지컬 중 하나예요. 전 그 뮤지컬에서 주인공 역할을 하는 것이 즐거웠어요.
W	I saw your performance in the musical last year. It was awesome!	여	전 작년에 선생님이 그 뮤지컬에서 하셨던 연기를 봤어요. 그것은 근사했어요!
M	Thanks. I can't wait to meet your students and get started.	남	감사합니다. 빨리 학생들을 만나서 시작하고 싶네요.
W	Let me show you around the auditorium. That's the stage where the students will perform.	여	강당을 구경시켜 드릴게요. 저것이 학생들이 공연할 무대예요.
M	Wow, that's a nice stage.	남	와, 저건 멋진 무대네요.
W	Thanks. Let's go backstage where the students are. I'll introduce you to them.	여	감사합니다. 학생들이 있는 무대 뒤로 가죠. 제가 선생님을 그들에게 소개시켜 드릴게요.
M	Okay.	남	좋습니다.

> **문제 해설** 여자는 자신의 음악 수업을 듣는 학생들에게 뮤지컬을 가르치기 위해 찾아온 남자에게 자신이 팬이라고 말하며 Fantasy라는 뮤지컬에서의 남자의 연기가 근사했다고 말하고 있다. 따라서 두 사람의 관계를 가장 잘 나타낸 것은 ③ '교사 – 뮤지컬 배우'이다.

> **어휘&어구** in person 직접, 몸소   mention 말하다, 언급하다   performance 연기, 공연   auditorium 강당   backstage 무대 뒤로

04 섬 여행
[정답] ⑤

W	Dad, we're approaching the island!	여	아빠, 우린 섬에 다가가고 있어요!
M	Yes, it's beautiful! The water is so clear.	남	그래, 아름답구나! 물이 매우 맑아.
W	And look at all of the fish swimming in the sea. I can't wait to go snorkeling.	여	그리고 바다에서 헤엄치는 저 모든 물고기들을 봐요. 빨리 스노클링을 하러 가고 싶어요.
M	Me, neither. But be careful when you walk on the sea walkway to the beach. It has no rail.	남	나도 그렇구나. 하지만 해변으로 가는 바다 위 보도를 걸을 때는 조심하렴. 그것은 난간이 없구나.
W	All right. So we have to go through the log cabin at the end of the walkway to get on the island?	여	알겠어요. 그럼 섬으로 가려면 바다 위 보도 끝에 있는 통나무집을 통과해야 하는 거죠?
M	Yes. Then we're going to check in to our rooms.	남	그래. 그다음에 우리 방에 투숙 수속을 할 거야.
W	Are we staying in one of those houses behind the trees?	여	우리는 나무들 뒤에 있는 저 집들 중 하나에 머무를 건가요?
M	Yeah. I think we can enjoy the ocean view from the house.	남	그래. 우리는 그 집에서 바다 경치를 즐길 수 있을 것 같구나.
W	Cool! And there are tables under the trees on the beach. One of them is free. Let's spend the afternoon there today.	여	멋져요! 그리고 해변에는 나무 아래에 탁자들이 있어요. 그중 하나가 비어 있어요. 우리 거기서 오후를 보내요.
M	That's a great idea.	남	그거 좋은 생각이구나.

> **문제 해설** 그림에서는 해변 나무 아래에 돗자리들이 놓여 있는데, 대화에서 여자는 탁자들이 있다고 말했다. 따라서 그림에서 대화의 내용과 일치하지 않는 것은 ⑤이다.

> **어휘&어구** approach 다가가다   can't wait to 빨리 ~하고 싶다   walkway 보도   log cabin 통나무집   check in 투숙 수속을 하다   ocean view 바다 경치   free 비어 있는

05 코딩 수업 등록
[정답] ①

M	Mom, take a look at this flyer.	남	엄마, 이 전단을 보세요.
W	What is it about?	여	무엇에 관한 것이니?
M	It's about summer vacation classes. Do you think I can take one?	남	그것은 여름 방학 수업에 관한 거예요. 제가 하나를 들어도 될까요?
W	Of course! Which one would you like to take?	여	물론이지! 어느 수업을 듣고 싶니?

M I'm thinking about the coding class. What do you think?

W That sounds good. But I heard that the coding class is difficult to enter because the class size is really small. When is the registration?

M It starts at 10 a.m. this Saturday. It's online and it's on a first-come, first-served basis.

W You have Taekwondo class at that time, right?

M Right. So I won't be able to register at that time.

W Then I'll do it for you. Don't worry.

M Really? Thank you so much, Mom.

남	코딩 수업을 생각하고 있어요. 어떻게 생각하세요?
여	좋은 것 같구나. 그런데 코딩 수업은 인원이 정말 적어서 들어가기 어렵다고 들었어. 등록이 언제니?
남	이번 주 토요일 오전 10시에 시작해요. 그것은 온라인이며 선착순이에요.
여	너는 그 시간에 태권도 수업이 있잖아, 그렇지?
남	맞아요. 그래서 제가 그 시간에 등록을 할 수가 없어요.
여	그러면 내가 너 대신 해 줄게. 걱정하지 마.
남	정말요? 정말 감사해요, 엄마.

문제 해설 여름 방학에 코딩 수업을 듣고 싶은 남자가 등록이 시작되는 시간에 태권도 수업이 있어 등록을 할 수가 없다고 하자 엄마인 여자가 대신 해 주겠다고 했다. 따라서 여자가 할 일로 가장 적절한 것은 ① '남자 대신 수업 등록하기'이다.

어휘&어구 registration 등록   on a first-come, first-served basis 선착순으로   register 등록하다

06 기념품 티셔츠와 향토 식품 구입 [정답] ④

W Hello. May I help you?

M Yes. I'd like to buy some souvenir T-shirts.

W You've come to the right place! That blue T-shirt with an ocean painting on it is very popular.

M That's a nice picture. How about the yellow one?

W Oh, yes. That one has handcrafted beads on it. It's $2 more expensive than our regular T-shirts, so $12.

M They're both nice. I'll take one of each, so one blue and one yellow.

W Okay. Can I interest you in any of our local food products?

M Yeah, how much are these packages of dried mango?

W They're $3 a package, but if you buy more than five, you get 10% off.

M Then I'll take 10 packages. Here's my credit card.

W Sounds good. I'll check you out over at the counter.

여	안녕하세요. 제가 도와드릴까요?
남	네. 기념 티셔츠를 좀 사고 싶어요.
여	제대로 찾아오셨습니다! 바다 그림이 그려진 저 파란색 티셔츠가 매우 인기가 있어요.
남	그거 멋진 그림이군요. 노란색인 것은 어때요?
여	아, 네. 그것은 그 위에 수제 구슬들이 달려 있어요. 그것은 저희 일반적인 티셔츠보다 2달러 더 비싸서, 12달러예요.
남	둘 다 멋져요. 각각 하나씩 살게요, 그래서 파란색 하나와 노란색 하나요.
여	알겠어요. 저희 향토 식품들 중 손님의 관심을 끌 만한 것이 있을까요?
남	네, 이 말린 망고 봉지들은 얼마예요?
여	그것들은 한 봉지에 3달러인데, 5개 넘게 사시면 10퍼센트 할인을 받으시게 돼요.
남	그럼 10봉지를 살게요. 여기 제 신용 카드가 있어요.
여	좋아요. 저기에 있는 계산대에서 계산해 드릴게요.

문제 해설 남자는 기념품으로 10달러짜리와 12달러짜리 티셔츠를 하나씩 구입하고, 한 봉지에 3달러짜리 말린 망고를 10봉지 사면서 10퍼센트 할인을 받았다. 따라서 남자가 지불할 금액은 ④ '49달러'이다.

어휘&어구 souvenir 기념품   popular 인기 있는   handcrafted 수제의, 수공예품인   bead 구슬, 비즈   local food 향토 식품   counter 계산대, 판매대

07 계주를 대신 뛸 친구 찾기 [정답] ③

M Hi, Karen. How's your day going?

W Hey, Jacob. It's going well. I heard that you've been practicing for the relay race for Sports Day.

M Yeah. We've been practicing every day after school.

W That's good. By the way, I heard that Jane twisted her ankle.

M Yeah. We didn't think it would be that bad, but she just texted me that she won't be able to participate in the relay.

W Oh, no! That's too bad.

남	안녕, Karen. 어떻게 지내니?
여	안녕, Jacob. 잘 지내고 있어. 체육 대회 계주를 위해 연습을 하고 있다고 들었어.
남	응. 우리는 방과 후에 매일 연습하고 있어.
여	좋네. 그런데 Jane이 발목을 삐었다고 들었어.
남	응. 우리는 그렇게 좋지 않을 거라고 생각은 못 했는데, 그녀가 방금 계주에 참가하지 못할 거라고 문자를 보냈어.
여	아, 저런! 그것참 안됐구나.
남	응. 실은 Jane 대신에 네가 계주를 뛸 수 있니?
여	이런, 그러고 싶지만, 그날 중국어 말하기 대회가 있어서 나는 학교

M	I know. Actually, can you run in the relay instead of Jane?
W	Gosh, I'd like to, but I won't be at school because I have a Chinese speaking contest that day.
M	Oh, I see. I'll ask someone else then.
W	Ask Amy. She's a really good runner.
M	Really? I'll talk to her then. Thanks.
W	No problem.

	에 없을 거야.
남	아, 그렇구나. 그러면 다른 사람에게 물어볼게.
여	Amy에게 물어봐. 그녀는 정말 달리기를 잘하거든.
남	정말? 그러면 내가 그녀와 이야기해 볼게. 고마워.
여	천만에.

문제 해설 체육 대회 계주에 출전하는 Jane이 발목을 다쳐 뛸 수가 없어 남자가 여자에게 계주를 뛸 수 있는지를 묻자 여자는 체육 대회 날 중국어 말하기 대회가 있어서 계주에 참가할 수 없다고 했으므로, 여자가 Jane 대신 계주에 참가할 수 없는 이유는 ③ '중국어 말하기 대회가 있어서'이다.

어휘&어구 twist 삐다, 접질리다 ankle 발목 text 문자를 보내다

08 자전거 타기 행사
[정답] ⑤

W	Joshua, what are you looking at?
M	A flyer for the Riverside Bike Ride, which is coming up.
W	Oh, cool. Is it nearby?
M	Yeah. It's going to be held near our school. The ride starts at River Port Plaza.
W	Great. That's not far from here. Look, the event follows the Riverside Bike Trail for 15 kilometers.
M	Plus, it says it's not a competition, just a leisurely ride.
W	Then, it'll take about one hour if we take our time.
M	It also says the trail has been recently renovated and repaved.
W	The trail must be in good condition.
M	For sure. And the timing is perfect! It's on November 27th, at 3 p.m.
W	Terrific! It's just after the final exams. Why don't we sign up?
M	Let's do it. How about asking Linda and Steve to join us?
W	Great idea!

여	Joshua, 뭘 보고 있는 거야?
남	다가오는 Riverside Bike Ride (행사) 전단이야.
여	오, 멋지다. 근처니?
남	응. 우리 학교 근처에서 열릴 거야. 이 자전거 타기는 River Port Plaza에서 시작해.
여	좋네. 여기서 멀지 않네. 봐, 이 행사는 Riverside Bike Trail을 따라 15킬로미터야.
남	게다가, 이건 시합이 아니라 그냥 여유롭게 타는 거라네.
여	그럼, 천천히 하면 한 시간 정도 걸릴 거야.
남	길이 최근에 보수되고 다시 포장되었다고도 하네.
여	길 상태는 좋을 것이 틀림없어.
남	물론이지. 그리고 시기도 완벽해! 11월 27일 오후 3시야.
여	좋네! 기말고사 직후야. 우리 신청하는 게 어때?
남	그렇게 하자. Linda와 Steve에게 우리와 함께하자고 하는 게 어때?
여	좋은 생각이야!

문제 해설 출발 장소(The ride starts at River Port Plaza), 코스 길이(the event follows the Riverside Bike Trail for 15 kilometers), 소요 예상 시간(it'll take about one hour), 행사 일시(on November 27th, at 3 p.m.)는 언급되었지만, ⑤ '신청 방법'은 언급되지 않았다.

어휘&어구 flyer 전단 nearby 근처의, 가까운 port 항구 plaza 광장 trail 길, 탐방로 competition 시합, 경쟁 leisurely 여유로운, 느긋한 take one's time 천천히 하다 renovate 보수하다 repave 다시 포장하다 sign up 신청하다, 등록하다 join ~과 함께하다

09 Stand-up Comedy with Funny Glen 프로그램 안내
[정답] ⑤

W	Attention, please. I'm Emma Jones, program coordinator at the Midtown Community Center. I'd like to tell you about a new program we're having: Stand-up Comedy with Funny Glen. Funny Glen is a local comedian with 5 years of teaching experience. Stand-up Comedy with Funny Glen is a 6-week program open to adults aged 20 and over. Participants will learn the art of stand-up comedy, including writing and telling jokes. The class

여	주목해 주시기 바랍니다. 저는 Midtown Community Center의 프로그램 기획 책임자 Emma Jones입니다. 저희가 가지고 있는 새 프로그램, Stand-up Comedy with Funny Glen에 대해 여러분께 말씀드리고자 합니다. Funny Glen은 5년의 강사 경력을 가진 지역의 코미디언입니다. Stand-up Comedy with Funny Glen은 20세 이상의 성인이 참가할 수 있는 6주짜리 프로그램입니다. 참가자들은 농담을 쓰고 말하는 것을 포함하여 단독 연기 코미디의 기술을 배울 것입니다. 수업은 1주일에 한 번 매주 목요일

will meet once a week, on Thursdays. The first class is Thursday, July 9th. You may register online or at the community center. The registration fee is $60, which doesn't include the workbook. We hope to see you there!

마다 있을 것입니다. 첫 수업은 7월 9일 목요일입니다. 온라인이나 커뮤니티 센터에서 등록하실 수 있습니다. 등록비는 60달러이며, 워크북이 포함되어 있지 않습니다. 여러분을 거기서 만나기를 희망합니다!

문제 해설 등록비가 60달러인데 워크북이 포함되어 있지 않다는 내용이 있으므로, 담화의 내용과 일치하지 않는 것은 ⑤ '등록비에 워크북이 포함되어 있다.'이다.

어휘&어구 coordinator 기획 책임자, 조정자 stand-up 단독 연기 코미디(의) comedian 코미디언 participant 참가자 art 기술 including ~을 포함하여 joke 농담, 조크, 우스개 register 등록하다 registration fee 등록비 workbook 워크북, 연습 문제집

---

10 태블릿 케이스 구입
[정답] ③

M What are you doing on your smartphone, Annie?

W Oh, hey, Andy. I'm looking for a case for my tablet. My current one is falling apart.

M Where are you going to buy a new one?

W Well, here. These five are on sale right now. I've ordered from this site before, so I'm thinking about getting one of those.

M Oh, they all look good. Do you have anything in mind?

W I like how this one looks, but it's nylon, which falls apart easily.

M Then, get one of the others. Which color do you want?

W Any of these would be okay except for yellow. That'd be hard to keep clean.

M Okay. These ones come with a stylus pen. Do you have one?

W No, but I've always wanted one. I'll get one of these that come with a stylus pen.

M Then there are two options left. Which one do you prefer?

W Hmm, they both look good. I was hoping to keep it less than $40, so I'll get the cheaper one.

M I think that's a good choice.

남 Annie, 스마트폰으로 뭘 하고 있니?

여 오, 안녕, Andy. 태블릿 케이스를 찾고 있어. 지금 있는 게 망가지고 있어서.

남 새것을 어디에서 살 예정이니?

여 음, 여기. 이 다섯 개가 지금 세일 중이야. 전에 이 사이트에서 주문한 적이 있어서, 그중에서 하나를 살까 생각 중이야.

남 오, 다 괜찮아 보여. 마음에 두고 있는 게 있니?

여 이 제품은 외관은 좋은데, 나일론이어서 쉽게 망가져.

남 그럼, 다른 것 중에서 하나 사도록 해. 어떤 색을 원하니?

여 노란색을 빼고는 아무거나 괜찮을 것 같아. 노란색은 깨끗하게 유지하기 힘들 거야.

남 그래. 이것들은 스타일러스 펜이 딸려 있네. 스타일러스 펜이 있니?

여 아니, 그런데 난 항상 하나 갖고 싶었어. 스타일러스 펜이 딸려 있는 이것들 중 하나를 사야겠어.

남 그럼 선택할 것이 두 개 남았네. 어떤 것이 더 좋아?

여 음, 둘 다 좋아 보여. 40달러가 넘지 않는 것으로 하려고 했으니, 더 저렴한 것으로 할게.

남 그게 좋은 선택이라고 생각해.

문제 해설 나일론이 아니면서, 노란색이 아니고, 스타일러스 펜이 딸려 있는 것들 중에서 40달러가 넘지 않는 더 저렴한 것을 구입하겠다고 했으므로, 여자가 주문할 태블릿 케이스는 ③이다.

어휘&어구 current 현재의, 통용의 fall apart 망가지다, 부서지다 come with ~이 딸려 있다 stylus pen 스타일러스 펜(모니터나 태블릿에서 그림을 그리거나 탭하여 선택하는 데 사용하는 작은 펜 모양의 도구) option 선택(할 것)

---

11 노숙자 쉼터에 옷 기부
[정답] ③

M Honey, what are you going to do with those clothes?

W I'm going to donate them to the homeless shelter downtown. They don't fit me anymore.

M That's a good idea. I have a lot of clothes that I don't wear often, too.

W Then put them with my clothes. I'll take them, too.

남 여보, 그 옷들을 어떻게 할 건가요?

여 그것들을 시내 노숙자 쉼터에 기부할 거예요. 내게는 더 이상 맞지 않아요.

남 좋은 생각이네요. 내게도 자주 입지 않는 옷들이 많이 있어요.

여 그럼 그것들을 내 옷과 함께 놓으세요. 그것들도 가져갈게요.

문제 해설 집에서 이루어지는 부부 사이의 대화로 더 이상 맞지 않는 옷을 노숙자 쉼터에 기부하려는 여자에게 남자는 자신도 자주 입지 않는 옷들이 많

이 있다고 말했다. 따라서 남자의 마지막 말에 대한 여자의 응답으로 가장 적절한 것은 ③ '그럼 그것들을 내 옷과 함께 놓으세요. 그것들도 가져갈게요.'이다.

① 맞아요. 당신에게 맞는 옷을 그곳에서 찾을 수 있어요.

② 난 그렇게 생각하지 않아요. 이 옷들을 돌려줘야 해요.

④ 좋아요. 언제 시내에 갈지 내게 알려만 주세요.

⑤ 좋아요. 다음에 거기에 갈 때, 내 것도 기부하세요.

어휘&어구 donate 기부하다   homeless shelter 노숙자 쉼터   fit 맞다

---

12 달리기를 통한 체중 감량
[정답] ①

W Hi, Mike. Long time no see. Wow, you've lost a lot of weight. You look great!	여 안녕하세요, Mike. 오랜만이에요. 와, 살이 많이 빠졌네요. 매우 좋아 보여요!
M Thanks. I went on a diet and started exercising a lot.	남 감사합니다. 다이어트를 시작했고 운동을 많이 하기 시작했어요.
W What kind of exercise? I know you're always busy.	여 어떤 운동이었는데요? 당신은 늘 바쁘신 걸로 아는데요.
M I go for a morning run before work.	남 출근 전에 아침 달리기를 하러 가요.

문제 해설 오랜만에 보는 남자가 다이어트와 운동을 해서 살을 많이 뺐다는 말을 듣고, 여자는 늘 바쁘게 사는 남자가 어떤 운동을 했는지 묻고 있다. 따라서 여자의 마지막 말에 대한 남자의 응답으로 가장 적절한 것은 ① '출근 전에 아침 달리기를 하러 가요.'이다.

② 빈속에 운동하지 마세요.

③ 포기하지 않으면 좋은 결과를 볼 거예요.

④ 수영은 재미있고 사람들을 만나는 매우 좋은 방법이에요.

⑤ 단기간에 체중을 줄이는 것은 쉽지 않아요.

어휘&어구 go on a diet 다이어트를 시작하다

---

13 아파트 카드키를 집에 두고 나온 할머니
[정답] ③

[Cell phone rings.]	[휴대 전화가 울린다.]
M Hello, Grandma?	남 여보세요, 할머니?
W Daniel, where are you now? You're not at home.	여 Daniel, 지금 어디 있니? 집에 없구나.
M I'm on my way now. Don't you remember I told you in the morning that I was supposed to have a job interview?	남 지금 가는 중이에요. 구직 면접을 보기로 되어 있다고 아침에 말씀드린 것이 기억나지 않으세요?
W Right. I remember now. I forget a lot these days. By the way, I have a problem.	여 맞다. 이제 기억이 나는구나. 요즘 많이 잊어버리네. 그건 그렇고, 문제가 생겼어.
M You have a problem? What is it?	남 문제가 생겼다고요? 뭔데요?
W I forgot to take the apartment complex key card when I went out for a walk. So I can't get into our apartment.	여 산책하려고 나올 때 아파트 카드키 챙기는 것을 잊어버렸단다. 그래서 우리 아파트에 들어갈 수가 없구나.
M Did you call the security office to open it?	남 경비실에 전화해서 그것을 열어 달라고 하셨어요?
W Sure, I did. But nobody answered.	여 물론, 그랬지. 하지만 아무도 받지 않았어.
M All right. Don't worry. I'm almost there.	남 알겠어요. 걱정 마세요. 거의 다 왔어요.
W How long do you think it'll take to get here?	여 여기에 도착하려면 얼마나 걸릴 것 같니?
M Well, I'll be there in just about 5 minutes.	남 음, 5분 정도면 거기에 도착할 거예요.
W Really? I'm relieved that you're not far from here.	여 그래? 네가 여기서 멀지 않은 데 있어서 다행이구나.

문제 해설 아파트 카드키를 집에 두고 온 여자가 지금 집에 오고 있는 남자(손자)에게 전화를 걸어 처해 있는 상황을 말하고 있는 대화로 남자에게 집에 오는 데 얼마나 걸릴지를 묻자 남자는 거의 다 왔으며 5분 정도면 도착할 거라 대답한다. 따라서 남자의 마지막 말에 대한 여자의 응답으로 가장 적절한 것은 ③ '그래? 네가 여기서 멀지 않은 데 있어서 다행이구나.'이다.

① 좋아, 지금부터는 내 카드키를 사용해도 좋다.

② 걱정하지 마. 그 카드키가 더 이상 필요하지는 않아.

④ 미안하지만, 그때는 너와 함께 갈 수가 없을 것 같구나.

⑤ 얘야. 인터뷰 결과에 대해 정말 듣고 싶구나.

어휘&어구 apartment complex 아파트 단지   security office 경비실   be eager to ~하기를 몹시 원하다

14 선물로 받은 물건 교환
[정답] ②

W	Hi. Can I help you, sir?	여	안녕하세요. 도와드릴까요, 손님?
M	Yes. I got this climbing hat as a gift, but it doesn't fit me.	남	네. 이 등산 모자를 선물로 받았는데, 제게 맞지 않아요.
W	Let me see it. *[Pause]* Oh, it's our brand.	여	어디 봅시다. *[잠시 후]* 아, 저희 브랜드군요.
M	Yes. I can exchange it without a receipt, right?	남	네. 영수증이 없어도 그것을 교환할 수 있어요, 그렇지요?
W	Sure. If it's our brand, we can do that. Would you like to change it to a bigger hat?	여	그럼요. 저희 브랜드면 그렇게 해 드릴 수 있어요. 그것을 더 큰 모자로 바꿔 드릴까요?
M	No, actually I have several hats. Can I change it to other items?	남	아니요, 사실 전 등산 모자는 여러 개 있어요. 그것을 다른 품목으로 바꿀 수 있나요?
W	Yes, you can. What did you have in mind?	여	네, 그러실 수 있어요. 무엇을 염두에 두고 계셨나요?
M	I'd like to change it to a climbing bag over there.	남	그것을 저기 있는 등산 가방으로 바꾸고 싶어요.
W	Does it matter that it's more expensive than the hat?	여	모자보다 더 비싼데 괜찮으시겠어요?
M	No. By the way, I saw a discount sign. Does the discount apply to this bag?	남	괜찮아요. 그런데 할인 표시를 봤어요. 그 할인이 이 가방에도 적용이 되나요?
W	Let me see. *[Typing sound]* Yeah, you can get 10% off the marked price.	여	어디 볼게요. *[타자 치는 소리]* 네, 표시된 가격에서 10퍼센트 할인을 받으실 수 있어요.
M	Okay. Then I'll pay the difference in cash.	남	좋아요. 그럼 차액은 현금으로 지불할게요.

문제 해설 선물로 받은 등산 모자를 다른 품목으로 교환하는 과정에서 여자는 남자가 사려는 상품이 더 비싸다고 말하지만 남자가 사겠다고 말하자 표시된 가격에서 10퍼센트 할인이 된다고 말한다. 따라서 여자의 마지막 말에 대한 남자의 응답으로 가장 적절한 것은 ② '좋아요. 그럼 차액은 현금으로 지불할게요.'이다.
① 좋네요. 그럼 그것을 환불받고 싶어요.
③ 좋아요. 그렇다면 가방도 살게요.
④ 물론이지요. 제 사이즈인 다른 모자를 찾아볼게요.
⑤ 그렇군요. 할인 중이 아닌 등산 가방을 찾아봐야 할 것 같아요.

어휘&어구 fit 맞다 receipt 영수증 apply to ~에 적용되다 refund 환불; 환불하다 as well 또한

15 호텔 방 교환 요청
[정답] ④

W	Jason is on the first day of a three-day trip by himself. He has booked a hotel with a beautiful beachfront view and is looking forward to getting some nice rest and relaxation. After checking in at the hotel, he goes to his room with great anticipation. He opens his hotel room door, but all he can smell is a thick smell of cigarettes. He specifically booked a nonsmoking room. He feels it is his right to ask for a room change. So, he directly goes down to the front desk to ask for it. In this situation, what would Jason most likely say to the hotel front desk agent?	여	Jason은 사흘간의 나 홀로 여행 중 첫날을 보내고 있습니다. 그는 아름다운 해변 전경을 가진 호텔을 예약했고 얼마간의 기분 좋은 휴식과 휴양을 하기를 기대하고 있습니다. 호텔에서 체크인한 후에, 그는 큰 기대를 안고 자신의 객실로 갑니다. 그가 호텔 객실 문을 여니, 그가 맡을 수 있는 것이라곤 짙은 담배 냄새뿐입니다. 그는 분명히 비흡연 객실을 예약했습니다. 그는 객실 교환을 요청하는 것이 자신의 권리라고 생각합니다. 그래서 그는 그것을 요청하기 위해 즉시 프런트로 내려갑니다. 이런 상황에서 Jason은 호텔 프런트 사무원에게 뭐라고 말하겠습니까?
Jason	I'd like to switch to another nonsmoking room.	Jason	다른 비흡연 객실로 바꾸고 싶습니다.

문제 해설 Jason은 휴가를 보내기 위해서 해변 전경을 가진 호텔의 비흡연 객실을 예약했으나, 객실에서 짙은 담배 냄새가 나서 객실 교환을 위해 프런트로 내려간 상황이다. 따라서 Jason이 호텔 프런트 사무원에게 할 말로 가장 적절한 것은 ④ '다른 비흡연 객실로 바꾸고 싶습니다.'이다.
① 이 객실 열쇠가 작동하지 않는 것 같습니다.
② 객실 등급을 높이는 데 얼마가 듭니까?
③ 이번 주말에 빈 객실이 있습니까?
⑤ 다음 주말 예약을 취소해야겠습니다.

어휘&어구 book 예약하다 look forward to -ing ~을 기대하다 relaxation 휴양 anticipation 기대 specifically 분명히, 특별히 agent 사무원, 직원 vacancy 빈 객실 cancel 취소하다

M Hello, everyone. I'm Dr. Johansson from the Salvia Medical Center. Many people with back pain believe that they should avoid exercising, but that's not completely true. There are some exercises that are good for individuals with back pain. First is swimming. This is a great exercise for people with back pain because it's low-impact, with minimal stress on the body. Cycling is also a low-impact activity that's good for individuals with back pain. It even helps strengthen the muscles around the back. Moving on, golf is great because it not only helps promote flexibility but also includes gentle stretching. And finally is yoga, which combines gentle movements and stretching, so it is an ideal choice. So even if your back hurts, you can safely stay active by doing these exercises.

남 안녕하세요, 여러분. 저는 Salvia Medical Center의 Dr. Johansson입니다. 허리 통증이 있는 많은 사람들은 본인들이 운동을 피해야 한다고 생각하지만, 이는 전적으로 사실인 것은 아닙니다. 허리 통증이 있는 사람에게 좋은 몇 가지 운동이 있습니다. 먼저 수영입니다. 이것은 몸에 미치는 압력이 아주 적은, 충격이 작기 때문에 허리 통증이 있는 사람들에게 훌륭한 운동입니다. 자전거 타기도 허리 통증이 있는 사람에게 좋은 충격이 작은 활동입니다. 그것은 허리 주위 근육을 강화하는 데도 도움이 됩니다. 계속해서, 골프는 유연성을 증진시키는 데 도움이 될 뿐만 아니라 부드러운 스트레칭도 포함하기 때문에 좋습니다. 그리고 마지막으로 요가는 부드러운 동작과 스트레칭이 결합되어 이상적인 선택입니다. 따라서 허리가 아프더라도 이러한 운동을 함으로써 여러분은 안전하게 활동을 유지할 수 있습니다.

[문제 해설] **16** 남자는 많은 사람들이 허리 통증이 있는 사람은 운동을 피해야 한다고 생각하지만 그런 사람들에게도 좋은 운동이 있다고 하면서 그 운동들을 소개하고 있으므로, 남자가 하는 말의 주제로 가장 적절한 것은 ① '허리 통증이 있는 사람들에게 좋은 운동'이다.
② 활동적인 생활 방식을 유지하는 것의 이점
③ 운동 전 스트레칭의 중요성
④ 많은 사람들이 허리 통증으로 고통받는 이유
⑤ 우울증으로 고통받는 사람들에게 도움이 되는 활동
17 허리 통증으로 고통받는 사람에게도 좋은 운동으로 수영, 자전거 타기, 골프, 요가는 언급되었지만, ④ '달리기'는 언급되지 않았다.

[어휘&어구] avoid 피하다 low-impact 충격이 작은 strengthen 강화하다 muscle 근육 flexibility 유연성 benefit 이점

4회 수능실전 대비연습   본문 62~63쪽

| 01 ④ | 02 ④ | 03 ③ | 04 ⑤ | 05 ② | 06 ④ | 07 ④ | 08 ⑤ | 09 ⑤ | 10 ② | 11 ⑤ | 12 ③ | 13 ① | 14 ⑤ |
| 15 ④ | 16 ④ | 17 ③ | | | | | | | | | | | |

---

01 무료 급식 자원봉사자 모집   [정답] ④

M Hello, my name is George Thompson, and I'm the owner of J&J Restaurant downtown. For over a year, we have been providing free lunches for homeless people at the restaurant once a month. This has become more and more popular, so we need to recruit some volunteers to help us out. Volunteers will help prepare meals, serve, and clean up. No prior experience is required. So if you're interested in helping people in need, please visit our homepage and apply. Your support can make a difference in the lives of the less fortunate in our community. Together, let's make a positive impact! Thank you.

남 안녕하세요, 제 이름은 George Thompson이고, 저는 시내에 있는 J&J Restaurant의 주인입니다. 일 년 넘게 우리는 한 달에 한 번 음식점에서 집 없는 사람들을 위해 무료 점심을 제공해 왔습니다. 이것이 점점 더 알려져서 우리는 우리를 도와줄 자원봉사자 몇 명을 모집해야 합니다. 자원봉사자들은 식사 준비, 서빙 및 청소를 돕게 될 것입니다. 사전 경험은 필요하지 않습니다. 그러니 도움이 필요한 사람들을 돕는 데 관심이 있으시다면, 우리 홈페이지를 방문해 신청해 주시기 바랍니다. 여러분의 도움이 우리 지역 사회에서 불우한 사람들의 삶에 차이를 만들 수 있습니다. 함께 긍정적인 영향을 주도록 합시다! 감사합니다.

[문제 해설] 남자는 자신의 음식점에서 일 년 넘게 집 없는 사람들에게 무료로 점심을 제공해 왔는데 그 일을 도와줄 자원봉사자를 모집하니 신청해 달라고 말하고 있다. 따라서 남자가 하는 말의 목적으로 가장 적절한 것은 ④ '무료 식사 나눔을 도울 봉사자를 모집하려고'이다.

[어휘&어구] downtown 시내에 recruit 모집하다, 뽑다 prior 사전의 apply 신청하다 support 도움, 지원

02 허락 없이 상대방의 사진을 찍는 것의 문제점 [정답] ④

W	Ian, can I talk to you for a minute?	여	Ian, 너랑 잠시 이야기할 수 있어?
M	Sure, Emily. What's up?	남	물론이지, Emily. 무슨 일이니?
W	I'm not sure if it's okay to tell you this, but since we're all friends I feel like I should. Did you know that Jane is upset with you?	여	너한테 이 말을 해도 될지 모르겠지만 우리가 모두 친구니까 그래야 할 것 같아. Jane이 너한테 마음이 상한 것을 알고 있었니?
M	Really? I didn't know that. Why is that?	남	정말? 몰랐어. 이유가 뭐지?
W	You took a picture of her the other day, right?	여	네가 저번에 그녀의 사진을 찍었잖아, 맞지?
M	Yeah. But as you know, I always take pictures when we hang out. What's the problem?	남	응. 하지만 네가 알고 있듯이 나는 우리가 어울릴 때 항상 사진을 찍잖아. 무슨 문제가 있니?
W	Well, some people may feel uncomfortable about having their photo taken without their permission.	여	음, 어떤 사람들은 자신들의 허락 없이 사진 찍히는 것에 대해 불편함을 느낄 수 있어.
M	Hmm, I haven't thought of that.	남	흠, 그건 미처 생각하지 못했어.
W	You and I don't mind having our picture taken, but some people don't like being photographed, especially without their permission.	여	너나 나는 우리 사진이 찍히는 것을 상관하지 않지만, 어떤 사람들은 특히 자신들의 허락 없이 사진 찍히는 것을 좋아하지 않아.
M	Ah, so that's why Jane is upset.	남	아, 그래서 Jane이 기분이 상했구나.
W	Right. She just hasn't told you directly because she doesn't want to offend you.	여	맞아. 그녀는 너의 기분을 상하게 하고 싶지 않아서 그냥 너에게 직접 말하지 않은 거야.
M	I see. Thanks for telling me. I'll talk to her about it.	남	그렇구나. 말해 줘서 고마워. 내가 그것에 대해 그녀와 이야기를 나눠 볼게.

문제 해설 대화하는 두 사람의 친구인 Jane이 남자에게 기분이 상한 이유에 대해 여자는 남자가 Jane의 사진을 찍었기 때문이라고 말하면서 어떤 사람들은 허락 없이 사진 찍히는 것을 좋아하지 않는다고 말하고 있다. 따라서 여자의 의견으로 가장 적절한 것은 ④ '허락 없이 상대방의 사진을 찍으면 그 사람이 불편해할 수도 있다.'이다.

어휘&어구 upset 마음이 상한, 속상한 uncomfortable 불편한 permission 허락, 허가 mind 상관하다 directly 직접 offend 기분 상하게 하다

03 주택 구입 [정답] ③

M	Hello, Ms. Anderson. Nice to see you again.	남	안녕하세요, Anderson 씨. 다시 만나서 반갑습니다.
W	Hello, Mr. Davis.	여	안녕하세요, Davis 씨.
M	Have you talked to your family about the three houses that you looked at last time?	남	지난번에 보신 집 세 채에 대해 가족들과 이야기해 보셨어요?
W	Yes. Thanks again for showing them to me.	여	네. 그것들을 제게 보여 주신 점에 대해 다시 한번 감사드려요.
M	No problem. I feel very rewarded by helping people find the right house. What do you think about them? I thought the one on the hill would be best for you.	남	천만에요. 저는 사람들이 적당한 집을 찾는 데 도움이 됨으로써 아주 보람을 느끼죠. 그것들에 대해 어떻게 생각하세요? 언덕 위의 것이 손님에게 가장 좋을 것이라고 생각했어요.
W	I love its interior design and the yard is beautiful. But its price is too high for our budget.	여	그것의 실내 장식이 마음에 들고 마당이 아름다워요. 하지만 우리 예산을 고려하면 그것의 가격이 너무 높아요.
M	Oh, I see. Then how do you like the one near the beach? That's within your budget range, right?	남	아, 그렇군요. 그러면 해변 근처의 것은 어떠세요? 그것은 손님의 예산 범위 안에 있지요, 그렇죠?
W	Yes. The house is nice too and its location is amazing. But I wish it had more bedrooms.	여	네. 그 집 또한 마음에 들고 위치가 아주 좋아요. 하지만 그 집에 침실이 더 많았으면 좋겠어요.
M	Okay. Then how about the one with four bedrooms?	남	좋아요. 그러면 침실이 4개인 것은 어떠세요?
W	I think that one is spacious enough, but it's too old. It needs lots of work to fix it up.	여	그것은 충분히 넓은 것 같은데, 너무 오래되었어요. 그것을 수리하기 위해 많은 일이 필요해요.
M	I see. Would you like to see any of them again?	남	알겠습니다. 그것들 중 다시 보고 싶은 게 있나요?
W	Yes, the beach house. I'd like to see if I could possibly add space to it by remodeling.	여	네, 해변의 집이요. 리모델링해서 그 집에 공간을 늘릴 수 있는지 알아보고 싶네요.
		남	좋습니다. 집주인에게 전화해서 그들에게 곧 우리가 들르고 싶다고

M	Great. I'll call the house owner and tell them we would like	말할게요.
	to stop by soon.	여 좋은 생각입니다.
W	Sounds good.	

여자는 집 세 채를 보여 준 남자에게 감사하면서 세 집의 장단점을 언급한 후에 해변 근처에 있는 두 번째 집을 다시 보고 싶다고 말하고 있고, 남자는 사람들이 좋은 집을 찾는 데 도움이 됨으로써 아주 보람을 느끼며 여자가 다시 보기를 원하는 집의 주인에게 전화를 하겠다고 말했다. 따라서 두 사람의 관계를 가장 잘 나타낸 것은 ③ '부동산 중개인 – 고객'이다.

feel rewarded 보람을 느끼다   **interior design** 실내 장식   **yard** 마당   **budget** 예산   **beach** 해변   **location** 위치   **spacious** 넓은   **fix up** ~을 수리하다   **remodel** 리모델링하다, 개조하다   **stop by** 들르다

04 집 체육관 소개   [정답] ⑤

M	So, Claudia, this is my home gym.	남	그래, Claudia, 이곳이 내 홈 짐이야.
W	Wow, this is awesome! It even has windows.	여	와, 이곳이 아주 멋지구나! 창문도 있네.
M	Yeah. So I open them up and let fresh air in while working out.	남	응. 그래서 나는 운동하는 동안에는 그것들을 열어서 신선한 공기가 들어오게 해.
W	That's good. I like the mirror next to the windows.	여	좋구나. 창문 옆에 있는 거울이 마음에 들어.
M	It helps to make sure I use the right form when exercising. And I just got this indoor bike a few days ago. It has a monitor so I can watch TV while riding it.	남	내가 운동할 때 올바른 자세로 하는지 확인하는 데 도움이 돼. 그리고 며칠 전에 이 실내용 자전거를 샀어. 모니터가 있어서 그것을 타면서 TV를 볼 수 있어.
W	Awesome. What do you do with the gym ball next to the bicycle?	여	멋지다. 자전거 옆에 있는 짐볼로는 무엇을 하니?
M	I use it for stretching.	남	나는 그것을 스트레칭에 사용해.
W	That's good. So how much do these dumbbells in front of the mirror weigh?	여	좋구나. 그런데 거울 앞에 있는 이 아령들은 무게가 얼마나 나가니?
M	They're 5 kg each. They're not too heavy, but they're good enough for the exercises I do.	남	각각 5킬로그램이야. 그것들이 아주 무겁지는 않은데, 내가 하는 운동에는 충분히 좋아.
W	This room is a perfect place to exercise alone.	여	이 방은 혼자 운동하기에 완벽한 장소야.
M	Exactly. Would you like to try the bicycle?	남	맞아. 자전거를 타 보겠니?
W	Sure.	여	그래.

남자의 홈 짐에서 거울 앞에 있는 아령의 무게가 얼마나 나가는지 여자가 묻자 남자는 각각 5킬로그램이라고 말했는데 그림에는 3킬로그램짜리 아령이 있으므로, 그림에서 대화의 내용과 일치하지 않는 것은 ⑤이다.

work out 운동하다   **dumbbell** 아령   **weigh** 무게가 ~ 나가다

05 자녀의 드레스 찾아오기   [정답] ②

[Cell phone rings.]		[휴대 전화가 울린다.]
M	Hello?	남	여보세요?
W	Honey, when do you get off work today?	여	여보, 오늘 언제 퇴근해요?
M	Pretty soon. Why? What's up?	남	곧 해요. 왜요? 무슨 일 있어요?
W	Well, Jill just messaged me and said her violin lesson is going to run a little late. She needs some extra practice for her performance tomorrow.	여	글쎄, Jill이 바이올린 연습이 조금 늦게까지 진행될 거라고 내게 방금 문자 메시지를 보냈어요. 그 애의 내일 연주회를 위해 약간의 추가 연습이 필요하대요.
M	Okay. So do you want me to pick her up on my way home?	남	알겠어요. 그래서 내가 퇴근하는 길에 그 애를 태워 가길 원해요?
W	No. I can take care of that.	여	아니요. 그건 내가 처리할 수 있어요.
M	Then is there anything else you want me to do?	남	그러면 내가 했으면 하는 무슨 일이 있나요?
W	Yes. I had her dress dry-cleaned at the dry cleaner's. Can you pick it up?	여	네. 내가 그 애의 드레스를 세탁소에 드라이클리닝을 해 달라고 맡겼어요. 그것을 찾아올 수 있어요?

M	Sure, no problem.	남	물론이죠, 걱정 말아요.
W	Thanks. Do you know where the dry cleaner's is?	여	고마워요. 세탁소가 어디에 있는지 알아요?
M	I think so. It's the one across from the library, right?	남	그런 것 같아요. 도서관 건너편에 있는 거 맞죠?
W	Yes. The dress is under my name. I'll pick up Jill after her violin practice.	여	네. 드레스는 내 이름으로 맡겼어요. Jill은 바이올린 연습이 끝난 후에 내가 데려올게요.
M	Okay. See you at home.	남	좋아요. 집에서 봐요.

문제 해설 여자가 딸의 드레스를 세탁소에서 찾아올 것을 남자에게 부탁하였고 남자가 이를 수락하였으므로, 남자가 할 일로 가장 적절한 것은 ② '드레스 찾아오기'이다.

어휘&어구 performance 연주회, 공연 take care of ~을 처리하다 dry cleaner's 세탁소

06 분갈이를 위한 재료 구입 [정답] ④

W	Honey, can you come here for a moment? I'm shopping online for what we need to repot the plant in the living room.	여	여보, 잠깐 여기로 와 줄래요? 거실에 있는 식물을 분갈이하기 위해 필요한 것들을 온라인으로 쇼핑하고 있어요.
M	Okay.	남	알았어요.
W	What do you think about this large white pot? It's $30.	여	이 커다란 하얀 화분에 대해 어떻게 생각해요? 그건 30달러예요.
M	Hmm.... I think this brown one is better.	남	음…. 이 갈색 것이 더 나은 것 같아요.
W	I agree. But it's $40.	여	나도 동의해요. 하지만 그것은 40달러예요.
M	It's $10 more, but I think it's worth it.	남	그것이 10달러 더 비싸지만, 그것이 그럴 만한 가치가 있다고 생각해요.
W	Okay. I'll buy it. And we need some potting soil, too.	여	좋아요. 그것을 살게요. 그리고 우리는 화분용 흙도 필요해요.
M	How much is a bag?	남	한 봉지에 얼마예요?
W	$5 each. I think we need two of them.	여	개당 5달러예요. 우리는 두 봉지가 필요한 것 같아요.
M	Okay, let's get two bags. And let's get a bag of pebbles to put on the soil. Look here. They're $4 a bag.	남	좋아요. 두 봉지를 사요. 그리고 흙 위에 놓을 조약돌을 한 봉지 삽시다. 여기 봐요. 그것은 한 봉지에 4달러예요.
W	That's a good idea. Pebbles will look nice. I'll get a bag of pebbles.	여	좋은 생각이에요. 조약돌이 멋져 보일 거예요. 조약돌 한 봉지를 살게요.
M	Okay. What's the shipping fee for all of them?	남	좋아요. 그 모든 것들을 위한 배송비가 얼마예요?
W	Normally it's $3, but I just got a membership, so the shipping is free. I'll pay for them by my credit card now.	여	보통 3달러인데, 방금 회원 자격을 얻어서 배송비가 무료예요. 이제 내 신용 카드로 그것들을 지불할게요.

문제 해설 여자는 40달러짜리 갈색 화분, 한 봉지에 5달러인 화분용 흙 두 봉지, 한 봉지에 4달러인 조약돌 한 봉지를 구입하기로 했고, 회원 자격을 얻어서 배송비는 무료인데 여자가 신용 카드로 물건값을 지불한다고 했으므로, 여자가 지불할 금액은 ④ '54달러'이다.

어휘&어구 repot 분갈이하다 soil 흙 pebble 조약돌, 자갈 membership 회원 자격

07 야구팀을 그만둔 이유 [정답] ④

W	What's up, Jeremy?	여	안녕, Jeremy?
M	Hey, Olivia. Where are you coming from?	남	안녕, Olivia. 어디에서 오는 길이니?
W	I was volunteering. My fellow book club members and I read books to kids at the library every Saturday.	여	봉사 활동을 했어. 동료 독서 동아리 회원들과 내가 매주 토요일 도서관에서 아이들에게 책을 읽어 줘.
M	Wow, that's really thoughtful.	남	와, 정말 사려 깊은 일이구나.
W	Thank you. By the way, what's all that?	여	고마워. 그런데 그게 다 뭐니?
M	Just stuff I'm throwing out. I don't need these things anymore.	남	그냥 내가 버리는 물건들이야. 이것들이 더 이상 필요 없거든.
W	You don't need your baseball glove? Aren't you on the school baseball team?	여	네 야구 글러브가 필요 없니? 너는 학교 야구팀원이지?
M	Well, this glove is really old. And I'm not on the team this year.	남	음, 이 글러브는 정말 낡았어. 그리고 나는 올해 팀에 속해 있지 않아.
		여	그래? 혹시라도 너랑 나머지 선수들 사이에 무슨 일이 있었니?
		남	아니야. 내가 다음 주에 조금 멀리 이사를 해서 방과 후 연습에 가

W	Really? Did something happen between you and the other players by any chance?
M	No. It's because I'm moving a little far away next week, so it'd be hard to make it to practice after school.
W	Oh, are you? I didn't know that. So are you changing schools?
M	No. I'm staying at the same school. My dad will give me a ride to school on his way to work.
W	That's nice.

	기가 어려울 것 같아서야.
여	아, 그래? 나는 몰랐어. 그러면 학교를 옮기니?
남	아니야. 나는 같은 학교에 있을 거야. 아빠가 출근길에 나를 학교에 태워다 주실 거야.
여	잘됐네.

문제 해설 야구 글러브를 버리려는 남자에게 여자가 그 이유를 묻자 남자는 자신이 더 이상 학교 야구팀에 속해 있지 않다고 하면서 다음 주에 이사를 해서 방과 후 연습에 참여하기가 어려워 팀을 떠났다고 했으므로, 남자가 야구팀을 그만둔 이유는 ④ '이사로 방과 후 연습에 갈 수 없어서'이다.

어휘&어구 fellow 동료의; 동료 thoughtful 사려 깊은, 친절한 stuff 물건 throw out ~을 버리다 by any chance 혹시라도 make it to ~에 가다 give ~ a ride ~을 태워 주다

08 Riverville Run [정답] ⑤

M	Judy, check out this flyer for the Riverville Run.
W	Oh, it's this year. It's held every two years.
M	Right. It's on Saturday, May 11th this year.
W	I'd love to run in it. How about you?
M	Sure. Let's do it together.
W	Great! It should be fun. By the way, is the starting point the same as in the past?
M	Yeah. It begins in front of the downtown library. It's a 10-kilometer loop, so the end is also at the library.
W	Okay. When is the registration deadline?
M	Next Friday. Let's register now. We just have to scan this QR code to register.
W	Perfect. I'll get my phone.
M	All right.

남	Judy, Riverville Run에 대한 이 전단을 확인해 봐.
여	아, 그것이 올해구나. 그것은 2년마다 개최되잖아.
남	맞아. 올해는 5월 11일 토요일이야.
여	거기서 뛰고 싶네. 너는 어때?
남	물론이야. 그것을 함께 하자.
여	좋아! 재미있을 거야. 그런데 출발지가 예전과 같니?
남	응. 그것은 시내에 있는 도서관 앞에서 시작해. 그것은 10킬로미터 순환 코스여서 도착지도 도서관이야.
여	알겠어. 등록 마감일은 언제니?
남	다음 주 금요일이야. 지금 등록하자. 등록하려면 이 QR 코드를 스캔하기만 하면 돼.
여	완벽해. 내 전화기를 가져올게.
남	알겠어.

문제 해설 대화에서 Riverville Run에 관해 개최 빈도, 개최일, 출발지, 등록 방법은 언급되었지만, ⑤ '참가비'는 언급되지 않았다.

어휘&어구 flyer 전단 loop 순환, (동그라미 모양의) 고리 registration 등록

09 GW Handwriting Contest 안내 [정답] ⑤

W Good morning, listeners! I'd like to tell you about the University of Greenwood's upcoming annual GW Handwriting Contest. The contest is open to all Greenwood residents, and there are three age categories: 12 and younger, ages 13–16, and ages 17 and older. Contestants will be given a text to copy and submit, and their submissions will be judged on the style, neatness, and layout of their handwriting. The submission deadline is March 31. Winners in each category will win a $200 cash prize and a trophy. The award-winning works will be posted on our website until April 30, 2019. For the official rules and the text to be copied, visit www.gwhc.org. Thank you.

여 안녕하세요, 청취자 여러분! 매년 개최되는 Greenwood 대학교의 다가오는 GW Handwriting Contest에 대해 말씀드리고 싶습니다. 이 대회는 Greenwood 주민 누구나 참가할 수 있으며, 12세 이하, 13세에서 16세, 17세 이상의 세 가지 연령 범주가 있습니다. 참가자에게는 옮겨 적어 제출할 글이 주어지며, 그들의 제출물은 필적의 스타일, 깔끔함 및 짜임새를 기준으로 심사를 받게 될 것입니다. 제출 마감은 3월 31일입니다. 각 연령 범주별 우승자는 200달러의 상금과 트로피를 받을 것입니다. 수상작은 2019년 4월 30일까지 저희 웹사이트에 게시될 것입니다. 공식적인 규칙과 옮겨 적을 글을 보시려면, www.gwhc.org를 방문해 주세요. 감사합니다.

문제 해설 수상작은 웹사이트에 4월 30일까지 게시될 것이라고 했으므로, 담화의 내용과 일치하지 않는 것은 ⑤ '수상작은 3월 31일까지 웹사이트에 게시된다.'이다.

어휘&어구 resident 주민, 거주민   contestant 참가자   submission 제출(물)   neatness 깔끔함   layout 짜임새   cash prize 상금

---

10 어머니날 선물 세트 주문
[정답] ②

W Dad, please come help me.	**여** 아빠, 와서 저 좀 도와주세요.
M Okay. What's up?	**남** 알았어. 무슨 일이야?
W I want to buy Mom a Mother's Day present from this online store, but I don't know which of these five gift sets to choose.	**여** 이 온라인 가게에서 엄마에게 어머니날 선물을 사 드리고 싶은데, 이 다섯 가지 선물 세트 중 어떤 것을 골라야 할지 모르겠어요.
M Let's see. All of them look nice. But I don't think your mom would use this silk pillowcase and sleeping mask.	**남** 어디 보자. 모두 멋져 보이네. 하지만 나는 네 엄마가 이 실크 베갯잇과 수면 마스크를 사용할 거라고 생각하지 않아.
W That's good to know. I'll buy one of these four sets then. Oh, I like this one, but it's out of my budget.	**여** 알게 돼서 다행이에요. 그럼 이 네 세트 중에서 하나를 사겠어요. 아, 저는 이게 마음에 드는데, 제 예산 밖이에요.
M What's your budget?	**남** 예산이 어떻게 돼?
W I don't think I can spend more than $40.	**여** 40달러 넘게 쓸 수 없을 것 같아요.
M Then you have to choose one of these three. What do you think of this set?	**남** 그럼 너는 이 세 가지 중에서 하나를 골라야 해. 이 세트에 대해 어떻게 생각하니?
W Oh, look at the delivery date. I want it to be delivered earlier than May 5 just in case. Mother's Day falls on May 8 this year.	**여** 오, 배송 날짜를 보세요. 혹시 모르니 5월 5일보다 빨리 배송되기를 원해요. 올해 어머니날은 5월 8일이에요.
M These two options are left then. I think your mom will like either of them. Why don't you go for the one with a higher customer rating?	**남** 그렇다면 이 두 개의 선택 사항이 남아 있어. 네 엄마는 어느 것이든 다 좋아할 거야. 더 높은 고객 평가를 받은 것으로 하는 게 어때?
W Okay, I'll order it. Thanks for your help.	**여** 네, 그것으로 주문할게요. 도와줘서 고마워요.
M No problem.	**남** 천만에.

문제 해설 여자는 어머니날 선물로 실크 베갯잇과 수면 마스크는 제외하고, 40달러가 넘지 않으며, 5월 5일 이전에 배송되는 것 중에서, 더 높은 고객 평가를 받은 선물 세트를 골랐으므로, 여자가 주문할 선물 세트는 ②이다.

어휘&어구 pillowcase 베갯잇   budget 예산   rating 평가, 등급, 순위

---

11 비행기에서 약품 요청
[정답] ⑤

M Excuse me, I'd like to know if you have a thermometer on this plane. My son seems to have a fever.	**남** 실례합니다. 이 비행기에 체온계가 있는지 알고 싶어요. 제 아들에게 열이 있는 것 같거든요.
W We should have one in the first-aid kit. I'll go bring it to you in a minute.	**여** 아마 구급상자에 있을 거예요. 곧 가서 가져다드리겠습니다.
M Thank you. And could I get some fever-reducing pills for children, too?	**남** 감사합니다. 그리고 어린이용 해열제도 좀 얻을 수 있을까요?
W Sure. Let me bring the medicine to you, too.	**여** 물론이죠. 제가 약도 가져다드리겠습니다.

문제 해설 남자는 비행기에서 열이 나는 아들을 위해 해열제를 좀 얻을 수 있는지 물었으므로, 여자의 응답으로 가장 적절한 것은 ⑤ '물론이죠. 제가 약도 가져다드리겠습니다.'이다.
① 네. 약을 구급상자에 넣으세요.
② 아니요. 그 알약을 두어 개 더 드셔야 해요.
③ 맞아요. 복용량을 기억하고 계셔야 합니다.
④ 보세요! 체온계를 보니 아드님에게 열이 있네요.

어휘&어구 thermometer 체온계   fever 열   first-aid kit 구급상자   fever-reducing 해열의, 열을 내리는   pill 약, 알약   keep track of ~을 기억하고 있다, ~에 대해 계속 알고 있다

12 연휴 동안 하고 싶은 일

[정답] ③

W Honey, we have a 4-day weekend at the end of this month. Is there anything special you'd like to do during the holiday?

M Well, it'd be nice to do something outdoors. It'd be boring to just stay inside for four days.

W I agree. Let me know if you have anything in mind.

M Going camping seems like a great plan.

여 여보, 우리가 이번 달 말에 4일간의 주말 휴가가 있어요. 휴가 동안 특별히 하고 싶은 일이 있어요?

남 음, 야외에서 뭔가를 하면 좋을 거 같아요. 4일 동안 안에만 있으면 지루할 거예요.

여 동의해요. 당신이 생각해 둔 것이 있으면 알려 줘요.

남 캠핑을 가는 것이 좋은 계획인 것 같아요.

문제 해설 4일간의 주말 휴가를 앞두고 휴가 동안 야외에서 무언가를 하고 싶다는 남자에게 여자가 생각해 둔 것이 있으면 알려 달라고 했다. 따라서 여자의 마지막 말에 대한 남자의 응답으로 가장 적절한 것은 ③ '캠핑을 가는 것이 좋은 계획인 것 같아요.'이다.

① 당신은 나만큼 외향적이잖아요.

② 나는 항상 너무 바빠서 지루함을 느끼지 않아요.

④ 4일은 어떤 계획을 세우기에는 너무 짧았어요.

⑤ 나는 주말에 집에서 좀 쉬었어요.

어휘&어구 holiday 휴가, 방학 outdoors 야외에서 have ~ in mind ~을 생각해 두다, ~을 염두에 두다 outgoing 외향적인

13 발표에 필요한 제품의 사진 촬영

[정답] ①

M Hey, Mary. What are you going to do after school?

W Hi, Daniel. I'm going to find some visual material for my science class presentation.

M What's the presentation topic?

W It's about AI and the Fourth Industrial Revolution. I want to add realistic pictures of the products used in everyday life besides the information online.

M You've already checked the school library, right?

W Yes, I went there, but I couldn't find the pictures I was looking for.

M That's too bad. Oh, when is your presentation? The 2022 AI Expo is at the civic center downtown this weekend, which exhibits many AI products.

W Really? The presentation is next Friday, so it sounds like the expo could be helpful for my presentation.

M Yeah. They even allow you to take pictures of the exhibits.

W I didn't know about that. I'm sure I'll go to the expo.

남 안녕, Mary. 방과 후에 무엇을 할 거니?

여 안녕, Daniel. 과학 수업 발표를 위해 시각 자료를 좀 찾을 거야.

남 발표 주제가 뭐니?

여 인공 지능과 4차 산업 혁명에 관한 거야. 온라인 정보 외에 일상생활에서 사용되는 제품의 실감 나는 사진을 추가하고 싶어.

남 학교 도서관은 이미 확인해 봤지, 그렇지?

여 응, 거기에 갔었지만, 내가 찾고 있던 사진들을 찾을 수 없었어.

남 그것참 안됐네. 아, 네 발표가 언제니? 2022 인공 지능 박람회가 이번 주말에 시내에 있는 시민 회관에서 열리는데, 많은 인공 지능 제품들을 전시해.

여 정말이니? 발표는 다음 주 금요일이어서, 박람회는 내 발표에 도움이 될 수 있을 것 같네.

남 그래. 그들은 심지어 네가 전시품들의 사진을 찍는 것을 허용해.

여 나는 그것에 대해 알지 못했어. 박람회에 꼭 가 볼 거야.

문제 해설 여자가 인공 지능과 4차 산업 혁명을 주제로 발표를 준비하면서 일상생활에서 사용되는 제품의 실감 나는 사진을 추가하고 싶지만 사진을 학교 도서관에서 찾을 수 없었다고 하자, 남자는 주말에 열리는 인공 지능 박람회에서 많은 인공 지능 제품들이 전시되고 사진 촬영도 가능하다고 말하고 있다. 따라서 남자의 마지막 말에 대한 여자의 응답으로 가장 적절한 것은 ① '나는 그것에 대해 알지 못했어. 박람회에 꼭 가 볼 거야.'이다.

② 문제없어. 나는 인터넷에서 조사하는 것에 능숙해.

③ 괜찮아. 네가 필요한 책들을 위해 다른 도서관을 확인해 봐.

④ 나는 동의해. 너는 일찍 시작해서 잘할 수 있을 거야.

⑤ 인공 지능에 관한 너의 지식이 내가 전시회를 하는 데 도움이 될 거야.

어휘&어구 material 자료 presentation 발표 AI 인공 지능(= artificial intelligence) the Fourth Industrial Revolution 4차 산업 혁명 realistic 실감 나는, 현실적인 expo 박람회, 전시회 civic center 시민 회관 exhibit 전시하다; 전시품 research 조사하다

14 박물관행 버스 타기 [정답] ⑤

W Excuse me. I'm touring the city and was wondering if I could ask you something.

M Sure. Go ahead.

W Can I catch a bus here which goes to the Pine Museum?

M Yes, you should take the number 10 bus and change buses at Oak Street.

W How many stops are there from here to Oak Street?

M About 15 stops. It takes about 30 minutes.

W Oh, I see. And how much is the fare?

M It's 1 dollar and 50 cents.

W Thank you.

M No problem. But you know you could also take the subway to the museum. You don't even have to transfer lines.

W Really? Can you tell me where the subway station is?

M It's simple. Just walk about ten minutes that way.

W Oh my! I've been walking around all day. I don't feel like walking anymore.

M Then I guess you should use the bus, not the subway.

여 실례합니다. 이 도시를 관광하고 있는 중인데 뭐를 여쭤봐도 되는지요.

남 그럼요. 말씀해 보세요.

여 여기서 Pine 박물관에 가는 버스를 탈 수 있나요?

남 네, 10번 버스를 타고 Oak 가에서 버스를 갈아타야 합니다.

여 여기서 Oak 가까지 몇 정거장인가요?

남 약 열다섯 정거장입니다. 30분쯤 걸립니다.

여 아, 알겠습니다. 그리고 요금은 얼마인가요?

남 1달러 50센트입니다.

여 감사합니다.

남 천만에요. 하지만 그 박물관까지 가는 지하철을 탈 수도 있습니다. 노선을 갈아탈 필요도 없고요.

여 정말로요? 지하철역이 어디인지 알려 줄 수 있나요?

남 간단해요. 저쪽으로 약 10분 걷기만 하면 됩니다.

여 이런! 하루 종일 걸어 돌아다니는 중이에요. 더 이상 걷고 싶지 않아요.

남 그러면 지하철이 아니라 버스를 타셔야 할 것 같아요.

문제 해설 도시를 관광하고 있는 중인 여자가 남자에게 Pine 박물관에 가는 버스 노선을 묻자, 남자는 버스 번호를 알려 주고 버스는 갈아타야 하지만 지하철은 갈아탈 필요가 없다고 말한다. 이어서 지하철역의 위치를 묻는 여자에게 남자가 걸어서 10분 거리라고 하자, 여자는 하루 종일 걸어 돌아다니는 중이어서 더 이상 걷고 싶지 않다고 말하고 있다. 따라서 여자의 마지막 말에 대한 남자의 응답으로 가장 적절한 것은 ⑤ '그러면 지하철이 아니라 버스를 타셔야 할 것 같아요.'이다.

① 아뇨. 복잡한 지하철을 타는 것을 좋아하지 않아요.

② 물론입니다. 당신은 여기서 거기까지 걸어갈 수 있어요.

③ 미안해요. 전에 그 박물관에 가 본 적이 없어요.

④ 맞아요. 당신은 버스 요금을 잔돈으로 가지고 있어야 해요.

어휘&어구 tour 관광하다 stop 정거장 fare 요금 transfer 갈아타다, 환승하다 feel like -ing ~하고 싶다 crowded 복잡한, 붐비는

15 집중력에 도움이 되는 아침 먹기 [정답] ④

M Emma is a high school student and she receives poor grades on her first exams. She didn't study that hard, which she regrets, so she decides to start studying hard. She begins waking up early every morning to study, but she has difficulty focusing on studying. She tells her friend Jeremy about her problem. Jeremy knows that Emma always skips breakfast, which he thinks is why she can't focus in the morning. He explains to Emma that eating breakfast is related to brain activity and concentration. Now Jeremy wants to suggest that Emma eat something in the morning to help her study. In this situation, what would Jeremy most likely say to Emma?

Jeremy Make sure you don't skip breakfast to concentrate better.

남 Emma는 고등학생인데 그녀는 첫 시험에서 낮은 성적을 받습니다. 그녀는 그렇게 열심히 공부하지 않은 것을 후회해서 열심히 공부를 시작하기로 결심합니다. 그녀는 공부를 하기 위해 매일 아침 일찍 일어나기 시작하지만, 공부에 집중하는 데 어려움을 겪습니다. 그녀는 친구인 Jeremy에게 자신의 문제에 대해 이야기를 합니다. Jeremy는 Emma가 항상 아침을 거른다는 것을 알고 있고, 그는 그것이 그녀가 아침에 집중하지 못하는 이유라고 생각합니다. 그는 Emma에게 아침을 먹는 것이 두뇌 활동 및 집중력과 관계가 있다고 설명합니다. 이제 Jeremy는 공부에 도움이 되려면 Emma가 아침에 무언가를 먹어야 한다고 제안하고 싶어 합니다. 이런 상황에서 Jeremy는 Emma에게 뭐라고 말하겠습니까?

Jeremy 더 집중을 잘할 수 있게 반드시 아침을 거르지 않도록 해.

문제 해설 고등학교 첫 시험에서 열심히 공부를 하지 않아 낮은 성적을 받은 Emma는 공부를 하기 위해 매일 아침 일찍 일어나기 시작하지만 집중이 잘 되지 않는다. 이에 친구인 Jeremy에게 조언을 구하자 그는 Emma가 아침을 먹지 않는 것이 문제라고 하면서 아침을 먹는 것이 두뇌 활동 및

집중력과 관계가 있으므로 아침을 먹으라고 조언하려는 상황이므로, Jeremy가 Emma에게 할 말로 가장 적절한 것은 ④ '더 집중을 잘할 수 있게 반드시 아침을 거르지 않도록 해.'이다.

① 아침을 그렇게 많이 먹는 것을 그만하도록 해.

② 네가 수업에 더 집중하는 것이 중요해.

③ 실수하지 않도록 너는 조심했어야 했어.

⑤ 성적이 네 학교생활에서 가장 중요한 것은 아니라는 것을 기억해.

어휘&어구 grade 성적 regret 후회하다 skip 거르다, 빼먹다 be related to ~과 관계가 있다 concentration 집중(력)

16~17 사물 인터넷(IoT) 기술을 사용한 제품

[정답] 16 ④ 17 ③

W Good afternoon, everyone. Last time, we talked about IoT, the Internet of Things, which refers to the connection of everyday objects to the Internet. Today, let me give you some examples of smart home appliances that use IoT technology. A smart refrigerator can create grocery lists and link to smartphone apps, allowing users to control the temperature remotely. Another example is a smart coffee maker, which makes it easy to schedule, monitor, and modify users' coffee brewing from anywhere. The next example is a smart washing machine. It can easily specify when users need their laundry done. Finally, a recently launched smart alarm clock, hidden in a stylish lamp, offers a refreshing wake-up experience through changing light and customized music. With these products, we can experience the IoT technology every day.

여 안녕하세요, 여러분. 지난 시간에 우리는 IoT, 즉 사물 인터넷에 대해 이야기했었는데, 그것은 일상의 물건들이 인터넷에 연결되어 있음을 일컫는 말입니다. 오늘은 IoT 기술을 활용하는 가정용 스마트 전자 기기의 예시를 들어 보겠습니다. 스마트 냉장고는 식료품 목록을 생성하고 스마트폰 앱과 연결하여 사용자가 온도를 원격으로 조정할 수 있습니다. 또 다른 예는 스마트 커피 메이커인데, 이것은 사용자의 커피 끓이기에 관해 어디서나 일정을 조정하고, 추적하며, 수정하는 것을 쉽게 만들어 줍니다. 다음 예는 스마트 세탁기입니다. 이것은 사용자가 빨래를 언제 해야 하는지를 쉽게 구체적으로 말을 해 줍니다. 마지막으로, 최근에 출시된 스마트 알람 시계는, 멋진 램프 안에 숨겨진 채로, 변화하는 조명과 개개인의 요구에 맞춘 음악을 통해 상쾌하게 잠에서 깨는 경험을 제공합니다. 이러한 제품들과 함께 우리는 IoT 기술을 매일 경험할 수 있게 됩니다.

문제 해설 16 여자는 지난 시간에 배웠던 사물 인터넷 기술이 적용된 가정용 전자 기기의 다양한 예시를 들며, 사물 인터넷을 활용한 제품들을 소개하고 있으므로, 여자가 하는 말의 목적으로 가장 적절한 것은 ④ '사물 인터넷 기술을 활용한 제품들을 소개하려고'이다.

17 냉장고, 커피 메이커, 세탁기, 알람 시계는 언급되었지만, ③ '공기 청정기'는 언급되지 않았다.

어휘&어구 home appliance 가정용 전자 기기 remotely 원격으로 modify 수정하다 brew (커피를) 끓이다 specify 구체적으로 말하다, 명확히 말하다 launched 출시된 customized 개개인의 요구에 맞춘

5회 수능실전 대비연습

본문 70~71쪽

| 01 ① | 02 ② | 03 ① | 04 ④ | 05 ③ | 06 ④ | 07 ⑤ | 08 ④ | 09 ④ | 10 ⑤ | 11 ③ | 12 ③ | 13 ② | 14 ① |
| 15 ① | 16 ⑤ | 17 ③ |

01 Little Fun Reading Club 책 배달 서비스

[정답] ①

M Hello, parents! Do you want your child to learn the enjoyment of reading? Then enroll them in the Little Fun Reading Club. Every month your child will receive a Little Fun Reading Club box containing three books. The books are matched to your child's age and interests that you check in the initial enrollment form. The books are selected through a rigorous review process, considering the subjects, authors, awards, and book reviews. And all the books are

남 안녕하세요, 부모님 여러분! 여러분의 자녀가 독서의 즐거움을 알기를 원하십니까? 그렇다면 그들을 Little Fun Reading Club 에 등록시키십시오. 매달 여러분의 자녀는 3권의 책이 들어 있는 Little Fun Reading Club 상자를 받게 될 것입니다. 그 책들은 여러분이 처음 등록 양식에 표시하는 자녀의 연령과 관심사에 맞춰집니다. 그 책들은 주제, 작가, 상, 책 후기를 고려한 철저한 검토 과정을 통해 선정됩니다. 그리고 모든 책들은 어떤 연령 범주이든 구독 상자에 포함되기 전에 Little Fun Reading Club 전문가가

read and discussed by the Little Fun Reading Club experts before they are included in a subscription box for any age category. For only $16.95 a month, give your child the meaningful gift of reading!

읽고 토론을 합니다. 한 달에 단지 16.95달러로 독서라는 의미 있는 선물을 여러분의 자녀에게 주십시오!

문제 해설 남자는 부모들에게 자녀가 독서의 즐거움을 알 수 있도록 매달 3권의 책을 배달해 주는 서비스를 홍보하고 있다. 따라서 남자가 하는 말의 목적으로 가장 적절한 것은 ① '자녀를 위한 책 배달 서비스를 홍보하려고'이다.

어휘&어구 enroll 등록시키다 initial 처음의, 초기의 enrollment 등록, 입학 rigorous 철저한 expert 전문가 subscription 구독

---

02 워크숍 계획 변경하기 [정답] ②

M Ms. Ellis, have you checked the weather forecast for this Saturday?

W No. That's the day of the company workshop. We're going hiking.

M Right. But it seems like it might rain that day.

W Really? Let me check. *[Pause]* Oh, no. There's a high chance of rain right now, but it could change. It's only Monday.

M That's true. But in case it does rain, we won't be able to go hiking.

W Hmm, you're right. Maybe we should plan something else.

M Yeah, we'd better change the place. It's better to be safe than sorry.

W Right. Let's talk about it together after lunch.

M Okay. Then we won't have to worry about whether it's going to rain or not.

W Exactly. I'll inform the others that we're going to meet at 1:30.

M Sounds good.

남 Ellis 씨, 이번 토요일 일기 예보를 확인해 보셨어요?

여 아니요. 그날은 회사 워크숍이 있는 날이네요. 우리는 하이킹을 가잖아요.

남 맞아요. 그런데 그날 비가 올 것 같네요.

여 정말요? 제가 확인해 볼게요. *[잠시 후]* 아, 저런. 현재로서는 비가 올 확률이 높기는 한데 바뀔 수 있어요. 아직 월요일이잖아요.

남 그건 사실이에요. 그렇지만 비가 정말 올 경우에는 우리는 하이킹을 갈 수가 없어요.

여 음, 맞는 말이에요. 아마도 다른 계획을 세워야 할 것 같네요.

남 네, 우리가 장소를 변경하는 게 낫겠어요. 후회하는 것보다 안전한 것이 더 낫잖아요.

여 맞아요. 점심 식사 후에 함께 그것에 대해 이야기해요.

남 알겠습니다. 그러면 우리는 비가 올지 안 올지에 대해 걱정할 필요가 없을 거예요.

여 맞아요. 다른 사람들에게 우리가 1시 30분에 만날 거라고 알릴게요.

남 좋습니다.

문제 해설 회사 워크숍으로 토요일에 하이킹을 가기로 한 상황에서 일기 예보에 따르면 그날 비가 올 가능성이 높자 남자는 나중에 후회하지 말고 장소를 변경하는 게 낫겠다고 말했다. 이에 여자도 동의하면서 다른 직원들과 의논하자고 했으므로, 남자의 주장으로 가장 적절한 것은 ② '날씨에 대비해 워크숍 장소를 변경하는 것이 좋다.'이다.

어휘&어구 weather forecast 일기 예보 chance 확률, 가능성 in case ~한 경우는 inform 알리다

---

03 사육사가 하는 일 [정답] ①

W Hello. I'm Sharon Baker. We talked on the phone yesterday.

M Hi, Ms. Baker. Come on in.

W Thanks for taking time out of your day for me. What were you doing?

M I was just cleaning up one of the cages, and now I'm getting food ready for the animals. I'm glad to have a chance to talk about my job with your readers.

W They'll love it. A lot of our young readers asked us to write about what it's like working with animals at a zoo.

M I'm so happy to let them know.

여 안녕하세요. 전 Sharon Baker입니다. 어제 전화로 말씀 나누었죠.

남 안녕하세요, Baker 씨. 들어오세요.

여 저를 위해 일과 중 시간을 내어 주셔서 감사합니다. 뭘 하고 계셨어요?

남 방금 우리들 중 하나를 청소하고 있었는데, 지금은 동물을 위한 먹이를 준비하고 있어요. 당신의 독자분들과 제 일에 대해 이야기할 수 있는 기회를 갖게 되어 기쁩니다.

여 독자들이 정말 좋아할 거예요. 저희의 많은 어린 독자들이 동물원에서 동물들과 일하는 것이 어떤 것인지 써 달라고 요청했거든요.

남 그들에게 알려 주게 되어 정말 기쁘네요.

W	Me, too. This will be in an article in the October issue of our magazine. Can I ask what the pills in this bowl are? Are they medicine for animals?	여	저도요. 이것은 저희 잡지의 10월호에 실릴 기사에 나올 거예요. 이 통에 담긴 알약이 뭔지 여쭤봐도 될까요? 동물들을 위한 약인가요?
M	They're animal vitamins. We put them in their food.	남	동물용 비타민이에요. 저희가 그것들을 먹이에 넣습니다.
W	Oh, I never knew that there were animal vitamins. Can I go with you when you feed the animals?	여	아, 동물용 비타민이 있다는 걸 몰랐네요. 동물들에게 먹이를 줄 때 함께 갈 수 있나요?
M	Of course. I'll show you how it's done.	남	물론이죠. 어떻게 하는지 보여 드리겠습니다.
W	Great! I'll take some pictures.	여	좋아요! 제가 사진 좀 찍을게요.

문제 해설 남자는 우리를 청소한 후 동물을 위해 먹이를 준비하고 있다고 했고, 여자는 남자가 하는 일에 관한 기사를 잡지에 실을 것이라고 말했다. 따라서 두 사람의 관계를 가장 잘 나타낸 것은 ① '잡지 기자 – 사육사'이다.

어휘&어구 cage 우리, 새장   issue (잡지 같은 정기 간행물의) 호   magazine 잡지   pill 알약   bowl (우묵한) 통, 그릇   feed 먹이다, 먹이를 주다

04 곧 태어날 아기의 방
[정답] ④

M	Look at our baby room, honey. I can't wait to see our baby.	남	우리 아기방을 좀 봐요, 여보. 얼른 아기를 만나고 싶네요.
W	I can't believe we're going to be parents soon.	여	우리가 곧 부모가 될 것이라는 게 믿어지지 않네요.
M	Me, neither. Those stars hanging from the ceiling make this room look peaceful.	남	나도 그래요. 천장에 매달려 있는 저 별들은 이 방이 평화로워 보이도록 해 줘요.
W	Yes. They look nice.	여	네. 좋아 보이네요.
M	Right. When our baby sees this drawing of a smiling sun on the wall, he will surely smile, too.	남	맞아요. 벽에 그려진 웃고 있는 이 해님 그림을 보면, 우리 아기도 틀림없이 미소를 지을 거예요.
W	It makes me so happy to picture our baby smiling in his bed. Honey, did you put this cushion in the bed? I haven't seen it before.	여	우리 아기가 침대에서 미소 짓고 있는 모습을 마음속에 그려 보니 무척 행복해지네요. 여보, 당신이 이 쿠션을 침대 안에 놓아두었나요? 전에 본 적이 없어요.
M	Yes, I did. Look! The letter "C" written on the cushion stands for "Chris", our baby's name.	남	네, 그래요. 봐요! 쿠션 위에 쓰인 'C'라는 글자는 우리 아기 이름 'Chris'를 뜻해요.
W	Good choice! And I like the round photo frame on the wall near the bed.	여	잘 골랐네요! 그리고 침대 근처 벽에 있는 둥근 사진 액자가 마음에 들어요.
M	I'm going to put our baby's first photo in the frame.	남	우리 아기의 첫 사진을 그 액자에 넣을 거예요.
W	I hope to see our baby crawl to the stuffed toy dog next to the bed and play with it soon.	여	우리 아기가 곧 침대 옆에 있는 봉제 강아지 인형으로 기어가서 그것을 가지고 노는 것을 보고 싶어요.

문제 해설 여자는 둥근 사진 액자가 마음에 든다고 했지만 그림의 액자는 네모이다. 따라서 그림에서 대화의 내용과 일치하지 않는 것은 ④이다.

어휘&어구 ceiling 천장   crawl 기어가다   stuffed toy 봉제 인형

05 발표 날짜 변경 부탁
[정답] ③

M	Charlotte, can I talk to you for a moment?	남	Charlotte, 잠시 이야기할 수 있니?
W	Sure, Ivan. Is it about the book I borrowed from you? I'm almost done with it.	여	물론이지, Ivan. 내가 너한테 빌린 책에 관한 것이니? 내가 거의 다 읽었어.
M	No, it's not about that. You can keep it for as long as you need it.	남	아니야, 그 얘기가 아니야. 네가 필요로 하는 동안은 그 책을 가지고 있어도 돼.
W	Okay. Then what's up?	여	알겠어. 그러면 무슨 일이니?
M	You're scheduled to give your history presentation next week, right?	남	네가 다음 주에 역사 발표를 하기로 예정되어 있잖아, 맞지?
W	Yeah. And aren't you the week after me?	여	응. 그리고 너는 나 다음 주 아니니?
		남	응. 그런데 내가 미술 대회에 참가하라는 요청을 받았는데, 그것이

M Yeah. But I was asked to participate in an art competition, which is on the same day as my presentation.

W Oh, so you need to change the date.

M Right. So could you switch presentation dates with me?

W Sure. No problem.

M Thank you so much. I'll tell the teacher about it.

W Okay. I hope you do well in the art competition.

M Thanks, Charlotte.

여 나의 발표일과 같은 날이야.

아, 그러면 날짜를 바꿔야겠구나.

남 맞아. 그래서 네가 나랑 발표 날짜를 바꿔 줄 수 있니?

여 물론이야. 괜찮아.

남 정말 고마워. 내가 선생님께 그것을 말씀드릴게.

여 알겠어. 미술 대회에서 좋은 결과 있기를 바랄게.

남 고마워, Charlotte.

문제 해설 미술 대회에 참가하라는 요청을 받은 남자는 대회 날짜가 역사 발표가 예정된 날짜와 같아 다음 주에 발표를 하기로 되어 있는 여자에게 발표 날짜를 바꿔 달라고 부탁하고 있으므로, 남자가 여자에게 부탁한 일로 가장 적절한 것은 ③ '발표 날짜 바꿔 주기'이다.

어휘&어구 as long as ~하는 동안은   be scheduled to ~할 예정이다   switch 바꾸다

06 신발 주문하기 [정답] ④

W Hello, how can I help you?

M Hi. Are all of the shoes you have out on the floor?

W No, we have some in the storeroom.

M Okay. Do you have this shoe in a size 7?

W Let me check the system. [Pause] I'm sorry, we don't. But I can order it for you though. You should get it in about 3 days.

M Is it possible to have the shoes delivered to my house?

W Yes, but there's a $5 delivery fee for that.

M That's okay. And the shoes are $90, right?

W Yes.

M I have this $5-off coupon. Can I use it for the shoes?

W I'm sorry, but the coupon can't be used on any new items like these shoes.

M No problem. I'll take the shoes and have them delivered to my house. Here's my credit card.

W Thank you. Just a moment.

여 안녕하세요, 어떻게 도와드릴까요?

남 안녕하세요. 가지고 있으신 신발들이 모두 바닥에 꺼내져 있나요?

여 아닙니다, 창고에도 좀 있습니다.

남 그렇군요. 이 신발 사이즈 7이 있나요?

여 시스템을 확인해 보겠습니다. [잠시 후] 죄송합니다, 없네요. 그렇지만 그것을 손님께 주문해 드릴 수 있습니다. 약 3일 후에 받으실 수 있습니다.

남 저의 집으로 신발을 배달시키는 것도 가능한가요?

여 네, 하지만 거기엔 5달러의 배달비가 있습니다.

남 괜찮습니다. 그리고 신발은 90달러네요, 그렇죠?

여 네.

남 이 5달러 할인 쿠폰이 저한테 있습니다. 신발에 그것을 사용할 수 있을까요?

여 죄송하지만, 이 신발과 같은 신상품에는 그 쿠폰을 사용할 수 없습니다.

남 괜찮습니다. 신발을 구매하고 저의 집으로 배달시키도록 할게요. 제 신용 카드가 여기 있습니다.

여 감사합니다. 잠시만요.

문제 해설 남자는 90달러인 신발이 매장에는 재고가 없어 배달비 5달러를 지불하고 집으로 배달을 요청하고 있다. 5달러 할인 쿠폰은 사용할 수가 없다고 했으므로, 남자가 지불할 금액은 ④ '95달러'이다.

어휘&어구 storeroom 창고, 저장실   order 주문하다   deliver 배달하다

07 온라인 IT 학회에 늦은 이유 [정답] ⑤

W Hi, Ben. I didn't think I saw you at the online IT conference. Were you there?

M Yes, but I was late, so I missed the first session.

W Oh, it's too bad you missed it. That was the best part of the conference. Did you forget the start time?

M No. I added a reminder on my phone with the right date and time. And I also made sure I had the right access link before the conference.

W Then why were you late?

여 안녕, Ben. 내가 온라인 IT 학회에서 널 못 본 것 같은데. 너 거기 있었어?

남 응, 하지만 늦어서, 첫 번째 시간을 놓쳤어.

여 아, 그것을 놓쳤다니 안타깝다. 그것이 학회 중 가장 좋은 부분이었거든. 시작 시간을 잊었니?

남 아니. 전화기에 정확한 날짜와 시간으로 알림을 추가했었어. 그리고 학회 시작 전에 접속 링크가 맞는지도 확인했어.

여 그럼 왜 늦었니?

남 컴퓨터 문제가 있었어.

M	I had a computer issue.	여	컴퓨터에 뭔가 문제가 있었니?
W	Was there something wrong with your computer?	남	아니. 내가 막 노트북을 켰을 때 자동으로 업데이트가 시작됐어. 그
M	No. Just when I turned on my laptop, it automatically started updating. It took around 30 minutes!		게 30분 정도 걸렸어!
W	Oh, no! And you can't restart your laptop while it's updating.	여	아, 이런! 그리고 업데이트 중에는 노트북을 다시 시작할 수 없잖아.
M	Right. So I had to just sit and wait.	남	맞아. 그래서 그저 앉아서 기다려야만 했지.
W	Sorry to hear that. But I heard they're going to upload a video of the entire conference later.	여	그랬다니 안됐다. 하지만 나중에 전체 학회 동영상을 업로드할 거라고 들었어.
M	Oh, good. I can watch the first session later then.	남	오, 다행이다. 그럼 나중에 첫 번째 시간을 볼 수 있겠네.

문제 해설 남자가 온라인 IT 학회에 접속하려고 노트북을 켰을 때 자동으로 업데이트가 시작되는 바람에 첫 번째 시간을 놓쳤다고 말하고 있다. 따라서 남자가 온라인 IT 학회에 늦은 이유는 ⑤ '노트북 자동 업데이트가 오래 걸려서'이다.

어휘&어구 conference 학회, 회의 miss 놓치다 session (특정한 활동을 위한) 시간, 모임 reminder 알림, 상기시키는 것 access 접속 automatically 자동적으로 entire 전체의

08 Doggy Palace [정답] ④

M	Hi, Debbie. I heard you're taking a family trip.	남	안녕, Debbie. 가족 여행을 떠난다고 들었어요.
W	Yes, next week. But I still haven't found anyone to take care of our dog.	여	네, 다음 주예요. 그런데 아직도 우리 개를 돌볼 사람을 찾지 못했어요.
M	Why don't you use a dog boarding service at Doggy Palace?	남	Doggy Palace에서 개 숙박 서비스를 이용해 보지 그래요?
W	What's that?	여	그게 어떤 거예요?
M	It's a place that looks after dogs. I took my dog there last month when I was out of town on business.	남	개를 돌보는 곳이에요. 전 지난달에 업무로 집을 비웠을 때 제 개를 그곳에 데려갔었어요.
W	That sounds good. Where is it?	여	괜찮은 것 같은데요. 그곳은 어디에 있어요?
M	It's on 42nd Avenue, just a few minutes from the airport.	남	42번가에 있는데, 공항에서 불과 몇 분 거리예요.
W	That's convenient. Do you remember the rates?	여	그거 편리하겠네요. 요금은 기억나세요?
M	It's $40 per night and $150 per week.	남	1박에 40달러이고, 1주일에 150달러예요.
W	Not bad. Are the facilities nice?	여	나쁘지 않네요. 시설은 좋은가요?
M	Yes. It's really clean, and they have a large outdoor park for the dogs to play in.	남	네. 정말 깨끗하고, 개들이 놀 수 있는 큰 야외 공원이 있어요.
W	How can I use the service?	여	그 서비스를 이용하려면 어떻게 해야 하죠?
M	You can make a reservation online or by phone.	남	온라인이나 전화로 예약할 수 있어요.
W	Great! That's where I'll take my dog. Thanks!	여	좋아요! 그곳에 제 개를 데려가야겠네요. 감사해요!

문제 해설 Doggy Palace에 관해 위치, 이용 요금, 시설, 예약 방법은 언급되었지만, ④ '영업시간'은 언급되지 않았다.

어휘&어구 boarding 숙박, 기숙 on business 업무로 convenient 편리한 facility 시설 outdoor 야외의 make a reservation 예약을 하다

09 로봇 경주 대회 [정답] ④

M	Hello, robot lovers! I'm Mr. Rodriguez, the school science teacher, with an announcement about the school robot racing competition. It's going to be held on Saturday, July 6th. Students build robots and race them in a 30-meter race. All students can participate, either individually or as a team. There are no restrictions on the size or shape of the robots. The three fastest robots will qualify to race	남	안녕하세요, 로봇을 사랑하는 여러분! 교내 로봇 경주 대회에 관한 발표를 하는 저는 학교 과학 교사 Mr. Rodriguez입니다. 대회는 7월 6일 토요일에 열릴 것입니다. 학생들은 로봇을 만들고 그것들이 30미터를 경주를 하게 합니다. 모든 학생은 개인 또는 팀으로 참가할 수 있습니다. 로봇의 크기나 형태에는 제한이 없습니다. 세 개의 가장 빠른 로봇은 8월에 열릴 전국 대회에 참가할 자격을 얻게 됩니다. 접수 마감은 다음 주 월요일까지이며, 1층에 비치된

in the national competition in August. The deadline to enter is next Monday, and you can enter by submitting a registration form located on the 1st floor to me. I look forward to your passionate participation!

신청서를 저에게 제출하면 참가할 수 있습니다. 여러분의 열정적인 참여를 기대합니다!

문제 해설 교내 로봇 경주 대회에서 세 개의 가장 빠른 로봇은 8월에 열릴 전국 대회에 참가할 자격을 얻게 된다고 했으므로, 담화의 내용과 일치하지 않는 것은 ④ '가장 빠른 로봇 하나가 전국 대회에 참가하게 된다.'이다.

어휘&어구 announcement 발표   individually 개인적으로, 개별적으로   restriction 제한   qualify 자격을 얻다   passionate 열정적인

10 자외선 차단제 구매하기 [정답] ⑤

W Honey, are you shopping for sunscreen?

M Yeah. Which one in this list do you think I should get?

W Didn't you have Green Life sunscreen before?

M Yeah. It felt a bit sticky, which I didn't like. I'll try a different brand this time.

W Okay. Look at this one's UV index. You should get one with a UV index of at least 7.

M Definitely. And this one is gel type. I don't like that.

W I agree. It can feel sticky. So either stick or spray would be better.

M Right. The difference between these last two is the amount.

W How about buying the larger one?

M That makes sense. I'm sure I'll use it a lot this summer.

W Then this is the sunscreen you should get.

M Right. I'll order it now.

여 여보, 자외선 차단제를 사려고요?

남 네. 이 목록에서 어느 것을 내가 사야 할까요?

여 전에 Green Life 자외선 차단제를 사용하지 않았나요?

남 맞아요. 그것은 약간 끈적거려서 내가 좋아하지 않았어요. 이번에는 다른 브랜드로 써 보려고요.

여 알겠어요. 이것의 자외선 지수를 봐요. 자외선 지수가 적어도 7인 것을 구입해야 해요.

남 물론이죠. 그리고 이건 젤 타입이네요. 나는 그것을 좋아하지 않아요.

여 동의해요. 그것은 끈적거리는 느낌이 들 수 있어요. 따라서 스틱이나 스프레이가 더 좋을 거예요.

남 맞아요. 이 마지막 두 제품의 차이점은 양이에요.

여 더 큰 것을 사는 게 어때요?

남 맞아요. 분명히 내가 이번 여름에 그것을 많이 사용하게 될 거예요.

여 그렇다면 이것이 당신이 사야 할 자외선 차단제예요.

남 맞아요. 지금 그것을 주문할게요.

문제 해설 남자는 자외선 차단제를 고르면서 지난번에 썼던 Green Life 브랜드는 제외하고 자외선 지수가 7 이상이면서 젤 타입이 아닌 남은 두 제품 중에서 여름에 많이 사용할 거여서 양이 더 큰 것으로 주문하겠다고 했으므로, 남자가 선택할 자외선 차단제는 ⑤이다.

어휘&어구 sunscreen 자외선 차단제   sticky 끈적거리는   UV index 자외선 지수

11 수선점에 맡긴 교복 바지 [정답] ③

M Mom, did you get the zipper on my school uniform pants repaired?

W I dropped them off at the repair shop yesterday. And I got a message a little while ago that they're ready to be picked up. What's wrong?

M My other pair of pants got too dirty to wear to school tomorrow.

W Then, I'll go to the repair shop and pick up your pants.

남 엄마, 제 교복 바지의 지퍼를 수선 맡기셨어요?

여 어제 수선점에 맡겼지. 그리고 조금 전에 찾아가도록 준비가 되었다는 메시지를 받았어. 뭐가 잘못된 게 있니?

남 제 다른 바지가 내일 학교에 입고 가기에 너무 더러워졌거든요.

여 그럼, 내가 수선점에 가서 네 바지를 찾아올게.

문제 해설 남자가 교복 바지를 수선 맡겼는지를 여자에게 묻자, 여자는 그것이 찾아가도록 준비되었다는 연락을 받았다고 대답하면서 무엇 때문인지 물었고, 이에 남자는 다른 바지가 너무 더러워져서 내일 학교에 입고 갈 수 없다고 말했다. 따라서 남자의 마지막 말에 대한 여자의 응답으로 가장 적절한 것은 ③ '그럼, 내가 수선점에 가서 네 바지를 찾아올게.'이다.

① 좋아. 내가 지금 네 바지 지퍼를 수선할게.

② 물론이지. 나는 스스로 나의 교복을 세탁할 수 있어.

④ 글쎄, 네 바지를 네 방 어디에서도 찾을 수가 없었어.

⑤ 미안해. 네 바지를 나중에 수선점에 맡길게.

어휘&어구 drop off ~을 맡기다, ~을 가져다 두다   repair shop 수선점, 수리점   pick up ~을 (되)찾아오다

12 Albany 산 터널 공사

W	Todd, did you hear the news that the city's going to make a tunnel through Albany Mountain?	여	Todd, 시에서 Albany 산을 뚫어서 터널을 만들 거라는 소식을 들었어요?
M	Yes. It's always bumper-to-bumper all the way to work due to the mountain.	남	네. 그 산 때문에 항상 출근길 교통이 줄곧 정체돼요.
W	When the tunnel is completed, you'll be able to go right through it.	여	터널이 완공되면, 그것을 바로 통과해서 갈 수 있겠네요.
M	I think that will cut my commuting time in half.	남	그것이 나의 통근 시간을 반으로 줄여 줄 것 같아요.

문제 해설 시에서 산을 뚫어 터널을 만들 거라는 소식을 들었는지 묻는 여자의 말에, 남자가 그 산 때문에 항상 출근길 교통이 줄곧 정체된다고 하자, 여자는 터널이 완공되면 남자가 터널을 바로 통과해서 갈 수 있을 거라고 말했다. 따라서 여자의 마지막 말에 대한 남자의 응답으로 가장 적절한 것은 ③ '그것이 나의 통근 시간을 반으로 줄여 줄 것 같아요.'이다.
① 우리는 출근하는 가장 빠른 방법을 찾아야 해요.
② 당신은 안전을 위해 산을 돌아가는 것이 더 나아요.
④ 새 터널 공사 때문에 도로가 폐쇄되어 있습니다.
⑤ 러시아워 동안 터널 안에 차량이 많이 있습니다.

어휘&어구 bumper-to-bumper 교통이 정체된, (자동차가) 꼬리를 문 commute 통근하다 construction 공사, 건설 traffic (특정 시간에 도로상의) 차량들, 교통(량)

13 망원경 추천 부탁

M	Ms. Green, can I ask you something?	남	Green 선생님, 뭐 좀 여쭤봐도 될까요?
W	Sure, Peter. Is it about today's class?	여	물론이지, Peter. 오늘 수업에 관한 것이니?
M	No, it's about stargazing. I've become really interested in it recently.	남	아니에요, 별 보기에 관한 것이에요. 제가 최근에 그것에 정말 관심이 생겼거든요.
W	That's cool. I got into stargazing when I was young, too.	여	멋지구나. 나도 어렸을 때 별 보는 것을 시작했단다.
M	That's what I thought since you're a science teacher. Could you recommend a good telescope for me to buy?	남	선생님께서 과학 선생님이셔서 그러셨을 거라고 생각했어요. 제가 살 만한 좋은 망원경을 추천해 주실 수 있을까요?
W	Hmm. Well, there's a wide variety of them with different functions and prices.	여	음. 글쎄, 기능과 가격이 다른 아주 다양한 제품들이 있거든.
M	I noticed that. I'm guessing that the more expensive, the better, right?	남	그렇더라고요. 비쌀수록 더 좋은 것 같은데, 맞죠?
W	Yes, in general. But for beginners like you, there's no need to buy an expensive one.	여	응, 일반적으론 그래. 하지만 너와 같은 초보자들에게는 비싼 것을 살 필요는 없어.
M	That's what I thought.	남	저도 그렇게 생각했어요.
W	So how about using some of my telescopes first to find out which one suits you best?	여	그러면 어떤 것이 너에게 가장 잘 맞는지 알아보기 위해 우선 내 망원경 중 몇 개를 사용해 보는 게 어떠니?
M	Oh, really? That'd be really helpful in making my decision.	남	오, 정말요? 그렇게 하면 제가 결정을 내리는 데 정말 도움이 될 거예요.
W	I'll bring some telescopes from my home for you.	여	널 위해 내가 집에서 망원경을 몇 개 가져올게.

문제 해설 최근 별 보기에 관심이 생긴 남자가 자신의 과학 선생님인 여자에게 좋은 망원경을 추천해 달라고 하자 여자는 비싼 것은 살 필요가 없다고 하면서 자신이 가지고 있는 망원경 중 몇 개를 우선 사용해 보라고 말하자 남자가 그러면 큰 도움이 될 거라고 말했다. 따라서 남자의 마지막 말에 대한 여자의 응답으로 가장 적절한 것은 ② '널 위해 내가 집에서 망원경을 몇 개 가져올게.'이다.
① 좋은 망원경은 더 비싼 경향이 있어.
③ 하늘은 별을 관찰할 수 있을 만큼 맑아야 해.
④ 네가 우선은 별 보기에 대한 지식을 어느 정도 가지고 있어야 해.
⑤ 이 망원경을 사용하는 제대로 된 방법을 내가 너에게 이미 보여 줬잖아.

어휘&어구 stargazing 별 보기, 천문학 telescope 망원경 function 기능 proper 제대로 된, 적절한 observe 관찰하다 knowledge 지식

14 전학생에게 학교 안내하기 [정답] ①

W	Paul, do you have a minute?	여	Paul, 시간 좀 있니?
M	Yes, Ms. Brown.	남	네, Brown 선생님.
W	A new student named Ben Jones is transferring to our school next week.	여	Ben Jones라는 전학생이 다음 주에 우리 학교로 전학을 올 거야.
M	Oh, that's great.	남	오, 잘됐네요.
W	So, I wonder if you can give him a school tour sometime before next Monday.	여	그래서, 네가 다음 월요일 전에 그에게 학교 견학을 시켜 줄 수 있는지 궁금해.
M	Sure, I'd love to. When would be good?	남	물론이죠, 그리고 싶어요. 언제가 좋을까요?
W	Ben said any time this weekend is possible. When is convenient for you?	여	Ben이 이번 주말이면 언제든지 가능하다고 했어. 너한테는 언제가 편하니?
M	Saturday morning is good. I work at the library in the afternoon. And I'm going on a picnic with my family on Sunday.	남	토요일 아침이 좋아요. 저는 오후에 도서관에서 일해요. 그리고 일요일에 가족들과 소풍 갈 거예요.
W	Okay. Saturday morning should be fine with Ben. Could you make plans with him? I'll give you his phone number.	여	좋아. Ben에게도 토요일 아침이 괜찮을 거야. 네가 그와 함께 계획을 세울 수 있니? 내가 그의 전화번호를 알려 줄게.
M	Sure. I'll call him to figure out the time and place to meet up.	남	물론이죠. 제가 그에게 전화해서 만날 시간과 장소를 알아볼게요.
W	That'd be great. He'll really appreciate your help.	여	잘됐네. 그는 너의 도움에 정말 고마워할 거야.
M	No problem. I'm happy to show him around the school.	남	괜찮아요. 제가 그에게 학교를 구경시켜 줄 수 있어서 기뻐요.

문제 해설 여자는 남자에게 새로 전학을 올 학생과 주말에 만나 학교 안내를 해 달라고 부탁하고, 남자가 전학생에게 전화를 걸어 만날 시간과 장소를 알아본다고 하자 여자는 전학생이 남자에게 고마워할 거라고 말하고 있다. 따라서 여자의 마지막 말에 대한 남자의 응답으로 가장 적절한 것은
① '괜찮아요. 제가 그에게 학교를 구경시켜 줄 수 있어서 기뻐요.'이다.
② 알겠어요. 제가 그에게 전화를 걸어 우리가 다음 주에 만날 수 있는지 물어볼게요.
③ 천만에요. 그가 이제는 우리 학교에 익숙하리라 생각해요.
④ 저도 그에게 고마워요. 그는 주말마다 제가 공부하는 것을 도와줘요.
⑤ 네. 저는 새 학교로 전학 가서 새 친구들을 사귀게 되어 너무 신나요.

어휘&어구 transfer 전학하다, 옮기다 convenient 편리한 figure out 알아내다 appreciate 고맙게 여기다 be familiar with ~에 익숙하다 grateful 고마워하는

15 경기장에 가기 위한 카풀 요청 [정답] ①

| W | Greg and Juan are neighborhood friends who go to the same college. They both play on the college football team and they have an early game tomorrow at a college about an hour away. Because the team bus broke down, the football players have to find their own way to the game. However, Greg is worried about driving to the game because he recently just got his driver's license, so he's not used to driving long distances. Luckily, he finds out that Juan is planning to drive to the game. So, he wants to ask Juan if he can go to the game with him. In this situation, what would Greg most likely say to Juan? | 여 | Greg와 Juan은 같은 대학에 다니는 이웃 친구입니다. 그들 둘 다 대학 미식축구팀에서 활동하며, 한 시간 정도 걸리는 대학에서 내일 일찍 경기가 있습니다. 그 팀의 버스가 고장 나서, 미식축구 선수들은 경기에 가는 방법을 각자 찾아야 합니다. 그런데, Greg는 최근에 막 운전면허증을 따서, 먼 거리를 운전하는 것이 익숙하지 않기 때문에, 경기까지 차를 몰고 가는 것이 걱정스럽습니다. 다행히, 그는 Juan이 경기까지 차를 몰고 갈 계획이라는 것을 알게 됩니다. 그래서 그는 Juan에게 함께 경기에 갈 수 있는지 묻고 싶습니다. 이런 상황에서 Greg는 Juan에게 뭐라고 말하겠습니까? |
| Greg | Do you mind if I ride with you tomorrow? | Greg | 내일 너와 같이 차를 타도 될까? |

문제 해설 Greg는 차를 몰고 한 시간 정도 걸리는 대학까지 갈 자신이 없어서, 차를 몰고 갈 계획이 있는 친구 Juan에게 함께 갈 수 있는지 물어보려 한다. 따라서 Greg가 Juan에게 할 말로 가장 적절한 것은 ① '내일 너와 같이 차를 타도 될까?'이다.

② 집에 가는 길에 나를 내려 줄 수 있니?

③ 너를 경기장에 데려다줄 운전기사를 배정해 줄게.

④ 내일 학교까지 택시를 같이 탈까?

⑤ 좋아. 부모님께 전화해서 우리를 경기까지 태워 달라고 할게.

어휘&어구 neighborhood 이웃 driver's license 운전면허증

16~17 모기 물린 데 바르면 좋은 천연 물질
[정답] 16 ⑤ 17 ③

M Hi, everyone! When the weather gets warmer, annoying mosquitoes come out. And with mosquitoes come itchy mosquito bites! So today I'd like to talk about natural substances you can apply to mosquito bites. First of all, you can try aloe vera. Known for its soothing effect, aloe vera gel can provide instant relief to your itchiness. You can also use witch hazel, which has cooling effects and can reduce itchiness. Apply it directly to mosquito bites using a cotton pad. Surprisingly, honey can also soothe skin irritated by mosquito bites and even prevent infection. Apply a little on the bites and leave it on for a while before rinsing. Lastly, soaking in an oatmeal bath or applying a paste of ground oatmeal mixed with water can provide relief from itching and promote healing. So the next time you become a victim of mosquitoes, skip going to the pharmacy and instead try these natural substances for some needed relief. Thank you for listening!

남 안녕하세요, 여러분! 날씨가 점점 더 따뜻해지면 성가신 모기들이 나옵니다. 그리고 모기와 함께 가려운 모기 물림도 생깁니다! 그래서 오늘은 제가 모기 물린 곳에 바를 수 있는 천연 물질에 대해 이야기하려고 합니다. 우선, 알로에베라를 사용하실 수 있습니다. 진정 효과가 있는 것으로 알려진 알로에베라 젤은 가려움을 즉각적으로 완화할 수 있습니다. 냉각 효과가 있고 가려움을 줄일 수 있는 위치 하젤도 사용하실 수 있습니다. 면 패드를 사용하여 모기 물린 곳에 직접 바르세요. 놀랍게도, 꿀도 모기에 물려 자극받은 피부를 진정시키고 심지어 감염을 예방할 수 있습니다. 물린 곳에 조금 바르고 잠시 그대로 두었다가 씻어 내세요. 마지막으로, 오트밀 목욕물에 담그거나 물과 섞은 간 오트밀 반죽을 바르면 가려움증이 완화되고 치유가 촉진될 수 있습니다. 그러므로 다음에 여러분이 모기의 희생자가 되면 약국에 가지 말고 대신 이러한 천연 물질을 써 보고 필요한 얼마간의 도움을 받으세요. 들어 주셔서 감사합니다!

문제 해설 16 남자는 모기에 물린 곳에 바르면 가려움을 누그러뜨릴 수 있는 좋은 천연 물질을 여러 가지 소개하고 있다. 따라서 남자가 하는 말의 주제로 가장 적절한 것은 ⑤ '모기 물림으로 인한 가려움을 줄이기 위한 천연 해결책'이다.

① 모기에 물리는 것을 피하는 방법

② 모기를 쫓아내는 생활용품

③ 가려운 피부에 바르면 안 되는 물질

④ 모기 물림에 대한 면역력을 키우기 위해 먹기 좋은 음식

17 모기 물린 데 바르는 천연 물질로 알로에베라 젤, 위치 하젤, 꿀, 간 오트밀은 언급되었지만, ③ '차 나무 오일'은 언급되지 않았다.

어휘&어구 itchy 가려운 substance 물질 soothe 진정시키다, 달래다 relief 완화, 경감 irritate 자극하다 rinse 씻어 내다, 헹구다 victim 희생자, 피해자 pharmacy 약국 immunity 면역력

6회 수능실전 대비연습
본문 78~79쪽

01 ③ 02 ① 03 ④ 04 ⑤ 05 ③ 06 ② 07 ⑤ 08 ⑤ 09 ④ 10 ② 11 ⑤ 12 ③ 13 ③ 14 ①
15 ① 16 ① 17 ⑤

---

01 옷 제작 동아리 가입 권유
[정답] ③

W Hello, Ariel High School freshmen. I'm Jeanie Morrison, the president of the Teen Designer Club. Are you interested in designing clothes? Well, the Teen Designer Club offers a fantastic opportunity to pursue your passion. You'll get to

여 안녕하세요, Ariel 고등학교 신입생 여러분. 저는 Teen Designer 동아리의 회장인 Jeanie Morrison입니다. 옷을 디자인하는 것에 관심이 있으신가요? 음, Teen Designer 동아리는 여러분의 열정을 추구할 수 있는 환상적인 기회를 제공합니다. 여러분은 완벽하

create your own custom clothes that fit you perfectly. You might be wondering if it's more difficult and expensive compared to buying regular clothes. Well, the answer is no! And not only is it cheaper, it's really fun and easy to learn. And hey, boys, don't worry! Our club warmly welcomes everybody! So if you're interested, feel free to reach out to us through our website, www.teendesigners.com, or just give us a call. Thank you!

게 맞는 맞춤형 옷을 만들어 볼 수 있습니다. 여러분은 아마도 일반적인 옷을 구매하는 것과 비교하면, 그것이 더 어렵고 비싸다고 생각할 수도 있습니다. 그런데, 답은 그렇지 않습니다! 그것은 비용이 더 저렴할 뿐만 아니라 정말 재미있고 쉽게 배울 수 있습니다. 그리고, 이봐요, 남학생들, 걱정하지 마세요! 우리 동아리는 모두를 따뜻하게 환영합니다! 그러니 관심이 있으시다면, 저희 웹사이트인 www.teendesigners.com을 통해 마음 놓고 연락해 주시거나 전화를 주시기 바랍니다. 감사합니다!

문제 해설 여자는 Ariel 고등학교 신입생들에게 맞춤형 옷을 디자인하는 동아리에 지원하라고 말하고 있으므로, 여자가 하는 말의 목적으로 가장 적절한 것은 ③ '옷 제작 동아리 가입을 권유하려고'이다.

어휘&어구 president 회장 compared to ~과 비교하여 regular 보통의, 일반적인 feel free to *do* 마음 놓고 ~하다 reach out to ~과 연락하다, ~과 접촉하다

02 추위가 건강에 좋은 이유　　　　　　　　　　[정답] ①

M	Look, it's snowing. I love winter weather so much.
W	Not me! I can't stand winter. It's so cold!
M	Probably you don't know that cold weather can be good for you.
W	No way! It always gives me a cold and makes me feel gloomy.
M	Of course, you can catch a cold, but cold weather can help make you stronger.
W	How's that?
M	The cold can kill harmful bacteria, which can boost your overall health.
W	Oh, I didn't know that. That sounds similar to cold therapy, which is commonly used to treat injuries.
M	Exactly. The cold can provide relief for certain conditions and regulate body temperature, leading to deeper and more restful sleep.
W	Wow. I guess I should try to start appreciating the cold weather in the winter.

남　보세요, 눈이 내리고 있어요. 전 겨울 날씨를 정말 좋아해요.
여　저는 그렇지 않아요! 겨울을 견딜 수가 없어요. 너무 추워요!
남　추운 날씨가 건강에 좋다는 걸 모르나 보네요.
여　그럴 리 없어요! 날씨 탓에 난 항상 감기에 걸리고 우울해져요.
남　물론 감기에 걸릴 수도 있지만, 추운 날씨는 강하게 만드는 데 도움을 줄 수 있어요.
여　어째서 그런가요?
남　추위는 해로운 박테리아를 죽일 수 있고, 그래서 전반적인 건강을 향상시킬 수 있어요.
여　오, 그건 몰랐네요. 그건 부상 치료에 일반적으로 사용되는 한랭 요법과 비슷한 얘기 같아요.
남　정확해요. 추위는 특정 질환을 완화해 주고, 체온을 조절하여 더 깊고 더 편안한 잠을 자게 해 줄 수 있어요.
여　와. 그럼 겨울에 추운 날씨의 진가를 알아보는 걸 시작해 봐야겠어요.

문제 해설 추운 날씨를 싫어한다는 여자의 말에 남자는 추운 날씨는 우리를 건강하게 만들어 준다고 하면서, 추위는 해로운 박테리아를 없애 주고, 통증을 덜어 주며, 체온을 조절해 주어서 숙면에 도움이 된다고 말한다. 따라서 남자의 의견으로 가장 적절한 것은 ① '추운 날씨는 건강에 이롭다.'이다.

어휘&어구 stand ~에 견디다, 참다 gloomy 우울한 cold therapy 한랭 요법 relief 완화, 경감 regulate 조절하다 appreciate 진가를 알아보다, 고마워하다

03 패션모델 사진 촬영　　　　　　　　　　[정답] ④

M	Good morning! How are you today?
W	Couldn't be better. I'm so happy to be working with you.
M	Likewise. We have some amazing outfits and locations planned for today's shoot.
W	I can't wait to get started.
M	Me too. And if you have any ideas or preferences, please let me know.

남　안녕하세요! 오늘 컨디션 어떠신가요?
여　최고예요. 함께 일할 수 있어서 너무 행복해요.
남　동감이에요. 오늘 촬영을 위해 멋진 의상들과 장소들을 계획했어요.
여　기대돼서 빨리 시작하고 싶어요.
남　저도요. 그리고 만약 아이디어나 더 좋아하는 것이 있으면, 꼭 말씀해 주세요.

W	I appreciate that. I'll definitely share my thoughts during the shoot.	여	감사해요. 촬영 중에 제 생각을 분명하게 공유할게요.
M	Perfect. Remember, when you're in front of my camera, show off your unique style and personality.	남	좋아요. 제 카메라 앞에서는 당신만의 독특한 스타일과 개성을 뽐내야 하는 것을 기억해 주세요.
W	Okay, I'll try to take poses that bring the outfits to life.	여	알겠어요. 의상을 생동감 있게 연출할 수 있는 포즈를 취해 볼게요.
M	Fantastic! Let's get started. Get ready to shine, and I will capture your brilliance.	남	멋지네요! 시작합시다. 빛날 준비하세요, 그러면 저는 당신의 빛나는 순간을 담아낼 거예요.
W	Yeah! Let's create some magic!	여	네! 함께 마법을 만들어 봐요!

문제 해설 남자는 여자에게 촬영을 위해 의상과 장소를 계획했다고 하면서 자신의 카메라 앞에 서면 여자만의 독특한 스타일과 개성을 뽐내 달라고 말하고 있으며, 여자는 남자에게 촬영 중에 자기 생각을 분명하게 공유할 것이고, 의상을 생동감 있게 보여 줄 포즈를 취하겠다고 말했다. 따라서 두 사람의 관계를 가장 잘 나타낸 것은 ④ '사진작가 – 패션모델'이다.

어휘&어구 couldn't be better 기분[상태]이 최고이다 Likewise. 나도 동감이야. location 장소 shoot 촬영 preference 더 좋아하는 것 show off 뽐내다, 자랑하다 personality 개성 outfit 의상 한 벌 capture 담아내다, 포착하다 brilliance 빛남, 광휘

04 책상 정리 [정답] ⑤

W	Dad, come and see how I've rearranged my study area.	여	아빠, 오셔서 제가 제 학습 공간을 어떻게 재배치했는지 보세요.
M	Okay, Sally. Oh, you put your desk under the window.	남	좋아, Sally. 아, 창문 아래로 책상을 옮겼구나.
W	Right. Now I can look outside when I study.	여	네. 이젠 공부할 때 밖을 내다볼 수 있어요.
M	That's nice. And you put your new laptop on the right side of the desk.	남	좋구나. 그리고 책상 오른편에는 새 노트북 컴퓨터를 놓았구나.
W	Yeah. I'm so happy to have my own laptop.	여	네. 제 노트북이 생겨서 정말 좋아요.
M	I bet! Oh, the lamp on the left side of the desk is also new.	남	좋겠구나. 아, 책상 왼편에 있는 램프도 새로운 거구나.
W	Right. It's adjustable.	여	맞아요. 조절할 수 있는 것이에요.
M	Good. Your pencil holder next to it has a unique shape. It looks like a soccer ball. That's really cool.	남	좋구나. 그 옆에 있는 네 연필꽂이는 모양이 독특하구나. 축구공 모양이네. 정말로 멋지구나.
W	Isn't it? My friend Jennifer gave it to me for my birthday.	여	그렇죠? 제 친구 Jennifer가 제게 생일 선물로 줬어요.
M	Oh, where did you put all your books that used to be on the bookshelf? It's almost empty now.	남	아, 책꽂이에 있던 네 책을 다 어디에 놓았니? 지금은 거의 비어 있네.
W	I put most of them on the bookshelf in the living room. Only these two books are the ones I need nowadays.	여	그것들 대부분을 거실 책꽂이에 두었어요. 요즘 필요한 책은 이 두 권뿐이에요.
M	Well, I really like what you've done here.	남	음, 네가 여기에 해 놓은 것이 정말 마음에 든다.

문제 해설 남자가 책꽂이가 거의 비어 있다고 말했는데 그림에서는 책꽂이에 책이 가득 차 있다. 따라서 그림에서 대화의 내용과 일치하지 않는 것은 ⑤이다.

어휘&어구 rearrange 재배치하다, 재정리하다 laptop 노트북 컴퓨터 adjustable 조절할 수 있는 pencil holder 연필꽂이 used to 한때[예전에] ~이었다 bookshelf 책꽂이

05 야영 여행 준비 [정답] ③

M	Honey, I'm so excited about going camping tomorrow.	남	여보, 나는 내일 야영 가는 것에 대해 정말 마음이 설레요.
W	Me, too. I especially like our plan of watching a movie outdoors by the campfire.	여	나도 그래요. 나는 모닥불 옆 야외에서 영화를 보려는 계획이 특히 좋아요.
M	Absolutely! I think it's a great idea.	남	그렇고말고요! 나는 그것이 정말 좋은 아이디어라고 생각해요.
W	It's going to be so romantic. Did you pack the projector and screen?	여	정말 낭만적일 거예요. 영사기와 스크린을 챙겼나요?
M	Of course. I've put them in the car.	남	물론이죠. 차에 그것들을 실었어요.
W	Great. Thanks.	여	좋아요. 고마워요.
M	Shall we take some blankets just in case it gets cold in the evening?	남	혹시라도 저녁때 추워질 경우를 대비하여 담요를 좀 가져가야 할까요?
		여	내가 이미 그것들을 우리 여행 가방에 쌌어요.

W	I've already packed them in our luggage.		남	잘했어요. 오, 우리는 내일 어떤 영화를 볼지를 아직 결정하지 않았어요. 한 편 골라 줄 수 있나요?
M	Good. Oh, we haven't decided which movie we're going to watch tomorrow. Could you pick one?		여	그럼요. 내가 영화 한 편을 선택할게요.
W	Sure. I'll choose a movie.		남	고마워요. 접이식 의자들이 어디 있는지 알아요?
M	Thanks. Do you know where the folding chairs are?		여	그것들을 마지막으로 트렁크에서 본 것 같아요.
W	I think I last saw them in the trunk.		남	알았어요. 여행 가방을 차에 실을 때 내가 점검할게요.
M	Alright. I'll check when I'm putting the luggage in the car.		여	좋아요. 내일이 정말 기대돼요!
W	Great. I cannot wait for tomorrow!			

문제 해설 내일 야영 가기로 한 두 사람이 야외에서 영화를 보기로 했는데, 남자가 여자에게 아직 볼 영화를 고르지 않았으니 골라 줄 수 있냐고 물었고, 여자는 한 편을 선택하겠다고 대답했으므로, 여자가 할 일로 가장 적절한 것은 ③ '영화 선택하기'이다.

어휘&어구 pack (짐을) 챙기다[싸다] projector 영사기, 프로젝터 just in case 혹시라도 ~할 경우를 대비하여 luggage (소형) 여행 가방 folding chair 접이식 의자

06 리조트에서의 활동　　　　　　　　　　　　　　　　　　　　　　　　　[정답] ②

W	Hello. How may I help you?		여	안녕하세요. 어떻게 도와드릴까요?
M	Hello. Could I book some activities here in this resort?		남	안녕하세요. 여기 이 리조트에서 몇 가지 활동을 예약할 수 있을까요?
W	Sure. For how many people? And what activities are you thinking of?		여	물론이죠. 몇 분이시죠? 그리고 어떤 활동을 생각하고 계세요?
M	There are three of us, and we'd like to go sea kayaking, tomorrow morning if possible. How much is that?		남	저희 셋이 있는데, 가능하면 내일 아침에 바다 카약을 타러 가고 싶어요. 그것은 얼마예요?
W	Sure, no problem. It's $20 per person, and it starts at 8 a.m.		여	물론이죠, 문제없어요. 그것은 1인당 20달러이고, 오전 8시에 시작해요.
M	Perfect. And how much are tickets for the aquarium and virtual reality game room?		남	좋아요. 그리고 수족관과 가상 현실 게임방 입장권은 얼마예요?
W	They're $30 for the aquarium and $10 for the virtual reality game room.		여	수족관은 30달러이고, 가상 현실 게임방은 10달러예요.
M	The virtual reality game room sounds exciting. How long would we get in the virtual reality game room?		남	가상 현실 게임방이 재밌을 것 같아요. 가상 현실 게임방에서 얼마 동안 있나요?
W	One hour.		여	한 시간이요.
M	Okay. I'll take 3 tickets for that, too. Oh! I have a 10% off coupon.		남	좋아요. 그것도 3장 살게요. 아! 10% 할인 쿠폰이 있어요.
W	Okay. So 3 tickets for sea kayaking and 3 tickets for the virtual reality game room. And you get 10% off the total price.		여	좋아요. 그러면 바다 카약 3장, 가상 현실 게임방 3장. 그리고 총가격에서 10%를 할인받으세요.
M	Yes. Here's my credit card.		남	네. 여기 제 신용 카드가 있어요.

문제 해설 남자는 리조트 활동 중 1인당 20달러인 바다 카약에 세 명을 예약하고, 1인당 10달러인 가상 현실 게임방 입장권 세 장을 사면서 총가격에서 10% 할인되는 쿠폰을 사용했다. 따라서 남자가 지불할 금액은 ② '81달러'이다.

어휘&어구 activity 활동 book 예약하다 aquarium 수족관 virtual reality 가상 현실

07 재충전을 위한 영화 관람 제안　　　　　　　　　　　　　　　　　　　　　[정답] ⑤

M	Hi, Jenny. How did your computer test go?		남	안녕, Jenny. 컴퓨터 시험은 어땠니?
W	Not very well. I studied a lot too. It's frustrating.		여	별로 좋지 않았어. 게다가 열심히 공부했는데. 속상하네.
M	I understand how you feel. It sounds like you could use a break to recharge. How about going to the movies tonight?		남	네 기분이 이해되네. 재충전할 수 있는 휴식이 필요한 것 같구나. 오늘 밤 영화를 보러 갈까?
W	Thanks for the offer, but I'm afraid I can't.		여	제안해 줘서 고마워, 하지만 아쉽게도 못 갈 것 같아.
M	Why not? Do you have your part-time job tonight?		남	왜? 오늘 밤 아르바이트가 있는 거야?

W	No, I only work during the week.	여	아니, 나는 주중에만 일해.	

W No, I only work during the week.

M I see. Well, if anything changes and you can go, let me know. There are some really good movies playing right now.

W Thanks, but I'm going to a special lecture on job interviews at the career center tonight.

M Oh, I see. That'll be really useful. I'll probably just go to the bookstore and look around.

W That sounds like a good plan.

여 아니, 나는 주중에만 일해.

남 알겠어. 만약 상황이 바뀌어서 갈 수 있게 된다면 알려 줘. 현재 상영 중인 정말 좋은 영화들이 있거든.

여 고마워, 그런데 나는 오늘 밤 취업 지원 센터에서 있는 취업 면접에 관한 특강에 갈 거야.

남 아, 알겠어. 정말 유용하겠다. 아마 나는 그냥 서점에 가서 둘러봐야 할 것 같아.

여 좋은 계획인 것 같은데.

문제 해설 남자가 재충전을 위한 영화 관람을 제안하자 여자는 갈 수 없다고 말해서 남자가 상황이 바뀌면 알려 달라고 했고, 여자가 취업 지원 센터에서 열리는 취업 면접 특강에 갈 것이라고 말하고 있다. 따라서 여자가 영화관에 갈 수 없는 이유는 ⑤ '취업 면접 특강을 들어야 해서'이다.

어휘&어구 frustrating 속상하게 하는, 좌절감을 갖게 하는 break 잠시의 휴식 recharge 다시 충전하다 lecture 강연 look around 둘러보다

---

08 배달 서비스 신청 [정답] ⑤

[Telephone rings.]

W Blue Quick Delivery Service. How can I help you?

M Hi. I'd like to have a small package delivered to San Francisco, California.

W All right. Can you please give me the receiver's name and address?

M Sure. John Faulk and 4512 West River Road, San Francisco, California.

W Thanks. And where can we pick up your package?

M 1414 University Ave., here in Berkeley.

W Okay. May I ask what you are sending?

M It's a camera.

W All right. I'll send somebody over to pick it up. He should be there in about an hour.

M Thank you. How much will it cost?

W Well, we have to weigh your package to decide the charge.

M I see. How long will it take for the package to be delivered?

W It'll take about two hours, I think.

M Okay, thanks.

[전화벨이 울린다.]

여 Blue Quick Delivery Service입니다. 어떻게 도와드릴까요?

남 안녕하세요. 작은 상자 하나를 California의 San Francisco로 배달하고 싶어요.

여 알겠습니다. 받는 분의 성함과 주소를 말씀해 주시겠습니까?

남 물론이지요. John Faulk이고 California, San Francisco, West River Road 4512입니다.

여 감사합니다. 그리고 상자를 어디로 받으러 갈까요?

남 여기 Berkeley, University Ave. 1414입니다.

여 알겠습니다. 무엇을 보내시는지 여쭤봐도 되겠습니까?

남 카메라 한 대입니다.

여 알겠습니다. 그것을 받으러 가기 위해 직원을 보내겠습니다. 한 시간 정도면 거기에 도착할 것입니다.

남 감사합니다. 요금은 얼마인가요?

여 음, 요금을 결정하기 위해서는 포장한 상품의 무게를 달아 봐야 합니다.

남 그렇군요. 그 포장한 상품이 배달되는 데 얼마나 걸릴까요?

여 두 시간 정도 걸릴 것 같습니다.

남 좋아요, 감사합니다.

문제 해설 상자 배달에 관해 배달지 주소, 배달 물품, 비용 산정 방법, 배달 소요 시간은 언급되었지만 ⑤ '배달 운송 수단'은 언급되지 않았다.

어휘&어구 delivery 배달 package 포장한 상품 weigh 무게를 달다 charge 요금

---

09 새로 출시된 피자 [정답] ④

M Tom's pizza just got better! We just introduced our brand-new creation, Tom's Double Pizza, on May 1st! Prepare yourself for an explosion of fiery flavors with our super spicy special garlic sauce. Topped with mouthwatering bacon, fresh tomatoes, and black olives, every bite will take you to pizza heaven. And if you order takeout in May, you get a 15% off your order and a free soft drink. Or if you order for delivery, your pizza will arrive at your

남 Tom's pizza가 방금 맛있어졌습니다! 우리는 5월 1일에 우리의 신상품인 Tom's Double Pizza를 막 출시했습니다! 우리의 초강력 매운 마늘 소스와 함께 폭발적인 얼얼한 맛을 경험할 준비를 하세요. 한 입씩 베어 먹을 때마다 토핑으로 올려진 군침 도는 베이컨, 신선한 토마토, 그리고 블랙 올리브가 당신을 피자 천국으로 데려갈 것입니다. 그리고 5월에 포장 주문을 하면 주문 금액에서 15% 할인과 무료 탄산음료를 제공합니다. 또는 배달 주문을 하면 정확히 20분 이내에 피자가 문 앞으로 배달됩니다! 그러니 새로운

doorstep within just 20 minutes! So, don't wait to enjoy the incredible taste of the new Tom's Double Pizza.

Tom's Double Pizza의 놀라운 맛을 지금 당장 즐기세요.

문제 해설 5월에 포장 주문을 하면 주문 금액에서 15% 할인을 제공한다고 했으므로, 담화의 내용과 일치하지 않는 것은 ④ '5월에 포장해 가면 주문 금액에서 10% 할인받는다.'이다.

어휘&어구 introduce (신제품을) 출시하다 brand-new 신상품의 prepare oneself for ~에 대해 준비하다 explosion 폭발 mouthwatering 군침을 흘리게 하는 incredible 놀라운, 믿을 수 없는

---

10 무선 포인터 구입 [정답] ②

W Honey, why are you looking at wireless pointers on the Internet? Are you going to buy one?

M Yes. I need one for my presentation next week.

W Have you ever used one before?

M No. I'm not sure which one to get. But I don't want to spend more than $40.

W I know a little about them. I suggest you get one with a control distance of at least 30 meters.

M Okay. Then I won't get this one.

W Do you have any preference for the laser color? Well, how about green?

M That'd be okay, but red is usually better for people to see.

W You might be right. How about battery life?

M I don't think I need this one with a longer battery life. I know I won't use it that often. I'll get this one.

W I think that's a good choice.

여 여보, 인터넷에서 무선 포인터를 왜 보고 있나요? 하나 살 건가요?

남 네. 다음 주 발표를 위해 하나가 필요해요.

여 전에 사용해 본 적이 있나요?

남 아니요. 어느 것을 사야 할지 모르겠어요. 하지만 나는 40달러 넘게 쓰고 싶지는 않아요.

여 난 그것들에 대해 조금 알아요. 통제 거리가 적어도 30미터가 되는 것을 사는 것을 제안해요.

남 알겠어요. 그럼 이것은 사지 않을게요.

여 더 좋아하는 레이저 색깔이 있나요? 음, 녹색은 어때요?

남 그것이 괜찮긴 한데 사람들이 보는 데에는 보통 빨간색이 더 나아요.

여 당신 말이 맞을 것 같네요. 배터리 수명은 어때요?

남 배터리 수명이 더 긴 이것이 필요할 것 같지는 않아요. 그것을 그렇게 자주 사용하지는 않을 것을 알아요. 이것을 살게요.

여 좋은 선택인 것 같아요.

문제 해설 남자는 40달러가 넘지 않으며, 통제 거리가 적어도 30미터가 되고, 레이저 색은 빨간색이며, 배터리 수명이 더 짧은 것을 사기로 했다. 따라서 남자가 구입할 무선 포인터는 ②이다.

어휘&어구 wireless 무선의 presentation 발표 distance 거리 preference 선호

---

11 동료 생일 선물 준비 [정답] ⑤

M Peggy, have you bought a surprise birthday present for your coworker yet?

W Yes. I bought a music CD. It's his favorite band's debut album.

M That's cool. But I think you need to check if he already has it.

W You're right. I'll find a way to look into it without revealing the surprise.

남 Peggy, 너 동료에게 줄 깜짝 생일 선물 샀어?

여 응. 음악 CD를 샀어. 그가 가장 좋아하는 밴드의 데뷔 앨범이야.

남 멋지네. 하지만 그가 이미 그것을 가지고 있는지 확인해 봐야 할 것 같아.

여 맞아. 깜짝 선물을 들키지 않으면서 알아보는 방법을 찾아보겠어.

문제 해설 여자가 동료의 생일 선물로 음악 앨범을 샀는데, 남자가 여자의 동료가 이미 갖고 있는 앨범인지 확인해 봐야 한다고 말하고 있으므로, 이에 대한 여자의 응답으로 가장 적절한 것은 ⑤ '맞아. 깜짝 선물을 들키지 않으면서 알아보는 방법을 찾아보겠어.'이다.
① 너무 안타깝다. 이번에는 꼭 성공했으면 좋았을 텐데.
② 정말 멋지다! 그의 열렬한 팬으로서 난 그의 앨범은 다 가지고 있어.
③ 미안해. 다음 주말까지 음악 CD를 얻을 수 있기를 바랄게.
④ 행운을 빌어. 분명 데뷔할 기회를 얻을 거라고 확신해.

어휘&어구 coworker 동료 debut 데뷔

12 안연고 구입

[정답] ③

W Excuse me, but I think you forgot to include the eye ointment.

M Let me check. Well, the eye ointment is not included in your prescription.

W Oh, my doctor must have forgotten to add it to the prescription. Can I buy it over the counter?

M I'm sorry, but you can't purchase it without a prescription.

여 죄송하지만, 안연고를 포함시키는 것을 잊으신 것 같아요.

남 확인해 보겠습니다. 음, 안연고는 고객님의 처방전에 포함되어 있지 않아요.

여 아, 의사 선생님이 그것을 처방전에 추가하는 것을 잊으신 것이 틀림없어요. 그것을 처방전 없이 살 수 있을까요?

남 죄송하지만, 처방전 없이는 그것을 구입할 수 없어요.

문제 해설 여자는 안연고를 처방전 없이 살 수 있는지 물어보고 있다. 따라서 남자의 응답으로 가장 적절한 것은 ③ '죄송하지만, 처방전 없이는 그것을 구입할 수 없어요.'이다.

① 다시 한번 봐 주세요. 분명히 제가 그것을 고객님께 드렸어요.

② 맞아요. 안연고가 알약보다 더 효과가 있어요.

④ 물론이죠. 고객님의 처방전을 제출하시고 나중에 다시 오세요.

⑤ 걱정하지 마세요. 이 연고는 콘택트렌즈와 함께 사용해도 안전해요.

어휘&어구 ointment 연고 prescription 처방전 over the counter 처방전 없이 (살 수 있는) purchase 구입하다

13 잘못 행동한 친구에게 조언하기

[정답] ③

W Hey, Brian. I saw something that bothered me yesterday.

M What did you see?

W I saw it in the park. Can you guess?

M Hmm. I'm not sure. Just tell me.

W I saw a boy littering in the park.

M Oh... I don't like when people throw trash.

W Right? And actually, that boy was you!

M You saw that? I just... I couldn't find a trash can anywhere. There should be more trash cans in the park.

W I understand but there might be better alternatives. You know our park is getting dirtier these days.

M It's not like I litter all the time. It was just a few times. I promise I'll never do it again.

W Okay. Keep your word. I'll be watching you.

여 얘, Brian. 나 어제 마음에 걸리는 걸 봤어.

남 뭘 봤는데?

여 그걸 공원에서 봤어. 맞춰 볼래?

남 음. 잘 모르겠어. 그냥 말해 봐.

여 공원에서 한 남자아이가 쓰레기를 버리는 걸 봤어.

남 아… 사람들이 쓰레기를 버리는 건 별로야.

여 그래? 그런데 사실 그 남자아이가 너였어!

남 네가 그걸 봤어? 그냥… 쓰레기통을 아무 데에서도 못 찾아서였어. 공원에 더 많은 쓰레기통이 있어야 해.

여 이해는 하지만 더 나은 대안이 있을 수도 있어. 너도 우리 공원이 요즘 점점 더 지저분해지는 거 알잖아.

남 내가 항상 쓰레기를 버리는 건 아니야. 나는 그냥 몇 번 정도였어. 다시는 그러지 않겠다고 약속할게.

여 좋아. 네 말 지켜. 내가 지켜볼 거야.

문제 해설 여자가 공원에 쓰레기를 함부로 버린 남자에게 공원이 더러워지고 있는 문제가 바로 남자의 행동 때문이라고 질책하자, 남자는 항상 그런 것이 아니고 몇 번뿐이었지만 다시는 그런 행동을 하지 않겠다고 말하고 있다. 따라서 이에 대한 여자의 응답으로 가장 적절한 것은 ③ '좋아. 네 말 지켜. 내가 지켜볼 거야.'이다.

① 정말 미안해. 절대로 일부러 한 건 아니야.

② 좋은 생각이야. 네가 자랑스러워.

④ 다행이다. 이걸 주인에게 돌려주자.

⑤ 아직 이해가 안 가. 예를 하나 들어 줘.

어휘&어구 litter 쓰레기를 버리다 trash can 쓰레기통 alternative 대안

14 한국 민속촌 방문

[정답] ①

W Hey, Joe. It's a perfect day to visit the Korean Folk Village, isn't it?

여 안녕, Joe. 한국 민속촌을 방문하기에 완벽한 날이야, 그렇지 않니?

M	Yeah. I'm so glad we came here today.	남	그래. 나는 우리가 오늘 여기 와서 너무 기분이 좋아.
W	Me too. Do you know where the ticket booth is?	여	나도 그래. 매표소가 어디에 있는지 아니?
M	It's over there. Wow, look at the long line.	남	저기에 있어. 와, 저 긴 줄을 봐.
W	Oh, it looks like there's a special event today.	여	아, 오늘 특별한 행사가 있는 것 같아.
M	Really?	남	정말?
W	Yeah. See the sign. There's a special festival related to the Joseon Dynasty today.	여	응. 표지판을 봐. 오늘 조선왕조와 관련된 특별한 축제가 있어.
M	That sounds really cool!	남	정말 멋질 것 같아!
W	Yeah! Let's get in line and get our tickets.	여	그래! 줄을 서서 표를 사자.
M	All right. Hey, do you see those people inside the village wearing hanboks?	남	좋아. 이봐, 너는 마을 안에 한복을 입고 있는 사람들이 보이니?
W	Yeah. I wonder if we can rent hanboks here.	여	응. 나는 우리가 여기에서 한복을 빌릴 수 있는지 궁금해.
M	Let's ask the person at the ticket booth.	남	매표소에 있는 사람에게 물어보자.
W	What if they say yes?	여	그렇다고 하면 어떻게 할 건데?
M	Then, we should rent hanboks and take some pictures.	남	그러면 우리는 한복을 빌리고 사진을 몇 장 찍어야지.

문제 해설 한복을 입고 있는 사람들이 민속촌에서 한복을 빌렸는지를 매표소에 있는 사람에게 물어보자는 남자의 말에 여자가 한복을 빌려준다고 하면 어떻게 할 건지 물었다. 따라서 남자의 응답으로 가장 적절한 것은 ① '그러면 우리는 한복을 빌리고 사진을 몇 장 찍어야지.'이다.

② 음, 오늘은 그냥 평범한 날인데도 줄이 길어.

③ 글쎄, 나는 한국 민속촌이 방문하기 가장 좋은 곳이라고 생각해.

④ 문제없어! 우리가 한복을 입고 있어서 할인받을 수 있어.

⑤ 걱정하지 마. 우리가 여기 일찍 와서 나는 우리가 앞줄에 앉을 수 있을 거로 생각해.

어휘&어구 folk 사람들, 민속 ticket booth 매표소 dynasty 왕조 rent 빌리다

15 역사 과제 수행 약속 취소하기

[정답] ①

W	Danny and Clara are middle school friends and classmates who are taking history class together. Their history teacher, Mr. Davidson, gave them a history report to do. Danny and Clara decided to work on it together, and made plans to meet at Clara's house the next evening to work on it. However, after Danny told his parents about the meeting at Clara's house, his parents informed him that they have a plan for the next evening, so he needs to stay home and take care of his baby sister that evening. Consequently, he wants to inform Clara that he cannot make it that day. In this situation, what would Danny most likely say to Clara?
Danny	Sorry. I can't come to your house for the history report as we planned.

여	Danny와 Clara는 함께 역사 수업을 듣고 있는 중학교 친구이자 동급생입니다. 역사 선생님인 Davidson 선생님이 그들에게 역사 보고서 과제를 내 주었습니다. Danny와 Clara는 함께 과제를 수행하기로 해서 다음 날 저녁 Clara의 집에서 만나기로 약속했습니다. 그러나 Danny가 그의 부모님께 Clara의 집에서 만나기로 한 사실을 말하자, 그의 부모님은 자신들이 다음 날 저녁에 계획이 있어서 Danny가 그날 저녁 집에 머물며 여동생을 돌봐야 한다고 알려 주었습니다. 따라서 Danny는 Clara에게 그날 약속을 지킬 수 없다는 것을 알려야 합니다. 이런 상황에서 Danny가 Clara에게 뭐라고 말하겠습니까?
Danny	미안해. 우리가 계획한 대로 역사 보고서를 쓰러 너의 집에 갈 수 없어.

문제 해설 내일 저녁 Clara의 집에서 역사 과제 수행을 같이 하기로 약속한 것을 지킬 수 없게 되었다는 것을 알려 주고 싶어 하는 Danny가 Clara에게 할 말로 가장 적절한 것은 ① '미안해. 우리가 계획한 대로 역사 보고서를 쓰러 너의 집에 갈 수 없어.'이다.

② 맞아. 내가 역사를 함께 공부할 더 좋은 장소를 계속 찾아볼게.

③ 너무 안됐다. 아기인 너의 여동생이 완전히 그리고 빨리 회복되길 바랄게.

④ 믿을 수 없어. 어떻게 네 부모님이 그런 무례한 행동을 참을 수 있을까?

⑤ 정확해. 선생님께 역사 보고서 마감일을 재조정해 달라고 말할게.

어휘&어구 plan 계획, 약속 take care of ~을 돌보다 consequently 따라서 inform ~에게 알리다 make it (모임에) 가다

W　Hello, students. Last class, we learned about national identity. National identity can be formed through national symbols. Every country in the world has numerous national symbols, such as a national anthem, flag, bird or flower. Today we're going to focus on national flowers. A large number of countries across the globe have national floral emblems. Some of them are chosen by the governments, while others are selected through public polls. Interestingly, some countries share the same national flower. Do you know what is the official flower in both the United States and England? The answer is the rose. Also, the tulip is the national flower of both Turkey and the Netherlands. And India and Egypt have the lotus as their national flower. The red poppy is the national flower for Belgium and Albania. Now let's take a look at some photos of floral emblems.

여　안녕하세요, 학생 여러분. 지난 수업에서 우리는 국가 정체성에 대해서 배웠습니다. 국가 정체성은 국가의 상징물을 통해서 형성될 수 있습니다. 세계의 모든 나라는 국가(國歌), 국기, 국조 또는 국화와 같은 많은 국가의 상징물을 가지고 있습니다. 오늘은 국화에 초점을 맞추겠습니다. 지구상의 여러 나라가 국가의 상징화를 가지고 있습니다. 그것 중 일부는 정부에 의해서 선택되고, 반면 다른 것들은 여론 조사를 통해서 선정됩니다. 흥미롭게도 몇몇 국가는 같은 국화를 갖고 있습니다. 여러분은 미국과 잉글랜드 두 나라에서 공식적인 꽃이 무엇인지 알고 있나요? 답은 장미입니다. 또한 튤립은 터키와 네덜란드 두 나라의 국화입니다. 그리고 인도와 이집트는 연꽃이 그들의 국화입니다. 개양귀비는 벨기에와 알바니아의 국화입니다. 이제 상징화의 몇몇 사진을 봅시다.

문제 해설　16 국화가 같은 나라를 소개하고 있으므로, 여자가 하는 말의 주제로 가장 적절한 것은 ① '같은 국화를 가진 나라'이다.
　② 국가 정체성에 관한 오해
　③ 국화의 예상치 못한 의미
　④ 국가의 상징물을 가지는 것의 중요성
　⑤ 국가 유산이 보존되어야 하는 이유
　17 잉글랜드, 인도, 이집트, 벨기에는 언급되었지만, 프랑스는 언급되지 않았으므로, 언급된 나라가 아닌 것은 ⑤이다.

어휘&어구　identity 정체성　national anthem 국가(國歌)　floral emblem 상징화　public poll 여론 조사　official 공식적인　lotus 연꽃　red poppy 개양귀비

7회　수능실전 대비연습

본문 86~87쪽

| 01 ⑤ | 02 ⑤ | 03 ① | 04 ③ | 05 ② | 06 ④ | 07 ② | 08 ④ | 09 ④ | 10 ② | 11 ② | 12 ⑤ | 13 ⑤ | 14 ④ |
| 15 ② | 16 ① | 17 ② |

01　학년 회장에 출마한 친구 지지

[정답] ⑤

M　Good morning, everyone. Thank you for the warm welcome. I'm standing here today on behalf of the strongest presidential candidate for our grade, Mark Jenson. The reasons I support him are simple. This year, there are two major events for us as seniors. First is the school festival and the second is the dance party at the end of the school year. They're the biggest and most important events of our high school lives, and they require a tremendous amount of time and planning to organize. So, we need a leader who can meet that challenge. And I think Mark is the most qualified candidate to be able to plan and put on these two major events. He has shown leadership in class, and he will do the same for the school if we elect him. So vote for Mark. Thank you.

남　안녕하세요, 여러분. 따뜻하게 환영해 주셔서 감사합니다. 저는 우리 학년을 위한 가장 강력한 회장 후보인 Mark Jenson을 위해 오늘 이곳에 서 있습니다. 제가 그를 지지하는 이유는 간단합니다. 올해, 졸업반인 우리에게 두 개의 중요 행사가 있습니다. 첫 번째는 학교 축제이고 두 번째는 학년말에 열리는 댄스파티입니다. 그것들은 우리의 고등학교 생활 중 가장 크고 가장 중요한 행사들이고, 준비하는 데 엄청난 양의 시간과 계획을 필요로 합니다. 그래서, 우리는 그 어려운 과제에 대처할 수 있는 리더가 필요합니다. 그리고 저는 Mark가 이 두 개의 중요 행사를 계획하고 실행할 수 있는 가장 적합한 후보라고 생각합니다. 그는 학급에서 리더십을 보여 주었고, 그리고 우리가 그를 선출한다면 그는 학교를 위해서도 같은 일을 할 것입니다. 그러니 Mark에게 투표해 주세요. 감사합니다.

문제 해설 남자는 학년 회장에 출마한 친구 Mark를 위해 지지 연설을 하면서 Mark에게 투표해 주기를 부탁하고 있다. 따라서 남자가 하는 말의 목적으로 가장 적절한 것은 ⑤ '학년 회장으로 출마한 친구에 대해 지지를 호소하려고'이다.

어휘&어구 on behalf of ~을 위해서, ~을 대표하여   candidate 후보자   tremendous 엄청난   organize 준비[조직]하다   meet 대처하다, 충족시키다, 만나다   qualified 적합한, 자격이 있는   put on ~을 실행하다   vote for ~에게 투표하다

02 여행지 선택 [정답] ⑤

W	Hi, Tom. Where are you headed?
M	Hi, Lily. I'm going to meet Jimmy and Tyler to plan for our summer trip.
W	Where are you guys going?
M	We haven't decided yet. Jimmy wants to travel to Rome again while Tyler firmly insists that we go to a country that we have not been to before like Nepal.
W	Why does Jimmy want to go to Rome again?
M	Because when we went there last time, we didn't have time to do everything we wanted.
W	What's Tyler's argument?
M	He thinks that traveling in developed countries doesn't challenge us enough. What do you think?
W	Hmm. If I had a vote, I'd go with Tyler.
M	Why is that?
W	First of all, when the culture is totally different, any experiences you have of the new culture will broaden your horizon.
M	Hmm, interesting.
W	Also, I think you'll learn a lot from a journey into a new country you've never been to.

여 안녕, Tom. 어디 가고 있니?

남 안녕, Lily. 여름 여행 계획을 짜기 위해 Jimmy와 Tyler를 만나러 가는 중이야.

여 너희들은 어디로 갈 거니?

남 아직 결정하지 못했어. Jimmy는 다시 로마를 여행하길 원하고 Tyler는 우리가 이전에 가 보지 않았던 네팔과 같은 나라에 가야 한다고 확고히 주장해.

여 Jimmy는 로마에 왜 다시 가길 원하니?

남 지난번에 로마를 방문했을 때 원하는 모든 것을 할 시간이 없었거든.

여 Tyler 주장의 근거가 뭐니?

남 그는 선진국으로의 여행은 우리에게 도전 의식을 충분히 북돋우지 않는다고 생각해. 너는 어떻게 생각하니?

여 음. 내가 투표권이 있다면 나는 Tyler 편을 들 거야.

남 왜 그러니?

여 무엇보다도, 문화가 완전히 다르면 그 새로운 문화에 대해 갖게 되는 경험이 너의 시야를 넓혀 줄 거야.

남 음, 흥미로운데.

여 또한 네가 가 보지 않은 새로운 나라로의 여행에서 많은 것을 배울 거로 생각해.

문제 해설 여자는 이전에 갔던 지역에 다시 여행을 가길 원하는 Jimmy와 이전에 가 보지 않은 지역에 가자는 Tyler의 의견이 서로 맞서고 있다는 것을 듣고, 문화가 낯선 지역에 가면 시야가 넓어지고 많은 것을 배울 거라는 의견을 말하고 있다. 따라서 여자의 의견으로 가장 적절한 것은 ⑤ '낯선 나라에서의 문화 체험은 시야와 견문을 넓혀 준다.'이다.

어휘&어구 firmly 확고히, 단호히   argument 주장의 근거, 주장   challenge 도전 의식을 북돋우다   broaden (경험·지식 등을) 넓히다   horizon 시야, 수평선

03 아이들의 동영상 시청이 안 좋은 점 [정답] ①

M Hello, I'm Steve Jennings from Ace Parents Academy. Kids can learn a lot from watching videos, but that doesn't mean watching videos is always beneficial for them. Above all, it takes away time from children that could be spent on reading books and prevents them from developing an interest in it. As a consequence, it can limit their imagination. When children read, they engage in imagining characters and scenes, which enhances their creativity. However, with videos such as movies and cartoons, everything is presented visually, so kids seldom use their imagination. Excessive video consumption can hinder their imaginative abilities, leaving minimal space for creative thinking.

남 안녕하세요, 저는 Ace Parents Academy의 Steve Jennings입니다. 아이들은 동영상 시청을 통해 많은 것을 배울 수 있지만, 그것이 항상 그들에게 유익하다는 뜻은 아닙니다. 무엇보다도, 그것(동영상 시청)은 아이들에게서 책을 읽는 데 쓰일 수 있던 시간을 빼앗으며, 아이들이 책을 읽는 것에 흥미를 갖지 못하도록 막습니다. 그 결과, 그것은 아이들의 상상력을 제한할 수 있습니다. 아이들이 책을 읽을 때는 등장인물과 장면을 상상하고, 이는 그들의 창의력을 향상합니다. 그러나 영화나 만화와 같은 동영상은 모든 것이 시각적으로 제시되어서 아이들은 자신의 상상력을 거의 사용하지 않습니다. 과도한 동영상 시청은 그들의 상상력을 제한하며, 이것으로 인해 창의적인 사고를 할 수 있는 여지가 거의 남지 않을 것입니다.

어휘&어구 beneficial 유익한 consequence 결과 enhance 향상하다 present 제공하다

04 심리 상태를 보여 주는 그림

[정답] ③

W	Hi, Mr. White. I'm Nancy Blake, Elin's mom.
M	Nice to meet you, Ms. Blake. Have a seat, please.
W	Thank you.
M	Last week I asked my students to draw a picture, and this is Elin's.
W	Oh, it's nice. She put the sun in the corner.
M	It's a common thing among kids. What is interesting is that Elin drew a house with a chimney.
W	You're right. Smoke is coming out of it. Does it mean anything special?
M	A smoking chimney means an expression of warmth and affection within the family.
W	That's a good sign.
M	And the wide-open door leading to the pathway shows her open mind to the outside world.
W	That makes sense. The girl who is jumping rope must be Elin.
M	Yes, I think so. And take a look at this tree. She drew branches and leaves on the tree. It means she has a well-rounded nature.
W	It's very interesting that we can read her mind just with a picture.
M	I hope it helps you understand a part of her psychological state.

여 안녕하세요, White 선생님. 저는 Elin의 엄마 Nancy Blake예요.
남 만나서 반갑습니다, Blake 씨. 앉으세요.
여 감사합니다.
남 지난주에 저는 학생들에게 그림을 그리라고 했는데, 이것이 Elin의 것입니다.
여 오, 멋지네요. 그녀는 태양을 모서리에 두었네요.
남 그것은 아이들 사이에서 흔한 일입니다. 흥미로운 점은 Elin이 굴뚝이 있는 집을 그렸다는 것입니다.
여 맞아요. 그것에서 연기가 나오고 있어요. 이것이 어떤 특별한 것을 의미하나요?
남 연기 나는 굴뚝은 가족 내에서의 따뜻함과 애정의 표현을 의미합니다.
여 그것은 좋은 징후네요.
남 그리고 좁은 길로 이어지는 활짝 열린 문은 외부 세계에 대한 그녀의 열린 마음을 보여 줍니다.
여 일리가 있네요. 줄넘기를 하는 소녀는 틀림없이 Elin이군요.
남 네, 그렇게 생각합니다. 그리고 이 나무를 보세요. 그녀는 나무에 가지와 잎들을 그렸어요. 그것은 그녀가 원만한 성품을 가졌다는 것을 의미합니다.
여 우리가 그녀의 마음을 단지 그림 한 장으로 읽을 수 있다는 것이 매우 흥미롭군요.
남 그것이 어머님께서 그녀의 심리 상태 일부를 이해하는 데 도움이 되기를 바랍니다.

어휘&어구 chimney 굴뚝 affection 애정, 애착 pathway 좁은 길, 오솔길 jump rope 줄넘기를 하다 well-rounded 원만한 psychological 심리적인, 정신적인

05 사촌 방문 맞이 준비하기

[정답] ②

W	Honey, do you remember that my cousin, Amy, will be arriving at the station at 10:00 a.m. this Saturday?
M	Sure. I'm going to pick her up. We haven't seen her for a long time since we moved here.
W	Yeah. She is going to stay with us all weekend. Let's plan a fun weekend for her.
M	Okay. Like I told you, I've already made a reservation at a fancy restaurant for her.
W	That's sweet. And let's decorate the house for her arrival.

여 여보, 내 사촌 Amy가 이번 토요일 오전 10시에 역에 도착할 거라는 거 기억하죠?
남 물론이죠. 내가 그녀를 마중 나갈 거예요. 우리가 여기로 이사한 이후로 오랫동안 그녀를 보지 못했어요.
여 그래요. 그녀는 주말 내내 우리와 함께 머무를 거예요. 그녀를 위해 즐거운 주말 계획을 세워 봐요.
남 좋아요. 말했던 것처럼 내가 이미 그녀를 위해 고급 레스토랑에 예약을 했어요.
여 정말 멋져요. 그러면 그녀의 도착에 맞게 집을 꾸며 볼까요?

M	Good idea. Let's get some flowers. I'll take care of that.	남	좋은 생각이에요. 꽃을 좀 사 오죠. 그건 내가 맡을게요.
W	Perfect. There's a nice flower shop near your workplace.	여	완벽해요. 당신 직장 근처에 좋은 꽃 가게가 있잖아요.
M	Exactly. I'll call them to see what they have. Also, I'll book a city bus tour before dinner on Saturday.	남	맞아요. 그들에게 전화해서 어떤 꽃이 있는지 확인해 볼게요. 그리고 토요일 저녁 식사 전에 도시 버스 관광도 예약할게요.
W	Sounds like a great plan. I wonder if there's anything I can do.	여	좋은 계획 같군요. 내가 할 수 있는 일이 있을지 모르겠어요.
M	Let's get her a small gift to celebrate her first visit to our home.	남	우리 집에 처음 방문한 것을 기념하기 위해 작은 선물을 준비해 봐요.
W	Good idea. I'll make a list of thoughtful presents for her.	여	좋은 생각이에요. 그녀를 위한 정성 어린 선물 목록을 만들게요.
M	Let's show Amy how much we're looking forward to seeing her.	남	Amy에게 우리가 얼마나 그녀를 기다리고 있는지 보여 주자고요.

> **문제 해설** 남자가 그들의 집에 처음 방문하는 여자의 사촌을 위해 선물을 준비할 것을 제안하자, 여자는 자신이 선물 목록을 만들겠다고 했으므로 여자가 할 일로 가장 적절한 것은 ② '선물 목록 만들기'이다.
>
> **어휘&어구** make a reservation 예약하다 fancy 고급의 decorate 꾸미다, 장식하다 workplace 직장 thoughtful 정성 어린

06 옷 쇼핑하기 [정답] ④

M	Hello. Is there anything I can help you with today?	남	안녕하세요. 오늘 제가 도와드릴 게 있나요?
W	Hi. Actually, yes. Do you have this shirt in a smaller size? I only see larges here.	여	안녕하세요. 실은 그래요. 이 셔츠를 더 작은 사이즈로 갖고 있나요? 여기서는 큰 것만 보이네요.
M	Yes, there are smalls and mediums in the back. What size would you like?	남	네, 작은 사이즈와 중간 사이즈는 뒤에 있습니다. 어떤 사이즈를 원하시나요?
W	A medium, please. And is it part of the sale?	여	중간 사이즈로 주세요. 그리고 할인 판매에 포함되는 건가요?
M	Yes. It's on sale for 30% off. It's now $28.	남	네. 30퍼센트 할인 판매 중입니다. 지금 28달러입니다.
W	Great! I'll buy it. What other things are on sale?	여	좋아요! 그걸로 사겠어요. 다른 물건들은 무엇이 할인 판매되나요?
M	All of the hats are 10% off. Would you like me to show you where they are?	남	모든 모자가 10퍼센트 할인하여 판매 중입니다. 어디에 있는지 보여 드릴까요?
W	Yes, please. My son actually needs a hat.	여	네, 부탁드립니다. 실은 제 아들이 모자가 필요해요.
M	Here they are. They're all on sale.	남	여기 있습니다. 모두 할인 판매 중입니다.
W	Oh, this one is perfect for my son. How much is it?	여	오, 이 모자가 제 아들에게 딱 맞네요. 얼마인가요?
M	It's originally $20. But you get 10% off.	남	원래는 20달러입니다. 그렇지만 10퍼센트 할인됩니다.
W	It's not expensive. I'll buy that, too.	여	가격이 비싸지 않군요. 그것도 제가 살게요.

> **문제 해설** 여자는 중간 사이즈의 셔츠를 30퍼센트 할인된 가격인 28달러에 구매하였고, 모자도 원래의 20달러에서 10퍼센트 할인받아 18달러에 구매하였다. 따라서 여자가 지불할 금액은 ④ '46달러'이다.
>
> **어휘&어구** medium 중간 on sale 할인 판매 중인 originally 원래

07 프랑스어 통역 요청하기 [정답] ②

W	Hey, Matthew. I've found a young French biomedical engineer.	여	안녕, Matthew. 젊은 프랑스 생의학 공학자를 찾았어.
M	Oh? That's great.	남	오? 잘됐네.
W	Yes. I believe she can play a big role in completing our company's new major project. So I want her to join our team.	여	그래. 나는 그녀가 우리 회사의 중요한 새 프로젝트를 마무리하는 데 큰 역할을 할 수 있다고 생각해. 그래서 나는 그녀가 우리 팀에 함께하기를 원해.
M	How are you going to get her to join us?	남	어떻게 그녀가 우리와 함께하도록 할 거니?
W	I will go to Daejeon to meet her this Saturday. She is working in a lab there.	여	나는 이번 토요일에 그녀를 만나러 대전에 갈 거야. 그녀는 그곳에 있는 실험실에서 일하고 있어.
M	Did you set up a time to meet her?	남	그녀와 만날 시간을 잡았니?
		여	응. 그녀에게 이메일을 보냈고, 그녀가 토요일에 나를 만날 수 있다

W   Yes. I sent her an email and she said she could meet me on Saturday.

M   I see. But do you think she will be interested?

W   I think I am going to have to persuade her to work with us.

M   Oh, really?

W   Yeah. But the biggest problem is she doesn't speak Korean well, and I only speak a little French.

M   Oh, that's a problem.

W   So, could you go see her with me? You speak French, don't you?

M   Yes, I do. But I'm afraid I can't. My older sister is getting married this Saturday.

W   Oh, I forgot. Anyway, I need to find someone to help me out.

고 했어.

남   알겠어. 그런데 그녀가 관심을 가질 거로 생각해?

여   그녀가 우리와 함께 일하도록 설득해야 할 거로 생각해.

남   아, 그래?

여   응. 하지만 가장 큰 문제는 그녀는 한국어를 잘하지 못하고 나는 프랑스어를 조금밖에 못 한다는 거야.

남   아, 그거 문제네.

여   그래서, 네가 그녀를 만나러 나와 함께 갈 수 있겠니? 너는 프랑스어를 하잖아, 그렇지?

남   그래. 하지만 갈 수 없을 것 같아. 누나가 이번 주 토요일에 결혼해.

여   아, 잊고 있었어. 아무튼, 나를 도와줄 누군가를 찾아야겠어.

문제 해설   여자는 남자에게 토요일에 프랑스인 생의학 공학자를 만나러 같이 가 달라고 부탁했으나 남자는 누나의 결혼식 때문에 함께 갈 수 없다고 말한다. 따라서 남자가 토요일에 여자와 함께 갈 수 없는 이유는 ② '누나 결혼식이 있어서'이다.

어휘&어구   biomedical 생의학의   complete 마무리하다   lab 실험실(laboratory)   persuade 설득하다

---

08 방과 후 학교 수학 수업   [정답] ④

W   Excuse me, Mr. Smith. May I talk to you for a minute?

M   Sure. What is it?

W   I'd like to get more information about the after school math class you mentioned yesterday.

M   Okay. It's targeted for students who are struggling in math.

W   I see. When does the class start?

M   It begins on May 3rd. And it'll meet after school on Mondays, Wednesdays, and Fridays.

W   All right. And how much does it cost?

M   Don't worry. It's free.

W   That's great. I have one more question. Who's going to teach it?

M   Probably a university student who graduated from our school.

W   Okay, Mr. Smith. Thank you so much for the detailed information.

M   You're welcome. Come to me anytime if you need my help.

여   실례합니다, Smith 선생님. 잠시 말씀을 드려도 되나요?

남   물론이지. 뭐지?

여   어제 선생님께서 말씀하신 방과 후 학교 수학 수업에 대한 정보를 더 얻고 싶습니다.

남   좋아. 그것은 수학에 애를 먹고 있는 학생들을 대상으로 해.

여   그렇군요. 그 수업은 언제 시작하나요?

남   5월 3일에 시작한단다. 그리고 월, 수, 금요일 방과 후에 진행돼.

여   알겠습니다. 그리고 수강료는 얼마인가요?

남   걱정하지 마. 무료란다.

여   좋네요. 질문드릴 게 하나 더 있어요. 누가 가르치시나요?

남   아마 우리 학교를 졸업한 대학생일 거야.

여   알겠습니다, Smith 선생님. 상세하게 알려 주셔서 대단히 감사합니다.

남   천만에. 도움이 필요하다면 언제든지 오거라.

문제 해설   방과 후 학교 수학 수업에 관해 수강 대상, 시작 날짜, 수강료, 강사는 언급되었지만, ④ '교재'는 언급되지 않았다.

어휘&어구   mention 말하다, 언급하다   target 대상[목표]으로 삼다   struggle 애먹다, 고군분투하다   detailed 상세한

---

09 엄격한 채식주의자를 위한 후식 만들기 대회   [정답] ④

W   Have you always wanted to show off your cooking skills? Think of a delicious dessert that is free of milk, butter, and eggs, and enter the Vegan Dessert Contest. Send us your recipe and a photo of your dish by April 21st. After all entries have been uploaded, visitors to our website can vote

여   여러분의 요리 솜씨를 항상 자랑하고 싶으셨나요? 우유와 버터 그리고 달걀이 들어가지 않은 맛있는 후식을 생각해 보고, Vegan Dessert Contest에 참여하세요. 여러분의 요리법과 요리 사진을 저희에게 4월 21일까지 보내 주세요. 모든 출품작이 업로드된 후에, 저희 웹사이트 방문자들은 자신들이 좋아하는 후식에

for their favorites. Last year, chefs assessed the entries, but this year is different. The winner will be chosen based only on the total number of votes each entry receives. The winner will receive $1,000, and will be announced on May 5th. Be creative and show us your best desserts for vegans!

투표할 수 있습니다. 지난해에는, 요리사들이 출품작을 평가했었는데, 올해는 다릅니다. 우승자는 각 출품작이 받은 총투표수만을 근거로 선정될 것입니다. 우승자는 1,000달러를 받게 될 것이고, 5월 5일에 발표될 것입니다. 창의력을 발휘해서 엄격한 채식주의자를 위한 여러분의 최고의 후식을 저희에게 보여 주세요!

문제 해설 요리사들이 출품작을 평가했던 지난해와는 달리 올해 우승자는 각 출품작이 받은 총투표수만을 근거로 선정될 것이라고 했으므로, 담화의 내용과 일치하지 않는 것은 ④ '요리사들의 평가가 심사에 반영될 것이다.'이다.

어휘&어구 show off ~을 자랑하다 vegan 엄격한 채식주의자(고기는 물론 우유, 달걀도 먹지 않음) recipe 요리법 entry 출품[참가/응모] vote 투표하다; 투표수 assess 평가하다

10 반려견 목줄 사기 [정답] ②

M	Honey, it looks like you're shopping for something online.
W	I am. I'm looking for a dog leash for Walnut. His leash is coming apart.
M	Good idea. I noticed that too. Have you found a good site?
W	Yeah. Here's a site selling leashes. What length do you think we should get?
M	This one seems too long. I think under 7 feet would be good.
W	I agree. And this one is too expensive. There's no need to spend more than $15.
M	Right. And look, these two have padded handles. Do you think that's necessary?
W	We go for long walks, so that would be much more comfortable.
M	Good point. So it's down to these two. What do you think about this one?
W	Hmm. Well, I think nylon comes apart pretty easily.
M	You're right. Let's order the other one then.

남 여보, 온라인으로 뭔가 쇼핑하고 있는 것 같군요.
여 네. Walnut을 위해 강아지 목줄을 찾고 있어요. 목줄이 끊어지고 있어서요.
남 좋은 생각이에요. 저도 그걸 봤거든요. 좋은 사이트를 찾았어요?
여 네. 여기 목줄을 판매하는 사이트가 있네요. 어떤 길이를 사야 할까요?
남 이건 너무 길어 보여요. 제 생각엔 7피트 미만이 좋을 것 같아요.
여 동감이에요. 그리고 이건 너무 비싸요. 15달러 이상 쓸 필요 없을 것 같아요.
남 맞아요. 그리고 보세요, 이 두 개는 패드를 덧댄 손잡이들이 있네요. 그게 필요할까요?
여 우리는 오래 산책하러 가니까, 그게 훨씬 더 편할 것 같아요.
남 좋은 지적이네요. 그러면 이 두 개가 남았네요. 이것에 대해 어떻게 생각하나요?
여 음. 나일론은 쉽게 끊어지는 것 같아요.
남 맞아요. 그럼 다른 것을 주문하죠.

문제 해설 여자는 반려견의 목줄로 7피트 이하의 길이에 15달러보다 저렴한 가격으로 패드를 덧댄 손잡이가 있는 것을 원하며, 나일론 소재인 모델은 사지 않겠다고 했다. 따라서 두 사람이 주문할 반려견 목줄은 ②이다.

어휘&어구 leash 목줄 come apart (조각조각) 끊어지다 padded 패드를 덧댄 nylon 나일론 leather 가죽

11 디지털카메라 수리 [정답] ②

M	Hi. The button on my digital camera is stuck. Would you be able to fix it?
W	Let me have a look. *[Pause]* I see what's wrong. I can fix it later today.
M	Okay. What time shall I come to pick it up?
W	Well, I'll give you a call when it's done.

남 안녕하세요. 제 디지털카메라의 버튼이 움직이질 않아요. 고치실 수 있나요?
여 제가 한번 보겠습니다. *[잠시 후]* 뭐가 문제인지 알겠네요. 오늘 이따가 고칠 수 있어요.
남 알겠습니다. 제가 몇 시에 그길 찾으러 올까요?
여 음, 그것이 다 되면 제가 전화드릴게요.

문제 해설 남자가 고장 난 디지털카메라를 여자에게 수리를 맡기고 나서 몇 시에 찾으러 오면 되겠는지 묻고 있다. 따라서 남자의 마지막 말에 대한 여자의 응답으로 가장 적절한 것은 ② '음, 그것이 다 되면 제가 전화드릴게요.'이다.
① 너무 늦으셨네요. 누군가 이미 그것을 찾아갔어요.
③ 죄송해요. 왜 버튼이 움직이지 않는지 모르겠어요.
④ 그건 제가 카메라를 떨어뜨린 후 어제부터 시작됐어요.

⑤ 오래되지 않았어요. 전 그 카메라를 겨우 한 달 동안 가지고 있었어요.

어휘&어구   digital camera 디지털카메라   be stuck 움직일 수 없다, 꼼짝 못 하다   fix 수리하다   pick up ~을 찾아오다

12   방향제를 뿌릴 때 주의 사항

[정답] ⑤

W   Jack, what did you spray in your room? The smell is really strong.

M   It's antibacterial spray. Mike, my friend, gave it to me. He said I should spray it to keep my room clean.

W   Yeah, but you should open the window so you're not breathing so much of it in.

M   You're right. I'll open the window right away.

여   Jack, 방에 뭘 뿌렸니? 냄새가 정말 강하구나.

남   항균 스프레이예요. 제 친구 Mike가 저에게 주었어요. 그 애 말이 방을 깨끗하게 하려면 그것을 뿌려야 한다고 했어요.

여   응, 하지만 그것을 그렇게 많이 들이마시지 않도록 창문을 열어야 해.

남   맞아요. 지금 바로 창문을 열게요.

문제 해설   남자가 방에 방향제를 뿌렸고, 여자가 그것을 그렇게 많이 들이마시지 않도록 창문을 열어야 한다고 말하고 있다. 따라서 여자의 마지막 말에 대한 남자의 응답으로 가장 적절한 것은 ⑤ '맞아요. 지금 바로 창문을 열게요.'이다.
① 괜찮아요. 전 긴장을 풀고 깊게 숨을 쉴 수 있어요.
② 물론이죠. 어제 창문을 닦았어요.
③ 걱정하지 마세요. 이미 손을 씻었어요.
④ 좋아요. 창문을 닦기 위해 창문에 그것을 뿌릴게요.

어휘&어구   antibacterial 항균성의   breathe ~ in ~을 들이마시다

13   베트남식 국수 요리 포

[정답] ⑤

W   We finally finished the project!

M   It feels so good! Now I'm as hungry as a bear. Let's grab something to eat.

W   Yeah. I could eat a horse! What do you want to eat?

M   How about pho?

W   Pho? What's that?

M   It's a Vietnamese noodle soup dish. You need to try it.

W   Well, it sounds good, but will that be enough? I normally don't get full off of just noodles.

M   But pho is different. There's meat and other ingredients in it.

W   Oh, meat? Then it definitely sounds like it'd be enough.

M   There are also different vegetables in it. I'm sure you'll love it.

W   Okay, let's go. I hope it's as delicious as you say.

여   우리 마침내 프로젝트를 끝냈어요!

남   기분이 너무 좋아요! 이제 몹시 배가 고파졌네요. 뭐 좀 먹죠.

여   좋아요. 저도 진짜 배고파요! 뭘 먹고 싶어요?

남   포를 먹는 건 어때요?

여   포? 그게 뭔가요?

남   베트남식 국수 요리예요. 꼭 한번 드셔 보세요.

여   음, 괜찮은 것 같긴 한데 그게 충분할까요? 전 보통 면만 먹으면 배가 부르지 않거든요.

남   그런데 포는 달라요. 그 안에 고기와 다른 재료들이 들어가 있어요.

여   오, 고기도 들어가요? 그럼 분명히 충분할 것 같군요.

남   거기에 채소도 다양하게 들어가 있어요. 분명히 맛있게 드실 거에요.

여   좋아요, 가 봅시다. 당신이 말씀하시는 것만큼 맛있기를 바랄게요.

문제 해설   프로젝트를 끝내고 배가 고픈 남자가 여자에게 베트남식 국수인 포를 제안하자 여자는 면 요리는 배가 부르지 않을 것 같다고 말했다. 남자는 포에는 고기와 채소 등이 들어 있고 여자가 그 맛을 아주 좋아할 것이라고 언급했다. 따라서 남자의 마지막 말에 대한 여자의 응답으로 가장 적절한 것은 ⑤ '좋아요, 가 봅시다. 당신이 말씀하시는 것만큼 맛있기를 바랄게요.'이다.
① 너무 많이 먹지 말아요. 배탈 나겠어요.
② 더는 못 먹겠어요. 남은 음식은 포장해 갑시다.
③ 정말 베트남에 가고 싶어요. 그곳에 한 번도 가 본 적이 없어요.
④ 감사해요. 당신이 추천한 포는 정말 맛있었어요.

어휘&어구   as hungry as a bear 몹시 배고픈   grab something to eat 간단히 먹다   I could eat a horse (말 한 마리라도 먹을 수 있을 것처럼) 진짜 배고프다   don't get full off of ~을 먹어도 배부르지 않다   ingredient 재료   definitely 분명히

14 싱가포르에 있는 펜팔 소개하기 [정답] ④

M	Hey, Gloria. You look really busy.	남	안녕, Gloria. 너 정말 바빠 보인다.
W	Yes. I have to write an essay about Singapore without the help of the internet, and it's driving me crazy.	여	맞아. 인터넷의 도움 없이 싱가포르에 대한 에세이를 써야 해서 정말 답답해.
M	Singapore? Do you know a lot about it?	남	싱가포르? 그 나라에 대해 많이 알고 있니?
W	No. That's the problem.	여	아니. 그게 문제야.
M	Then why do you have to write about it?	남	그러면 왜 그 나라에 관해서 써야 해?
W	The teacher randomly gave us our topic. There's so much research I need to do.	여	선생님께서 우리에게 무작위로 주제를 주셨거든. 해야 할 조사가 너무 많아.
M	If you want, I can introduce you to Tracy?	남	원하면 Tracy에게 너를 소개해 줄까?
W	Who's Tracy?	여	Tracy가 누구야?
M	She's my Singaporean pen pal. Maybe she can help you.	남	그녀는 나의 싱가포르인 펜팔 친구야. 아마 그녀가 도움을 줄 수도 있을 거야.
W	Oh, that would be great. So is she your girlfriend?	여	오, 그러면 좋겠다. 그래서 그녀는 네 여자친구야?
M	No, she's just a friend. She's really nice. And she even enjoys collecting coins like you.	남	아니, 그냥 친구야. 그녀는 정말 착해. 게다가 너처럼 동전 수집도 즐기거든.
W	Cool! Can she become my friend too?	여	멋지다! 그녀가 나의 친구가 될 수 있을까?
M	Yes. You can make a new friend and get help with your essay.	남	그럼. 넌 새 친구를 사귈 수 있고, 에세이에 도움을 받을 수 있어.

문제 해설 여자가 싱가포르에 대해 에세이를 쓰느라 정신없이 바쁜 모습을 보고 남자가 여자를 Tracy에게 소개해 주겠다고 말한다. 여자가 Tracy가 누구인지 묻자 남자는 Tracy는 자신의 싱가포르인 펜팔 친구이며, 그녀가 여자에게 (에세이에) 도움을 줄 수 있다면서, Tracy 역시 여자처럼 동전 모으기를 좋아한다고 말한다. 이에 여자는 Tracy가 자신과 친구가 될 수 있을지 묻는다. 따라서 여자의 마지막 말에 대한 남자의 응답으로 가장 적절한 것은 ④ '그럼. 넌 새 친구를 사귈 수 있고, 에세이에 도움을 받을 수 있어.'이다.

① 그래. 네가 펜팔 프로그램을 통해 연락할 수 있어.

② 아니. 난 내가 에세이 쓰는 것을 도와줄 친구가 없어.

③ 아니. 스마트 기기를 사용하지 않으면 많은 것을 얻을 수 없어.

⑤ 그래. 내 이메일을 네게 문자로 보낼 테니 그녀에게 그것을 전해 줘.

어휘&어구 drive ~ crazy ~을 답답하게[미치게] 하다 randomly 무작위로 introduce 소개하다 pen pal 펜팔, 편지 친구

15 실내용 화초 키우기 [정답] ②

W	Joshua and Maya are friends. Joshua is good at taking care of plants. Whenever Maya visits his house, she compliments him on all of his nice houseplants. So Joshua decides to give Maya a potted houseplant for her birthday. After a few weeks, Maya notices some of the leaves on the plant turning yellow. She's worried and asks Joshua what could be the problem. After asking her how she's taken care of the plant, Joshua concludes that Maya is overwatering the plant. Joshua wants to tell Maya that if she keeps doing that, it could be deadly. In this situation, what would Joshua most likely say to Maya?	여	Joshua와 Maya는 친구 사이입니다. Joshua는 식물 돌보는 것을 잘합니다. Maya는 그의 집을 방문할 때마다, 그의 멋진 실내용 화초 모두에 대해 칭찬합니다. 그래서 Joshua는 그녀의 생일 선물로 화분에 심은 실내용 화초를 Maya에게 주기로 합니다. 몇 주 후에, Maya는 화초의 잎 중 일부가 노랗게 변하고 있는 것을 알아차립니다. 그녀는 걱정스러워서 무엇이 문제일 수 있는지 Joshua에게 묻습니다. 그녀가 화초를 어떻게 돌보았는지 물어본 후에, Joshua는 Maya가 화초에 물을 지나치게 많이 주고 있다고 결론짓습니다. Joshua는 Maya에게 그녀가 계속 그렇게 하면 치명적일 수 있다고 말해 주고 싶습니다. 이런 상황에서 Joshua는 Maya에게 뭐라고 말하겠습니까?
Joshua	Try not to water the plant too much or it will die.	Joshua	화초에 물을 지나치게 많이 주지 않도록 해. 그러지 않으면 그것은 죽을 거야.

문제 해설 Joshua는 자신이 Maya에게 준 화초의 잎이 노랗게 변하는 이유가 물을 지나치게 많이 줘서 그렇다고 결론짓고 물을 지나치게 많이 주면 화초에 치명적일 수 있다고 말하고 싶어 하는 상황이므로, Joshua가 Maya에게 할 말로 가장 적절한 것은 ② '화초에 물을 지나치게 많이 주지 않도록 해. 그러지 않으면 그것은 죽을 거야.'이다.

① 화초는 생존하는 데 햇빛이 필요하다는 걸 잊지 마.

③ 화초는 시원하고 그늘진 곳에 두어야 해.
④ 가능한 한 자주 화초에 신선한 공기를 꼭 공급하도록 해.
⑤ 화초가 웃자라는 것을 막기 위해서는 가지를 쳐야 해.

어휘&어구 compliment 칭찬하다 houseplant 실내용 화초 potted 화분에 심은 notice 알아차리다 conclude 결론짓다 overwater 물을 지나치게 많이 주다 deadly 치명적인 shaded 그늘진 trim 가지를 치다 overgrow 웃자라다

16~17 감기 예방 수칙

[정답] 16 ① 17 ②

M Hello, Class. The cold season is just around the corner. Nine out of ten people catch a cold once a year, and during the change of seasons, people catch colds more easily. So, what can we do to prevent catching a cold? Let's talk about some basic rules to do. First, maintain a balanced diet. Extreme diets weaken your body, which can make you catch a cold more easily. Second, strengthen your immune system through exercise. With a strong immune system, you're less likely to catch a cold. Third, lower the temperature of your house by 9 to 11 degrees Fahrenheit. Temperatures that are too high or too low can have a bad effect on your body's defense. Lastly, be sure to get enough rest and sleep. You're more likely to catch a cold when you're tired, so enough rest and sleep are extremely important. Keep all of this in mind for the upcoming winter season!

남 안녕하세요, 학생 여러분. 추운 계절이 곧 다가오고 있습니다. 열 명 중 아홉은 일 년에 한 번은 감기에 걸리는데, 환절기에는 사람들이 더 쉽게 감기에 걸리게 됩니다. 그래서 감기에 걸리는 것을 예방하기 위해 우리는 무엇을 할 수 있을까요? 몇 가지 해야 할 기본 수칙을 이야기해 보겠습니다. 첫째, 균형 잡힌 식단을 유지하세요. 극단적인 식이 요법은 여러분의 신체를 약화시키고, 이것으로 인해 감기에 더 쉽게 걸리게 할 수 있습니다. 둘째, 운동을 통해 면역 체계를 강화하세요. 강한 면역 체계를 가지고 있으면 감기에 걸릴 확률이 줄어듭니다. 셋째, 집 온도를 화씨로 9~11도 낮추세요. 너무 높거나 낮은 온도는 신체의 방어 기능에 나쁜 영향을 줄 수 있습니다. 마지막으로, 충분한 휴식과 수면을 취하세요. 피곤할 때 감기에 걸릴 가능성이 더 높으므로, 충분한 휴식과 수면은 극히 중요합니다. 이 모든 것을 겨울이 다가오는 계절을 위해 명심하세요!

문제 해설 16 남자는 우리 대다수가 일 년에 한 번은 감기에 걸리고 환절기에는 더 쉽게 걸린다고 하면서 감기에 걸리지 않고 예방하는 방법들을 설명하고 있다. 따라서 남자가 하는 말의 주제로 가장 적절한 것은 ① '감기 예방을 위한 다양한 방법들'이다.
② 사람들의 건강에 위험한 습관들
③ 감기와 독감의 흔한 징후와 증상
④ 인간 생명에 위협이 되는 환경적 요인들
⑤ 규칙적인 운동 루틴의 중요성

17 극단적 식이요법을 하지 않기, 운동하기, 온도 알맞게 조절하기, 충분한 수면하기는 언급되었지만, ② '손 씻기'는 언급되지 않았다.

어휘&어구 just around the corner 바로 다가와서, 임박하여 prevent 예방하다 maintain 유지하다 immune system 면역 체계 temperature 온도 degree (온도·각도·경위도 따위의) 도 Fahrenheit 화씨온도

8회 수능실전 대비연습

본문 94~95쪽

01 ④ 02 ② 03 ⑤ 04 ⑤ 05 ④ 06 ③ 07 ⑤ 08 ② 09 ④ 10 ④ 11 ② 12 ② 13 ⑤ 14 ⑤
15 ② 16 ② 17 ④

01 주차장 도색 작업 안내

[정답] ④

W Hello, residents! I'm Jennifer Jones, the apartment maintenance office manager, and I have an important announcement about the repainting of the parking lot. It's scheduled for June 18th. We do this every four years to

여 안녕하세요, 입주민 여러분! 저는 아파트 유지 보수 담당자인 Jennifer Jones이고, 주차장 재도색에 관한 중요한 공지 사항이 있어서 알려 드리려고 합니다. 작업은 6월 18일에 예정되어 있습니다. 우리는 4년마다 이렇게 하여 주차장의 외관과 기능성을 개선

improve the parking lot's appearance and functionality. And this time, we're also painting the expanded parking area for the disabled. During the painting process, some areas of the parking lot may be temporarily unavailable. If you have any concerns or require assistance, please contact the management office. We're here to help. Thank you for your attention, and have a wonderful day!

합니다. 이번에는 확장된 장애인 주차 공간도 도색하고자 합니다. 도색 과정 중에는 일부 주차장 공간이 일시적으로 사용이 제한될 수 있습니다. 염려되는 부분이 있거나 도움이 필요하신 경우 관리실로 연락해 주시기를 바랍니다. 저희는 도움을 드리기 위해 여기에 있습니다. 집중해서 들어 주셔서 감사합니다. 즐거운 하루 보내세요!

문제 해설 여자는 아파트 입주민들에게 주차장의 재도색 작업이 6월 18일에 예정되어 있으며 4년에 한 번씩 하는 이 작업으로 주차장의 외관과 기능성이 개선될 것이라고 말하고, 이번에는 확장된 장애인 주차 구역도 도색할 것이라고 안내하고 있다. 따라서 남자가 하는 말의 목적으로 가장 적절한 것은 ④ '주차장 재도색 작업 시행을 알려 주려고'이다.

어휘&어구 maintenance 유지, 보수 announcement 공지 사항 appearance 외관 functionality 기능성 the disabled 장애인 temporarily 일시적으로 concern 염려, 걱정

---

02 봉사 활동 참여

[정답] ②

W Hey, Mark, I saw you in front of the library in a group of people yesterday. You were all wearing green shirts.

M Yeah. We met there and then went to McCalister Park.

W What did you do there?

M We handed out food to homeless people. It's an activity of the volunteer club I'm in. We do it every week.

W That's great. How long have you been in the club?

M I actually just joined a few weeks ago.

W That's so cool. I didn't think you were interested in doing anything like that.

M I wasn't until I read a book about the happiness of helping people a couple months ago. It really changed me.

W Awesome! So, you must feel really happy while passing out food.

M Definitely. You should actively engage in helping people whenever you have the opportunity.

W Absolutely. Your story actually encourages me to explore similar opportunities.

M I'm glad to hear that! Trust me. Don't miss the chances to help out in your community.

W Okay. I will.

여 안녕, Mark. 어제 도서관 앞에서 여러 사람과 함께 있는 너를 보았어. 모두 초록색 셔츠를 입고 있더라고.

남 응. 거기서 사람들과 만나서 McCalister Park로 갔어.

여 거기서 무엇을 했니?

남 노숙자분들께 음식을 나눠 주었어. 내가 속한 자원봉사 동아리의 활동이야. 우리는 매주 이렇게 하고 있어.

여 진짜 대단하다. 그 동아리에 얼마나 오래 있었지?

남 사실 몇 주 전에 가입했어.

여 정말 멋지다. 난 네가 그런 일을 하는 데에 관심이 있는 줄 전혀 몰랐는데.

남 두어 달 전에 사람들을 돕는 행복에 관해 쓴 책을 읽을 때까지는 그 관심이 없었어. 그 책이 나를 정말로 바꾸었어.

여 대단해! 그러니까 너는 음식을 나눠 주면서 정말 행복한 기분을 느끼고 있음이 틀림없구나.

남 확실히 그래. 너도 기회가 있을 때마다 사람들을 돕는 일에 적극적으로 참여해야 할 거야.

여 당연하지. 네 이야기를 들으니 나도 비슷한 기회를 찾아야겠다는 생각이 들었어.

남 그 말을 들으니 참 기쁘다! 날 믿어 봐. 지역 사회에 도움을 주는 기회를 놓치지 마.

여 알았어. 그래 볼게.

문제 해설 남자는 여자에게 노숙자에게 음식을 나눠 주는 등의 봉사 활동을 통해 사람들을 도와주면서 자신도 행복한 기분을 느끼고 있으며, 여자에게도 기회가 있을 때마다 남을 돕는 일에 적극 참여해야 한다고 권하고 있으므로, 남자의 주장으로 가장 적절한 것은 ② '기회가 될 때마다 사람들을 적극적으로 도와야 한다.'이다.

어휘&어구 hand out ~을 나눠 주다, ~을 건네주다 homeless 노숙하는 engage in ~에 참여하다

---

03 무용 오디션 참가

[정답] ⑤

W Are you ready, Mr. Simpson?

M I'm pretty nervous, but yes, I'm ready.

W Just relax and do your best.

M Thank you. Could I take a quick sip of water first?

W Sure. Begin when you are ready.

여 준비되었나요, Simpson 씨?

남 매우 긴장되지만, 네, 준비되었어요.

여 긴장을 풀고 최선을 다하세요.

남 감사합니다. 먼저 물 한 모금 빨리 마셔도 될까요?

여 물론이지요. 준비되면 시작하세요.

M	Okay, I'm ready. I'll start now.
W	[Pause] Oh, that was wonderful!
M	Thank you.
W	You performed it so smoothly even with your ankle bandaged up.
M	My ankle is still sore from performing in Swan Lake in the international dance festival last week.
W	Part of being a dancer is performing through the pain, and you just did that. You moved so effortlessly that I couldn't even tell your ankle was hurting.
M	Once I start to dance, I don't even notice the pain.
W	Based on your audition today, I can tell you are extremely talented and dedicated.
M	Thank you for saying that. If I get the part, I will do my best to put on a great production.

남	네, 준비되었어요. 지금 시작합니다.
여	[잠시 후] 아, 멋졌어요!
남	감사합니다.
여	발목에 붕대를 감고도 매우 부드럽게 춤을 추는군요.
남	지난주 국제 무용 축제 때, '백조의 호수' 공연에서 춤을 추었는데 발목이 아직 아픕니다.
여	무용수가 되는 일의 일부는 고통을 참고 춤을 추는 것인데, 당신이 바로 그것을 하신 겁니다. 아주 수월하게 움직이셔서 발목이 아프다는 것을 알 수도 없었네요.
남	일단 춤을 추기 시작하면, 고통을 느끼지도 못해요.
여	오늘 당신의 오디션을 보니, 당신은 매우 재능 있고 헌신적이십니다.
남	그렇게 말해 주셔서 감사합니다. 그 배역을 맡는다면, 좋은 작품을 무대에 올리도록 최선을 다하겠습니다.

문제 해설 남자는 지난주 국제 무용 축제 때 '백조의 호수' 공연에서 춤을 추었다고 했으므로 무용수임을 알 수 있다. 여자는 남자의 오디션을 보고 남자의 실력을 평가하고 있으므로 심사 위원임을 알 수 있다. 따라서 두 사람의 관계를 가장 잘 나타낸 것은 ⑤ '심사 위원 – 무용수'이다.

어휘&어구 sip 한 모금 perform 공연하다 bandage up ~에 붕대를 감다 sore 아픈, 쑤시는 effortlessly 수월하게, 힘들이지 않고 dedicated 헌신적인 production 작품

04 자녀 방 꾸미기 [정답] ⑤

W	Honey, look at the picture in this interior design book. I want to decorate Mike's room like this.
M	Let me see. Wow, it's wonderful. The first thing that gets my attention is the world map on the wall.
W	I think world maps are great because they allow us to dream of far-off places.
M	This big bookshelf beside the window is nice. It would make organizing all of Mike's books easier.
W	Yes, it would. I like how the desk is placed in front of the window.
M	Me, too. Let's move Mike's desk like that. It'll be a more comfortable place for him to do his homework.
W	And look how they have storage boxes under the bed. That's a good way to create more storage.
M	If we do that, we could stop worrying about him leaving his stuff all over the room.
W	That'd be great. And look at the plant hanging from the ceiling. Some greenery in a room is always a mood booster.
M	Right. Plants can have a positive effect on a child's emotional well-being.
W	I can't wait to start redecorating his room.

여	여보, 이 실내 디자인 책에 있는 사진을 보세요. Mike의 방을 이렇게 꾸미고 싶어요.
남	어디 봅시다. 와, 멋지군요. 내 눈길을 끄는 첫 번째 것은 벽에 붙은 세계 지도예요.
여	세계 지도는 우리가 멀리 떨어진 곳을 꿈꾸게 해 줄 수 있어서 멋지다고 생각해요.
남	창문 옆에 있는 이 커다란 책꽂이가 멋지네요. 그것은 Mike의 모든 책을 정리하는 것을 더 쉽게 해 줄 거예요.
여	네, 그럴 거예요. 창문 앞에 책상이 배치된 것이 마음에 드는군요.
남	나도요. Mike의 책상을 그렇게 옮깁시다. 그곳이 그가 숙제하기에 더 편안한 장소일 거예요.
여	그리고 침대 밑에 보관함을 둔 것을 보세요. 더 많이 보관하기 위한 좋은 방법이네요.
남	그렇게 하면, 그가 온 방 안에 물건을 놔두는 것에 대해서 걱정을 그만할 수 있겠어요.
여	좋을 것 같군요. 그리고 천장에 매달린 식물을 보세요. 방 안에 화초가 좀 있는 것이 언제나 분위기를 돋워 주지요.
남	맞아요. 식물은 아이의 정서적 행복에 긍정적인 영향을 미칠 수 있어요.
여	빨리 그의 방을 다시 꾸미는 것을 시작하고 싶네요.

문제 해설 대화에서는 식물이 천장에 매달려 있다고 했으나 그림에서는 침대 발치 쪽 바닥에 놓여 있으므로, 대화의 내용과 일치하지 않는 것은 ⑤이다.

어휘&어구 interior 실내의 decorate 꾸미다 organize 정리하다 storage box 보관함 stuff 물건 greenery 화초 mood booster 분위기를 돋우는 것

05 집들이 파티 준비하기

[정답] ④

W	Ted. I'm really excited about having my own studio in our new house.
M	That's going to be really nice. So have you thought about when we should have our housewarming party?
W	Yeah. How about in two weekends?
M	That works. Then I'll start writing the invitations.
W	Sounds good. And how about setting up a photo booth so people can take funny pictures.
M	I love that idea! I'll see if we can borrow some fun costumes from the local theater.
W	That's sounds awesome! Everybody will have so much fun dressing up.
M	And as far as food goes, let's just keep it simple and get a variety of finger foods.
W	Good idea! Can you look for a restaurant that we can order from?
M	Sure. I'll find a few places that we can choose from.
W	And I'll also do some research to find different indoor games for us to play.
M	Great. I can't wait for the housewarming party.

여	Ted. 우리 새집에 나 자신만의 작업실을 갖게 되어 정말 기뻐요.
남	정말 좋을 거예요. 그럼 언제 집들이 파티해야 할지 생각해 봤나요?
여	네. 이주 후 주말은 어때요?
남	괜찮아요. 그럼 내가 초대장을 쓰기 시작할게요.
여	좋아요. 그리고 사람들이 재미있는 사진을 찍을 수 있도록 포토 부스를 설치해 보는 건 어떨까요?
남	그 아이디어 정말 마음에 들어요! 지역 극장에서 재미있는 의상을 빌릴 수 있는지 확인해 볼게요.
여	정말 멋지겠어요! 모두가 변장하고 재미있게 놀게 될 거예요.
남	그리고 음식은 간단하게 손으로 먹을 수 있는 음식을 다양하게 준비해 봐요.
여	좋은 생각이에요! 음식을 주문할 수 있는 식당을 찾아봐 줄래요?
남	좋아요. 우리가 고를 수 있도록 몇 군데 장소를 찾아볼게요.
여	그럼 나도 우리가 할 수 있는 여러 실내 게임을 찾으려 조사를 좀 해 볼게요.
남	좋아요. 집들이 파티가 정말 기대되는군요.

문제 해설 집들이 파티를 준비하는 여자가 남자에게 음식을 주문할 수 있는 식당을 찾아봐 줄 수 있냐고 묻자 남자는 그렇게 하겠다고 말했다. 따라서 여자가 남자에게 부탁한 일로 가장 적절한 것은 ④ '음식 주문할 식당 찾기'이다.

어휘&어구 studio 작업실 housewarming party 집들이 파티 invitations 초대장 costume 의상 dress up 변장하다 a variety of 다양한 finger food 손으로 (쉽게) 집어 먹을 수 있는 음식 indoor 실내의

06 엄마를 위한 꽃 선물 사기

[정답] ③

M	Good morning! How may I help you?
W	I'm looking for some flowers for my mom. Can you give me some suggestions?
M	Certainly! How about these charming egg cup roses? They're adorable.
W	Oh, they're lovely. How much are they?
M	They're four dollars each.
W	Then I'll take one egg cup rose.
M	I recommend these carnations too. They're two dollars each.
W	That's good. And can I choose different colors?
M	Of course! You can mix and match the colors as you like.
W	Perfect. I'll take five carnations then: three red and two pink.
M	Would you like them arranged as a bouquet? It's free.
W	Thank you very much. Here's my credit card.

남	안녕하세요! 무엇을 도와드릴까요?
여	엄마를 위한 꽃을 찾고 있어요. 제안 좀 해 주시겠어요?
남	물론이죠! 이 매력적인 에그 컵 장미는 어떠세요? 사랑스럽거든요.
여	아, 정말 예쁘네요. 얼마인가요?
남	하나에 4달러입니다.
여	그럼 에그 컵 장미 하나 살게요.
남	이 카네이션도 추천할게요. 한 송이에 2달러예요.
여	좋네요. 그러면 다른 색상을 선택할 수 있나요?
남	물론이죠! 마음대로 색상을 혼합해서 맞추실 수 있어요.
여	완벽해요. 그럼 카네이션을 빨간색 3송이, 분홍색 2송이로 5송이 구매할게요.
남	꽃다발로 정리해 드릴까요? 무료입니다.
여	감사합니다. 카드 여기 있어요.

문제 해설 여자는 어머니에게 선물할 꽃을 사는데 개당 4달러인 에그 컵 장미를 1개 샀고, 송이당 2달러인 카네이션을 5송이 샀으므로, 여자가 지불할 금액은 ③ '14달러'이다.

어휘&어구 suggestion 제안 adorable 사랑스러운 recommend 추천하다 carnation 카네이션 arrange 정리하다 bouquet 꽃다발

M	Hi, Monica! Have you heard that our club is organizing a special camp this summer?	남	안녕, Monica! 우리 동아리가 이번 여름에 특별한 캠프를 준비 중이라는 소식 들었어?
W	Oh, really? I don't know that. What's the plan for the camp?	여	아, 정말? 전혀 몰랐어. 캠프 계획이 어떻게 되는 거야?
M	They're planning to visit the City Museum, which exhibits Korean traditional things. They'll do historical research there.	남	동아리에서는 시립 박물관을 방문할 계획인데, 그곳은 한국 전통 물건들을 전시하고 있어. 거기서 역사 연구를 진행할 계획이야.
W	I'd really like to go. How can I apply?	여	나는 꼭 가고 싶어. 어떻게 신청할 수 있을까?
M	Just talk to the club president. But there's one requirement you should know about.	남	그냥 동아리 대표에게 얘기해 봐. 하지만 하나 알아 둬야 할 조건이 있어.
W	What's that?	여	뭐지?
M	You need to submit a research proposal related to the theme of the camp.	남	캠프 주제와 관련된 연구 제안서를 제출해야 해.
W	No problem. There're so many things that I really want to know about Asian history. And what's your research topic?	여	문제없어. 난 아시아 역사에 대해서 꼭 알고 싶은 것이 많으니까. 그래서 네 연구 주제는 뭐니?
M	Unfortunately, I won't be able to participate this time. I've already committed to a volunteering opportunity at an animal shelter.	남	유감스럽게도 나는 이번에는 참여할 수 없어. 이미 동물 보호소에서의 자원봉사 기회를 맡기로 약속되어 있거든.
W	Still, volunteering at an animal shelter is a wonderful thing. It's going to be a rewarding experience.	여	그래도 동물 보호소 봉사 활동은 정말 좋은 일이야. 보람 있는 경험이 될 거야.

문제 해설 두 사람이 동아리의 캠프 참가 신청에 대해 나누는 대화인데, 여자가 남자의 연구 제안서 주제를 묻자, 남자가 자신은 캠프에 참가할 수 없다고 하면서 동물 보호소 봉사를 하기로 되어 있다고 했다. 따라서 남자가 동아리 봉사 활동에 참여할 수 없는 이유는 ⑤ '동물 보호소 봉사 활동을 해야 해서'이다.

어휘&어구 organize (계획·모임을) 준비하다 exhibit 전시하다 traditional 전통적인 requirement (필요) 조건 research proposal 연구 제안서 commit 약속하다 animal shelter 동물 보호소

08 영어 시험 세부 사항 [정답] ②

W	Hey, Evan. Why don't you stop drawing and study for the English test on Friday?	여	저기, Evan. 그림 그리는 거 그만두고 금요일에 있는 영어 시험을 위해 공부하는 게 어때?
M	Wait, what? There's an English test on Friday? Isn't it next week?	남	잠깐, 뭐라고? 금요일에 영어 시험이 있는 거야? 다음 주 아닌가?
W	There is a test this Friday.	여	이번 주 금요일에 시험이 있어.
M	Oh my gosh. I must not have been paying attention when the teacher told us that. So the test is this Friday?	남	오, 안 돼. 선생님이 말씀하실 때 내가 집중하지 않은 모양이야. 그러니까 시험이 이번 주 금요일에 있다는 거지?
W	Yes. It starts at 1 p.m. and lasts for an hour and a half.	여	맞아. 오후 1시에 시작해서 1시간 반 동안 진행돼.
M	How many questions are there?	남	문제가 몇 문제인데?
W	The test has 25 simple questions and one essay writing task.	여	시험은 간단한 25문제와 에세이 쓰기 한 개가 있어.
M	So, a total of 26 questions. What is the essay about?	남	그러니까 총 26문제네. 그 에세이 주제가 뭐지?
W	You can choose between two topics: friends and your future.	여	친구와 너의 미래, 이 두 가지 주제 중에 선택할 수 있어.
M	Great. I'll choose the topic of my best and kindest friend, you.	남	좋아. 난 내 최고의 친구이자 가장 친절한 친구인 너에 대한 주제로 선택하겠어.
W	Stop joking around. This test is really important for this term. You'd better start studying.	여	장난치지 마. 이번 학기에 이 시험은 정말 중요해. 너는 공부를 시작해야 해.
M	I know, you're right. I'm going to start studying hard today.	남	알아, 네 말이 맞아. 오늘부터 열심히 공부할 거야.

문제 해설 두 사람이 영어 시험에 관해 대화를 나누고 있는데, 실시 요일, 시험 시간, 총문항 수, 에세이 주제는 언급되었지만, ② '시험 범위'는 언급되지 않았다.

어휘&어구 **pay attention** 집중하다, 주의하다 **last** 지속하다 **joke around** 우스갯소리를 하다

09 Kensington 세계 축제 [정답] ④

M Welcome to Kensington World Festival. I'm Larry Johnson, the head organizer of the festival. This festival is a celebration of various cultures and traditions. This year, students from different countries have prepared exciting programs. First, there will be a book display in the library, where students will exhibit books from their countries at each booth. Lunch will be from 11 to 1. In the student cafeteria, various kinds of Asian foods will be served, all for free! After lunch, starting at 1:30, there will be a fashion show featuring traditional African clothing in the student hall. At 4, there will be a traditional music performance in the Kensington Concert Hall. Students from twenty countries will showcase their incredible musical and dancing skills together. I hope you have a great time at the festival.

남 Kensington World Festival에 오신 것을 환영합니다. 저는 페스티벌의 주최자인 Larry Johnson입니다. 이 페스티벌은 다양한 문화와 전통의 기념행사입니다. 올해에는 여러 나라의 학생들이 흥미로운 프로그램을 준비했습니다. 먼저, 도서관에서 책 전시가 있을 것인데, 각 부스마다 학생들이 그들의 나라에서 온 책들을 전시할 예정입니다. 점심은 11시부터 1시까지입니다. 학생 식당에서 다양한 종류의 아시아 음식이 제공될 것이며, 모두 무료로 즐길 수 있습니다! 점심 이후로는 1시 30분부터 학생회관에서 전통 아프리카 의상을 선보이는 패션쇼가 있을 예정입니다. 오후 4시에는 Kensington 콘서트홀에서 전통 음악 공연이 이뤄질 것입니다. 20개국의 학생들이 함께 놀라운 음악과 춤 실력을 선보일 예정입니다. 페스티벌에서 즐거운 시간을 보내시기 바랍니다.

문제 해설 점심 식사 후 1시 30분부터 전통 아프리카 의상을 선보이는 패션쇼가 있을 예정이라고 했으므로, 담화의 내용과 일치하지 않는 것은 ④ '오후 2시에 아프리카 전통 패션쇼가 있을 예정이다.'이다.

어휘&어구 **organizer** 주최자 **celebration** 기념[축하]행사 **display** 전시 **exhibit** 전시하다 **student cafeteria** 학생 식당 **featuring** 특집으로 다루는

10 스마트폰 구입 [정답] ④

M Honey, what are you looking at?

W A website that sells smartphones. It's about time to get a new one.

M I agree. Yours is ancient! Let's see those. What do you think about this model?

W It's good, but I want at least 64 GB of storage.

M Yeah, right. Oh, these models have a lot of camera lenses. That'd be good for taking pictures for social media.

W Right. I want a smartphone with four lenses or more.

M And I'm sure when it comes to color you don't want black or gray.

W Yeah. You know me. I like bright colors.

M Then, it comes down to these two models. What's your price range?

W I'd like to spend less than $900.

M Then, this is the one to choose.

W Yup. I'll get it.

남 여보, 무엇을 보고 있어요?

여 스마트폰을 파는 웹사이트요. 새것을 하나 살 때가 됐어요.

남 맞아요. 당신 스마트폰은 너무 오래됐어요! 저것들을 보죠. 이 모델은 어때요?

여 좋지만 적어도 64GB의 저장 공간을 원해요.

남 네, 맞아요. 아, 이 모델들은 많은 카메라 렌즈들을 가지고 있어요. 그것은 소셜 미디어를 위해 사진을 찍는 데 좋을 거예요.

여 맞아요. 나는 네 개 이상의 렌즈가 있는 스마트폰을 원해요.

남 그리고 색깔에 관한 한 당신은 분명 검은색이나 회색을 원하지 않아요.

여 네. 나를 잘 알고 있네요. 나는 밝은 색깔이 좋아요.

남 그럼, 이 두 개의 모델로 좁혀지네요. 당신이 원하는 가격대는 얼마인가요?

여 900달러 미만을 쓰고 싶어요.

남 그럼, 이것이 선택할 것이네요.

여 네. 그것을 살게요.

문제 해설 여자는 64GB 이상의 저장 공간을 원했고, 적어도 네 개의 렌즈가 있는 스마트폰을 원했으며, 밝은색이 좋다고 말했고, 가격대는 900달러 미만을 쓰고 싶다고 말했으므로, 여자가 구입할 스마트폰은 ④이다.

어휘&어구 **ancient** 아주 오래된 **storage** 저장 공간, 저장 **when it comes to** ~에 관한 한 **price range** 가격대

11 우비 챙기기 [정답] ②

M	Honey, are you ready to leave for Jenny's soccer game?	남	여보, Jenny의 축구 시합을 보러 갈 준비됐어요?
W	Yeah, let's go. It's not raining outside, is it?	여	네, 가요. 밖에 비 안 오죠, 그렇죠?
M	Not now. But the weather forecast said it might rain later. Did you put the umbrellas in the car?	남	지금은 아니에요. 하지만 일기 예보에서 나중에 비가 올 수도 있다고 했어요. 차에 우산들을 두었나요?
W	No, I didn't. I packed the raincoats instead.	여	아니요, 안 두었어요. 대신 우비를 챙겼어요.

문제 해설 남자가 여자에게 일기 예보에서 비가 올 수 있다고 했는데 차에 우산을 두었느냐고 묻고 있다. 따라서 남자의 마지막 말에 대한 여자의 응답으로 가장 적절한 것은 ② '아니요, 안 두었어요. 대신 우비를 챙겼어요.'이다.
① 제가 말했잖아요. 그 우산은 구하기 쉽지 않아요.
③ 걱정하지 말아요. 비가 전처럼 많이 내리고 있지는 않아요.
④ 네, 날씨가 경기를 보는 데 완벽했어요.
⑤ 물론이죠. 당신은 일기 예보를 확인했어야 했어요.

어휘&어구 weather forecast 일기 예보　raincoat 우비

12 감기 처방 약 [정답] ②

W	Oh, gosh. I don't feel well at all. My coughing is getting worse and worse.	여	오, 세상에. 몸이 전혀 안 좋네요. 기침이 점점 심해지고 있어요.
M	Sorry to hear that. Are you taking any medicine?	남	안됐군요. 약은 먹고 있나요?
W	Yes. I've been taking some cold medicine for the past couple days.	여	네. 요 며칠째 감기약을 먹고 있어요.
M	That's good. Don't forget to get enough rest, too.	남	잘했어요. 충분한 휴식을 취하는 것도 잊지 마세요.

문제 해설 몸이 안 좋고 기침도 점점 심해지고 있는 여자에게 남자가 감기약을 먹고 있는지 묻자, 여자는 요 며칠 동안 약을 먹고 있다고 말했다. 따라서 여자의 마지막 말에 대한 남자의 응답으로 가장 적절한 것은 ② '잘했어요. 충분한 휴식을 취하는 것도 잊지 마세요.'이다.
① 믿을 수 없어요. 감기를 아주 빨리 극복하셨네요.
③ 맞아요. 저는 요즘 거의 감기에 걸리지 않아요.
④ 아쉽네요. 문을 연 병원을 찾기가 쉽지 않아요.
⑤ 절대 아니에요. 진통제가 두통을 줄이는 데 더 좋아요.

어휘&어구 feel well 몸(컨디션)이 좋다　coughing 기침(하기)　get worse and worse 점점 나빠지다[심해지다]　medicine (먹는) 약

13 학교 신문 기사 분량 조절하기 [정답] ⑤

M	Olivia, here's the first draft of the school newspaper. I just got it from the print shop.	남	Olivia, 여기 학교 신문 초안이야. 방금 인쇄소에서 가져왔어.
W	Nice. How does it look?	여	멋지다. 어때 보여?
M	Pretty good, but Ms. Manning's article seems a little long.	남	꽤 좋은데 Manning 씨의 기사가 좀 긴 거 같아.
W	It's her article about being a cartoonist, right?	여	그거 만화가가 되는 것에 관한 그분의 기사지, 맞지?
M	Yeah. It's really good, but it's almost two whole pages.	남	응. 정말 좋은데, 거의 두 페이지 전체야.
W	That's because she included some of her illustrations.	여	본인의 삽화를 좀 넣으셔서 그렇구나.
M	Hmm, they seem important, so I don't think we should take them out.	남	음, 그것들은 중요해 보여서 난 우리가 그것들을 빼서는 안 될 거 같아.
W	Then should we ask the print shop to make the font size smaller?	여	그러면 글씨 크기를 더 작게 해 달라고 인쇄소에 요청해야 할까?
M	That's one option, but it's already pretty small. If she could cut about 200 words, it'd be perfect.	남	그게 하나의 선택 사항인데, 이미 꽤 작아. 그분이 200단어 정도 줄여 주시면 완벽할 거 같아.
W	That'd work. How about asking her? She's really nice. You have her email address.	여	그러겠네. 그분에게 요청하는 건 어떨까? 그분은 정말 좋으셔. 너 그분 이메일 주소 갖고 있잖아.
		남	할 수는 있는데. 하지만 그분이 그것을 좀 무례하다고 할 것 같니?
		여	전혀 아니야. 그분은 자기 기사를 좀 수정하는 것을 기꺼이 해 주실

M I could. But do you think she'd find that a little impolite?

W Not at all. She won't mind making some changes to her article.

거야.

문제 해설 남자와 여자가 학교 신문 초안을 보면서 Manning 씨의 기사가 조금 긴 거 같아 여자가 Manning 씨에게 기사를 줄여 달라고 요청하자고 제안하자 남자가 무례해 보일 것 같은지 묻고 있다. 따라서 남자의 마지막 말에 대한 여자의 응답으로 가장 적절한 것은 ⑤ '전혀 아니야. 그분은 자기 기사를 좀 수정하는 것을 기꺼이 해 주실 거야.'이다.

① 문제없어. 네가 요청하면 그녀는 만화를 그려 주실 거야.

② 동의해. 넌 네 기사를 제시간에 끝내야 해.

③ 말도 안 돼. 그녀는 이 기사에 전혀 책임이 없어.

④ 걱정하지 마. 넌 지금 바로 학교 신문을 인쇄할 수 있어.

어휘&어구 draft 초안, (아직 완성본이 아닌) 원고 print shop 인쇄소 illustration 삽화 impolite 무례한, 실례되는

---

14 직장 동료의 오해
[정답] ⑤

M Agnes, you look upset. Is there something wrong?

W Yes. Benny, can we talk for a moment?

M Of course. What's the matter?

W Well... actually, it's about Ellen. She seems to have some type of misunderstanding about me.

M Really? What do you mean?

W She seems to think she received the poor evaluation on her last annual report because of me.

M What? That's not true, you know.

W That's what I mean. I can't believe she's been making those false claims without talking to me first.

M That's strange. She's usually communicative and sensible. If she had thought you were the reason for her bad evaluation, she would've discussed it with you.

W I think so, too. I don't know what to do.

M Why don't you have an honest talk with Ellen about the problem?

남 Agnes, 기분이 안 좋아 보이네요. 잘못된 일이라도 있어요?

여 네. Benny, 잠깐 동안 얘기 나눌 수 있을까요?

남 물론이지요. 뭐가 문제인가요?

여 저… 실은, Ellen에 관한 일이에요. 그녀가 저에 관해서 어떤 종류의 오해를 하는 것 같아요.

남 정말인가요? 무슨 뜻이에요?

여 그녀는 저 때문에 지난 연차 보고서에서 안 좋은 평가를 받았다고 생각하는 것 같아요.

남 뭐라고요? 당신도 알다시피, 그건 사실이 아니잖아요.

여 제 말이 바로 그거예요. 그녀가 저에게 먼저 얘기하지도 않고, 그런 잘못된 주장을 하고 있다니 믿을 수가 없어요.

남 그거 이상하네요. 그녀는 보통 솔직하고 분별이 있지요. 만일 그녀가 자신에 대한 안 좋은 평가가 당신 때문이라고 생각했다면, 그것에 대해 당신과 논의했을 거예요.

여 저도 역시 그렇게 생각해요. 어떻게 해야 할지 모르겠어요.

남 그 문제에 대해서 Ellen과 솔직한 대화를 나눠 보는 것이 어때요?

문제 해설 직장 동료 Ellen이 자신에 관해 오해하는 것 같다는 여자의 말에 남자가 Ellen은 솔직하고 분별이 있다고 하면서 Ellen에 대한 안 좋은 평가가 여자 때문이라고 생각했다면 그것에 대해 Ellen이 여자와 논의했을 거라고 말한다. 여자가 남자의 생각에 동의하면서 어떻게 해야 할지 모르겠다고 말하고 있으므로, 이에 대한 남자의 응답으로 가장 적절한 것은 ⑤ '그 문제에 대해서 Ellen과 솔직한 대화를 나눠 보는 것이 어때요?'이다.

① 최근 당신의 형편없는 업무수행에 관해서 당신에게 얘기하고 싶습니다.

② 당신이 먼저 그녀에게 가서 사과해야 한다고 생각하지 않으세요?

③ 아, 안 돼요. 누구나 자신의 의견을 표현할 권리를 가지고 있어요.

④ Ellen의 연차 보고서에 대해 공정한 평가를 했어야 했어요.

어휘&어구 for a moment 잠깐 동안 misunderstanding 오해 evaluation 평가 annual report 연차 보고서 false 잘못된, 거짓된 claim 주장; 주장하다, 요구하다 communicative 솔직한, 터놓고 이야기하는 sensible 분별[양식]이 있는

---

15 분실한 지갑 습득 확인하기
[정답] ②

M Austin stops at a grocery store on his way home to pick up some milk. To pay for the milk, he takes his wallet out of his pocket and hands the cashier his credit card. The cashier

남 Austin은 우유를 좀 사기 위해 집으로 가는 도중에 식료품점에 잠시 들릅니다. 우윳값을 내기 위해 그는 자신의 주머니에서 지갑을 꺼내고 계산대 직원에게 자신의 신용 카드를 건네줍니다. 계산대

gives Austin his credit card back, and Austin puts his wallet in his pocket. When he gets home, he puts his hand in his pocket to take out his wallet. Suddenly, he realizes that his wallet isn't in his pocket. He searches his other pockets and can't find it. He thinks about when he last used his wallet and remembers it was at the grocery store, so he quickly goes back to the store. At the grocery store, Austin wants to ask the cashier if he has seen his wallet. In this situation, what would Austin most likely say to the cashier?

Austin Excuse me, have you seen a wallet here?

직원은 Austin에게 신용 카드를 돌려주고, Austin은 지갑을 주머니에 넣습니다. 집에 도착했을 때 그는 지갑을 꺼내기 위해 자기 손을 주머니에 넣습니다. 갑자기 그는 자기 지갑이 주머니에 없다는 것을 알게 됩니다. 그는 다른 주머니들을 뒤져 보지만 그것을 찾을 수 없습니다. 그는 자신이 언제 마지막으로 지갑을 사용했는지 생각하고 그것이 식료품점에서였다고 기억해 내서 재빨리 그 가게로 돌아갑니다. 식료품점에서 Austin은 계산대 직원에게 그가 자기 지갑을 보았는지 물어보고 싶습니다. 이런 상황에서 Austin은 계산대 직원에게 뭐라고 말하겠습니까?

Austin 실례합니다, 여기서 지갑 하나를 보셨습니까?

문제 해설 식료품점에서 마지막으로 주머니에서 지갑을 꺼냈던 Austin이 집에 도착했을 때 지갑이 없어진 것을 알고 식료품점으로 다시 가서 계산대 직원에게 자기 지갑을 보았는지 물어보고 싶어 한다. 따라서 Austin이 계산대 직원에게 할 말로 가장 적절한 것은 ② '실례합니다, 여기서 지갑 하나를 보셨습니까?'이다.
① 나 대신 식료품점에 갈 수 있나요?
③ 그것을 분실물 보관소에 두어야 한다고 생각해요.
④ 아까 여기 왔을 때 깜빡 잊고 제 우유를 안 가져갔어요.
⑤ 바닥에서 발견한 이 지갑을 어떻게 해야 하나요?

어휘&어구 stop at ~에 잠시 들르다 pick up ~을 사다 wallet 지갑 cashier 계산대 직원 lost and found 분실물 보관소 floor 바닥

16~17 멸종 위기에 처한 식품

[정답] 16 ② 17 ④

W Hello, everyone. Last class, we learned about the causes of climate change. Today we're going to talk about how climate change will have a negative impact on our food production. Endangered lists are no longer just for animals. The following foods are so-called "endangered foods." One of them is coffee. Coffee plantations in South America, Africa, and `Hawaii are being threatened by rising air temperatures and unstable rainfall patterns. Second, peanuts require consistently warm temperatures and 20 to 40 inches of rain over five months. Because of long-term droughts, these plants are finding it very difficult to stay alive. Third, wheat is becoming endangered, too. In the coming decades, at least one-quarter of the world's wheat production will be lost. Lastly, climate change is affecting the world's aquaculture as well. As the water temperature rises, salmon populations will decline because they depend on cold water for reproduction. Now let's have a look at some graphs of recent global changes in temperature.

여 안녕하세요, 여러분. 지난 수업 시간에 우리는 기후 변화의 원인에 대해 학습했습니다. 오늘은 기후 변화가 우리의 식품 생산에 어떻게 부정적인 영향을 미치게 될 것인지에 대해 이야기해 보겠습니다. 멸종 위기 목록은 더 이상 동물에게만 해당하지 않습니다. 다음의 식품은 이른바 '멸종 위기 식품'입니다. 그중 하나는 커피입니다. 남아메리카, 아프리카, 그리고 하와이의 커피 농장은 대기 온도 상승과 불안정한 강우 패턴으로 위협받고 있습니다. 둘째, 땅콩은 지속해서 따뜻한 온도와 5개월 넘게 20에서 40인치의 비가 필요합니다. 장기간의 가뭄 때문에, 이 식물은 연명하기에 매우 어려움을 겪고 있습니다. 셋째, 밀 또한 멸종 위기에 처해 있습니다. 앞으로 수십 년 후에, 세계 밀 생산의 최소 4분의 1은 사라질 것입니다. 마지막으로, 기후 변화는 세계의 수산 양식에도 또한 영향을 미치고 있습니다. 수온이 올라감에 따라, 연어 개체 수가 감소할 것인데, 그것들은 번식을 위해 차가운 물에 의존하기 때문입니다. 이제 최근의 세계 기온 변화에 대한 그래프를 좀 살펴봅시다.

문제 해설 **16** 기후 변화가 식품 생산에 어떻게 부정인 영향을 미치는지에 관해 설명하고 있으므로, 여자가 하는 말의 주제로 가장 적절한 것은 ② '기후 변화로 위협받는 식품'이다.
① 식품 생산을 증가시키는 방법
③ 유기농 식품을 먹는 영양상의 이점
④ 기후 변화가 인간의 건강에 미치는 영향
⑤ 기후 변화와 해수면 상승의 세계적인 추세
17 커피, 땅콩, 밀, 연어는 언급되었지만, 쌀은 언급되지 않았으므로, 언급된 식품이 아닌 것은 ④ '쌀'이다.

어휘&어구 endangered 멸종 위기에 처한 plantation (커피, 설탕 등을 재배하는 대규모) 농장 unstable 불안정한 rainfall 강우 consistently 지속해서, 끊임없이 drought 가뭄 wheat 밀 aquaculture 수산 양식 salmon 연어 reproduction 번식, 생식

9회 **수능실전 대비연습**

01 ②　02 ⑤　03 ⑤　04 ④　05 ③　06 ④　07 ②　08 ④　09 ⑤　10 ③　11 ①　12 ④　13 ④　14 ⑤
15 ④　16 ①　17 ④

---

01 스쿨버스 안전 수칙 관련 설문지 응답 요청 [정답] ②

M Hello, students. I'm John Edwards from the school office. We're always trying to find ways to improve your safety during your school bus commute. So we would appreciate it if you could fill out a survey about your school bus experience. The survey sheet has been mailed to your home. It consists of 20 questions that ask about your perception of safety rules related to waiting for the bus, boarding the bus, being on the bus, and getting off the bus. Your answers will be very helpful in determining how we can make riding the bus safer for you. After filling out the survey, please submit it to your homeroom teacher. Thank you for your cooperation.

남 안녕하세요, 학생 여러분. 저는 교무실의 John Edwards입니다. 우리는 여러분이 스쿨버스로 통학하는 동안 여러분의 안전을 개선할 방법을 찾으려고 항상 노력하고 있습니다. 그래서 여러분의 스쿨버스 경험에 관한 설문에 응답해 주면 고맙겠습니다. 설문지는 여러분 가정으로 우송되었습니다. 그것은 버스를 기다리는 것, 버스 타는 것, 버스에 있는 것, 그리고 버스에서 내리는 것과 관련된 안전 수칙에 관한 여러분의 인식에 대해 묻는 20개의 질문으로 구성되어 있습니다. 여러분의 응답이 우리가 어떻게 여러분을 위해 버스에 타는 것을 더 안전하게 만들 수 있는지를 알아내는 데 아주 도움이 될 것입니다. 설문에 응답한 후에 그것을 담임 선생님께 제출해 주십시오. 협조에 감사드립니다.

문제 해설 남자는 학생들에게 스쿨버스의 안전 수칙과 관련된 설문지를 이미 가정으로 우송했으며 설문에 응답한 후에 담임 선생님께 제출해 달라고 요청하고 있다. 따라서 남자가 하는 말의 목적으로 가장 적절한 것은 ② '스쿨버스 안전 수칙 관련 설문지 응답을 요청하려고'이다.

어휘&어구 school office 교무실　improve 개선하다　safety 안전　commute 통학, 통근　appreciate 고마워하다　fill out (~의 기재 사항을) 기입하다, (서류 양식을) 작성하다　survey 설문, 조사　sheet (종이) 한 장　consist of ~로 구성되다　perception 인식　related to ~과 관련된　board (버스·배·비행기 등에) 타다　homeroom teacher 담임 교사　cooperation 협조, 협력

---

02 그림을 그려 주는 대신 아이가 직접 느낀 것을 표현하도록 돕기 [정답] ⑤

W Alex, how's your son these days?

M He's into drawing, so he often asks me to draw pictures. This morning I drew trees for him.

W I don't think it's a good idea to draw pictures for him. Instead, you should help him express what he feels for himself.

M What do you mean?

W Children learn the world through direct experiences by exploring with their eyes, their hands, and their senses.

M Right. But I still don't understand why drawing trees for him is a problem.

W Imagine how children will feel the tree. Leaves, trunks, branches.... Each child will feel the tree in his own way.

M You mean the tree the child experiences is different from the tree I draw?

W Exactly. When you draw a tree for him, he'll practice imitating his father's tree, not the tree he felt.

M You've got a point.

W The next time he asks you to draw something, encourage him to express his feelings for himself instead of saying

여 Alex, 당신의 아들은 요즘 어떻게 지내요?

남 그 애는 그림 그리는 데 빠져 있어서, 자주 저한테 그림을 그려 달라고 부탁해요. 오늘 아침에는 개한테 나무를 그려 주었어요.

여 아이에게 그림을 그려 주는 것은 좋은 생각이 아닌 것 같아요. 대신, 개가 느끼는 것을 자신이 직접 표현하도록 도와주어야 해요.

남 무슨 말씀이시죠?

여 아이들은 자신의 눈과 자신의 손, 그리고 자신의 감각들을 가지고 탐구함으로써 직접 경험을 통해 세상을 배우잖아요.

남 맞아요. 하지만 개한테 나무를 그려 주는 것이 왜 문제가 되는지 여전히 이해가 되지 않네요.

여 아이들이 나무를 어떻게 느낄지 상상해 보세요. 나뭇잎, 나무의 몸통, 가지…. 아이들은 각자 저마다의 방식으로 나무를 느낄 거예요.

남 아이가 경험하는 나무는 제가 그리는 나무와 다르다는 말씀인가요?

여 바로 그거예요. 당신이 아이에게 나무를 그려 주면, 개는 자기가 느낀 나무가 아니라, 아빠의 나무를 모방하는 연습을 할 거예요.

남 당신 말씀이 일리가 있네요.

여 다음에 아이가 뭔가를 그려 달라고 할 때는 '그래'라는 말 대신 아이가 스스로 자신의 감정을 표현할 수 있도록 격려해 주세요.

남 알겠어요.

"yes."

M I got it.

문제 해설 여자는 아들에게 나무를 그려 주었다는 남자의 말에, 그것은 좋은 생각이 아니며 아이가 직접 느낀 것을 표현하도록 도와주어야 한다고 하면서, 나무를 그려 주면 아이는 자기가 느낀 나무가 아니라 아빠의 나무를 모방하는 연습을 할 거라고 말한다. 따라서 여자의 의견으로 가장 적절한 것은 ⑤ '그림을 그려 주는 대신 아이가 느낀 것을 스스로 표현하게 도와야 한다.'이다.

어휘&어구 be into ~에 빠져 있다 explore 탐구하다, 탐험하다 trunk 나무의 몸통, 줄기 imitate 모방하다, 흉내 내다

03 남편의 생명을 구해 준 택시 기사   [정답] ⑤

[Cell phone rings.]

M Hello?

W Hello. May I speak to Mark Green?

M Speaking. May I ask who's calling?

W My name is Amy. You're the taxi driver who found the man who fainted on the street and reported it to 911, right?

M Yes, I'm him.

W I'm his wife. I called 911 and found out your phone number because I really wanted to thank you.

M Oh, I'm glad to have helped. How is your husband?

W He's okay thanks to you. The doctor said my husband might have been in big trouble if he had arrived a little later.

M I'm glad to hear he's better.

W My husband also wants to send you a thank-you gift.

M He doesn't have to do that. I just did what I had to do.

W Hmm, really?

M Of course. I just hope your husband keeps getting better.

[휴대 전화가 울린다.]

남 여보세요?

여 안녕하세요. Mark Green 씨와 통화할 수 있을까요?

남 접니다. 전화하신 분은 누구시죠?

여 제 이름은 Amy입니다. 길에서 기절한 남자를 발견하고 911에 신고해 주신 택시 기사님, 맞으시죠?

남 네, 제가 그 사람입니다.

여 저는 그 사람의 아내입니다. 감사 인사를 정말 드리고 싶어서 제가 911에 전화해서 기사님 전화번호를 알아냈습니다.

남 아, 도움을 드려서 기쁘네요. 남편은 어떠신가요?

여 기사님 덕분에 괜찮습니다. 조금 더 늦게 도착했으면 그 사람이 큰 곤경에 처했을지도 모른다고 의사 선생님께서 말씀하셨습니다.

남 남편께서 나아지셨다니 기쁘네요.

여 제 남편도 감사 선물을 기사님께 보내드리고 싶어 합니다.

남 그러실 필요 없습니다. 제가 해야 할 일을 했을 뿐입니다.

여 음, 정말이세요?

남 물론입니다. 저는 그저 남편분께서 계속 더 좋아지시기를 바랄 뿐입니다.

문제 해설 여자는 길에서 기절한 남편을 911에 신고해 줘서 도움을 준 택시 기사의 전화번호를 911을 통해 알아낸 뒤 그에게 전화를 걸어 감사 인사를 전하고 있다. 따라서 두 사람의 관계를 가장 잘 나타낸 것은 ⑤ '응급 환자 신고자 – 환자 가족'이다.

어휘&어구 faint 기절하다 report 신고하다, 알리다 keep -ing 계속해서 ~하다

04 산 밑에 있는 식당   [정답] ④

W Tommy, we made it back to the foot of the mountain. That was a fun hike, wasn't it?

M Yeah, I loved it. Now I'm starving. How about eating at this restaurant?

W Okay. They have a menu on the outside wall. They serve various kinds of food.

M That's great. And there is a tree in the dining area. It seems to block out the sun.

W Yes. Why don't we take the empty round table surrounding the tree?

M All right. Look, the bear statue is holding a welcome sign.

W The statue is fitting because there used to be a lot of bears in this area.

M I didn't know that. Look at the vegetable garden with the fence. They probably cook with what they grow here.

W The food must be really fresh.

여 Tommy, 우린 산 밑으로 돌아왔어요. 재미있는 하이킹이었어요, 그렇죠?

남 그래요, 정말 좋았어요. 이제 몹시 배고프군요. 이 식당에서 식사하는 게 어때요?

여 좋아요. 바깥벽에 메뉴판이 있어요. 다양한 음식이 제공되네요.

남 그거 좋네요. 그리고 식사 공간에 나무가 한 그루 있네요. 그것이 햇빛을 차단하는 것 같아요.

여 맞아요. 그 나무를 둘러싸고 있는 빈 둥근 식탁에 앉는 것이 어때요?

남 좋아요. 보세요, 곰 조각상이 환영 표지판을 들고 있어요.

여 이 지역에는 곰이 많았으니 그 조각상이 잘 어울리네요.

남 저는 그것을 몰랐어요. 울타리가 있는 채소밭을 보세요. 아마 그들이 여기에서 재배하는 것을 가지고 요리하나 봐요.

여 음식이 정말 신선하겠어요.

남 그래요, 어서 먹어 보고 싶군요. 우리 이제 식탁에 앉아요.

여 좋아요.

M Yeah, I can't wait to try it. Let's get seated at the table now.

W Okay.

문제 해설 남자는 곰 조각상이 환영 표지판을 들고 있다고 말했는데, 그림에는 곰 조각상이 환영 표지판을 들고 있지 않다. 따라서 그림에서 대화의 내용과 일치하지 않는 것은 ④이다.

어휘&어구 starving 몹시 배고픈 statue 조각상 vegetable garden 채소밭

---

05 과학 박람회 준비 [정답] ③

M Hi, Ms. Kane. How's everything going for tomorrow's science fair?	남 안녕하세요, Kane 선생님. 내일 과학 박람회 준비는 어떻게 되어 가고 있나요?
W Hi, Mr. Anderson. I just finished confirming the project display areas with the school administration.	여 안녕하세요, Anderson 선생님. 저는 방금 학교 행정부와 프로젝트 전시 구역 확인을 마쳤어요.
M Would you like me to help you with anything?	남 제가 뭐라도 도와드릴까요?
W That'd be fantastic. Thanks. There are still a few more things that need to be done.	여 그래 주신다면 정말 좋을 것 같아요. 감사합니다. 아직 해야 할 일이 몇 가지 더 있어요.
M Okay. Have the tables for the project displays been set up yet?	남 네. 프로젝트 전시를 위한 테이블이 설치되었나요?
W Not yet. But some students are going to do that later today.	여 아직은 아니에요. 하지만 몇몇 학생들이 오늘 늦게 그걸 할 거예요.
M All right. I noticed that none of the signs directing people where to go have been put up. Should I put them up?	남 좋아요. 제가 보니 사람들이 어디로 가야 하는지 알려 주는 표지판이 하나도 게시되어 있지 않은데요. 그것들을 게시할까요?
W I'll take care of that. Actually, it'd be really helpful if you could set up the audio equipment for the presentations.	여 제가 그걸 처리할게요. 실은, 발표를 위한 오디오 장비를 설치해 주시면 정말 도움이 될 것 같아요.
M Sure, I can handle that.	남 물론이죠, 제가 처리할 수 있어요.
W Great! Thanks so much for the help!	여 좋아요! 도와주셔서 정말 감사합니다!

문제 해설 발표를 위한 오디오 장비를 설치해 달라고 부탁하는 여자에게 남자가 자신이 처리할 수 있다고 했으므로, 남자가 할 일로 가장 적절한 것은 ③ '오디오 장비 설치하기'이다.

어휘&어구 science fair 과학 박람회 confirm 확인하다 administration 행정부 set up 설치하다 put up 게시하다 equipment 장비

---

06 애니메이션 센터 표 구매 [정답] ④

M Welcome to the Lindenberg Animation Center. Do you need tickets?	남 Lindenberg 애니메이션 센터에 오신 것을 환영합니다. 표가 필요하십니까?
W Hi. Yes, I do. I need three tickets. How much are they?	여 안녕하세요. 네, 그렇습니다. 표가 세 장 필요해요. 얼마인가요?
M General admission tickets are $10 for adults and $15 for children under 13.	남 일반 입장권은 성인이 10달러, 13세 미만 어린이는 15달러입니다.
W I need two adult tickets and one child ticket.	여 성인 표 두 장과 어린이 표 한 장이 필요해요.
M All right, so that's three tickets in total.	남 좋아요, 그럼 총 세 장이군요.
W Yes. We're also interested in the Stop Motion Animation Workshop. Is that included with general admission?	여 네. 저희는 스톱 모션 애니메이션 워크숍에도 관심이 있어요. 그것도 일반 입장권에 포함되어 있나요?
M No, it's not. It's an extra $5 per person.	남 아닙니다. 1인당 5달러 추가예요.
W Okay. I'd also like three tickets to the workshop.	여 네. 워크숍 표도 3장 주세요.
M All right. So, two adult and one child general admission tickets, and three workshop tickets, right?	남 좋습니다. 그러면 일반 입장권 성인 2장, 어린이 1장, 그리고 워크숍 표 3장이죠, 그렇죠?
W Yes, that's correct. Here's my credit card.	여 네, 맞습니다. 여기 제 신용 카드가 있습니다.

문제 해설 여자는 10달러짜리 성인 일반 입장권 2장과 15달러짜리 어린이 입장권 1장, 5달러짜리 워크숍 표 3장을 샀다. 따라서 여자가 지불할 금액은 ④ '50달러'이다.

07 취업 박람회
[정답] ②

W	Hi, Jack. Where are you going?	여	안녕, Jack. 어디 가는 중이니?
M	Hi, Sandra. I'm on my way to the school gym.	남	안녕, Sandra. 학교 체육관에 가는 중이야.
W	Oh, for your basketball club?	여	아, 네 농구 동아리 때문에?
M	No. I actually quit the basketball club.	남	아니. 실은 농구 동아리를 그만뒀어.
W	Really? I thought you really liked basketball.	여	정말이니? 네가 정말로 농구를 좋아한다고 생각했었는데.
M	I did. And I still like it. But I quit to join the soccer club. I recently realized how much I love playing soccer.	남	그랬었지. 그리고 아직도 좋아해. 하지만 축구 동아리에 가입하기 위해 그만뒀어. 최근에 내가 축구를 하는 것을 얼마나 많이 좋아하는지 깨달았어.
W	That's cool. Then why are you going to the gym?	여	그거 멋지네. 그러면 체육관에는 왜 가니?
M	There's a job fair today and tomorrow. Don't you know about it?	남	오늘과 내일 취업 박람회가 있어. 그것에 대해 모르니?
W	Oh, yeah, that's right. I know about it.	여	아, 응, 맞아. 그것에 대해 알고 있어.
M	I just want to see what it's like. Maybe I'll find something I'm interested in.	남	그것이 어떤지 그저 보고 싶어. 어쩌면 내가 관심 있는 것을 찾을지도 몰라.
W	That's a good idea. I'd also like to go, but I have to finish a big history report by Monday.	여	좋은 생각이네. 나도 가고 싶지만, 중요한 역사 보고서를 월요일까지 끝내야 해.
M	I see. See you later.	남	알겠어. 나중에 보자.

문제 해설 여자가 남자에게 체육관에 가는 이유를 묻자, 남자는 취업 박람회가 있어서 보고 싶어서 간다고 말하고 있으므로 남자가 체육관에 가는 이유는 ② '취업 박람회를 둘러보려고'이다.

어휘&어구 gym 체육관 (= gymnasium) quit 그만두다 job fair 취업 박람회 big 중요한

08 Old Town Trolley Tour
[정답] ④

W	Honey, since we're going to Queen's City next week, I was thinking it'd be fun to take the Old Town Trolley Tour.	여	여보, 우리 다음 주에 Queen's City에 가니까, Old Town Trolley Tour를 하는 것이 재미있을 것 같아요.
M	That's a fantastic idea! Do you have any details about the tour?	남	멋진 생각이에요! 투어에 대한 세부 사항을 알고 있어요?
W	Yeah, I checked their website. The tour covers the main attractions of Queen's City. It takes you around the historic downtown area, the waterfront, and other popular landmarks.	여	네, 그 웹사이트를 확인했어요. 그 투어는 Queen's City의 주요 명소를 포함해요. 그걸로 역사적인 도심 지역, 해안가, 그리고 다른 유명한 랜드마크들을 돌아볼 수 있어요.
M	Cool! How long does the tour last?	남	멋져요! 투어는 얼마나 걸리죠?
W	It lasts about 90 minutes.	여	90분 정도 걸려요.
M	That's perfect. And how much does it cost?	남	완벽해요. 그리고 그것의 요금은 얼마죠?
W	Tickets are $50 per person.	여	표는 1인당 50달러예요.
M	That's not bad at all. How do we get tickets for the tour?	남	전혀 나쁘지 않네요. 투어 표는 어떻게 구하나요?
W	We can book them on their website. Should we do that now?	여	그 웹사이트에서 예약할 수 있어요. 지금 할까요?
M	Sure! I'm already looking forward to the tour!	남	물론이죠! 벌써부터 투어가 기대되네요!

문제 해설 Old Town Trolley Tour에 관해 경유지, 소요 시간, 요금, 예약 방법에 대해서는 언급되었으나, ④ '참가 가능 인원수'는 언급되지 않았다.

어휘&어구 cover 포함하다, 다루다 attraction 명소 historic 역사적인 waterfront 해안가 landmark 랜드마크, 주요 지형지물 book 예약하다 look forward to ~을 기대하다

09 Benton Cheese Village Experience

[정답] ⑤

W Attention, everyone! I'm Sarah Lee, the manager of Benton Cheese Village, and I'm excited to tell you about our Benton Cheese Village Experience. Starting in August, we're inviting you to join us every Saturday for an exciting adventure. The day starts off with a hands-on cheese-making experience where you'll learn how to milk the cows and mold the cheese! Sounds fun, right? But that's not all! You'll also have a chance to feed the adorable animals in our village. Delicious pizza will be provided for lunch, and you'll be able to try a variety of our cheeses. Wondering how to get tickets? You must book them online. Tickets are not sold on site. So visit our website at www.bentoncheesevillage.com, today!

여 모두 주목하세요! 저는 Benton Cheese Village의 관리자 Sarah Lee이며, 저희 Benton Cheese Village Experience에 대해 알려 드리게 되어 기쁩니다. 8월부터 시작하여, 매주 토요일에 신나는 모험을 즐기실 수 있도록 여러분을 초대합니다. 소의 우유를 짜고 치즈를 만드는 방법을 배울 수 있는, 치즈 만들기를 직접 해 보는 체험으로 하루가 시작됩니다! 재미있겠죠, 그렇죠? 하지만 그게 다가 아닙니다! 여러분은 또한 우리 마을의 사랑스러운 동물들에게 먹이를 줄 수 있는 기회를 가질 것입니다. 점심 식사로 맛있는 피자가 제공되며, 여러분은 우리의 다양한 치즈를 맛볼 수 있을 것입니다. 입장권을 어떻게 구하는지 궁금하신가요? 온라인으로 그것을 예약해야 합니다. 입장권은 현장에서 판매하지 않습니다. 그러니 오늘 저희 웹사이트 www.bentoncheesevillage.com을 방문하세요!

문제 해설 입장권은 현장에서 판매하지 않는다고 했으므로, 담화의 내용과 일치하지 않는 것은 ⑤ '입장권은 온라인 예매와 현장 구매 모두 가능하다.' 이다.

어휘&어구 manager 관리자 adventure 모험 hands-on 직접 해 보는 mold (부드러운 재료를 단단히 다지거나 틀에 넣어) 만들다 feed 먹이를 주다 adorable 사랑스러운 provide 제공하다 a variety of 다양한 on site 현장에서

10 창문 블라인드 주문

[정답] ③

M Hi, Amy. I'm trying to buy window blinds for my bedroom on this website. Can you help me?

W Sure. Do you have a particular material in mind?

M Not really. I just don't want wood. It's weak to moisture and humidity.

W I agree. It can also split over time. And what's your budget?

M I don't want to spend more than $60.

W Okay. And there are two types, horizontal or vertical. It depends on the size of your window and how it opens.

M My bedroom window is really big and wide, and it slides open.

W A vertical one will be better, then.

M Okay. I'll go with a vertical type.

W Do you think you need light-blocking blinds?

M Definitely. I want to be able to keep my bedroom dark in the morning.

W Then you should go with this model.

M Good. I'll order it right now. Thanks.

남 안녕하세요, Amy. 제가 이 웹사이트에서 침실용 창문 블라인드를 구입하려고 하는데요. 절 도와주실 수 있나요?

여 그럼요. 생각해 두고 계신 특정한 소재가 있나요?

남 그렇지는 않아요. 그저 나무는 아니면 좋겠어요. 그것은 수분과 습기에 약해서요.

여 동의해요. 그것은 시간이 지나면서 갈라질 수도 있어요. 그리고 예산은 어느 정도예요?

남 60달러 넘게 쓰고 싶지 않아요.

여 좋아요. 그리고 가로형 또는 세로형의 두 가지 유형이 있네요. 그것은 창문의 크기와 열리는 방법에 의해 결정되죠.

남 제 침실 창문은 정말로 크고 넓고, 미닫이로 열려요.

여 그럼 세로형이 더 좋을 거예요.

남 좋아요. 세로형을 선택할게요.

여 빛을 차단하는 블라인드가 필요하다고 생각하세요?

남 물론이에요. 전 아침에 침실을 어둡게 유지할 수 있기를 바라요.

여 그럼 이 모델로 선택하셔야겠네요.

남 좋아요. 지금 바로 그것을 주문할게요. 고마워요.

문제 해설 남자가 블라인드 소재가 나무는 아니면 좋겠다고 했고, 예산은 60달러 넘게 쓰고 싶지 않다고 했으며, 여자가 세로형을 추천하자 남자가 그것을 선택했고 빛 차단 기능을 원한다고 말했다. 따라서 남자가 주문할 창문 블라인드는 ③이다.

어휘&어구 particular 특정한 material 소재, 재료 moisture 수분 humidity 습기 split 갈라지다, 쪼개지다 over time 시간이 지나면서 budget 예산 horizontal 가로의 vertical 세로의 light-blocking 빛을 차단하는

11 계란 구매

M	Sandy, I'm going to head over to the farmers' market in a little bit. Is there anything you need?
W	Oh, actually, there is. Would you mind picking up some eggs for me?
M	Not at all. Any specific type of eggs you prefer?
W	Not really. Just regular ones will do.

남	Sandy, 조금 있다가 제가 농산물 직판장에 갈 거예요. 뭐 필요한 것 있나요?
여	아, 사실 있어요. 계란 좀 사다 주시겠어요?
남	그럼요. 선호하는 특정 종류의 계란이 있나요?
여	그런 건 아니에요. 그냥 일반적인 것이면 돼요.

문제 해설 농산물 직판장에 가려고 하면서 필요한 게 있는지 묻는 남자에게 여자는 계란을 사다 달라고 하고, 이에 남자가 선호하는 특정 종류의 계란이 있는지 물었다. 따라서 이에 대한 여자의 응답으로 가장 적절한 것은 ① '그런 건 아니에요. 그냥 일반적인 것이면 돼요.'이다.

② 네. 오늘은 농산물 직판장이 열렸어요.
③ 좋아요. 제가 꼭 큰 것들로 가져다드릴게요.
④ 말도 안 돼요. 아침 식사로 계란을 먹고 싶지 않아요.
⑤ 신경 쓰지 마세요. 저는 이런 것들을 먹어 본 적이 없어요.

어휘&어구 head over to ~로 가다   farmers' market 농산물 직판장   specific 특정한

12 휴대용 컴퓨터 수리

W	I've had nothing but problems with my new laptop. It keeps shutting down unexpectedly.
M	Really? And you just got it a few weeks ago. Have you taken it to a repair shop?
W	Yes, I have. But they said they couldn't find any issues with it and said it's functioning properly.
M	That's frustrating. Maybe you should ask for a replacement.

여	저의 새 휴대용 컴퓨터에 문제만 있어 왔어요. 예기치 않게 계속 종료돼요.
남	그래요? 몇 주 전에 그것을 샀잖아요. 그걸 수리점에 가져가 봤나요?
여	네, 가져가 봤어요. 하지만 그들은 그것에 대한 어떤 문제도 찾을 수 없었고 제대로 작동하고 있다고 말했어요.
남	그거 답답하군요. 당신은 교환을 요청해야 할 것 같네요.

문제 해설 새 휴대용 컴퓨터가 예기치 않게 종료된다는 여자에게 남자는 그것을 수리점에 가져가 봤는지 묻고, 여자는 가져가 봤지만 그들이 문제를 찾을 수 없다고 말했다고 답했다. 따라서 이에 대한 남자의 응답으로 가장 적절한 것은 ④ '그거 답답하군요. 당신은 교환을 요청해야 할 것 같네요.'이다.

① 멋져요! 그 휴대용 컴퓨터가 제대로 작동하고 있다니 기쁘네요.
② 안됐군요. 당신은 즉시 수리점에 가야 해요.
③ 왜 아니죠? 당신의 새 휴대용 컴퓨터가 예전 것보다 더 좋아요.
⑤ 걱정하지 마세요. 수리하는 데 단지 이틀 정도 걸릴 거라고 확신해요.

어휘&어구 unexpectedly 예기치 않게   repair shop 수리점   issue 문제   function 작동하다   properly 제대로

13 농장 체류 프로그램

W	Honey, come and look at this ad. It's about a farm stay program.
M	Let me see. Oh, the farm is not far from here.
W	Yeah. Moreover, this overnight program costs only $300 per family, including 3 meals.
M	Sounds great! What can we do there?
W	We can dig out sweet potatoes, pick corn, make cheese, and so on. Also, we can catch fish in the nearby river.
M	Perfect! Our kids will like it.
W	Yeah. They'll have lots of fun there and learn to enjoy nature.

여	여보, 와서 이 광고를 좀 봐요. 농장 체류 프로그램에 관한 거예요.
남	한번 볼게요. 아, 농장이 여기서 멀지 않네요.
여	그래요. 게다가 이 1박 프로그램은 세 끼 식사를 포함해서 가족당 비용이 겨우 300달러예요.
남	좋아요! 우리는 거기서 무엇을 할 수 있나요?
여	고구마 캐기, 옥수수 따기, 치즈 만들기 등을 할 수 있어요. 또한, 우리는 근처에 있는 강에서 물고기를 잡을 수도 있어요.
남	완벽하네요! 우리 아이들이 그것을 좋아할 거예요.
여	그래요. 아이들은 거기서 무척 재미있는 시간을 보내고 자연을 즐기는 것을 배울 거예요.
남	틀림없이 그럴 거예요. 여보, 이번 토요일과 일요일로 그 프로그램

M I'm sure they will. Honey, why don't we apply for the program for this Saturday and Sunday?

W Okay. Let me check on the Internet if there's room left. *[Typing sound]* Hmm.... It's all booked up for this weekend.

M Would you check if there are any places left next weekend?

W There are a few available. I'll make a reservation.

을 신청하는 게 어때요?

여 좋아요. 남은 자리가 있는지 인터넷으로 확인해 볼게요. *[자판 두드리는 소리]* 흠…. 이번 주말에는 예약이 끝났네요.

남 다음 주말에 남은 자리가 있는지 확인해 줄래요?

여 (예약) 가능한 자리가 몇 개 있어요. 예약할게요.

문제 해설 두 사람은 농장 체류 프로그램이 마음에 들어 이번 토요일과 일요일로 신청을 하고자 했으나, 여자가 인터넷 검색 후 이번 주말에는 예약이 끝났다고 하자 남자가 다음 주말에 남은 자리가 있는지 확인해 달라고 했다. 따라서 여자의 응답으로 가장 적절한 것은 ④ '(예약) 가능한 자리가 몇 개 있어요. 예약할게요.'이다.

① 그래요. 다음 주말에 당신과 함께 할 수 있어요.
② 내 잘못이에요. 곧 다른 호텔을 찾아볼게요.
③ 가능해요. 당신 대신 내가 아이들을 돌볼게요.
⑤ 미안해요. 난 농장 체류 프로그램에 관심이 없어요.

어휘&어구 overnight 1박의 be all booked up 예약이 끝나다

---

14 스토리텔링이 마케팅에 미치는 영향력   [정답] ⑤

W Dave, I saw a really good documentary on TV last night.

M Oh, really? What was the name of it?

W The Age of Storytelling. It was about an experiment a journalist conducted. It was super interesting.

M What was the experiment about?

W Well, a journalist bought some objects, like a little toy, a mug, and an old pepper shaker, for about $1 each.

M They are cheap objects.

W Right. And he had creative writers invent stories about them. Then he resold the items online with their stories posted on a website.

M Ah, so he gave the items a special meaning.

W Yeah. And he could resell the items for a much higher price than he bought them for. He sold one of the items for more than $100!

M Wow! That's so amazing!

W I think the results of the experiment provide insights into marketing.

M For sure. They show the power of storytelling in marketing.

여 Dave, 어젯밤 TV에서 정말 좋은 다큐멘터리를 봤어.

남 어, 그래? 그것의 제목이 뭐였어?

여 The Age of Storytelling이었어. 그것은 한 언론인이 했던 실험에 관한 거였어. 정말 흥미로웠지.

남 무엇에 관한 실험이었니?

여 음, 한 언론인이 작은 장난감, 머그 컵, 오래된 후추통 같은 몇 개의 물건들을 개당 1달러 정도에 샀어.

남 그것들은 값싼 물건들이네.

여 맞아. 그리고 그는 창의적인 작가들에게 그것들에 대한 이야기를 지어내게 했어. 그런 다음 그는 한 웹사이트에 그 이야기들을 게시하면서 그 물품들을 되팔았지.

남 아, 그럼 그가 그 물품들에 특별한 의미를 부여했네.

여 응. 그리고 그는 그 물품들을 자기가 샀던 것보다 훨씬 더 높은 가격에 재판매할 수 있었어. 그는 그가 산 물건 중 하나를 100달러가 넘는 가격에 팔았지!

남 와! 그거 너무 놀랍다!

여 그 실험 결과가 마케팅에 관한 통찰력을 제공해 주는 것 같아.

남 물론이야. 그것이 마케팅에서의 스토리텔링의 힘을 보여 주네.

문제 해설 여자는 남자에게 값싼 물품들에 이야기로 특별한 의미를 부여하여 더 비싼 값에 판매했던 한 언론인의 실험에 대한 이야기를 들려준 후 그 실험 결과가 마케팅에 관한 통찰력을 제공해 주고 있는 것 같다고 말하고 있다. 따라서 여자의 마지막 말에 대한 남자의 응답으로 가장 적절한 것은 ⑤ '물론이야. 그것이 마케팅에서의 스토리텔링의 힘을 보여 주네.'이다.

① 물론이야. 물건을 온라인으로 사는 것이 더 편리해.
② 괜찮아. 난 곧 그 다큐멘터리를 직접 볼 거야.
③ 걱정 마. 우리는 그 품목들을 더 비싼 가격에 되팔 수 있어.
④ 맞아. 그 물건들에 대해 이야기를 지어내는 건 틀림없이 어려울 거야.

어휘&어구 documentary 다큐멘터리 journalist 언론인 conduct (특정한 활동을) 하다, 수행하다 object 물건 invent 지어내다, 발명하다 resell 되팔다 item 물품 insight 통찰력

M Cathy's family recently moved to a new house, so she had to transfer to a new high school. Her new friends are really kind, so she's happy. But there's one disappointing thing about her new school. She likes physics and wants to major in it when she goes to college, but her new school doesn't have advanced physics classes she wants to take. One day, she tells Mr. Carpenter, her science teacher, about her disappointment. He tells her that the city provides online courses for students, including advanced physics courses. Cathy decides to sign up for the online advanced physics course, so she wants to ask Mr. Carpenter the way she can take the course. In this situation, what would Cathy most likely say to Mr. Carpenter?

Cathy Could you tell me how to take the online advanced physics course?

남 Cathy의 가족은 최근에 새집으로 이사를 하였고, 그래서 그녀는 새로운 고등학교로 전학을 가야만 했습니다. 그녀의 새 친구들은 정말 친절해서, 그녀는 행복합니다. 하지만 그녀의 새 학교에는 한 가지 실망스러운 점이 있습니다. 그녀는 물리학을 좋아하고 대학에 가면 물리학을 전공하고 싶어 하지만, 그녀의 새 학교에는 그녀가 수강하고 싶은 고급 물리학 과목이 없습니다. 어느 날, 그녀는 과학 선생님인 Carpenter 선생님에게 그녀의 실망에 대해 이야기합니다. 선생님은 시에서 고급 물리학 과목을 포함한 학생들을 위한 온라인 강좌를 제공한다고 그녀에게 말합니다. Cathy는 온라인 고급 물리학 강좌를 신청하기로 결심해서 Carpenter 선생님에게 그 강좌를 수강할 수 있는 방법을 여쭤보기를 원합니다. 이런 상황에서 Cathy는 Carpenter 선생님에게 뭐라고 말하겠습니까?

Cathy 온라인 고급 물리학 강좌를 수강하는 방법을 저에게 알려 주시겠어요?

문제 해설 Cathy의 가족이 새집으로 이사하여, 그녀는 전학을 가게 되었는데, 새 학교에는 그녀가 수강하고 싶은 고급 물리학 수업이 없다. 그래서 과학 선생님인 Carpenter 선생님에게 이것에 대해 말했더니, 선생님은 시에서 운영하는 온라인 강좌를 수강하면 된다는 사실을 알려 주었다. 이에 Cathy는 그 강좌를 수강하는 방법을 Carpenter 선생님에게 묻고 싶어 한다. 이런 상황에서 Cathy가 Carpenter 선생님에게 할 말로 가장 적절한 것은 ④ '온라인 고급 물리학 강좌를 수강하는 방법을 저에게 알려 주시겠어요?'이다.

① 어느 대학에 가장 좋은 물리학 프로그램이 있다고 생각하세요?

② 온라인 강좌가 저에게 너무 어려울 것 같은가요?

③ 선생님의 물리학 강좌를 위한 교재를 저에게 알려 주시겠어요?

⑤ 고급 물리학 강좌에서 더 좋은 성적을 얻으려면 어떻게 해야 하나요?

어휘&어구 transfer 전학하다 disappointing 실망스러운 advanced 고급의 physics 물리학

16~17 식물의 환경 적응 [정답] 16 ① 17 ④

W Hello, students. Have you ever wondered how plants can survive in extreme conditions? Today, we're going to explore the amazing ways in which plants adjust and thrive in various environments. First, water lilies have adapted to live in aquatic habitats. Their wide leaves and air-filled spaces allow them to float, while their roots absorb nutrients from the water. Second, aloes are plants that thrive in dry conditions. They have adapted by storing water in their thick leaves, allowing them to survive long periods of drought. Third, mangroves are trees that grow in saltwater environments along coastlines. They have roots that can tolerate high salt concentrations and specialized structures to get oxygen from soil soaked with water. Lastly, Joshua trees can be found in vast, extremely dry deserts. With reduced leaves and an extensive root system, Joshua trees can efficiently collect water from deep underground. Now let's watch a short video about these amazing plants.

여 안녕하세요, 학생 여러분. 식물이 극한의 조건에서 어떻게 살아남을 수 있는지 의문을 가져 본 적이 있으신가요? 오늘, 우리는 식물이 다양한 환경에서 적응하고 번성하는 놀라운 방법을 탐구할 것입니다. 첫째, 수련은 수생 서식지에서 살도록 적응했습니다. 그것들의 넓은 잎과 공기로 가득 찬 공간은 뿌리가 물에서 영양분을 흡수하는 동안 그것들이 떠 있을 수 있게 해 줍니다. 둘째, 알로에는 건조한 환경에서 잘 자라는 식물입니다. 그것들은 긴 기간의 가뭄에서 살아남을 수 있도록 두꺼운 잎에 물을 저장함으로써 적응했습니다. 셋째, 맹그로브는 해안선을 따라 해수 환경에서 자라는 나무입니다. 그것들은 높은 염분 농도를 견딜 수 있는 뿌리와 물에 적셔진 흙에서 산소를 얻기 위해 특화된 구조를 가지고 있습니다. 마지막으로, Joshua 나무는 광대한, 매우 건조한 사막에서 발견될 수 있습니다. 작아진 잎과 광범위한 뿌리 시스템으로, Joshua 나무는 지하 깊은 곳에서 효율적으로 물을 모을 수 있습니다. 이제 이 놀라운 식물들에 대한 짧은 비디오를 봅시다.

문제 해설 **16** 여자는 몇 가지 예를 통해 다양한 식물들이 각각 다양한 환경에서 어떻게 적응하는지 설명하고 있으므로, 여자가 하는 말의 주제로 가장 적

절한 것은 ① '식물이 다양한 환경에 적응하는 방법'이다.

② 식물이 동물로부터 자신을 보호하는 방법

③ 실내용 화초를 건강하게 유지하기 위해 해야 할 일

④ 식물이 환경에 중요한 이유

⑤ 실외 식물이 실내 식물보다 더 잘 자라는 이유

17 수련, 알로에, 맹그로브, Joshua 나무는 언급되었지만, ④ '단풍나무'는 언급되지 않았다.

어휘&어구 survive 살아남다 extreme 극한의 thrive 번성하다 adapt 적응하다 float 뜨다 absorb 흡수하다 nutrient 영양분 drought 가뭄 tolerate 견디다 concentration 농도 specialized 특화된 oxygen 산소 soaked with ~로 적셔진 vast 광대한 reduced 작아진, 감소한 extensive 광범위한 efficiently 효율적으로

10회 수능실전 **대비연습**

본문 110~111쪽

01 ⑤	02 ⑤	03 ③	04 ④	05 ②	06 ④	07 ④	08 ④	09 ④	10 ③	11 ④	12 ⑤	13 ⑤	14 ④
15 ③	16 ④	17 ④											

---

01 살충제 살포에 따른 주민 협조 요청

[정답] ⑤

M Attention, residents. This is Klaudio Rodriguez from the maintenance office. Due to the recent unusually wet and hot weather, we've noticed an increase in the number of insects and pests within the apartment complex. To deal with this problem, we've hired a pest control company to spray pesticide around the complex. This will take place next Monday during the day. Pesticides are chemicals that can be harmful if taken in or absorbed through the skin. Therefore, we kindly ask that you avoid touching any flowers, trees, or other vegetation for a couple of days after the spraying. Your cooperation is greatly appreciated. If you have any questions or concerns, don't hesitate to contact us. Thank you.

남 주목해 주세요, 주민 여러분. 저는 관리 사무소의 Klaudio Rodriguez입니다. 최근 평소와 달리 습하고 더운 날씨로 인해 아파트 단지 내에 곤충과 해충의 수가 증가한 것이 목격되고 있습니다. 이 문제를 해결하기 위해 단지 주변에 살충제를 살포하도록 해충 방제 회사를 고용했습니다. 이는 다음 주 월요일 낮 동안에 실시될 것입니다. 살충제는 섭취되거나 피부를 통해 흡수될 경우 유해할 수 있는 화학 물질입니다. 따라서 살포 후 2~3일 동안은 꽃, 나무 또는 다른 식물을 만지지 마시기를 정중히 요청드리는 바입니다. 협조해 주셔서 정말 감사합니다. 질문이나 우려 사항이 있으시면 주저하지 말고 저희에게 문의해 주십시오. 감사합니다.

문제 해설 남자는 아파트 단지 내에 최근 늘어난 곤충과 해충 때문에 단지 주변에 살충제를 살포할 것이기 때문에 살포 후 2~3일 동안 꽃, 나무 또는 다른 식물을 만지지 말 것으로 요청하고 있다. 따라서 남자가 하는 말의 목적으로 가장 적절한 것은 ⑤ '살충제를 뿌린 단지 주변의 수목을 만지지 말 것을 요청하려고'이다.

어휘&어구 resident 주민, 거주자 unusually 평소와 달리, 특이하게 pest 해충 apartment complex 아파트 단지 hire 고용하다 pesticide 살충제 chemical 화학 물질 absorb 흡수하다 vegetation 식물, 초목

---

02 목표 실천에 도움이 되는 방법

[정답] ⑤

M Stacy, what have you been up to lately?

W Hi, Tom. I've been planning to start an exercise routine because I've been feeling a little stiff.

M Oh, what exercises are you thinking of?

W I'm thinking of doing a 30-minute stretch routine every day, but I'm not sure if I'll be able to stick to it.

M Try not to doubt yourself like that. You can do it.

W Thanks, but I've set similar goals in the past and ended up giving up. I really hope I can stick to it this time.

남 Stacy, 요즘 잘 지내니?

여 안녕, Tom. 몸이 좀 뻣뻣한 느낌이 들어서 운동 루틴을 시작하려고 계획을 세우고 있어.

남 아, 어떤 운동을 생각하고 있니?

여 매일 30분씩 스트레칭 루틴을 할 생각인데, 내가 그것을 지킬 수 있을지 잘 모르겠어.

남 그렇게 자신을 의심하지 않도록 해. 넌 할 수 있어.

여 고마워, 그렇지만 나는 과거에 비슷한 목표를 세웠는데 결국 포기했었어. 이번에는 내가 그것을 지킬 수 있기를 정말 바라.

M	I know of a method you should try. I used it to develop a habit of reading.	남	네가 시도해야 할 한 가지 방법을 내가 알고 있어. 나는 독서 습관을 기르기 위해 그것을 사용했었어.
W	Oh, what is it?	여	오, 그게 뭐니?
M	You write down your goal on pieces of paper and place them around your house where you can see them.	남	네 목표를 종이에 적어 집안 곳곳에 잘 보이는 곳에 그것을 두는 거야.
W	Ah, that way I'll constantly be reminded of my plan.	여	아, 그렇게 하면 내 계획이 끊임없이 생각나겠구나.
M	Exactly. Wherever you go, you'll see those papers and remember to take action right away.	남	맞아. 어디를 가든지 그 종이들을 보고 즉시 행동해야 하는 것을 기억하게 될 거야.
W	That's a great idea. Thank you.	여	그거 좋은 생각이네. 고마워.

문제 해설 매일 30분씩 스트레칭 루틴을 시작하기로 계획한 여자가 그 계획을 잘 지킬 수 있을지 걱정하자 남자는 목표를 종이에 적어 집안 곳곳에 잘 보이는 곳에 두면 그것을 볼 때마다 즉시 행동해야 한다는 것을 기억할 수 있어서 도움이 될 것이라고 조언하고 있다. 따라서 남자의 의견으로 가장 적절한 것은 ⑤ '목표를 눈에 보이는 곳에 적어 두면 실천하는 데 도움이 된다.'이다.

어휘&어구 stiff 뻣뻣한 stick to ~을 지키다, ~을 고수하다 end up -ing 결국 ~하게 되다 constantly 끊임없이 be reminded of ~이 생각나다

03 아이가 책 읽기를 좋아하게 만드는 법

[정답] ③

W	Hello, I'm Jane Brown, a librarian with over 20 years of experience in various schools. A lot of parents have told me they're concerned that their children don't enjoy reading books. One key characteristic I've noticed in people who love reading is that they read whatever interests them. This goes against what I see some parents do: they force their children to read particular genres or topics of books. This usually leads to negative outcomes. Instead, it's important to encourage your children to read their favorite books, whatever they are. I believe that this is the best way to turn your kids into lifelong readers.	여	안녕하세요. 저는 여러 학교에서 20년이 넘는 경험을 가진 사서 Jane Brown입니다. 많은 부모들은 그들의 자녀가 책 읽기를 즐기지 않아 걱정이라고 저에게 말씀하셨습니다. 책 읽기를 즐기는 사람들에게서 제가 발견한 한 가지 주된 특징은 그들은 자신들이 흥미를 느끼는 것은 무엇이든 읽는다는 것입니다. 이것은 일부 부모가 하는 것과는 반대되는 것입니다. 즉, 그들은 자녀에게 특정 장르나 주제의 책을 읽도록 강요합니다. 이것은 일반적으로 부정적인 결과를 초래합니다. 대신 여러분의 자녀가 무엇이든지 간에 그들이 가장 좋아하는 책을 읽도록 격려하는 것이 중요합니다. 저는 이것이 여러분의 자녀를 평생 책 읽는 사람으로 변화시키는 가장 좋은 방법이라고 믿습니다.

문제 해설 여자는 부모가 그들의 자녀에게 특정 장르나 주제의 책을 읽도록 강요하는 것이 부정적인 결과를 초래할 수 있다고 하면서 자녀가 가장 좋아하는 책이 무엇이든지 간에 읽도록 격려하는 것이 책 읽기를 즐기게 변화시킬 수 있다고 했으므로, 여자가 하는 말의 요지로 가장 적절한 것은 ③ '좋아하는 책을 마음껏 읽게 해야 아이가 책을 즐기게 된다.'이다.

어휘&어구 librarian (도서관의) 사서 characteristic 특징 interest ~의 관심[흥미]을 끌다 outcome 결과 encourage 격려하다 lifelong 평생의

04 부모님 댁 마당 모습

[정답] ④

M	Hey, Ms. Anderson, did you have a good weekend?	남	안녕하세요, Anderson 씨, 주말 잘 보내셨어요?
W	Hi, Mr. Robinson. Yeah, my family visited my parents' house.	여	안녕하세요, Robinson 씨. 네, 우리 가족은 제 부모님 댁을 방문했습니다.
M	Ah, you said your parents live in the countryside.	남	아, 부모님이 시골에 사신다고 하셨잖아요.
W	Yes. In fact, here's a picture from the weekend.	여	네. 사실, 주말에 찍은 사진이 여기 있어요.
M	Oh, cool. Your parents have a pond in the yard. And there are even fish in it.	남	오, 멋지네요. 부모님 댁 마당에 연못이 있군요. 그리고 그 안에 물고기도 있어요.
W	Yeah. My son is the boy wearing a hat, feeding the fish.	여	네. 제 아들은 물고기에게 먹이를 주고 있는 모자 쓴 남자아이예요.
M	He must have loved it! These two big trees in the yard must be really old. I'm sure they provide some nice shade.	남	그 애가 그것을 틀림없이 좋아했겠네요! 마당에 있는 이 두 그루의 큰 나무는 정말 오래된 것임이 틀림없네요. 그것들이 좋은 그늘을 분명히 제공하겠어요.
W	Right. That's why my parents set up the hammock between the trees. The person lying on the hammock is my husband.	여	맞아요. 그래서 제 부모님이 그 나무들 사이에 해먹을 설치하셨어요. 해먹에 누워 있는 사람이 제 남편이에요.
M	It looks so relaxing.		

W	We also put up this tent in front of the pond to sleep in at night, but it got pretty chilly at night, so we didn't actually sleep in it.	남	정말 편안해 보여요.

W We also put up this tent in front of the pond to sleep in at night, but it got pretty chilly at night, so we didn't actually sleep in it.

M I see. Your parents' place is really cool.

W Yeah, we love visiting there.

남 정말 편안해 보여요.

여 우리는 밤에 자려고 연못 앞에 이 텐트도 쳤는데, 밤에 날씨가 꽤 쌀쌀해져서 실제로 거기서 자지는 않았어요.

남 그렇군요. 부모님의 집이 정말 멋져요.

여 네, 우리는 그곳에 방문하는 걸 아주 좋아해요.

문제 해설 부모님 집 마당에 걸린 해먹에서 여자의 남편이 누워 있다고 말했는데 그림에서는 남편이 해먹에 걸터앉아 차를 마시고 있으므로, 그림에서 대화의 내용과 일치하지 않는 것은 ④이다.

어휘&어구 countryside 시골 feed 먹이를 주다 must have p.p. ~했음에 틀림없다 set up ~을 설치하다 relaxing 편안한 chilly 쌀쌀한

05 삼촌에게 발표에 대한 도움 부탁하기 [정답] ②

W Hey, Justin, how are the preparations for the presentation going?

M They're going fine. How about your group?

W We've decided on everybody's roles and started gathering materials.

M It sounds like your group is making progress. Actually, our team is having some difficulties.

W Ah, is someone in your group causing problems?

M That's not it. We're doing a presentation on robots, and surprisingly, we haven't been able to find examples of robots that we're looking for.

W You've tried searching online, right?

M Of course. It seems that we're looking for things that aren't very common.

W I see. Actually, my uncle is a robot engineer. He might know about uncommon robots. I could ask him if he could help.

M Oh, could you do that? It'd be really helpful if I could talk to him.

W Sure. I'll talk to him over the phone and let you know.

M Thank you so much, Amy.

여 이봐, Justin, 발표 준비는 어떻게 되어 가고 있니?

남 잘되고 있어. 너희 조는 어떠니?

여 우리는 모두의 역할을 정하고 자료를 수집하기 시작했어.

남 너희 조는 진전을 보이고 있는 것 같구나. 사실 우리 팀은 어려움을 좀 겪고 있어.

여 아, 너희 조에서 누군가가 문제를 일으키고 있어?

남 그건 아니야. 우리는 로봇에 대해 발표를 할 건데, 놀랍게도 우리가 찾고 있는 로봇의 예를 찾을 수 없었어.

여 온라인으로 검색은 해 봤겠지, 그렇지?

남 물론이지. 우리가 아주 흔하지 않은 것들을 찾고 있는 것 같아.

여 그렇구나. 사실 우리 삼촌은 로봇 공학자셔. 그가 흔하지 않은 로봇에 대해 알고 계실지도 몰라. 그가 도움을 줄 수 있는지 내가 물어볼 수 있어.

남 오, 그렇게 해 줄 수 있니? 그와 이야기를 나눌 수 있으면 정말 도움이 될 거야.

여 물론이지. 내가 전화로 그와 이야기하고 너한테 알려 줄게.

남 정말 고마워, Amy.

문제 해설 조원들과 로봇에 관해 발표를 하려는 남자가 흔하지 않은 로봇의 예를 찾고 있는데 잘 찾을 수 없다고 하자 여자는 로봇 공학자인 자신의 삼촌에게 도움을 줄 수 있는지 전화를 걸어 물어봐 주겠다고 했으므로, 여자가 할 일로 가장 적절한 것은 ② '삼촌과 통화해 보기'이다.

어휘&어구 role 역할 make progress 진전을 보이다 present 발표하다 common 흔한 uncommon 흔하지 않은, 드문

06 PT 과정 등록 및 셔츠 구매 [정답] ④

W Welcome to King's Fitness Center. How can I help you today?

M Hi, I'd like to register for a PT course.

W Okay. We have a 3-month course and a 6-month course.

M How much does each course cost?

W The 3-month course is $400, and the 6-month course is $600.

M The 6-month course is a better deal. I'll go with that one.

여 King's 피트니스 센터에 오신 것을 환영합니다. 오늘 어떻게 도와드릴까요?

남 안녕하세요, PT 과정에 등록하고 싶어요.

여 네. 저희는 3개월 과정과 6개월 과정이 있어요.

남 각 과정의 비용은 얼마인가요?

여 3개월 과정은 400달러이고, 6개월 과정은 600달러입니다.

남 6개월 과정이 더 좋은 거래인 것 같군요. 그걸로 할게요.

여 좋습니다. 그리고 신규 회원이시니까 PT 과정에서 10% 할인을

W	Sounds good. And you'll get 10% off the PT course as a new member.	받으실 거예요.	
M	That's great. I'd also like to buy this fitness center running shirt. How much is it?	남	잘됐네요. 저는 이 피트니스 센터 러닝셔츠도 사고 싶습니다. 그것은 얼마인가요?
W	It's normally $20, but it's $10 off for new members.	여	보통 20달러인데, 신규 회원에게는 10달러 할인해 드립니다.
M	Good. I'll take it. Here's my credit card.	남	좋아요. 그것을 살게요. 여기 제 신용 카드입니다.
W	Thank you.	여	감사합니다.

문제 해설 남자는 600달러인 6개월 PT 코스를 10퍼센트 신규 할인을 받고 등록하기로 했으며, 20달러인 러닝셔츠를 10달러 할인받아 사기로 했으므로, 남자가 지불할 금액은 ④ '550달러'이다.

어휘&어구 register for ~에 등록하다

07 피아노 콘서트 관람 약속 [정답] ④

M	Hi, Kate. How did your math test go yesterday?	남	안녕, Kate. 어제 수학 시험은 어땠니?
W	Not very good. I didn't study enough for it.	여	별로 좋지 않았어. 그것을 위해 공부를 충분히 하지 못했거든.
M	Was there any particular reason?	남	특별한 이유라도 있었니?
W	Well, I caught a cold last week and had a hard time concentrating.	여	음, 나는 지난주에 감기에 걸려서 집중하는 데 어려움을 겪었어.
M	Sorry to hear that. So are you going to tennis practice after school today?	남	안됐구나. 그래서 오늘 방과 후에 테니스 연습을 하러 갈 거니?
W	I'd like to, but I can't.	여	그러고 싶지만, 그럴 수가 없어.
M	Why? Did your knee start hurting again?	남	왜 그러니? 무릎이 또 아프기 시작한 거니?
W	No. Ever since I saw the doctor, it's been a lot better.	여	아니야. 진료받은 이후로 훨씬 더 좋아졌어.
M	That's good to hear. So, do you have to practice for your school festival performance with the dance team?	남	다행이구나. 그래서, 너는 댄스팀과 함께 학교 축제 공연을 위해 연습해야 하는 거니?
W	No. I'm meeting my cousin after school. We're going to a piano concert together.	여	아니. 방과 후에 사촌을 만나기로 했어. 우리는 함께 피아노 콘서트에 갈 거야.
M	I see. Sounds like fun. Have a great time.	남	그렇구나. 재미있겠구나. 좋은 시간 보내.
W	Thanks! I'll definitely make it to the next tennis practice.	여	고마워! 다음 테니스 연습에는 꼭 참석할게.

문제 해설 방과 후에 테니스 연습을 하러 갈 것인지를 묻는 남자의 말에 여자는 방과 후에 사촌을 만나 피아노 콘서트에 갈 것이라고 했으므로, 여자가 오늘 테니스 연습을 하러 갈 수 없는 이유는 ④ '피아노 콘서트에 가야 해서'이다.

어휘&어구 particular 특별한 have a hard time -ing ~하는 데 어려움을 겪다 concentrate 집중하다 performance 공연 cousin 사촌 definitely 꼭, 반드시 make it to ~에 참석하다[도착하다]

08 Bently Drama Festival [정답] ④

M	Ms. Anderson, what are you busy with these days?	남	Anderson 선생님, 요즘 무슨 일로 바쁘세요?
W	Hello, Mr. Smith. I'm in charge of organizing the Bently Drama Festival this year, so I've been working on that.	여	안녕하세요, Smith 선생님. 저는 올해 Bently Drama Festival을 기획하는 일을 맡고 있어서, 그것에 관한 일을 하고 있어요.
M	Ah, I see. That's the annual citywide student drama festival, right?	남	아, 그렇군요. 그것은 매년 시 전역에서 열리는 학생 연극 축제죠, 그렇죠?
W	Right. It starts next Wednesday, and it lasts three days.	여	네. 다음 주 수요일에 시작해서 3일 동안 계속되지요.
M	I see. How many teams are participating?	남	그렇군요. 몇 팀이 참가하나요?
W	There are nine teams participating this year, with three teams performing on each day.	여	올해는 아홉 개의 팀이 참가하고, 하루에 세 개의 팀이 공연해요.
M	And where will it take place?	남	그럼 그것은 어디에서 개최되나요?
W	Finding a proper place wasn't easy, but fortunately, I was able to reserve the auditorium at the city's education office.	여	적절한 장소를 찾기가 쉽지 않았지만, 다행히 시 교육청의 강당을 예약할 수 있었어요.
		남	그곳은 축제를 위한 완벽한 장소네요.

M That's a perfect place for the festival.	**여** 동의해요. 그리고 저는 오늘 아침에 두 개의 고등학교가 지역 쇼핑몰과 함께 그 축제를 후원하리라는 것을 알게 되어 기뻐요.
W I agree. And I'm happy because I just found out this morning that two high schools are going to sponsor the festival along with a local shopping mall.	**남** 그 말을 들으니 저도 기뻐요. 축제 기획을 정말 잘하신 것 같군요.
M I'm also glad to hear that. Sounds like you've done an amazing job with organizing the festival.	**여** 고마워요, Smith 선생님.
W Thank you, Mr. Smith.	

문제 해설 Bently Drama Festival에 관해 개최 기간, 참가 팀 수, 장소, 후원 기관은 언급되었지만, ④ '상품'은 언급되지 않았다.

어휘&어구 in charge of ~을 맡고 있는 organize 기획하다, 준비하다 annual 매년의 participate 참가하다 perform 공연하다 take place 개최되다, 발생하다 reserve 예약하다 auditorium 강당 education office 교육청 sponsor 후원하다

---

09 World Spirit Music Concert 안내 [정답] ④

M Hello, listeners! I'm David Richardson from the National Traditional Music Center, and I'm thrilled to announce the World Spirit Music Concert, a spectacular concert focusing on traditional music from around the world! After the concert was not held last year, many countries reached out to participate this year. So, this year there will be traditional bands from 12 countries performing. The concert's next Friday from 7 to 10 p.m. at the National Traditional Music Concert Hall. At the end, all the music bands will join together for an amazing harmonious finale. To attend the concert, simply purchase tickets on our website. Don't miss out on this unique event combining traditional cultures around the world!	**남** 안녕하세요, 청취자 여러분! 저는 국립 전통 음악 센터의 David Richardson이며, 세계 각국의 전통 음악에 초점을 맞춘 화려한 콘서트인 World Spirit Music Concert를 알리게 되어 매우 기쁩니다! 작년에 콘서트가 개최되지 않고 나서, 많은 나라들이 올해 참가하기 위해 손을 뻗었습니다. 그래서, 올해는 12개국의 전통 음악단이 공연할 것입니다. 그 콘서트는 다음 주 금요일 오후 7시부터 10시까지 국립 전통 음악 콘서트홀에서 열립니다. 마지막에는, 모든 음악단이 놀라운 조화로운 피날레를 위해서 함께할 것입니다. 콘서트에 참석하시려면 저희 웹사이트에서 관람권을 사기만 하면 됩니다. 전 세계의 전통문화를 결합한 이 독특한 행사를 놓치지 마세요!

문제 해설 마지막에는 피날레를 위해 모든 음악단이 함께할 것이라고 했으므로, 담화의 내용과 일치하지 않는 것은 ④ '마지막 순서로 개최국이 단독 공연을 할 것이다.'이다.

어휘&어구 thrilled 매우 기쁜 announce 알리다 spectacular 화려한, 멋진 reach out 손을 뻗다 perform 공연하다 harmonious 조화로운 finale 피날레, 마지막 부분 purchase 사다 combine 결합하다

---

10 딸기잼 주문 [정답] ③

W Honey, we're completely out of strawberry jam.	**여** 여보, 딸기잼이 다 떨어졌어요.
M I know. I'll order some online right now. Take a look. Which one of these should we buy?	**남** 알아요. 내가 지금 바로 온라인으로 주문할게요. 이거 봐요. 이것들 중 어떤 것을 사야 할까요?
W Let me see. [Pause] This one's pretty big. Do we need that much?	**여** 어디 봐요. [잠시 후] 이건 꽤 크네요. 우리가 그렇게 많이 필요한가요?
M I don't think so. It's over 300 g. That's a lot. Let's get a smaller size.	**남** 그렇게 생각하지 않아요. 300g이 넘잖아요. 무척 많아요. 좀 더 작은 사이즈로 사요.
W All right. Whoa, look at this one. It's over $20!	**여** 좋아요. 와, 이것 좀 봐요. 20달러가 넘어요!
M Oh, that's too pricey.	**남** 오, 그건 너무 비싸요.
W I agree. Let's choose one of the other three options.	**여** 동의해요. 다른 세 가지 선택 중 하나를 골라 봐요.
M Look at the customer ratings. These two have a higher customer rating than this one.	**남** 고객 평가를 보세요. 이 두 가지는 이것보다 고객 평가가 더 높아요.
	여 그럼 고객 평가가 더 높은 것으로 사요.

W	Then let's get one with a higher customer rating.
M	Okay. How about we try a tube this time?
W	Sounds good. It should be convenient to use.
M	Right. Then I'll go ahead and order this one.

남	좋아요. 이번에는 튜브를 써 보는 게 어때요?
여	좋은 것 같아요. 그게 사용하기에 편리할 거예요.
남	맞아요. 그럼 이것을 주문할게요.

문제 해설 남자는 300g보다 작고, 가격이 20달러가 넘지 않으며, 남은 세 가지 중에 고객 평가가 더 높고, 튜브에 담긴 것을 주문하겠다고 했으므로, 남자가 주문할 딸기잼은 ③이다.

어휘&어구 be out of ~이 떨어지고 없다 pricey 비싼 customer rating 고객 평가 convenient 편리한

---

11 캠핑 준비 [정답] ④

M	Hey, Cathy, do you have any plans for the upcoming long weekend?
W	Yeah. I'm going camping with my friend at Mt. Emerton.
M	Sounds fun! But it's supposed to be pretty cold this weekend, so make sure you prepare for that.
W	I will. I'm going to bring a really warm sleeping bag.

남	안녕, Cathy, 다가오는 긴 주말에 무슨 계획 있어요?
여	네. 나는 친구와 Emerton 산으로 캠핑을 갈 거예요.
남	재밌겠군요! 하지만 이번 주말에는 꽤 춥다고 하니, 그에 대한 대비를 꼭 하셔야겠어요.
여	그럴게요. 저는 정말 따뜻한 침낭을 가지고 갈 거예요.

문제 해설 긴 주말 동안 친구와 산으로 캠핑을 갈 거라고 여자가 말하자, 남자는 이번 주말에 꽤 추울 것이니 이에 대비하라고 조언하고 있으므로, 이에 대한 여자의 응답으로 가장 적절한 것은 ④ '그럴게요. 저는 정말 따뜻한 침낭을 가지고 갈 거예요.'이다.
① 고마워요. 당신의 스웨터가 저를 따뜻하게 해 주었어요.
② 정말 잘됐네요! 그것은 매우 흥미로운 경험이었어요.
③ 확실해요. 우리는 더위를 식히기 위해 호수로 수영하러 갈 거예요.
⑤ 걱정하지 마세요. 우리는 캠핑 여행을 위해 충분한 음식을 살 거예요.

어휘&어구 upcoming 다가오는 prepare for ~에 대비하다 sleeping bag 침낭

---

12 점심 약속 연기 [정답] ⑤

W	Chris, I'm terribly sorry, but could we reschedule our lunch appointment? I won't be able to make it today.
M	Of course. I was really looking forward to our lunch though. Is everything all right?
W	Unfortunately, a family emergency came up. I should be free to meet any day after Tuesday.
M	All right. I'll check my calendar and get back to you.

여	Chris, 정말 미안하지만, 우리 점심 약속 일정을 변경할 수 있을까요? 오늘은 못 갈 것 같아요.
남	물론이에요. 하지만 우리의 점심을 정말 기대하고 있었어요. 모든 게 괜찮으신 거예요?
여	유감스럽게도, 급한 집안일이 생겼어요. 저는 화요일 이후라면 언제든지 시간이 될 거예요.
남	알겠어요. 제 달력을 확인하고 다시 연락드릴게요.

문제 해설 여자가 오늘 점심 약속 시간에 못 갈 것 같다고 말하며 일정을 변경하자고 말하자 남자는 모든 게 괜찮은지 묻고, 이에 여자가 급한 집안일이 생겼다고 말하며 화요일 이후에는 시간이 된다고 답했다. 이에 대한 남자의 응답으로 가장 적절한 것은 ⑤ '알겠어요. 제 달력을 확인하고 다시 연락드릴게요.'이다.
① 좋아요. 오늘 점심 식사 때 뵐게요.
② 맞아요. 당신과 함께 점심을 먹어서 정말 즐거웠어요.
③ 네. 당신이 가족과의 계획을 취소해야 했다니 유감입니다.
④ 아닌 것 같아요. 오늘은 이미 제 일정이 꽉 찼습니다.

어휘&어구 reschedule 일정을 변경하다 unfortunately 유감스럽게도 family emergency 급한 집안일

13 과학 프로젝트 회의

[정답] ⑤

[Cell phone rings.]

W Hi, Mark.

M Sarah, why didn't you answer your phone when I called a little while ago?

W Sorry. I had it on silent because I was studying. What's up?

M Remember our meeting with Mr. Stevens about our science project today? It was supposed to start an hour ago. We waited for you in his office for 20 minutes before canceling the meeting.

W Oh, no. I completely forgot about it. I'm so sorry.

M It's disappointing that you forgot. We've been preparing for this meeting for weeks!

W I know. I've just been so overwhelmed with exams that it slipped my mind. I sincerely apologize.

M Well, I accept your apology. But Mr. Stevens was pretty let down.

W I should personally apologize to him right away.

M I agree. And you should ask him if he's willing to reschedule the meeting for some time next week.

W Okay. I'll go see him now to apologize and discuss a new meeting time.

[휴대 전화가 울린다.]

여 안녕, Mark.

남 Sarah, 내가 조금 전에 전화했을 때 왜 전화를 안 받았어?

여 미안해. 공부하느라 무음으로 해 뒀어. 무슨 일이야?

남 오늘 우리 과학 프로젝트에 대해 Stevens 선생님과 만나기로 한 거 기억해? 한 시간 전에 시작하기로 되어 있었어. 우리는 선생님 사무실에서 너를 20분 동안 기다리다가 회의를 취소했어.

여 오, 이런. 그것에 대해 까맣게 잊고 있었어. 정말 미안해.

남 잊어버렸다니 실망스러워. 우리는 몇 주 동안 이 회의를 준비해 왔는데!

여 알아. 그저 시험 때문에 내가 너무나도 갈피를 못 잡아서 깜빡 잊어버렸어. 진심으로 사과할게.

남 음, 사과를 받아들일게. 하지만 Stevens 선생님께서 꽤 실망하셨어.

여 내가 선생님께 개인적으로 즉시 사과드려야겠어.

남 맞아. 그리고 선생님께 다음 주 중으로 회의 일정을 다시 잡으실 의향이 있는지 네가 여쭤봐야 해.

여 알겠어. 지금 선생님을 찾아뵙고 사과드리고 새로운 회의 시간을 논의할게.

문제 해설 선생님과 친구와 함께 하기로 했던 과학 프로젝트 회의에 대해 완전히 잊은 채 회의에 가지 않은 여자에게 남자는 선생님께서 꽤 실망하셨다고 말하고, 이에 여자는 선생님께 즉시 사과드리겠다고 한다. 남자가 이에 동의하며 다음 주 중으로 회의 일정을 다시 잡으실 의향이 있는지도 여쭤봐야 한다고 덧붙였으므로, 남자의 마지막 말에 대한 여자의 응답으로 가장 적절한 것은 ⑤ '알겠어. 지금 선생님을 찾아뵙고 사과드리고 새로운 회의 시간을 논의할게.'이다.

① 맞아. 선생님이 오늘 너무 바쁘셔서 우리를 만날 수 없다고 말씀하셨어.

② 모르겠어. 내가 사과할 필요는 없어.

③ 맞아. 오늘 회의는 정말 유익하고 도움이 되었어.

④ 그렇게. 다만 다시는 우리의 회의에 대해 잊지 않도록 확실히 해.

어휘&어구 on silent 무음의 be supposed to *do* ~하기로 되어 있다 overwhelmed 갈피를 못 잡는, 압도당한 slip one's mind 깜빡 잊다 apologize 사과하다 let down ~을 실망시키다

14 간식 먹는 습관 고치기

[정답] ④

M Emily, you just had dinner a little while ago, and now you're eating something again.

W Dad, I've been snacking too much lately. I want to stop.

M I can help you with that. Have you heard of the habit loop?

W No. What is it?

M It's the basic structure of every habit. It consists of three parts: the cue, the routine, and the reward. Identifying the parts can help you break your habit.

W Okay. I assume the routine is eating snacks.

M Exactly. So then you need to figure out what triggers your snack eating.

남 Emily, 너 조금 전에 저녁을 먹었는데, 지금 또 무언가를 먹고 있구나.

여 아빠, 제가 요즘 간식을 너무 많이 먹고 있어요. 멈추고 싶어요.

남 내가 도와줄 수 있단다. 습관 고리에 대해 들어 본 적 있니?

여 아니요. 그게 뭐예요?

남 그건 모든 습관의 기본 구조란다. 신호, 루틴, 보상이라는 세 가지 요소로 이루어져 있어. 이 요소들을 확인하는 것이 습관을 버리는 것을 도울 수 있단다.

여 알겠어요. 제 생각엔 루틴은 간식 먹기인 거 같아요.

남 정확해. 그럼 이제 간식 먹는 것을 유발하는 것을 찾아야 해.

여 음, 저는 아무것도 할 일이 없을 때나 바쁠 때 간식을 먹는 경향이

W Hmm. I tend to eat snacks when I have nothing else to do or when I'm really busy. I usually don't eat snacks otherwise.

M It sounds like your cue is an emotional state.

W You're right. I eat snacks because I feel bored.

M Right. So now let's focus on the reward. I think the reward is that you feel less bored when you're eating snacks.

W That's true. So, do you know of a plan to help me break my snacking habit?

M Sure. You have to find something else to remove your boredom.

있어요. 그 외에는 별로 간식을 먹지 않아요.

남 너의 (습관의) 신호는 감정의 상태인 것 같구나.

여 맞아요. 저는 심심해서 간식을 먹는 거예요.

남 그렇구나. 이제 보상에 초점을 맞춰 보자. 간식을 먹을 때 덜 심심하다고 느끼는 것이 보상인 것 같구나.

여 사실 그래요. 그래서, 간식 먹는 습관을 버리기 위해 어떤 방법이 있는지 알고 계시나요?

남 <u>물론이지. 너는 심심함을 해소하기 위해 다른 것을 찾아야 해.</u>

문제 해설 여자가 남자에게 간식 먹는 습관을 멈추고 싶다고 말하자, 남자는 여자에게 신호, 루틴, 보상이라는 습관 고리의 세 가지 요소를 확인하는 것으로 습관을 버릴 수 있다고 말한다. 남자가 루틴은 간식을 먹는 것이고, 신호는 감정 상태인 것으로 확인한 후 먹을 때 덜 심심하다고 느끼는 것이 보상인 것 같다고 말하자 여자는 세 가지를 알게 되었으니 간식 먹는 습관을 버리는 방법을 아는지를 남자에게 묻는다. 따라서 여자의 마지막 말에 대한 남자의 응답으로 가장 적절한 것은 ④ '물론이지. 너는 심심함을 해소하기 위해 다른 것을 찾아야 해.'이다.

① 그래. 우리가 네 습관 고리의 세 단계를 모두 알아내 보자.

② 미안해. 좋은 습관을 지니는 것은 인생에서 성공을 위해 중요해.

③ 아니야. 가끔은 지루함이 뇌에 필요한 휴식을 줘.

⑤ 정확해. 그것은 체중 증가로 이어지고 비만의 위험을 높일 수 있어.

어휘&어구 snack 간식; 간식을 먹다 loop 고리 consist of ~로 구성되다 reward 보상 identify 확인하다 break the habit ~하는 습관을 버리다 assume 추측하다 trigger 유발하다

15   인간의 부주의로 일어나는 산불   [정답] ③

W Kelly and Andy are a mother and son with a strong passion for protecting the Earth. They are currently watching a news report on TV about intense wildfires in another region of the country. The news states that the wildfires have burned over one million acres of land and are still spreading, leading to the death and destruction of wildlife and their habitats. The news reporter attributes the cause of the wildfire to reckless logging by humans. Andy is deeply upset about the way humans are harming the environment. He wants to express his anger to Kelly. In this situation, what would Andy most likely say to Kelly?

Andy <u>I'm so angry, Mom. How could people let that happen?</u>

여 Kelly와 Andy는 지구를 보호하는 데 강한 열정을 가진 어머니와 아들입니다. 그들은 현재 그 나라의 다른 지역에서 발생한 강렬한 산불에 대한 뉴스 보도를 텔레비전으로 시청하고 있습니다. 뉴스에 따르면 산불로 인해 백만 에이커 이상의 땅이 타 버렸고, (산불은) 여전히 퍼져 나가고 있으며, 야생 동물의 죽음과 서식지의 파괴로 이어지고 있다고 합니다. 뉴스 기자는 산불의 원인을 인간들의 무분별한 벌목 탓이라고 이야기합니다. Andy는 인간들이 환경을 해치고 있는 방식에 대해 매우 속상합니다. 그는 Kelly에게 자신의 분노를 표현하고 싶어 합니다. 이런 상황에서 Andy는 Kelly에게 뭐라고 말하겠습니까?

Andy <u>정말 화가 나요, 엄마. 사람들이 어떻게 그런 일이 벌어지게 할 수 있어요?</u>

문제 해설 Andy와 Kelly가 뉴스를 통해 어느 지역에서 산불이 발생해서 아주 넓은 땅이 타 버렸고, 그로 인해 많은 야생 동물이 죽고, 그들의 서식지가 파괴되고 있음을 알게 된다. 그리고 이러한 산불의 원인이 인간의 무분별한 벌목 때문이란 것을 알게 되자 Andy는 그의 엄마인 Kelly에게 지금의 화가 난 심정을 말하고 싶어 하는 상황이므로, Andy가 Kelly에게 할 말로 가장 적절한 것은 ③ '정말 화가 나요, 엄마. 사람들이 어떻게 그런 일이 벌어지게 할 수 있어요?'이다.

① 엄마, 채널을 바꿔요. 이 뉴스는 따분해요.

② 믿기지 않아요. 엄마. 산불이 이렇게 쉽게 꺼지다니요.

④ 그건 터무니없어요, 엄마. 그런 질문을 하지 말아야 해요.

⑤ 정말 창피해요, 엄마. 제가 생각하지 않고 행동하고 말았어요.

어휘&어구 passion 열정 currently 현재 intense 강렬한, 심한 wildfire 산불 region 지역 destruction 파괴 habitat 서식지 attribute ~ to ... ~을 …의 탓으로 생각하다 reckless 분별없는 logging 벌목

16~17 행운과 불운에 관련된 미신

[정답] 16 ④ 17 ④

M Welcome to the Jacky-Wicky horror show! I'm Taylor. Have you ever wondered why on some days nothing goes your way, while on others everything goes our way? People have varying reasons as to why. In our show, we take a look at the mysteries of superstitions passed down through the ages. Let's begin learning about different situations. First is wearing a rabbit's foot, which is believed to bring good luck. Hanging up a horseshoe is thought of similarly, as it's a way to collect good luck for future use. However, if you hang it upside down, all the luck will pour out, leaving you with none! Breaking a mirror is also believed to bring seven years of bad luck! Walking underneath a ladder may lead to something unfortunate. And it's often advised not to open an umbrella indoors, unless you want bad luck for the rest of the day. Throughout our show, you will learn about more beliefs and warnings that people follow.

남 Jacky-Wicky horror show에 오신 것을 환영합니다! 저는 Taylor입니다. 어떤 날은 우리에게 모든 것이 순조롭게 흘러가고, 반면 어떤 날은 좋은 일이 별로 일어나지 않는다는 것에 대해 여러분은 궁금해했던 적이 있으신가요? 사람들은 그에 대한 가지각색의 이유를 갖고 있습니다. 우리 쇼에서는, 세월에 따라 전해진 신비로운 미신적 관습에 대해 알아보려고 합니다. 이제 다양한 상황에 대해 배워 봅시다. 첫 번째로 토끼의 발을 착용하는 것인데, 이는 행운을 가져다준다고 믿어집니다. 말굽을 걸어놓는 것도 비슷한 의미로, 행운을 모아 나중에 사용하는 방식입니다. 하지만 그것(말굽)을 거꾸로 걸어 놓으면 모든 행운이 쏟아져 나와 아무것도 남지 않게 됩니다! 거울을 깨뜨리는 것 또한 7년 동안 불운이 따른다고 믿어집니다! 사다리 아래로 걸어가면 불운한 일이 생길 수도 있습니다. 그리고 종일 불운이 닥치길 바라지 않는다면 실내에서 우산을 펼치지 말라고 자주 권고됩니다. 우리 쇼를 보는 내내 여러분은 더 많은 믿음과 사람들이 따라야 할 주의 사항에 대해 배우게 될 것입니다.

문제 해설 **16** 남자가 여러 물건을 언급하며 행운과 불운에 관련된 미신적 관습에 관해 설명하고 있으므로, 남자가 하는 말의 주제로 가장 적절한 것은 ④ '행운과 불운에 관련된 미신적 관습'이다.
① 인간들이 미신을 거부하는 이유
② 인생에서 어려움을 다루는 팁
③ 미신의 위험에 대한 경고
⑤ 가정용 물건을 적절히 사용하는 방법
17 말굽, 거울, 사다리, 우산은 언급되었으나 ④ '양초'는 언급되지 않았다.

어휘&어구 horror 공포 go one's way 일이 진행되다 varying 가지각색의 superstition 미신, 미신적 관습 horseshoe 말굽 underneath 아래에 ladder 사다리 warning 경고

11회 수능실전 **대비연습**

본문 118~119쪽

01 ① 02 ⑤ 03 ② 04 ④ 05 ⑤ 06 ④ 07 ④ 08 ④ 09 ④ 10 ⑤ 11 ⑤ 12 ④ 13 ④ 14 ②
15 ① 16 ② 17 ③

---

01 놀이공원 퍼레이드 시간 연장

[정답] ①

W Hello, Blue Moon Amusement Park visitors. Based on the cheers and laughs we're hearing, it sounds like you're having a great time at the park today! And we want to enhance your joy and excitement even more! Starting today, we're extending the parade time from 30 minutes to 45 minutes, giving you more time to enjoy it. So, grab your spot along the parade route and get ready to be amazed by the outstanding performers and beloved characters filling the streets with music and magic for an extended duration. I hope you enjoy the rest of your day here at Blue Moon Amusement Park!

여 Blue Moon 놀이공원 방문객 여러분, 안녕하세요. 우리가 듣는 환호와 웃음소리로 미루어 볼 때, 여러분이 오늘 공원에서 즐거운 시간을 보내고 있는 것처럼 들립니다! 그리고 우리는 여러분의 기쁨과 즐거움을 훨씬 더 크게 만들고 싶습니다! 오늘부터 퍼레이드 시간을 30분에서 45분으로 연장해서, 여러분이 그것을 즐길 수 있는 시간을 더 드립니다. 그러니, 퍼레이드 길을 따라 자리를 잡으시고, 더 길어진 시간 동안 뛰어난 공연자들과 사랑받는 캐릭터들이 거리를 음악과 마술로 가득 채우는 것에 놀랄 준비를 하세요. 여기 Blue Moon 놀이공원에서 남은 하루를 즐기시길 바랍니다!

문제 해설 여자는 놀이공원 방문객에게 퍼레이드 시간이 30분에서 45분으로 연장되었음을 알리고 있다. 따라서 여자가 하는 말의 목적으로 가장 적절한 것은 ① '퍼레이드 시간 연장을 알리려고'이다.

어휘&어구 cheer 환호 enhance 더 크게 만들다, 높이다 extend 연장하다 grab 잡다 route 길, 경로 performer 공연자 beloved 사랑받는 duration 기간, 지속

02 음악 줄넘기의 체중 감량 효과
[정답] ⑤

W Hi, Jeremy. It seems like you've lost some weight.

M I have lost a little. Thanks for noticing.

W That's great to hear! What have you been doing?

M I've been taking daily walks. But honestly, it's pretty boring, so I want to find something else to do.

W How about jumping rope? It can be a great exercise for weight loss.

M Really? It can be?

W Yeah. It's a high-intensity exercise that burns calories quickly, which helps lose weight.

M I see. But that sounds pretty boring and monotonous.

W That's why it's good to jump rope while listening to music. You jump to the beat of the music, so it's way more enjoyable.

M Ah, that could keep me motivated.

W Absolutely! Jumping rope to music is great for losing weight.

M I'll definitely give it a try. Thanks for the recommendation!

여 안녕, Jeremy. 살이 좀 빠진 것 같아요.

남 조금 빠졌어요. 알아봐 줘서 고마워요.

여 잘됐네요! 뭘 하고 있었던 거예요?

남 매일 산책을 하고 있어요. 하지만 솔직히 꽤 지루해서 다른 할 일을 찾고 싶어요.

여 줄넘기는 어때요? 그것은 체중 감량에 좋은 운동이 될 수 있어요.

남 그래요? 그럴 수도 있어요?

여 네. 칼로리 소모가 빠른 고강도 운동이라서, 체중 감량에 도움이 돼요.

남 그렇군요. 하지만 꽤 지루하고 단조롭게 들려요.

여 그래서 음악을 들으면서 줄넘기를 하는 것이 좋아요. 음악의 박자에 맞춰 점프하기 때문에 훨씬 더 즐거워요.

남 아, 그러면 내게 계속 동기 부여가 될 수 있겠네요.

여 물론이에요! 음악에 맞춰 줄넘기를 하는 것은 체중을 감량하는 데 좋아요.

남 반드시 한번 해 볼게요. 추천해 줘서 고마워요!

문제 해설 여자는 줄넘기가 칼로리 소모가 빠른 고강도 운동이고, 음악을 들으면서 음악의 박자에 맞춰 점프하면 계속 동기 부여가 될 수 있다고 하면서, 음악에 맞춰 줄넘기를 하는 것은 체중을 감량하는 데 좋다고 말한다. 따라서 여자의 의견으로 가장 적절한 것은 ⑤ '음악을 들으면서 줄넘기하는 것이 체중 감량에 좋다.'이다.

어휘&어구 jumping rope 줄넘기 weight loss 체중 감량 high-intensity 고강도(의) monotonous 단조로운 motivated 동기 부여가 되는 definitely 반드시, 분명히 recommendation 추천

03 능률 유지 비결
[정답] ②

M Hello, viewers! Thank you for tuning in to my video channel. As you might know, I juggle multiple roles as a content creator, freelance writer, and fitness instructor. I'm often asked how I manage to stay efficient with such a busy schedule. My secret is prioritizing tasks in the morning. Let's say you have to study for a math test, deal with urgent emails, and prepare for a school club meeting. In that case, it's a good idea to create a to-do list in your head and set your priorities in the morning. This way, you can stay efficient and might even have some spare time to do things you love. Thanks again for watching!

남 안녕하세요, 시청자 여러분! 제 동영상 채널에 맞추어 주셔서 감사합니다. 아시다시피, 저는 콘텐츠 제작자, 프리랜서 작가, 그리고 운동 강사로서 여러 역할을 솜씨 있게 해내고 있습니다. 이렇게 바쁜 일정 속에서 어떻게 능률을 유지해 낼 수 있는지 저는 자주 질문을 받습니다. 저의 비결은 아침에 일의 우선순위를 정하는 것입니다. 여러분이 수학 시험공부를 하고, 긴급한 이메일을 처리하고, 학교 동아리 회의를 준비해야 한다고 가정해 봅시다. 그럴 때는 머릿속에 할 일 목록을 만들고 아침에 우선순위를 정하는 것은 좋은 생각입니다. 이런 식으로, 여러분은 능률을 유지할 수 있고 심지어 여러분이 좋아하는 것들을 할 수 있는 여가를 가질지도 모릅니다. 시청해 주셔서 다시 한번 감사드립니다!

문제 해설 바쁜 일정 속에서 능률을 유지해 낼 수 있는 비결은 아침에 일의 우선순위를 정하는 것이라는 내용이므로, 남자가 하는 말의 요지로 가장 적절한 것은 ② '아침에 일의 우선순위를 정하면 능률을 유지할 수 있다.'이다.

어휘&어구 tune in to ~에 맞추다 juggle (여러 일을) 솜씨 있게 해내다 instructor 강사 manage to do ~을 해내다 prioritize 우선순위를 정하다 deal with ~을 처리하다 urgent 긴급한 spare time 여가

04 주립 공원에서 보트 타기 [정답] ④

M	Hey, Ellie. What are you looking at on your phone?
W	Hey, Sebastian. It's a picture of my brother Sean and me at Wheeler State Park.
M	Let me see. *[Pause]* Wow, there's a windmill in the background.
W	Pretty cool, right?
M	Yeah. And I really like the bench between the trees. It's a cozy place to sit.
W	Do you see the teddy bear on the bench? It's Sean's. He accidentally left it there, so we had to go back and get it.
M	Thank goodness nobody took it! I see you and Sean in a boat.
W	We rented it. It was fun, and I wore my striped hat because it was really sunny.
M	Oh, look. These two ducks were swimming behind you.
W	Aren't they adorable? They followed us the whole time we were in the boat. It was a great time.

남	안녕, Ellie. 휴대 전화로 무엇을 보고 있니?
여	안녕, Sebastian. Wheeler 주립 공원에 있는 나와 내 동생 Sean의 사진이야.
남	어디 보자. *[잠시 후]* 와, 배경에 풍차가 있네.
여	꽤 멋지지, 그렇지?
남	응. 그리고 나무 사이에 있는 벤치가 정말 좋아. 앉기에 아늑한 곳이야.
여	벤치에 있는 곰 인형 보여? 그건 Sean 거야. 걔가 실수로 그것을 거기에 두고 와서, 우리는 다시 가서 그것을 가져와야 했어.
남	아무도 안 가져가서 다행이다! 너와 Sean이 보트에 타고 있는 게 보여.
여	우리는 그걸 빌렸어. 재미있었고, 햇빛이 정말 세서 나는 내 줄무늬 모자를 썼어.
남	오, 봐. 이 두 마리의 오리가 네 뒤에서 헤엄치고 있어.
여	귀엽지 않니? 그것들은 우리가 보트에 타고 있는 동안 줄곧 우리를 따라다녔어. 멋진 시간이었어.

문제 해설 여자는 줄무늬 모자를 썼다고 말했는데, 그림에는 모자에 물방울무늬가 있다. 따라서 그림에서 대화의 내용과 일치하지 않는 것은 ④이다.

어휘&어구 windmill 풍차 cozy 아늑한 accidentally 실수로, 우연히 rent 빌리다 adorable 귀여운, 사랑스러운

05 할머니 생신 파티 준비 [정답] ⑤

M	Mom, I'm really excited for grandma's birthday party tomorrow.
W	Me, too. It's going to be fun. I just finalized the menu with the caterer.
M	That's good. As far as the cake, are you baking one?
W	No. I ordered one from the bakery.
M	That's easier. Is there anything I can do to help? I could vacuum the floors.
W	That's not necessary. Your dad will take care of that later today.
M	Okay. I think it'd be nice to decorate the table with flowers and family photos.
W	That's a great idea. We can use the family photos in the master bedroom.
M	Yeah. I'll go grab them right now.
W	Perfect! While you do that, I'll call the flower shop.

남	엄마, 내일 할머니 생신 파티가 있어서 정말 기대돼요.
여	나도 그렇단다. 재미있을 거야. 내가 방금 요리사와 함께 메뉴를 마무리했단다.
남	좋네요. 케이크에 관해서라면, 엄마가 하나 구우실 건가요?
여	아니. 빵집에서 하나 주문했어.
남	그게 더 쉽죠. 제가 도울 일이 있나요? 제가 바닥을 진공청소기로 청소할 수 있어요.
여	그럴 필요 없어. 아빠가 오늘 나중에 그걸 처리하실 거란다.
남	네. 테이블을 꽃과 가족사진으로 장식하면 좋을 것 같아요.
여	좋은 생각이야. 부부용 침실에 있는 가족사진을 사용할 수 있겠다.
남	네. 지금 바로 가서 그것들을 가지고 올게요.
여	완벽해! 네가 그걸 할 동안 나는 꽃집에 전화해 볼게.

문제 해설 할머니 생신 파티를 준비하는 상황에서 남자가 테이블을 꽃과 가족사진으로 장식하면 좋을 것 같다고 하자 여자가 부부용 침실에 있는 가족사진을 사용할 수 있겠다고 하고, 이에 남자가 지금 바로 가서 가지고 오겠다고 했으므로, 남자가 할 일로 가장 적절한 것은 ⑤ '가족사진 가져오기'이다.

어휘&어구 finalize 마무리하다 caterer (행사·연회 등의) 출장 요리사 vacuum 진공청소기로 청소하다 decorate 장식하다 master bedroom 부부용 침실 grab 서둘러 가져오다

M	Welcome to Aqua Splash Water Park.	남	Aqua Splash 워터 파크에 오신 것을 환영합니다.
W	Hi, I need four admission tickets. How much are they?	여	안녕하세요, 입장권 4장이 필요합니다. 얼마예요?
M	They're $30 for adults and $20 for children under 12.	남	성인은 30달러이고, 12세 미만의 어린이는 20달러입니다.
W	Okay. I'll take two adult tickets and two child tickets, please.	여	네. 성인 표 두 장과 어린이 표 두 장 주세요.
M	All right. Would you like to rent a locker as well? It's a secure way to store your belongings while you enjoy the park.	남	알겠습니다. 사물함도 대여하시겠습니까? 공원을 즐기는 동안 소지품을 보관하는 안전한 방법입니다.
W	How much does it cost?	여	비용이 얼마나 드나요?
M	It's $10 to rent a locker for the day.	남	사물함 한 개를 하루 동안 대여하는 데 10달러입니다.
W	Sounds good. I'll rent one locker.	여	좋습니다. 사물함 하나를 빌릴게요.
M	So, that's two adult tickets, two child tickets, and one locker rental, correct?	남	그럼 성인 표 2장, 어린이 표 2장, 사물함 1개 대여군요, 맞죠?
W	That's right. Oh, and I saw something on your social media about a 10%-off promotional event.	여	맞아요. 아, 그리고 저는 소셜 미디어에서 10% 할인 홍보 행사에 관한 무언가를 봤는데요.
M	I'm sorry, but that event ended last week.	남	죄송하지만, 그 행사는 지난주에 끝났어요.
W	I see. No problem. Here's my credit card.	여	알겠습니다. 괜찮아요. 여기 제 신용 카드입니다.

문제 해설 여자는 30달러인 성인 표 2장과 20달러인 어린이 표 2장, 10달러인 사물함을 1개 대여하고, 10% 할인은 받지 못했다. 따라서 여자가 지불할 금액은 ④ '110달러'이다.

어휘&어구 admission 입장 secure 안전한 store 보관하다 belongings 소지품 promotional 홍보의

W	Hey, Sam. How have you been?	여	안녕, Sam. 어떻게 지냈어요?
M	Pretty good. But busy. Being a dad and a graduate student isn't easy.	남	잘 지냈어요. 하지만 바빴죠. 아빠이면서 대학원생인 건 쉽지 않아요.
W	I can only imagine. But you've been doing really great in our classes. Now that our mid-terms are over, John and I are planning to go hiking this Friday. Would you like to join us?	여	전 겨우 짐작만 갈 뿐이에요. 하지만 당신은 우리 수업에서 정말 잘 해 왔어요. 이제 중간고사가 끝났으니, John과 저는 이번 주 금요일에 하이킹을 갈 계획이에요. 같이 가실래요?
M	I wish I could, but I can't.	남	그러고 싶지만 그럴 수가 없어요.
W	Why not? Are you going to start working on your research project?	여	왜요? 당신의 연구 프로젝트 작업을 시작하실 건가요?
M	No. Since it's not due until the end of the semester, I plan on starting it sometime next week.	남	아니요. 학기가 끝날 때까지는 마감이 아니라서, 다음 주 중에 시작할 계획이에요.
W	Then why can't you come?	여	그럼 왜 못 오시는 거예요?
M	It's about my daughter.	남	제 딸과 관련이 있어요.
W	Do you have to visit her school on Friday?	여	금요일에 딸의 학교를 방문하셔야 하나요?
M	No. I'm attending a parenting workshop conducted by Dr. Paul Johnson.	남	아뇨. Paul Johnson 박사님이 진행하는 육아 워크숍에 참석할 거예요.
W	Oh, he's a parenting expert, right?	여	아, 그는 육아 전문가죠, 그렇죠?
M	Yeah. I think it's going to be really informative.	남	네. 정말 유익할 것 같아요.
W	I'm sure it will be.	여	틀림없이 그럴 거예요.

문제 해설 여자가 남자에게 하이킹을 갈 수 없는 이유를 묻자, 남자는 육아 전문가가 진행하는 육아 워크숍에 참석할 거라고 말하고 있으므로 남자가 하이킹을 갈 수 없는 이유는 ④ '육아 워크숍에 참석해야 해서'이다.

어휘&어구   graduate 대학원의   attend 참석하다   parenting 육아   conduct 진행하다, 처리하다   expert 전문가   informative 유익한, 유용한 정보를 주는

08 가족 춤 활동

[정답] ④

[Telephone rings.]	*[전화벨이 울린다.]*

W Hello, Gardner Community Center. How may I help you?

M Hi, I'd like to get some information about your family dance activity.

W You mean the one held in Gardner Park?

M That's right. When is it held?

W It's every Saturday, starting at 10 a.m.

M Great! What types of dances does it focus on?

W It focuses on a variety of dance styles, including hip-hop and salsa. Everybody I've talked to who's attended the activity said it's really fun.

M That sounds fantastic! Can I just show up, or do I need to sign up in advance?

W We encourage participants to sign up in advance, but on-site registration is also possible.

M That's good to know. Thank you for the information.

W You're welcome. Have a great day. Bye.

여 안녕하세요, Gardner 커뮤니티 센터입니다. 무엇을 도와드릴까요?

남 안녕하세요, 가족 춤 활동에 관한 정보를 좀 얻고 싶습니다.

여 Gardner 공원에서 열리는 것 말씀인가요?

남 맞아요. 그것은 언제 하나요?

여 매주 토요일에, 오전 10시에 시작합니다.

남 좋아요! 어떤 종류의 춤에 중점을 두나요?

여 힙합과 살사를 포함한 다양한 춤 스타일에 초점을 맞추고 있습니다. 그 활동에 참가한 사람들 중 제가 이야기를 나눠 본 모두가 정말 재미있다고 말했어요.

남 환상적으로 들리네요! 그냥 가도 되나요, 아니면 미리 등록해야 하나요?

여 저희는 참가자들이 사전에 등록할 것을 권장하지만, 현장 등록 또한 가능합니다.

남 좋은 정보네요. 정보 감사합니다.

여 천만에요. 좋은 하루 되세요. 안녕히 계세요.

문제 해설   가족 춤 활동에 관한 장소, 시작 시간, 춤의 종류, 현장 등록 가능 여부에 대해서는 언급되었으나, ④ '참가비'는 언급되지 않았다.

어휘&어구   focus on ~에 중점[초점]을 두다[맞추다]   attend 참가하다   sign up 등록하다   in advance 미리

09 Sanford 학교 동영상 콘테스트

[정답] ④

W Hello, students. I'm Melanie Brown, director of the Sanford Public School Foundation. This year, we have something exciting for you: the Sanford School Video Contest! It's a fantastic opportunity for students of all ages. We're seeking short videos, thirty seconds or less, showcasing your school. You can create a video of fun moments you've recorded throughout your school years, introduce your teachers, or capture new memories with your friends. Multiple winners will be selected, and each of them will receive a cash prize of $100. Each person is allowed to submit only one video, and the submission deadline is September 1st. For more information, please visit our website at www.sanfordpsf.org.

여 안녕하세요, 학생 여러분. 저는 Sanford 공립 학교 재단의 이사인 Melanie Brown입니다. 올해, 우리는 여러분을 위해 신나는 것을 준비했습니다. 바로 Sanford 학교 동영상 콘테스트입니다! 모든 연령대의 학생들에게 환상적인 기회입니다. 30초 이하의 짧은, 여러분의 학교를 소개하는 동영상을 찾고 있습니다. 여러분은 학창 시절 내내 녹화한 재미있는 순간들의 동영상을 만들거나, 선생님들을 소개하거나, 친구들과의 새로운 추억을 담을 수 있습니다. 여러 명의 수상자가 선정되며, 각 수상자에게는 100달러의 상금이 수여됩니다. 영상은 1인당 한 개씩만 제출할 수 있으며, 제출 마감일은 9월 1일입니다. 더 많은 정보를 원하시면, 저희 웹사이트 www.sanfordpsf.org를 방문해 주세요.

문제 해설   영상은 1인당 한 개씩만 제출할 수 있다고 했으므로, 담화의 내용과 일치하지 않는 것은 ④ '한 사람이 여러 개의 동영상을 제출할 수 있다.'이다.

어휘&어구   seek 찾다   showcase 소개하다, 전시하듯 보여 주다   capture 담다, 붙잡다   submit 제출하다

10 여름 캠프 등록

W Honey, it's time to decide on a summer camp for Annie and Tom.

M You're right. *[Typing Sound]* Let me pull up the website that shows the summer camps in town.

W All right. Let's see. Which theme sounds best?

M I think all of them except science would be okay. They did the science camp last summer.

W Yeah, they wouldn't want to do that again. And we want them to attend the same camp, so we need to consider their ages too.

M Right. We need a camp for both 8- and 10-year-olds. Then there's the price.

W Since there's the two of them, let's keep it under $200.

M Okay. Hmm. Then should we choose this camp that includes lunch?

W No, I'll pack their lunches. I'm concerned about Annie's allergies.

M Good point. Then in that case, let's choose this camp.

W All right. I'm sure they'll like it.

여 여보, Annie와 Tom을 위한 여름 캠프를 결정할 때예요.

남 맞아요. *[타자 치는 소리]* 동네 여름 캠프를 보여 주는 웹사이트를 띄울게요.

여 좋아요. 어디 봅시다. 어떤 주제가 가장 좋을 것 같아요?

남 과학을 제외하면 모든 게 괜찮을 것 같아요. 애들이 지난여름 과학 캠프를 했잖아요.

여 네, 애들이 그걸 다시 하고 싶지는 않을 거예요. 그리고 우리는 애들이 같은 캠프에 참가하기를 원하니까, 애들 나이도 고려해야 해요.

남 맞아요. 우리는 8살과 10살 둘 다를 위한 캠프가 필요해요. 그리고 가격이요.

여 둘이 있으니까, 200달러 아래로 합시다.

남 좋아요. 흠. 그럼 점심이 포함된 이 캠프를 선택할까요?

여 아니요, 내가 도시락을 쌀 거예요. 저는 Annie의 알레르기가 걱정돼요.

남 좋은 지적이에요. 그렇다면, 이 캠프를 선택합시다.

여 알겠어요. 애들이 좋아할 거예요.

문제 해설 두 사람은 주제가 과학이 아니고, 8살과 10살이 모두 참가할 수 있고, 200달러 미만이며, 점심이 포함되지 않은 캠프를 선택했다. 따라서 두 사람이 자녀를 위해 선택한 여름 캠프는 ⑤이다.

어휘&어구 pull up (화면 등을) 띄우다   be concerned about ~에 대해 걱정하다   allergy 알레르기

11 토마토소스 만들기

M Oh, no. We're all out of tomato sauce. I was planning to cook pasta for dinner.

W Don't worry. We have tomatoes in the refrigerator. We can make it from scratch.

M I've never done that. Do you think it's difficult?

W Not really. We can just follow a recipe I found in a magazine.

남 오, 이런. 토마토소스가 다 떨어졌어요. 저는 저녁으로 파스타를 요리할 계획이었는데요.

여 걱정하지 마세요. 우리는 냉장고에 토마토가 있어요. 맨 처음부터 만들 수 있어요.

남 저는 한 번도 그걸 해 본 적이 없어요. 그건 어려울까요?

여 그렇지는 않을 거예요. 우리는 제가 잡지에서 찾은 요리법대로만 하면 돼요.

문제 해설 저녁에 파스타를 요리할 계획이었지만 토마토소스가 다 떨어졌다고 말하는 남자에게 여자가 냉장고에 토마토가 있으니 맨 처음부터 만들 수 있다고 말하고, 이에 남자가 한 번도 해 본 적이 없다고 하며 그게 어려울지 여자에게 물었다. 따라서 이에 대한 여자의 응답으로 가장 적절한 것은 ⑤ '그렇지는 않을 거예요. 우리는 제가 잡지에서 찾은 요리법대로만 하면 돼요.'이다.

① 네. 당신의 파스타는 훌륭했고 완벽하게 요리되었어요.
② 아닌 것 같아요. 하지만 토마토소스를 대신 사용합시다.
③ 물론이에요. 샐러드에 익은 토마토가 좀 필요할 거예요.
④ 안됐군요. 냉장고에 토마토가 하나도 남아 있지 않아요.

어휘&어구 from scratch 맨 처음부터

12 긁힌 자국이 있는 가방 구매

W Did you find everything okay, sir?

M Well, I'd like to purchase a bag like this, but this one is scratched right here. Do you happen to have a new one?

여 원하시는 거 모두 잘 찾으셨나요, 손님?

남 음, 저는 이런 가방을 사고 싶은데, 이것은 바로 여기가 긁혔어요. 혹시 새것이 있습니까?

| W | I'm sorry, but that's the last one we have in stock. But I can offer you a 15% discount. | 여 | 죄송하지만, 그것이 우리가 가진 마지막 재고입니다. 하지만 제가 손님께 15% 할인을 해 드릴 수 있어요. |
| M | That sounds fair. I'll take it even with the scratch. | 남 | 괜찮은 것 같네요. 긁힌 자국이 있더라도 그것을 살게요. |

문제 해설 가방을 사고 싶지만 긁힌 자국이 있어 새것이 있는지 묻는 남자에게 여자는 그것이 마지막 재고이지만 15% 할인을 해 주겠다고 말했다. 따라서 이에 대한 남자의 응답으로 가장 적절한 것은 ④ '괜찮은 것 같네요. 긁힌 자국이 있더라도 그것을 살게요.'이다.
① 감사합니다. 그러면 새것을 기다릴게요.
② 걱정하지 마세요. 할인은 판매를 증가시킬 것입니다.
③ 신경 쓰지 마세요. 다음 주에는 재고가 더 있을 겁니다.
⑤ 맞아요. 긁힌 자국을 제거해 주셔서 감사합니다.

어휘&어구 purchase 사다 scratch 긁다 happen to *do* 혹시 ~하다 have in stock 재고가 있다 offer 제공하다 fair 괜찮은, 타당한

13 제로 웨이스트 가게 [정답] ④

M	Hi, Janet. What are you doing on your phone?	남	안녕하세요, Janet. 휴대 전화로 뭐 하고 있어요?
W	I'm trying to find an eco-friendly cleaning product.	여	친환경적인 청소용품을 찾고 있어요.
M	Have you heard about the zero-waste store in town? They have sustainable alternatives for everyday items.	남	시내에 있는 제로 웨이스트 가게에 대해 들어 봤어요? 거기엔 일상용품에 대한 지속 가능한 대안이 있어요.
W	No, I haven't. What exactly is a zero-waste store?	여	아니요, 들어 본 적 없어요. 제로 웨이스트 가게가 정확히 뭐죠?
M	It's a store that tries to minimize packaging waste and promote reusable products.	남	포장 폐기물을 최소화하고 재사용 가능한 제품을 홍보하기 위해 노력하는 가게예요.
W	That's great! I've been getting more concerned about climate change lately. It's really serious.	여	잘됐네요! 저는 최근에 기후 변화에 대해 점점 더 걱정하고 있거든요. 정말 심각해요.
M	Absolutely. It's important we make sustainable choices in our daily lives.	남	맞아요. 우리가 일상생활에서 지속 가능한 선택을 하는 것은 중요해요.
W	Definitely. So do they have cleaning products at the zero-waste store?	여	그럼요. 그래서 제로 웨이스트 가게에 청소용품이 있나요?
M	Yes. I actually bought a cleaning spray with a reusable aluminum bottle last week.	남	네. 실은 제가 지난주에 재사용 가능한 알루미늄 병으로 된 세척 스프레이를 샀어요.
W	That's exactly what I'm looking for. Can you tell me where the store is?	여	그게 바로 제가 찾고 있는 거예요. 가게가 어디에 있는지 알려 주실 수 있어요?
M	Of course. We can even go there together. I'm planning on going there tomorrow.	남	물론이죠. 우리가 그곳에 함께 갈 수도 있어요. 저는 내일 그곳에 갈 계획이에요.
W	Perfect. I'll get that sustainable cleaning spray there.	여	완벽하네요. 저는 거기서 그 지속 가능한 세척 스프레이를 살래요.

문제 해설 친환경적인 청소용품을 찾는 여자에게 남자는 제로 웨이스트 가게에 대해 알려 주고, 거기에서 자신이 친환경적인 세척 스프레이를 샀다고 말했다. 이에 여자가 그게 자신이 찾는 것이라며 가게 위치를 묻고, 남자가 자신이 내일 거기에 갈 계획이니 함께 갈 수도 있다고 말했으므로, 남자의 마지막 말에 대한 여자의 응답으로 가장 적절한 것은 ④ '완벽하네요. 저는 거기서 그 지속 가능한 세척 스프레이를 살래요.'이다.
① 괜찮아요. 병은 제가 직접 재활용할게요.
② 물론이죠. 새로운 가게를 연 것을 축하해요.
③ 죄송해요. 저는 차라리 시내에 있는 제로 웨이스트 가게에 갈래요.
⑤ 아닌 것 같아요. 그 가게는 청소용품을 팔지 않아요.

어휘&어구 eco-friendly 친환경적인 sustainable 지속 가능한 alternative 대안 minimize 최소화하다 promote 홍보하다 reusable 재사용 가능한 concerned about ~에 대해 걱정하는 lately 최근에

14 학교 국제 관계 동아리 모임 [정답] ②

W	What are you reading, Jay?	여	Jay, 뭘 읽고 있어?
M	Hi, Irene. It's a news article about international affairs.	남	안녕, Irene. 국제 문제에 관한 뉴스 기사야.
W	I didn't know you enjoyed reading such news articles.	여	네가 그런 뉴스 기사를 읽는 것을 좋아하는지 몰랐어.

M	Yeah, I do. But sometimes they're a little challenging to understand. I wish I had some people to talk to about them.	남	응, 좋아해. 하지만 때때로 이해하기가 조금 어려워. 그것들에 대해 이야기할 사람이 있었으면 좋겠어.
W	I had no idea you were interested in something like that. You should join the school International Relations Club. I'm in it.	여	나는 네가 그런 것에 관심이 있는지 전혀 몰랐어. 학교의 국제 관계 동아리에 가입해. 나는 회원이야.
M	Oh, do you discuss news articles about international affairs?	남	오, 국제 관계에 관한 뉴스 기사에 대해 토론하니?
W	Yeah. We meet every Thursday. It'd be a great chance for you to have meaningful conversations.	여	응. 우리는 매주 목요일에 모여. 네가 의미 있는 대화를 할 수 있는 좋은 기회가 될 거야.
M	That's perfect. So I can join the club?	남	그거 완벽하네. 내가 동아리에 가입할 수 있니?
W	Of course! You should come this week. I can send you the article that we'll talk about so you can read it in advance.	여	물론이지! 이번 주에 와. 네가 미리 읽어 볼 수 있도록 우리가 이야기할 기사를 보내 줄 수 있어.
M	Sounds good. What's the article about?	남	좋아. 그 기사는 무엇에 관한 거야?
W	It's about Korea's diplomatic strategy. I'll send it to you right away.	여	한국의 외교 전략에 관한 거야. 지금 바로 보내 줄게.
M	Thanks. I'll make sure to read it before the meeting.	남	고마워. 모임 전에 꼭 읽어 볼게.

문제 해설 뉴스 기사를 읽는 것에 관심이 있지만 이해하기 어려울 때가 있어서 같이 이야기할 사람이 있으면 좋겠다는 남자에게 여자가 자신이 회원인 국제 관계 동아리를 소개한다. 이에 남자가 호응하며 자신이 동아리에 가입할 수 있는지 묻자 여자는 이번 주 모임에 올 것을 권하면서 모임 전에 미리 읽어 볼 수 있도록 기사를 보내 주겠다고 했다. 따라서 여자의 마지막 말에 대한 남자의 응답으로 가장 적절한 것은 ② '고마워. 모임 전에 꼭 읽어 볼게.'이다.
① 좋아. 지난주에 그걸 읽지 못해서 미안해.
③ 알겠어. 나에게 맞는 동아리를 찾으면 알려 줘.
④ 알겠어. 내가 그것에 대해 좋은 기사를 쓸 수 있는지 보자.
⑤ 걱정할 필요 없어. 틀린 부분이 있으면 수정해서 돌려줄게.

어휘&어구 article 기사 international affairs 국제 문제 challenging 어려운 meaningful 의미 있는 in advance 미리 diplomatic 외교의 strategy 전략

15 주말 가족 활동 계획 [정답] ①

M	Jim and Adrian are married and have a 15-year-old son named Ethan. They're currently planning some family activities for the upcoming weekend. Adrian suggests they go to a nearby shopping mall to have lunch and enjoy the indoor amusement park there. These days, Jim is concerned about Ethan's lack of exposure to nature. Basically, all Ethan has been doing lately is spending most of his time indoors studying for his mid-term exams and attending academies. Jim thinks it's really important for him to connect with nature, breathe in some fresh air, and experience the beauty of the natural surroundings. So Jim wants to suggest to Adrian that they arrange some things to do outside. In this situation, what would Jim most likely say to Adrian?	남	Jim과 Adrian은 결혼했고 Ethan이라는 이름의 15세 아들을 두고 있습니다. 그들은 현재 다가오는 주말을 위해 가족 활동을 계획하고 있습니다. Adrian은 그들이 근처의 쇼핑몰에 가서 점심을 먹고 거기에 있는 실내 놀이공원을 즐길 것을 제안합니다. 요즘, Jim은 Ethan이 자연에 노출되지 않는 것에 대해 걱정하고 있습니다. 기본적으로, 최근 Ethan은 대부분의 시간을 실내에서 중간고사 공부를 하고 학원에 다니는 것만 해 왔습니다. Jim은 그가 자연과 관계를 맺고, 신선한 공기를 좀 마시고, 자연환경의 아름다움을 경험하는 것이 정말 중요하다고 생각합니다. 그래서 Jim은 Adrian에게 밖에서 할 수 있는 일들을 준비하자고 제안하고 싶어 합니다. 이런 상황에서 Jim은 Adrian에게 뭐라고 말하겠습니까?
Jim	Why don't we plan some outdoor activities?	Jim	야외 활동을 계획해 보는 게 어때요?

문제 해설 부부가 주말을 위한 가족 활동을 계획하고 있다. Adrian은 실내 활동을 제안하지만, Jim은 실내에서 공부하고 학원에 다니는 것만 해 오고 자연에 노출되지 않은 아들에 대해 걱정하면서 밖에서 할 수 있는 일들을 준비하자고 제안하고 싶어 한다. 이런 상황에서 Jim이 Adrian에게 할 말로 가장 적절한 것은 ① '야외 활동을 계획해 보는 게 어때요?'이다.
② 우리가 그의 학원 수업을 취소해야 할 것 같아요.

③ 점심 먹으러 다른 쇼핑몰로 갑시다.

④ 우리는 Ethan에게 그가 무엇을 하고 싶은지 물어봐야 해요.

⑤ Ethan을 위해 시골에 있는 집으로 이사 가는 게 어때요?

어휘&어구 **currently** 현재 **nearby** 근처의 **indoor** 실내의 **amusement park** 놀이공원 **lack of** ~이 없는 것 **exposure** 노출 **surrounding** 환경 **arrange** 준비하다

16~17 해양 동물 보호를 위한 관광 관행

[정답] 16 ② 17 ③

W Hello, everyone. While encountering sea animals during vacation is extremely exciting, it's important that these animals be protected. So today we're going to talk about responsible travel measures being used to protect some of these animals. First, in Costa Rica, tour operators are working together to protect the nesting beaches of marine turtles. They ensure there are minimal disturbances to the nesting turtles during tours. Next, in the Maldives, educational sessions are provided for visitors to raise awareness about whale sharks. Tourists are taught how to prevent any direct contact with them that could harm them. Moving on, there are travel measures that emphasize protecting seahorses' habitats in the Philippines. Tourists are encouraged to not disturb seahorse habitats, such as coral reefs and seagrass beds. Lastly, in New Zealand, dolphin watching tours operate under strict guidelines to maintain a safe distance from dolphins. Also, marine research institutions often work closely with tour operators to develop guidelines that prioritize the well-being of dolphins. Now let's watch a short video.

여 안녕하세요, 여러분. 휴가 중에 해양 동물들을 만나는 것은 매우 흥미롭지만, 이 동물들을 보호하는 것은 중요합니다. 그래서 오늘 우리는 이 동물들 중 일부를 보호하기 위해 사용되는 책임 있는 여행 조치에 대해 이야기할 것입니다. 첫째, 코스타리카에서, 관광 운영자들은 바다거북이 둥지를 트는 해변을 보호하기 위해 함께 일하고 있습니다. 그들은 둥지를 트는 거북들에게 투어 중에 방해가 최소화되도록 확실히 합니다. 다음으로, 몰디브에서는 고래상어에 대한 인식을 높이기 위해 방문객들을 위한 교육 시간이 제공됩니다. 관광객들은 고래상어에게 해를 끼칠 수 있는 직접적인 접촉을 방지하는 방법을 배웁니다. 다음으로, 필리핀에서 해마의 서식지 보호를 강조하는 여행 조치들이 있습니다. 관광객들은 산호초와 해초 바닥과 같은 해마 서식지를 방해하지 않도록 권장됩니다. 마지막으로, 뉴질랜드에서 돌고래 관찰 투어는 돌고래들로부터 안전한 거리를 유지하기 위해 엄격한 지침에 따라 운영됩니다. 또한, 해양 연구 기관들은 돌고래들의 안녕을 우선시하는 지침을 개발하기 위해 자주 관광 운영자들과 긴밀히 협력합니다. 이제 짧은 비디오를 하나 보겠습니다.

문제 해설 **16** 여자는 몇 가지 예를 통해 해양 동물을 보호하기 위해 사용되는 책임 있는 여행 조치에 대해 이야기하고 있으므로, 여자가 하는 말의 주제로 가장 적절한 것은 ② '해양 종을 보존하기 위한 관광 관행'이다.

① 기후 변화가 해양 종에 미치는 영향

③ 멸종 위기에 처한 해양 종을 구하는 것에 있어서의 어려움

④ 해양 보존을 위한 기술 혁신

⑤ 해양 생태계에 대한 외래 동물 종의 위협

17 바다거북, 고래상어, 해마, 돌고래는 언급되었지만, ③ '바다사자'는 언급되지 않았다.

어휘&어구 **encounter** 만나다 **measure** 조치 **operator** 운영자 **nest** 둥지를 틀다 **minimal** 최소한의 **disturbance** 방해 **raise awareness** 인식을 높이다 **prevent** 방지하다 **contact** 접촉 **emphasize** 강조하다 **habitat** 서식지 **coral reef** 산호초 **seagrass** 해초 **strict** 엄격한 **guideline** 지침 **prioritize** 우선시하다

MEMO

MEMO

미리 준비하는 중학생을 위한

영어듣기

✛ 수학 전문가 100여 명의 노하우로 만든
　수학 특화 시리즈

✛ 연산 ε ▸ 개념 α ▸ 유형 β ▸ 고난도 Σ 의
　단계별 영역 구성

✛ 난이도별, 유형별 선택으로
　사용자 맞춤형 학습

연산 ε(6책) ｜ 개념 α(6책) ｜ 유형 β(6책) ｜ 고난도 Σ(6책)

EBS No.1 과목 특화 브랜드

✦ 원리 학습을 기반으로 한
  중학 과학의 새로운 패러다임

✦ 학교 시험 족보 분석으로
  내신 시험도 완벽 대비

원 리 학 습 으 로 완 성 하 는 과 학

비욘드

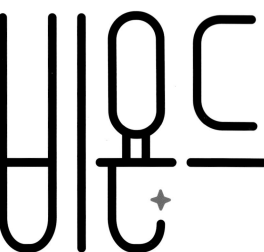

개념 탐구 적용 실전   **체계적인 실험 분석 + 모든 유형 적용**

✦ **시리즈 구성** ✦

중학 과학 1-1	중학 과학 1-2
중학 과학 2-1	중학 과학 2-2
중학 과학 3-1	중학 과학 3-2